Frommer's®

Barcelona

4th Edition

by Peter Stone

WILEY

A John Wiley and Sons, Ltd, Publication

Published by:

WILEY PUBLISHING, INC.

Copyright © 2011 John Wiley & Sons Ltd, The Atrium, Southern Gate, Chichester, West Sussex PO19 8SQ, UK

Telephone (+44) 1243 779777

Email (for orders and customer service enquiries): cs-books@wiley.co.uk. Visit our Home Page on www.wiley.com

UK Publisher: Sally Smith

Project Manager: Daniel Mersey

Commissioning Editor: Fiona Quinn

Development Editor: Sasha Heseltine

Content Editor: Erica Peters

Cartography: Andrew Dolan

Photo Editor: Jill Emeny

Front cover photo: © Art Kowalsky / Casa Batlló

Back Cover photo: © Photos to Go / Carved doorway in the Passion façade, La Sagrada Família

Wiley also publishes its books in a variety of electronic formats. Some content that appears in print may not be available in electronic books.

For information on our other products and services or to obtain technical support, please contact our Customer Care Department within the U.S. at 877/762-2974, outside the U.S. at 317/572-3993 or fax 317/572-4002.

British Library Cataloguing in Publication Data: A catalogue record for this book is available from the British Library

ISBN 978-0-470-71124-8 (pbk), ISBN 978-1-119-99200-4 (ebk), ISBN 978-1-119-99449-7 (epub), ISBN 978-1-119-99465-7 (emobi)

Typeset by Wiley Indianapolis Composition Services

Printed and bound in the United States of America

5 4 3 2 1

CONTENTS

LIST OF MAPS

LIST OF MAPS

ABOUT THE AUTHOR

Born in London, England, **Peter Stone** started his working life in the Foreign Office in Downing Street before moving on to translating and journalism. Over the last 31 years he has resided in different areas of Spain, including Málaga, Barcelona, Alicante, Palma de Mallorca, and Las Palmas de Gran Canaria, and also lived in Greece and North Africa. A lifelong lover of Spanish culture, history and language, he made Madrid his home in 1998, and his publications on the Spanish capital include *Madrid Escapes* and *Frommer's Madrid*. He has also contributed to a wide variety of international magazines and guidebooks, including *Time Out, Insight, Intelliguide, Spain Gourmetour,* and *Pauline Frommer's Spain*.

HOW TO CONTACT US

In researching this book, we discovered many wonderful places—hotels, restaurants, shops, and more. We're sure you'll find others. Please tell us about them, so we can share the information with your fellow travelers in upcoming editions. If you were disappointed with a recommendation, we'd love to know that, too. Please email frommers@wiley.co.uk or write to:

Frommer's Barcelona, 4th Edition
Wiley Publishing, Inc. • 111 River St. • Hoboken, NJ 07030-5774

AN ADDITIONAL NOTE

Please be advised that travel information is subject to change at any time—and this is especially true of prices. We therefore suggest that you write or call ahead for confirmation when making your travel plans. The authors, editors, and publisher cannot be held responsible for the experiences of readers while traveling. Your safety is important to us, however, so we encourage you to stay alert and be aware of your surroundings. Keep a close eye on cameras, purses, and wallets, all favorite targets of thieves and pickpockets.

FROMMER'S STAR RATINGS, ICONS & ABBREVIATIONS

Every hotel, restaurant, and attraction listing in this guide has been ranked for quality, value, service, amenities, and special features using a **star-rating system.** In country, state, and regional guides, we also rate towns and regions to help you narrow down your choices and budget your time accordingly. Hotels and restaurants are rated on a scale of zero (recommended) to three stars (exceptional). Attractions, shopping, nightlife, towns, and regions are rated according to the following scale: zero stars (recommended), one star (highly recommended), two stars (very highly recommended), and three stars (must-see).

In addition to the star-rating system, we also use **seven feature icons** that point you to the great deals, in-the-know advice, and unique experiences that separate travelers from tourists. Throughout the book, look for:

special finds—those places only insiders know about

fun facts—details that make travelers more informed and their trips more fun

kids—best bets for kids and advice for the whole family

special moments—those experiences that memories are made of

overrated—places or experiences not worth your time or money

insider tips—great ways to save time and money

great values—where to get the best deals

The following **abbreviations** are used for credit cards:

AE   American Express   DISC   Discover   V   Visa

DC   Diners Club   MC   MasterCard

TRAVEL RESOURCES AT FROMMERS.COM

Frommer's travel resources don't end with this guide. Frommer's website, **www.frommers. com,** has travel information on more than 4,000 destinations. We update features regularly, giving you access to the most current trip-planning information and the best airfare, lodging, and car-rental bargains. You can also listen to podcasts, connect with other Frommers. com members through our active-reader forums, share your travel photos, read blogs from guidebook editors and fellow travellers, and much more.

THE BEST OF BARCELONA

Barcelona is unlike any other Spanish city. Its entrepreneurial energy and artistic creativity have shone through even in the hardest times, and its complex and brilliant cultural world is the envy of the country, although arch-rival Madrid would be the last to admit this. Gothic buildings and world-class museums fill the historic center, while the whimsical creations of the *modernisme* movement and cutting-edge contemporary architecture line the wide boulevards of the newer city.

You'll find more sophisticated shops, avant-garde restaurants, and sleek hotels here than anywhere else in Spain, plus an eclectic nightlife that extends way around the clock.

Nature, too, plays a surprisingly prominent role. Wooded hills enclose the Catalan capital, oasis-like parks alleviate the urban sprawl, and sandy beaches extend north from Barcelona's lively port area. North toward France the cove-indented Costa Brava offers what many regard as the loveliest scenery in all the Mediterranean, while inland the towering Pyrénées boasts some of the finest mountain walks and skiing in Europe.

So what really rates as the "best" in and around this ever-changing, 21st-century city? Where are the real high spots among all those Gothic and *moderniste* gems? Where can you savor a truly fabulous meal? Where's the chicest place to bed down? Which nightspot is the place of the moment? Where to shop until you drop? And which particular aspect of Barcelona's magical Mediterranean setting stays with you forever?

Here are our personal choices.

THE most unforgettable
BARCELONA EXPERIENCES

○ **Strolling Along La Rambla:** Barcelona's most famous promenade pulses with life. The array of living statues, street musicians, performers, hustlers, and eccentrics ensures there is never a dull moment during your kilometer-long stroll. Don't forget to stop and drink the water at the historic Canaletas fountain halfway down. It's said those who drink here will return to the city. See p. 62.

○ **Having a Drink on the Beach at Sunset:** The Catalan capital's 6km (4 miles) stretch of new city beaches, where the promenade, jetties, and marinas are lapped by inviting Mediterranean waters, have been transformed from a once-neglected area into a round-the-clock international playground. Their atmospheric *chiringuitos* (waterside bars and eating spots specializing in seafood dishes) are perfect spots for either lunch or a relaxing end-of-day drink, often accompanied by the music of an in-house DJ. See p. 76.

○ **Exploring the El Born Neighborhood:** This compact medieval quarter just inland from Barceloneta was once a labyrinth of earthy artisan workshops. Now a cool crowd converges on its narrow tangle of streets lined with renovated old mansions: by day to check out top museums like the Picasso and smart shops exhibiting the latest in cutting-edge fashion and design; at night to enjoy the plethora of bars and restaurants offering the ultimate in New Catalan cuisine. See p. 204.

○ **Attending a Concert at the Palau de la Música Catalana:** This masterpiece of *moderniste* (Art Nouveau) architecture must be one of the most lavish concert halls in the world. All strains of classical and jazz are played, but even the most finicky music lover will be moved by the Palau's onslaught of decorative detail. See p. 240.

○ **Eating Breakfast at the Boqueria:** There are about a dozen bars and restaurants in the city's main food market, one of the largest and most colorful in Spain. It's the height of fashion these days, and in the early morning you can rub shoulders with Barcelona's top chefs and gourmands over coffee and croissants as you watch the day's deliveries coming in. See p. 226.

○ **Bar-Hopping in the Barri Gòtic:** Whether it's an iconic tapas bar, a traditional *cava* bar, or a cocktail lounge filled with minimalist furniture and minimally clad patrons, Barcelona's Ciutat Vella (Old City) is a watering-hole mecca, bar none. One of the best choices is Mam i Teca, a dinky Raval delight with the accent on revamped Catalan specialties. See p. 243.

○ **Spending a Sunday on Montjuïc:** The sharply rising hill of Montjuïc is the first sight that greets visitors arriving at the port. Behind the rocky slopes facing the sea are acres of pine-dotted parkland beloved by cyclists, joggers, and strollers on the weekend. Topped by the castle-museum of El Museu Militar de Montjuïc, which has stunning city views, its slopes provide a tranquil alternative to the hustle of the city below and offer welcome breathing space. The most exhilarating way to get up there is by the spectacular Transbordador Aeri cable car (p. 189), which swings high above the harbor from Barceloneta, giving views over sea and city. See p. 183.

- **Taking a Trip to Tibidabo by Tram and Funicular:** The summit of the city's distinctive inland backdrop is reached in two stages: first by the Tramvía Blau (Blue Tram), which winds past the Sarrià district's elegant houses, and then by a creaky Art Deco funicular lift, which rattles its way up the mountainside to reveal increasingly breathtaking views of the city below. Both of these vintage forms of transport were built over a century ago to transport people to the church and the Parc d'Atraccions del Tibidabo, Barcelona's famous amusement park, on the mountain's peak. The exhilarating journey up to the top is all part of the fun. See p. 48.

- **Dining at Els Quatre Gats:** The original bar at Els Quatre Gats acted as a fraternity house for late-18th-century dandies. It later became the preferred hang-out for the young Picasso and his bohemian contemporaries. While most of the art adorning the walls is now reproduction, this classic Catalan restaurant is still alive with history. The resident pianist and general formality only add to the atmosphere. See p. 127.

- **Taking Your First Glance at the Sagrada Família:** Nothing quite prepares you for the first glimpse of Gaudí's most famous work; the cathedral erupts from the center of a suburban city block like some retro-futurist grotto. Look closely at the facade covered in religious symbolism and before stepping over the threshold into the undulating, unfinished interior. See p. 176.

- **People-Watching outside the Museu d'Art Contemporani de Barcelona (MACBA):** The forecourt of the Museum of Contemporary Art is a snapshot of the new multicultural Barcelona. Spend some time at one of its outside bars watching the multinational local kids playing cricket, soccer, and skateboarding in a fascinating melting pot of recreational activity. See p. 173.

- **Staying Up Until Dawn:** A long dinner, a few drinks at a bar, on to a club, and then before you know it the sun is rising over the Mediterranean's party capital, throwing a warm glow over Barcelona's palm-filled plazas and streets. Nothing beats a lazy walk home through the Ciutat Vella (Old City) at this magical hour. See p. 236.

- **Seeing the Torre Agbar Lit Up by Night:** Even more controversial than the Sagrada Família when it first appeared, this 140-m (460-feet)-high, multi-hued, phallic-shaped tower erupts surreally from the otherwise bland cityscape around the Plaça de les Glòries. The tower was built by architect Jean Nouvel in honor of the city's Forum, the conference center that opened to great fanfare in 2004. It has over 4,000 multiform, light-reflecting windows and currently houses the offices of the Barcelona Water Board. You get a great view of it from the top of Montjuïc. See p. 24.

- **Walking in the Collserola Hills:** You'd think you were a hundred miles from the city as you wander along endless trails through lush oak and pine forests. That is, until you get one of those breathtaking views of the city way below through the trees. Tucked away in the midst of all the greenery is a tiny museum, once the summer villa of 19th-century Catalan poet Jacint Verdaguer. A half-hour FGC train ride to Baixada de Vallvidrera drops you right on the edge of this leafy wonderland. See p. 81.

o **Taking a Day Trip to Tossa de Mar:** This quintessential Costa Brava resort, complete with tiny intact old town and a perfect pine-fringed crescent beach, has kept its character in spite of the tourist invasion. Some of the Mediterranean magic that the likes of Marc Chagall, Ava Gardner, and James Mason found here in the 1950s still lingers on. It's only an hour away by bus from the Estació Nort, so you'll even have time to take in a short *crucero* (boat trip) along the rugged coast, popping in and out of sea caves lapped by pellucid waters. See p. 287.

THE best SPLURGE HOTELS

o **Hotel Arts Barcelona,** Marina 19–21 (𝄢 **93-221-10-00;** www.hotelarts barcelona.com): The preferred choice of top models and temperamental rock stars, the Hotel Arts has remained a jet-set playground and symbol of "cool Barcelona" for well over a decade. See p. 115.

o **Hotel Casa Fuster,** Passeig de Gràcia 132 (𝄢 **93-225-30-00;** www.hotel escenter.es/casafuster): This *moderniste* masterpiece was an emblematic building before it was converted into this luxury five-star hotel. The rooms have been restored to turn-of-the-20th-century opulence, and its clubby VIP ambience makes you feel very special. Impeccable service and extra touches like fresh flowers in your room add to the agreeable sensation of being pampered. See p. 98.

o **Hotel España,** Sant Pau 9-11 (𝄢 **93-318-17-58;** www.hotelespanya.com): This hotel combines comfort and luxury with the evocation of a bygone age. Designed by a contemporary of Gaudí's, the street-level dining room, filled with florid motifs and brass fixtures, will whisk you back to the early 1900s, when it was filled with chattering patrons taking supper after a trip to the opera house next door. See p. 97.

o **Mandarin Oriental,** Passeig de Gràcia 38-40 (𝄢 **93-151-88-88;** www. mandarinoriental.com/barcelona): One of the newest additions to the city's truly luxurious waterholes, this elegant "East meets West" hostelry is part of the famed worldwide Mandarin chain. The sumptuous interiors were created by top Spanish designer Patricia Urquiola, and its Thai-style spa facilities are among the best in town. See p. 103.

THE best MODERATELY PRICED HOTELS

o **Gat Raval,** Joaquin Costa 44, 1st floor (𝄢 **93-481-66-70**): Cool, chic and stylish (although you may have to share a bathroom), the spotless and colorful Gat Raval is a great bargain stopover choice in the Ciutat Vella's liveliest and most richly international quarter. See p. 96.

o **Hostal D'Uxelles,** Gran Vía 688 and 667 (𝄢 **93-265-25-60;** www.hotel duxelles.com): This *hostal* looks like it has stepped straight off the pages of one of those rustic-interiors magazines. Located on the first floor of two adjacent buildings, each of the 14 rooms has a distinct character, but all include canopied beds, antique furniture, and Andalusian-style ceramic bathrooms. See p. 109.

○ **Hotel Peninsular,** Sant Pau 34 (© **93-302-31-38;** www.hotelpeninsular.net): Serenity and character abound in this nunnery-turned-hotel. Located on a colorful street just off La Rambla, it features an Art Nouveau elevator and a lush inner courtyard that make it feel like a refuge from the hustle and bustle outside. It's understandably popular, so book ahead. See p. 97.

○ **Marina Folch,** Carrer del Mar 16, principal (© **93-310-37-09;** www.hotelmarina folchbcn.com): This small family-run hotel is your best low-cost option in the beachside neighborhood of Barceloneta, where there are plenty of outdoor bars and open spaces for the kids to run wild. Ask for a room at the front for a balcony with a view of the port. See p. 116.

THE most unforgettable
DINING EXPERIENCES

○ **Having a Paella Overlooking the Harbor:** Ignore the pushy neighboring eating spots on Barceloneta's main portside boulevard and give yourself to a seafood treat at the homely, laidback Puda Can Manel, Passeig Don Joan Borbó Comte 60 (© **93-221-50-13**). The succulent paellas and *fideuàs* (seafood with noodles instead of rice) are the genuine article and also excellent value, which is why you see so many locals here, especially on Sundays. See p. 157.

○ **Tasting the Cuisine of Catalonia's Top Chef:** Still the talk of the town, Carles Abellán has long been hailed as one of the most innovative chefs of New Catalan cuisine. His restaurant, **Comerç 24,** Comerç 24 (© **93-319-21-02,** comerc24.com.mialias.net), was conceived as a playful take on all that's hot in the tapas world. Delights such as "kinder egg surprise" (a soft-boiled egg with truffle-infused yolk) and an intensely flavored mini-*suquet* (fish stew) continue to exert their gourmet siren appeal. See p. 133.

○ **Partaking in a Sunday Dining Tradition:** The lines say it all: **7 Portes,** Passeig Isabel II 14 (© **93-319-30-33;** www.7portes.com), one of the oldest restaurants in Barcelona, is a Sunday institution. Extended families dine on excellent meat and fish dishes in a turn-of-the-20th-century atmosphere. See p. 154.

○ **Sampling the Finest Regional Dishes:** In spite of its Italian name, the **Via Veneto,** Ganduxer 10 (© **93-200-72-44;** www.viavenetorestaurant.com), is traditional to the core, serving up some of the finest Catalan cooking in the land. The restaurant exudes old-fashioned class. The serving methods, such as the sterling-silver duck press, seem to belong to another century—as do some of the clients. See p. 150.

○ **Eating the Freshest Seafood in Barcelona:** You'll find it at **Els Pescadors,** Plaça Prim 1 (© **93-225-20-18;** www.elspescadors.com), in the atmospheric working-class beachside suburb of Poble Nou. People come here for the food—not the view—to sample prawns, whitebait, or *dorada* (bream). They serve whatever has been caught that day. Book ahead on weekends. See p. 153.

○ **Trying a Tasting Menu:** Tasting menus, a series of small gourmet dishes resembling deluxe tapas, are all the rage. They can be expensive, though, so if you want the best value head to **Coure,** Pasaje Marimón 20 (© **93-200-75-32**), in Gràcia and sample chef Albert Ventura's offerings, which include such exquisite delights as lime-flavored tuna and eucalyptus *helado*—ice cream. See p. 148.

THE best THINGS TO DO FOR FREE

○ **Enjoying the Freebie Cultural Treats:** Top visits here are the **Foment de les Arts i del Disseny (FAD)** cultural center, where you can view exhibitions and sometimes buy bargain paintings by promising young unknowns; and **Caixaforum** art gallery, which has an ever-changing trio of stimulating exhibitions. Around the city you'll find an impressive variety of open-air public art displays: Antoni Llena's bizarre metal *David i Goliat* in Plaça dels Volontaris, Frank Gehry's copper *Peix* (Fish) in Port Olímpic, and Colombian sculptor Fernando Botero's rather chubby *Gat* (Cat) in El Raval. There's also Roy Lichtenstein's trademark comic-strip-style *Barcelona Head,* near the Columbus statue down by the harbor, and Joan Miró's *Dona i Ocell* (Woman and Bird), finished in 1981 just before his death, and located in the park named after him in Sants. See chapter 7, "What to See & Do."

○ **Wandering Around the Parks:** Despite its densely urban appearance, Barcelona is actually filled with parks where you can relax, stroll, and in many cases enjoy fun amenities. Visit the website www.bcn.es/parcsijardins for the full list. Parc de la Ciutadella, just to the east of the Old City, with its fountains and statues, is a relaxing respite from the adjoining claustrophobic medieval labyrinth, while Parc Güell, higher up in Gràcia district, delights visitors of all ages with its fairy-tale Gaudí structures. In Montbau, the **Parc de la Crueta del Coll** has a playground and public summer pool, which in winter reverts to being an artificial lake. To the west, rambling hilltop **Montjuïc**—with its marvelous harbor views, jogging paths, the Fundació Joan Miró, Botanical Gardens, and illuminated Font Màgica (Magic Fountain)—is a spacious kaleidoscope of greenery and cultural and sporting attractions. Less well known and more rural is the **Parc d'en Castell de l'Oreneta,** just above the Monastir (monastery) de Pedralbes, where you can enjoy marvelous panoramic city and coastal views as you wander along signposted trails among meadows. See chapter 7, "What to See & Do."

○ **Taking in the Ecclesiastical Gems:** The city is full of amazing historical and religious monuments, and many of them are free. For example, unlike in most of Spain's major cities, there is no charge for visiting the **Catedral,** although there is a fee for its museum. Other monumental treats are the **Capella de Sant Jordi,** and the churches of **La Mercè** and **Santa María del Pi,** each of which makes its own special contribution to the spiritual and architectural beauty of the city and shows you another aspect of its rich history. Another marvel is the Santa María del Mar church in the Born section of La Ribera. See chapter 7, "What to See & Do."

THE best STUFF TO BRING HOME

- **Leather:** Leather is one of Spain's most highly valued products, and best buys range from stylish belts and handbags to handmade shoes and fine jackets. The top spot for such purchases in Barcelona is **Loewe** (p. 228). An economy-conscious choice is **Acosta** at Avinguda Diagonal 262. This family-run chain offers a well-priced selection of leather goods. See p. 228.
- **Ceramics & Pottery:** Though this is not a Barcelona specialty, you'll find a wide selection of ceramic vases, dishes, and jugs from Valencia, some of which have the style and finesse of fine art. There are also plenty of choices from areas such as Toledo and Seville. **Artesania i Coses** near the Picasso Museum is a good place to browse. See p. 231.
- **Porcelain:** The most popular and widely available ornaments in this field are made by the Valencian company **Lladró,** similar in style to the Italian Capodimonte. Though considered rather twee by some, they're extremely popular with the majority of visitors. **Kastoria,** at Avinguda Catedral, is the place to check out statuettes and friezes. See p. 231.
- **Antiques:** If you're looking for some interesting traditional engravings, carvings, or just simple bric-a-brac to take home, you have plenty of options. The best (and most expensive) option is the three-story **Sala d'Art Artur Ramón** in the Ciutat Vella. See p. 218.
- **Hats:** If you yearn to stroll around at home in a genuine Catalan *barretina* (cap) or a traditional low-key campesino's beret, the place to look is **Sombrería Obach** in the old Jewish quarter of El Call. See p. 227.

THE best ACTIVITIES FOR FAMILIES

- **In the City:** Anything by Antoni Gaudí, the city's most famous architect, immediately appeals to young eyes and imaginations. His whimsical **Parc Güell,** with its imagery from the animal kingdom and hidden grottoes, is a particular favorite. Speaking of animals, the city's world-class Aquarium, with its walk-through tunnels and superb collection of Mediterranean marine life, is also a good bet. The **Parc Zoológic** has a fantastic primate collection and is located in the **Parc de la Ciutadella,** which also boasts a lake with rowboats for hire, swings, and other assorted kiddies' attractions. Museum-wise, a trip to the Maritime Museum, with its 16th-century galley and early submarine, could be combined with a jaunt on **Las Golondrinas**—quaint, double-decker pleasure boats that take you from the port to the breakwater. The **Museu de la Cera** (Wax Museum) may not be up to the standard of its counterpart in London, but is interesting enough to make it worth a visit. Older children will also find the **Museu de la Xocolata** (Chocolate Museum) enticing, and the **Museu de la Ciència** (Science Museum) has excellent hands-on exhibits for all ages. Then, of course, there are the beaches—most with showers, toilets, bars, and recliners for hire. **Happy Park** in L'Eixample, just off the Passeig de Gràcia, is a vast indoor all-weather fun park where tots can enjoy twister slides, ball pools, and other fun activities. There's also a day-care center for tots. See chapter 7, "What to See & Do."

o **On the Outskirts:** An all-time favorite is the **Parc d'Atraccions Tibidabo.** This veteran amusement park, perched on top of the city's highest peak, provides death-defying attractions and a few gentler ones from bygone days. The **Parc del Laberint d'Horta,** meanwhile, is a neoclassical park on the outskirts of the city; and up in the Zona Alta above Pedralbes, the **Parc del Castell de l'Oreneta** has miniature train rides, weekend pony canters, and playgrounds with games for kids. See chapter 7, "What to See & Do."

o **Further Afield:** In Torrelles de Llobregat, just 8km (5 miles) out of town, you'll find **Catalunya en Miniatura,** a Lilliputian mock-up of Barcelona and its province that includes a tiny Sagrada Família and Girona cathedral. A suitably dwarf-size train transports young passengers, and there are daily shows by clowns. At Vilassar de Dalt, 24km (15 miles) north of Barcelona, is the **Illa Fantasia** (Fantasy Island), a lively and spacious aquatic park with water slides, picnic areas, and a host of children's games and competitions; visit www.illa fantasia.com for more information. **Montserrat,** Catalonia's "spiritual heart," offers plenty of walking tracks amid its phantasmagoric terrain of huge rocks and outcrops, caves, and, of course, the monumental monastery. See chapter 11, "Side Trips In Catalonia."

THE best MUSEUMS

o **Fundació Joan Miró:** This museum contains Spain's best collection of the famed surrealist Catalan's works, all donated by the great man himself. The museum is tucked away on Montjuïc hill in a location that enjoys marvelous vistas of port and city from its roof terrace, where there's an attractive sculpture garden. Concerts take place here in summer. Highlights are the Foundation Tapestry and Mercury Fountain, by his American sculptor friend Alexander Calder. See p. 184.

o **Museu d'Art Contemporani de Barcelona (MACBA):** This is Catalonia's answer to Paris's Pompidou Centre, and it's right in the heart of the earthy yet partially gentrified Raval district, beside a lively square filled with students, passersby, and noisy skateboard fans. It has one of the best collections of modern art in Spain, featuring works by Tàpies and Barceló; there's also a library, bookshop, and cafe. See p. 173.

o **Museu Frederic Marès:** This charming old palace of secret patios and high ceilings houses one of the most richly varied collections of medieval sculpture in the world, all donated by Marés—a talented sculptor himself. Exhibits can be viewed on two floors, which open on alternative days and range from polychromatic Roman crucifixes and Gothic statues to a Ladies' Room filled with Victorian knick-knacks, and a Museu Sentimental dedicated to Barcelona over the past 2 centuries. See p. 166.

- **Museu Nacional d'Art de Catalunya (MNAC):** Located in the imposing Palau Nacional on the northern edge of Montjuïc, this museum overlooks the Font Màgica (Magic Fountain, p. 188) and is arguably one of the greatest repositories of Romanesque religious works in the world. Many of the icons and frescoes have been moved here from tiny churches high up in the Pyrénées, where replicas now fill the spaces they originally occupied. Gothic styles are also well represented, and more recently there have been *moderniste* additions—many taken from the Manzana de la Discordia. See p. 186.

- **Museu Picasso:** One of the most visited cultural spots in the city, this museum is mainly dedicated to works by the younger Picasso, which have been collected and assembled by his friend Jaume Sabartés y Gual. It spreads through a quintet of medieval palaces in La Ribera's atmospheric Calle Montcada. The artist donated many of the works himself, and highlights include the famed *Las Meninas* and *The Harlequin*. See p. 169.

BARCELONA IN DEPTH

Barcelona is dynamic, restlessly creative, constantly changing, always looking beyond Spain—into Europe or even across the Atlantic—for inspiration, yet for centuries it was scantly regarded.

Then came two unconnected events that together reversed the outside world's perception of the city. The first occurred in 1975 when General Francisco Franco—who had systematically and often brutally tried to eradicate the treasured Catalan language and culture for 4 long decades—died, and the city and province started to live and breathe independently again. The second came with the 1992 Summer Olympics, which brought a fever of renovation work that radically transformed Barcelona from a drab, gray industrial city to a gleaming new metropolis.

The medieval facades of the Barri Gòtic, which for centuries had been coated in a thick layer of grime, were sandblasted, cleaned, and restored to their pristine glory. The city swung with intoxicating speed from being ignored to being awesomely revered. Word had spread and suddenly Barcelona was "in." The media baptized Barcelona the coolest rendezvous in Europe, saying that the city boasted some of the most inventive restaurants, bars, shops, and hotels on the continent. Such is the city's fame that today no fewer than eight million visitors arrive annually to explore its delights. And such is the Catalans' pride and ambition that they are preparing it for an even greater role: As capital of a separate nation, independent of Spain.

BARCELONA TODAY

Today's multitudes of tourists flock to Barcelona for a number of very good reasons: To view the Picassos, Dalís, Tàpies, and Mirós; to marvel at its historic UNESCO-awarded sites (10 in all), and at the *moderniste* extravaganzas of Antoni Gaudí and the modern eccentricities of Frank Gehry and Jean Nouvel; to sample the New Catalan cuisine of Carlos Abellán and Sergi Arola (both disciples of the pioneering foodie guru Ferran Adrià), who are spearheading a culinary revival that's resulted in half a dozen Michelin-rated restaurants; and to spend money in some of Europe's most sophisticated shops and stores, especially in L'Eixample's Passeig de Gràcia—Barcelona's riposte to Paris's Champs Elysées.

Today thousands of tourists crowd the delightful narrow lanes of the Ciutat Vella (Old City), eager to view its many historic attractions, and pack La Rambla, the most colorful and fascinating avenue in the whole Mediterranean. Local residents, alas, have to wait until winter to see their favorite promenade returned to a more peaceful state.

Some (spoilsport) critics have expressed the concern that the city is currently more interested in its surface image and in packaging itself as a sellable commodity than in dealing with practical matters, such as more judicious city planning. Heavyweight luminaries such as art critic Robert Hughes—who wrote the definitive in-depth portrait of the city at the time of the 1992 Olympics (see "Barcelona in Popular Culture," p. 24)—have been particularly disappointed, and many fear that in the quest for media approval, the city will become a virtual theme park for tourists.

Regardless, the Catalan metropolis has certainly experienced many changes for the better—starting with the fact that today it's even easier to get to and get around the city. By train, visitors can travel from Madrid to Barcelona's main Sants station in just under 3 hours, thanks to a high-speed (300km/h or 190 mph) AVE train service. The lightweight tram, TGV, and Metro services that can get you around the city quickly and efficiently also continue to expand and improve.

Like many forward-thinking cities, Barcelona is becoming more eco-friendly. Following Amsterdam's model, the city has implemented a bike-rental plan which encourages residents and visitors alike to use a **bike-sharing system** in which red *bicicletas* (6,000 in all) are available for free from a variety of bus and Metro stations for up to 30 minutes to those who want to make short trips along some of the city's new cycle lanes.

Barcelona is home to some beautiful parks, ranging from the much-loved veteran **Parc de la Ciutadella** to the sprawling pine-covered **Parc de Collserola** and the eccentric fairyland **Parc Güell.** There are expansive grassy areas on **Montjuïc,** above the port. But there are also newcomers, like **Parc Diagonal Mar** and Poble Nou's **Parc Central,** both of which opened in 2008 and which filled in wastelands left by departing industries. However, these parks tend to be more designer-conscious, stylishly laid out and resembling modern works of art rather than places to relax amid soothing greenery.

In the past, a wealth of architectural styles, from medieval Gothic to 19th-century *moderniste,* made Barcelona famous. Today, ultra-modern, mold-breaking buildings also dominate the skyline, from Jean Nouvel's **Torre Agbar** on the eastern edge of L'Eixample to Norman Foster's **"Needle"** tower high on the wooded hills near Tibidabo. A typical example of Barcelona's ability to convert the conventional into something exceptional is La Ribera's **Santa Caterina** food market, where the avant-garde roof, designed by Enric Miralles (who was responsible for the Parc Diagonal Mar, mentioned above), gives truth to writer V. S. Pritchett's saying that Catalans "live artwardly" even when it comes down to workaday matters.

How Tibidabo Got Its Name

Only in author Dan Brown's wildest imagination would Jesus Christ and the Devil have found themselves chatting to each other on top of the great hill behind the city. But locals love to tell you it was here that the Devil tried to tempt Christ by offering him all he could see—in this case, the lovely coastline all the way north toward the Costa Brava and (on a clear day) the Pyrénées mountains—if he would renounce God's ways and follow him. *Ti dabo* means "I give to you" in Latin and represents the Devil making his offer. The story may be an unlikely myth, but try telling that to the Catalans.

With the increase in tourism, traditional industries such as car and textile production have declined in the city and relocated out of town, where they continue to flourish. High-tech companies have sprung up in areas such as the Llobregat Delta, near the airport. Within the city, old working-class areas are definitely changing, mostly for the better. Neighborhoods like **Poble Sec,** where girls used to work on assembly lines in calico factories, and **Poble Nou,** where the old chimneys of the former textile works still stand beside warehouses converted into trendy pads for high-income executives, are exchanging their gritty proletarian look for stylish gentrification. Call it a theme park if you want, but it sure looks better.

Today Barcelona is a multicultural, polyglot city and home to various international communities. There is a large and industrious Chinese community, who ironically flourish around the misnamed Barri Xino (Chinese Quarter), even though immigrant Asians lived there for decades in the past. The name Barri Xino was inspired by a lurid crime book called *Sangre en las Atarazanas* (Blood in the Dockyards), written by Francisco Madrid in 1926 and set in an imaginary version of Los Angeles' Chinatown. There are also thriving Arab, Eastern European, South American, and African communities, some of whom live in the once-seedy but now up-and-coming Raval quarter.

Despite all these changes, the native Barcelonans remain what they have always been: Practical, businesslike, proletarian, nonconformist, rebellious, artistic, and hedonistic. They embody a complex and contradictory blend of traits that at least partly explain how the city perpetually manages to experiment, adapt, and use its amazing natural energy and creativity to reinvent itself.

LOOKING BACK AT BARCELONA
Early Days: Iberians, Greeks & Romans (5th century B.C.–4th century A.D.)

Long before any conquerors arrived, the plains surrounding the spot where Barcelona now stands were populated by peaceful, agrarian people known as the **Laetani,** while other parts of Catalonia were settled by the **Iberians.** The **Greeks** were the region's first real immigrants, setting up a sizeable trading colony on the northern coast at Empúries, whose remains can still be seen today. Empúries was also the entry point for the Romans, who were at war with North African power

Carthage for dominance over the western Mediterranean. Their base on the Peninsula was down the coast at New Carthage (Cartagena), a city rich in silver and bronze mines that the Romans saw as prime booty. In response to an attack on Rome by Hannibal, the Romans set about subjugating the Peninsula using Tarraco (Tarragona) as a base. Barcino (Barcelona) at that time had no harbor and served merely as a port of call between Tarraco and Narbonne in France. But a growing town quickly mushroomed out from Mons Taber, the highest point of today's city, where the cathedral now stands. You can still see traces of Roman civilization in Barcelona today, though they're eclipsed by smaller Tarragona's surprising wealth of monuments.

Visigoths & Moors

When Rome was crushed by the Barbarians in the 5th century, the Visigoths pounced on this northeastern corner of Spain, taking a broad swath stretching from the eastern Pyrénées to Barcelona. The chaotic rule of the Visigoth kings, who imposed their sophisticated set of laws on existing Roman ones, lasted about 300 years. They were prolific church builders, and Visigothic fragments still survive in Barcelona and, again more vividly, in Tarragona's cathedral.

In A.D. 711, Moorish warriors led by Tarik crossed over into Spain and conquered the country. Three years later, they controlled most of it, except for a few mountain regions around Asturias. Their occupation of Barcelona was short-lived, though, which explains why the city has virtually no vestiges of Moorish architecture compared to al-Andalús (Andalucia), where their culture flourished.

Christian Count Wilfred (The Hairy) Takes Over

Up in the Pyrénées, Catalonia's heartland, the Moors clashed head-on with the Franks led by Charlemagne, who drove them back south. In 801, Louis the Pious, son of Charlemagne, took Barcelona and set up a buffer state, marking the territorial boundaries (known as the Marcha Hispánica) of what was to become medieval Catalonia and endowing the local language with elements of his own (Provençal). Local counts were awarded various territories. **Guifré el Pilós** (Wilfred the Hairy; 878–97) acquired several regions, including Barcelona, and managed to unite the area through a bloody battle that history has earmarked as the birth of Catalonia. Mortally wounded in a battle against the Moors, the Frankish emperor

---

Down Among the Romans

A big surprise for many visitors to Barcelona is the remarkably intact layout of Julia Faventia Agusta Pia Barcino (or Barcino for short), the old Roman city lying directly under the **Museu d'Història de la Ciutat de Barcelona** (City History Museum) in the heart of the Barri Gòtic. Descend a few steps and all around you are the foundations of its villas, temples, and squares, clearly marked and evocative enough for you to imagine life as it was then. This spot puts you within reach of three worlds: Beside you are the Roman remains, on the surface is medieval architecture, and contemporary hotels, office blocks, and stores are nearby.

dipped Wilfred the Hairy's fingers in his own blood and traced them down his shield, creating the Quatre Barres, the future flag of Catalonia. There followed a 500-year-long dynasty of Catalan count-kings with the power to forge a nation.

The Golden Age & Decline

Catalonia entered the 11th century as a series of counties operating under the feudal system. It was growing stronger politically, and artistic and artisan disciplines were beginning to flourish. Under **Ramón Berenguer III** (1096–1131) and his son, the region annexed the southern Tarragonese territories and neighboring Aragón as well. Then came **Jaume I** (1213–76), whose powerful navy conquered Sicily and the Balearic Islands and established Catalonia as the principal maritime power in the Mediterranean. Under his long reign, the second city walls (more extensive than the old Roman ones) and the massive *drassanes* (shipyards) were built, and a code of sea trade and local parliament were established. Merchants grew rich and contributed toward the building of Gothic edifices such as the church of **Santa María del Mar** and its surrounding mansions, the **Saló del Tinell** at the Royal Palace, and the **Saló del Cent.** Catalan literature and language flourished alongside the city's continuing prosperity.

BARCELONA: A BRIEF HISTORY

550 B.C. Greeks settle at Empúries in northern Catalonia.	**719** Moorish invasion of Iberian Peninsula reaches Barcelona.
212 B.C. The Romans, using Empúries as an entry point, subjugate Spain.	**878** Guifré el Pilós (Wilfred the Hairy) defeats Moors and founds dynasty of Counts of Barcelona (5-century-long autonomous rule).
206 B.C. Romans defeat Carthaginians.	
1st C. A.D. Christians spread throughout Catalonia.	**1064** The *Usatges,* the first Catalan Bill of Rights, is drafted.
15 Barcino founded by Romans.	**1137** A royal marriage unites Catalonia and the neighboring region of Aragón.
70 First Jewish settlements in Barcino.	
415 Barcelona occupied by the Visigoths; capital until 554.	**1213–35** Jaume I consolidates empire, conquers Mallorca, Ibiza, and Valencia.

In 1479, however, this was interrupted by the most far-reaching of all royal unions, that of **Fernando II** of Catalonia-Aragón to **Isabel of Castile.** Spain was united, but Catalonia lost its autonomy in the shift. The pious "Catholic Kings" roughly expelled all the Muslims and Jews from Spain, including those living in Barcelona's tiny El Call quarter. And even though Columbus was received in Barcelona upon his return from the discovery of America, Catalans were not allowed to trade with the New World. In the early 17th century, under the rule of **Felipe IV** (1605–55), anti-centralist feeling was further agitated by Spain's Thirty Years' War with France, Catalonia's neighbor, with which Catalonia soon allied. The most emotive of all uprisings, the so-called Guerra dels Segadors (Harvesters' War) was squashed by Spanish troops, and as a final blow, in 1650 **Felipe** ceded Catalan lands north of the Pyrénées to France.

In 1700, a Bourbon prince, **Philip V** (1683–1746), became king, and the remainder of Catalonia fell under French influence. An Austrian Hapsburg archduke then challenged Philip V's right to the throne, precipitating the War of the Spanish Succession. Catalonia gambled on the archduke's victory by supporting him, and lost. Philip V, after taking the city on September 11, 1714 (still celebrated as the Diada,

---

💬 Santa María del Mar: From Jousting to Hobnobbing

The short, broad *paseo* that leads from the magnificent Santa María del Mar cathedral to the market of El Born (currently under renovation) is a trendy passage, lined with chic cafes and bars. Today, it is difficult to imagine that a few centuries ago these cafes would have been in the path of a heavily armored *caballero* (knight) charging at his opponent with a lance. But jousting was commonplace in this area during the Middle Ages. In fact, the word *born* is Catalan for *joust.*

1249 Barcelona forms the *Consell de Cent* (Council of 100) municipal government.	**1494** Catalonia falls under Castilian rule.
1283 Corts (Parliament) to govern Catalonia created.	**1522** Under the rule of Charles V, Catalans refused permission to trade in the New World.
1347–59 The Black Plague halves the city's population. The *Generalitat* (autonomous government) is founded.	**1640–50** Catalan revolt known as the *Guerra dels Segadors* (Harvesters' War); Catalonia declares itself a republic, allied with France.
1469 Fernando II, monarch of Catalonia-Aragón, marries Isabel, queen of Castile, uniting all of Spain.	**1701–13** Spanish War of Succession.
1492 Columbus discovers America. The "Catholic Monarchs" expel all remaining Jews and Muslims.	**1759** Barcelona falls to Franco-Spanish army; the Catalan language is banned.
	1808–14 French occupy Catalonia in Peninsular War with England.

continues

> ### Parc de la Ciutadella: From Prison to Playground
>
> Few corners of the city are as serene and relaxing as **Parc de la Ciutadella.** Lakes, fountains, shrubs, flowers, palms, and quaint statues greet people as they wander its winding paths. Yet for the best part of 2 centuries, these were the grounds of the citadel that housed Barcelona's political prisoners, many of whom met a bad end in there.
>
> In 1888, the prison was run by the notorious military commander General Prim, when the city fathers took the decision to demolish it and hold the city's first Universal Exhibition in the grounds. These were accordingly turned into the spacious park you see today—a happy change from the horrors of the past.

the Catalan national day), punished the province by outlawing the Catalan language, closing all universities, and building a citadel (on the site of the Ciutadella Park) to keep an eye on the rowdy population.

In 1808, during the Peninsula War, came a 5-year French occupation that covered the whole of Spain, after which the Spanish king **Ferdinand VII** was restored to the throne. Two decades later the first glimmerings of a Catalan renaissance appeared when the poet Carles Aribau published his highly romantic work *Oda a la Patria*. Between 1854 and 1859 the old city walls were demolished and Ildefonso Cerdá's plans for today's wide-laned Eixample were given the go-ahead. The new city was on its way, and no amount of civil unrest—strikes and anarchic demos prevailed during this politically unsettled period—could stop it.

The Renaixença & Modernism

Backed by a hardworking populace, Barcelona was the first Spanish city to embrace the Industrial Revolution. Textiles, with raw materials being brought in from the

1832	The Industrial Revolution begins in Barcelona with the first steam-driven factory.	1924	Dictatorship established by General Primo de Rivera; Catalan language banned.
1854–65	Old City walls torn down; work begins on the "new city", expansion called *L'Eixample.*	1929	Second International Exhibition held, on Montjuïc.
1873	First Spanish Republic established.	1931	Francesc Marcià negotiates autonomy for Catalonia during the Second Republic and declares himself president.
1888	First Universal Exposition in Barcelona held at *Parc de la Ciutadella.*		
1892–93	Collectives demand Catalan autonomy. Anarchist throws bomb in the Teatre Liceu Opera House.	1936–39	Spanish Civil War; ends with anarchist-occupied Barcelona taken by Franco's army.
		1960s	Package tourism boom takes off on Catalonia's Costa Brava.
1909	*Setmana Tràgica* (Tragic Week); anarchists go on anticlerical rampage in Barcelona.	1975	Franco dies; Juan Carlos becomes king.

New World, became big business, and the city gained a reputation as the "Manchester of the South." This new-found wealth led to the 19th-century *Renaixença* (Renaissance), a heady time of artistic and economic growth that returned Barcelona to its medieval heights of great prosperity.

Catalonia rejoiced in this resurgence in a variety of ways. It revived the Jocs Florals, a poetry competition celebrating the Catalan language, demolished the city walls, built L'Eixample (Catalan for "extension," or "new city"), and launched the landmark *moderniste* movement, in which Antoni Gaudí and his architectural contemporaries held sway. The **Universal Exhibition** of 1888, a showcase for the glories of the new, cashed-up Catalonia, drew over two million visitors. The Lliga de Catalunya, the province's first pro-independence political party, was founded.

Anarchist and communist groups were convening underground and acting out above ground; in 1893 a guerrilla extremist threw bombs into the audience at the Gran Teatre de Liceu, to the horror of the rest of Europe, creating widespread panic and disarray. As in most periods of rapid growth, the gap between rich and poor was becoming increasingly evident, and a subculture grew, planting the seeds of the city's reputation for excess, seediness, and political action.

In 1876, Spain became a constitutional monarchy. But labor unrest, disputes with the Catholic church, and war in Morocco combined to create further political chaos throughout the country. The political polarization of Barcelona and Madrid erupted in 1909. Furious that the national government had lost the colonies of Cuba and Puerto Rica (and therefore valuable trade) and was conscripting Catalans for an unwanted war in Morocco, rabble-rousers set fire to

1978	King Juan Carlos grants Catalonia autonomous rule; Catalan language restored.
1981	Coup attempt by right-wing officers fails; democracy prevails.
1982	Socialists gain power after 43 years of right-wing rule.
1986	Spain joins the European Community (now the European Union)
1992	Barcelona hosts the 25th Summer Olympic Games.
1998	Generalitat introduces "linguistic normalization" laws to strengthen Catalan as the region's primary language.

| 2004 | Spanish Prime Minister José Luis Zapatero officially requests that Catalan, along with Basque and Galician, be recognized as working languages of the E.U. |
| 2006 | A new *Estatut* (Statute) granting Catalonia additional autonomous powers is passed by the Spanish Socialist government. |

dozens of religious institutions in the city. Known as the Setmana Tràgica (Tragic Week), this period of rioting caused the deaths of over 100 people and injured many more. All suspected culprits, even some who had not been in Barcelona at the time, were executed.

The 20th Century: Republican Strife & Civil War

On April 14, 1931, a revolution occurred, the second Spanish Republic was proclaimed, and **King Alfonso XIII** (1886–1941) and his family were forced to flee the country. Initially, the liberal constitutionalists took control, but they were swiftly pushed aside by the socialists and anarchists. They adopted a constitution separating church and state, secularizing education, and containing several other radical provisions, including autonomous rule for Catalonia. In 1931, **Francesc Macià** (1859–1933) declared himself president of the Catalan republic.

But the extreme nature of these reforms fostered the growth of the conservative Falange party (*Falange española,* or "Spanish Phalanx"), modeled after Italy's and Germany's fascist parties. By the time of the 1936 elections, the country was split politically, with Catalonia firmly to the left. In Barcelona, attacks on bourgeois symbols (and people) and the occupation of public buildings by collectives were common. On July 18, 1936, the Spanish army, supported by Mussolini and Hitler, tried to seize power, igniting the **Spanish Civil War.** General **Francisco Franco** flew from Morocco to Spain in a tiny Dragon Rapide aircraft and led the Nationalist (rightist) forces in fighting that instantly ravaged the country. By October 1, Franco was clearly in charge of the leadership of nationalist Spain, abolishing popular suffrage and regional autonomy—in effect, establishing totalitarian rule. Over the next 3 years, Barcelona and the Catalan coast were bombed by German and Italian fighter planes, untold numbers of citizens were executed, and thousands fled across the Pyrénées into France. Then Franco's forces marched into Barcelona under the banner "Spain is here." The Catalan language and culture were once again forced underground, and Francesc Macià was sentenced to 30 years in prison.

Spurred on by even worse conditions in the south around Andalucia, where hunger and poverty were an everyday threat, millions of immigrants arrived in Barcelona in mid-century. The 1960s saw another economic boom, this time led by tourism, which grew into an important industry on the Costa Brava and Costa Daurada. Communists formed militant trade unions, and the working class was embittered by decades of repression.

Before his death in November 1975, General Franco selected as his successor Juan Carlos de Borbón y Borbón, son of the pretender to the Spanish throne. The electorate eagerly approved a new constitution and the king was crowned. This fledgling democracy guaranteed human and civil rights, as well as free enterprise, and ended the status of the Catholic church as the church of Spain. It also granted limited autonomy to several regions, including Catalonia and the Basque provinces. In 1980 the conservative **Convergènica i Unio** party, with **Jordi Pujol** (b. 1930) at the helm, was voted in, initiating a series of negotiations for greater self-rule that still continue today.

In 1981, a group of right-wing military officers seized the Cortés (parliament) in Madrid and called upon King Juan Carlos to establish a Francoist state. The king refused and the conspirators were arrested. The fledgling democracy had overcome its first test, and Catalonia's morale and optimism were boosted even further when the Socialists won the national elections a year later. Catalanista liberals, such as the Gauche Divine (Divine Left) party, dominated the city's counterculture for the rest of the decade, as engineers and town planners at the Socialist-led city hall prepared Barcelona for the 1992 Olympic Games and its new, modern era. In 1998 Catalan became the official language of education and the judiciary, with quotas imposed on the media, who had to present a proportion of news in Catalan. The following year more than 43,000 adults enrolled for free Catalan language courses supplied by the **Generalitat** (Catalan Regional Government).

The 21st Century

In 2003, after 20 years as head of the Generalitat, the conservative Jordi Pujol lost to Socialist **Pasqual Maragall,** who had served as mayor of Barcelona during the Olympic years. In coalition with the left-wing ERC (Esquerra Republicana de Catalunya, or Republican Left of Catalan) party, whose aim is *total* independence for Catalonia, Maragall has been accused of placing emotive issues of a nationalist nature before policymaking. But the fact remains that Catalonia contributes more to the central government's tax coffers than any other region—and receives less in paybacks. The following year, in 2004, the Spanish Socialist government in Madrid, led by the pragmatic José Luis Zapatero, gave the official seal of approval for Catalan to be a written and spoken language within the European Union, and in 2006 helped pass a new *estatut* (statute) granting the province more autonomy.

The region's eventual goal, however, is to have a totally self-governing Catalonia. In July 2010, the city staged its biggest demonstration yet in favor of declaring the province a fully fledged **nation,** independent of Spain. At least a million Catalans participated, flooding La Rambla, Plaça de Catalunya, and the Passeig de Gràcia.

And that same month saw the local parliament pass an historic bill banning all **bullfights** in the city and province from 2012 onwards. More and more, it seems, the Catalans are turning their back on the erstwhile dictatorial motherland and all things "Spanish." (See also "Animal-Rights Issues," chapter 3).

Nationalistic and provincial priorities apart, Barcelona—like many other European cities—is facing another quite different social issue. Today, immigrants make up 5% of the city's total population of just over four million, rocketing to 50% in some inner-Barcelona pockets. The government now recognizes the need to provide education for immigrants, emphasize religious and cultural tolerance, regulate the foreign workforce, and implement the immersion of Catalan language and culture, despite cries from the right that Catalan culture and language will be lost if Catalonia absorbs any more foreigners. Immigrants are essential, however, for the region's primary industry. South Americans and North Africans are now employed in the vast acres of vineyards, olive groves, and other agrarian pursuits that surround the city. Secondary industry sectors include chemical, car, and textile manufacturing, with a massive Internet and technology sector. Tourism employs a huge number of temporary workers during the summer, but unemployment currently hovers, as in the rest of the country, at around 5%.

BARCELONA'S ART & ARCHITECTURE

Barcelona's Art through the Ages

From the cave paintings discovered at Lleida to several true giants of the 20th century—**Picasso, Dalí,** and **Miró**—Catalonia has had a long and significant artistic tradition. Today it is the Spanish center of the plastic arts and design culture. One of Catalonia's leading 21st-century designers is Barcelona-born **Alfredo Arribas,** who has won a variety of international prizes. His work varies from creating striking bar and restaurant interiors to collaborating with Sir Norman Foster on innovative city piazzas in Germany.

The first art movement to attract attention in Barcelona was **Catalan Gothic sculpture,** in vogue from the 13th to the 15th centuries and producing such renowned masters as Mestre Bartomeu and Pere Johan. Sculptors working with Italian masters brought the Renaissance to Barcelona, but few great Catalonian legacies remain from this period. The rise of baroque art in the 17th and 18th centuries saw Catalonia filled with several impressive examples, but nothing worth a special pilgrimage; the great masters El Greco and Velázquez worked in Toledo and Madrid, respectively.

In the neoclassical period of the 18th century, Catalonia—and particularly Barcelona—arose from an artistic slumber. Art schools opened and foreign painters arrived, exerting considerable influence. The 19th century produced many Catalan artists who followed general European trends without forging any major creative breakthroughs.

The 20th century brought renewed artistic ferment to Barcelona, as reflected by the arrival of Málaga-born **Pablo Picasso**—Barcelona is today the site of a major Picasso museum (p. 169). The great surrealist painters of the Spanish school, **Joan Miró** (who also has an eponymous museum in Barcelona) and **Salvador Dalí** (whose fantastical museum is along the Costa Brava, north of Barcelona), also came to the Catalan capital.

Many Catalan sculptors achieved acclaim in the 20th century, including Enric Casanovas, Josep Llimona, and Miquel Blay. The Spanish Civil War brought cultural stagnation, yet against all odds many Catalan artists continued to make bold statements. **Antoni Tàpies** was one of the principal artists of this period (the Fundació Tàpies in Barcelona is devoted to his work). Among the various schools formed in Spain at the time was the **neo-figurative band,** which included such artists as Vásquez Díaz and Pancho Cossio. The Museum of Modern Art in the neighborhood of El Raval (p. 172) illustrates the various 20th-century Catalan artistic movements, including the Dau al Set, the surrealist movement started in the 1940s by the "visual poet" Joan Brossa. His art

> ### Picasso & *Les Demoiselles*
>
> Biographers of the 20th century's greatest artist, Spanish-born Pablo Picasso, claim that the artist was inspired to paint one of his masterpieces, *Les Demoiselles d'Avignon,* after a "glorious night" spent in a notorious bordello on Barcelona's Carrer D'Avinyó.

and many other works by leading sculptors dot the streets of Barcelona, making it a vibrant outdoor museum. Watch out for Roy Lichtenstein's *Barcelona Head* opposite the main post office in the Plaça d'Antoni López, Joan Miró's phallic *Dona i Ocell* in the park of the same name, and Fernando Botero's giant cat on the Rambla del Raval.

Today many Barcelona artists are making major names for themselves, and their works are sold in the most prestigious galleries of the Western world. Outstanding among these is sculptor **Susana Solano,** who ranks among the most renowned names in Spanish contemporary art, and the neo-expressionist Miguel Barceló. Design and the graphic arts have thrived in Barcelona since the heady days of *modernisme*. It seems that nothing in Barcelona, from a park bench to a mailbox, escapes the "designer touch." Leading names include the architect and interior designer Oscar Tusquets, and the quirky graphic artist Javier Mariscal, whose work can be seen in many of the city's designer houseware stores. The most important plastic-arts schools in Spain are located in Barcelona, and the city acts as a magnet for young European creatives who flock here to set up shop.

Barcelona's Architecture

Like many other cities in Spain, Barcelona claims its share of Neolithic dolmens and ruins from the later Roman periods. Relics of the Roman colony of Barcino can be seen beneath the Conjunt Monumental de la Plaça del Rei (and more are being found all the time), as can monuments surviving from the Middle Ages, when the Romanesque solidity of no-nonsense barrel vaults, narrow windows, and fortified design were widely used.

In the 11th and 12th centuries, religious fervor swept through Europe, and pilgrims began to flock to Barcelona on their way west to Santiago de Compostela, bringing with them French building styles and the need for new and larger churches. The style that emerged, called Catalan Gothic, had harsher lines and more austere ornamentation than traditional Gothic. Appropriate for both civic and religious buildings, it used massive *ogival* (pointed) vaults, heavy columns, gigantic sheets of sheer stone, clifflike walls, and vast rose windows set with colored glass.

One of Barcelona's purest and most-loved examples of this style is the **Basilica of Santa María del Mar** (p. 207), northeast of the city's harbor. Built over 54 years, it is the purest example of Catalan Gothic in the city. Other examples include the Church of Santa María del Pi, the Saló del Tinell (part of the Museu de la Ciutat), and, of course, the mesmerizing Barri Gòtic itself. The Barri Gòtic (Gothic Quarter) forms the central part of the Ciutat Vella (Old City) and is the largest, best-preserved medieval urban district in Europe.

In 1858 the expansion of Barcelona into the northern **Eixample** district provided a blank canvas for *moderniste* architects. The gridlike pattern of streets was intersected by broad diagonals. Although it was never endowed with the more radical details of its original design, it provided a carefully planned, elegant path in which a growing city could showcase its finest buildings. Today L'Eixample boasts the highest concentration of *moderniste* architecture in the world.

Modernisme is a confusing term, as "modernism" generally denotes 20th-century functionality. It is best known as Art Nouveau, a movement that took hold of Europe in the late 1800s in the arts. In Barcelona, it shone in the city's architecture, and its shining star was **Antoni Gaudí.**

The *modernistes* were obsessed with detail. They hailed the past in their architectural forms (from Arabic to Catalan Gothic) and then sublimely sprinkled them with nature-inspired features employing iron, glass, and florid ceramic motif, all of which are seen in dazzling abundance in the city. Other *moderniste* giants were **Domènech i Montaner** and **Puig i Cadafalch,** whose elegant mansions and concert halls were perfectly suited to the enlightened, sophisticated prosperity of the 19th-century Catalonian bourgeoisie. An economic boom coincided with the profusion of geniuses who emerged in the building business. Entrepreneurs made their fortunes in the fields and mines of the New World and went on to commission some of the beautiful and elaborate villas in Barcelona and nearby Sitges. There were also lesser-known designers, such as **Pere Falqués,** whose wrought-iron lampposts line parts of the Passeig de Gràcia, and **José María Jujol i Gibert,** responsible for the beautiful *trencadis* (colorful broken mosaic patterns) that adorn Parc Güell.

Consistent with the general artistic stagnation in Spain during the Franco era (1939–75), the 1950s and 1960s saw a tremendous increase in the number of anonymous housing projects around the periphery of Barcelona and, in the inner city, eyesore-ridden decay. But as the last tears were being shed over the death of General Franco elsewhere in the country, Barcelona's left-wing intelligentsia were envisioning how to regenerate their city after decades of physical degradation under the dictator.

When Barcelona won its bid to host the Summer Olympic Games in 1992, work on their vision of "New Barcelona" accelerated. City planners made possible the creation of smart new urban beaches, a glitzy port and marina, traffic-reducing ring roads, daring public sculptures and parks, plus promenades and squares weaving through the Old City. The area has successfully evolved thanks to planners dividing it into small zones and developing each of them so cleverly that they blend into a seamlessly united whole.

The objective was to rejuvenate the *barri,* the distinct village-neighborhoods of Barcelona that denote income or political stance (sometimes even the language or the soccer team) and make up the city's peculiar territoriality. This radical and ingenious approach did not go unnoticed by the rest of the world. In 1999 the Royal Institute of British Architects presented Barcelona's city council with their Gold Medal, the first time a city (as opposed to an architect, such as previous winners Le Corbusier and Frank Lloyd Wright) had received the accolade. Barcelona is now used as a model across Europe for town planners wishing to overhaul their own downtrodden cities.

Over 15 years after the city's Olympic Year, the physical face of Barcelona is still changing in leaps and bounds. With an engaged local government still at the helm, broad swaths of industrial wasteland have been reclaimed north of the city for parkland, a new marina, and the emergence of dot-com areas such as 22@Barcelona and ritzy residential neighborhoods. A new city nucleus in the north has been created around the new AVE high-speed train terminal that links Madrid to Barcelona in a 3-hour journey. Still a city that's not afraid to take risks with its architecture, Barcelona's skyline has been enhanced by French architect Jean Nouvel's daring and

MY place IS HERE, WITH THE POOR

June 7, 1926, started much as any other day in the life of the architect **Antoni Gaudí i Cornet.** Leaving his humble studio at his work in progress, the Temple of the Sagrada Família, the old man shuffled through the Eixample district with the help of his cane, on his way to evening vespers. He did not hear the bells of the no. 30 tram as it came pelting down the Gran Vía. While waiting for an ambulance, people searched the pockets of his threadbare suit for some clue as to his identity but none was to be found. The great architect was mistaken for a vagrant and taken to the nearby public hospital of Santa Creu.

For the next 3 days, Gaudí lay in agony. Apart from occasionally opening his mouth to utter the words, "Jesus, my God!" his only other communication was to protest a suggestion that he be moved to a private clinic. "My place is here, with the poor," he is reported to have said.

Gaudí was born in 1852 in the rural township of Reus. The son of a metalworker, he spent long hours studying the forms of flora, fauna, and topography of the typically Mediterranean agrarian terrain. "Nature is a great book, always open, that we should make ourselves read," he once said. As well as using organic forms for his lavish decorations (over 30 species of plant are seen on the famous Nativity Facade of the Sagrada Família), he was captivated by the structure of plants and trees. As far as he was concerned, there was no shape or form that could be devised on an architect's drawing table that did not already exist in nature. "All styles are organisms related to nature," he claimed.

Apart from Mother Nature, Gaudí's two other guiding lights were religion and Catalan nationalism. When the *moderniste* movement was in full swing, architects such as Luis Domènech i Montaner and Josep Puig i Cadafalch were designing buildings and taking florid decoration and detail to the point of delirium. Gaudí, in the latter half of his life, disapproved of their excess and their capricious, outward-reaching (that is, European) notions. He even formed a counterculture, the Artistic Circle of Saint Luke, a collective of pious creatives with a love of God and the fatherland equal to his own.

He never married and was close to 50 when he moved into a house in the Parc Güell, the planned "garden city" above Barcelona, with his ailing niece and his housekeeper. After they both died, his dietary habits, always seen as somewhat eccentric by the carnivorous Catalans (Gaudí was a strict vegetarian), became so erratic that the Carmelite nuns who lived in the park made sure he was properly nourished. His appearance took on a bizarre twist; he let his beard and hair grow for months, forgot to put on underwear, and wore old slippers both indoors and out.

What became apparent by the end of his life was that Gaudí was one of the greatest architects the world has known, whose revolutionary techniques are still the subject of theory and investigation and whose vision was an inspiration for some of today's top architects, including Spain's own Santiago Calatrava, designer of Montjuïc's Torre de Comunicaciones. In 2002, **Año Gaudí** (the year of Gaudí), the celebration of the 150th anniversary of his birth, saw an equal number of tourists flock to Barcelona as Paris for the first time ever. At the time of writing it was hoped that 2010 would see the completion of the Sagrada Família's roof. Expect even greater crowds if Sagrada Família is finally completed, as predicted, for the centenary of Gaudí's death in 2026.

controversial **Torre Agbar** in the outer suburb of Glòries, which has become the towering symbol of a city embracing the future with bravado.

The inventiveness continues unabated, although some modern projects have been temporarily held up for economic reasons. These include Norman Foster's ambitious plan to remodel and expand the city's **Camp Nou** soccer stadium, and Anglo-Iraqi Zaha Hadid's steel and glass **Torre Espiral** (Spiral Tower), which is aimed to dominate the coastline just north of the city. Both are tentatively expected to be given the green light by 2011.

BARCELONA IN POPULAR CULTURE

Literature

NON-FICTION For a first-hand account of the Spanish Civil War and its devastating effects on Barcelona and Catalonia, George Orwell's *Homage to Catalonia* remains a classic. Irish writer Colm Tóibín takes a more lighthearted look at post-Orwell Barcelona, with plenty of anecdotes and colors through the eyes of a *güiri* (foreigner) in *Homage to Barcelona*.

Palafrugell-based writer **Josep Pla** produced a number of first-rate travel books on the whole region, but his masterpiece is generally acknowledged to be the *Cuadern Gris*, about his experiences as a very young man launching a local newspaper and dividing life and work between his hometown and Barcelona in the 1920s. *Twelve Walks Through Barcelona's Past* by James Amelang covers a dozen hikes with historical themes and is a good companion to chapter 8, "Strolling Around Barcelona."

Strictly for soccer enthusiasts, *Barça: A People's Passion,* by Jimmy Burns, is a dramatic history of the city's much-loved soccer team, the richest and possibly most politically charged soccer club in the world. Fans will also love the newly published *Barça, the Year of Living Gloriously* by sports enthusiast David Ross.

Barcelona by art critic Robert Hughes is a well-versed and witty articulation of the city's architectural and cultural legacy. According to the *New York Times,* the book is probably destined to become "a classic in the genre of urban history." To prepare for a visit to Barcelona's Museu Picasso, read *Picasso, Creator and Destroyer* by Arianna Stassinopoulos Huffington and *Picasso: A Biography* by Patrick O'Brian, which is the most comprehensive examination yet of the artist and his work.

In *Salvador Dalí: A Biography*, author Meryle Secrest asks: Was he a mad genius or a cunning manipulator? Spanish resident-chronicler Ian Gibson scrutinized Dalí from a racier angle in his book, *The Shameful Life of Salvador Dalí*. In *Gaudí: A Biography,* by Gijs van Hensbergen, the author claims that Gaudí was "drunk on form," and that the architect still has not lost his power to astonish with his idiosyncratic and innovative designs.

FICTION An important classic novel is Joanot Martorell's *Tirant lo Blanc,* the Catalan language's lesser-known 15th-century equivalent of *Don Quijote,* a knights-and-fair-damsels saga.

For a realistic account of what it was like to grow up in the austere days of post–Civil War Barcelona, read *La Plaça del Diamant* (Diamond Square) by Merce

Rodoreda, set in the formerly working-class and now trendy area of Gràcia, and *Nada* by Carmen Laforet, which describes the hardships of growing up in a tyrannical household in L'Eixample.

Eduardo Mendoza's *The City of Marvels* tells a rags-to-riches story of a young farmer who arrives in Barcelona at the time of the 1888 Universal Exhibition and becomes one of the city's richest and most influential businessmen. Juan Marsé's *Shanghai Nights*, in contrast, depicts the disillusioned existences of failed anarchists after the Civil War in the grittier corners of Barcelona and Toulouse, and of their children who dream of a more glamorous world in an imaginary Shanghai.

The city's most prolific writer, poet, and essayist was **Manuel Vázquez Montalbán,** who died in 2003. He wrote *The Angst-Ridden Executive, Murder in the Central Committee,* and other popular works featuring the food-loving Barcelonan private eye Pepe Carvalho. In between describing Calvalho's unorthodox methods of solving his fictional cases, Vázquez Montalbán inserts an enticing number of (real-life) gourmet spots that make the reader's mouth water. Vázquez Montalbán also wrote *Barcelonas,* an in-depth insider guidebook that combines lively accounts of Catalan history, character, and culture with scathing wit and insight.

One of the most recent portraits of the city is *A Short History of Sant Cugat* by local English resident Michael Costello. It recounts (in just 90 pages) the story of one of Barcelona's most attractive suburbs, Sant Cugat del Vallès, a 20-minute train ride from the city center.

Film

Many film directors have been enamored with Barcelona, and as a result the city plays a major role in several films. *Barcelona* (1994), directed by American Whit Stillman, is based on the director's own experiences in the city during the final stages of the Cold War. Susan Seidelman's mystery-comedy *Gaudí Afternoons* (2001) made less of an impact, in spite of some more colorful location work around the city and a star cast, including Marcia Gay Harden and Juliette Lewis.

All About My Mother (1999), an Oscar-winning film directed by Pedro Almodóvar, set many scenes in a surrealistically marginal Barcelona, which was in reality the seedy Camp Nou area. A recent film in which the city virtually plays a main character is Woody Allen's *Vicky Cristina Barcelona* (2008), featuring Scarlett Johansson, Penélope Cruz, and Javier Bardem (Cruz and Bardem are now married); this film depicts a highly romanticized version of the city.

Taking a polar opposite view of the city, but again starring the chameleon-like Bardem, is *Biudiful* (2010), directed by the no-holds-barred Mexican Alejandro González Iñárritu of *Amores Perros, 21 Grams,* and *Babel* fame. This movie depicts the seedy underbelly of the Catalan capital with the director's familiar gritty realism, focusing on a sub-world of petty criminals and drug pushers. Funded by the Barcelona Tourist Board it is not, but as a movie on a distinctly minority section of the population it rings a far truer note than Woody Allen's rose-tinted-specs tale.

The picturesque Costa Brava has also found its place in film history. British heart-throb James Mason and screen goddess Ava Gardner starred in *Pandora and the Flying Dutchman* (1951), which was filmed along the Costa Brava, focusing on Tossa de Mar (see p. 257 in chapter 11, "Side Trips In Catalonia"). *Los Pianos Mecánicos* (1965) recounts the intrigues and affairs of a small idyllic Spanish village.

It was filmed in Cadaqués (known in the movie as Caldeya) by Spanish director J. A. Bardem (the ubiquitous Javier's uncle), and several colorful scenes were also shot in Barcelona.

Catalan Music

The two most famous Catalan **composers** of the late 19th and early 20th centuries were Camprodón-born **Isaac Albéniz**—a child prodigy who played in piano concerts at the age of four—who is known for his *Iberia* suite, and **Enrique Granados** from Lleida, who is best known for the lively *Goyescas*. **Federico Mompou** was an unassuming composer whose works include *Charmes* and *Impressions Intimes*.

The region's greatest creator of operas was the 19th-century composer **Felipe Pedrell;** his two prime achievements, *Los Pirineos* and *La Celestina*, are occasionally performed in the Palau de la Música. Barcelona's leading **opera singer** is **Josep Carreras,** who successfully survived leukemia in the late 1980s to become, alongside Placido Domingo, one of Spain's greatest tenors.

Pablo (Pau) Casals was one of Spain's most talented cellists before his death in 1973. You can visit his house-museum at El Vendrell near Tarragona (see p. 257 in chapter 11, "Side Trips In Catalonia"). **Joan Manuel Serrat** is the region's most noted *cantautor* (singer-songwriter), and a champion for the region's rights. He sings many of his songs in Catalan.

One of Catalonia's most successful pop singers is Sabadell-born **Sergio Dalma,** who sings in Spanish and Castilian. His upbeat 2008 album "A Buena Hora" won him a platinum disc.

EATING & DRINKING IN BARCELONA

Eating is an extremely important social activity in Catalonia. Eating out remains a major pastime, whether in the evening with friends, at lunch in a local bar with colleagues, or with the traditional Sunday family feast. Although Barcelona is a fast-paced city, mealtimes, especially lunchtime, are still respected, with the whole city shifting into low gear between the hours of 2 and 4pm. Many people either head home or crowd into a local eatery for a three-course *menú del día* (lunch of the day).

Catalan grub is quite different from the food of the rest of the Spain. In Barcelona, the mainstay diet is typically Mediterranean, with an abundance of fish, legumes, and vegetables, the latter often served simply boiled with a drizzle of olive oil. Pork, in all its forms, is widely eaten, whether as grilled filets, the famous Serrano ham, or delicious *embutidos* (cold cuts) from inland Catalonia. Another local characteristic is the lack of tapas bars. Very good ones do exist but not in the same abundance as in the rest of Spain. Instead Catalans tend to go for *raciones* (plates of cheese, pâtés, and cured meats) if they want something to pick at.

Many restaurants in Barcelona close on Sunday and Monday, so check ahead of time before heading out. Hotel dining rooms are generally open 7 days a week, and there's always something open in the touristy areas. If you really want to get a true taste of Catalan cuisine, stay away from places in La Rambla and check chapter 6, "Where To Dine," or ask your hotel concierge for recommendations. Dining in

Though foodie frontiers in the city are not absolute, there are certain areas that are known for certain types of food. The heart of the Barri Gòtic quarter is, for example, one of the best spots to sample good old-fashioned **Catalan cooking** (as at **Can Culleretes;** p. 126), while Barceloneta is an unrivaled location for gorging on Mediterranean **seafood.** In sophisticated L'Eixample, the food is as richly inventive and innovative as the *moderniste* architecture it touts. Eat lunch at a key spot like **Gaig** (p. 142) and you'll get the picture. Also don't miss L'Eixample's elegant **Toc** (p. 145), which offers the classiest traditional *escalivadas* (grilled peppers and egg-plants/aubergines marinated in olive oil) and *esqueixadas* (shredded salt cod salad) in town.

In polyglot El Raval you'll not only find cheap and cheerful Middle Eastern, Mexican, and Filipino joints, but also some stunningly stylish **Mediterranean "fusion"** establishments (check out the delectable **Lupino,** p. 136). Although Barcelona is not traditionally known for its tapas, you'll find some highly imaginative versions all over, but especially in a chic La Ribera bar like **Comerç 24** (p. 133) and in the delectable **Mam i Teca,** back in El Raval (p. 136).

You can find excellent country cooking without heading out into the lovely Catalan countryside in the **Pedralbes** district, where, high above the city beside a serenely beautiful monastery, the homely **Matóde Pedralbes** (p. 148) offers rustic *venta* (country inn) style dishes such as *anclas de ranas* (frog's legs) and *cargols a la llauna* (snails). If seafood takes your fancy (and where better to enjoy it than beside the Med?) then **Barceloneta's Mondo** and **Lluçanes** are just two of the newer incentives among the veritable sea of *marisquerías* and *tabernas* that fill this uniquely nautical quarter.

The traditional covered markets are a must-see for foodies. They were built in the city's *moderniste* heyday and are worth visiting as historic monuments as much as exotic food emporiums. Top markets are the famed **Boqueria, Santa Caterina, Sant Antoni,** and **Barceloneta.** Feast your eyes on their curving arches and high ceilings before savoring the colorful cornucopia of local produce filling the stalls.

Barcelona can range from memorable to miserable (or memorable for all the wrong reasons!), so it pays to do a bit of research. If possible, always book ahead for reputable restaurants, especially on the weekends.

BREAKFAST In Catalonia, as in the rest of Spain, the day starts with a light continental breakfast, often in a bar. Most Spaniards have coffee, usually strong, served with hot milk—either a *cafe con leche* (half coffee, half milk) or a *cortado* (a shot of espresso "cut" with a dash of milk). If you find these too strong or bitter for your taste, ask for a more diluted *cafe americano*. Most people just have a croissant (*cruasan*), doughnut, or *ensaimada* (a light, sugar-sprinkled pastry). If you want something more substantial, ask for a *bocadillo* (roll) with cheese or grilled meat or cold cuts, or ask to see the list of *platos combinados* (combination plates). These consist of a fried egg, french fries, bacon, and a steak or a hamburger. A *bikini* is an old-fashioned toasted ham-and-cheese sandwich.

Barcelona for Foodies

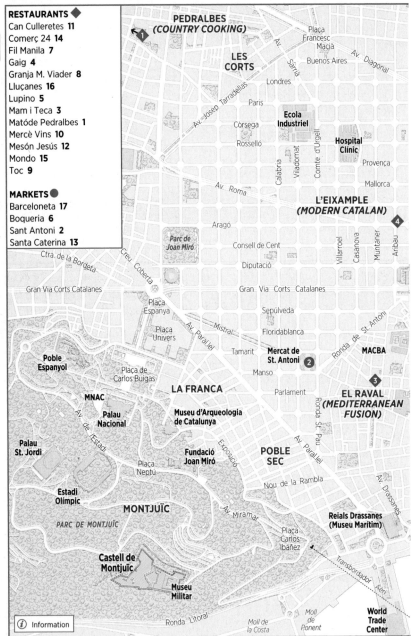

RESTAURANTS ◆
Can Culleretes **11**
Comerç 24 **14**
Fil Manila **7**
Gaig **4**
Granja M. Viader **8**
Lluçanes **16**
Lupino **5**
Mam i Teca **3**
Matóde Pedralbes **1**
Mercè Vins **10**
Mesón Jesús **12**
Mondo **15**
Toc **9**

MARKETS ●
Barceloneta **17**
Boqueria **6**
Sant Antoni **2**
Santa Caterina **13**

PEDRALBES
(COUNTRY COOKING)

Plaça
Francesc
Macià
Av. Diagonal
Buenos Aires

LES
CORTS

Londres

Av. Josep Tarradellas

Paris

Còrsega

Ecola
Industriel

Rosselló

Hospital
Clínic

Provença

Mallorca

Av. Roma

L'EIXAMPLE
(MODERN CATALAN)

Aragó

Parc de
Joan Miró

Consell de Cent

Diputació

Ctra. de la Bordeta

Creu Coberta

Gran Via Corts Catalanes

Gran Via Corts Catalanes

Plaça
Espanya

Av. Paral·lel

Mistral

Sepúlveda

Floridablanca

Plaça
Univers

Tamarit

Mercat de
St. Antoni

MACBA

Poble
Espanyol

Plaça de
Carlos Buigas

Manso

LA FRANCA

Parlament

EL RAVAL
*(MEDITERRANEAN
FUSION)*

MNAC

Palau
Nacional

Museu d'Arqueologia
de Catalunya

Av. de l'Estadi

Ronda St. Pau

Palau
St. Jordi

Fundació
Joan Miró

Plaça
Neptú

Exposició

POBLE
SEC

Av. Paral·lel

Estadi
Olímpic

MONTJUÏC

Nou de la Rambla

Av. Drassanes

PARC DE MONTJUÏC

Av. Miramar

Castell de
Montjuïc

Plaça
Carlos
Ibáñez

Reials Drassanes
(Museu Marítim)

Transbordador Aeri

Museu
Militar

Ronda Litoral

Moll de
la Costa

Moll
de
Ponent

World
Trade
Center

ⓘ Information

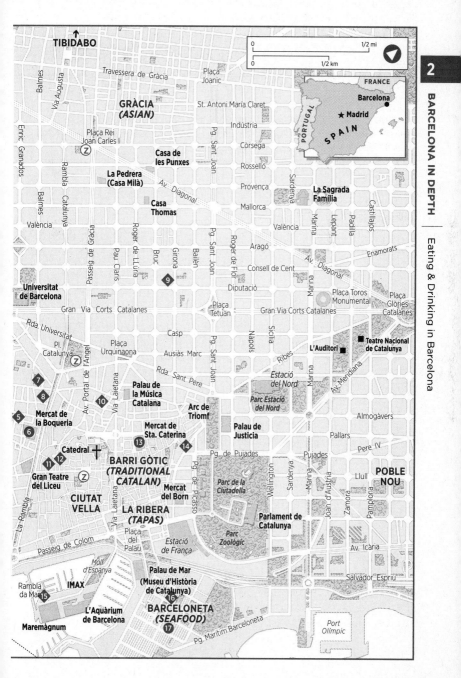

LUNCH This is the most important meal of the day in Barcelona. Lunch usually includes three or four courses, although some smart eateries in the Old City are now offering one course with dessert for lighter eaters. It begins with a choice of soup, salad, or vegetables. Then follows the meat, chicken, or fish dish, simply grilled or in a rich stew or casserole. At some point, meat eaters should definitely try *botifarras,* the locally made sausages. Desserts are (thankfully) light: Fruit, yogurt, or a *crema catalana* (crème brûlée). Wine and bread are always part of the meal. Lunch is served from 1:30 to 4pm, with "rush hour" at 2pm.

DINNER If you had a heavy or late lunch, you may want to go for tapas or a few *raciones* in a wine bar; this is the perfect time to try the quintessential Catalan snack *pa amb tomàquet* (rustic bread rubbed with olive oil and tomato pulp, served with cheese, pâté, or cold cuts). If you choose a restaurant, expect a slightly finer version of what you had at lunch but with a larger bill, as the set-menu deal is a lunchtime-only thing. The chic dining hour is 10 or 10:30pm. In touristy areas and hardworking Catalonia, you can dine at 8pm, but you may find yourself alone in the restaurant.

What to Eat

As well as producing many dishes that are uniquely its own, Barcelona looks toward France and central Spain for some of its culinary inspiration. Its *bullabesa* (bouillabaisse), *cargols* (snails), and *anclas de ranas* (frog's legs) are clearly Gallic-influenced, while a classic stew like *escudella i carn d'olla*—viewed by singer-songwriter Lluis Llach as "reflecting all the wisdom of Catalan people"—is really a blend of the French *pot au feu* and Madrileño *cocido,* and the ubiquitous *lechona* (suckling pig) is an import from central Castile. In countryside inns (or *ventas*) you'll often find game like hare and pheasant, which again show influences from the rest of Spain.

But the real traditional cuisine throughout Barcelona and its inland areas is rather like the inhabitants: Solid and gutsy. Meaty dishes such as veal and blood sausage are accompanied by hearty *garbanzos* (chickpeas), *lentejas* (lentils), *mongetes* (white beans), or *judias blancas y negras* (white- and black-eyed beans). And the traditional fishy paella of southerly neighbor Valencia is often transformed into noodle-based *fideuà* containing rabbit, chicken, and rich regional *botifarra* sausage.

Since Barcelona is right beside the Mediterranean, conventional seafood and rice paellas also abound. The long Catalan coast shelters over 30 fishing ports and fish is a supreme passion with local gourmets; the choice highly varied. A popular local dish is *suquet de peix,* a rich fish-and-potato stew that was once a favorite breakfast of fishermen who'd been out on the water with their nets all night. Another master-piece is *zarzuela,* a stew that combines an extraordinarily wide range of Mediterra-nean fish, from *salmonetes* (red mullet) and *besugo* (bream) to *mejillones* (mussels) and *gambas* (prawns). *Sardinas* (sardines) are particularly scrumptious—and inex-pensive—when grilled over a pine-wood fire. Squid, octopus, and *sepia* (cuttlefish) feature heavily, from *calamares romana* (deep-fried squid) to *chipirones* (bite-size baby octopus, also fried) to squid cooked in its own ink. Basque-style *bacallà* (salted cod), originating from chillier Northern Atlantic waters, is another favorite, whether it's simply baked (*a la llauna*) or forms the base of a cold garlicky hors d'oeuvre called *esqueixada.* (Don't confuse this, by the way, with the similar-sounding *escalivada,*

Frommer's Favorite Local Spots

Mercè Vins (Calle Amargos 1; $\mathcal{C}$ 93-302-60-56) is a colorful little spot that is essentially a breakfast bar serving great coffee and huge *ensaimadas* (cholesterol-charged Majorcan buns). It's especially good for bargain set lunches (8.50€) that may include generous salads, *sopa de calabaza* (pumpkin soup), and *longaniza picante* (spicy local sausage). Its *coups de grâce* are the criminally rich sweets (try the chocolate flan or rich fig pudding).

Don't be put off by the cutesy faux-rustic decor that features pitchforks, wagon wheels, and gingham tablecloths at **Mesón Jesús** (Cecs de la Boqueria 4; $\mathcal{C}$ 93-317-46-98). The staff is so friendly and the delicious, simple food is so cheap that it's a must. Try the bargain *gambas* (prawns) or *suquet* (fish stew) and we guarantee you'll be back.

A favorite with all the family is the 80-year-old Catalan cafe-creamery **Granja M. Viader** (Xucla 46; $\mathcal{C}$ 93-318-34-86; www.granjaviader.cat), set in a former farmhouse dating from the days when Raval was surrounded by fields. Its specialties range from milk shakes and *horchatas* (a rice and almond drink flavored with cinnamon) to chocolate drinks, accompanied by rich pastries and cakes.

If huge menus don't terrify you, head for **Fil Manila** (Carrer Ramelleres 2; $\mathcal{C}$ 93-318-64-87), a nifty Philippine-run spot in the heart of multiethnic Raval. When you are tired of reading the menu, just stab your finger at random and trust luck. You're unlikely to go wrong and could end up with anything from sour fish soup to pork with noodles, all good and inexpensive.

which consists of strips of chargrilled sweet peppers and eggplant/ aubergine, and is also served cold.)

Catalans are particularly inventive with their tortillas (egg, not corn variety), and these can include white beans, asparagus, and garlic shoots, often served with *pa amb tomàquet,* that Catalan gem of simplicity consisting of bread, garlic, crushed tomato, and generously applied olive oil. (Some of Spain's very best oil comes from Catalonia's Lleida province.) A pungent white sauce that adds an extra dimension to any meal is *alioli,* made from garlic, salt, and mayonnaise.

Vegetables are not common accompaniments to main courses, but an *ensalada catalana*—a salad of lettuce, tomato, onions, and olives—is invariably available, with the added bonus of local cold cuts like *mortadella* or mountain ham. Vegetarians and vegans should always check that no meat is included in what appears to be a vegetable dish or salad on the menu. Desserts are more modest and include the nifty milk-and-egg-based flan (caramel custard) and *crema catalana* (crème brûlée). Probably the best local cheese-based dessert is *mel i mató* (*mel* is honey and *mató* a very soft goat's cheese almost resembling yogurt: Quite delicious). Another popular creamy goat's cheese is *garrotxa,* which comes from inland Catalunya; while a more conventional dry tangy goat's cheese is *serrat* from the Pyrénées.

What to Drink

Catalan wines, though less world-renowned than the northerly Riojas, are in fact among Spain's best—particularly in the southerly Penedès wine region where enologist Miguel Torres produces rich Corona reds and Viña Sol whites. Penedès also accounts for about 75% of all the *cava* (sparkling wine) made in Spain, and the infinitely different varieties range from small family-made "garage" bodega wines to international brands like Freixenet and Codorníu, produced in *cava* capital Sant Sadurni d'Anoia. Codorníu is housed in a spectacular *moderniste* building that is part of the Spanish heritage trust, with 15km (9⅓ miles) of underground tunnels to explore while you learn about the *cava*-making process.

The jewel in Catalonia's winemaking crown, however, is Tarragona province's deep, dark red—and impressively expensive—Priorat. Its most notable promoter was Carles Pastrana of Clos L'Obac, who set about establishing a set of D.O. (*denominación de origen*) standard rules and regulations.

The famed *sangria*, a red-wine punch that combines wine with oranges, lemons, *gaseosa* (seltzer), and sugar, was originally conceived as a refreshing summer drink blending cheap wine with *gaseosa* or lemonade, though today's spirit- and additive-boosted touristy versions tend to be artificially stronger, so take care.

If you prefer something lighter, there's lager-like San Miguel *cerveza* (beer), which, though originally from the Philippines, has been produced for decades in inland Lleida. This is by far the province's most popular beer. All beer tends to be lighter, more like the U.S. version than the British. A *clara* is a glass of beer mixed with lemon soda. A small bottle of beer is called a *mediana,* and a glass is a *caña.*

Although water is safe to drink, many find the taste of Barcelona's tap water unpleasant. Mineral water, in bottles of .5 to 5 liters, is available everywhere. Bubbly water is *agua con gas;* noncarbonated is *agua sin gas.* Vichy Catalan, salty carbonated water that many people believe acts as a digestive aid, is very popular. Soft drinks are also popular, and standard, nationally produced versions of cola are widely available.

The coffee you have with your breakfast or after your meal is invariably first-class, rich, and strong, and if you've waded through a particularly large lunch or dinner, a *carajillo,* coffee containing a dash of cognac (Catalonia's top cognac brand is Mascaró), will either finish you off or help it go down.

PLANNING
YOUR TRIP TO
BARCELONA

The delights of a visit to Barcelona, with its glorious architecture and enviable seaside setting, are made easy for visitors to experience, despite its three million inhabitants, sometimes humid climate, congested streets, and inevitable rush-hour traffic jams. You don't need to bother with the hassle of arranging visas before you set off, and once you arrive, there's an abundance of helpful *oficinas de turismo* (tourist information offices) to ensure you're briefed on what to see and do.

A very good local transportation system includes buses, the Metro (subway), *tramvías* (the new, streamlined trams), and *rodalíes* (suburban train services); plus the cost of travel is extremely low—particularly if you purchase the 10-tickets-in-one deal (p. 45) available on all transport. Additionally, there is an ever-increasing number of amenities for travelers with disabilities.

The benign Mediterranean climate ensures Barcelona is rarely uncomfortably cold, even in winter. Summers can be hot and humid, though, and this may restrict mobility for older visitors when they're touring the sights. But you can always take a break and relish verdant shady areas like Parc de la Ciutadella, Montjuïc, and Tibidabo, which have panoramic Mediterranean and city vistas.

Violent **crime** is fairly uncommon, but you should definitely watch out for potential bag snatchers and muggers in the narrow lanes around La Rambla and around the Plaça Reial—especially late at night.

If you take your laptop you'll find a choice of places where you can connect to the **Internet.** Most of the more expensive hotels are equipped with Wi-Fi, and there are plenty of cybercafes throughout the city. For additional help in planning your trip and for more on-the-ground resources in Barcelona, please turn to chapter 13, "Fast Facts."

WHEN TO GO

Climate

Barcelona is blessed with a benign Mediterranean climate. Early summer and fall are ideal times to visit, especially May to June and September to October. Even in the winter, days are crisp to cold (due to its proximity to the mountains) but often sunny. Snow is rare and never lasts more than a day or two.

Most of the rainfall occurs in April, but some quite spectacular storms, as is typical of the Mediterranean, can occur all year round. July and August are hot and humid, even at night, as the temperature often only drops minimally. The surrounding sea is warm enough to swim in from the end of June to early October. Inland, the temperatures drop slightly, as does the humidity. North on the Costa Brava, a strong wind known as the *tramontana* often blows, refreshing in summer, chill in winter.

August is the major vacation month in Europe. The traffic to Spain from France, the Netherlands, and Germany becomes a veritable migration, and low-cost hotels along the coastal areas are virtually impossible to find unless booked well in advance. To compound the problem, many restaurants and shops also decide it's time for a vacation, thereby limiting the visitors' selections for both dining and shopping.

That said, Barcelonans also head out of town for cooler climes, leaving tourists to enjoy the city for themselves. Barcelona is also a major international trade fair and conference destination. These happen throughout the year, so if you plan to stay in a mid- to high-range hotel book ahead of time. In fact, Barcelona is officially Spain's most popular destination, so tourism is pretty much all year round.

Barcelona's Average Daytime Temperatures & Rainfall

	JAN	FEB	MAR	APR	MAY	JUNE	JULY	AUG	SEPT	OCT	NOV	DEC
Temp. (°F)	48	49	52	55	61	68	73	73	70	63	55	50
Temp. (°C)	9	9	11	13	16	20	23	23	21	17	13	10
Rainfall (in.)	1.7	1.4	1.9	2	2.2	1.5	.9	1.6	3.1	3.7	2.9	2
Rainfall (cm)	4.3	3.6	4.8	5.1	5.6	3.8	2.3	4.1	7.9	9.4	7.4	5.1

Catalan & National Holidays

Holidays observed are January 1 (New Year's Day), January 6 (Feast of the Epiphany), March/April (Good Friday and Easter Monday), May 1 (May Day), May/June (Whit Monday), June 24 (Feast of St. John), August 15 (Feast of the Assumption), September 11 (National Day of Catalonia), September 24 (Feast of Our Lady of Mercy), October 12 (Spain's National Day), November 1 (All Saints' Day), December 6 (Constitution Day), December 8 (Feast of the Immaculate Conception), December 25 (Christmas), and December 26 (Feast of St. Stephen).

If a holiday falls on a Thursday or Tuesday, many people also take off the weekday in between, creating an extra-long weekend. While this only really affects those doing business in the city, you should book hotels well ahead of time on these popular *puentes* (bridges).

Barcelona Calendar of Events

For an exhaustive list of events beyond those listed here for the city of Barcelona, check http://events.frommers.com, where you'll find a searchable, up-to-the-minute roster of what's happening in cities all over the world.

Saint George Conquers the World

Barcelona—like Seville and Madrid—is a big fiesta city; whether it's a rip-roaring street carnival or a culture fest, the year's calendar is sprinkled with events to keep in mind when planning your trip. Note that on official holidays (see above) shops, banks, and some restaurants and museums close for the day.

The dates for festivals and events given below may not be precise. Sometimes the exact days are not announced until 6 weeks before the actual festival. Also, days allotted to celebrate Easter, Carnaval and some other religious days change each year. Check with the Barcelona tourist office (see "Visitor Information," later in this chapter) if you're planning to attend a specific event.

JANUARY

Día de los Reyes (Three Kings Day). Parades are held around the country on the eve of the Festival of the Epiphany, which is traditionally when Christmas gift-giving is done (the concept of "Santa Claus" has crept into the culture now, so people also exchange gifts at Christmas). In Barcelona, the three "kings" arrive by boat in the evening to dispense gifts to all the excited children. January 6.

FEBRUARY

Carnaval. Carnaval in Barcelona is a relatively low-key event. The most dressing up you will see is by groups of children or stall owners in the local markets who organize a competition between themselves for "best costume" (buying fresh fish off a woman dressed in full Louis VI regalia is one of those "only in Barcelona" experiences you will treasure), as well as the city's main Carnaval parade. Just south of the city, however, in the seaside town of Sitges, locals, especially the local gay community, go all out and many Barcelonans take the short train ride to celebrate along with them. Just before Lent.

MARCH/APRIL

Semana Santa (Holy Week). Catalonia has some Easter traditions not found in the rest of the country. The Mona is a whimsical chocolate and pastry creation given in the same way we give Easter eggs. On Palm Sunday, palm leaves are blessed in Gaudí's Sagrada Família and the city's main cathedral celebrates with the curious l'ou com balla—a hollowed-out egg shell placed on top of a fountain in the city's cathedral's cloister to bob around and "dance." Out of town, the ominously named Dansa de la Mort (Dance of Death) sees men dressed as skeletons performing a "death" dance in the village of Verges near Girona, and various Passion Plays are also performed, the most famous in the village of Esparraguera, 40km (25 miles) outside of Barcelona. One week before Easter.

La Diada de St. Jordi. Saint George (St. Jordi in Catalan) is the patron saint of Catalonia, and his name day coincides with the death of Don Quijote author Miguel Cervantes. On this day men give a single red rose to the significant women in their lives (mother, girlfriend, sister, and so on), and women give a book in return (although many men now give women a book). This is one of the most colorful days in Catalonia, as thousands of rose-sellers take to the streets and bookshops set up open-air stalls along the major thoroughfares. April 23.

May Day. Also known as Labor Day, this day sees a huge march by the city's trade union members. Dozens of herbs, natural remedies, and wholesome goodies are sold along the Carrer de l'Hospital in the Fira de Sant Ponç. May 1.

Corpus Christi. During this festival, solemn processions trudge through Barcelona, while the streets of Sitges are carpeted in flowers. Can fall in May or June.

JUNE

Sónar. This dance-music and multimedia festival has gained a reputation as one of the best on the world circuit. Thousands from all over Europe descend on the city for the DJs, live concerts, and other related events. During the day events are held at the Museum of Contemporary Art; at night, they move to the enormous trade-fair buildings. Purchase tickets to this wildly popular festival well in advance at www.sonar.es. Early to mid-June.

Verbena de Sant Juan. Catalonia celebrates the Twelfth Night with fiery activities that can keep even grannies up till dawn. Families stock up on fireworks a week in advance before setting them off in streets and squares and even off balconies. Bonfires are lit along the beachfront, and the sky is ablaze with smoke and light. Lots of *cava* is consumed, and it is traditional to have the year's first dip in the sea at dawn (officially the first day of summer). Madcap fun. June 23.

JULY

El Grec. International names in all genres of music and theater come to the city to perform in various open-air venues, including the mock-Greek theater, namesake of the city's main culture fest. Beginning of July.

AUGUST

Festa Major de Gràcia. This charming week-long fiesta is held in the village-like neighborhood of Gràcia. All year long, the residents of Gràcia work on elaborate decorations with themes such as marine life, the solar system, or even local politics, to hang in the streets. By day, long trestle tables are set up for communal lunches and board games; at night, thousands invade the tiny streets for outdoor concerts, dances, and general revelry. Early to mid-August.

SEPTEMBER

La Diada de Catalunya. This is the most politically and historically significant holiday in Catalonia. Although it celebrates the region's autonomy, the date actually marks the day the city was besieged by Spanish and French troops in 1714 during the War of Succession. Demonstrations calling for greater independence are everywhere; wreath-laying ceremonies take place at tombs of past *politicos;* and the *senyera,* the flag of Catalonia, is hung from balconies. Not your typical tourist fare, but interesting for anyone who wishes to understand Catalan nationalism. September 11.

La Mercè. This celebration honors Our Lady of Mercy (La Mercè), the city's patron saint. Legend has it she rid Barcelona of a plague of locusts, and the Barcelonese give thanks in rip-roaring style. Free music concerts, from traditional to contemporary, are held in the plazas (particularly Plaça de Catalunya and Plaça Sant Jaume), and folkloric figures such as the *gigants* (giants) and *cap grosses* (fatheads) take to the streets. People come out to perform the *sardana* (the traditional Catalan dance) and to watch the nail-biting *castellers* (human towers). Firework displays light up the night, and the hair-raising *correfoc,* a parade of firework-brandishing "devils" and dragons, is the grand finale. One of the best times to be in Barcelona. September 24.

OCTOBER

Dia de la Hispanitat. Spain's national day (which commemorates Columbus' "discovery" of the New World) gets a mixed reception in Catalonia, due to the region's overriding sense of independence. The only street events you are likely to see are demonstrations calling for exactly that, or low-key celebrations from groups of people from other regions of Spain. October 12.

NOVEMBER

All Saints' Day. This public holiday is reverently celebrated, as relatives and friends

> ## 💬 The Pooping Catalan (Caganer)
>
> When you visit December's Fira de Santa Lucia (see above), look out for one particular personage among all the Magi, farm animals, and other *pessebre* figurines for sale on the stalls. The *caganer* is a small fellow, usually dressed as a peasant farmer (but who can be seen in anything from formal attire to the Barcelona Football Club uniform). He is squatting with his pants down, and a stream of excrement connects his bare buttocks to the earth. His origins are lost in folklore, but it is generally believed that he sprang from the Catalan philosophy of "giving back to the earth what one takes from it." Catalan artist Joan Miró placed the *caganer* in *La Granja* (The Farm), which is on display at Barcelona's Miró Foundation.

lay flowers on the graves (or *nichos*—in Spain, people are buried one on top of another in tiny compartments) of the dead. The night before, some of the bars in the city hold Halloween parties, another imported custom that seems to be catching on. November 1.

DECEMBER

Nadal (Christmas). In mid-December stall-holders set up Fira de Santa Lucia, a huge open-air market held in the streets around the main cathedral. Thousands come to buy handicrafts, Christmas decorations, trees, and the figurines for their *pessebres* (nativity dioramas) that are hugely popular here. The Betlem Church on La Rambla holds an exhibition of them throughout the month, and a life-size one is constructed outside the city hall in the Plaça Sant Jaume. December 25.

VISITOR INFORMATION

TOURIST OFFICES   You can begin your info search with Spain's tourist offices located in the following places:

In Canada   Contact the **Tourist Office of Spain,** 102 Bloor St. W., Suite 3402, Toronto, Ontario, M5S 1M9 (✆ **416/961-3131**). Online details and information can be found at www.spain.info/en_CA/index.html.

In the United Kingdom   The **Spanish National Tourist Office** is at 22–23 Manchester Sq., London, W1M 5AP (✆ **020/7486-8077**). Visit online at www.tourspain.co.uk.

In the United States   For information before you go, contact the **Tourist Office of Spain,** 666 Fifth Ave., Fifth Floor, New York, NY 10103 (✆ **212/265-8822**). It can provide sightseeing information, events calendars, train and ferry schedules, and more. Elsewhere in the United States, branches of the Tourist Office of Spain are located at 8383 Wilshire Blvd., Suite 956, Beverly Hills, CA 90211 (✆ **323/658-7188**); 845 N. Michigan Ave., Suite 915E, Chicago, IL 60611 (✆ **312/642-1992**); and 1221 Brickell Ave., Suite 1850, Miami, FL 33131 (✆ **305/358-1992**). Check online for more details of the above offices and general information on Barcelona at www.okspain.org.

Spain

DESTINATION BARCELONA: pre-departure CHECKLIST

- If you're flying, are you carrying a current passport? The citizens of Schengen Agreement European Union countries can cross into Spain without photo ID, but citizens of other countries, including the U.S., Canada, Australia, New Zealand, and the U.K., must have a passport.
- If you're driving, did you pack your driver's license? Did you buy road maps online?
- Do you have the address, phone number, and website of your country's embassy or consulate with you?
- Did you find out your daily ATM withdrawal limit?
- Do you know your credit card PINs?
- To check in for your flight with an e-ticket, do you have the credit card you used to buy your ticket?
- If you purchased traveler's checks, have you recorded the check numbers and stored the documentation separately from the checks?
- Did you bring ID cards, such as student ID, that could entitle you to discounts?
- Did you leave a copy of your itinerary with someone at home?
- Do any theater, restaurant, or travel reservations need to be booked in advance?
- Is your favorite attraction open? Call ahead for opening and closing times. Bear in mind that most museums close on Monday in Barcelona.

WEBSITES   You can find lots of great information at the following sites: **Tourist Office of Spain** (www.okspain.org), **All About Spain** (www.red2000.com), and **CyberSp@in** (www.cyberspain.com).

Find Catalonia-specific information online at **www.barcelonaturisme.com**, **www.hotel-barcelona.com/tours.html**, and **www.barcelona-tourist-guide.com**. The official site of city hall, **www.bcn.es,** is useful for details such as opening times and upcoming events written in English. The local English-language magazine *Barcelona Metropolitan* (**www.barcelona-metropolitan.com**) is aimed mainly at expats, but will appeal to the visitor who wants more of an insider look at the city. For one-stop tour, hotel, and activity booking try **www.barcelona.com**. If you want to pre-book train tickets, **www.renfe.es** is the official site of Spain's rail network.

ENTRY REQUIREMENTS

Passports

A valid passport is all that an American, British, Canadian, Australian, or New Zealand citizen needs to enter Spain. It is important to note when your passport expires. If you're not traveling from within the European Union, Spain requires your passport to have at least 6 months left before its expiration date. For information on how to obtain a passport, go to "Passports" in chapter 13, "Fast Facts" (p. 324).

Visas

No visas are required for American, British, Canadian, Australian, or New Zealand visitors to Spain, providing your stay does not exceed 90 days. For specifics on getting a visa, go to "Visas" in chapter 13, "Fast Facts" (p. 324).

Medical Requirements

For information on medical requirements and recommendations, see "Health," p. 51.

Customs

WHAT YOU CAN TAKE HOME FROM BARCELONA

For information on what you're allowed to bring home from Barcelona, contact one of the following agencies:

Australian Citizens: Australian Customs Service, Customs House, 5 Constitution Ave., Canberra City, ACT 2601 (✆ **1300/363-263;** from outside Australia, ✆ 612/6275-6666; www.customs.gov.au).

Canadian Citizens: Canada Border Services Agency, Ottawa, Ontario, K1A 0L8 (✆ **800/461-9999** in Canada, or 204/983-3500; www.cbsa-asfc.gc.ca).

New Zealand Citizens: New Zealand Customs, The Customhouse, 17–21 Whitmore St., Box 2218, Wellington 6140 (✆ **04/473-6099** or 0800/428-786; www. customs.govt.nz).

U.K. Citizens: HM Customs & Excise, Crownhill Court, Tailyour Road, Plymouth, PL6 5BZ (✆ **0845/010-9000;** from outside the U.K., ✆ 020/8929-0152; www. hmce.gov.uk).

U.S. Citizens: U.S. Customs & Border Protection (CBP), 1300 Pennsylvania Ave. NW, Washington, DC 20229 (✆ **877/287-8667;** www.cbp.gov).

GETTING THERE & GETTING AROUND

Getting To Barcelona

BY PLANE

FROM NORTH AMERICA   Flights from the U.S. East Coast to Spain take 6 to 7 hours. The Spanish national carrier **Iberia Airlines** has routes into Spain, with daily services from most major U.S. cities (New York, Washington, Chicago, Atlanta) either direct to Barcelona (BCN) or via Madrid (MAD). Other major U.S. and Spanish airlines also fly from all over the U.S. daily.

FROM THE U.K.   Major British carriers, budget, and charter airlines serve Barcelona from airports throughout the United Kingdom.

Charter and budget flights to the regional Catalan airports of Reus (REU) and Girona (GRO) leave from many British regional airports. Girona is located about 90 minutes outside Barcelona and connected by train. Girona also serves travelers heading to the Costa Brava, north of Barcelona, while Reus is mainly used by holidaymakers to the resorts of the Costa Daurada, in the south.

The websites www.flightcentre.co-uk, www.cheapflights.co.uk, and www.expedia.co.uk are good sources of cheap travel tickets.

FROM AUSTRALIA & NEW ZEALAND From Australia and New Zealand, there are a number of major carriers flying to Spain via stopovers in several Asia countries and London Heathrow.

To find out more details about which airlines travel to Barcelona, please see "Airline Websites," p. 329.

Getting into Town from the Airport

El Prat, Barcelona's airport, is 13km (8 miles) from the city center and there are several options you can use to get into town.

BY CAR

Many of the world's biggest car-rental companies, including Avis, Budget, and Hertz, maintain offices throughout Spain and in all the airports around Barcelona as well as the city center. For listings of the major car-rental agencies in Barcelona, see chapter 13, "Fast Facts" (p. 324).

The usual minimum-age limit for car rentals in Spain is 21 for compact or intermediate-size cars, but some van or larger car rentals require drivers to be 25 years of age. Upper-age requirements reach 70 to 75 for certain vehicles. Book ahead online to be sure of getting the best hire rates and make sure that comprehensive insurance is included in your deal. For details of driving in Catalonia and Spain, please see p. 44.

Most cars hired in Spain are stick-shift (i.e. with gears), not automatic. Most are air-conditioned and nearly all use unleaded fuel.

BY BUS

Aerobús services A1 and A2 travel between the airport and the city center. Buses leave from outside Arrivals at all three terminals every 15 minutes from 6am to midnight, and stop at Plaça Espanya, Gran Vía de les Corts Catalanes, Plaça Universitat, and Plaça de Catalunya. Journey time is about 40 minutes to the last stop.

BY TRAIN

The half-hourly RENFE **rail service** departs between 6:15am and 11:15pm from the El Prat **train station** to Estació Barcelona-Sants (Plaça dels Paisos Catalans), taking 25 minutes. On the way the trains stop at Plaça de Catalunya, Arc de Triomf, and Clot-Aragó. From these stations there are connections with the Metro and bus services.

BY TAXI

There are black-and-yellow **taxi** ranks outside all three airport terminals. They should be metered. Don't use the ticket touts in the Arrivals halls. Tip between 5% and 10% of the fare. There's a supplement from the airport after 10pm.

Getting to Barcelona

BY CAR

If you're touring Europe in a rented car, the routes to Barcelona by road from France are: Via Toulouse, take the A-61 to Narbonne, and then the A-9 to the border crossing at La Junquera, crossing the Pyrénées. You can also take the RN-20, with a border station at Puigcerdà.

- Your choice of airline and airplane will affect your legroom. Skytrax has posted a list of average seat pitches at **www.airlinequality.com.**
- Emergency exit and bulkhead seats have the most legroom.
- If you're traveling with a companion, book an aisle and a window seat. Middle seats are usually booked last, so chances are good you'll end up with three seats to yourselves.
- Reserve a window seat so you can sleep and avoid your head being bumped in the aisle.

- Get up, walk around, and stretch every 60 to 90 minutes to keep your blood flowing.
- Drink water before, during, and after your flight to combat the lack of humidity in airplane cabins. Avoid alcohol, which will dehydrate you.
- If you're flying with kids, take toys and books to entertain them, and pastilles and chewing gum to help relieve ear pressure during ascent and descent.
- Reset your watch to your destination time when you board the plane.

Barcelona is tucked away in the northeast corner of Spain, just south of the Pyrénées. Main highways within Spain from the city run west and south and the best connections are with Madrid (N11) and Valencia (E15).

Ferries link Portsmouth and Plymouth in the U.K. with Santander and Bilbao. The quickest way to get to Barcelona from these north-coast ports is to take the A68 to Zaragoza and then the A2 to Barcelona center. From Santander or Bilbao allow 12–15 hours for the drive across the Basque Country and Aragón to Barcelona.

If you're driving to Spain from the U.K., book the cross-channel ferry well in advance, as traffic is very heavy, especially in summer. The major crossings between the U.K. and France connect Dover and Folkestone with Dunkirk, Calais, and Boulogne. Newhaven is connected to Dieppe and Plymouth to Roscoff. The shortest crossing is from Dover to Calais on **P&O Ferries** (www.poferries.com) and takes 1¼ hours. **Norfolkline** (www.norfolkline.com) operates a ferry service from Dover to Dunkirk that takes 2 hours. The drive from Calais to the Spanish border takes about 15 hours.

The Channel Tunnel links the U.K. (Folkestone) and France (Calais) by road and rail. Tickets for train services between London and Paris or Brussels are available from Eurostar (www.eurostar.com). From Calais, it's about an 18-hour drive to Barcelona.

DRIVING RULES   As in all mainland European countries, Spaniards drive on the right-hand side of the road, overtaking on the left. On highways and toll roads, impatient local drivers may flash their lights at you if they feel you are driving too slowly, even if you're in the inside land. At roundabouts, vehicles already circling from your left have the right of way.

After Greece and Portugal, Spain has the highest driving-accident rates in Europe, but figures have dropped in recent years thanks to strict breathalyzer tests and a points deduction scheme for traffic infringements. Spain's highways are among the best in the world, making cross-country journeys a positive pleasure. Less advisable is trying to negotiate the traffic in congested Barcelona. Here public transport—in particular the Metro—comes into its own.

If you must drive through Barcelona, try to avoid morning and evening rush hours. Never park your car facing oncoming traffic, as that is against the law. If you are fined by the highway patrol (*Guardia Civil de Tráfico*), you must pay on the spot. Penalties for drinking and driving are very stiff (**breathalyzers** are now being far more strictly used than in the past). The limit is now 0.5 milligrams per milliliter of blood. That's just one glass of wine or a *caña* (small beer); better still, drink no alcohol at all if you're driving.

BY TRAIN

All trains in Catalonia are operated by **Spanish State Railways** (**RENFE, © 90 224 0202.** www.renfe.com). For day and overnight trips, the comfortable TALGO, TER, and Electrotren high-speed trains are in operation.

Catalonia itself has a comprehensive network of rail lines. Hundreds of trains arrive every day at Barcelona's Sants (Plaça dels Països Catalans. Metro: Sants Estació) and França (Avinguda Marquès de l'Argentera, 6-12. Metro: Barceloneta) railway stations from towns around the region and far-flung destinations including Paris, Madrid, southern Spain, and Milan.

For long-distance and overnight journeys on Spanish trains, seat and sleeper reservations are mandatory. See www.renfe.com for more information.

In the U.S. or Canada, tickets for travel around Catalonia can be purchased at any reputable travel agent or online at www.renfe.com.

To get from London to Barcelona by rail, take Eurostar (www.eurostar.com) to Paris's Gare du Nord before traveling across Paris to Gare d'Austerlitz. Trip time from London to Paris is 2 hours 20 minutes; from Paris to Barcelona is about 12 hours, which includes 2 hours spent in Paris changing stations.

A variety of **InterRail Passes** are available, and the most practical and economical of them all for Spain is the **One Country Pass,** which allows various numbers of days of travel within any month. See www.raileurope.co.uk for instructions on how to book them.

If you're already in Europe, traveling to Spain by train is easy and cheap, especially if you have a Eurail Pass (www.eurail.com). Rail passengers visiting from France should make *couchette* (bunk beds in a sleeper car) reservations as far in advance as possible, especially during the peak summer season. Book online through ACP International: www.acprail.com/tickets-and-reservations/europe.

Driving in Catalonia

Signs are standardized all over Europe, but here are some pointers for Catalonia. Roads marked **A** are *autopistas* (toll-paying express routes), those marked **N** are highways or *autovías*, while those marked **E** are standard main highways. To leave the *autopista*, look for signs saying "salida" in Spanish, "sortida" in Catalan. On most express highways, the speed limit is 120km/h (75 mph). On other roads, speed limits range from 90km/h (56 mph) to 100km/h (62 mph). There is often scant regard for the speed limit.

Getting There & Getting Around | PLANNING YOUR TRIP TO BARCELONA

The Spanish railway system is getting faster and more efficient by the year. The **AVE high-speed train service,** launched in 2007, now connects Barcelona with Madrid in 2¾ hours, stopping en route at Lleida and Zaragoza. The train travels at a speed of up to 300km/h (190 mph). Also increasing in speed and frequency is the rail service to neighboring **France.** From 2012 there will be eight AVE trains a day (in addition to the current 10 slower trains) from Barcelona's Estació de França via Figueres to **Perpignan:** 150km (93 miles) and a mere 45 minutes away.

BY BUS

Bus travel to Spain is possible but not popular—it's quite slow. Coach services operate regularly from the major capitals of western Europe to Barcelona. The busiest routes are from London and are run by **Eurolines,** 52 Grosvenor Gardens, London, SW1W 0AU (② **0990/143-219;** www.eurolines.co.uk). The journey from London's Victoria Station to Barcelona takes around 27 hours, with a stop at Lyons in France.

Getting Around Barcelona
BY SUBWAY (METRO)

Barcelona has an excellent underground public transport system. The **Metro** goes pretty much any place in the city you will need to get to. It is run by the **TMB** (Transports Metropolitans de Barcelona; www.tmb.net), who also manages the bus and tram network and the FGC (Ferrocarrils de la Generalitat), a pre-Metro, part-underground-part-overground system.

It is the efficient Metro system, however, that most visitors to the city will use. There are five color-coded and numbered lines that fan out from the center of the city. Stations are recognizable by a red diamond-shaped sign with the letter M in the center. Maps are available from the stations and from tourist information offices. The stations at Plaça de Catalunya, Sants, and Passeig de Gràcia connect with RENFE or overground trains. When you purchase a ticket for another part of Spain or Catalonia (which you can do from RENFE offices at Sants and Passeig de Gràcia stations or online at www.renfe.com) make sure you ask which station it leaves from.

Metro tickets can be bought on the day of your journey or beforehand from inside the station, either at the ticket office or from touch-screen vending machines, which have English instructions. Various options are available. A single (*senzill* or *sencillo*) ticket in central zone 1 costs 1.40€. More economic options include a T-10 at 7.85€, which offers 10 journeys that can be shared by two or more people, or a T-Día for unlimited 24-hour transport in central Barcelona for 5.90€. Travel cards valid for 2 or 3 days are also available for 11.20€ to 15.90€. You can buy reduced-price tickets valid for longer periods, but for most short visits the T-10 is your best bet, with the T-Día in reserve for extra-busy days. All these tickets are valid for the FGC and bus systems as well as the Metro.

When a *sencillo* ticket is activated, it is valid for up to 75 minutes on a different form of transport if you need to do a combined Metro/bus journey. The Metro runs 5am to midnight Sunday to Thursday and 5am to 2am Friday and Saturday. TMB's

Barcelona Public Transportation

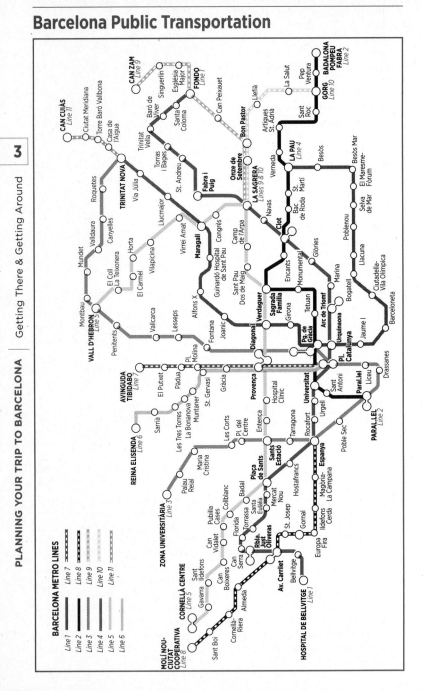

easy-to-navigate website (www.tmb.net) has information on the city's transport system in English, including which Metro stations and buses are equipped to take wheelchairs. The customer service number is ℰ **93-318-70-74;** there are also customer service centers at Universitat, Sagrada Família, Sants, and Diagonal stations. While it's tempting to hop on and off the Metro to see the sights, remember that Metro stations are often only about a 5- to 10-minute walk apart; a good pair of shoes is the best way around central Barcelona!

The Metro system continues to expand. The biggest development is the extension of **line 9,** which will be the longest single line in Europe when it is finished, running a total of 48km (30 miles) from Can Zam in Santa Coloma to the Zona Franca at El Prat airport. Its 52 stations have each been designed by a different architect and at the time of writing (2010) six have already been finished. The whole project is due for completion by 2014 at a total estimated cost of 6.5 billion euros.

Also newly completed is the **L10** extension from Gorg in Badalona to the Nova Estació in Poligon Pratenc.

BY BUS & TRAM

Sleek new *tramvías* **(trams)** ply the main routes through the city alongside the buses, which are plentiful but less convenient, being at the mercy of the city's infamous traffic snarls. Most bus and tram routes stop at Plaça de Catalunya, also the stop-off point for the Aerobús service from the airport and the Bus Turístic (see below). Routes are clearly marked at each stop, as are timetables. However, most buses and trams stop running well before the Metro closes. One bus service that is particularly useful is the **Nitbus,** which runs from 11pm to 4am and is the only valid alternative to the 2 to 3am taxi drought. These are bright yellow, clearly marked with an N, and most leave from Plaça de Catalunya. Note that while travel cards and other TMB passes are valid for daytime buses they're not valid on Nitbuses. Tickets cost 1.25€ one-way and are bought directly from the driver.

BY TAXI

Yellow-and-black taxis are plentiful and reasonably priced. You can hail one in the street if its green light is on. Taxis have meters, but don't make the mistake of

---

 All Aboard!

The most convenient way to see Barcelona, especially if your time is limited, is to hop on (and off) the **Bus Turístic** (ℰ 93-318-70-74; www.barcelonabus turistic.cat). This double-decker, open-top tourist bus travels to all the major sights; either disembark or stay on and continue on to the next hotspot. There are two routes—the red or Nord (North) route, which covers L'Eixample and Tibidabo with Gaudí's main works (including the Sagrada Família) as the highlights, or the blue or Sur (South) route, which allows you to see the Old City and Montjuïc; both have multilingual commentary along the way. The main point of embarkation is Plaça de Catalunya, outside the El Corte Inglés department store. Cost is 22€ for a one-day pass (14€ for children 4–12) and 29€ for a 2-day pass (18€ for children 4–12). Tickets can be purchased onboard or at the tourist information office at Plaça de Catalunya. The service operates daily, except Christmas and New Year's Day, from 9am to 9:30pm.

Here are the most useful Metro stops for sightseeing:

○ **Paral.lel** (lines 2 and 11) connects with the funicular line up to **Montjuïc** (p. 183), where you can explore the castle and see some of the city's best museums.

○ **Avinguda Tibidabo** (line 7), behind L'Eixample, where you hop directly onto the Tramvía Blau (Blue Tram) to connect with the funicular up to **Tibidabo's** (p. 47) mountain-top fun-fair and church.

○ **Lesseps** (line 11) takes you close to the village-like quarter of **Gràcia** (p. 181)

and within strolling distance of enchanting **Parc Güell** (p. 181).

○ **Sagrada Família** (lines 5 and 6), where you can visit the famed Gaudí temple (p. 176) and climb one of its spires.

○ **Liceu** (line 5) deposits you in bustling La Rambla (p. 66), midway between the labyrinthine medieval Ciutat Vella (p. 160) and multi-ethnic Raval quarter (p. 172).

○ **Barceloneta** (line 4) in the former fishermen's quarter (p. 151), with its market, fish restaurants, port, and beach areas.

confusing the cheaper day rate (Tariff 2, starting at 2€) with the more expensive post-8pm night rate (Tariff 1, starting at 3.10€). A list of prices and surcharges is (by law) on display on the back passenger window. There have been recent reports of taxi drivers charging exorbitant fares for short distances, so always make sure that the meter is turned on when you start your journey. To book a cab, either the next available one or for the next day, call the **Institut Metropolità del Taxi** (℡ 93-223-51-51; www.taxibarcelona.cat). They can also give you information about booking wheelchair-adapted taxis.

BY BICYCLE

One growing form of transport in the city is the bicycle. There are a number of bicycle lanes in the center of the city and a few firms that rent them, including **Un Coxte Menys,** Esparteria 3 (℡ 93-268-21-05), and **Biciclot,** Verneda 16 (℡ 93-307-74-75). The city now has a **bike-sharing system** in which red *bicicletas* (6,000 in all) are available for free from bus and Metro stations for up to 30 minutes for short trips. You are required by law to wear a helmet.

OTHER FORMS OF TRANSPORT

At some point in your visit to Barcelona, you may want to visit the mountain of Tibidabo for the views and fun-fair. A century-old tram called the **Tramvía Blau** (Blue Tram) goes from Plaça Kennedy to the bottom of the funicular to Tibidabo. It operates daily from 10am to 8pm from mid-June to mid-September and 10am to 6pm on weekends only the rest of the year.

At the end of the run, you can go the rest of the way by funicular to the top of Tibidabo, at 503m (1,650 feet), for a stunning panoramic view of Barcelona. The funicular operates only when the fun-fair at Tibidabo is open (p. 48). Opening times vary according to the time of year and the weather conditions. As a rule, the funicular starts operating 20 minutes before the fun-fair opens and runs every half-hour; during peak visiting hours, it runs every 15 minutes. The fare is 2.80€ one-way and 4.30€ round-trip.

The **Tibibus** goes from Plaça de Catalunya, in the center of the city, to Tibidabo at limited times, again depending on when the park opens and closes. The one-way fare is 2.30€.

Barcelona's newest form of public transport is the sleek and comfortable Tramvía Baix, a modern tram that mainly services the outer suburbs. It is handy, however, for reaching the outer limits of the Diagonal and the Palau de Pedralbes (p. 70). Hop on at Plaça Francesc Macià.

BY CAR

A car offers the greatest flexibility while you're touring, even if you're just doing day trips from Barcelona. Don't drive *in* Barcelona; it's too congested, street parking is a nightmare, and garage or lot parking is expensive. Theoretically, rush hour is Monday through Saturday from 8 to 10am and 4 to 7:30pm. In reality, it's always busy.

On the other hand, if you're touring Catalonia province, a car is useful to get off the beaten track independently—although bus and train transport to all the main places of interest, such as Tarragona, Montserrat, Girona, and the Costa Brava, is extremely efficient and economical (see chapter 11, "Side Trips In Catalonia").

MONEY & COSTS

Currency

The **euro** (€) is the single European currency. Exchange rates of participating countries are locked into the common currency, fluctuating against the dollar. Unfortunately for U.K and U.S. visitors, in the last couple of years the euro has gone from basically a one-to-one exchange rate with the dollar to a much stronger position.

Spain is no longer a budget destination and Barcelona itself is often quoted as being the most expensive city in the country. Compared to other major European cities such as London or Paris, however, it can still be a bargain, but if you're not used to big-city prices, you could have a bit of shock.

Reflecting a modern, cosmopolitan city that has to cater to all budgets, you can go up- or down-market in your choice of dining and accommodations. Often the most memorable experience is not dependent on the price tag. Staying away from the tourist traps and seeking out family-run restaurants will make you inclined to hand over your credit card with a smile when the check comes. In a climate of stiff competition (especially from the holiday apartment sector), hotels are usually clean and comfortable. Trains are very reasonably priced, fast, and on time, and most service personnel treat you with respect. And once you move beyond Barcelona into the rural areas you will find that the price of hotels and restaurants drops noticeably.

In Spain, prices for children aged 6 to 17 are often lower than for adults. Entrance fees for children under 6 are generally waived.

THE VALUE OF THE EURO V. OTHER POPULAR CURRENCIES

Euro €	U.S. $	U.K. £	Can $	Aus $	NZ $
1.00	1.38	.87	1.42	1.42	1.84

WHAT THINGS COST IN BARCELONA

Cup of coffee	1.40€–2€
Glass of beer (half pint)	2.50€
Glass of Rioja wine	2.50€–2.80€
Movie ticket	7.50€
Taxi from airport to center	30€–35€
Three-course meal for one with wine	25€–35€

This guide lists exact prices in the local currency. The currency conversions quoted above were correct at press time. However, rates fluctuate, so before departing consult a currency-exchange website such as **www.xe.com/ucc** or **www.oanda.com/convert/classic** to check up-to-the-minute rates.

Exchange rates may be more favorable when you arrive in Barcelona but it's helpful to have at least some money in local currency when you get there. Currency and traveler's checks can be changed at all the local airports.

When you get to Barcelona, it's best to exchange currency or traveler's checks at a bank, not a *cambio* (exchange bureau), hotel, or shop as rates and commission fees are high. Most Barcelona hotels accept major credit and debit cards.

ATMs

The easiest and best way to get cash while away from home is from ATMs (automated teller machines), also called "cashpoints."

Maestro (www.mastercard.com) and **Visa** (www.visa.com) both have credit card networks spanning the globe; look on the back of your bank card to see which network you're on and check online for ATM locations in Barcelona. Be sure you know your PIN and daily withdrawal limit before you depart. Most banks impose a fee every time you use a card at another bank's ATM, and that fee is higher for international transactions than for domestic ones. In addition, the bank from which you withdraw cash may charge its own fee. For international withdrawal fees, ask your bank.

Credit Cards

Credit cards are the safest way to carry money. They provide a record of all your expenses, and offer relatively good exchange rates. You can get cash advances on your credit cards at banks or ATMs, provided you know your PIN. You'll pay interest from the moment of withdrawal, even if you pay your monthly bill on time.

Check with your credit or debit card issuer to see what fees will be charged for overseas transactions. Recent reform legislation in the U.S., for example, has curbed some exploitative lending practices. But many banks have responded by increasing fees in other areas, including fees for customers who use credit and debit cards while out of the country. Fees can amount to 3% or more of the purchase price. Check before departing to avoid any surprise charges on your statement.

American Express, Diners Club, MasterCard, and Visa credit cards are all widely accepted in Spain.

Traveler's Checks

Traveler's checks are not now widely used but are accepted in Barcelona at banks and travel agencies. Buy them from your bank before you leave home.

They are offered in various denominations, and you'll pay a service charge of between 1% and 4%.

American Express, MasterCard, Thomas Cook, and **Visa** offer **foreign currency traveler's checks,** which are useful if you're traveling to the euro zone; they're accepted at locations where dollar checks are not.

If you carry traveler's checks, keep a record of their serial numbers separate from your checks in the event that these are stolen or lost. You'll get a refund faster if you know the numbers.

HEALTH
Staying Healthy

Spain does not pose any major health hazards. The rich cuisine—garlic, olive oil, and wine—may give some travelers mild diarrhea, so take some anti-diarrhea medicine, moderate your eating habits, and, even though the water is safe, drink mineral water only. If you are visiting Barcelona over the summer, limit your exposure to the sun, especially during the first few days of your trip and, thereafter, from 11am to 3pm. Use a sunscreen with a high protection factor and apply it liberally. Remember that children need more protection than adults do.

GENERAL AVAILABILITY OF HEALTH CARE
No shots of any sort are required before traveling to Spain. Once there, medicines for a wide variety of common ailments, from colds to diarrhea, can be obtained over the counter at local *farmacias* (pharmacies/drugstores). Generic equivalents of common prescription drugs are also usually available in Spain. However, it does no harm to bring over-the-counter medicines with you to be on the safe side.

Common Ailments

CHANGE OF DIET No need to go on a tempting cholesterol binge if you really don't want to. Vegetarians can follow their usual diet pattern in Barcelona, as there is an increasing number of vegetarian eating spots available (p. 159) as well as a multitude of *herbolarios* (health food shops).

SUN EXPOSURE   In the hot weather, do as the locals do and avoid the sun between 11am and 3pm. Use a high-protection sunscreen and reapply after swimming in the sea. Take care with kids; give them a sunhat and reapply suncream often.

SEA HAZARDS   Urban beaches in Barcelona have lifeguards on duty and are marked by flags: Green is safe, yellow means you should take caution, and red means stay out of the sea. Where there are no guards on duty, use your common sense, especially north of Barcelona along the Costa Brava, where the seabed is rocky. Over the past few years the standard of Spain's beaches in terms of water pollution has improved, leading to a consistently high rating in terms of cleanliness. At the onset of summer, jellyfish can be a problem in the sea. They are not poisonous but do have a nasty sting. If you get stung, get help from the nearest *farmacia* (pharmacy/drugstore).

RESPIRATORY ILLNESSES   Lodged between the mountains and the sea, Barcelona often traps smog from its nearby industrial belt. While the quality of the air is monitored, local media do not publish "high risk" days. Common sense is required for people with respiratory illnesses.

What to Do If You Get Sick Away from Home

Spanish medical facilities are among the best in the world. If a medical emergency arises, your hotel staff can put you in touch with a reliable doctor. If not, contact your embassy or consulate; each one maintains a list of English-speaking doctors, as does the website http:\\barcelona.angloinfo.com. Medical and hospital services aren't free, so take out adequate medical insurance before you travel. In Barcelona you may have to pay your medical costs upfront and be reimbursed later.

If you suffer from a chronic illness, consult your doctor before your departure. Pack all your prescription medications in your carry-on luggage. Carry written prescriptions in generic, rather than brand-name, form, in case a local pharmacist is unfamiliar with the brand. Bring copies of your prescription in case you lose your pills or run out.

We list **emergency numbers** and insurance information in chapter 13, "Fast Facts" (p. 324).

Avoiding "Economy-Class Syndrome"

Deep vein thrombosis, or, as it's known in the world of flying, "economy-class syndrome," is a blood clot that develops in a deep vein. It's a potentially deadly condition that can be caused by sitting in cramped conditions—such as an airplane cabin—for too long. During a long-haul flight, get up, walk around, and stretch your legs every 60 minutes or so to keep your blood flowing. Other preventive measures include frequent flexing of the legs while sitting, drinking lots of water, and avoiding alcohol and sleeping pills. If you have a history of deep vein thrombosis, heart disease, or other condition that puts you at high risk, experts recommend wearing compression stockings or taking anticoagulants before you fly; ask your physician about the best course for you. Symptoms of deep vein thrombosis include leg pain or swelling, and shortness of breath.

Healthy Travels to You

The following government websites offer up-to-date health-related travel advice.

o **Australia:** www.smartraveller.gov.au
o **Canada:** www.hc-sc.gc.ca/index_e.html
o **U.K.:** www.nhs.uk/healthcareabroad
o **U.S.:** www.cdc.gov/travel

CRIME & SAFETY

TERRORISM The bomb attacks on three suburban trains in Madrid on March 11, 2004, resulted in the deaths of 200 people; a direct or indirect consequence of the massacre was that after a massive protest demonstration of two million people in the streets of Madrid, voters unexpectedly returned the left-wing PSOE, or *Partido Socialista Obero Español* (Spanish Socialist Workers' Party) to power in the 2004 general elections, after more than a decade of right-wing rule under the PP (Partido Popular, or Peoples' Party). The policy of the prime minister, Rodríguez Zapatero, had always been to oppose the war in the Middle East, and one of his first acts was to authorize the full withdrawal of Spanish troops from Iraq just over 3 months later.

So there is nothing to suggest that terrorism constitutes a more serious threat in Barcelona than in any other major world city. Travelers to Spain should refer to the guidance offered by their own countries. For U.S. travelers, visit www.state.gov; for U.K. visitors, advice is provided by the Foreign Office at www.fco.gov.uk.

The more local threat comes from **ETA,** the Basque separatist-terrorist organization. Negotiations between the PSOE government, helmed by Zapatero, and the outlawed Herri Batasuna party—the front for ETA—led to cautious optimism for a peaceful settlement. Of late ETA has become notably silent. Whether this heralds the beginning of the end for them as a purported "political force" remains to be seen.

CONVENTIONAL CRIME While most of Spain has a moderate crime rate and most visitors have trouble-free visits, the principal tourist areas have experienced an increase in violent crime. Barcelona has reported a growing incidence of violent attacks, with older tourists particularly at risk. Criminals frequent tourist areas and major attractions such as museums, monuments, restaurants, hotels, beach resorts, trains, train stations, airports, subways, and ATMs.

Muggings and pickpocketing are commonplace in La Rambla and the narrow lanes of the Barri Gòtic. Travelers should exercise caution, carry limited cash and credit cards, and leave extra cash, credit cards, passports, and personal documents in a safe location. Crimes occur at all times of day and night, although visitors—and residents—are more vulnerable in the early hours of the morning.

Thieves often work in teams. In most cases, one person distracts a victim while the accomplice performs the robbery. A stranger might ask for directions or "inadvertently" spill something on you. While your attention is diverted, an accomplice makes off with your valuables. Attacks may also be initiated from behind, with the victim being grabbed around the neck and choked by one assailant while others rifle through their belongings. A group of assailants may surround a victim in a crowded tourist area or on public transportation, and only after the group has departed does the person realize they've been robbed. Some attacks have been so violent that people have needed to seek medical attention afterward.

Luggage, cameras, or laptops are commonly stolen from parked cars. Don't leave anything in a parked car, and keep doors locked, windows rolled up, and valuables out of sight when driving. "Good Samaritan" scams are also frequent. The driver of a passing car tries to divert your attention by indicating that you have a mechanical problem. If you stop to check your vehicle, accomplices steal from you as you check the engine. As a rule of thumb, don't accept help from anyone other than a uniformed member of the police or Guardia Civil.

The loss or theft abroad of a passport should be reported to the local police and your embassy or consulate. **For U.S. visitors,** refer to the Department of State's pamphlet, *A Safe Trip Abroad,* for ways to promote a more trouble-free journey. It's available online at http://bookstore.gpo.gov or via the Bureau of Consular Affairs home page at http://travel.state.gov.

U.K., Australian, New Zealand, and Canadian citizens who lose their passport must also report it to the local police and to their local Consulate as follows. **For Britons:** British Consulate General (Edificio Torre de Barcelona, Avinguda Diagonal 477, Barcelona. ✆ 93-366-62-00. www.ukinspain.com). **For Australians:** Honorary Consul for Australia, Avinguda Diagonal 45, 3°, Barcelona. ✆ 93-490-9013. **For New Zealanders:** Consulate of New Zealand, Travessera de Gràcia 64, 2°, Barcelona. ✆ 93-202-0890. **For Canadians:** Consulate of Canada, Plaça de Catalunya 9, 1°, 2ª, Barcelona. ✆ 93-412-7236.

Dealing with Discrimination

As Barcelona's population slowly becomes more international, overt racial prejudice appears to be diminishing. But there is still a small fringe of hard-core racists.

Since the Madrid bombings of 2004, there has been a slight hardening of mood toward Arabs by certain members of the community; and some residents' attitudes toward Latin Americans have been soured by the appearance (in small numbers) of young criminal gangs in the outer suburbs of the city.

Barcelona is as liberal as any other city in its acceptance of gays and lesbians, including homosexual marriages (see "Gay & Lesbian Travelers," below).

Solo female travelers can expect a reasonably hassle-free trip (see "Women Travelers," below).

SPECIALIZED TRAVEL RESOURCES

In addition to the destination-specific resources listed below, please visit www.frommers.com for other specialized travel resources.

Travelers with Disabilities

Disabilities shouldn't stop anyone from traveling. There are more options and resources out there than ever before.

Because of the endless flights of stairs in most buildings in Barcelona, visitors with disabilities may have difficulty getting around the city, but conditions are slowly improving: Newer hotels are sensitive to the needs of people with disabilities, and the more expensive restaurants are generally wheelchair-accessible. However, since most places have very limited, if any, facilities for people with disabilities, you might consider taking an organized tour specifically designed to accommodate such travelers.

For the names and addresses of such tour operators as well as other related information, contact the **Society for Accessible Travel and Hospitality (SATH;** www.sath.org). Annual membership dues are $50 for seniors and students. **Air AmbulanceCard.com** is now partnered with SATH and allows you to pre-select top-notch hospitals in case of an emergency. Another organization that offers assistance to travelers with disabilities is **MossRehab** (www.mossresourcenet.org).

For the visually impaired, the best resource is the **American Foundation for the Blind (AFB;** www.afb.org), offering information on travel and various requirements for the transport of, and border formalities for, Seeing Eye dogs. It also issues identification cards to travelers who are blind.

Some travel agencies offer customized itineraries for travelers with disabilities. One of the best organizations is **Flying Wheels Travel** (www.flyingwheelstravel.com), which offers escorted tours and cruises. Others include **Access-Able Travel Source** (www.access-able.com) and **Accessible Journeys** (www.disabilitytravel.com).

If you're flying to Barcelona, airline and ground staff will help you on and off planes and reserve seats with sufficient legroom, but you must arrange this assistance *in advance* of travel by contacting your airline by phone or through its website.

Avis has an "Avis Access" program that offers such services as a dedicated 24-hour toll-free number (✆ **888-879-42-73;** www.avis.es) for customers with special travel needs; special car features such as swivel seats, spinner knobs, and hand controls; and accessible bus service.

Check out the quarterly *Emerging Horizons* (www.emerginghorizons.com) and SATH's *Open World* magazine.

FOR BRITISH TRAVELERS WITH DISABILITIES   Disabled travelers from the U.K. can book trips through **Enable Holidays** (www.enableholidays.com) in Bristol or the Glasgow-based **Disabled Access Holidays** (www.disabledaccess holidays.com).

The **Royal Association for Disability and Rehabilitation (RADAR;** www.radar.org.uk) provides a number of information packs on sports and outdoor vacations, insurance, financial arrangements for disabled people, and accommodations in nursing care units for groups or for the elderly.

For more on organizations that offer resources to travelers with disabilities, go to www.frommers.com/planning.

Gay & Lesbian Travelers

In 1978 Spain legalized homosexuality among consenting adults, and in 2005 parliament legalized marriage between same-sex couples. Catalonia has helped pave the way in rights for gay couples, pre-empting national laws by granting same-sex couples the same official status and conjugal rights as heterosexuals, and has given the green light for changes in the law that would facilitate adoption by same-sex couples. Barcelona is one of the major centers of gay life in Spain, and two of the most popular resorts for gay travelers, Sitges (south of Barcelona) and the island of Ibiza, are in close proximity.

Lesbians and gays can pick up a copy of *Gay Travel A to Z* on www.amazon.com; this gives general information as well as listings for bars, hotels, restaurants, and places of interest for gay travelers throughout the world.

The **International Gay & Lesbian Travel Association (IGLTA;** www.iglta. com) specializes in connecting travelers with the appropriate gay-friendly tour specialists. It offers a quarterly newsletter, marketing mailings, and a membership directory that is updated four times a year. For an online directory of gay- and lesbian-friendly travel businesses, go to their website and click on "Members."

Many agencies offer tours and travel itineraries specifically for gay and lesbian travelers. Among them are **Above and Beyond Tours** (www.abovebeyondtours. com); **Now, Voyager** (www.nowvoyager.com); and **Olivia** (www.olivia.com).

Websites www.gay.com/view/travel and www.gaytravel.co.uk provide up-to-date information about gay-owned, gay-oriented, and gay-friendly lodging, dining, sightseeing, nightlife, and shopping establishments in every important destination worldwide.

The following travel guides are available at bookstores and online booksellers: *Spartacus International Gay Guide* (Bruno Gmünder Verlag; www.spartacus world.com/gayguide); *Odysseus: The International Gay Travel Planner* (Odysseus Enterprises Ltd); and the *Damron* guides (www.damron.com), with separate, annual books for gay men and lesbians.

For more gay and lesbian travel resources, visit www.frommers.com/planning.

Senior Travel

Many discounts are available for seniors traveling to Barcelona, but often you need to be a member of an association to obtain them.

For information before you go, download the free booklet, *101 Tips for the Mature Traveler,* available from **Grand Circle Travel** (www.gct.com).

One of the most dynamic travel organizations for seniors is **Elderhostel** (www. elderhostel.org). Established in 1975, it operates courses throughout Europe, including Spain. Most last around 3 weeks and prices include airfare, accommodation in student dormitories or modest inns, all meals, and tuition. Courses are usually liberal arts oriented. These are not luxury vacations, but they are fun and fulfilling. Participants must be at least 55 years old. **ElderTreks** (www.eldertreks. com) offers small-group tours to off-the-beaten-path or adventure-travel locations, restricted again to travelers aged 50 and older.

Recommended publications offering travel resources and discounts for seniors include the quarterly magazine *Travel 50 & Beyond* (www.travel50andbeyond. com); *Travel Unlimited: Uncommon Adventures for the Mature Traveler* (Avalon); *101 Tips for Mature Travelers,* available from Grand Circle Travel (*©* **800/221-2610** or 617/350-7500; www.gct.com); and *Unbelievably Good Deals and Great Adventures That You Absolutely Can't Get Unless You're Over 50* (McGraw-Hill), by Joan Rattner Heilman.

For more information and resources on travel for seniors, see www.frommers.com/planning.

Family Travel

Barcelona is a lively and very crowded city that also happens to be a very good destination for families with **children.** From the peaceful **Parc Güell** to the **Parque**

Zoológico, as well as fun spots like **Happy Park Port Aventura** and **Catalunya en Miniatura,** there's plenty to choose from.

To locate accommodations, restaurants, and attractions that are particularly kid-friendly, refer to the "Kids" icon throughout this guide.

For some general tips on family travel check our very own *Frommer's 500 Places to Take Your Kids Before They Grow Up,* which can be purchased via www.amazon.com.

Note that children traveling to Spain with companions other than their own parents should have a notarized letter from their parents to this effect. For full entry requirements to Spain check www.travel.state.gov.

For a list of more family-friendly travel resources, visit www.frommers.com/planning.

Women Travelers

In Barcelona women are as emancipated as in any other main European city. If a degree of machismo still exists it is minimal, and women are reaching high positions in all walks of life. Women exploring the city on their own will not be hassled.

For general advice to female travelers check out the award-winning website **Journeywoman** (www.journeywoman.com), a women's travel-information network where you can sign up for a free e-mail newsletter and get advice on everything from etiquette and dress to safety; or the travel guide *Safety and Security for Women Who Travel,* by Sheila Swan and Peter Laufer (Travelers' Tales, Inc), offering sensible tips on safe travel.

For general travel resources for women, go to www.frommers.com/planning.

Multicultural Travelers

As Barcelona becomes increasingly multicultural, particularly in areas of the Old City such as El Raval, visitors and residents of all nationalities are naturally accepted by a fairly open-minded society. A person of a different race or skin color rarely draws even a second glance, unlike a few decades back when Barcelona was a 99% *castizo* (locals) city.

That said, instances of racial conflict are not unknown, though these tend to be with African, Arabic, and Latin American locals rather than foreign visitors (see "Dealing with Discrimination," above).

Student Travel

Check out the **International Student Travel Confederation** (**ISTC;** www.istc.org) website for comprehensive travel services information and details on how to get an **International Student Identity Card (ISIC),** which qualifies students for savings on rail passes, plane tickets, and entrance fees. It also provides them with basic health and life insurance and a 24-hour helpline. The card is valid for a maximum of 18 months. Apply for the card in person at any **STA Travel** bureau (this is the biggest student travel agency in the world) or online at www.statravel.com; check out the website to locate STA Travel offices worldwide. If you're no longer a student but still under 26, you can get an **International Youth Travel Card** (**IYTC**) from the STA, which entitles you to discounts. **Travel CUTS** (www.travelcuts.com) offers similar services for both Canadians and U.S. residents. Irish students can try **USIT** (www.usit.ie), an Ireland-based specialist in student, youth, and independent travel.

Single Travelers

On package vacations, single travelers are often hit with a "single supplement" to the base price. To avoid this, agree to share a room with other single travelers or find a compatible roommate before you go, from one of the many online roommate-locator agencies such as www.singlestravelcompany.com.

For more information on traveling single, go to www.frommers.com/planning.

For Vegetarian Visitors

There is an increasing choice of vegetarian restaurants in Barcelona. For lots of veggie restaurants, check chapter 6, "Where To Dine."

THE GREENING OF BARCELONA
Responsible Tourism

Responsible tourism is conscientious travel. It means being careful with the environments you explore, and respecting the communities you visit. Two overlapping components of sustainable travel are **ecotourism** and **ethical tourism. The International Ecotourism Society (TIES)** defines ecotourism as responsible travel to natural areas that conserves the environment and improves the well-being of local people. TIES suggests that ecotourists follow these principles:

- Minimize environmental impact.
- Build environmental and cultural awareness and respect.
- Provide positive experiences for both visitors and hosts.
- Provide direct financial benefits for conservation and for local people.
- Raise sensitivity to host countries' political, environmental, and social climates.
- Support international human rights and labor agreements.

You can find eco-friendly travel tips and statistics, as well as touring companies and associations—listed by destination under "Travel Choice"—at the TIES website, www.ecotourism.org.

Although Barcelona gives the impression of being a sprawling, congested city surrounded by industry, its political leaders have thankfully become increasingly ecology-conscious in recent years.

Over 150,000 trees now line its streets and its multifaceted **parks,** which range from high sprawling Collserola and Montjuïc down to magical Güell and cosy Ciutadella, are all managed by the punctilious local Parcs i Jardins Institut Municipal (Parks and Gardens Municipal Department), which prioritizes a **sustainable gardening** scheme in which local plants resistant to environmental diseases are planted and irrigated by an automatic money- and water-saving system.

All sorted **waste** is selectively composted and there are **recycling bins** widely dispersed throughout the city: They are colored green for glass, yellow for unperishable plastic, and orange for general rubbish.

As a viable means of getting around noiselessly and without polluting the air there's **free bicycle hire** (with over 6,000 bikes on the streets, it's already a highly popular option), and there are also serious plans for **electrical vehicles,** still at the experimental stage, to be operating in the near future. Even the **lighting** has seen radical changes, with an increase in the number of self-standing energy-saving **solar lamps** lining the streets.

There is a surprising number of beautiful and untouched eco-friendly regions near Barcelona that you can easily get to by bus or local train (*cercanías*). The **Illes Medes** is a group of seven minuscule islets close to the fishing port and resort of Estartit; the clear waters here are ideal for boating and scuba-diving excursions to see the water's rich variety of plant and marine life. The **Parc Natural del Delta del Ebre,** near Tortosa, is a salty and fertile region of marshes, dunes, and rice paddies that is great for bird-watching, sailing, and cycling along reed-lined waterside paths.

Animal-Rights Issues
A LOAD OF BULL

Spain is not a country that has been noted for its kindness to animals in the past. Fiestas that include piercing bulls with lances in the Castilian town of Tordesillas still prevail (although the annual throwing-a-donkey-off-a-tower shebang in an Extremaduran village has happily disappeared).

The main bone of contention is, of course, the **bullfight,** which has slowly but surely lost popularity in Catalunya, although in most of Spain it remains a treasured event unique in Europe (in Portugal and southern France they have bullfights but don't kill the bull). It's also a very big moneymaker, with an estimated revenue of 300 million euros a year!

Unswayed by cash incentives on this particular occasion, the usually pragmatic burghers of Barcelona **banned** bullfighting altogether on July 28, 2010, when an historic regional parliamentary decision officially prohibited the colorful spectacle from 2012 onwards. The decision contrasts with policies in steadfastly traditional cities like Madrid, Seville, Valencia, and Murcia, all of which are determined to retain their Spanish "sport." The sole exception here is the Canary archipelago, which abolished bullfighting back in the 1990s.

Reasons for Barcelona's decision to ban bullfighting have ranged from condemning *la corrida* for its cruelty to animals to a downright rejection of anything 100% Spanish. Whatever's "in" with Madrid is "out" with Barcelona, from using the Castilian language to accepting the intractable policies of the right-wing PP (Partido Popular) who run Madrid.

So the fabled *neo-mudejar*-styled Monumental Plaza de Toros to the east of L'Eixample is on the verge of formally ending decades of legendary *corridas* featuring Spain's top *toreros*, many of them nigh-mythical figures like Luis Dominguín and Antonio Ordoñez, who reached their peak of popularity in the Catalan capital in the 1950s. What this emblematic building will be used for after 2012 remains to be seen.

Meanwhile the more functional looking **Plaça Espanya** bullring, one of Barcelona's two former *corrida* icons, has long been closed in readiness for transformation into a commercial center, although work has been held up until funds prove available in the current economic uncertainty.

ESCORTED GENERAL-INTEREST TOURS

There are many escorted-tour companies to choose from, each offering transportation to and within Barcelona, prearranged hotel space, and bilingual tour guides and lectures. Expensive and luxurious tours are run by **Abercrombie & Kent International** (www.abercrombiekent.com), including a deluxe 11-day "Highlights of Spain" tour that spends 4 days in Barcelona. **Trafalgar Tours** (www.trafalgartours.com) offers a number of tours of Spain, with Barcelona on several itineraries. **Insight Vacations** (www.insightvacations.com) has an 11-day "Highlights of Spain" tour that begins in Madrid and sweeps along the southern and eastern coasts, stopping in Barcelona. Tours from **Petrabax Tours** (www.petrabax.com) travel by bus and feature stays in *paradores* (high-standard, state-run hotels—some modern, some in historic buildings).

SPECIAL-INTEREST TOURS

The **Barcelona Information Office** (www.barcelonaturisme.com) provides several detailed walks covering different architectural and aesthetic aspects of the city (Gothic, *modernisme,* gourmet, and Picasso). They depart from the Plaça de Catalunya, last between 1½ and 2 hours, and cost between 12€ and 15€ per adult.

More personal and expensive walking trips are arranged by **My Favourite Things** (www.myft.net). These cover more offbeat and idiosyncratic aspects of Barcelona and cost from 30€ per adult.

STAYING CONNECTED
Cellphones (Mobile Phones)

All European cellphone networks are GSM (Global System for Mobiles), so if your cellphone is on a GSM system, you will be fine in Barcelona. If you are unsure how to set up your phone for overseas use, call your wireless operator and ask for "international roaming" to be activated on your account. Per-minute roaming charges are high in Europe, so it's a good idea to buy a prepaid SIM card from a local retailer in Barcelona. This will get you a local phone number and much, much lower calling rates.

If you are staying in Barcelona for more than a few days, **renting** a phone might be the answer. You can rent from kiosks at the local airports but in Barcelona itself there is only one company that offers this service: **Rent A Phone,** Carrer Numància 212 (© **93-280-21-31**). They charge per call. A call to another cellphone in Spain will cost around .80€ per minute, and up to 1.50€ per minute for calls to the States or the U.K.

Buying a phone is a good idea if you're staying in Spain long-term. Find a local mobile shop and get the cheapest package; you'll probably pay less than 60€ for a phone and SIM card. Local calls are as low as 10¢ per minute, and incoming calls are free. Don't forget that in Spain you have to show your passport when you buy a phone and SIM card.

Internet

Travelers in Barcelona can check e-mail and access the Internet from their laptop or PDA, or at cybercafes found all over town. Many hotels, and all three local airports, have Wi-Fi access too. If you have Web access while traveling, use a broadband-based telephone service like Skype (www.skype.com) or Vonage (www.vonage.com) to make free international calls from your laptop or at a cybercafe.

Telephones

Be wary of using the telephone in your room as hotels impose a surcharge on calls, sometimes as high as 40%. On the street, *cabinas* (phone booths) have dialing instructions in English, and you will need to buy a *tarjeta telefónica* (phonecard) from a newsstand or tobacconist. To make a long international call, a *locutorio* (call center; there are lots in the Old City) offers cheap rates. They also sell phone cards that work with both landlines and mobiles and must be used within a month of the first call.

All telephone numbers in Spain operate on a nine-digit system. Each number is preceded by its provincial code for local, national, and international calls. So whether you are calling Barcelona from within the city or from another province within Spain, you must dial 93-XXX-XX-XX.

To call Barcelona from the United States:

1. Dial the international access code: **011.**
2. Dial the country code for Spain: **34.**
3. Dial **93** for Barcelona and then the number. So the whole number you'd dial would be 011-34-93-XXX-XX-XX.

To call Barcelona from the United Kingdom:

1. Dial the international access code: **00.**
2. Dial the country code for Spain: **34.**
3. Dial **93** for Barcelona and then the number. So the whole number you'd dial would be 00-34-93-XXX-XX-XX.

To make international calls from Barcelona: Dial 00 and then the country code (U.S. or Canada 1, U.K. 44, Ireland 353, Australia 61, New Zealand 64). Dial the area code and number. Knock the first "0" off the area code when calling the U.K.

For directory assistance: Dial ☎ **11818** if you're looking for a number inside Spain, or ☎ **11825** for numbers in all other countries.

For operator assistance: For assistance in making an international call, dial ☎ **1008** (for Europe, Morocco, Tunisia, Libya, and Turkey) or **1005** (for the U.S. and all other countries); for assistance in calling a number in Spain, dial ☎ **1009.**

SUGGESTED BARCELONA ITINERARIES

You're completely spoiled in Barcelona. It offers not just one but many different worlds to explore. The famous narrow alleys of Barri Gòtic (the Gothic Quarter), with its magnificently preserved monuments, is a complete medieval town come to life, throbbing with vitality. The wide-laned Eixample above it, conceived in the 19th century and dotted with inimitable *moderniste* architectural gems, is more spacious and elegant, to be wandered around and explored at leisure.

At a pinch, you can cover the main highlights of both these very different areas in just a day. But the more time you have available, the more justice you can do to this unique city's multitude of contrasting sights. Here are our recommendations on how to spend your time. See chapter 8, "Strolling Around Barcelona," for more detailed routes you can follow; and chapter 7, "What To See & Do," for in-depth information on the monuments themselves.

CITY LAYOUT

Plaça de Catalunya (**Plaza de Cataluña** in Spanish) is the city's heart, the world-famous **La Rambla**—also known as Las Ramblas—its main artery. La Rambla begins at the Plaça Portal de la Pau, with its 49-m (160-feet)-high monument to Columbus opposite the port, and stretches north to the Plaça de Catalunya. Along this wide promenade you'll find newsstands, stalls selling birds and flowers, portrait painters, and cafe tables and chairs, where you can sit and watch the passing parade. Such is its popularity with visitors today that during the summer months you'll be hard pressed to spot a genuine local. Moving northward along La Rambla, the area on your left is **El Raval,** the largest neighborhood in Barcelona, and to your right is the **Barri Gòtic (Gothic Quarter).** These two neighborhoods, plus the area of **La Ribera,** which lies further to your right across another main artery, the Vía Laietana, make up the sizeable **Ciutat Vella (Old City).** Within these three neighborhoods are two subregions. One is the notorious **Barri Xinès** or **Barrio Chino** (literally, **Chinese Quarter,** although this is no Chinatown; see below) near the eastern end of El Raval, bordering La Rambla. The other is **El Born**—prosperous in the Middle Ages and today Barcelona's bastion of cool—in the lower, port-side pocket of La Ribera. As this whole condensed, character-filled area is large—though not as large as sprawling but amorphous L'Eixample (see below)—I have subdivided all its attractions into El Raval, Barri Gòtic, and La Ribera.

Across the **Plaça de Catalunya,** La Rambla becomes **Rambla Catalunya,** with the elegant **Passeig de Gràcia** running parallel to the immediate right. These are the two main arteries of **L'Eixample** (Catalan for "extension"). This is where most of the architectural jewels of the *modernisme* period, including key works by Antoni Gaudí, dot the harsh grids of this graceful, middle-class neighborhood. Both end at the **Diagonal,** a major cross-town artery that also serves as the city's business and commercial hub. Northward across the Diagonal is the suburb of **Gràcia.** Once a separate village, it makes up in atmosphere for what it lacks in notable monuments.

The other areas of interest for the visitor are **Montjuïc,** the bluff to the southwest of the city, and the maritime area of **Barceloneta** and the beaches. The first is the largest green zone in the city, contains some of its top museums, and was the setting for the principal events of the 1992 Summer Olympic Games. The second is a peninsula that has long been the city's populist playground, with dozens of fish restaurants, some facing the beaches that sprawl northward along the coast. Behind the city to the northwest, higher than Montjuïc, is **Tibidabo,** looming like a sentinel and enjoying great views of the city and the Mediterranean. It also has a veteran amusement park and a kitsch pseudo-Gothic church, which aspires to emulate Paris's Sacré Coeur.

FINDING AN ADDRESS/MAPS Finding a Barcelona address doesn't generally pose too many problems. The Eixample district is built on a grid system, so by learning the cross-street you can easily find the place you are looking for. Barcelona is hemmed in on one side by the sea (*mar*) and by the mountain of Tibidabo (*montaña*) on the other, so often people just describe a place as being on the *mar* or *montaña* side of the street in L'Eixample. The Ciutat Vella, or Old City, is a little more confusing, and you will need a good map (available from news kiosks along La Rambla) to find specific places. However, the new city abounds with long boulevards and spacious squares, making it easy to navigate. The designation "s/n" (*sin número*) means that the building has no number; however, this is mainly limited to large buildings and monuments, so it's pretty obvious once you get there where it is. In built-up Barcelona, the symbol "°" designates the floor (for example, the first floor is 1°). Street names are in Catalan. Some people still refer to them in Spanish, but there is very little difference between the two so it shouldn't cause any confusion. The word for "street" (*carrer* in Catalan and *calle* in Spanish) is nearly always dropped; that is, Carrer Ferran is simply referred to as "Ferran." *Passeig* (or *paseo* in Spanish) and *avinguda* (or *avenida* in Spanish), meaning respectively "boulevard" and "avenue," are nearly always kept, as in Passeig de Gràcia and Avinguda de Tibidabo. *Rambla* means a long, pedestrianized avenue and *plaça* (or *plaza* in Spanish) a square.

Greater Barcelona

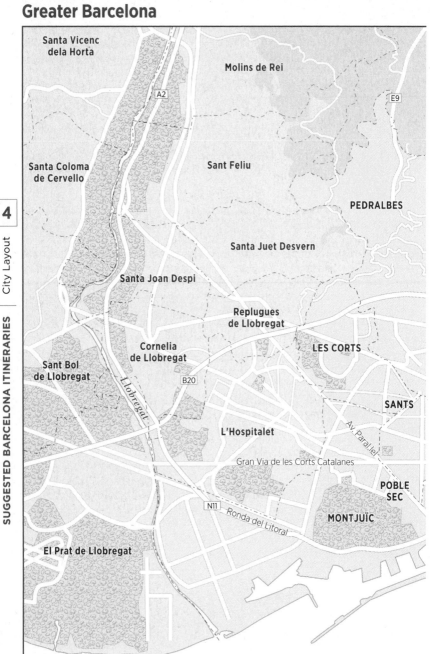

Santa Vicenc dela Horta

Molins de Rei

A2

E9

Santa Coloma de Cervello

Sant Feliu

PEDRALBES

Santa Juet Desvern

Santa Joan Despi

Replugues de Llobregat

LES CORTS

Cornelia de Llobregat

Sant Bol de Llobregat

Llobregat

B20

SANTS

L'Hospitalet

Av. Paral·lel

Gran Via de les Corts Catalanes

POBLE SEC

N11

Ronda del Litoral

MONTJUÏC

El Prat de Llobregat

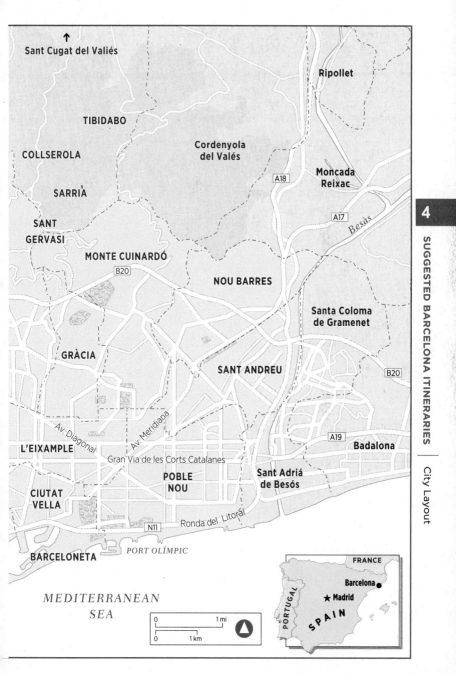

Sant Cugat del Valiés

Ripollet

TIBIDABO

COLLSEROLA

Cordenyola del Valés

Moncada Reixac

A18

SARRIÀ

A17

Besàs

SANT GERVASI

MONTE CUINARDÓ

B20

NOU BARRES

Santa Coloma de Gramenet

GRÀCIA

SANT ANDREU

B20

Av. Diagonal

Av. Meridiana

A19

Badalona

L'EIXAMPLE

Gran Via de les Corts Catalanes

POBLE NOU

Sant Adriá de Besós

CIUTAT VELLA

Ronda del Litoral

N11

BARCELONETA

PORT OLÍMPIC

MEDITERRANEAN SEA

0   1 mi

0   1 km

FRANCE

Barcelona

PORTUGAL

★ Madrid

S P A I N

Neighborhoods in Brief

CIUTAT VELLA (OLD CITY)

Barri Gòtic Next to the excesses of the 19th-century *moderniste* period, Barcelona's golden age was between the 13th and 15th centuries, the Gothic period. The city expanded rapidly in medieval times, so much so that it could no longer be contained within the old Roman walls. So new ones were built. They originally ran from the port northward along what was to become La Rambla, down the Ronda Sant Pere to Calle Rec Comtal, and back to the sea again. Except for a few remaining sections along the Vía Laietana, most of them have now been destroyed. But the ensemble of 13th- to 15th-century buildings (or parts of) that remain make up the most complete Gothic quarter on the continent. These include government buildings, churches (including the main cathedral), and guild houses.

Guilds *(gremis)* were a forerunner of the trade unions and the backbone of Barcelona medieval life. Many of their shields, which would have denoted the headquarters of each particular trade, can be seen on buildings dotted around the Barri Gòtic. Tiny workshops were also enclosed in the area, and even now many street names bear the name of the activity that went on there for centuries—such as Escudellers (shield makers), Assaonadors (tanners), Carders (wool combers), and Brocaters (brocade makers), to name a few.

El Call, the original Jewish quarter, is also located within the Barri Gòtic. A tiny area around the Carrer del Call and L'Arc de Sant Ramón del Call was the scene of the sacking of the Jews by Christian mobs in the late 1400s.

Apart from the big attractions such as the **Cathedral de la Seu,** the **Plaça Sant Jaume** (which contains the two organs of Catalan politics, the Ajuntament and the Generalitat, p. 166), and the medieval palace of the **Plaça del Rei,** where Columbus was received after returning from the New World, the Barri Gòtic's charm lies in its details. Smaller squares, such as the **Plaça Felip Neri** with a central fountain, the oasis-like courtyard of the **Frederic Marès Museum,** gargoyles peering down from ancient towers, and small chapels set into the sides of medieval buildings—this is what makes the area so fascinating. Most of them can only be discovered on foot, ideally at sunset when the fading Mediterranean light lends the stone buildings a warm hue, and musicians, mainly of the classical nature, jostle for performance spaces around the cathedral.

Some of the sites in the Barri Gòtic are not medieval at all (architecture and history purists argue that the name has remained simply for the sake of tourism) but of no less merit. The most famous of these is the so-called Bridge of Sighs (nothing like the Venetian original) in Carrer del Bisbe, built during the city's Gothic revival in the 1920s. But even modern additions do nothing to diminish the character of the Barri Gòtic. The abundance of specialist shops, from old fan and espadrille makers to more cutting-edge designer ware, is another attraction, as are the dozens of outdoor eateries where you can enjoy a coffee or two looking out onto an ancient edifice.

The sprawling Barri Gòtic is hemmed in on one side by the ugly, ever-busy Vía Laietana and on the other by **La Rambla.**

The most famous promenade in Spain, ranking with Madrid's Paseo del Prado, was once a riverbed. These days, street entertainers, flower vendors, news vendors, cafe patrons, and strollers flow along its length. The gradual 1.5km (1 mile) descent toward the sea has been called a metaphor for life because its bustling action combines cosmopolitanism and crude vitality.

La Rambla actually consists of five sections, each a particular *rambla*—Rambla de Canaletes, Rambla dels Estudis, Rambla de Sant Josep, Rambla dels Caputxins, and Rambla de Santa Mónica. The shaded pedestrian esplanade runs from the Plaça de Catalunya to the port—all the way to the

Columbus Monument. Along the way you'll pass the **Gran Teatre del Liceu,** on Rambla dels Caputxins, one of the most magnificent opera houses in the world, restored to its former glory after a devastating fire in 1994. Watch out for the giant sidewalk mosaic by Miró halfway down at the Plaça de la Boqueria.

El Raval On the opposite side of La Rambla lies El Raval, Barcelona's largest inner-city neighborhood. This is where the ambitious plans for the post-Olympic "New Barcelona" are at their most evident as entire blocks of dank apartment buildings were bulldozed to make way for sleek new edifices, squares, and boulevards. El Raval has recently been cited as the neighborhood with the greatest multicultural mix in Europe, some still living in the old buildings, some renovated, some untouched. A quick stroll around its maze of streets, where Pakistani fabric merchants and South American spice sellers stand side by side with traditional establishments selling dried cod and local wine, confirms the fact. The *adhan* (the Muslim call to prayer) wafts from ground-floor mosques next to neo-hippie bars, yoga schools, and contemporary art galleries. The largest of the galleries is the **MACBA (Museum of Contemporary Art),** a luminous white behemoth designed by the American architect Richard Meir. It resides on a huge concrete square that has, since its opening in 1995, become the neighborhood's most popular playground. At any time of the day, the space will be inundated by kids playing cricket and soccer, skateboarders cruising the ramps of the museum's forecourt, and housewives on their way to the nearby **Boqueria** market. Another favorite stomping ground is the Rambla del Raval—a wide, airy pedestrianized avenue dating from 2000 and lined with cafes and multinational (mainly Asian) eating spots.

The signs of gentrification are everywhere, and while this still attracts its fair share of criticism, no one can deny the life-enhancing benefits of the above-mentioned developments for a neighborhood that has been historically deprived of light and breathing space. The neighborhood's former reputation as a seedy inner-city slum is gradually receding, though the area still has its rough edges.

Change has been slower to come to the so-called **Barri Xinès** or **Barrio Chino,** the lower half of El Raval between the waterfront and Carrer de l'Hospital. Despite the name ("Chinese Quarter"), this isn't Chinatown. In fact, most attribute its nickname to an imaginative writer by the name of Francisco Madrid who, influenced by a fellow journalist who'd just returned from a visit to the States where he felt New York's Chinatown reminded him of this area, published a 1926 book on these lines called *Sangre en las Atarazanas* (Blood on the Dockyards). A decade later the French writer Jean Genet (p. 77) wrote *A Thief's Journal* during a stint in one of its peseta-a-night whorehouses. In some pockets of the Chino, little has changed: While drug dealing has been largely shipped out to the outer suburbs, prostitution still exists openly, as does the general seediness of many of the streets. But, as with all of the Old City, the times they are a-changin' and you may find yourself wandering down here at night to attend the opening of a new bar or club. Petty thieves, prostitutes, drug dealers, and purse-snatchers are just some of the neighborhood "characters," so exercise caution. Although Barri Xinès has a long way to go, an urban renewal program has led to the destruction of some of the rougher parts of the barrio.

La Ribera Another neighborhood that stagnated for years but is now well into a renaissance is La Ribera. Across the noisy artery Vía Laietana and southward from Calle Princesa, this small neighborhood is bordered by the **Port Vell** (Old Port) and the **Parc de la Ciutadella.** Like the Barrio Chino (see above), **El Born** is La Ribera's "neighborhood within a neighborhood." But far from being a rough diamond, El Born is a polished pastiche of the Ciutat Vella where designer clothing and houseware showcases occupy medieval buildings and workshops.

The centerpiece is the imposing **Santa María del Mar,** a stunningly complete Gothic basilica built with funds from cashed-up merchants who once lived here. Many lived in the mansions and palaces along the Carrer de Montcada, today home to a trio of top museums including the **Museu Picasso.** Most of the mansions here were built during one of Barcelona's major maritime expansions, principally in the 1200s and 1300s. During this time, El Born was the city's principal trade area. The refurbished **La Llotja,** the city's first stock exchange, lies on its outer edge on the Plaça Palau; although the facade dates from 1802, the interior is pure Catalan Gothic.

The central **Passeig del Born** got its name from the medieval jousts that used to occur here. "Born" is Catalan for "lists" in the sense of "jousting tournament lists (i.e. competitions)." At the northern end, the wrought-iron Mercat del Born was the city's principal wholesale market until the mid-1970s. Recent excavation work has revealed entire streets and houses dating back to the 18th century, sealing the edifice's fate as a new museum where these ruins can be viewed via glass flooring and walkways. Behind the Mercat del Born, the **Parc de la Ciutadella** is a tranquil oasis replete with a manmade lake; wide, leafy walkways; and yet more museums.

THE PORT & WATERFRONT

Barceloneta, the Beaches & the Harbor Although Barcelona has a long seagoing tradition, its waterfront stood in decay for years. Today, the waterfront promenade, **Passeig del Moll de la Fusta,** bursts with activity. The best way to get a bird's-eye view is to take an elevator up the Columbus Monument in Plaça Portal de la Pau, at the port end of La Rambla.

Near the monument are the **Reials Drassanes** (Royal Shipyards), a booming place during the Middle Ages. Years before Columbus landed in the New World, ships sailed around the known world from here, flying the yellow-and-red flag of Catalonia. These days, the shipyards are home to the excellent Museu Marítim. Across the road,

the wooden swing bridge known as the Rambla del Mar takes you across the water to the Maremagnum entertainment and shopping complex.

To the east, the glitzy **Port Vell** (Old Port) was one of the main projects for the city's Olympic renewal scheme. Its chic yachting marina is similar to those of other great Mediterranean ports like Marseilles and Piraeus, and there are large expanses of open recreational areas where people get out and enjoy the sun. It is also home to the city's Aquarium. On one side it is flanked by **Passeig Joan de Borbón,** the main street of **Barceloneta** (Little Barcelona). Formerly a fishing district dating from the 18th century, the neighborhood is full of character and is still one of the best places in the city to eat seafood. The blocks here are long and narrow—architects planned them that way so that each room in every building fronted a street. The streets end at Barceloneta beach. Like all of the city's beaches, this was neglected to the point of nonexistence pre-1992. The harborfront was clogged with industrial buildings—many of them abandoned—and tatty but well-patronized *chiringuitos* (beach bars). Today these are some of the finest urban beaches in Europe. From Barceloneta, separated by breakwaters, no fewer than seven of them sprawl northward. The **Port Olímpic,** dominated by a pair of landmark, sea-facing skyscrapers (one accommodating the five-star Hotel Arts and the city's casino), boasts yet another marina and a host of restaurants and bars. Take them all in at your leisure as you stroll along the Passeig Marítim (seafront promenade).

CITY-CENTER BARCELONA

L'Eixample To the north of the Plaça de Catalunya is the massive section of Barcelona (known as the *Ensanche* in Spanish) that grew beyond the old medieval walls. In the mid-1800s, Barcelona was bursting at the seams. The dank, serpentine streets of the old walled city were breeding grounds for cholera and typhoid and habitual mass rioting. Rather than leveling the Ciutat Vella, the city's authorities had a sloping sweep of land just outside the walls at their disposal and contracted the socialist engineer Idelfons Cerdà to offer a solution. His subsequent 1856 work, *Monograph on the Working Class of Barcelona,* became the first-ever attempt to study the living, breathing landscape of a city: Urbanization to you and me, a term Cerdà himself coined in the process.

Cerdà visited hundreds of Old City hovels before he drew up plans for Barcelona's New City. Needless to say, his fact-checking led him to the bowels of human suffering; he discovered that life expectancy for the proletariat was half that of the bourgeoisie, they were paying exorbitant rents to ruthless landlords for their decaying houses, and mortality rates were lower in the narrower streets. Above all, he concluded that air and sunshine were vital to basic well-being.

Today little is in evidence of Cerdà's most radical plans for L'Eixample, apart from the rigorous regularity of its 20-m (66-feet)-wide streets and famous chamfered pavements. The *modernistes* were the neighborhood's earliest architects, filling the blocks with their labored fantasies, such as Gaudí's La Sagrada Família, Casa Milà, and Casa Batlló. His works aside, L'Eixample is a living, breathing museum piece with an abundance of Art Nouveau architecture and details not found anywhere else in Europe. **La Ruta del Modernisme** is a specially designed walking tour that guides you to the best of them. See walking tour 4 in chapter 8, "Strolling Around Barcelona."

In accordance with Cerdà's basic plan, avenues form a grid of perpendicular streets, cut across by a majestic boulevard— **Passeig de Gràcia,** a posh shopping street ideal for leisurely promenades. L'Eixample's northern boundary is the **Avinguda Diagonal** (or simply the *El Diagonal*), which links the expressway and the heart of the city and acts as Barcelona's business and banking hub.

Gràcia This charming neighborhood sprawls out northward of the intersection of the **Passeig de Gràcia** and the **Diagonal.**

Its contained, village-like ambience stems from the fact that it was once a separate town, only connected to central Barcelona in 1897 with the construction of the Passeig de Gràcia. It has a strong industrial and artisan history, and many street-level workshops can still be seen. Gràcia's charm lies in its low-level housing and series of squares—the Plaça del Sol and Plaça Ruis i Taulet are two of the prettiest—rather than in monuments or museums. The residents themselves have a strong sense of neighborhood pride and a marked independent spirit, and their annual fiestas (p. 181) are some of the liveliest in the city. For the casual visitor, Gràcia is a place to wander through for a slice of authentic *barri* life.

Montjuïc & Tibidabo Locals call them "mountains," and while northerly Tibidabo does actually rise to over 488m (1,600 feet), the port-side bluff of Montjuïc is somewhat lower. Both are great places to go for fine views and cleaner air. The most accessible, Montjuïc (Catalan for "Hill of the Jews," after a Jewish necropolis that once stood there), gained prominence in 1929 as the site of the World's Fair and again in 1992 as the site of the Summer Olympic Games. Its major attractions are the **Fundacíon Miró,** the Olympic installations, and the **Poble Espanyol** (Spanish Village), a 2-hectare (5-acre) site constructed for the World's Fair. Examples of Spanish art and architecture are on display against the backdrop of a traditional Spanish village. Opposite the village lies the **CaixaForum,** one of the city's newer contemporary art showcases, housed in a converted *moderniste* textile factory. In a recent push to raise Montjuïc's status even further, new parks and gardens (such as the Jardí Botanic) have been laid out. At the base of Montjuïc is the working-class neighborhood of Poble Sec and the Ciutat del Teatre, location of the city's theatrical school and a conglomeration of performing-arts spaces.

Tibidabo (503m/1,650 feet) is where you should go for your final look at Barcelona. On a clear day you can see the mountains of Majorca, some 210km (130 miles) away. Reached by train, tram, and cable car, Tibidabo is a popular Sunday excursion in Barcelona, when whole families head to the fun-fair of the same name.

OUTER BARCELONA

Pedralbes At the western edge of El Diagonal, next to the elite districts of Sant Gervasí and Putxet, is the equally posh residential area where wealthy Barcelonans live in stylish blocks of apartment houses, 19th-century villas behind ornamental fences, or stunning *moderniste* structures. Set in a park, the **Palau de Pedralbes** (Av. Diagonal 686) was constructed in the 1920s as a gift from the city to Alfonso XIII, the grandfather of King Juan Carlos. Today it has a new life, housing the Ceramic and Decorative Arts Museums. The Finca Güell is also part of the estate, the country home of Gaudí's main patron, Eusebi Güell. Although not open to the public, the main gate and gatehouse, both designed by Gaudí, are visible from the street. The pride of this zone is the 14th-century Gothic church-cum-convent of **Monestir de Pedralbes,** where you can view lovely cloisters and well-preserved kitchens.

THE BEST OF BARCELONA IN 1 DAY

This is going to be a very full day, so make an early start at the **Plaça de Catalunya.** Spend the morning wandering down **La Rambla** to the **Mirador de Colón** beside the port. Return via the **Plaça Reial** and explore the neighboring **Barri Gòtic** with its central **Catedral.** Then walk across to the Raval and Poble Sec districts on the western side of La Rambla. From there, take the funicular to the top of **Montjuïc** for a fine view of Barcelona and its harbor. Explore the gardens and castle museum and, if there's time, pop into the Museu Nacional d'Art de Catalunya for a glimpse of the finest collection of Romanesque relics in Spain. In the evening travel by Metro to visit Antoni Gaudí's unfinished masterpiece, **La Sagrada Família,** and the **Parc Güell.**

1 Plaça de Catalunya

Located at the top end of La Rambla and midway between the medieval Old City and the 19th-century Eixample, this circular plaça, with its fountains and sculptures, is the cultural hub of Barcelona. Surrounded by large stores, open-air cafes, and hotels, it's a place to watch passersby, listen to the Latino buskers, feed the pigeons, and even try to join in and dance the *sardana* on festive occasions. As the afternoon proceeds it gets increasingly crowded and colorful (p. 62).

2 La Rambla ★★★

Also known as Las Ramblas, this mile-long avenue is divided into five distinct sections named, successively, Canaletes, Estudis, Sant Josep, Caputxins, and Santa Mónica. It's a stage-set of human statues, jugglers, singers, eccentrics, misfits, transvestites, caged small animals, kiosks, cafes, and vibrant flower stalls, all shaded by a leafy canopy of huge plane trees. Originally called *ramla* (riverbed) by the Arabs, it's the favorite evening stroll for Barcelonans and visitors alike. For year-round atmosphere, there's nowhere else like it in Spain.

3 Mirador de Colón

Situated at the port end of La Rambla, this ornate bronze statue in honor of the Genovese sailor who discovered you-know-where was built during Barcelona's 19th-century industrial boom. After 10am you can get to the top by elevator and enjoy marvelous views of the harbor and Ciutat Vella. Spot the deliberate mistake: Columbus is pointing east across the Mediterranean to Mallorca instead of west toward the Atlantic (p. 165).

4 Café de l'Opera 🍵

Halfway down La Rambla, Café de l'Opera, La Rambla 74 (📞 93-317-75-85; www.cafe operabcn.com) is a 19th-century Parisian-style cafe. Its murals, iron columns, and wall mirrors with etchings evoke a more elegant age, as waiters with bow ties serve you with commendable indifference. It's the ideal spot to sit back, enjoy a quality coffee, and watch the non-stop activity outside.

5 Plaça Reial ★

This is one of the city's great old squares, with neoclassical pillars and archways, 19th-century lampposts, slender ageing palm trees, and enough semi-resident marginals—from drug addicts to transsexuals—to do justice to any Almodóvar movie worth its salt. More ominous in the past, today it is virtually a tourist attraction. Watch out for pickpockets, though.

6 Barri Gòtic ★★★

Said to be the largest inhabited (and probably most densely populated) medieval quarter in Europe, the narrow-alleyed Barri Gòtic really needs a minimum of a half a day's leisurely exploration, so if you're in town for more than 3 days, come back again (and again) to do it full justice. At night its illuminated streets and buildings give it a magical touch. If you're only here a day, then the **Catedral** (see below) is an absolute must. Also not to be missed are the central **Plaça del Rei,** with its two key monuments, and the **Museu d'Historia de la Ciutat,** built over a complete subterranean Roman township. Another must-see is the **Palau del Rei,** where Columbus introduced American Indians to Spain's monarchs for the first time in its **Salódel Tinell** (p. 164).

7 Catedral ★★★

Originally built on the site of the old Roman town, this monumental place of worship was begun in the 13th century and finished in the 15th. (No hurry in those days!) It has seen many changes over the centuries, although it was mercifully one of the few buildings to be spared the destructive fury of the Civil War. Here the young Santa Eulàlia—cruelly martyred for protesting her Christianity during Dacian's repressive rule—is buried. Don't miss the 14th-century choir stalls, chapter house, and roof, or the delightful cloister, which bucolically hides tall palms, a cluster of orange trees, and a pond with geese amid the surrounding Gothic and Renaissance splendor (p. 265).

8 Can Culleretes 🍵

For an atmospheric lunch, you can't beat Barcelona's oldest restaurant (established in 1786), Can Culleretes, Quintana 5 (📞 93-317-64-85; www.culleretes.com). It's tucked away in a secretive lane in the heart of the Barri Gòtic. You won't be the only non-Catalan

The Best of Barcelona in 1 Day

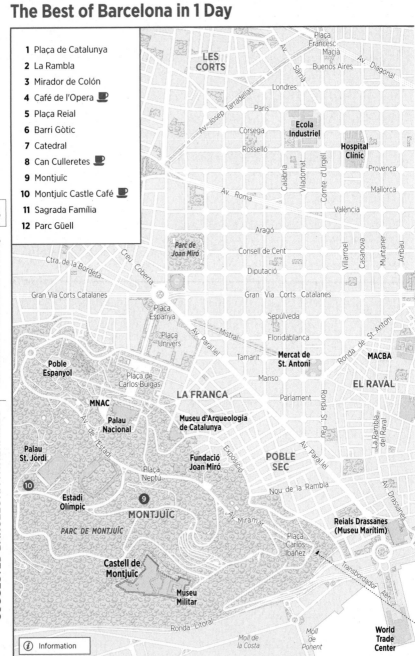

1 Plaça de Catalunya
2 La Rambla
3 Mirador de Colón
4 Café de l'Opera
5 Plaça Reial
6 Barri Gòtic
7 Catedral
8 Can Culleretes
9 Montjuïc
10 Montjuïc Castle Café
11 Sagrada Família
12 Parc Güell

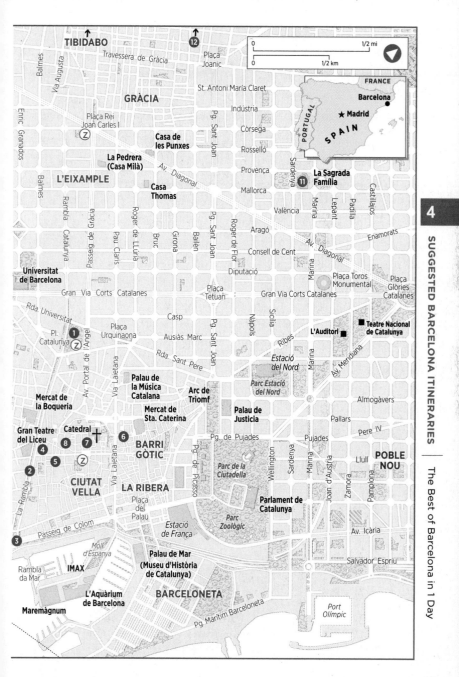

visitor—the place is in too many guidebooks—but the restaurant is a monument, the service and decor from another age, and the traditional food and wine pretty good (p. 126).

9 Montjuïc ★★

Topped by an imposing castle, which is now a military museum, this distinctive hill on the city's west flank offers some of the best vistas of the Catalan capital. After the radical improvements prior to the 1992 Olympics (don't forget to take an outside peep at the stadium), it's now also the city's greatest green zone, with a wealth of walkways, parklands, leisure areas, and cultural attractions to explore. Get there by the funicular from Poble Sec or by the more vertiginous Telefèric de Montjuïc, which carries you high above the harbor (p. 183).

10 Montjuïc Castle Café 🍽

This unpretentious self-service cafe, tucked away inside the castle with a patio section where you can sit outside in good weather, is a great spot for relaxing and savoring the old *"castell"* ambience.

11 Sagrada Família ★★

In the evening, cross the city by Metro Line 5 to the Sagrada Família, abandoned for decades and still unfinished. The cathedral finally saw restoration and expansion work carried out when its hermit-like architect, Antoni Gaudí (who was killed by a tram in 1926—p. 23—and whose tomb can be viewed in the crypt), came back into fashion in the 1990s. The four original spires—by the master himself—are generally acknowledged to be far superior to the additional quartet designed by modern architects. Take a ride up to the top of one of the towers and enjoy the fine view. Loved and reviled in equal measure, the building remains unique. Current construction progress is slow, however, and even the most optimistic forecaster doesn't see the whole thing reaching completion for at least another decade (p. 176).

12 Parc Güell ★★

Take Metro Line 5 to Diagonal and Line 3 to Lesseps, and walk up to Parc Güell in time for sunset. You can imagine gremlins living in this unique fairy-tale park located high up in the city and loved by children and adults alike. Look out for its mosaic serpent and Hansel-and-Gretel houses at the entrance (one of which is a tiny museum, the Centre d'Interpretacióí Acollida, devoted to describing creator Gaudí's building methods). At its center, up some steps, the Banc de Trencadís—a multi-colored ceramic bench—curves around a spacious esplanade, while behind it footpaths climb into the pine woods of Vallcarca and Monte Carmel, offering scenic views through the trees of the city below (p. 181).

THE BEST OF BARCELONA IN 2 DAYS

On the first day follow the itinerary described above. On the second day stroll through the pond- and garden-filled **Parc de la Ciutadella** and visit the zoo, time permitting. Then explore the narrow-laned *barrio* of **La Ribera,** with its **Museu Picasso** and imposing **Santa María del Mar** church, and walk down to the old (but gentrified) maritime quarter and beachfront of **La Barceloneta** with its modern adjoining Port Olímpic area. It's the ideal spot for an atmospheric seafood lunch. In the afternoon wander around **Port Vell** and explore the regenerated **El Raval** district.

1 Parc de la Ciutadella ★★

Once the site of a fort (*ciutadella* is Catalan for "citadel"), this verdant park is the most attractive and popular spot in lower Barcelona, complete with two lush but small botanical gardens, a Gaudí-designed fountain (*La Cascada*) with a huge statue of a primeval elephant, and a quiet lake where you can go rowing. Other attractions include the Castell dels Tres Dragons (Castle of the Three Dragons) and the Parlament de Catalunya (Catalan Parliament; Passeig de Pujades; ✆ **93-304-65-00;** www.parlament.cat), which you can visit for free if you have time to make an appointment. The zoo's well worth a look; it has a charming park setting, and houses hippos, elephants, komodo dragons, and dolphins. Kiddies enjoy the zoo "train" rides and play areas (p. 16).

2 La Ribera ★★

The western part of Ciutat Vella is really two districts, El Born and Sant Pere (referring to the area's oldest square and church, respectively). Its name, La Ribera, actually means "the shore," as the sea once reached its southern edge. The central Carrer Montcada is lined with museums and the whole former medieval merchants' quarter is packed with traditional shops, tiny squares, and narrow streets named after various local trades that were carried out here— hence Carrer Cotoners (weavers), Carrer Corders (rope makers), Carrer Mirallers (mirror makers), and Carrer Vidrieria (glazers).

3 Museu Picasso ★★★

By far the most popular art museum in town, the Picasso is tastefully spread throughout a quintet of fine old mansions in the heart of La Ribera. Be prepared for a long wait, but if you do manage to squeeze it into your time-challenged schedule, don't miss the Malagueño artist's version of Velazquez's *La Meninas*. The museum concentrates on more conventional works and etchings of the adolescent artist, who arrived in town with his family in 1895 and wasted no time in opening his first (very modest) studio in Carrer de la Plata (p. 169).

4 Tèxtil Café 🍵

Tèxtil Café, Carrer Montcada 12 (✆ 93-268-25-98), is a charming spot nestled in the patio of the 14th-century mansion containing the Museu Tèxtil, just a few steps away from the Museu Picasso. Enjoy coffee and pastries in an elegant year-round setting. Even in winter—apart from on rare rainy days—you can sit outside under gas heaters.

5 Santa María del Mar ★

Once upon a time this magnificent church, with its soaring vaults and wonderful stained-glass windows, stood right on the shore of the Mediterranean (*ribera* is Spanish for "shore"). It was the focal point of a then-vibrant seafaring and trading quarter, which eventually receded, as did the sea. Today it's one of the best-preserved Gothic monuments in the city, most evocative for being less crowded than some of the better-known sights.

The Best of Barcelona in 2 Days

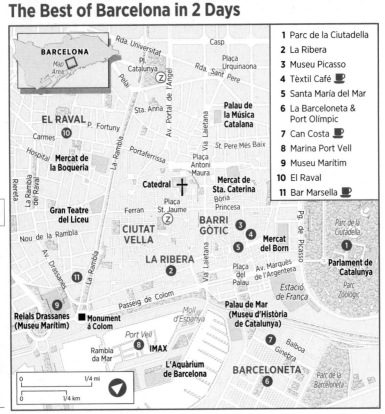

1 Parc de la Ciutadella
2 La Ribera
3 Museu Picasso
4 Tèxtil Café
5 Santa María del Mar
6 La Barceloneta & Port Olímpic
7 Can Costa
8 Marina Port Vell
9 Museu Marítim
10 El Raval
11 Bar Marsella

6 La Barceloneta & Port Olímpic ★

Built on the compact triangle of land (reclaimed from marshes) between the Port Vell and the first of the city beaches (Sant Sebastiá), this 18th-century working-class zone—which is built in a formal grid system of lanes around a central market—has today become more gentrified and sought-after by visitors and residents alike. Its once-neglected beach is now well cared for and has a palm-lined promenade where folks walk their pooches. The original, tatty, much-loved *chiringuitos* (shacks) that bordered the shore, serving delicious seafood dishes, were demolished pre-1992 to make way for today's more acceptably salubrious establishments (still known as *chiringuitos*), which sell exactly the same food at much increased prices. Moving with the times, it remains a great location and a fun spot for paella, as does the vibrant adjoining Port Olímpic with its long promenade, beaches, yachting marinas, and trendy eating spots and nightclubs.

7 Can Costa

You can't pass though Barceloneta without sampling one of its finest—and definitely oldest—seafood eating spots, Can Costa, Passeig de Joan de Borbón (✆ 93-221-59-03;

www.cancosta.com). It's located a block back from the waterfront, as all the genuine locals are. This is the real thing, with excellent *fideuà de paella* (made with noodles, not rice) and baby *calamares* that are worth leaving home for. It can get busy for lunch, so arrive early—and that's anytime before 2pm in Spain (p. 151).

8 Marina Port Vell ★

The main port is the most visibly changed part of Barcelona's waterfront, which for decades notoriously "turned its back on the sea." Today the once-drab industrial zone, where piles of containers brooded under sad-looking palms, has been cleansed, revitalized, and transformed. At its northern end, the large yachting marina beside the older Moll de Barceloneta is lined with international vessels of all shapes and sizes. A smart promenade with public seats runs southward around the harbor past two large, modern jetties: the Moll d'Espanya, whose exclusive Club Marítim, aquarium, IMAX cinema, and Maremagnum zone of trendy shops and nightspots are all linked to the promenade by the curving Rambla de Mar footbridge; and the Moll de Barcelona, with its high, modern World Trade Center and Torre de Jaume I, opposite the 14th-century Reials Drassanes (Royal Shipyards), housing the Museu Marítim (p. 190).

9 Museu Marítim

The Gothic arches inside the Royal Shipyards loom impressively over what's probably the best nautical museum in the Mediterranean: A superb testament to Barcelona's great naval past. Check out the marvelous "Great Adventure of the Sea" collection, with its full-scale replica of Don Juan of Austria's Royal Galley from the decisive 16th-century Battle of Lepanto, when Spain defeated the Ottomans. There are smaller models of Magellan's world-navigating *Santa María*, and one of the earliest submarines, the *Ictíneo;* and just outside you can go on board the old *Santa Eulàlia* sailing ship moored in Moll de la Fusta (p. 190).

10 El Raval

Once largely a seedy, run-down district, with red-light sections (some of which still exist) and many buildings little more than slums, this is another rejuvenated corner of the city, more polyglot than most due to the large number of immigrant residents. In 2000, the center was bulldozed to provide much-needed breathing space in the form of a brand-new Rambla, complete with trees, benches, and kiddies' play areas—part of an ambitious *"Ravall obert al cel"* (Ravall open to the sky) project. Around it some of the city's most stimulating new art galleries sprang up, spearheaded by the **MACBA** (Museum of Contemporary Art of Barcelona, p. 173). The continuing proliferation of rough edges enhances the *barrio's* appeal, giving it massive street cred. A few classic local buildings like Gaudí's **Palau Güell** (p. 174) and the Romanesque **Sant Pau del Camp** (p. 175) retain a real sense of history in this atmospheric western corner of the Ciutat Vella.

11 Bar Marsella 🍷

It's the end of your second day, so why not treat yourself to a well-earned snifter of cloudy anise-flavored pastis at Bar Marsella, Carrer Sant Pau 65 (✆ 93-442-72-63)? A Provençal-cum-Catalan landmark to hedonism, it's a 19th-century oasis of huge mirrors, heavy drapes, creaky rafters, and high chandeliers. The place has been run by the same family for five generations. Among its first customers was young French poet Jean Genet, who in the 1930s reveled in the degeneracy of those early Raval days.

THE BEST OF BARCELONA IN 3 DAYS

Spend the first 2 days as described in the above itineraries. On Day 3 make a leisurely morning exploration of **L'Eixample,** the 19th-century district that expanded the city away from the congested Barric Gòtic and Ciutat Vella in general. This is where you'll find Barcelona's widest avenue, the **Passeig de Gràcia,** and greatest concentration of *moderniste* (Art Nouveau) architecture, highlighted by the **Manzana de la Discordia** zone (covered in detail in chapter 8, "Strolling Around Barcelona"), where Gaudí's **Casa Batlló,** Puig i Cadafalch's **Casa Amatller,** and Domènech i Muntaner's **Casa Lleo Morera** are all so close they virtually shake hands with each other. Most famous of all is another Gaudí gem, **Casa Milà** (popularly known as **La Pedrera**), further along the *paseo.* Pop into Vinçon, the city's famed design emporium, for a descent to relative normality, and then continue up to the village-like district of **Gràcia** at the northern edge of L'Eixample. Return to have lunch in **Casa Calvet,** a restaurant housed in an early work of the omnipresent Gaudí.

In the afternoon catch the Metro up to **Pedralbes** to visit the monastery and palace. Then continue up to **Tibidabo** by funicular for the best panoramic views of the city and coast stretching north toward the Costa Brava. In the evening wander into the adjoining **Collserola Park** (see below), still high above the city.

1 Passeig de Gràcia

Compared to the color and life of La Rambla, this 60-m (200-feet)-wide avenue, with its traffic-filled center, two pedestrian mini-*paseos,* and four rows of trees, is both more urban and more cosmopolitan. It is known locally as "Queen of Paseos" and is lined with elegant buildings, sought-after eating spots, and high-end shops like **Adolfo Dominguez** for stylish clothing, **Josep Font** for Art Nouveau pieces, and **Tous,** which sells spectacular jewelry. The street rises gently from Plaça de Catalunya through the heart of the 19th-century Eixample to the village-like district of Gràcia. See chapter 8, "Strolling Around Barcelona."

2 Manzana de la Discordia ★★★

A short way up the *paseo* you'll find this remarkable block, with its trio of architectural standouts designed by maestros of the *moderniste* movement: The inimitable Gaudí's frilly and curvaceous **Casa Batlló** was built 1904–6, Puig i Cadafalch's staid Flemish-style **Casa Amatller** in 1898–1900, and Domènech i Muntaner's decidedly eccentric **Casa Lleo Morera** in 1902, compared by some to a collapsed wedding cake. *Manzana* means both "block" and "apple" in Spanish, so the double meaning could also refer to the mythical golden Apple of Discord, which was to be given to the winner of a beauty contest judged by Paris. Decide for yourself which building comes out on top.

3 Casa Alfonso 🍷

Casa Alfonso, Roger de Llúria 6 (✆ 93-301-97-83; www.casaalfonso.com) is a great tapas bar that serves a wide enough variety of mouth-watering snacks and *raciones* to satisfy anyone with an early-morning appetite. Their Jabugo ham from the Huelva province is

The Best of Barcelona in 3 Days

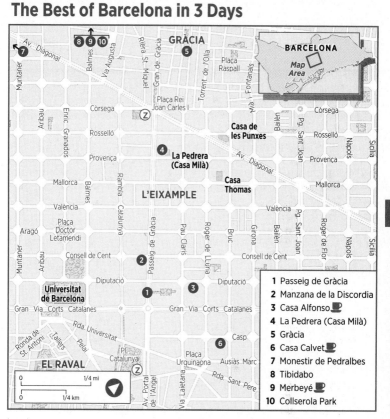

BARCELONA
Map Area

GRÀCIA

1 Passeig de Gràcia
2 Manzana de la Discordia
3 Casa Alfonso
4 La Pedrera (Casa Milà)
5 Gràcia
6 Casa Calvet
7 Monestir de Pedralbes
8 Tibidabo
9 Merbeyé
10 Collserola Park

considered by many to be Spain's best. At this hour, though, you may simply prefer to settle for a cafe con leche and admire the aromatic rows of hanging hams (p. 146).

4 La Pedrera (Casa Milà) ★★★

You've not finished with *moderniste* architecture by a long shot. On its own some 457m (1,500 feet) further up the avenue is what many feel to be the most striking building of all: **Casa Milà** (by Gaudí again), also known as "La Pedrera" (the rock quarry) since its twisted verandas and frivolous chimneys are all made of bizarrely sculptured limestone from Montjuïc hill. It's really a block of apartments (one is open to the public), the most original in the entire city, and the high point of any visit comes when you get onto the roof and enjoy the Mary Poppins cityscape visible past those astonishing chimneys (p. 175).

5 Gràcia

This intimate district at the northern end of the Passeig de Gràcia, just past the Avinguda Diagonal, started life as a small village built around an 18th-century convent; during Barcelona's Industrial Revolution in the late 1880s, it became a working-class zone where a famed revolt over the reintroduction of the military draft is commemorated by a tall bell tower that stands in Plaça Ruis i Taulet. Today it's a sought-after and slightly gentrified corner of the city in which many traditional features, such as vintage *herbolarios* (health-cure shops) and fortune-telling palm readers, have lingered on amid the abundance of tiny squares and narrow lanes. Its mood is vaguely bohemian, and many artists have chosen to establish their workshops here. The August **Festa Major de Gràcia** is a riot of street fun that lasts a week; don't miss it if you're here then (p. 181).

6 Casa Calvet ☕

Head back down into the lower Eixample for an indulgent (but not too indulgent if you want to get through the afternoon) lunch at Casa Calvet, Carrer Casp 48 (✆ 93-412-40-12; www.casacalvet.es), a Gaudí-designed ground-floor restaurant. The *moderniste* setting is complemented by a new-and-old blend of top Catalan cuisine (p. 141).

7 Monestir de Pedralbes ★★

Take Metro Line 6 from Plaça de Catalunya to Reina Elisenda and walk to the monastery. Situated high up in one of the city's classiest suburbs alongside the Catalan Gothic monastery church, this 14th-century gem founded by Queen Elisenda is one of Barcelona's oldest and most attractive religious buildings. Once inside, take a peep at its secluded garden and fountain; explore the beautiful three-floored cloister; and visit the pharmacy, kitchen, and high-vaulted refectory with restored artifacts of daily convent life (p. 193).

8 Tibidabo ★★

You can arrive at this strange mixture of the ecclesiastic and the brassy either by Tramvía Blau (Blue Tram; weekends only in winter) and funicular lift, or by taking a bus all the way up from Plaça Doctor Andreu. At the top, 488m (1,600 feet) above the sea and enjoying sensational views of the city and coast, is one of the few places in the world you'll find a church next to a fun-fair. The church, named Sagrat Cor (Holy Heart), is built in an unattractive gray neo-Gothic style. It was designed by Enric Sagnier and built between 1902 and 1961; its silhouette can be seen from so many miles away that it's become one of the city's most familiar landmarks. The fun-fair's been in operation for over 80 years and its vintage attractions include the wheezy Aeromàgic mountain ride and a 1928 flight simulator. See chapter 7, "What To See & Do."

9 Merbeyé ☕

Merbeyé, Plaça Doctor Andreu, Tibidabo (✆ 93-417-92-79; www.torredecollserola.com), is a showy and colorful cocktail-bar-cum-cafe. It has a plush jazz-oriented lounge, with cool background music, plus a tranquil open-air terrace to sit and unwind after the day's sightseeing over a daiquiri or *cafe con leche* and enjoy the great view.

10 Collserola Park

To the southwest of Tibidabo, on the same high massif, is this splendid 8,000-hectare (19,800-acre) area of wild countryside where footpaths meander amid the oak forests and offer occasional spectacular vistas. Within the park are farmhouses, chapels, and springs, including the charming Font de la Budellera. Along the way you'll also see plaques with verses by the Catalan poet Jacint Verdaguer. See the small museum dedicated to him inside the 18th-century Villa Joana. A far more recent eye-catcher is the Norman Foster–designed Torre de Collserola, shaped like a giant syringe, which is just 5 minutes' stroll away from Tibidabo (see above). There's an unbeatable view from the top, accessible by a vertigo-inducing elevator. At night you can see its lights flashing from way below.

WHERE TO STAY

Economic crisis or no, Barcelona is still managing to hold on to its position as Europe's favorite city-break destination, as well as expanding its ever-eclectic range of accommodations in the process. At the top end of the market are first-class and deluxe hotels, which are reasonably priced compared to similar lodgings in Paris or London, giving you a chance to splurge—especially over weekends—on bargains. Scour the Internet for deals and find out about special offers. Even visitors on a budget have ample choice.

Attractive changes have taken place in many of the older establishments in Barcelona. Traditionally—and especially in the heart of the Ciutat Vella quarter—these old *hostales* are centered around a well or patio and may have seemed dark, gloomy, and almost claustrophobic in the past. Today, however, many have been renovated and transformed into bright, appealing places to sleep. Some have gardens and patios to look out on. One thing that has not changed, however, is the noise (especially from weekend revelers), though mercifully more rooms are soundproofed these days. 1920s' *moderniste* facades and original tiled floors have also been retained in many hotels, and the city's increasing number of boutique establishments are decorated with all the stylistic inventiveness you'd expect in such a famously avant-garde metropolis.

Keeping pace with the times, nearly all Barcelona hotels—including even the most budget-oriented ones—offer broadband and Wi-Fi.

An appealing new trend is the modest but gradual increase in quality hotels close to the city's Mediterranean shoreline, an area as inexplicably neglected in the Catalan capital as it was in other Spanish ports from Valencia to Málaga until the beginning of the 1990s. Now, as we enter the second decade of the 21st century, visitors in search of adventurous new coastal watering holes can choose between, among others, Port Olímpic's luminous **Pullman Barcelona Skipper** (p. 115) and the striking but controversial harborside **W Barcelona** (p. 115), which resembles a huge sail from a distance. In the opinion of some diehard locals, it jars with the port's layout, but we'll leave you to judge for yourself.

Exotic new hostelries also continue to appear in the ever-booming heart of the city, highlighted most recently by L'Eixample's world-class **Mandarin Oriental** (p. 103), opened in 2008, and the ultra-chic **Murmuri** (p. 107). Meanwhile the Barri Gòtic entices anew with offbeat attractions like the gay-friendly **Curious** (p. 95) and elegant innovations such as the refurbed **Advance** and **Praktik Rambla** hotels (both transformed from traditional mansions into chic 21st-century accommodations with all mod cons (p. 105 and 103).

Still awaited with eager anticipation is the supremely nautical **Sunborn Yacht Hotel** (www.sunborninternational.com), where you'll actually bed down on a ship. The vessel was built in Malaya by the Finnish company Sunborn and, at the time of writing, is due to sail at the end of 2010 to Barcelona, where it will be berthed permanently in the Port El Forum along the coast from Port Olímpic.

Saving on Your Hotel Room

The **rack rate** is the maximum rate a hotel charges for a room. *Hardly anybody pays rack rates* and, with the exception of smaller B&Bs, you can usually pay quite a bit less than the rates shown below. If you come to Barcelona during the very hot months of July and August (in reality, the city's "low season") you'll usually pick up bargains in the higher-priced hotels, at lower rates than those we officially list here. Check online with the hotel, or visit the booking websites **www.venere.com**, **www. fastbooking.com**, and **www.hotelsonline.com**, which have some of the most competitive rates available. High-price times in Barcelona are Easter and New Year, so avoid those periods if you can.

Here's how I've organized the price categories:

- **Very expensive,** 300€ and up
- **Expensive,** 200€ to 299€
- **Moderate,** 100€ to 199€
- **Inexpensive,** under 100€

These are high-season prices with no discounts applied. *Always* peruse the category above your target price—you might just find the perfect match, especially if you follow the advice below. ***Note to single travelers:*** Rates for singles may be available in some of the accommodations listed in this chapter—call the hotel directly for specific rates. To lower the cost of your room:

- **Ask about special rates or other discounts:** Always ask whether a cheaper room is available, or whether any special rates apply. You may qualify for corporate, student, military, senior, or other discounts. Find out the hotel policy on children—do kids stay free in the room or is there a special rate?
- **Dial direct:** When booking a room in a chain hotel, you'll often receive a better deal by calling the individual hotel's reservation desk rather than the chain's main number.
- **Book online:** Many hotels offer Internet-only discounts, or supply rooms to websites such as Priceline, Hotwire, or Expedia at specially discounted online rates. Shop around. And if you have particular needs—a quiet room, a room with a view—call the hotel directly to make your needs known after you've booked online.

- **Remember the law of supply and demand:** Resort hotels are most crowded and therefore most expensive on weekends, so discounts are usually available for mid-week stays. Business hotels in downtown locations are busiest during the week, so expect big discounts over the weekend. Many hotels have high-season and low-season prices, and booking the day after high season ends can mean big discounts.
- **Look into group or long-stay discounts:** If you come as part of a large group, you should be able to negotiate a bargain rate, since the hotel can then be sure of occupancy in a number of rooms. Likewise, if you're planning a long stay (at least 5 days), you may qualify for a discount. As a general rule, expect 1 night free after a 7-night stay.
- **Avoid excess charges and hidden costs:** When you book a room, ask if the hotel charges for parking. Use your own cellphone, pay phones, or prepaid phone cards instead of hotel phones, which have exorbitant charges. And don't be tempted by the room's minibar offerings: Most hotels charge through the nose for water, soda, and snacks. Finally, check out local taxes and service charges, which can increase the cost of a room by 15% or more.
- **Book an apartment:** A room with a kitchenette allows you to shop for groceries and cook for yourself. This is a big money-saver for families on long stays.
- **Think about eating options:** To save money and enjoy the maximum amount of time eating out, opt for a **room-only** stay. Alternatively, there's a variety of combined room and meal options, which vary according to the amount of time you want to spend eating in the hotel. They range from **bed-and-breakfast** (room with breakfast only) to **half-board** (room, breakfast, and one meal, usually dinner) or **full-board** (room, breakfast, lunch, and dinner). If you choose half-board it's often possible to switch dinner in the hotel for lunch if you decide to eat out.
- **Enroll in frequent-stay programs:** These programs are upping the ante lately to win the loyalty of repeat customers. Frequent guests accumulate points or credits to earn free hotel nights, airline miles, in-room amenities, merchandise, tickets to concerts and events, or discounts on sporting facilities. Perks are awarded by many major chain hotels and some have reciprocal arrangements with other hotels, car-rental firms, airlines, and credit card companies to give consumers an additional incentive to repeat business.

Which Quarter Suits You?

The **Barri Gòtic** (Gothic Quarter) is good for *hostales* (not to be confused with hostels) and guesthouses. You can live and eat less expensively here than in any other part of Barcelona and save money on transport, as most sights are within walking distance. Keep an eye on your belongings, since bag snatchings can occur here, especially in the narrow, alleyed Old Quarter. By and large, though, Barcelona is a safe city to wander round.

More modern and more expensive accommodations are found north of the Barri Gòtic in the **Eixample** district, centered on the Metro stops Plaça de Catalunya and Universitat. Many buildings are in the *moderniste* style from the last decades of the 19th

The official ban on smoking is due to cover all public places from January 1, 2011 (unless the authorities chicken out). At the time of writing, almost all hotels have non-smoking rooms; by the time this book is published, all hotels will be obliged to be smoke-free, both in public areas and in all rooms.

century; sometimes the elevators and plumbing are of the same vintage. However, L'Eixample is a desirable and safe neighborhood, especially along its wide boulevards, and is excellent for eating out. Traffic noise is the only problem you might encounter.

The area around **Sants** and **Plaça Espanya** is the main hub of business hotels, and convenient for conferences, meetings, and trade shows. Families also enjoy its easy access to the parks and leisure attractions of Montjuïc, 5 minutes' stroll away. It's also convenient for the airport (just 20 minutes by taxi) and the hotels here tend to be good if you require a family-size room. However, most leisure travelers will probably find Sants too far away from the city center.

Farther north, above the Avinguda Diagonal, you enter the **Gràcia** area, where you can enjoy distinctively Catalan neighborhood life. It has a village feel, low-rise buildings, and plenty of sunny plazas populated by students. The main attractions are a bit distant but easily reached by public transportation, and the barrio has an eclectic feel that makes it worth exploring. Above this the neighborhoods of **Sarrià** and **Sant Gervasi** are mainly upper-class residential areas, with plenty of top-end bars and restaurants.

Barcelona's multi-faceted **portside** and **seafront** area offers an attractive blend of seaside and city lifestyles. Hotels here range from five-star monuments to luxury to the odd bed-and-breakfast, and its quieter, still-burgeoning neighbour Poble Nou is an increasingly popular beachside choice.

Another option is to look at **aparthotels** and short-term rented **apartments** (self-catering accommodations), which are becoming increasingly popular. They give you independence, a kitchen to cook for yourself, and the sensation of a home-away-from-home.

Finally, there is a new wave in **bed-and-breakfast** accommodations. Virtually unheard of until 2 or 3 years ago, these family-run guesthouses (often with just two or three rooms) offer a personal and cheap alternative to mainstream chains.

Whichever option you choose, book well ahead to secure your accommodations. Don't even think of rolling into town without a booking in hand or you will find yourself looking for a room in the outer suburbs or out of Barcelona altogether. This is not just true of the summer months: Tourism here is non-stop, year-round.

Not many of Barcelona's hotels have garages. When parking is available at the hotel, the price is indicated; otherwise, the hotel staff will direct you to a garage. Expect to pay upwards of 16€ for 24 hours, and if you do have a car, you might as well park it and leave it there, because driving around the city can be excruciating. If you don't plan to leave the city, there is little point in hiring a car at all.

5

WHERE TO STAY

Introduction

BEST HOTEL BETS

- **Best for a Romantic Getaway:** Lovebirds have good reasons not to leave the confines of **Gran Hotel La Florida,** Carretera Vallvidrera al Tibidabo s/n (✆ **93-259-30-00;** www.HotelLaFlorida.com), a fabulous historic hotel—and not all of those reasons are to be found in the bedrooms. The stainless-steel lap pool, spa, and gardens offering sweeping views of the city are enticement enough to keep you holed up for days. See p. 117.

- **Best for Art Lovers:** As stylish as anywhere in the city, the **Hotel Claris,** Pau Claris 150 (✆ **93-487-62-62;** http://claris.barcelonahotels.it), has rooms and foyers dotted with early Egyptian art and artifacts, 19th-century Turkish kilims, and even some Roman mosaics, fruits of the owner's passion for collecting. See p. 98.

- **Best for Business Travelers: Catalonia Barcelona Plaza,** Plaça Espanya 6-8, ((✆ **93-426-26-00;** http://barcelonaplaza.barcelonahotels.it). Ideally located near Sants railway station, in easy reach of the airport and close to a wide range of conference halls and exhibition centers, this immaculate hotel boasts some of the most sophisticated business amenities in town. See p. 111.

- **Best for Celebrity Spotting:** Preferred choice of top models and temperamental rock stars, the **Hotel Arts,** Marina 19–21 (✆ **93-221-10-00;** www.hotelartsbarcelona.com), has remained a jet-set playground and symbol of "cool Barcelona" for more than a decade. See p. 115.

- **Best for Service:** As well as being a highly regarded hotel, the **Prestige,** Passeig de Gràcia 62 (✆ **93-272-41-80;** www.prestigepaseodegracia.com), offers a unique service to its clients. The role of the concierge is replaced with "Ask Me"—specially trained information officers on call to find the answers to the most challenging queries, from scoring soccer tickets to finding halal restaurants. See p. 101.

- **Best In-House Restaurant:** When celebrated chef Fermin Puig took over the food department of the highly regarded **Majestic,** Passeig de Gràcia 68 (✆ **93-488-17-17;** www.splendia.com/Hotel-Majestic), he not only revolutionized what clients receive on their breakfast tray but also created **Drolma,** one of the country's most celebrated haute cuisine restaurants. Puig's take on traditional Catalan and southern French cooking has impressed even the most demanding gourmand. See p. 139.

- **Best Historic Hotel:** The *moderniste* masterpiece **Hotel Casa Fuster,** Passeig de Gràcia 132 (✆ **93-225-30-00;** http://Hotels.com/Casa-Fuster-Hotel), was an emblematic building *before* it was converted into a luxury residence. The rooms have been restored to turn-of-the-20th-century opulence, but with all the mod cons expected by today's high society. See p. 98.

- **Best Modern Design:** Its once-staid interiors now imaginatively revamped and transformed into a luminous and relaxing blend of grays and whites, hotel **Curious,** Carmé 25 (✆ **93-301-44-84;** www.hotelcurious.com), has the coolest and sleekest minimalist decor of any traditional building in the Ciutat Vella. See p. 95.

- **Best for Sheer Atmosphere:** If faded glory is your thing, then look no further than the **Hotel España,** Sant Pau 9-11 (☏ **93-318-17-58;** www.hotelespanya. com). Designed by a contemporary of Gaudí's, the street-level dining room, filled with florid motifs and brass fixtures, will whisk you back to the early 1900s, when it was filled with chattering patrons taking supper after a trip to the opera house next door. See p. 97.

- **Best for Architecture Buffs:** The very best of modern and traditional architectural styles and decor meet in the gay-friendly **Advance Design Collection Hotel,** Sepúlveda 180 (☏ **93-289-28-92;** www.hoteladvance.com), an atmospheric former 19th-century mansion, which has been magically transformed by some of the city's top designers. See p. 105.

- **Best Boutique Hotel:** As boutique-hotel fever sweeps the city, the ultra-chic **Soho,** Gran Vía de les Corts Catalanes 543 (☏ **93-552-96-10;** www.hotelsoho barcelona.com), located near the lively Plaça Espanya corner of town, emerges as the new *numero uno,* thanks to the joint creative work of its inimitably cool Catalan and Danish designers. See p. 113.

- **Best Small Hotel: Hostal D'Uxelles,** Gran Vía 688 and 667 (☏ **93-265-25-60;** www.hotelduxelles.com), looks like it has stepped straight off the pages of one of those rustic-interiors magazines. Located on the first floor of two adjacent buildings, each of the 30 rooms has a character all of its own, but all include canopied beds, antique furniture, and Andalusian-style ceramic bathrooms. See p. 109.

- **Best for Sea Views:** You can't get nearer to the Med than the new, iconic **W Barcelona,** Plaça de la Rosa dels Vents 1 (☏ **93-295-28-00;** www.starwood hotels.com). Designed by top architect Ricardo Bofill in the shape of a vast sail, it towers on the very edge of Barcelona's busy and colorful harbor, visible from far off and already an essential part of the city's coastal profile. See p. 115.

- **Best for City Views:** The **Hotel Miramar,** Plaça Carlos Ibañez 3 (☏ **93-281-16-00;** www.hotelmiramarbarcelona.com), perched on the northeasterly flank of Montjuïc hill and surrounded by attractive gardens, enjoys magnificent bird's-eye views of the city, inland hills, and the coastline below. See p. 112.

- **Best Inexpensive Hotel:** Serenity and character abound in **Hotel Peninsular,** Sant Pau 34 (☏ **93-302-31-38;** www.hotelpeninsular.net), a nunnery-turned-hotel. Located on a colorful street just off La Rambla, the hotel—with its Art Nouveau elevator, long hallways in tones of green and white, and lush inner courtyard—is an oasis from the hustle and bustle outside. Book ahead. See p. 97.

- **Best for Families Who Don't Want to Break the Bank:** The family-run **Marina Folch,** Carrer del Mar 16, principal (☏ **93-310-37-09**), is the only hotel in the beachside neighborhood of Barceloneta, with plenty of open space for the kids to run wild. Ask for a room at the front for a balcony with a view of the port. See p. 116.

- **Best Hostal:** Forget faded curtains and floral wallpaper. **Gat Raval,** Joaquín Costa 44 (☏ **93-481-66-70;** www.gatrooms.es), is a streamlined *hostal* fitted out in acid green and black that has been conceived for the modern world traveler on a budget. On-demand Internet access and touches of abstract art add to its contemporary ambience, and the foyer is always abuzz with travelers exchanging information. See p. 96.

CIUTAT VELLA

The **Ciutat Vella** (Old City) forms the monumental center of Barcelona, taking in Les Ramblas, Plaça de Sant Jaume, Vía Laietana, Passeig Nacional, the Passeig Colón, and the colorful Raval and La Ribera neighborhoods. It contains some of the city's best hotel bargains. Most of the glamorous, and more expensive, hotels are located in L'Eixample and beyond. For convenience, we have split the Ciutat Vella into three areas: **Barri Gòtic, La Ribera,** and **El Raval.**

Barri Gòtic

EXPENSIVE

Duquesa de Cardona ★★★ 📷   This small boutique hotel—popular with honeymooners—is across the road from the harbor of Port Vell, and the rooftop terrace and small plunge pool with Jacuzzi have splendid views of the pleasure and party boats that dock here year-round. The hotel occupies what was once a 19th-century palace, and many of its original Art Deco features have been preserved and mixed with elements of modern style to ensure maximum comfort. The bedrooms have an intimate, romantic feel but they seem a little cramped (especially those at the back), and it is worth paying the extra money to get a front-facing room with views of the harbor. Communal areas include a stylish living room with deep, cream-colored sofas and a smart Mediterranean restaurant with original marble tiles.

Passeig Colom 12, 08002 Barcelona. ✆ **93-268-90-90.** Fax 93-268-29-31. www.hduquesadecardona. com. 44 units. 275€ double; 395€ junior suite; 55€ sea-view supplement. AE, DC, MC, V. Public parking nearby 20€. Metro: Jaume I or Drassanes. **Amenities:** Restaurant; babysitting; outdoor pool; room service; spa. *In room:* A/C, TV, hair dryer, minibar, Wi-Fi.

Hotel Colón ★★ ☺   The long-established Colón, with its dignified neoclassical facade, is located in the heart of Barcelona's Ciutat Vella, right opposite the main entrance to the cathedral. Inside, you'll find comfortingly traditional public lounges, a helpful staff, and good-sized guest rooms filled with cozy furnishings. Despite renovations over the years, the decor remains strongly focused on sturdy Catalan-patterned drapes and upholstery. The sixth-floor rooms with tiny balconies overlooking the square and cathedral are the most desirable, while back rooms are quieter and lower rooms are rather dark. Upon request, families can often be given more spacious rooms. The hotel regularly offers attractive Christmas, New Year, and summer-season deals.

Av. de la Catedral 7, 08002 Barcelona. ✆ **800/845-0636** in the U.S., or 93-301-14-04. Fax 93-317-29-15. www.hotelcolon.es. 141 units. 285€ double; from 450€ suite. AE, DC, MC, V. Bus: 16, 17, 19, or 45. **Amenities:** Restaurant; bar; babysitting; room service. *In room:* A/C, TV, hair dryer, minibar, high-speed Internet.

Rivoli Ramblas ★   Within a dignified Art Deco town house on the upper section of La Rambla, a block south of the Plaça de Catalunya, this well-renovated hotel incorporates many fine examples of avant-garde Catalan design in its stylish interior. The communal areas have acres of polished marble, and it's a popular choice for guests in town on business. One of the Rivoli's highlights is the handsome, wood-decked roof terrace—a pleasant place to start the day. Guest rooms are carpeted, soundproofed, and elegant, and range from cozy and compact to large and quite spacious.

Ciutat Vella Accommodations

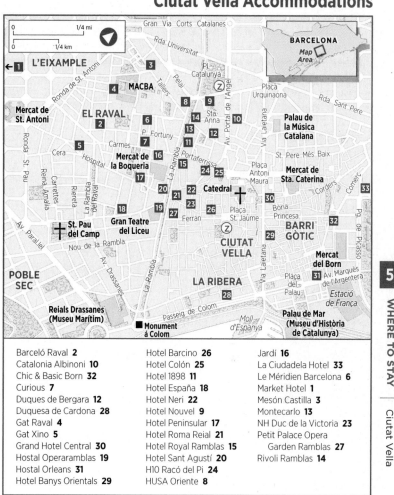

Barceló Raval **2**
Catalonia Albinoni **10**
Chic & Basic Born **32**
Curious **7**
Duques de Bergara **12**
Duquesa de Cardona **28**
Gat Raval **4**
Gat Xino **5**
Grand Hotel Central **30**
Hostal Operaramblas **19**
Hostal Orleans **31**
Hotel Banys Orientals **29**

Hotel Barcino **26**
Hotel Colón **25**
Hotel 1898 **11**
Hotel España **18**
Hotel Neri **22**
Hotel Nouvel **9**
Hotel Peninsular **17**
Hotel Roma Reial **21**
Hotel Royal Ramblas **15**
Hotel Sant Agustí **20**
H10 Racó del Pi **24**
HUSA Oriente **8**

Jardí **16**
La Ciudadela Hotel **33**
Le Méridien Barcelona **6**
Market Hotel **1**
Mesón Castilla **3**
Montecarlo **13**
NH Duc de la Victoria **23**
Petit Palace Opera
  Garden Ramblas **27**
Rivoli Ramblas **14**

La Rambla 128, 08002 Barcelona. ✆ **93-481-76-76.** Fax 93-317-50-53. www.hotelriviolliramblas.com. 129 units. 265€ double; 320€–775€ suite. AE, DC, MC, V. Metro: Plaça de Catalunya or Liceu. **Amenities:** Restaurant; bar; babysitting; health spa; sauna; solarium; limited room service. *In room:* A/C, TV, hair dryer, minibar, Wi-Fi.

MODERATE

Catalonia Albinoni ★★ An ideal choice for shopaholics, the Albinoni is situated halfway up the Portal de l'Angel, where you'll find shoulder-to-shoulder Spanish fashion stores like Zara and Mango, and El Corte Inglés (Spain's major department store), at one end, and boutiques and trinket shops at the other. Housed in a former palace dating back to 1876, it was converted into a hotel in 1998 and totally refurbished—while carefully retaining all its traditional highlights—in 2007. It remains on Barcelona's artistic-heritage list and many of the original romantic and baroque features have been beautifully preserved. Not least impressive is the elegant marble lobby and stately interior courtyard where the bar and reception area are located. All of the 74 plush bedrooms have polished wood floors and comfortable beds. Breakfast (although overpriced) is served on the terrace under awnings.

Av. Portal de l'Angel 17, 08002 Barcelona. © **93-318-41-41.** Fax 93-301-26-31. www.hoteles-catalonia. es. 74 units. 150€–185€ double. AE, DC, MC, V. Public parking nearby 20€. Metro: Plaça de Catalunya. **Amenities:** Cafe; babysitting; high-speed Internet; room service. *In room:* A/C, TV, hair dryer, minibar.

Duques de Bergara ★★

This upscale hotel occupies a town house built in 1898 for the Duke of Bergara by the architect Emilio Salas y Cortés (a protégée of Gaudí). Plenty of elegant *moderniste* touches remain, including the original molded-wood ceiling with a rose dome on the first floor, and a handful of original artworks from the era. In the reception area, look for stained-glass panels displaying the heraldic coat of arms of the duke. Guest rooms throughout have the same conservative, traditional comforts. Each unit has large, comfortable beds with first-rate mattresses, elegant fabrics, and good lighting. The original five-story structure more than doubled in size in 1998 with the addition of a seven-story tower.

Bergara 11, 08002 Barcelona. © **93-301-51-51.** Fax 93-317-34-42. www.hoteles-catalonia.es. 149 units. 190€–255€ double; 285€–325€ triple. AE, DC, MC, V. Public parking nearby 20€. Metro: Plaça de Catalunya. **Amenities:** Restaurant; cafe/bar; outdoor pool; room service; high-speed Internet. *In room:* A/C, TV, hair dryer, minibar.

Hotel Barcino ★ 🏨

Still one of the city's undiscovered four-star gems, the hospitable Barcino is located right in the heart of the Old Quarter close to a wealth of stylish eating spots and key historic monuments. Its rooms are classically decorated and the best have whirlpool baths (big enough for sharing) and private terraces with views over the rooftops and the cathedral, perfect for a pre-dinner drink. The hotel's buffet breakfast is pricey but comprehensive and filling enough to satisfy all tastes. If you want something less extravagant, there are plenty of local cafes serving coffee and croissants or *ensaimadas* (local pastries) a stone's throw from the front door.

Jaume I no. 6, 08002 Barcelona. © **93-302-20-12.** Fax 93-301-42-42. www.hotelbarcino.com. 53 units. 275€ double. AE, DC, MC, V. Public parking nearby 18€. Metro: Jaume I or Plaça de Catalunya. **Amenities:** Restaurant; cafe/bar; babysitting; room service. *In room:* A/C, TV, hair dryer, minibar, high-speed Internet.

Hotel 1898 ★

Located right beside the upper stretch of La Rambla in an emblematic 19th-century building that was the former headquarters of the Philippine Tobacco Company, this is one of the city's most deluxe new hotels. Vintage *moderniste* outside, it's lively and abrasively 21st-century inside, with each floor decorated in different arrays of dazzling striped colors. There are also ceiling fans, brick walkways, and jet-black leather couches filling the communal areas. The rooms are stylishly and comfortably furnished, and pricier units have terraces with wooden floorboards. Accommodations are also available for visitors with disabilities.

La Rambla 109, 08002 Barcelona. © **93-552-95-52.** www.nnhotels.es. 169 units. 185€–505€ double. Parking 25€. AE, DC, MC, V. Metro: Liceu. **Amenities:** Restaurant; bar; health club and spa; outdoor and indoor pools w/solarium. *In room:* A/C, TV, hair dryer, minibar, Wi-Fi.

Hotel Neri ★★★ 📷   The captivating Neri is located in a former Gothic palace close to the cathedral and the charming little square, Plaça Felip Neri. Its interior features gold-leaf decor, red velvet drapes, and soft-lit, echoing hallways, while the bedrooms are plush with high-thread-count cotton sheets, shot-silk pillowcases, throws, and rugs. The minibar has all the usual tipples plus exotic extras like incense and candles. Relaxing bonuses are a coffee and cocktail terrace right on the plaza and a rooftop garden resplendent with jasmine plants and creepers. There are also two spacious suites, which have in the past attracted illustrious visitors such as John Malkovich. The Neri's restaurant features Mediterranean cuisine and is another favored rendezvous for followers of the—trendily expensive—Catalan gourmet scene.

Sant Sever 5, 08002 Barcelona. ✆ **93-304-06-55.** Fax 93-304-03-37. www.hotelneri.com. 22 units. 180€–220€ double; 220€–285€ suite. AE, DC, MC, V. Public parking nearby 24€. Metro: Jaume I or Liceu. **Amenities:** Restaurant; cafe/bar; babysitting; room service. *In room:* A/C, TV, hair dryer, minibar, Wi-Fi.

Hotel Nouvel 📷   A smartly renovated hotel that dates back to 1917 and retains plenty of its original atmospheric *moderniste* flourishes, the Nouvel is a charming retreat right in the heart of the Old City. It's wonderful for lovers of the Art Deco style, with many of the original carved wood panels, smoked-glass partitions, and elaborate floor tiles. The bedrooms offer a mix of newly renovated accommodations, though the rooms with the most character are the more old-fashioned kind with the original tiles. The best have balconies, and it's worth asking for a room at the rear if street noise bothers you.

Santa Ana 18-20, 08002 Barcelona. ✆ **93-301-82-74.** Fax 93-301-83-70. www.hotelnouvel.com. 78 units. 160€–235€ double. Rate includes breakfast. MC, V. Public parking nearby 25€. Metro: Plaça de Catalunya. **Amenities:** Restaurant (lunch daily, dinner Thurs–Sat); babysitting; Wi-Fi. *In room:* A/C, TV, minibar.

Hotel Royal Ramblas 🍴   The flat-packed, office-block look of this hotel—all concrete and glassed-in balconies—doesn't compare too well with the striking period architecture in many other parts of the city, but don't let that put you off. Tastefully stylish refurbishments have resulted in a decidedly more attractive interior, which offers spacious rooms with comfortable beds and furnishings, and modern facilities. The better bedrooms have balconies offering fabulous views over Barcelona's real-life street theater: La Rambla.

La Rambla 117, 08002 Barcelona. ✆ **93-301-94-00** or 93-304-12-12 (reservations). Fax 93-317-31-79. www.royalramblashotel.com or www.hroyal.com. 119 units. 160€–235€ double. AE, DC, MC, V. Parking 20€. Metro: Plaça de Catalunya. **Amenities:** Restaurant; cafe/bar; babysitting; room service. *In room:* A/C, TV, hair dryer, minibar, Wi-Fi.

H10 Racó del Pi ★   Locations don't get much better than this one, right next to the Old City's prettiest plaza, which is bustling most days with pavement cafes, weekend produce markets, street performers, and artists. The hotel itself has plenty of character; it's small and intimate, with helpful staff who provide some nice touches like offering a glass of *cava* (sparkling wine) to guests on arrival. The rooms tend to be compact and dark (one disadvantage of the Barri Gòtic), but this seems a small price to pay for staying in such a cozy place and in such a desirable corner of the town center. All have en-suite, mosaic-tiled bathrooms. The hotel also serves a good breakfast buffet offering a range of homemade products.

Del Pi 7, 08002 Barcelona. ✆ **93-342-61-90.** Fax 93-342-61-91. www.hotelracodelpi.com. 37 units. 205€ double. AE, DC, MC, V. Public parking nearby 22€. Metro: Liceu. **Amenities:** Restaurant; cafe/bar; limited room service. *In room:* A/C, TV, hair dryer, minibar, high-speed Internet.

Montecarlo ★★★ The fabulously ornate facade of this La Rambla hotel dates back 200 years to the days when it was an opulent private home, and later the head-quarters of the Royal Artistic Circle of Barcelona. Public areas include some of the building's original accessories, with carved doors, a baronial fireplace, and crystal chandeliers. In the 1930s, it became the comfortably unpretentious hotel you'll find today. A legend in its own lifetime, the Montecarlo combines traditional comforts with modern amenities like free Internet connection. You'll find each of the midsize guest rooms smartly decorated, with extras that make all the difference, such as adjustable beds and large marble bathrooms with Jacuzzi tubs, bathrobes, and slippers. The service is exemplary and nothing is too much trouble, whether you want to book a winery excursion or simply park your car.

La Rambla 124, 08002 Barcelona. ✆ **93-412-04-04.** Fax 93-318-73-23. www.montecarlobcn.com. 55 units. 175€–375€ double; 475€ suite. AE, DC, MC, V. Parking 18€. Metro: Plaça de Catalunya. **Amenities:** Bar; babysitting; room service. *In room:* A/C, TV, hair dryer, minibar, Wi-Fi (free).

NH Duc de la Victoria 🏄 Part of the NH Hotel Chain that aims to provide smooth, seamless comfort in mid-price accommodations, this smart hotel is well situated on a quiet pedestrianized street in the heart of the Barri Gòtic. It's of a somewhat higher standard than most *hostales* in the area and makes a great base for discerning visitors who want to have all central amenities, from shops and restau-rants to historical monuments, right on their doorstep. Spotlessly clean throughout, it provides continental breakfasts but no main meals. Bedrooms are of a decent size with cool parquet floors, and all have compact bathrooms. Fifth-floor rooms with private balconies are the best.

Duc de la Victoria 15, 08002 Barcelona. ✆ **93-270-34-10.** Fax 93-412-77-47. www.hotelnhducdela victoria.com. 156 units. 190€ double; 265€ suite. AE, DC, MC, V. Public parking nearby 18€. Metro: Plaça de Catalunya. **Amenities:** Restaurant; cafe/bar; babysitting; room service; Wi-Fi. *In room:* A/C, TV, hair dryer, minibar.

Petit Palace Opera Garden Ramblas ★ 🏨 This well-appointed member of the Petit Palace high-tech hotel chain is conveniently located in the heart of La Rambla, close to two famous Barcelona landmarks: The Liceu Theater (p. 240) and the Boqueria covered market (p. 226). The hotel is an ideal choice both for business travelers and for leisure travelers who want to keep in touch, as the neatly furnished modern rooms all have laptops with free Wi-Fi connections. Accommodations cover everyone from single executives to families of four (with king-size beds) and all have hydromassage showers (larger rooms also have saunas). Facilities include a business center in the main hall, a bar/cafeteria, and a gourmet dining room.

Boqueria 10, corner of La Rambla 78, 08002 Barcelona. ✆ **93-302-00-92.** Fax 93-302-15-66. www. operagarden.barcelonahotels.it. 70 units. 150€–220€ single; 220€–300€ double; 280€–340€ quad. Metro: Liceu. **Amenities:** Restaurant; bar/cafe. *In room:* A/C, TV, minibar, Wi-Fi (free).

INEXPENSIVE

Hotel Roma Reial This is a good choice for youngsters who want to be out bar-hopping and clubbing long into the night and who don't mind a bit of background noise from the Plaça Reial, which is a magnet for budding songsters and partygoers unwilling to go home. Located in an attractive traditional building that blends perfectly with its historic neighbors around the plaza, it's a friendly and well-located bargain. The compact and comfortable rooms come with additional facilities such as air-conditioning and TV. Some have good views of the lively square itself.

Plaça Reial 11, 08002 Barcelona. ℂ **93-302-03-66.** Fax 93-301-18-39. www.hotel-romareial.com. 61 units. 80€ double; 95€ triple. Rates may include breakfast, depending on season. MC, V. Metro: Liceu. **Amenities:** Cafe. *In room:* A/C, TV.

La Ribera
EXPENSIVE

Grand Hotel Central   Avant-garde and with an astute blend of hedonistic and practical amenities, this dazzling 1920s' office conversion—located between Santa Caterina market and the cathedral—is one of the latest fashionable hostelries to hit town. Rooms, designed by the prestigious local Sandra Tarruella and Isabel López design team, are spacious and coolly furnished in subtle grays, light browns, and creams, with shiny pinewood flooring. The executive rooms and suites are even more spectacularly comfortable, and there are rooms available for visitors with disabilities. A big draw is the rooftop's infinity swimming pool and adjoining solarium. Generous buffet breakfasts are served in the mornings; at night you can dine in the **Ávalon** restaurant, presided over by top chef Ramón Freixa.

Via Laietana 30, 08003 Barcelona. ℂ **93-295-79-00.** Fax 93-268-12-15. www.grandhotelcentral.com. 147 units. 185€–220€ double; 275€–625€ suite. AE, MC, V. Parking 25€. Metro: Jaume I. **Amenities:** Restaurant; bar; babysitting; infinity pool; room service. *In room:* A/C, TV, DVD player, hair dryer, minibar, Wi-Fi.

MODERATE

Chic & Basic Born ★   Set in an old Born-district building that's retained its grand old stairway and lounge furnishings, this modern hotel-apartment concept (the coolest and most self-contained of the five now spread throughout the city) offers dazzling self-contained units that are anything but traditional in design and decor. Each apartment room is ravishingly colored in a different monochromatic hue, from suave gray to virgin white, and has its own small, relaxing lounge area complete with fridge, microwave, and coffee-making facilities. The one- or two-bedroom apartments have fully equipped kitchens and access to a small terrace as well as truly gorgeous bathrooms with power showers; the pristinely white bedrooms all have mood lighting to reflect your state of mind.

Calle Princesa 50, 08003 Barcelona. ℂ **93-295-46-52.** Fax 93-295-46-53. www.chicandbasic.com. 31 units. 185€ double; 220€–250€ apt. AE, DC, MC. Metro: Arc de Triomf or Jaume I. **Amenities:** Restaurant; exercise room. *In room:* TV, Wi-Fi.

Market Hotel   Located on the western side of the Ciutat Vella close to the city's traditional covered Sant Antoni market, this chic new hotel deftly combines style and economy. Run by the owners of the Quinze Nits chain of attractively priced hotels and eateries, it provides mostly small but comfortable rooms coolly decorated in minimalist whites, blacks, grays, and touches of red. Suites have large bathrooms with waterfall showers and tubs. Two of the rooms have been adapted for guests with disabilities.

Passeig Sant Antoni Abat 10, 08015 Barcelona. ✆ **93-325-12-05.** Fax 93-424-29-65. www.markethotel. com.es. 47 units. 100€–160€ double. AE, MC, V. Metro: Sant Antoni. **Amenities:** Restaurant; Wi-Fi. *In room:* A/C, TV.

INEXPENSIVE

Hostal Orleans 🍴   Tucked away in the Born district just across the street from one of Barcelona's oldest and most imposing churches, Santa María del Mar (p. 75), is a modest hotel that combines a desirable location with highly affordable rates. Rooms are spotlessly clean, and the hotel is filled with artifacts and color schemes that take you back to the 1970s. Bedrooms are mainly compact, with comfortable beds, and bathrooms have a half-size bath and shower. Some have balconies overlooking the street, which are great for people-watching, although often noisy at night as revelers wend their way between the lively local bars. The communal sitting room is well stocked with English-language magazines, and is a good place to meet other guests. Other pluses are the friendly service and a genuinely Catalan vibe.

Av. Marquès de l´Argentera 13, 1st floor, 08003 Barcelona. ✆ **93-319-73-82.** Fax 93-319-22-19. www. hostalorleans.com. 27 units. 70€–80€ double. MC, V. Metro: Barceloneta or Jaume I. *In room amenities:* 8€ supplement for A/C, TV.

Hotel Banys Orientals ★★ 🛍   Set in a 19th-century mansion adjoining the chic **Senyor Parellada** eatery (which partly acts as the hotel's own restaurant), this hip haven lies in the heart of the lively—and often noisy—Born district. The variably sized, minimalist-style rooms have been very tastefully renovated and all have either a spacious walk-in shower or full bathroom (the latter must be pre-booked). A buffet breakfast is served on its mezzanine and guests can run up a tab for lunch/evening meals as well. A wealth of cool shops and bars is right on your doorstep, but be sure to ask for a room at the back if you want to enjoy a relatively peaceful night's sleep.

Argenteria 37, 08003 Barcelona. ✆ **93-268-84-60.** Fax 93-268-84-61. www.hotelbanysorientals.com. 43 units. 110€ double. AE, DC, MC, V. Public parking nearby 20€. Metro: Jaume I. **Amenities:** Restaurant; limited room service; free minibar. *In room:* A/C, TV, hair dryer, high-speed Internet.

La Ciudadela Hotel ★ 🛍   This small, homely, family-run pension provides good-value accommodations and parking in a quiet zone on the northern edge of the Parc de la Ciutadella. From here, you can simply cross the road into the park or wander minutes west into the popular La Ribera district. Beside the hotel's eponymous restaurant (which has been going for 30 years), there's a terrace where you can relax in the sun in summer. Rooms are unpretentious but cozy, and all have en-suite bathrooms. This genial spot is remarkable value.

Paseo Lluis Companys 2 (corner of Passeig de Pujades), 08018 Barcelona. 13 units. ✆ **93-309-95-57.** Fax 93-528-63-35. www.ciudadelaparc.com. 75€–85€ double; 95€–100€ triple. MC, V. Public parking. Metro: Arc de Triomf. **Amenities:** Restaurant; cafe w/terrace. *In room:* A/C, TV, Wi-Fi (free).

El Raval

VERY EXPENSIVE

Le Méridien Barcelona ★★★   Elegantly renovated in recent years, this is the finest hotel in the Ciutat Vella, as the long roster of internationally famous guests testifies. It's even superior in comfort to its two closest—and highly regarded—rivals in the area, the Colón and the Rivoli Ramblas (p. 88). Its impeccable suites are, understandably, the most expensive in town. Guest rooms are spacious and comfortable, with extra-large beds and heated bathroom floors. Staff are attentive and hospitable, with a free guided walking tour of the El Raval area operated every Thursday at 10am. The Discovery Spa offers a superb selection of massages and beauty treatments. An added bonus for working travelers is the well-equipped Renaissance Club, an executive floor providing a wide range of business facilities.

La Rambla 111, 08002 Barcelona. ℭ **93-318-62-00.** Fax 93-301-77-76. www.lemeridien-barcelona.com. 233 units. 400€–495€ double; 560€–2,100€ suite. AE, DC, MC, V. Parking 22€. Metro: Liceu or Plaça de Catalunya. **Amenities:** Restaurant; bar; babysitting; health club & spa; room service. *In room:* A/C, TV, hair dryer, minibar.

MODERATE

Barceló Raval   This striking purple-hued, cylindrical building, looming above the Raval's main thoroughfare, epitomizes the adventurous new face of this regenerated, multi-ethnic district of the old town. The chic luminous rooms are equipped with state-of-the-art amenities such as iPod links and flatscreen plasma TVs, and the rooftop terrace enjoys stunning 360-degree views of the city. There's around-the-clock cafeteria service, and the hotel's cosmopolitan Review restaurant provides a full menu of breakfasts, light lunches, and stylishly inventive dinners. A gloriously sybaritic spa also has a gym and fitness machines. Everyone is well catered for here, from hedonistic tourist to keep-fit enthusiast and business visitor.

Rambla del Raval 17-21, 08001 Barcelona. ℭ **93-320-14-90.** http://barcelo-raval.hotel-rez.com. 186 units. 125€–160€ double. AE, DC, MC, V. Metro: Jaume I. **Amenities:** Bar; restaurant; health club and spa; outdoor pool; Wi-Fi. *In room:* A/C, TV, minibar, MP3 docking station.

Curious   This friendly hotel, refurbished from an original Barri Gòtic building and decorated in a minimalist style dominated by cool grays and whites (with occasional touches of mauve and ochre), has a switched-on yet relaxing feel. It stands in the narrow-laned heart of Raval a few minutes' stroll away from La Rambla, within easy reach of all central amenities. All rooms have 21st-century touches such as Wi-Fi connections and satellite TVs, and there are large black-and-white photos of the city pasted on the walls to get you in the mood for exploring. Spacious family units are also available.

Carmé 25, 08001 Barcelona. ℭ **93-301-44-84.** www.hotelcurious.com. 24 units. Metro: Liceu. 100€–120€. Rate includes breakfast. **Amenities:** Bar; cafe; non-smoking rooms; Internet. *In room:* A/C, TV, hair dryer, Wi-Fi (free).

Hotel Sant Agustí   Dating from 1720—when it first saw life as a convent—this tastefully renovated five-story hotel stands in the center of the Ciutat Vella on a pretty square near the Boqueria market (p. 226), overlooking the brick walls of an unfinished Romanesque church. The sandstone facade is dominated by large curving windows, while the interior hall and lounge feature a lush blend of emerald-hued furnishings and rose-pink decor. The small guest rooms are comfortable and modern. The outdoor cafe is a good place to chill on a hot afternoon and the immediate vicinity is full of the funky character that has made El Raval the city's grittiest bohemian retreat. Some units are equipped for travelers with disabilities.

Plaça de Sant Agustí 3, 08001 Barcelona. ℭ **93-318-16-58.** Fax 93-317-29-28. www.hotelsa.com. 77 units. 110€–160€ double; 175€–200€ triple; 185€–205€ quad; 225€–275€ 2-bedroom family unit. Rates include breakfast. AE, DC, MC, V. Metro: Liceu. **Amenities:** Restaurant; room service; Wi-Fi (free). *In room:* A/C, TV, hair dryer.

HUSA Oriente Situated on the site of a Franciscan monastery right beside the bustling Rambla, the Oriente was one of the original "grand hotels" of Barcelona and dates back to 1842. Such was its prominence by the 1950s that it attracted the likes of Toscanini, Maria Callas, and Errol Flynn (who once passed out drunk and was put on public display in his room—unconscious and in the nude—by a somewhat unscrupulous manager). Renovations have improved the hotel's amenities but it lacks the style and charisma of its former glory days, today attracting mainly frugal travelers. The arched ballroom of yesterday has been turned into an atmospheric lounge, and the dining room still has a certain grandeur. The rooms are simple but comfortable.

La Rambla 45, 08002 Barcelona. ✆ **93-302-25-58.** Fax 93-412-38-19. www.hotelhusaoriente.com. 142 units. 205€ double; 225€ triple. AE, DC, MC, V. Metro: Liceu. **Amenities:** Restaurant (summer only); bar. *In room:* A/C, TV, Wi-Fi (free).

Mesón Castilla ★ This government-rated two-star hotel, a former apartment building now owned and operated by the Spanish hotel chain HUSA, has a Castilian facade with a wealth of Art Nouveau detailing on the interior. Filled with antiques and quirky trinkets, it's one of the most atmospheric spots to stay in town. It's also handily located close to the hip second-hand stores and record shops of the upper Raval, as well as the modern art galleries—the MACBA (p. 173) and the CCCB (p. 172). The midsize rooms are comfortable—beds have ornate Catalan-style headboards—and some open onto large terraces.

Valldoncella 5, 08001 Barcelona. ✆ **93-318-21-82.** Fax 93-412-40-20. www.mesoncastilla.com. 57 units. 150€ double; 200€ triple. Rates include breakfast. AE, DC, MC, V. Parking 20€. Metro: Plaça de Catalunya or Universitat. **Amenities:** Breakfast room; babysitting; room service. *In room:* A/C, TV, hair dryer, minibar.

INEXPENSIVE

Gat Raval ★★ From grim and grungy to green and groovy, the Gat Raval is the first in this extraordinary little chain's mini-empire and has been pioneering in giving *hostal* accommodations a much-needed facelift. The Gats (Catalan for "cats") is notably both cool and economical, although guests may find it a bit noisy when that coolness occasionally yields to unrestrained hedonistic exuberance. Decorated in bright acid greens with black trim, the neat bedrooms are adorned with original works from the local art school, which give them an upbeat bohemian vibe. Only some of the bedrooms have en-suite bathrooms (stipulate when booking) and communal arrangements are so clean you could eat your dinner off the floor.

Joaquín Costa 44, 1st floor, 08001 Barcelona. ✆ **93-481-66-70.** Fax 93-342-66-97. www.gatrooms.es/en. 24 units. 80€ double w/sink; 95€ double w/bathroom. MC, V. Metro: Universitat. **Amenities:** Wi-Fi. *In room:* A/C, TV.

Gat Xino ★★ Those wishing to experience the same Gat über-coolness as the Gat Raval, but with a dash more luxury, can opt for the Gat Xino, which caters to a slightly more grown-up and affluent visitor. This hip guesthouse has a sleek breakfast room, and there's a wood-decked terrace and a roof terrace for soaking up the rays. All of the rooms have their own apple-green bathrooms, and there are a few added extras like flatscreen TVs, and light-boxes above the beds giving abstract photographic views of the city.

Hospital 155, 1st Floor, 08001 Barcelona. ✆ **93-324-88-33.** Fax 93-324-88-34. www.gatrooms.es/en. 35 units. 95€–120€) double. Rate includes breakfast. MC, V. Metro: Liceu. **Amenities:** Wi-Fi. *In room:* A/C, TV.

Hostal Operaramblas ⚓

Cheap and cheerful, this safe, well-maintained *hostal*, located almost next to the Opera House (and not to be confused with the Petit Palace chain's more swish Opera Garden Ramblas on the other side of the city's liveliest *paseo*—see p. 236) is good for those traveling on a tight budget or alone. Be warned, though: This is basic, no-frills accommodations, with notably thin walls (light sleepers might do well to travel with earplugs) and no luxuries. Plus factors are its friendly and obliging staff and upbeat personality. Some rooms are better than others, however, and if you arrive without a reservation, ask to look around first. Otherwise, opt for something at the back with a private bathroom (shower only), as the street outside—just off La Rambla—can be noisy until the early hours.

Sant Pau 20, 08001 Barcelona. ✆ **93-318-82-01.** www.operaramblas.com. 69 units. 60€ single; 80€–90€ double. MC, V. Metro: Liceu. **Amenities:** High-speed Internet. *In room:* A/C.

Hotel España ⚓

Set just off the Lower Rambla in an historic building constructed in 1902 by fabled architect Domènech i Montaner (designer and architect of the Palau de la Música, p. 240), the España still boasts a classically styled foyer and highly elegant dining room evoking the heyday of Barcelonan *modernisme*. The renovated rooms, while less classical, are quite spacious, with neat but functional furnishings, comfortable beds, attractive tiled floors, and mellow drapes over the high windows. Some rooms are equipped for travelers with disabilities. An old elevator serves the building's four floors, and genial, hardworking staff are always eager to converse with non-Spanish-speaking visitors.

Sant Pau 9-11, 08001 Barcelona. ✆ **93-318-17-58.** Fax 93-317-11-34. www.hotelespanya.com. 80 units. 130€ double; 150€ triple. AE, DC, MC, V. Metro: Liceu or Drassanes. **Amenities:** 3 restaurants. *In room:* A/C, TV, hair dryer.

Hotel Peninsular ⚓

Along the same street as the España, this Art Nouveau–style hotel is a welcoming haven for the budget traveler. Constructed within the shell of a monastery that used to have a passageway connection with Sant Agustí church, the hotel was modernized in the early 1990s. Its use of wicker furnishings and cream-and-green decor gives it a colonial air, and its inner tiled courtyard, lined with plants, is its most charming feature. In the typical *moderniste* style of its era, the Peninsular has long hallways and high doorways and ceilings. The bedrooms are basic but clean, and the better ones have en-suite bathrooms.

Sant Pau 34, 08001 Barcelona. ✆ **93-302-31-38.** Fax 93-412-36-99. www.hotelpeninsular.net. 70 units. 90€ double; 120€ triple. Rates include breakfast. MC, V. Metro: Liceu. **Amenities:** Breakfast bar; Wi-Fi. *In room:* A/C.

Jardí ⚓

Enjoying one of Barcelona's most favored locations, this friendly five-story hotel opens onto the tree-shaded Plaça Sant Josep Oriol, whose cafes huddle around the Gothic medieval church of Santa María del Pi in the heart of the Ciutat Vella. More recent touches include a modern elevator and some rather over-enthusiastic lighting (which for some dissipates the historic charm of the building), but much of the original architectural charm still remains. The rooms themselves are austerely atmospheric, with comfortable beds and en-suite bathrooms with tub and shower. The quieter units are at the top and five of the accommodations have private terraces, while 26 have small balconies. Under separate management, **Bar del Pi,** on the ground floor, is a favorite of artists and students who live nearby.

Plaça Sant Josep Oriol 1, 08002 Barcelona. ☏ **93-301-59-00.** Fax 93-342-57-33. www.hoteljardi-barcelona.com. 40 units. 90€–110€ double. MC, V. Metro: Liceu. *In room amenities:* A/C, TV.

L'EIXAMPLE

If *moderniste* architecture, designer shopping, and high-class restaurants are your bag, then the Eixample ("extension" in Catalan) is the place to be. The area was built in the mid-19th century to cope with the overflow from the Ciutat Vella, and has retained its middle-class, residential flavor.

VERY EXPENSIVE

Hotel Casa Fuster ★★★ 📷   Located in one of the city's most emblematic buildings, the meticulously renovated Casa Fuster (originally built in 1908 by key *moderniste* architect Domènech i Muntaner) blends sheer luxury with first-rate state-of-the-art amenities. Traditional highlights from its great *moderniste* era include the elegant foyer and downstairs Vienna cafe, once a well-known meeting spot for the city's intelligentsia, while many of the Belle Epoque-style rooms—all lavishly decorated in mauve, magenta, and mellow gray-brown—have balconies overlooking the wide cosmopolitan Passeig de Gràcia. Marble structures, drapery, cushions, and padding generously abound while other luxuries range from Loewe toiletries to hydromassage bathtubs and an extremely high staff-to-guest ratio. If you can tear yourself away from all these pampering comforts, some of L'Eixample's very best shops and historical monuments are virtually on your doorstep.

Passeig de Gràcia 132, 08008 Barcelona. ☏ **90-220-23-45** for reservations, or 93-255-30-00. Fax 93-255-30-02. www.hotelcasafuster.com. 105 units. 400€–525€ double; 600€–2,500€ suite. AE, DC, MC, V. Valet parking 25€. Metro: Diagonal. **Amenities:** Restaurant; bar; babysitting; pool; health club and spa, room service. *In room:* A/C, TV, hair dryer, minibar, high-speed Internet.

Hotel Claris ★★★   This landmark seven-story, 19th-century building is a genuine luxurious treat. Furnishings and decor throughout are a lavish amalgam of teak, marble, steel, and glass while the opulent blue-violet guest rooms feature wood marquetry and paneling, custom furnishings, safes, and some of the city's most sumptuous beds. State-of-the-art electronic accessories are in turn complemented by exotically unusual artwork ranging from Turkish kilims to Hindu sculptures, and the immaculate marble tiled bathrooms are roomy and filled with deluxe toiletries and tub/shower combos. If money is no object, book one of the 20 individually designed duplex units. Other pluses include a small second-floor museum of Egyptian antiquities (from the owner's personal collection) and a rooftop swimming pool and garden with panoramic city views.

Pau Claris 150, 08009 Barcelona. ☏ **93-487-62-62.** Fax 93-215-79-70. www.derbyhotels.com. 120 units. 325€–450€ double; 500€–525€ suite. AE, DC, MC, V. Self/valet parking 20€. Metro: Passeig de Gràcia. **Amenities:** 2 restaurants; 2 bars; babysitting; fitness center; sauna; outdoor pool; room service. *In room:* A/C, TV, hair dryer, minibar, Wi-Fi.

Hotel Condes de Barcelona ★   Situated on the wide shop-filled Passeig de Gràcia, this former private villa (1895) is one of Barcelona's most popular and glamorous

L'Eixample Accommodations

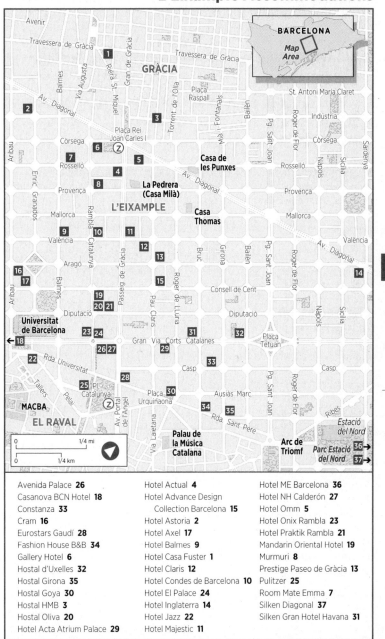

Avenir
Travessera de Gràcia
GRÀCIA
Travessera de Gràcia
St. Antoni Maria Claret
Plaça Raspall
Indústria
Còrsega
Plaça Rei Joan Carles I
Còrsega
Casa de les Punxes
Rosselló
Rosselló
Provença
La Pedrera (Casa Milà)
Provença
L'EIXAMPLE
Casa Thomas
Mallorca
Mallorca
València
València
Aragó
Consell de Cent
Universitat de Barcelona
Diputació
Diputació
Gran Via Corts Catalanes
Plaça Tetuan
Rda. Universitat
Casp
Casp
MACBA
EL RAVAL
Plaça Catalunya
Ausiàs Marc
Palau de la Música Catalana
Arc de Triomf
Estació del Nord
Parc Estació del Nord
BARCELONA
Map Area

0 1/4 mi
0 1/4 km

Avenida Palace **26**	Hotel Actual **4**
Casanova BCN Hotel **18**	Hotel Advance Design Collection Barcelona **15**
Constanza **33**	Hotel Astoria **2**
Cram **16**	Hotel Axel **17**
Eurostars Gaudí **28**	Hotel Balmes **9**
Fashion House B&B **34**	Hotel Casa Fuster **1**
Gallery Hotel **6**	Hotel Claris **12**
Hostal d'Uxelles **32**	Hotel Condes de Barcelona **10**
Hostal Girona **35**	Hotel El Palace **24**
Hostal Goya **30**	Hotel Inglaterra **14**
Hostal HMB **3**	Hotel Jazz **22**
Hostal Oliva **20**	Hotel Majestic **11**
Hotel Acta Atrium Palace **29**	

Hotel ME Barcelona **36**
Hotel NH Calderón **27**
Hotel Omm **5**
Hotel Onix Rambla **23**
Hotel Praktik Rambla **21**
Mandarin Oriental Hotel **19**
Murmuri **8**
Prestige Paseo de Gràcia **13**
Pulitzer **25**
Room Mate Emma **7**
Silken Diagonal **37**
Silken Gran Hotel Havana **31**

quality hotels. It boasts a unique neo-medieval facade that shows strong Gaudí influences, and has modern attractions that include having supper on the roof with a live jazz accompaniment. The comfortable, midsize guest rooms all contain marble bathrooms, reproductions of Spanish paintings, and soundproof windows. Unfortunately, the 74-room extension across the street (**Carrer Majorca**)—although comfortable and well equipped—doesn't quite capture the uniquely exotic flair of the original, so make sure you get a room in the main hotel.

Passeig de Gràcia 73-75, 08008 Barcelona. ✆ **93-445-00-00.** Fax 93-445-32-32. www.condesde barcelona.com. 235 units. 185€–325€ double; 420€–535€ suite. AE, DC, MC, V. Parking 20€. Metro: Passeig de Gràcia. **Amenities:** Restaurant; cafe; bar; babysitting; outdoor pool; room service. *In room:* A/C, TV, hair dryer, minibar, Wi-Fi.

Hotel El Palace ★★★ Formerly the legendary Ritz, and now a member of Spain's top HUSA chain, this Art Deco hotel—which dates back nearly a century—was totally refurbished in 2009 and now has a newly dazzling interior. The glorious character of the hotel has been retained, and original features such as the cream-and-gilt neoclassical lobby remain. The restaurants, lobby, and public areas are a study in cream, gold, and blue, and the high-ceilinged rooms are elegantly decorated with quality furnishings; some have mosaic patterns in the bathrooms. The superb restaurant continues in the hands of the Michelin-awarded chef, Romain Fornell.

Gran Vía de les Corts Catalanes 668, 08010 Barcelona. ✆ **93-510-11-30.** Fax 93-318-01-48. www. hotelpalacebarcelona.com. 125 units. 295€–400€ double; from 525€ junior suite; 1,000€–1,200€ suite. AE, DC, MC, V. Parking 22€. Metro: Passeig de Gràcia. **Amenities:** Restaurant; 2 bars; babysitting; health club; room service. *In room:* A/C, TV, DVD player, hair dryer, minibar, Wi-Fi.

Hotel Majestic ★★ This hotel has been one of Barcelona's most visible landmarks since 1918, when it was built in this highly sought-after location just 10 minutes' stroll away from Plaça de Catalunya. In the early 1990s it was radically renovated and upgraded to deluxe status while retaining the dignified stateliness of the public areas, but adding a sense of color and contemporary drama in the bedrooms. Today, each is outfitted in a different, mainly monochromatic color scheme, with carpets, artwork, and upholsteries. Staff members are hardworking and conscientious, albeit sometimes swamped with tour buses containing dozens of guests arriving all at once. Its **Drolma** restaurant (p. 139) has a Michelin star.

Passeig de Gràcia 68, 08007 Barcelona. ✆ **93-488-17-17.** Fax 93-488-18-80. www.hotelmajestic.es. 303 units. 220€–595€ double; 575€–750€ suite; de luxe "Sagrada Família" suite 1,000€–1,600€. AE, DC, MC, V. Parking 18€. Metro: Passeig de Gràcia. **Amenities:** 2 restaurants; 2 bars; fitness center and sauna; outdoor pool; room service. *In room:* A/C, TV, hair dryer, minibar, Wi-Fi.

Hotel Omm ★★★ Chic, intelligent, and strikingly executed, the hyper-trendy Omm has become a modern city landmark thanks to its "wafers of stone" facade. Inside, the dark, atmospheric communal halls and lounges are skillfully contrasted with bright, naturally lit bedrooms. All rooms feature ample but nonintrusive cupboard and wardrobe space and a variety of state-of-the-art modern conveniences, including flatscreen TVs and DVD and CD players. Kimonos are provided for guests wishing to pass directly to the spa or rooftop lap pool, from where you can see the roof of Gaudí's La Pedrera (p. 175). The chic sundeck is another privileged spot where you can laze away languid Barcelonese evenings. The Omm is owned by Grupo Tragaluz, one of Barcelona's most famous restaurateurs, and the hotel's restaurant **Moo** (p. 143) is an "in" spot for a pre-dinner drink.

Rosselló 265, 08008 Barcelona. ✆ **93-445-40-00.** Fax 93-445-40-04. www.hotelomm.es. 91 units. 300€–450€ double; 570€ suite. AE, DC, MC, V. Parking 22€. Metro: Diagonal. **Amenities:** Restaurant; cocktail bar; babysitting; health club; room service. *In room:* A/C, TV, DVD player, hair dryer, minibar, Wi-Fi.

Prestige Paseo de Gràcia ★★★ Restyled by top Catalan architect Josep Sant-pere from a 1930s' building, the Prestige is one of the most fashionable hotels in town. It has some nice touches, such as the **Zeroom** breakfast bar and library where you can enjoy laid-back mornings, and the Oriental garden where you can also sip coffee amid ivory sun loungers and bamboo planters. There's an "Ask Me" service—a kind of human-genie-in-a-bottle who hunts down information on the city for you, whether it's the opening hours of a museum or the nearest kosher restaurant. And the Japanese-inspired bedrooms are sleek and spacious, with all the added extras one could possibly need for a good night's sleep. All that's missing is a fancy restaurant with a celebrity chef at the helm.

Passeig de Gràcia 62, 08007 Barcelona. ✆ **93-272-41-80.** Fax 93-272-41-81. www.prestigepaseode gracia.com. 45 units. 225€–375€ double; from 450€ suite. AE, DC, MC, V. Valet parking 2.50€ per hr. Metro: Diagonal. **Amenities:** Cafe/bar; babysitting; health club and spa; room service. *In room:* A/C, TV, hair dryer, minibar, high-speed Internet.

Pulitzer ★★ 👜 Another stalwart addition to Barcelona's designer hotel scene, the super-trendy Pulitzer is a mere stone's throw from the Plaça de Catalunya. Its stylish lounge area is a comfortable oasis of white leather sofas, black marble trim, and floor-to-ceiling bookshelves lined with tomes such as *California Homes, Moroc-can Interiors,* and *The World's Greatest Hotels.* There's also a smart restaurant and a candle-lit roof terrace furnished with loungers where you can relax over a coffee or cocktail as you admire the fabulous day and night city vistas. The variably sized bedrooms are decorated in inky-black and charcoal-gray hues and are big on sump-tuous fabrics—leather, silk, and down pillows.

Bergara 8, 08002 Barcelona. ✆ **93-481-67-67.** Fax 93-481-64-64. www.hotelpulitzer.es. 92 units incl. 1 suite. 155€–245€ double. AE, DC, MC, V. Public parking nearby 25€. Metro: Plaça de Catalunya. **Amenities:** Restaurant; cocktail bar; babysitting; solarium; room service. *In room:* A/C, TV, hair dryer, minibar, Wi-Fi.

Silken Gran Hotel Havana ★ The Havana occupies a 19th-century building (Casa L. Fradera) that first opened its doors to the public as a hotel in 1991. It was completely redecorated in 2009 but still retains much of its original *moderniste* architecture and design. Rooms here are spacious and well equipped, with vast Italian-marble bathrooms. The best and priciest rooms are the executive suites on the sixth floor, which have private terraces with stunning views. Although all rooms are soundproofed, those facing the ever-busy Gran Vía still suffer from a certain amount of traffic noise; if you're a light sleeper it's best to ask for a room at the rear. The rooftop pool and sun terrace are an added bonus.

Gran Vía de les Corts Catalanes 647, 08010 Barcelona. ✆ **93-412-11-15.** Reservations 93-341-70-00. Fax 93-412-26-11. www.silken-granhavana.com. 145 units. 160€–205€ double; 220€–380€ suite. AE, DC, MC, V. Parking 20€. Metro: Passeig de Gràcia, Tetuan, or Girona. **Amenities:** Restaurant; bar; pool; babysit-ting; room service. *In room:* A/C, TV, hair dryer, minibar, Wi-Fi.

EXPENSIVE

Avenida Palace ★★ This superb hotel stands behind a pair of mock-fortified towers in an enviable 19th-century neighborhood filled with elegant shops and

FAMILY-FRIENDLY hotels

Citadines An in-house kitchen and maid service takes some of the hassle out of catering for little ones. See p. 119.

Fashion House B&B This individual but small-scale B&B boasts a studio apartment (La Suite) tailor-made for independent family needs. Book early to get this one. See p. 109.

Hotel Colón Opposite the cathedral in the Gothic Quarter. There are spacious rooms for traveling families. See p. 88.

Hotel Fira Palace At the base of the city's most expansive green zone, Montjuïc. Areas where the kids can run wild are only a short distance away. See p. 112.

apartment buildings. Although it was actually constructed in 1952, it manages to evoke an old-world sense of charm, partly because of the attentive staff and partly because of the flowers, antiques, and mid-20th-century accessories that fill the public rooms. Celebrity guests have been coming for decades, and the Beatles stayed in the master suite after their summer concert in 1965. The soundproofed rooms range from midsize to spacious and have comfortable beds, solidly traditional decor, and mainly dark wood furnishings.

Gran Vía de les Corts Catalanes 605 (at Passeig de Gràcia), 08007 Barcelona. (✆) **93-301-96-00.** Fax 93-318-12-34. www.avenidapalace.com. 160 units. 175€–275€ double; 300€–350€ suite. AE, DC, MC, V. Parking 18€. Metro: Passeig de Gràcia. **Amenities:** 2 restaurants; bar; babysitting; room service. *In room:* A/C, TV, hair dryer, minibar, Wi-Fi.

Hotel ME Barcelona Located at the eastern end of L'Eixample, close to the landmark Torre Agbar (p. 11) and the junction of Diagonal and Pere IV avenues, this cutting-edge, 24-story hotel is one of the best equipped for both leisure and business travelers. Accommodations vary from standard rooms to lofts and suites, all immaculately furnished in minimalist style with state-of-the-art communications facilities and en-suite bathrooms. There are also top-quality conference rooms, health facilities that include hydrotherapy and aromatherapy, and stylish eating spots headlined by the top-floor Dos Cielos restaurant, which has adjoining terraces offering stunning panoramic views of the city.

Av. Diagonal/Pere IV 272–286, 08005 Barcelona. (✆) **93-367-20-50** or 902-14-44-40. www.me-barcelona.com. 259 units. 245€–335€ double. AE, DC, MC, V. Metro: Poble Nou. **Amenities:** 3 restaurants; bars; babysitting; health club & spa; room service. *In room:* A/C, TV, minibar, Wi-Fi (free).

Hotel NH Calderón ★★ Efficiently maintained and well staffed with a multilingual corps of employees, this hotel delivers exactly what it promises: Comfortable accommodations in a well-conceived, standardized format that's akin to many other modern hotels around the world. Originally built in the 1960s, this 10-story hotel wasn't particularly imaginative then, but was greatly improved in the early 1990s after its acquisition by the NH Hotel Group and has been renovated at regular intervals since then. Rooms have comfortable, contemporary-looking furnishings with hints of high-tech design, good lighting, lots of varnished hardwood, and colorful fabrics.

WHERE TO STAY | L'Eixample

Rambla de Catalunya 26, 08007 Barcelona. ☏ **93-301-00-00.** Fax 93-412-41-93. www.nh-hoteles.com. 253 units. Mon–Thurs 285€ double; Fri–Sun 205€ double. AE, DC, MC, V. Parking 20€, Passeig de Gràcia. **Amenities:** Restaurant; bar; health club; sauna; outdoor pool; room service. *In room:* A/C, TV, hair dryer, minibar, Wi-Fi.

Hotel Praktik Rambla   This eminently jet-age concept—in previous existences the Palacios Hotel and the Climent Arola House—is located in the lower part of L'Eixample in an early 19th-century mansion designed by eminent architect **Francesc de P. Villar i Carmona.** He also designed the province's imposing Montserrat and Sant Cugat monasteries. Refurbished and renamed the Praktik Rambla in 2009, the hotel has been dragged into the 21st century while retaining original *moderniste* elements like the ornate Ionic columns that support the first-floor gallery. The spacious library features many of the architect's original sketches of the building, and leads to a secluded solarium. The brightly hued rooms have minimalist, cool furnishings that blend with the original exotic floor tiles. The staff is friendly in the extreme, and if you're feeling peckish the contemporary, industrial-chic Piscolabis restaurant offers innovative tapas and nouveau Catalan dishes.

Rambla de Catalunya 27, 08007 Barcelona. ☏ **93-343-66-90.** Fax: 93-304-33-32. www.hotelpraktik rambla.com. 43 units. 180€–210€ double. AE, MC, V. Metro: Passeig de Gràcia. **Amenities:** Restaurant. *In room:* A/C, TV, Wi-Fi (free).

Mandarin Oriental Hotel ★★   A member of the highly prestigious Asian chain, this exotic and long-awaited hotel burst on the Catalan scene in November 2009 when it opened its doors in a key location overlooking the city's finest boulevard, the Passeig de Gràcia. Seamlessly blending Eastern and Western styles, it boasts innovative interiors by Patricia Urquiola, one of Spain's most creative designers. Both accommodations and dining facilities are first-rate, as you would expect from Mandarin Oriental, and the hotel also houses one of the finest and best-equipped spas in the city, with body-enhancing experiences including Thai massage and "rainforest experience" showers. For business travelers in turn there are sophisticated amenities of the highest order, including fiber-optic technology and multi-line IP connections with private voice mail.

Passeig de Gràcia 38-40, 08007 Barcelona. ☏ **93-151-88-88.** www.mandarinoriental.com/barcelona. 98 units. 250€–300€ double. AE, DC, MC, V. Metro: Passeig de Gràcia. **Amenities:** Reception; restaurant; bar; babysitting; health club and spa; outdoor pool; room service. *In room:* A/C, TV, DVD player, hair dryer, minibar, Wi-Fi (free).

MODERATE

Casanova BCN Hotel ★   A member of the avant-garde Rafael chain, this flamboyantly attractive hotel has been tastefully converted from an 18th-century limestone mansion. Special features include an inner patio that's been tastefully converted into a garden spa and an eccentrically lit, cream interior that features sculpture-style seating. The cuisine served in its Mexiterranée restaurant is unconventional, offering a daring fusion of spicy Mexican and garlicky Catalan dishes. Guest rooms tastefully blend traditional and minimalist styles and range from comfortable doubles to plush junior suites with polished hardwood floors. Some have their own terrace, enjoying good views of this university corner of the city.

Gran Vía de les Corts Catalanes 559, 08011 Barcelona. ☎ **93-396-48-00.** Fax 93-396-48-10. www. casanovabcnhotel.com. 124 units. 133€–253€ double; 299€–358€ junior suite. MC, V. Parking 30€. Metro: Universitat. **Amenities:** Restaurant; bar; spa; room service. *In room:* A/C, TV, hair dryer, minibar, Wi-Fi (15€).

Constanza ★★★ 👫   A smart boutique hotel located within easy walking distance of La Ribera's shopping, cultural, and culinary attractions, the Constanza combines style and comfort with a young vibe and an upbeat, trendy ambience. The lobby is filled with white, boxy couches and red trim, and beyond it there's a minimalist breakfast room decorated with a continually changing program of flower images. The first-floor bedrooms are bright and fresh with leather-trimmed furniture and white cotton sheets. Some are rather small, and those at the front can be noisy, but if you can book a room with a private terrace, the place offers very good value.

Bruc 33, 08010 Barcelona. ☎ **93-270-19-10.** Fax 93-317-40-24. www.hotelconstanza.com. 20 units. 125€–150€ double. AE, MC, V. Public parking nearby 20€. Metro: Urquinaona. **Amenities:** Restaurant; health club; non-smoking rooms; room service. *In room:* A/C, TV, hair dryer, minibar; high-speed Internet.

Cram ★★ 👫   This eminently stylish addition to the hip Barcelona scene is not as crowded as its name implies, and has a special appeal to cool 30-somethings. It's located in a 19th-century mansion in the heart of L'Eixample, and while the original rose-pink facade has been retained, the interior lounges have been tastefully refurbished with dark-red cushions, gleaming black surfaces, and futuristic disc-shaped chairs. The elegant bedrooms have mirrored walls, amber-wood floors, and mellow gold-and-burgundy decor, and some bathrooms have Jacuzzis. The cosmopolitan shops and cafes of the Passeig de Gràcia can be reached on foot in 5 to 10 minutes, and gourmets will delight in the on-site presence of the long-established Gaig restaurant.

Aribau 54, 08011 Barcelona. ☎ **93-216-77-00.** Fax 93-216-77-07. www.hotelcram.com. 67 units. 155€–290€ double; 250€–475€ executive and privilege units; 290€–545€ suite. AE, MC, V. Parking 18€. Metro: Universitat. **Amenities:** Restaurant; bar; outdoor pool; spa; solarium; room service. *In room:* A/C, TV, hair dryer, Wi-Fi.

Eurostars Gaudí   This sleek member of the highly regarded Eurostars group is located in the heart of L'Eixample, just northwest of the city's main bullring. It's a highly contemporary hotel with a relaxing decor of richly textured color schemes. Staff members are friendly and attentive, and the bright, spacious dining room provides quality international cuisine and buffet breakfasts. Couples staying in the romantic double rooms receive a complimentary bottle of *cava* on arrival. From the rooftop sun terrace you get great city views that take in the nearby Sagrada Família (p. 176).

Consell de Cent 498–500, 08013 Barcelona. ☎ **93-232-02-88,** reservations 93-902-24-24. Fax 93-232-02-87. www.eurostarshotels.com/gaudi. 45 units. 140€–240€ double. AE, DC, MC, V. Metro: Monumental. **Amenities:** Restaurant; bar. *In room:* A/C, TV, hair dryer, minibar, Wi-Fi (free).

Gallery Hotel ★ 👫   Named after a nearby district of major art galleries, this stylishly decorated, modern hotel lies between the Passeig de Gràcia and Rambla de Catalunya, just below the wide Diagonal avenue in the upper district of L'Eixample. It's a long-established choice for both business and leisure visitors; its guest rooms are mainly midsize and tastefully furnished with pleasing touches such as fresh flowers and crisp bed linen. All have rather small en-suite bathrooms. Some have facilities for disabled guests. The on-site Cafe del Gallery restaurant is renowned for its savory Mediterranean cuisine.

Calle Roselló 249, 08008 Barcelona. ✆ **93-415-99-11.** Fax 93-415-91-84. www.galleryhotel.com. 115 units. Mon–Thurs 180€–200€ double, 350€ suite; Fri–Sun 150€–160€ double, 175€ suite. AE, DC, MC, V. Parking 18€. Metro: Diagonal. **Amenities:** Restaurant; bar; babysitting; health club; sauna; solarium; room service. *In room:* A/C, TV, hair dryer, minibar, high-speed Internet.

Hotel Acta Atrium Palace ★★★ 🎁

This high-tech designer hotel, with its sleek lines and oatmeal-marble decor, stylishly combines business and pleasure. Facilities range from a library-cum-business center to a softly lit restaurant and an indoor swimming pool with an adjoining Jacuzzi. The spacious bedrooms have comfortable beds with quilted throws and small sitting areas. Other touches include a free daily quota of mineral water and fruit juice. Top-floor suites offer maximum comfort; they feature a separate living room, two TVs, and a private terrace with deck chairs, a temperature-controlled hot tub, and great views.

Gran Vía de les Corts Catalanes 656, Eixample Esquerra, 08010 Barcelona. ✆ **93-342-80-00.** Fax 93-342-80-01. www.hotel-atriumpalace.com. 71 units. 145€–260€ double; 275€–350€ suite. AE, DC, MC, V. Parking 22€. Metro: Passeig de Gràcia or Plaça de Catalunya. **Amenities:** Restaurant; bar; babysitting; health club; pool; room service. *In room:* A/C, TV, hair dryer, minibar, Wi-Fi (free).

Hotel Actual 🗡

Situated across the road from the ultra-hip Hotel Omm (p. 100), the contemporary Actual nevertheless manages to hold its own, offering a smart and highly respectable money-saving alternative. And of course you can still make use of the Omm's wonderful bar and restaurant. Small but perfectly formed wood paneling, brushed steel, and large windows give the hotel a light, airy feel with a designer edge. Bedrooms are simply but elegantly decorated with chocolate-brown soft furnishings and white walls and bed linen. The staff is helpful and obliging and amenities include a pool for relaxed summertime swimming.

Rosselló 238, Eixample Esquerra, 08008 Barcelona. ✆ **93-552-05-50.** Fax 93-552-05-55. www.hotel actual.com. 29 units. 175€–200€ double. AE, DC, MC, V. Public parking 22€. Metro: Diagonal. **Amenities:** Cafe; babysitting; outdoor pool; room service. *In room:* A/C, TV, hair dryer, minibar, Wi-Fi.

Hotel Advance Design Collection Barcelona ★ 🎁

Located in a renovated 19th-century mansion formerly known as the Casa de los Marqueses de Framis, within easy reach of all central attractions, this elegant, gay-friendly hotel is one of the most atmospheric in the Eixample district. Its eclectic blend of stylish modern and colorful period decor was the work of top designer Santi Nin. All guest rooms are spacious, comfortable, and elegantly furnished, and most enjoy fine city views from their high windows. Half a dozen have their own private terrace. Service is attentive and very welcoming.

Sepúlveda 180, 08011 Barcelona. ✆ **93-289-28-92.** Fax 93-289-30-24. www.hoteladvance.com. 36 units. 139€–333€ double; 503€ triple. Rates include breakfast. AE, MC, V. Metro: Urgell. **Amenities:** Breakfast room. *In room:* A/C, TV, hair dryer, minibar, Wi-Fi (free).

Hotel Astoria ★ 🗡

This renovated 1950s' member of the distinguished Derby Hotel chain is located high up in L'Eixample, close to the junction of Carrer Enric Granados and the wide shop- and restaurant-filled Avinguda Diagonal. Retained features include the Art Deco facade, high ceilings, glossy tiled floors, marble pillars, geometric designs, and brass-studded detail in the public rooms—all strongly influenced by Moorish and Andalusian styles. The guest rooms are comfortable, midsize, and soundproofed, with slick louvered closets and gleaming white walls. All rooms have private bathrooms containing showers. Older units have warm textures of exposed cedar, and pristine modern accessories. Recent welcome additions are the rooftop pool and sauna.

París 203, 08036 Barcelona. ✆ **93-209-83-11.** Fax 93-202-30-08. www.derbyhotels.es. 117 units. 140€–185€ double; 225€–255€ suite. AE, DC, MC, V. Parking nearby 18€. Metro: Diagonal. **Amenities:** Restaurant; bar; health club; sauna; outdoor pool; room service. *In room:* A/C, TV, hair dryer, minibar, Wi-Fi.

Hotel Axel ★★★ 📷 Located in a fine *moderniste* building in a zone known as "Gaixample," this boutique hotel has widened its original single-sex net to embrace heteros and gays alike. The staff is hip, and amenities range from a cool, scarlet-colored cocktail bar and restaurant in the lobby to a trendy rooftop pool, bar, sauna, and sundeck. For dress-conscious visitors there's a men's designer clothing store next door (run by the Axel). All bedrooms have soundproofed windows, king-size beds covered with large soft pillows, a subtly erotic decor, and smart en-suite bathrooms—designed for two—some with Jacuzzis. An extra touch is the provision of free bottled mineral water in fridges on every floor. There are also a few rooms for visitors with disabilities.

Aribau 33, 08011 Barcelona. ✆ **93-323-93-93.** Fax 93-323-93-94. www.axelhotels.com. 66 units. 160€–275€ double; from 300€ suite. AE, DC, MC, V. Parking 16€. Metro: Universitat. **Amenities:** Restaurant; bar; health club; outdoor pool; room service. *In room:* A/C, TV, hair dryer, minibar, Wi-Fi.

Hotel Balmes Set in a seven-story structure built in the late 1980s, this chain hotel successfully combines conservative decor with modern accessories. It has a well-trained and friendly staff. Bedrooms have a warm color scheme of rich terra cottas and sunset yellows that brighten an otherwise white interior, allowing residents—many of whom are in town on business—to live and work comfortably. Marble-trimmed bathrooms are equipped with tub/shower combinations. If you're looking for peace and quiet, rooms at the back of the hotel overlook a small garden and swimming pool and are calmer and more relaxing than those facing the busy street. Check the website out of season, when rates can drop as low as 25%.

Majorca 216, 08008 Barcelona. ✆ **93-451-19-14.** Fax 93-451-00-49. www.derbyhotels.com/balmes. 100 units. 150€–230€ double. AE, DC, MC, V. Parking 16€. Metro: Diagonal. **Amenities:** Restaurant; bar; outdoor pool; room service. In room: A/C, TV, hair dryer, minibar, Wi-Fi.

Hotel Inglaterra ⚑ Despite the name, this quietly elegant hotel mainly features exotic Japanese-inspired decor. One of the very first boutique hotels in town, it provides spacious communal areas that include comfortable lounges, a snazzy breakfast room and bar, a well-equipped roof terrace for sunbathing and reading, and spacious minimalist rooms. All in all, this quality, chilled-out hotel provides excellent value for your money.

Pelai 14, 08001 Barcelona. ✆ **93-505-11-00.** Fax 93-505-11-09. www.hotel-inglaterra.com. 60 units. 210€–300€ double. AE, DC, MC, V. Public parking nearby 25€. Metro: Plaça de Catalunya or Universitat. **Amenities:** Restaurant; room service. *In room:* A/C, TV, hair dryer, minibar, Wi-Fi.

Hotel Jazz Just around the corner from Plaça de Catalunya, the Jazz is located in an enclave of design-led hotels. It has a low-key and downbeat decor that includes bleached-wood floors and oatmeal paintwork, which blends with a cool mix of gray and beige, and is interspersed with odd splashes of brighter colors. The large, soundproofed rooms all have immaculate, black-tiled bathrooms. The big plus comes on the roof, where you'll find a swimming pool and a wooden deck, with some impressive views over the urban rooftops. If you're here on a working trip there's also a well-equipped business center and free Wi-Fi.

Pelai 3, 08001 Barcelona. ✆ **93-552-96-96,** 0870/120-1521 (U.K.) or 207/580-2663 (U.S.). Fax 93-552-96-97. www.hoteljazz.com. 108 units. 180€–220€ double; 280€–330€ suite. AE, DC, MC, V. Parking 20€. Metro: Plaça de Catalunya or Universitat. **Amenities:** Cafe; babysitting; solarium; outdoor pool; room service. *In room:* A/C, TV, hair dryer, minibar, Wi-Fi (free).

Hotel Onix Rambla ★ 🔧   An oasis of modernity in the midst of Gothic-quarter mansions, the elegantly minimalist Onix Rambla is an excellent choice for anyone who wants to stay in a designer hotel without paying designer prices. The hotel is filled with discreetly tasteful works of modern art, and communal amenities include a pleasant breakfast room and snack bar. There are also bonuses such as the large rooftop sun terrace and plunge pool. Bedrooms are tastefully decorated with natural materials such as wood and leather.

Rambla de Catalunya 24, Eixample Esquerra, 08007 Barcelona. ✆ **93-342-79-80.** Fax 93-342-51-52. www.hotelonixrambla.com. 40 units. 140€–175€ double. AE, DC, MC, V. Metro: Passeig de Gràcia or Universitat. **Amenities:** Cafe; babysitting; health club; outdoor pool; room service; Wi-Fi (free). *In room:* A/C, TV, hair dryer, minibar, high-speed Internet.

Murmuri ★★   Small in size but big on style, the Murmuri is as hip and luxurious a base as you'll find, even in this switched-on city. Conveniently located in L'Eixample and close to all central facilities, it's noted for its discreetly welcoming staff. The spacious, immaculately furnished guest rooms have twin- or queen-size beds, luminous gray-and-white decor, and mod cons including adjustable lights, Wi-Fi, and MP3 docking stations. All have soundproofed, double-glazed windows and most enjoy fine views of the bustling Rambla de Catalunya. The hotel's elegantly minimalist restaurant serves some of the best Asian dishes in town and the cocktail bar is a popular rendezvous spot for Barcelona's cool people.

Rambla de Catalunya 104, 08008 Barcelona. ✆ **93-550-06-00.** www.murmuri.com. 7 units. 350€–600€ double; 600€–750€ suite. AE, MC, V. Parking 24€. Metro: Diagonal. **Amenities:** Restaurant; bar; room service. *In room:* A/C, TV, hair dryer, MP3 docking station, Wi-Fi (15€).

Room Mate Emma ★   The newest addition to Barcelona's homely and innovative chain of Room Mate hostelries, this one is located in the heart of L'Eixample, close to the shopper's haven of Passeig de Gràcia. The sleek, futuristic-style rooms, created by top interior designer Tomás Aliá and resembling one of the more imaginative sets of a Kubrick movie, are elegant and comfortable, though a tad on the compact side. There are slightly more expensive attic suites with terraces if you fancy a bit more space, and three rooms are equipped for disabled travelers.

Rosselló 205, 08008 Barcelona. ✆ **93-238-56-06.** www.room-matehotels.com. 56 units. 90€–140€ double; 150€–175€ attic suite. AE, DC, MC, V. Metro: Diagonal. **Amenities:** breakfast bar. *In room:* A/C, TV, hair dryer, minibar, Wi-Fi.

Silken Diagonal   Located next to the extraordinary Torre Agbar (p. 11) in the southeast corner of L'Eixample, the Silken Diagonal was designed by distinguished local architect Juli Capella. It features a striking black-and-white facade that conceals an unexpectedly bright and naturally lit interior. Its spacious public areas include four lounges, a designer-cuisine restaurant (Piano) providing top Catalan

BARCELONA'S self-catering SCENE

If you're intrigued by the cute-looking apartment blocks in the Ciutat Vella with their curved-beamed ceilings and balconies brimming with ferns, or the tiled-entrance apartments with Art Nouveau facades in L'Eixample, now's your chance to get up close and personal. Wander around the Barri Gòtic these days, and many of the apartments are available for rent at reasonable prices, enabling visitors to get a taste of what it's like to live in the city, shop in its markets, cook its food, and make merry over glasses of wine around the dinner table.

There's no shortage of properties you can rent. Two agencies that offer rentals in Barcelona are **Visit Barcelona** (www.visit-bcn.com), which has many Barri Gòtic properties for rent, and **Friendly Rentals** (www.friendlyrentals.com), which is a bit pricier.

If you're looking for something cultural and unconventional, one of the most interesting of these is **La Casa de les Lletres** (House of Letters; ℰ **93-226-37-30,** reservations 93-319-37-23; www.cru2001.com), with themed apartments paying homage to writers George Orwell and Catalan journalist and foodie Josep Pla. Accommodations mix state-of-the-art facilities with an intellectual bohemian vibe. Poetry and prose are literally written on the walls. Situated in an elegant town house on the handsome Plaça Antonio López, the location couldn't

be better, just minutes from Barceloneta and the Barri Gòtic. The nearby **Casa de l'Argent,** run by the same people, offers similar accommodations.

More basic apartments are found at www.nivellmar.net, which offers seaside lets—no more than 200m (660 feet) from the beach—all the way from Barceloneta to Poble Nou. The places on their books are functional rather than beautiful, but are well decorated, clean, and fairly priced. They are ideal for young travelers, or families with kids who want to be close to the sea. **Soho Rooms** (ℰ **63-008-82-44;** www.sohorooms bcn.com) rents tiny but atmospheric studios in a traditional Barri Gòtic building located in a narrow alley a short walk from the port.

For character apartments that won't break the bank, check out www.visit-bcn.com, which offers a wide range of different apartments, from classic Barri Gòtic town houses—such as the lovely Dos Amigos in the heart of the Old City, with its gorgeous tiles, warm paintwork, and small terrace—to loft-style apartments.

You can also rent a **casa rural** (country cottage) in the mountains or wooded valleys of the Catalan countryside around Barcelona. This provides a relaxing break from the stimulations of the big city and gives you a taste of rural life in Catalonia. Check **www.casasruralesbarcelona.com** for more information.

and Basque specialties, and a cozy cafe (the Tecla) where full buffet breakfasts are served. There is a small but popular rooftop swimming pool and surrounding wooden-floored solarium, which offers splendid city views. The stylish, comfortable rooms and suites are decorated in luminous whites and grays, and some have facilities for guests with disabilities.

Av. Diagonal 205, 08018 Barcelona. ℰ **93-489-53-09.** Fax 93-489-53-09. www.hoteldiagonal barcelona.com. 240 units. 160€–285€ double. AE, DC, MC, V. Metro: Glòries. **Amenities:** Restaurant; cafe/bar; rooftop pool; solarium. *In room:* A/C, TV, hair dryer, minibar, high-speed Internet.

INEXPENSIVE

Fashion House B&B ★ 🎁 One of the increasing number of hostelries in the center of Barcelona offering quality bed-and-breakfast, the Fashion House is located in an elegantly restored 19th-century town house decorated with stylish stuccoes and friezes. Two bedrooms share a bathroom, and all are bright and decked out in pastel colors. The best have verandas. La Suite, which doubles as a self-catering apartment, is an ideal choice for families who need more space and independence; it has private access to the communal terrace, which is well supplied with shaded tables and chairs, and plenty of greenery. Breakfast is served here in the summer.

Bruc 13 Principal, 08010 Barcelona. ℭ **63-790-40-44.** Fax 93-165-15-60. www.bcn-fashionhouse.com. 8 units. 80€–85€ double; 95€–100€ double w/balcony; 90€–110€ triple; 125€ triple w/balcony; 135€ suite. Extra bed 25€ per night. Rates include breakfast. 12€ supplement in high season. MC, V. Metro: Urquinaona. **Amenities:** Breakfast room. *In room:* A/C, TV (suite only), kitchenette (suite only).

Hostal d'Uxelles ★ 🎁 A picture-postcard hotel with helpful staff, the genteel Hostal d'Uxelles is well located in the busy heart of L'Eixample. Pastel hues and beatific sculptures of angels enhance its rustic charm, and all rooms are individually designed with ornate Art Deco wood paneling and romantic flourishes such as cupid's-bow drapes above the bed. Each comes with a bathroom resplendent with Andalusian tiling, and the best have private, plant-filled balconies big enough to hold a table and two chairs.

Gran Vía de les Corts Catalanes 667 (Hostal 2) and 668 (Hostal 1), 08010 Barcelona. ℭ **93-265-25-60.** Fax 93-232-85-67. www.hotelduxelles.com. 30 units. 80€–95€ double; 100€–135€ triple; 150€–200€ quad. AE, DC, MC, V. Parking nearby 18€. Metro: Tetuan or Girona. **Amenities:** Room service. *In room:* TV.

Hostal Girona ★★ 🍴 Designed in the 1860s by leading *moderniste* architect Ildefons Cerda, this is one of the most character-filled *hostales* in town. Its wall hangings, rugs, gilded picture frames, and teardrop chandeliers offset the period decor to perfection, creating a nostalgia-invoking ambience that's transformed it into a highly sought-after city-center retreat. It offers a variety of bedrooms, from singles without bathrooms to more plush doubles with en-suite bathrooms. Some have balconies overlooking the street or a quiet rear patio. All are comfortable and freshly painted, with plain white linen bedspreads. It's an individual gem and a bargain at that.

Girona 24 1-1, 08010 Barcelona. ℭ **93-265-02-59.** Fax 93-246-12-54. www.hostalgirona.com. 19 units. 60€–90€ double. MC, V. Metro: Girona or Urquinaona. *In room amenities:* A/C, TV.

Hostal Goya ★★ 🎁 A superior *hostal* largely patronized by a young and lively clientele, the traditional yet tastefully refurbished Goya is noted for its charming service and colorful *moderniste* decor, which includes magnificent original tiled floors. It offers a range of warmly furnished doubles, some with large, sunny balconies. Bonuses include a comfortable, Scandinavian-influenced sitting room/TV lounge where free tea, coffee, and hot chocolate are available throughout the day. Its homely character and convenient central location have made it a popular choice, so book early if you want to stay here.

Pau Claris 74, 08010 Barcelona. ℭ **93-302-25-65.** Fax 93-412-04-35. www.hostalgoya.com. 19 units. 100€–125€ double; 135€ suite w/bathroom and private terrace. MC, V. Metro: Urquinaona or Plaça de Catalunya. *In room amenities:* A/C in some units.

Hostal HMB   One of the more recent, welcome additions to Barcelona's low-cost hotel scene is this nifty and stylish little establishment, which offers just 13 compact but high-ceilinged rooms painted in bright blues and greens and with polished wooden floors. All rooms have flatscreen TVs. Furnishings are modestly comfortable throughout, and the public areas and corridors feature contemporary works of art. The location at the northern end of L'Eixample ensures that a wide variety of shops and city monuments—especially the *moderniste* gems (p. 179)—is within easy reach.

Calle Bonavista 21 Principal, 08012 Barcelona. ✆ **93-368-20-13.** Fax 93-368-19-95. www.hostalhmb. com. 28 units. 50€–60€ single; 75€–90€ double. MC, V. Metro: Diagonal. *In room amenities:* A/C, TV, Wi-Fi (free).

Hostal Oliva 🔑   This unpretentious hotel is a genuine Eixample original, dating from the 1930s; its vintage attractions include high ceilings, tiled floors, and a period wooden elevator with bench-style seats and a mirror. The neatly refurnished rooms are simple and rather basic, but the best ones overlook Barcelona's smartest shopping street and most have their own bathrooms. All are well priced, and if you're on a strict budget the cheapest of all are the darker interior rooms which share bathroom amenities with others on the same floor. The downside is that it can get noisy at times—especially over weekends, when revelers return late.

Passeig de Gràcia 32, 08007 Barcelona. ✆ **93-488-01-62** or 93-488-17-89. Fax 93-487-04-97. www. hostaloliva.com. 16 units. 45€–50€ single; 66€ double without bathroom; 85€ double w/bathroom. No credit cards. Metro: Passeig de Gràcia. *In room amenities:* A/C, TV, Wi-Fi.

SANTS, PARAL.LEL & MONTJUÏC

A favorite district for business travelers, this is the hub of Barcelona's out-of-towner meeting district with practical four-star accommodations galore, the Fira exhibition centers on Plaça Espanya, and the World Trade Center at the bottom of Paral.lel. There are leisure amenities in the immediate vicinity, and the art galleries, museums, and scenic parklands of Montjuïc are 10 minutes' walk away.

VERY EXPENSIVE

Barcelona Hilton ★★   This 11-floor, five-star property, located on one of the city's main arteries, is part of a huge commercial complex with an adjoining office tower. The lobby is impressively sleek with lots of velvet chairs. Public area furnishings are Hilton-standardized, but most of the large and well-equipped rooms feature thick carpets, rich wood decor, and some of the best bathrooms in the city, with dual basins and robes.

Av. Diagonal 589–591, 08014 Barcelona. ✆ **93-495-77-77.** Fax 93-495-77-00. www.barcelona.hilton. com. 287 units. 320€–395€ double; 350€–475€ suite. AE, DC, MC, V. Parking 36€. Metro: María Cristina. **Amenities:** 3 restaurants; bar; cafe; babysitting; health club; room service. *In room:* A/C, TV, hair dryer, minibar, Wi-Fi.

Rey Juan Carlos I ★★★   Named after the Spanish king who attended its opening and has visited it several times since, this five-star competes effectively with other legendary top-notch hostelries such as El Palace, Claris, and Hotel Arts. Opened in time for the Barcelona Olympics in 1992, it rises 17 stories at the northern end of the Diagonal in a wealthy neighborhood filled with corporate headquarters, banks, and upscale stores. It's a 15-minute Metro ride from the city's top central

Sants, Paral.lel & Montjuïc Accommodations

Barcelona Hilton **1**
Barcelona Universal Hotel **8**
B-Hotel Barcelona **5**
Catalonia Barcelona Plaza **4**
Gran Hotel Torre Catalunya **3**
Hotel Fira Palace **7**
Hotel Miramar **9**
Rey Juan Carlos I **2**
Soho Hotel **6**

attractions. Among its more striking design features is a soaring inner atrium with glass-sided elevators. The midsize to spacious guest rooms contain electronic extras, conservatively comfortable furnishings, and oversize beds. Many have views over Barcelona to the sea. Thoughtful touches include good lighting, adequate work-space, spacious closets, and blackout draperies.

Av. Diagonal 671, 08028 Barcelona. (℃) **800/445-8355** in the U.S., or 93-364-40-40. Fax 93-364-42-64. www.hrjuancarlos.com. 412 units. 250€–395€ double; 525€–1,400€ suite. AE, DC, MC, V. Parking 15€. Metro: Zona Universitària. **Amenities:** 2 restaurants; 2 bars; babysitting; fitness center; indoor & outdoor pool; salon; room service. *In room:* A/C, TV, hair dryer, minibar, Wi-Fi.

EXPENSIVE

Catalonia Barcelona Plaza ★   Located on a busy plaza overlooking a shopping mall converted from the former Arenas bullring, this large hotel caters mainly to business travelers attending the various conference and convention halls across the street, and its standard amenities include meeting rooms, an in-house travel agency, and bank. It's very convenient for the airport (about 20 minutes by taxi) and can host meetings of up to 700 people. The comfortable rooms are smartly furnished, but be warned that lower units get a certain amount of traffic noise. The rooftop swimming pool (covered in winter) and its adjoining sun terraces offer fine panoramic views that take in Montjuïc and distant Tibidabo.

Plaça Espanya 6–8, 08014 Barcelona. ✆ **93-426-26-00.** Fax 93-426-04-00. http://barcelonaplaza. barcelonahotels.it. 347 rooms. 185€–320€ double; 310€–410€ suite. AE, DC, MC, V. Parking 18€. Metro: Plaça Espanya. **Amenities:** Restaurant; bar; babysitting; health club; rooftop pool; solarium; room service. *In room:* A/C, TV, hair dryer, minibar, Wi-Fi (free).

Gran Hotel Torre Catalunya ★★

A vast skyscraper-style hotel close to Sants railway station and the Plaça Espanya, this modern four-star is far and away the most deluxe in the area, offering sizeable bedrooms, excellent service, and modern amenities. Added extras include turndown service, chocolates on the pillows, and huge marble bathrooms. Ciudad Condal, the restaurant on the 23rd floor, has awesome views over the city and is worth the visit for these alone. There are also excellent spa facilities with massage cabins, Jacuzzi, Turkish bath, and an indoor pool, as well as a business center for working travelers. Hardy guests can follow a sauna session with an immersion in an artificially-produced shower of snow, to help get the blood circulating.

Av. Roma 2–4, 08014 Barcelona. ✆ **93-600-69-99.** Fax. 93-325-51-78. www.torrecatalunya.com. 272 units. 120€–275€ double; 180€–320€ suite. AE, DC, MC, V. Free parking. Metro: Sants Estació de Sants. **Amenities:** Restaurant; bar; gymnasium; indoor swimming pool; spa and sauna; room service. *In room:* A/C, TV, CD player, hair dryer, minibar, Wi-Fi (free).

Hotel Fira Palace ★★ ☺

Popular among business travelers for its plush conference facilities and easy access to the exhibition centers of Plaça Espanya, this well-equipped hotel is another reliable all-round choice. If you are traveling with kids, the Fira offers some of the best family accommodations around, including huge, comfortable rooms. Communal facilities include a relaxing piano bar and two first-rate— but rather expensive—restaurants, a selection of health and fitness facilities, and an indoor swimming pool (closed on Sunday). Montjuïc's gardens, parks, and rambling footpaths are within easy strolling distance, and the main central sights can be easily reached by frequent bus and Metro services in about 10 minutes.

Av. Ruis i Taulet 1–3, 08004 Barcelona. ✆ **93-426-22-23.** Fax 93-424-86-79. www.fira-palace.com. 294 units. 225€–325€ double; 350€–450€ suite. AE, DC, MC, V. Parking 20€. Metro: Plaça Espanya. **Amenities:** 2 restaurants; bar; babysitting; health club; indoor pool; sauna; room service. *In room:* A/C, TV, hair dryer, minibar, Wi-Fi.

Hotel Miramar ★★

One of the most prestigious members of the SLH (Small Luxury Hotels of the World) group, the Miramar is attractively located right next to the Montjuïc i Llobera Botanical Gardens, overlooking both the city and the port. Built by distinguished architect Oscar Tusquets for the 1929 World's Fair, it was recently restored and converted into a hotel, retaining the style and charm of the original while introducing bright, avant-garde decor and state-of-the-art amenities that include well-equipped conference rooms, one of which is integrated into the hotel's gardens. The comfortable and tastefully furnished rooms all have en-suite bathrooms and terraces and enjoy garden or panoramic sea views. Some have wheelchair accessibility. At mealtimes the Forestier restaurant, adjoining the former palace's Patio de los Naranjos, filled with orange trees, provides a creative blend of Catalan and international dishes.

Plaça Carlos Ibañez 3, 08068 Barcelona. ✆ **93-281-16-00.** Fax 93-281-16-01. www.hotelmiramar barcelona.com. 75 units. 250€–280€ double; 400€–750€ suite. Extra beds 150€, cots free. AE, DC, MC, V. Nearby parking 20€. Metro: Paral.lel. **Amenities:** Restaurant; bar; indoor and outdoor swimming pools; spa; room service. *In room:* A/C, flatscreen TV, minibar, CD/DVD player, iPod docking station, Wi-Fi.

MODERATE

Barcelona Universal Hotel Predominantly catering to business travelers attending company meetings, the well-appointed Universal offers stylish, modern facilities within easy reach of the World Trade Center and the exhibition sites at Plaça Espanya. Pluses include a small rooftop terrace with raised wooden decking and a sunken pool. Bedrooms are spacious and comfortable, and although they are soundproofed, noise from the busy street can be a problem for many guests, so ask for something at the rear of the building, where you're less likely to be disturbed.

Av. Paral.lel 76–78, 08001 Barcelona. ✆ **93-567-74-47.** Fax 93-567-74-40. www.hotelbarcelonauniversal. com. 169 units. 140€–220€ double; 240€–320€ suite. AE, DC, MC, V. Parking 22€. Metro: Paral.lel. **Amenities:** Restaurant; bar; babysitting; fitness center; pool; solarium; room service. *In room:* A/C, TV, hair dryer, minibar, Wi-Fi.

B-Hotel Barcelona Owned by the same innovative group that created the stylish Hotel Jazz, this modern low-key hotel is a comfortable and affordable alternative to the high-priced business hotels that proliferate in the Sants area. The decor is modern minimalist with polished floorboards and a cool blue-gray color scheme. Those at the front have particularly good views of the Plaça Espanya. On-site communal facilities include a bar/cafeteria serving snacks and full buffet breakfasts. There's also an outdoor rooftop swimming pool and gym. For families with children, Montjuïc has ample gardens and parks, and is just a quick walk away.

Gran Vía de les Corts Catalanes 389-391, 08015 Barcelona. ✆ **93-552-95-00.** Fax 93-552-95-01. www.b-hotelbarcelona.com. 84 units. 140€–195€ double. AE, DC, MC, V. Metro: Plaça Espanya. **Amenities:** Bar/cafe; rooftop pool; fitness center; solarium. *In room:* A/C, TV, hair dryer, minibar, Wi-Fi.

Soho Hotel ★★ Barcelona's latest and most striking boutique hotel, the Soho is largely the work of two highly talented Catalans, Alfredo Arribas and Franc Aleu, who are jointly responsible for its on-trend style. The offbeat interior design includes mural depictions of various parts of the human body plus unique globular lights created by the late innovative Danish designer Verner Panton. Located in a lively stretch of the city between Plaça Espanya and the university, it's close to all central attractions. Most of the comfortable and well-furnished bedrooms overlook the Gran Vía, but aim for a seventh-floor room as these are quieter and have balconies. Rooms on lower levels can be noisy because of the traffic in the adjoining Gran Vía. In summer take a swim, sunbathe, or admire the panoramic city views from the roof-terrace pool.

Gran Vía de les Corts Catalanes 543. ✆ **93-552-96-10.** Fax 93-552-96-11. www.hotelsohobarcelona. com. 51 units. 140€–295€ double. MC, V. Free parking. Metro: Plaça de Catalunya. **Amenities:** Bar; outdoor pool. *In room:* A/C, TV, hair dryer, minibar, Wi-Fi (free).

BARRIO ALTO & GRÀCIA

The Alto represents the *pijo* (posh) part of town, with swanky restaurants and cocktail bars, millionaires' mansions, and lots of expensive cars, contrasting with the more eclectic, villagey atmosphere of Gràcia with its two-story houses, sunny plazas, and student/bohemian vibe.

EXPENSIVE

Meliá Barcelona ★   One block from the junction of the Avinguda Sarrià and the Avinguda Diagonal in the heart of the business district, this long-established member of the illustrious Meliá chain offers a wide range of leisure and business amenities. The comfortably upholstered, carpeted guest rooms and suites are done in neutral international modern style, and all have wide beds with firm mattresses, with a pillow menu and an aroma menu. The best rooms are in the first-floor section, known as "The Level," which was totally renovated in 2007 and offers a personalized concierge service. Another big new attraction is the Espai Sarrià conference center, which houses up to 700 delegates in seven individual salons equipped with state-of-the-art communications technology.

Av. Sarrià 50, Barrio Alto, 08029 Barcelona. ✆ **93-410-60-60.** Fax 93-321-51-79. www.solmelia.com. 333 units. 220€–325€ double; 350€–475€ suite. AE, DC, MC, V. Parking 20€. Metro: Hospital Clínic. **Amenities:** 2 restaurants; bar; babysitting; concierge; fitness center; spa; room service. *In room:* A/C, TV, hair dryer, minibar, Wi-Fi.

INEXPENSIVE

Acropolis Guest House ★ 🖾   The quirky and slightly chaotic Acropolis, with its crumbling columns and peeling paint work, has an eccentric charm. If you're a lover of truly original (yet modest) "new experience" hotels, you shouldn't miss it. The nostalgically well-worn bohemian aura is too good to pass up. Though it's not likely you'll be traveling with your pet abroad, you may be interested to know that this is also one of the few places that welcomes them. The overgrown garden and rustic kitchen are communal, and the bedrooms are simply but comfortably decorated. Half of them have en-suite bathrooms, but the place is spotlessly clean and sharing shouldn't be a problem. The best room has its own terrace with wonderful views.

Verdi 254, Gràcia, 08024 Barcelona. ✆/fax **93-284-81-87.** e-mail acropolis@telefonica.net. 8 units. 60€–70€ double w/bathroom; 50€–55€ double without bathroom. No credit cards. Metro: Lesseps. **Amenities:** TV lounge.

BARCELONETA, VILA OLÍMPICA & POBLE NOU

VERY EXPENSIVE

Eurostars Grand Marina Hotel ★★★   Superbly located in the World Trade Center on the large jetty at Moll de Barcelona and opposite the Drassanes Reials Maritim Museum (p. 190), right beside the city's harbor waters, this innovative circular-shaped hotel was designed by Henry Cobb and I. M. Pei (the man behind the pyramid at the Louvre). Its bright, airy, and spacious interior is filled with a 21st-century blend of avant-garde and minimalist artworks, plus sculptures that are offset by marble and glass architectural details. The bedrooms, all of which have en-suite bathrooms and hydro-massage bathtubs, are discreetly lit and sleekly designed with warm, plush ochre and orange-brown decor. The Presidential Suite on the roof enjoys magnificent views across the port to the city.

World Trade Center, Moll de Barcelona, 08039 Barcelona. ☎ **93-603-90-00.** Fax 93-603-90-90. www.
grandmarinahotel.com. 278 units. 175€–375€ double; 395€–890€ suite. AE, DC, MC, V. Parking 20€.
Metro: Drassanes. **Amenities:** Restaurant; cafeteria; piano bar; babysitting; health club; outdoor pool;
room service. *In room:* A/C, TV, hair dryer, minibar, high-speed Internet.

Hotel Arts ★★★   Managed by the Ritz-Carlton chain, this beachfront hotel
occupies 33 floors in one of Barcelona's landmark skyscrapers, directly facing the sea
and the Vila Olímpica, 2.5km (1½ miles) northwest of Barcelona's historic core. The
decor is contemporary and the spacious, well-equipped guest rooms have built-in
furnishings; generous desk space; and large, sumptuous beds. Four rooms are
equipped for guests with disabilities. Clad in pink marble, the deluxe bathrooms
have fluffy robes, Belgian towels, dual basins, and phones. The hotel possesses the
city's only beachside pool—overlooking Frank Gehry's bronze *Peix* (fish) sculpture—
and its new in-house bars and restaurants, such as **Arola** (p. 155), are jump-starting
nightlife in the neglected Olympic Marina. The young staff are polite and hardworking, the product of Ritz-Carlton training.

Carrer de la Marina 19–21, 08005 Barcelona. ☎ **93-221-10-00.** Fax 93-221-10-70. www.hotelarts
barcelona.com. 483 units. 350€–850€ double; 495€–2,200€ suite. AE, DC, MC, V. Parking 20€. Metro:
Ciutadella–Vila Olímpica. **Amenities:** 4 restaurants; cafe; 2 bars; babysitting; health club & spa; outdoor
pool; room service. *In room:* A/C, TV, hair dryer, minibar, high-speed Internet.

Pullman Barcelona Skipper ★   Since its opening in 2009, this elegantly contemporary hotel has become one of the favorite places to stay in Port Olímpic, a
stone's throw from the beach and colorful yachting harbor. Located beside the Hotel
Arts (p. 115), it has its own garden, complete with secluded swimming pool. The
roof terrace boasts another pool with panoramic coastal views, so you're not short on
places to swim. The hotel itself has a variety of amenities including Wi-Fi in all the
soundproofed guest rooms plus charming individual touches such as baths filled
with flowers (if you so choose) and top-quality cotton drapes on the beds. The junior
executive suites have a distinctly nautical motif and were especially designed to
resemble yacht cabins. Choose between the hotel's chic minimalist Syrah Mediter-
ranée, noted as much for its fine wines as its nouveau Catalan specialties, or simply
have a relaxing brunch beside the garden pool.

Litoral 10, 08005 Barcelona. ☎ **93-221-65-65.** www.pullman-barcelona-skipper.com. 150 units. 180€–
578€ double; from 750€ executive junior suite; from 1,450€ suite. AE, DC, MC, V. Metro: Ciutadella–Vila
Olímpica. **Amenities:** Restaurant; bar; babysitting; bikes; concierge; health club & spa; 2 outdoor pools;
room service. *In room:* A/C, TV, DVD player, hair dryer, minibar, Wi-Fi.

W Barcelona   Seen from above, this mold-breaking 26-story hotel, designed by
one of Catalunya's most innovative architects, Ricardo Bofill, is known locally as "La
Vela" because of its resemblance to a huge sail, dominating the port horizon.
Perched close to the sea's edge, overlooking the harbor's yachts and steamers, it
offers a wide selection of immaculately furnished rooms and suites, all coolly
designed in subtle grays and creams and providing luxurious comfort in a dream
nautical setting. The main restaurant, Bravo, provides top-quality Catalan and international cuisine, and at sunset you can climb to the Eclipse Bar to enjoy stunning
views as you sip your martini sangria. Swimmers can choose between the pool and
the immaculate manmade beach, and there's also a well-equipped spa and yoga area
to cater for mind and body. A member of the highly prestigious Starwood chain, the
standards of service and attention are all you'd expect and then some.

Plaça de la Rosa dels Vents 1, 08039 Barcelona. ℰ **93-295-28-00.** www.w-barcelona.com. 473 rooms including 67 suites. 250€–300€ double; 350€–500€ suite. **Amenities:** Restaurants; bar; cafe; health club and spa; outdoor pool; room service. *In room:* A/C, TV, DVD player, MP3 docking station, minibar, Wi-Fi.

MODERATE

Hotel Front Marítim ★ 🌮   The renovated Front Marítim is the centerpiece of a major tourist development bordering the Nueva Mar Bella beach, a 10-minute walk from Port Olímpic. The guest rooms are midsize and attractively and comfortably decorated. The hotel offers a range of facilities, including a lounge with large-screen TV, an a la carte restaurant, and a well-equipped fitness center. And the prices are affordable.

Paseo García Faria 69, 08019 Barcelona. ℰ **93-303-44-40.** Fax 93-303-44-41. www.hotelfrontmaritim. com. 177 units. 100€–140€ double; 160€ superior double. AE, DC, MC, V. Parking 15€. Metro: Selva de Mar. **Amenities:** Restaurant; bar; gym; sauna; room service; Wi-Fi. *In room:* A/C, TV, hair dryer, high-speed Internet.

Vincci Marítimo ★★ 🏨   This genuine 21st-century hotel with an emphasis on interior design—lots of glass panels, polished wood, and brushed steel—is located at the quieter, lesser-known eastern beachside end of the city, close to the traditional Poble Nou suburb and a 30-minute Metro ride from the historic center. Many of the sleekly spacious bedrooms enjoy excellent sea views. Communal facilities include a Japanese garden for relaxing breakfasts and early evening cocktails, and a smart, inventive restaurant. A couple of good beaches are close by, and other amenities in walking distance include the well-equipped Diagonal Shopping and Leisure Center and quaint local bars and cafes.

Llull 340, 08019 Barcelona. ℰ **93-356-26-00.** Fax 93-356-06-69. www.vinccihoteles.com. 144 units. 150€–220€ double; 210€–275€ suite. AE, DC, MC, V. Parking 16€. Metro: Selva de Mar. **Amenities:** Restaurant; bar; non-smoking floor; room service. *In room:* A/C, TV, hair dryer, minibar, high-speed Internet.

INEXPENSIVE

Marina Folch ★ 🏨   This small, informal guesthouse has earned itself a loyal following among visitors who want to be close to the sea without paying the usual high prices of the now "tastefully reinvented" former fishermen's district of Barceloneta. All 10 comfortable rooms have private bathrooms and are simply furnished. It's exactly what cheap, no-nonsense accommodations should be: A genuine retreat from the bustle of daily life minus the sometimes-tiring whistles and bells of more upmarket accommodations. The only drawback is that it is located above Restaurant Perú, run by the hotel management, so certain times of the day are noisy.

Carrer del Mar 16, 08003 Barcelona. ℰ **93-310-37-09.** Fax 93-310-53-27. 10 units. 60€–80€ double. AE, DC, MC, V. Parking 20€. Metro: Barceloneta. **Amenities:** Restaurant; room service. *In room:* A/C, TV.

Marina View B&B   Just in front of the Port Vell (Old Port) and halfway between the Vía Laietana and La Rambla, this homely bed-and-breakfast is in a top spot for making the most of the city's prime sights and beaches. Bedrooms are fairly small but pleasantly decorated, with some bonus extras like complimentary tea and coffee. Owner José María is a friendly and accommodating host, and will even provide breakfast in bed for those who want it.

Passeig de Colom s/n, 08002 Barcelona. ℰ **66-646-39-91** or 60-920-64-93. www.marinaviewbcn.com. 5 units. 125€–145€ double; 185€ triple. Rates include breakfast. MC, V for down-payment only. Public parking nearby 20€. Metro: Drassanes. *In room amenities:* A/C, TV, minibar, high-speed Internet.

If you're looking for a swim with your hotel, consider the following, which also offer beautiful views:

- **Barcelona Universal Hotel** (p. 113), which enjoys panoramic vistas of both Montjuïc and the port.
- **Hotel Arts** (p. 115), the city's only beachside hotel.
- **Hotel Balmes** (p. 106) for a garden oasis in the middle of L'Eixample.
- **Hotel Claris** (p. 98) for high-tech design, acres of steel, and wooden decking.
- **Hotel Duquesa de Cardona** (p. 88) for rooftop views over the boats and gin palaces of the Port Vell.
- **Hotel Omm** (p. 100) for unbeatable views of Gaudí's rooftops.

ON THE OUTSKIRTS

VERY EXPENSIVE

Gran Hotel La Florida ★★★ This former fashionable 1920s' hostelry—a firm favorite with Spanish celebrities, from movie idols to monarchy—was transformed into a hospital during World War II before reemerging as a stylishly renovated hotel a few years ago. Filled with works of art that would not be out of place in a high-profile city gallery, it offers an array of immaculately furnished rooms and suites. Since the hotel sits high up on Tibidabo hill, most rooms boast magnificent views. Communal amenities include a world-class restaurant, L'Orangerie, a spa and infinity pool, and terraced gardens. Service is courteous and attentive, and—a small but gracious personal touch—guests are welcomed with glasses of rose-petal water on arrival.

Carretera Vallvidrera al Tibidabo 83–93, 08035 Barcelona. ✆ **93-259-30-00.** Fax 93-259-30-01. www. hotellaflorida.com. 74 units. 295€–610€ double; 660€–950€ suite. AE, DC, MC, V. Parking 20€ 7km (4⅓ miles) from Barcelona. **Amenities:** Restaurant; nightclub; babysitting; health club; indoor & outdoor pool; room service. *In room:* A/C, TV, hair dryer, minibar, Wi-Fi.

MODERATE

abba Garden Hotel This big, terracotta-red hilltop hotel is less than a mile from Barcelona Football Team's Camp Nou, making it a top choice for Barça *fútbol* fans and visiting sports enthusiasts. Its distance from the center means that it enjoys plenty of space, with landscaped gardens, tennis courts, and a large outdoor swimming pool. It's also well located if you plan to spend your time ferrying to and from golf courses outside Barcelona. The downside is that its slightly isolated location can mean expensive taxi rides into town. If you're eating in, there's a reasonably good restaurant in the hotel, called Amalur, plus a bar. Bedrooms are spacious and freshly done out with flower-print fabrics.

Santa Rosa 33, Esplugues de Llobregat, 08950 Barcelona. ✆ **93-503-54-54.** Fax 93-503-54-55. www.abbagardenhotel.com. 138 units. 95€–195€ double. AE, DC, MC, V. Parking 18€. Metro: Zona Universitària. RENFE: Reina Elisenda. From Barcelona take Av. Diagonal out of the center to the Pedralbes area and look for signs to Hospital S. Jean de Deu next to hotel. **Amenities:** Restaurant; cafe; bar; babysitting; health club; 2 tennis courts; room service; Wi-Fi. *In room:* A/C, TV, hair dryer, minibar, high-speed Internet.

House-swapping is becoming popular: You stay in their place, they stay in yours, and you both get an authentic and personal view of the area. Try **HomeLink International** (www. homelink.org), the largest and oldest home-swapping organization, founded in 1952, with more than 11,000 listings worldwide. It has a number of apartments available for exchange in Barcelona. You could also check the corresponding Spanish website, www. spainlink.net. **HomeExchange.com** and **Intervac.com** are also reliable. There are house swaps on **Craigslist** (www. craigslist.org), too, although the offerings cannot be vetted or vouched for. Swap at your own risk.

Hesperia Sarrià ★ ☺   This hotel on the northern edge of the city, a 10-minute taxi ride from the center, sits in one of Barcelona's most pleasant residential neighborhoods. Built in the late 1980s, the hotel was last renovated before the 1992 Olympics. You'll pass a Japanese rock formation to reach the stone-floored reception area with its adjacent bar. Sunlight floods the monochromatic guest rooms (all doubles—prices for singles are the same). Although most rooms are midsize, they have enough space for an extra bed, which makes this a good choice for families. Beds have quality mattresses and fine linen. The uniformed staff offers a fine service.

Los Vergós 20, 08017 Barcelona. ℂ **93-204-55-51.** Fax 93-204-43-92. www.hoteles-hesperia.es. 140 units. 155€–230€ double; 190€–260€ suite. AE, DC, MC, V. Parking 16€. Metro: Tres Torres. **Amenities:** Restaurant; bar; room service. *In room:* A/C, TV, hair dryer, minibar, high-speed Internet.

Tryp Barcelona Aeropuerto   As the name suggests, the main reason for staying at this hotel is to be close to the airport. Tryp (part of the Sol Meliá group) is a reliable, four-star chain and excellent in terms of business facilities. This one has modern amenities with hardwood floors, and the comfortable spacious bedrooms all have large marble bathrooms. A buffet breakfast is included in the room price, and there's a free 24-hour airport shuttle bus.

Parque de Negocios Mas Blau II, Prat de Llobregat, 08820 Barcelona. ℂ **93-378-10-00.** Fax 93-378-10-01. www.trypbarcelonaaeropuerto.solmelia.com. 205 units. 120€–175€ double; 245€ suite. AE, DC, MC, V. Valet parking 18€. 1.5km (1 mile) from airport; 10km (6¼ miles) from Barcelona. **Amenities:** Restaurant; cafe; bar; health club; airport shuttle service; room service. *In room:* A/C, TV, hair dryer, minibar, high-speed Internet.

APARTMENTS & APARTHOTELS

Aparthotel Silver ★★ 📋   Located in the heart of Gràcia, the Silver apartments are a perfect base for those looking to remove themselves a little from the hustle and bustle of the city center. With its low-rise houses, cute sunny plazas, eclectic bars and restaurants, and bohemian vibe, Gràcia is one of Barcelona's least-discovered *barrios* and well worth getting to know. Silver's 49 studio apartments are smartly kitted out with plenty of storage space and comfortable beds. They come with a kitchenette with a small electric stove and a fridge, and all have private bathrooms with tub/shower combos. The building also has a private garden and lawn equipped with tables and chairs, and parking facilities. This place is a bargain, especially for couples seeking a little independence.

Bretón de los Herreros 26, Gràcia, 08012 Barcelona. ℂ **93-218-91-00.** Fax 93-416-14-47. www.hotel silver.com. 49 units. 80€–150€ apt. AE, DC, MC, V. Metro: Fontana. Parking 14€. **Amenities:** Cafe; bar; high-speed Internet; room service. *In room:* A/C, TV.

Citadines ☺   Modern, clean, and bright, this apartment-hotel is a good choice for those who want to be right on La Rambla with the option to cook for themselves (the wonderful fresh-produce market, La Boqueria, is just up the street). This is especially popular with groups and with families with children, providing fully equipped kitchens, optional maid service, and large, comfortable bedrooms with sofa beds in the living area. One thing that gives the Citadines an edge over many similar self-catering places in town is the ninth-floor roof terrace, offering 360-degree views over the whole city.

La Rambla 122, 08002 Barcelona. ℂ **93-270-11-11.** Fax 93-412-74-21. www2.citadines.com. 115 studios; 16 apts. 190€–225€ 2-person apt; 250€–290€ 4-person apt. AE, DC, MC, V. Metro: Plaça de Catalunya. Parking 20€. **Amenities:** Bar; solarium. *In room:* A/C, TV, DVD player, hair dryer, high-speed Internet.

Hispanos Siete Suiza ★★★   Of all the aparthotels in Barcelona, the Suiza is far and away the most individually glamorous—a real home-away-from-home combined with the comforts of a luxury hotel. The wooden-floored apartments all have two bedrooms, two bathrooms, a plush cozy living room, and a kitchen. Continental breakfast is included in the price, and the in-house restaurant, **La Cupula,** is overseen by Carles Gaig, the prestigious Michelin-starred Catalan chef. The original house was owned by a Catalan doctor, writer, poet, and philanthropist who was obsessed with the arts and vintage cars (a collection of seven beautiful 1920s' automobiles, from which the hotel gets its name, sits in the lobby). When his wife died of cancer, he set up a foundation in her memory and part of the hotel's profits go to this cause.

Sicilia 255, Eixample Dreta, 08025 Barcelona. ℂ **93-208-20-51.** Fax 93-208-20-52. www.hispanos 7suiza.com. 19 units. 200€–225€ 2-bedroom apt for 2; 40€ supplement for 3 or 4 guests. AE, DC, MC, V. Metro: Sagrada Família. Parking 16€. **Amenities:** Restaurant; cocktail bar; room service. *In room:* A/C, TV, minibar, high-speed Internet.

Hotel Boria-BCN 🛏   Built in 1800 as a traditional Barri Gòtic *palacete* (small palace) and imaginatively reformed with all mod cons 250 years later, the Boria enjoys the best of both hotel and self-catering worlds. Its atmospheric attic rooms have warm wooden flooring, cosy rugs, and nifty kitchen areas that fit snugly into the intimate layout of the building. There's communal access to a roof terrace with good views of the district's medieval skyline, and a library where you can browse through a small, multinational choice of books.

Boria 24-26, 08003 Barcelona. ℂ **93-315-07-42.** www.boriabcn.com. 12 units. 2-person apt 125€–300€ (60€ for additional adult). AE, DC, MC, V. Metro: Jaume I. **Amenities:** Solarium; Wi-Fi (free). *In rooms:* A/C, TV, minibar.

WHERE TO DINE

Barcelona's cuisine shot into the limelight with the media's celebration of local man Ferran Adrià as the "greatest chef in the world." But, alas, the great man won't be around for much longer. In 2010 he announced that his famed El Bulli restaurant would be closing for 2 years in 2011, and when it eventually reopens it will be as a school for restaurateurs.

The good news is that the way is now clear for other talented chefs to make their mark: Gifted professionals like Jordi Ruiz, Carles Abellán (owner of Comerç 24; p. 133), and Sergi Arola (who runs top eating spots in Madrid and Barcelona). They've long been making their own considerable waves, aided by the rich supply of fresh market produce, high-quality regional wines, and an instinctive savvy in the world of eating and drinking by both purveyors and consumers. As a result, these chefs are free to experiment, mingling traditional local dishes like pigeon with pears, cherries with anise, or pig's trotters with crab. The resultant hybrid *plato* is usually a delicious new taste experience.

Of course, not everyone aspires to such dizzying heights when eating out, so it's nice to see the trickle-down effect of all these top culinary concepts reaching more modest and affordable dining spots. Whether you're dining in an old-style tavern, having a late supper in one of the new cutting-edge eateries, picking at tapas at a bar, or launching into an alfresco paella, the quality of the food is usually high and the variety imaginative. Vegetarians can dine in an increasing number of creative spots, especially in the Old City. There are lots of modest international restaurants in the earthy South American, Greek, and Middle Eastern areas of El Raval.

Our new inclusions include a trio of nautical gems: **Lluçanes, Mondo,** and the aptly named **Big Fish** are all consolidating Barcelona's reputation as a great place for top-quality seafood. Add to these the chic **Atril,** minimalist cool **Toc,** veggie haven **La Báscula,** and uniquely homely **Granja M. Viader** and you have an eclectic cross section of the best that the Ciudad Condal has to offer. There's great tapas too at the fashionable **Mam i Teca.**

FOOD FOR THOUGHT
What Makes Catalan Cuisine?

Much of what Barcelona's feted new chefs do is put an avant-garde twist on traditional Catalan cuisine. But what is that exactly? Like its language, what Catalans eat is different from the rest of Spain and varies within the region, from the Mediterranean coastline and islands to the inland villages and Pyrénées mountains. Like Catalan culture, the cuisine looks out toward the rest of Europe (especially France) and the Mediterranean arc, rather than inward toward Castile. Many of the techniques and basic recipes can be traced back to medieval times, and as any Catalan is only too willing to point out, the quality of the produce proceeding from the *Països Catalans* (Catalan Countries) is some of the best available. The same goes for the locally produced wine. The D.O.s *(domaines ordinaires)* of the Penedès and Priorat regions are now as internationally renowned as La Rioja, and the local *cava* (sparkling, champagne-type wine) is consumed at celebratory tables from Melbourne to Manchester.

If there is one food dish that symbolizes Catalan cuisine, it is *pa amb tomàquet*. Invented as a way of softening stale bread during the lean years of the Civil War, there is barely a restaurant in Catalonia, from the most humble workman's canteen to the Michelin-starred palace, that does not have this on their menu. In its simplest form, *pa amb tomàquet* is a slice of rustic white bread rubbed with the pulp of a cut tomato and drizzled with olive oil. Top the bread with cheese, pâté, chorizo, or Iberian ham—this is then called a *torrada*. The idea is ingeniously simple, and like most ingeniously simple ideas, it works wonderfully. Catalans wax lyrical about it, and you will soon be hooked.

Catalan cuisine is marked by taste combinations that seem at odds with each other; red meat and fish are cooked in the same dish, nuts are pulped for sauces, poultry is cooked with fruit, pulse (bean) dishes are never vegetarian, there is not one part of a pig that is not consumed, and imported, salted cod is the favorite Catalan fish. Concoctions popping up on menus time and time again include *zarzuela* (a rich fish stew), *botifarra amb mongetes* (pork sausage with white beans), *faves a la catalana* (broad beans with Iberian ham), *samfaina* (a sauce of eggplant/aubergine, peppers, and zucchini/courgette), *esqueixada* (a salted cod salad), *fideuà* (similar to a paella, but with noodles replacing the rice), and *mel i mato* (a soft cheese with honey). It's hearty and more elaborate than other food of southern Spain. In its most traditional form, Catalan cuisine doesn't suit light appetites, which is why many locals have only one main meal a day, normally at lunchtime, with perhaps a supper of a *torrada* in the evening. Breakfast is also a light affair: A milky coffee (*café con leche* in Spanish, *café amb llet* in Catalan) with a croissant or doughnut.

Eating in Barcelona

Catalans generally lunch between 2 and 4pm and dine after 9pm. Most restaurant kitchens stay open in the evenings until about 11pm. Try making lunch your main meal and take advantage of the *menú del día* (lunch of the day) offered in the majority of eateries. It normally consists of three courses (wine and/or coffee and dessert included) and, at between 8€ and 14€ per head, is a cost-effective way of trying out pricier restaurants.

Tipping always confuses visitors as some restaurants list the 7% IVA (sales tax) separately on the bill. This is *not* a service charge; in fact, it is illegal for restaurants in Barcelona to charge for service. As a general rule, tips (in cash) of about 5% should be left in cheap to moderate places and 10% in expensive ones. In bars, leave a few coins or round your bill up to the nearest euro.

Vegetarian restaurants are on the increase. Some, like **Organic** (p. 137) and **La Báscula** (p. 128), even aspire to a degree of creative cooking. Contemporary places such as **Pla** (p. 129), **Anima** (p. 136), and **Juicy Jones** (p. 129) always have a couple of vegetarian options on offer. Apart from tortillas, few traditional tavernas serve veggie food, and always double-check: The Catalan word *carn* (*carne* in Spanish) only refers to red meat. Asking for a dish "without" (*sens* in Catalan, *sin* in Spanish) does not guarantee that it will arrive fish-or chicken-free.

Nonsmoking sections in restaurants and bars are, at the time of writing, fairly nonexistent. On January 1, 2011, however, a new law is scheduled to come into force that will completely ban smoking in restaurants. That is if the city authorities manage to go through with changing the law in the face of stiff opposition from the restaurant trade.

Below is a small selection of the hundreds of Barcelona restaurants, cafes, and bars. The constant influx of tourists means that many places on and around La Rambla now offer microwaved paella and charge 10 times over the average for a coffee. But in the small streets of the Barri Gòtic and the blocks of L'Eixample (which has largely escaped the side effects of mass tourism), there are plenty of value-for-money establishments that take enormous pride in introducing you to the delights of the local cuisine. Around El Raval, the city's most multicultural neighborhood, you will find dozens of cheap places serving ethnic cuisines, should you get tired of the local grub. *¡Bon profit!*

BEST RESTAURANT BETS

- **Hottest Chef:** Carles Abellán is today's wunderkind of New Catalan cuisine. His restaurant, **Comerç 24,** Comerç 24 (𝄐 **93-319-21-02;** www.comerc24.com) was conceived as a playful take on all that's hot in the tapas world. Delights such as "kinder egg surprise" (a soft-boiled egg with truffle-infused yolk) and tuna sashimi pizza await the adventurous. See p. 133.

- **Best Newcomer:** Opened in late 2009 in the heart of the Barri Gòtic's trendy Born district, the smart, minimalist **Big Fish,** Calle Comercial 9 (𝄐 **93-268-17-28;** www.bigfish.net) is overseen by chef Antonio Peláez and offers supremely good seafood dishes in a Mediterranean-cum-Oriental setting where extra attractions include a sushi bar. See p. 132.

- **Best Place for a Business Lunch:** "The incomparable haute cuisine of the elegant Micheline award-winning **La Dama** in L'Eixample has long attracted civic dignitaries and top executives. See p. 139.

- **Best Spot for a Celebration:** You can make as much noise as you like at **Mesón David,** Carretes 63 (𝄐 **93-441-59-34;** www.mesondavid.com), an old-school eatery with a vast menu of dishes from all regions of Spain. Chances are you will sit next to a raucous group celebrating a birthday or engagement, with waiters joining in the revelry too. See p. 137.

- **Best Wine List:** You're spoiled for choice at **La Vinya del Senyor,** Plaça Santa María 5 (© **93-310-33-79**) a gorgeous wine bar opposite the towering Santa María del Mar (p. 75). Mull over the 300 vintages on offer while taking in the facade from the outside terrace; then order some of their delicious tapas to accompany your choice. See p. 158.

- **Best for Paella:** A paella on the beach is a quintessential Barcelona experience and there is no place better to do it than **Can Majó,** Almirall Aixada 23 (© **93-221-54-55;** www.canmajo.es). Right on the seafront, this restaurant prides itself on its paellas and *fideuàs* (which use noodles instead of rice) and is an established favorite among the city's well-heeled families. See p. 156.

- **Best Modern Catalan Cuisine:** In the compact avant-garde **Manairó,** Diputació 424 (© **93-231-00-57;** www.manairo.com) at the eastern end of L'Eixample, adventurous chef Jordi Herrera goes where no Catalan has gone before with his boundary-crossing combinations of sea- and land-based dishes. See p. 144.

- **Best Traditional Catalan Cuisine: Via Veneto,** Ganduxer 10 (© **93-200-72-44;** www.viavenetorestaurant.com) exudes old-fashioned class and serves up some of the finest Catalan cooking in the land. Some of the serving methods, such as the sterling-silver duck press, seem to belong to another century (as do some of the clients). See p. 150.

- **Best for Kids:** Children are welcome almost everywhere in Spanish restaurants, but why not give them a real treat by heading for **La Paradeta,** Comercial 7 (© **93-268-19-39;** www.laparadeta.com)? This is the Catalan version of a British fish-and-chip shop, with all kinds of seafood laid out on ice greeting you as you walk in. Pick what you want and *bingo!* Out it comes, hot and steaming, in a cardboard box. See p. 133.

- **Best Fusion Cuisine:** Born in Catalonia but raised in Canada, chef Jordi Artal instinctively knows how to fuse old- and new-world cuisines. The five-course tasting menu in his upscale **Cinc Sentits,** Aribau 58 (© **93-323-94-90;** www.cincsentits.com) is a memorable way to sample this expertise. See p. 142.

- **Best for Tapas: Taller de Tapas,** L'Argentaria 51 (© **93-268-85-59;** www.tallerdetapas.com) was conceived to take the mystery out of tapas. Multilingual staff and menus ensure you don't get pig's cheeks when you order green leeks, and the rest of the delectable dishes are a perfect initiation for the tapas novice. See p. 135.

- **Best for People-Watching:** The food may not win any awards but that doesn't stop soccer stars, models, and other assorted semi-celebs from flocking to **CDLC,** Passeig Marítim 32 (© **93-224-04-70;** www.cdlcbarcelona.com) on the waterfront in the Vila Olímpica and decked out in fashionable faux-Thai chic. The real fun starts with the post-dinner disco, and you're not sure whether it's the breeze rolling in off the Mediterranean or the sound of thousands of air kisses. See p. 156.

- **Best Outdoor Dining Area:** As well as being one of the best-value restaurants in the city, the **Café de L'Acadèmia,** Lledó 1, Plaça Sant Just (© **93-319-82-53**) is blessed with one of the prettiest settings: A charming square in the Old Town flanked by Gothic buildings and an ancient water fountain. At night the warm glow of the table candles bounces off the stone walls, ensuring you linger long after the last drink. See p. 125.

- **Best View:** Dine on top of the world, or at least 75m (250 feet) up, in **Torre d'Alta Mar,** Passeig Don Joan Borbó Comte 88 (*© 93-221-00-07;* www.torre dealtamar.com) located in a cable-car tower. The view couldn't be more mesmerizing, allowing you an almost 360-degree view of the city's skyline and the surrounding sea in one swoop. See p. 155.

- **Best for Seafood:** Although good seafood is abundant in Barcelona, many swear that the best catches end up in **Cal Pep,** Plaça des les Olles 8 (*© 93-310-79-61;* www.calpep.com) a tiny bar near the port. Mountains of the stuff are prepared in front of your eyes by lightning-quick staff, and your dexterity is put to the test as you try not to elbow your neighbor while peeling your prawns. See p. 132.

- **Best Wine Bar:** Bathed in Bordeaux red, with large arched windows looking out onto a tranquil square, **Vinissim,** Sant Domenec del Call 12 (*© 93-301-45-75*) has a mind-boggling array of wines from all corners of the globe, plus a scrumptious array of tapas to soak them up. It offers a pleasing experience for all the senses. See p. 131.

- **Best for Sunday Lunch:** The lines say it all: **7 Portes,** Passeig Isabel II 14 (*© 93-319-30-33;* www.7portes.com) one of the oldest restaurants in Barcelona, is a Sunday institution. Extended families dine on excellent meat and fish dishes in turn-of-the-20th-century surroundings. See p. 154.

- **Best Vegetarian Restaurant:** Though veggie newcomers are sprouting up all over town, our favorite spot remains the established **Organic,** Junta de Comerç 11 (*© 93-301-09-02;* www.antoniaorganickitchen.com) a barnlike place with communal wooden tables; an all-you-can-eat salad bar; and tempting rice, pasta, and tofu dishes. See p. 137.

- **Best for a Sweet Tooth:** Sweet but never sickly, **Espai Sucre,** Princesa 53 (*© 93-268-16-30;* www.espaisucre.com) is perhaps the world's only restaurant that offers a menu made up entirely of desserts. Foodies rave about it and its reputation has spread far and wide as a once-in-a-lifetime gastronomic experience. Some savory dishes are available. See p. 133.

- **Best for Morning or Afternoon Tea: Granja Dulcinea's** hot chocolate is widely acknowledged to be the richest and most delicious of them all. See p. 128.

- **Best for Consistency: Pla,** Bellafila 5 (*© 93-412-65-52;* www.pla-repla.com) strikes that right balance between hip and highly creative without scaring you off. The menu focuses on local market produce with a touch of Asian and Arabic, and the staff members are very friendly and helpful. See p. 129.

- **Best Snack on the Go:** Before you embark on a visit to the Museum of Contemporary Art, fuel up at **Foodball,** Elisabets 9 (*© 93-270-13-63*) a specialist in inventive forms of fast food. Whole-grain rice balls filled with tofu, wild mushrooms, chickpeas, and the like, plus fresh juices and smoothies, are served in a quirky setting; you can also eat in. See p. 131.

- **Best Retro Interior:** As well as providing some of the most imaginative seafood dishes in town, **Big Fish,** Calle Comercial 9 (*© 93-268-17-28;* www.bigfish. net) in the trendy heart of El Born, makes its second appearance in this list with a striking New York-meets-Tokyo minimalist interior designed by Lazaro Rosa Violán, also responsible for the avant-garde Market Hotel (p. 93). The dazzlingly stark white walls and pillars are warmly offset by polished wood flooring, cosy leather Chesterfield chairs, and an ornate fireplace. See p. 132.

CIUTAT VELLA

Barri Gòtic

EXPENSIVE

Agut d'Avignon ★ SPANISH   One of my favorite restaurants in Barcelona is in a tiny alleyway near the Plaça Reial. It's still going strong after 40 years, and has a dedicated following. Mercedes Giralt Salinas and her son, Javier Falagán Giralt, have run the restaurant since 1983. A small 19th-century vestibule leads to the multilevel dining area, which has two balconies and a main hall evoking a hunting lodge. The menu is only in Catalan but the staff is happy to translate. The traditional specialties could include acorn-squash soup served in its shell, fisherman's soup with garlic toast, haddock stuffed with shellfish, sole with *nyoca* (a medley of nuts), large shrimp with aioli, duck with figs, or filet beefsteak in sherry sauce.

Trinitat 3, at Carrer d'Avinyó. ⓒ **93-302-60-34.** Reservations recommended. Main courses 18€–28€; lunch menu 18€. AE, DC, MC, V. Daily 1–4:30pm and 9pm–12:30am. Metro: Jaume I or Liceu.

MODERATE

Agut ★ 🎁 SPANISH   In an historic building three blocks from the harborfront, Agut epitomizes the bohemian atmosphere surrounding this gritty area. For three-quarters of a century this has been a family-run business, with María Agut García now at the helm. The aura evokes the 1950s, and the inventive dishes are served at reasonable prices. Begin with *mil hojas de botifarra amb zets* (layers of pastry filled with Catalan sausage and mushrooms) or the *terrine de albergines amb fortmage de cabra* (terrine of eggplant/aubergine with goat's cheese gratinée). One of my favorite dishes is *soufle de rape amb gambes* (soufflé of monkfish with shrimp). If you are ravenous, attempt the *chuletón de buey* (loin of ox) for two, which comes thick and juicy and accompanied by fresh vegetables. For dessert, order *sortido* for an assortment of dainty cakes made in-house.

Gignàs 16. ⓒ **93-315-17-09.** Reservations required. Main courses 12€–20€; fixed-price lunch menu Tues–Fri 15€. AE, DC, MC, V. Tues–Sun 1:30–4pm; Tues–Sat 9pm–midnight. Closed Aug. Metro: Jaume I.

Atril ★ SPANISH   Opened in 2008 and located in a tastefully converted building whose homely interior features a blend of modern and rustic-style furnishings, this charming bistro-restaurant offers a small but eclectic range of dishes, including kangaroo hamburgers and mussels cooked in Belgian beer. It also serves simple but delicious breakfasts and is an ideal spot to kick off your day's sightseeing. At midday there's a bargain lunch menu and on Sunday evenings you can enjoy acoustic music concerts while tapas and drinks are served.

Carders 23. ⓒ **93-310-12-20.** www.atrilbarcelona.com. Mains 12€–14€. Weekday lunch 10€–12€; weekend lunch 12€–14€. AE, DC, MC, V. Tues–Sat 1pm–midnight. Sunday noon–11:30pm. Closed Mon. Metro: Jaume I.

Café de L'Acadèmia ★★ 🍴 SPANISH   A short walk from Plaça Sant Jaume, this 28-table restaurant looks expensive but is actually one of the best and most affordable in the Barri Gòtic. Dishes of this quality usually cost three times as much in Barcelona. The chef is proud of his "kitchen of the market," suggesting that only the freshest ingredients from the day's shopping are featured. Try such delights as *bacallà gratinado i musselina de carofes* (salt cod gratinée with an artichoke mousse) or *terrina d'berengeras amb fortmage de cabra* (terrine of eggplant/aubergine with

Ciutat Vella Dining

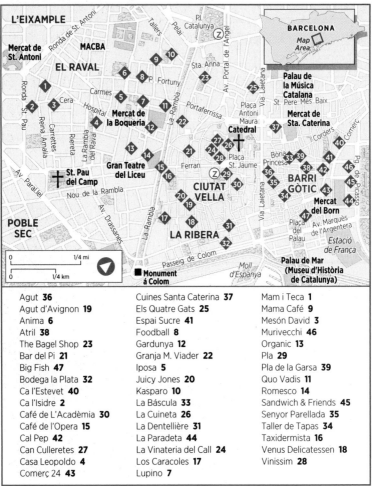

Agut **36**	Cuines Santa Caterina **37**	Mam i Teca **1**
Agut d'Avignon **19**	Els Quatre Gats **25**	Mama Café **9**
Anima **6**	Espai Sucre **41**	Mesón David **3**
Atril **38**	Foodball **8**	Murivecchi **46**
The Bagel Shop **23**	Gardunya **12**	Organic **13**
Bar del Pi **21**	Granja M. Viader **22**	Pla **29**
Big Fish **47**	Iposa **5**	Pla de la Garsa **39**
Bodega la Plata **32**	Juicy Jones **20**	Quo Vadis **11**
Ca l'Estevet **40**	Kasparo **10**	Romesco **14**
Ca l'Isidre **2**	La Báscula **33**	Sandwich & Friends **45**
Café de L'Acadèmia **30**	La Cuineta **26**	Senyor Parellada **35**
Café de l'Opera **15**	La Dentellière **31**	Taller de Tapas **34**
Cal Pep **42**	La Paradeta **44**	Taxidermista **16**
Can Culleretes **27**	La Vinateria del Call **24**	Venus Delicatessen **18**
Casa Leopoldo **4**	Los Caracoles **17**	Vinissim **28**
Comerç 24 **43**	Lupino **7**	

goat's cheese). A delectable specialty sometimes available is *codorniz rellena en cebollitas tiernas y foie de pato* (partridge stuffed with tender onions and duck liver). On warm evenings, go for one of the candle-lit tables outside on the atmospheric square dominated by a Gothic church.

Lledó 1, Plaça Sant Just. ✆ **93-319-82-53.** Reservations required. Main courses 10€–18€; fixed-price lunch menu 12€–16€. AE, MC, V. Mon–Fri 9am–noon, 1:30–4pm, 9–11:30pm. Closed 2–3 weeks in Aug. Metro: Jaume I.

Can Culleretes SPANISH Founded in 1786 as a *pastelería* (pastry shop), Barcelona's oldest restaurant retains many original architectural features. All three dining rooms are decorated with tile dadoes and wrought-iron chandeliers. The well-prepared food features authentic dishes from northeastern Spain, including sole Roman style, *zarzuela a la marinera* (shellfish stew), cannelloni, and paella and special game dishes, including *perdiz* (partridge). The service is old-fashioned, and sometimes it's filled more with tourists than locals, but it retains enough authentic touches to make it feel like the real McCoy. Signed photographs of visiting celebrities, flamenco artists, and bullfighters decorate the walls.

Quintana 5. © **93-317-64-85.** www.culleretes.com. Reservations recommended. Main courses 10€–18€; fixed-price menu Tues–Fri 18€. MC, V. Tues–Sun 1:30–4pm; Tues–Sat 9–11pm. Closed July. Metro: Liceu. Bus: 14 or 59.

Els Quatre Gats ★ 📷 SPANISH   This tastefully restored Barcelona legend has been around since 1897. The "Four Cats" (Catalan slang for "just a few people") was a favorite of Picasso and Rusiñol, who once hung their works on its walls. Now they are reproductions. On a narrow cobblestone street, this *fin-de-siècle* cafe was a base for members of the *moderniste* movement, and poetry readings by Joan Maragall and piano concerts by Isaac Albéniz and Enric Granados were regular events. The fixed-price meal is one of the better bargains in town. The homespun Catalan cooking is called *cucina de mercat* (based on whatever looked fresh at the market) but always includes such classics as *suquet de peix* (a fish and potato hot-pot) and *faves a la catalana* (baby broad beans with Serrano ham). Come at lunchtime, as it gets very crowded at night, when musicians play banal 1960s' pop songs.

Montsió 3. © **93-302-41-40.** www.4gats.com. Reservations required. Main courses 18€–28€; fixed-price lunch menu 15€. AE, DC, MC, V. Daily 1pm–1am; cafe daily 8am–2am. Metro: Plaça de Catalunya.

Gardunya ★★ SPANISH   This is the most famous restaurant in Barcelona's covered food market, La Boqueria (p. 226). Originally conceived as a hotel, it has concentrated on food since the 1970s. Battered, somewhat ramshackle, and a bit claustrophobic, it's fashionable with the trendy, bohemian artistic set. Gardunya is near the back of the market, so you'll pass endless rows of fresh produce, cheese, and meats on your way. You can dine downstairs, near the crowded bar, or more formally upstairs. Food is ultrafresh—the chefs certainly don't have to travel far for the ingredients. Try "hors d'oeuvres of the sea," cannelloni Rossini, grilled hake with herbs, *rape* (monkfish) *marinera,* paella, brochettes of veal, filet steak with green peppercorns, seafood rice, or a *zarzuela* (stew) of fresh fish with spices.

Jerusalem 18. © **93-302-43-23.** Reservations recommended. Main courses 10€–28€; fixed-price lunch 12.50€; fixed-price dinner 20€. DC, MC, V. Mon–Sat 1–4pm, 8pm–midnight. Metro: Liceu.

Granja M. Viader ★ SPANISH   This much-loved Catalan creamery, located in a 1931 edifice occupying the site of 19th-century *granja* (farmhouse) and dairy, is a mecca for lovers of rich, milky drinks. It claims to have created the first *cacaolat,* Spain's classic chocolate beverage, and provides an impressive range of *batidos* (milk shakes) and *horchatas* (a coconut-milk drink of Valencian origin, flavored with ground almonds or sesame). With its colorful tiled floors, simple bare tables, starkly functional lighting, paintings, and photo-studded white walls, this is a blend of the ornate and the semi-austere. Come for the goodies, not the decor. There's even a counter selling yogurts, cheeses, honey, olive oils, and calorie-shattering pastries.

Xuclà 4.6. © **93-318-34-86.** www.granjaviader.cat. Main courses 8€–12€. AE, DC, MC, V. Tues–Sat 9am–1:30pm, 5–8:30pm; Mon 5–8:30pm. Metro: Liceu.

La Báscula ★ 🍴 VEGETARIAN   This veggie haven has great character, in an atmospheric, narrow-laned corner of the former tradesman's district of Sant Pere. One of its prime attractions, apart from the ultra-healthy green menu, is an exceptionally wide choice of herbal teas and Argentinian *mate* (a sort of tea). Enjoy the excellent rice fishes, salads, and stuffed pita-bread delights in a spacious dining area to the rear of the space. The eclectic drinks menu includes iced tea, chai, and *glühwein* as well as *mate*.

Flassaders 30. ℃ **93-319-98-66.** Main courses 10€–18€. DC, MC, V. Tues–Sat 1pm–11:30pm. Metro: Jaume I.

La Cuineta 🍴 SPANISH   This restaurant near the Catalan government offices is a culinary highlight of the Barri Gòtic. Decorated in typical regional style, it favors local cuisine. The fixed-price menu is good value, or you can order a la carte. The most expensive appetizer is *bellota* (acorn-fed ham), but I suggest a market-fresh Catalan dish such as *favas* (broad beans) stewed with *botifarra,* a tasty, spicy local sausage.

Pietat 12. ℃ **93-315-01-11.** Reservations recommended. Main courses 16€–35€; fixed-price menu 15€–30€. AE, DC, MC, V. Daily 1–4pm, 8pm–midnight. Metro: Jaume I.

Los Caracoles ▣ SPANISH   As you walk down Escudellers, one of the Old Quarter's most seedily atmospheric lanes, you are drawn on by the aroma of roasting chickens rotating on an outside spit built into the side of the building. Enter through the main kitchen, complete with steaming pots and hot-under-the-collar cooks. Inside, the restaurant is a labyrinth—stairways lead to more dining rooms; private one-table nooks are hidden under stairs; and there are colorful tiles, wooden beamed ceilings, and antique fittings everywhere. The place positively oozes with character, and the cuisine is mainly Catalan comfort food: *Arroz negre* (rice cooked in squid ink), grilled squid, and, of course, roast chicken. There's a fair share of tourists and the food isn't always up to what it should be, but as an authentic slice of local culture it's definitely worth a visit.

Escudellers 14. ℃ **93-302-31-85.** www.loscaracoles.es. Reservations recommended. Main courses 10€–32€. AE, DC, MC, V. Daily 1pm–midnight. Metro: Drassanes.

🎁 **Calling All Chocoholics!**

Established in 1930, **Granja Dulcinea,** Petritxol 2 (℃ **93-302-68-24),** is the most famous chocolate shop in Barcelona. The specialties are *melindros* (sugar-topped soft-sided biscuits), and regulars dunk them into the very thick hot chocolate—so thick that it feels like eating a melted chocolate bar. A cup of hot chocolate with cream costs 3.50€ and a *ración* of *churros* (a deep-fried pastry), which also can be dipped in the hot chocolate, goes for 1.80€. No credit cards are accepted. Dulcinea is open daily from 9am to 1pm and 5:30 to 9pm (closed in Aug). In the same street you'll find the simple, brightly lit **Granja Pallaresa,** Petritxol 11 (℃ **93-302-20-36),** equally famous for its thick and rich chocolate drinks. There's a good choice of pastries, including calorie-laden *ensaimadas* (Mallorcan pastries filled with lard!) too. It opens daily from 9am to 1pm and 4 to 9pm. Take the Metro to Liceu for both cafes.

MAKE IT snappy

Fast-food establishments are ever on the increase, from prime-positioned McDonald's and Dunkin' Donuts to local takeouts. **Pans & Company** and **Bocata** both dispense freshly made *bocatas* (crusty rolls) filled with tasty hot and cold combinations. You'll also see branches of **La Baguetina Catalana** everywhere; this is a fantastic, franchised fueling-stop with mountains of carb-ridden cakes and pastries to go. A favorite with health-conscious backpackers, **Maoz** churns out freshly made falafels, which you top up yourself with as much salad as you can fit into the pita. Along **La Rambla** and the streets to either side, there are dozens of places to buy enormous *shwarmas:* Giant sandwiches filled with spit-roasted chicken or lamb and salad. Another great pitstop, **Milk** is at Gignas 21 (© **93-268-09-22;** www.milk-barcelona.com) and has great-value Thursday to Sunday brunches, serving pancakes, smoothies, and basic fried dishes to suit the leaner wallet. If you want to splash out, try one of its inventive cocktails (4€ upwards).

Pla ★★ MEDITERRANEAN   This cool Barri Gòtic eating spot has been a solid hit with locals and visitors alike since its 1998 opening, thanks to the consistently high standard of *carpaccios;* wide selection of market-fresh salads exposing tasty combinations such as spinach, mushrooms, and prawns; and main dishes with Asian and Arabic touches, that nearly always include a curry or a Moroccan couscous dish. The candle-lit setting and cozy atmosphere are complemented by the amiable, bilingual, and informal waiting staff, who take the time to talk you through their menus.

Bellafila 5. © **93-412-65-52.** www.pla-repla.com. Reservations required. Main courses 10€–18€. DC, MC, V. Sun–Thurs 9pm–midnight; Fri–Sat 9pm–1am. Closed Dec 25–27. Metro: Jaume I.

Taxidermista MEDITERRANEAN   This popular restaurant, located on the bustling Plaça Reial, has high ceilings, tall narrow pillars, and attractively tiled floors. Originally it was the 19th-century Gran Café Espanyol and later a natural history museum, with a taxidermy workshop that featured stuffed beasts from insects to lions (some were sold to Salvador Dalí). Today it's a chic restaurant renowned for its two- or three-course set lunches, but traces of its history still exist (bear and deer heads decorate one wall of the salon). A la carte specialties include crayfish ravioli with shellfish sauce and a great steak tartare, plus there's an extensive cellar of wines and *cavas.*

Plaça Reial 8. © **93-412-45-36.** www.taxidermistarestaurant.com. Main courses 16€–24€; set lunch 10€–14€. AE, DC, MC, V. Tues–Sun 1:30–4pm, 8:30pm–12:30am. Closed 3 weeks in Jan. Metro: Liceu.

INEXPENSIVE

Juicy Jones VEGETARIAN   A brightly colored blend of cartoon-strip and children's nursery decor greets you in this chummy, Danish-run place, where the young international waiters are friendly but sometimes give the impression they're just passing through. Hardly conventional either in style or choice of food, it offers a reasonably priced couscous and rice-accompanied range of inventive dishes, ranging from bean sprouts and *escalivada* (grilled onion, eggplant/aubergine, and red and green peppers) to tofu and ginger salads. The marvelous selection of fresh fruit juices includes pear, mango, and grapefruit; there are also soy milk shakes, organic wines, and beer available. Sit at the narrow counter near the entrance or in the secluded sunken restaurant at the back.

Cardenal Casañas 7. ℂ **93-302-43-30.** Main courses 7€–12€; lunch 9€ on weekdays. No credit cards. Daily noon–midnight. Metro: Liceu.

La Dentellière ★ 🍴 FRENCH   Charming, and steeped in the French aesthetic, this bistro is imbued with a modern, elegant decor. Inside, you'll find a small corner of provincial France, thanks to the dedicated effort of Evelyne Ramelot, the French writer who owns the place. After an aperitif at the sophisticated cocktail bar, order from an imaginative menu including lasagna made from strips of salt cod, peppers, and tomato sauce, and a delectable *carpaccio* of filet of beef with pistachios, lemon juice, vinaigrette, and Parmesan cheese. The wine list is particularly imaginative, with worthy vintages mostly from France and Spain.

Ample 26. ℂ **93-319-68-21.** Reservations recommended on weekends. Main courses 8€–22€. MC, V. Tues–Sun 8:30pm–midnight. Metro: Drassanes.

Romesco 🌶 SPANISH   Frequented by locals and travelers on a budget, Romesco will never win any Michelin stars, but it offers the sort of homemade food that is rapidly disappearing around touristy La Rambla. The lighting is bright, the tables are laminated, and the waiters and food are both no-nonsense and generously proportioned. You will find healthy, fresh dishes like grilled tuna served with a simple salad, or hearty delights such as *arroz a la cubana* (white rice, tomato sauce, a fried egg, and a fried banana). Desserts include a creamy *crema catalana* (crème caramel) and *arroz con leche* (rice pudding). Finish off with a strong black coffee like the locals.

Sant Pau 28. ℂ **93-318-93-81.** Main courses 8€–16€. No credit cards. Mon–Fri 1pm–midnight; Sat 1–6pm, 8pm–midnight. Closed Aug. Metro: Liceu.

SNACKS, TAPAS & DRINKS

The Bagel Shop CAFE   If you are craving a bagel, head for this simple cafe just off the top end of La Rambla. All the staples are here: Sesame, poppyseed, blueberry, plus a few European versions such as black olive. Fillings range from honey to salmon and cream cheese, and they also have a yummy selection of cheesecakes.

Canuda 25. ℂ **93-302-41-61.** www.thebagelshopbcn.com. Bagels 2.25€–7.50€. No credit cards. Mon–Sat 9:30am–9:30pm; Sun 11am–4pm. Metro: Liceu.

Bar del Pi SPANISH   One of the most famous bars in the Barri Gòtic, this tiny establishment is midway between two medieval squares opening onto a Gothic church. Typical tapas, canapés, and rolls are available. Most visitors come to drink coffee, beer, or local wines, sangrias, or *cavas*. In summer refresh yourself with a *horchata* milk shake flavored with almonds or sesame, or a slushy ice drink. Sit inside at one of the cramped bentwood tables, or stand at the crowded bar. In warm weather, take a table beneath the single plane tree on the landmark square. The plaza draws an interesting group of young bohemian sorts, travelers, and musicians.

Plaça Sant Josep Oriol 1. ℂ **93-302-21-23.** www.bardelpi.com. Tapas 2.75€–10€. No credit cards. Mon–Fri 9am–11pm; Sat 9:30am–10:30pm; Sun 10am–10pm. Metro: Liceu.

Bodega la Plata ★ SPANISH   Established in the 1920s, La Plata is one of a trio of famous bodegas on a narrow medieval street, occupying a corner building—where two open sides allow aromatic cooking odors to permeate the neighborhood—and containing a marble-topped bar and cramped tables. The culinary specialty comprises *raciones* (small plates) of deep-fried sardines—head and all. Make a meal for two by ordering the house's tomato, onion, and fresh anchovy salad. The highly quaffable and affordable Penedès house wine comes in three varieties: *Tinto, blanco,* and *rosado.*

Mercé 28. ✆ **93-315-10-09.** Tapas/*raciones* 2.50€–5€. No credit cards. Mon–Sat 1–3:45pm, 8pm–midnight. Metro: Drassanes.

Café de l'Opera ★ SPANISH   A 1920s' *moderniste*-era gem and one of the few emblematic cafes in the city that has resisted the ravages of "gentrification." The name comes from the Liceu Opera House, located directly opposite, across La Rambla, and once upon a time patrons gathered here for a pre-performance aperitif. Although the cafe has been renovated over the years, the interior still retains Belle Epoque details. It's a great place to hang out with a book during quieter daytime moments, and there is a terrace if people-watching is more your thing. Tapas are limited, but the cakes are divine. Service is brusque, exuding a jaded formality in keeping with the surroundings.

La Rambla 74. ✆ **93-317-75-85.** www.cafeoperabcn.com. Tapas from 3.50€; cakes from 4€. No credit cards. Daily 8:30am–2:30am. Metro: Liceu.

Foodball ★ HEALTH FOOD   Foodball is another concept from hyper-successful shoe company **Camper** (p. 232). It's a cafe and takeout joint located near the MACBA museum, and the clientele reflects the neighborhood's neo-hippie vibe. The foodballs in question are whole-grain macrobiotic rice balls stuffed with organic mushrooms, chickpeas, tofu and alga, or chicken. Take them out in stylish recycled lunchboxes or park yourself on the grandstand-style seating. Besides the foodballs, the only other produce available is fresh or dried fruit, juices, and purified water. If all this sounds just a bit too smug, don't be put off: Healthy fast food is scarce in Barcelona, and the foodballs are very, very tasty.

Elisabets 9. ✆ **93-270-13-63.** Foodballs 2.75€ each; menu 10€. Daily noon–11pm. Metro: Liceu.

La Vinateria del Call BAR   A tiny, traditional nocturnal bar right in the heart of the Barri Gòtic, close to Plaça de Sant Jaume. It serves delicious snacks and desserts that range from basic cheeses and homemade sausages to a variety of ice creams (try out the fig flavor) and has a good stock of wines, from low-cost Valdepeñas to pricey Riojas. Loud music enlivens the evenings, especially on boozy "bachelor nights" (be warned!).

Domènec del Call 9. ✆ **93-302-60-92.** MC, V. Daily 8:30pm–1am. Metro: Jaume I.

Venus Delicatessen CAFE   This pleasant cafe is on one of the inner city's alternative fashion shopping streets. It's a good stopping point for tea or coffee, cakes, and pastries. The "delicatessen" in the name is a bit misleading (there's not a deli counter in sight), but what it does do very well are light meals such as salads and quiches from midday to midnight. There is a ton of international press to thumb through and work by local artists on the wall to gaze at.

Avinyó 25. ✆ **93-301-15-85.** Main courses 8€–12€; fixed-price lunch 12€. No credit cards. Mon–Sat noon–midnight. Metro: Jaume I.

Vinissim ★★ SPANISH   A warm burgundy and exposed-brick interior is the perfect backdrop for this cozy wine bar on a pretty square in El Call. Here over 50 carefully selected wines—available by glass or bottle—come from all regions of Spain. Portions range from small tapas of ham, fish, or olives to *ración*-size combos like artisan goat's cheese, sun-dried tomatoes, caramelized onions, and potato and cheese *raclette*. One of their best white wines is Finca Lobeira Albariño from Galicia. Rich desserts include sticky date pudding and delicious white chocolate cheesecake. All in all, this is an absolute gem of a wine bar, with dishes to match.

Sant Domenec del Call 12. © **93-301-45-75.** Tapas/*raciones* 3.50€–15€; tasting menu 28€; fixed-price weekday lunch 16€. AE, DC, MC, V. Mon–Sat noon–4pm, 8pm–midnight. Metro: Liceu.

La Ribera

EXPENSIVE

ABaC ★ 🏛 SPANISH   This is the showcase of a personality chef, Xavier Pellicer, who creates a self-termed *cuisine d'auteur,* meaning a menu of completely original dishes. His minimalist restaurant has even attracted members of the Spanish royal family, eager to see what Pellicer is cooking up. A few of his dishes may be too experimental for some tastes, but for me he's a master in balancing flavors, and his dishes perk up the taste buds. His plates emphasize color and texture and his sauces are perfectly balanced. Menus change nightly according to Pellicer's culinary inspiration. Perhaps a mushroom tartare will be resting on your plate, or a velvety-smooth steamed foie gras. Roasted sea bass appears with sweet pimientos and oyster plant, and Iberian suckling pig is cooked and flavored to perfection, as is fennel ravioli with "fruits of the sea."

Av. Tibidabo 1. © **93-319-66-00.** www.abacbarcelona.com. Reservations required. Main courses 25€–40€; tasting menu 90€. AE, DC, MC, V. Tues–Sat 1:30–3:30pm, 8:30–11pm. Closed Aug. Metro: Jaume I or Barceloneta.

MODERATE

Big Fish ★★★ 🏛 SEAFOOD   This spacious, high-ceilinged addition to the Born's array of chic eating spots is one of the best new seafood restaurants in town. It was designed by Lazaro Rosa Violán, who created the Market Hotel (p. 93). The decor is offbeat, with small tables, polished wood floorboards, and bright white walls and pillars. The food is supreme: An inventive blend of Mediterranean and Atlantic catches with Japanese minimalism. Outstanding are the *veieras gallegas a la plancha* (Galician scallops cooked on a hotplate), *gambas de Palamós* (prawns from Palamós), and *lubina a la brasa con mermelada de tomates y esparragos* (charcoal-grilled sea bass with tomato and asparagus jam). For dessert try the white chocolate brownie or bite into a dainty Tokyo-style *kudamono* fruit dish. There's a non-stop sushi bar and cocktail area that stays open until 3am.

Calle Comercial 9. © **93-268-17-28.** www.bigfish.net. Main courses 17€–35€; lunch menu (mid-week) 14€. Daily 1:30–4pm, 8:30pm–midnight. Fri–Sat 8:30pm–12:30am. Metro: Jaume I.

Cal Pep ★ 🏛 SPANISH   Cal Pep lies just north of the Plaça de Palau, nestled beside a tiny postage-stamp square. It's generally packed, and the food is some of the tastiest in La Ribera. There's actually a Pep himself, and he's a great host, going around to see that all diners are happy. In the rear is a small dining room (book if you intend to eat there), but most patrons like to sit at the counter seats up front. Try the fried artichokes or the mixed seafood dish that includes tiny sardines. Clams come swimming in a well-seasoned broth given extra spice by a sprinkling of hot peppers. A delectable tuna dish is served with a sesame sauce, and fresh salmon is flavored with basil—sublime.

Plaça des les Olles 8. © **93-310-79-61.** www.calpep.com. Reservations required. Main courses 15€–25€. AE, DC, MC, V. Mon 8:30–11:30pm; Tues–Sat 1–4:30pm, 8:30–11:30pm. Closed Aug. Metro: Barceloneta or Jaume I.

Comerç 24 ★★ 🎁 SPANISH   The renowned chef at this avant-garde restaurant is Carles Abellán, a disciple of the famed Ferran Adriá of El Bulli. Abellán uses fresh seasonal ingredients, balanced sauces, and bold but never outrageous combinations, and he believes in split-second timing. Samples of his most imaginative dishes include freshly diced tuna marinated in ginger and soy sauce, and fresh salmon "perfumed" with vanilla and served with yogurt. His baked eggplant (aubergine) with Roquefort, pine nuts, and fresh mushrooms from the countryside is another treat. He also serves an old-fashioned snack that Catalan children ate when they came home from school—a combination of chocolate, salt, and bread flavored with olive oil. It's surprisingly good!

Comerç 24. 📞 **93-319-21-02.** www.comerc24.com. Reservations required. Main courses 12€–28€; tasting menu 50€. AE, DC, MC, V. Tues–Sat 1:30–3:30pm, 8:30pm–12:30am. Closed last 3 weeks in Aug and Christmas week. Metro: Jaume I.

Cuines Santa Caterina ★ 🎁   MEDITERRANEAN   This spacious spot adjoining the Santa Caterina market couldn't be better located for fresh local produce, with samples displayed enticingly along the large front windows. Designed by top architects Enric Miralles and Benedetta Tagliabue, the CSC—as it's popularly known—features an open kitchen, subtle back lighting, and ficus trees planted in between the long olive-wood tables. Lunch is particularly good value and the place is noisily packed as locals call out their choices from the chalkboard menu. Fusion, vegetarian, and down-to-earth dishes range from fresh sushi and green asparagus to baked potato with cheese and sausage. There's also a tapas bar with a fresh-juice section.

Mercado de Santa Caterina, Av. Francesc Cambó 1. 📞 **93-268-99-18.** www.grupotragaluz.com. Main courses 10€–24€. MC, V. Mon–Sat 1–4pm, 8–11:30pm. Metro: Jaume I.

Espai Sucre ★★ 🎁 DESSERT   Espai Sucre (Sugar Space) is Barcelona's most unusual dining room, with minimalist decor and seating for 30. The menu is entirely devoted to desserts. There is a shortlist of so-called salty dishes, like ginger couscous with pumpkin and grilled stingray, or artichoke cream with a poached quail egg and Serrano ham. A "salad" might contain small cubes of spicy milk pudding resting on apple matchsticks with baby arugula (rocket) leaves, peppery caramel, dabs of kafir lime and lemon curd, and a straight line of toffee. There are constant surprises. Ever had a soup of li chi, celery, apple, and eucalyptus? Try it here! If some of these concoctions frighten your palate, you'll find comfort in the more familiar—vanilla cream with coffee sorbet and caramelized banana. Every dessert comes with a recommendation for the appropriate wine to accompany it.

Princesa 53. 📞 **93-268-16-30.** www.espaisucre.com. Reservations required. Main courses 10€–22€; 3-dessert platter 34€. MC, V. Tues–Sat 9–11:30pm. Closed Aug and Christmas week. Metro: Arc de Triomf.

La Paradeta 🍴 ☺ SEAFOOD   Most *marisco* (seafood) meals can set you back a ton in Barcelona. Not so at this busy restaurant, which is more like a fish market than the trendy eateries of La Ribera's El Born district. The seafood—crabs, prawns, squid, and so on—is displayed in large plastic tubs. Pick out what you want at the counter and it's weighed up and cooked and you pick it up crisp and steaming on a platter. The same scenario goes for the drinks, which include some excellent Albariño whites and other good, reliable local wines. It's loads of fun, but order everything at once, as you'll have to wait in line, especially at the weekend.

Comercial 7. 📞 **93-268-19-39.** www.laparadeta.com. Fish charged per kilo. Average price 18€–30€. No credit cards. Tues–Thurs 8–11:30pm; Fri 8pm–midnight; Sat–Sun 1–4pm. Closed Dec 22–Jan 22. Metro:

Arc de Triomf. There are branches, with the same menus and opening hours, beside the Sagrada Família (Pasaje Simó 18; ☎ **93-450-01-91**) and in Sants (Carrer Riego 27; ☎ **93-431-90-59**).

Senyor Parellada SPANISH   The glossy, contemporary-looking interior of this restaurant is in distinct contrast to the facade of its century-old home. Inside, in a pair of lemon-yellow and blue dining rooms, you'll find menu items such as Italian-style cannelloni, stuffed cabbage, cod "as it was prepared by the monks of the Poblet monastery," baked monkfish with mustard and garlic sauce, and roasted rack of lamb with red-wine sauce. Patrons flock here faithfully, knowing they'll be served a traditional cuisine of northeast Spain created with fine local produce. The chefs know how to coax the flavor out of the premium ingredients.

Argenteria 37. ☎ **93-310-50-94.** www.senyorparellada.com. Reservations recommended. Main courses 10€–20€. AE, DC, MC, V. Daily 1–4pm, 8:30pm–midnight. Metro: Jaume I.

INEXPENSIVE

Bar del Pla ★★ SPANISH   Such was the popularity of the Pla (p. 129) in the Barri Gòtic that its owner opened a second branch in La Ribera, on the same street as the Museu Picasso. It's close to Santa Caterina market, which provides the fresh produce. Unlike the intimate original restaurant, this is a brash, down-to-earth bodega-style place, specializing in regional tapas and *raciones* like *jamón Serrano, croquetas,* and *tortillitas de champiñones* (tiny mushroom omelets). There's a good choice of local and Spanish wines, especially from the Penedès. Stylishly renovated, it's one of the area's brightest and most bustling eating spots.

Montcada 2. ☎ **93-268-30-03.** www.elpla.cat. Tapas/*raciones* 4€ –10€; main courses 12€–18€. Daily noon–11:30pm Fri–Sat to midnight). DC, MC, V. Closed Dec 25–27. Metro: Jaume I.

Murivecchi 🍴 ITALIAN   If this family-run restaurant was in the thick of the trendy El Born neighborhood, you would probably never get a table. The unassuming decor doesn't do it any favors either, but the food is excellent and good value for the money. There is a wood-fired oven for fans of real Neapolitan pizza, and the pasta dishes are no less delectable: *Tagliatelle al funghi porcini, spaghetti vongole,* and *linguini al pesto* are just a few. Add to this a list of *antipasti, risotti,* and *carpacci;* daily specials; and a sinful tiramisu—and you have some of the best Italian cuisine this side of Rome.

Princesa 59. ☎ **93-315-22-97.** Reservations recommended on weekends (☎ 93-218-30-00). Main courses 10€–18€; fixed-price lunch Mon–Fri 12€. MC, V. Daily 1–4pm, 8pm–midnight. Metro: Arc de Triomf.

Pla de la Garsa ★ 🍴 SPANISH   Located on the east of La Ribera, this historic building is fully renovated but still retains its 19th-century cast-iron spiral staircase leading to the dining area upstairs. The ground floor is more interesting. Here you'll encounter the owner, Ignacio Sulle, an antiques collector who has filled his establishment with an intriguing collection of *objets d'art.* The menu boasts one of the city's best wine lists and features a daily array of favorite traditional Catalan dishes. Begin with pâté, confit of duck, or terrine with black olives and anchovies. For a main course order a perfectly seasoned beef bourguignon or *fabetes fregides amb menta i pernil* (beans with meat and Serrano ham). The cheese selection is one of the finest in town, especially bountiful in Catalan goat's cheese, including Serrat Gros from the Pyrénées.

Assaonadors 13. ☎ **93-315-24-13.** www.pladelagarsa.com. Reservations recommended on weekends. Main courses 8€–16€. AE, DC, MC, V. Daily 8pm–1am. Metro: Jaume I.

SNACKS, TAPAS & DRINKS

Sandwich & Friends CAFE   Located on the main drag of El Born, Sandwich & Friends stands out from its fast-food rivals thanks to its huge wall mural by the famous illustrator Jordi Labanda. His portrayal of a social gathering of bright young things echoes the clientele itself, who come to enjoy the cafe's awesome selection of over 50 sandwiches, all named after "friends": *Marta* is a pork filet, tomato, and olive oil sandwich; *Daniel* is filled with frankfurter, bacon, and mustard. There is a selection of salads if you are calorie counting, which, going by the size of the staff, is the norm here. There are four other branches scattered throughout the city, one in Raval and three in L'Eixample, but this is the coolest.

Passeig del Born 27. ✆ **93-310-07-86.** www.sandwichandfriends.com. Sandwiches 5.25€–10€. MC, V. Daily 9:30am–1am. Metro: Jaume I or Barceloneta.

Taller de Tapas ★★ SPANISH   For a foreigner, ordering tapas can be daunting. Making yourself heard above the noise is one problem, and there is also the lack of written menus. The Born district's Taller de Tapas (Tapas Workshop) takes the trouble out of *tapeando*. Patrons sit at a table and order from a trilingual menu. The tapas are prepared in an open kitchen, with not a microwave in sight. The owners are always on the lookout for new ingredients that will work in tapas, so every week there is a board of specials. The tapas come from all over Spain: Marinated anchovies from L'Escala on the Costa Brava, Palamós prawns with scrambled eggs, grilled duck foie, and sizzling chorizo cooked in cider. For those who like a substantial breakfast, they do a morning tortilla menu.

L'Argentaria 51. ✆ **93-268-85-59.** www.tallerdetapas.com. Tapas 3.50€–12€. AE, DC, MC, V. Mon–Thurs 8:45am–midnight; Fri–Sat 8:45am–12:30am; Sun noon–midnight. Metro: Jaume I. There's another location at Plaça Sant Josep Oriol 9, Barri Gòtic (✆ **93-301-80-20;** Metro: Liceu).

El Raval

EXPENSIVE

Ca l'Isidre ★ SPANISH   In spite of its seedy location in the gritty Parel.lel district (take a cab at night!), this is perhaps the most sophisticated Catalan bistro in Barcelona. Opened in 1970, King Juan Carlos and Queen Sofía, Julio Iglesias, and the famous Catalan bandleader Xavier Cugat have all eaten here. Isidre Gironés, helped by his wife, Montserrat, is known for his fresh cuisine, which is beautifully prepared and served. Try spider crabs and shrimp, foie gras salad, sweetbreads with port and flap mushrooms, or carpaccio of veal. The selection of Spanish and Catalan wines is excellent.

Les Flors 12. ✆ **93-441-11-39.** www.calisidre.com. Reservations required. Main courses 18€–50€. AE, DC, MC, V. Mon–Sat 1:30–4pm, 8:30–11pm. Closed Sat–Sun June–July and all Aug. Metro: Paral.lel.

Casa Leopoldo ★★ 🍴 SEAFOOD   An excursion through the earthy streets of the Barri Xino is part of the Casa Leopoldo experience. At night it's safer to come by taxi. Founded in 1939, this colorful restaurant, with attractive tiled walls and wood-beamed ceilings, serves some of the freshest seafood in town. There's a popular stand-up tapas bar out front plus two dining rooms. Specialties include *rodaballo* (fresh grilled turbot), *anguila con gambas* (eel with shrimp), *percebes* (goose barnacles), *sepia* (cuttlefish), *sopa de mariscos* (seafood soup with shellfish), and *anguilas fritas* (deep-fried inch-long eels).

Sant Rafael 24. ☏ **93-441-30-14.** www.casaleopoldo.com. Reservations recommended. Main courses 25€–55€; tasting menu 50€. AE, DC, MC, V. Tues-Sun 1:30–4pm; Tues-Sat 9–11pm. Closed Aug and Easter. Metro: Liceu.

Quo Vadis ★ SPANISH   Elegant and impeccable, this is one of the finest restaurants in Barcelona and a favorite with the opera crowd from the Liceu Opera House next door. In a century-old mansion near the open stalls of the Boqueria food market, it was established in 1967 and has done a discreet but thriving business ever since. The four paneled dining rooms exude conservative charm. Culinary creations include a ragout of seasonal mushrooms, fried goose liver with prunes, filet of beef with wine sauce, and a variety of grilled or flambéed fish. There's a wide choice of desserts made with seasonal fruits imported from all over Spain.

Carme 7. ☏ **93-302-40-72.** www.restaurantquovadis.com. Reservations recommended. Main courses 18€–30€; fixed-price menu 35€. AE, DC, MC, V. Mon-Sat 1:15–4pm, 8:30–11:30pm. Closed Aug. Metro: Liceu.

MODERATE

Anima MEDITERRANEAN   Located near the MACBA, Anima is of the new breed of Raval eateries. Inside it's all bright colors and minimalism, and a glance at the menu would lead you to think that the cuisine also skimps on the trimmings. But the food here is highly satisfying, especially when you eat it on their outdoor terrace in the summer. Under the plane trees, you can dine on *rape con ajillo de pistachio y granizado de algas* (monkfish in pistachio garlic and iced liquidized seaweed), mozzarella balls swimming in gazpacho, ostrich steak with caramelized cranberries, and crystalized chocolate truffles for dessert. If all this sounds a bit too heavy, take a gamble with the great-value set-lunch menu instead.

Angels 6. ☏ **93-342-49-12.** Reservations recommended. Main courses 10€–20€; fixed-price lunch 14€. AE, DC, MC, V. Mon-Sat 1–4pm, 9pm–midnight. Dinner only in Aug. Metro: Liceu.

Lupino MEDITERRANEAN   Set in the heart of El Raval, the Lupino is renowned for its cool catwalk-like decor and an eclectically inventive cuisine that effortlessly blends Mediterranean, French, Creole, and North African dishes. Typical favorites are grilled entrecôte with couscous, cod with ratatouille and coconut emulsion, and pork stuffed with goat's cheese with cassava chips on the side. It's all very good and the lunchtime set menu is one of the best deals around. A rear terrace overlooks the back of the Boqueria market (in reality a parking lot, but oversize parasols block out the unsightly bits). Friday and Saturday are late-night cocktail nights when a DJ makes an appearance.

Carme 33. ☏ **93-412-36-97.** Reservations recommended on weekends. Main courses 14€–22€; fixed-price lunch Mon-Fri 11€, Sat-Sun 15€. AE, MC, V. Mon-Thurs 1–4pm, 9pm–midnight; Sat-Sun 1:30–4:30pm, 9pm–3am. Metro: Liceu.

Mam i Teca 🍴 SPANISH   A diminutive Raval tapas delight boasting a handful of tables. Mam i Teca is among the smallest eating spots in town, although the high ceilings obligingly create a sense of more space. The menu here is a combination of the highly imaginative and traditional Catalan (try the pungent organic *botifarra* sausage) and accompanying drinks include a range of interesting wines as well as the yeasty, locally made Almogáver beer.

Lluna 4. ☏ **93-441-33-35.** Main courses 10€–15€. MC, V. Mon, Wed-Fri, Sun 1–4pm, 8:45pm–midnight; Sat 8:45pm–midnight. Closed 2 weeks in Aug. Metro: Sant Antoni.

Mama Café MEDITERRANEAN   Also located in the thick of El Raval's hub of funky eateries, this is one of the more reliable bets where style doesn't overtake substance. The boho crowd is greeted by an urban-savvy staff, who churn out the dishes from a frantic open kitchen. The quality of the hamburgers here is unusually good (for Barcelona), the salads (nearly always with a fruit or goat's cheese) are market-fresh, and the pastas (such as salmon and capers) are more than acceptable. Mama Café is one of the few inner-city restaurants open on Monday (the only day when fish is not available on the menu, by the way, in case you're a seafood lover).

Doctor Dou 10. (C) **93-301-29-40.** www.mamacaferestaurant.com. Reservations recommended on weekends. Main courses 10€–18€; fixed-price lunch 12.50€. AE, MC, V. Daily 1–4pm, 9pm–midnight. Metro: Liceu.

INEXPENSIVE

Ca l'Estevet 🎁 SPANISH   This century-old eating spot is a veritable institution in El Raval, where the Estevet family has been welcoming a mixture of students, journalists, and intrepid tourists for decades. The warm, homely ambience is matched by traditional Catalan dishes such as *exqueixada* (shredded salt cod salad), *botifarra negre* (black sausage), *cargols a llauna* (snails), and *conill* (rabbit). Weekday lunches are the main thing here, and it gets very crowded, so turn up early by Spanish standards (that is, around 1:30pm).

Valdonzella 46. (C) **93-302-41-86.** Main courses 10€–16€; set lunch 14€. Mon 1–4pm, Tues–Sat 1–4pm, 8–11pm. Metro: Universitat.

Iposa 🌶 MEDITERRANEAN   Iposa is a cheap and cheerful Raval hangout with an outside leafy terrace that is coveted on sunny Saturday afternoons. The resident French chef ensures there is always something a little different on offer beyond the usual "Mediterranean" fare. If you're on a budget—and not too hungry—order the bargain lunchtime menu, but bear in mind that the portions are small and that you get just one main course, a dessert, and a drink. The food changes daily and includes dishes like a vegetable couscous, fresh grilled fish, and hot "hummus" soup.

Floristes de La Rambla 14. (C) **93-318-60-86.** Main courses 8€–12€; fixed-price lunch 7.50€. V. Aug daily 9pm–midnight; Sept–July Mon–Sat 1:30–4pm, 9pm–midnight. Metro: Liceu.

Mesón David ★ 🌶 SPANISH   Don't come here for a quiet evening. Mesón David is an absolute riot: Waiters scream at each other, tips are acknowledged by the ringing of a cowbell, crowds of diners sing, and somehow you have to make yourself heard. But the effort is worth it. The food is fast, furious, and excellent, with regional specialties from Navarran trout stuffed with Serrano ham and Galician-style broiled octopus to traditional Castilian roast suckling pork. Obviously, this isn't the place for a light meal. But it is enormous fun for a price that's unbelievably low for inner Barcelona. On busy nights you may have to wait for a table at the bar, and be shown the door on your last gulp of coffee.

Carretes 63. (C) **93-441-59-34.** www.mesondavid.com. Reservations recommended. Main courses 8€–12€; fixed-price lunch Tues–Fri 10€. AE, DC, MC, V. Tues–Sun 12:30–4pm, 8pm–1am. Metro: Paral.lel or Sant Antoni.

Organic 🌶 VEGETARIAN   Hip and hippie, Organic is one of the brightest vegetarian restaurants in town. At lunchtime, the happy waiting staff will show you to large communal tables and explain the system; the first course is a help-yourself soup and salad bar, all tasty and organically grown. The second (which you order from them) could be a vegetarian pizza, pasta, or perhaps a stir-fry. The self-serve desserts include apple cake, carob mousse, and fresh yogurt. At night the menu is a la carte and at the weekends there is live Brazilian music. A small selection of health foods is also available, including homemade bread, and a local masseuse offers her services to the lunchtime crowd.

Junta de Comerç 11. ☎ **93-301-09-02.** www.antoniaorganickitchen.com. Main courses 8€–14€; fixed-price lunch 8€–12€. AE, DC, MC, V. Daily noon–midnight. Metro: Liceu.

SNACKS, TAPAS & DRINKS

Kasparo CAFE This place has one of my all-time favorite terraces: A leafy, porti-coed affair a stone's throw from the MACBA (p. 173). It's so popular that you often see people milling around, waiting to pounce on the next free table. A wide range of tapas—which varies daily—is marked up on a blackboard, and there's a good

---

tapas TIME

Traditionally, the Barcelonese don't go for the tapas crawl like their cousins in Madrid or Andalucia. They prefer to sit down over three courses, acres of linen, and a bottle of chilled white wine. But the trend for eating small portions, and the influence of new chefs such as Carles Abellán at **Comerç 24** (p. 133), has re-awakened local interest in eating tapas.

For classic Spanish tapas in the heart of the Old City, try **Taller de Tapas**, Calle de l'Argenteria 51 (☎ **93-268-85-59;** p. 135). For a 50-strong list of snacks all freshly made on the spot, **Cal Pep**, Plaça de les Olles 8 (☎ **93-310-79-61;** p. 132), comes close to godliness when you're talking spanking-fresh seafood; or there's **Bar Celta**, Calle Mercè 16 (☎ **93-315-00-06**)—one of the oldest tapas joints in town—for purple octopus tentacles and delightful green peppers known as *pimientos del padrón*. On the same street you can down rustic farm-house ciders, flaming chorizo, and dark, deeply satisfying slivers of *cecina* (cured beef) at a smattering of *sidrerías* (Asturian tapas bars).

In La Ribera and the Born, **Mosquito**, Calle Carders 46 (☎ **93-268-75-69**), does a well-executed range of Indian, Thai, Malaysian, and Indonesian dishes, along with *gyoza* dumplings and organic beers at unbeatable prices. More

up-market fare can be had from the ever-inventive hands of Paco Guzmán at **Santa María,** Calle Comerç 17 (☎ **93-315-12-27**). Think Spanish–Asian fusion, with local fruits stuffed with Thai spiced pea-nuts; raw sea bass with passion fruit, tomato, and lime vinaigrettes; and suck-ling pig with wasabi and soy.

If you're heading uptown, avoid the monster barns on the Passeig de Gràcia and opt instead for **Ciudad Condal,** Ram-bla de Catalunya 18 (☎ **93-318-19-97**), arguably the city's most visited tapas bar for *patatas bravas,* fried fish, and ancho-vies. Push on up the road to **Cervecería Catalana,** Carrer Majorca 236 (☎ **93-216-03-68**), for juicy slices of filet beef skewered with peppers, and giant prawn brochettes. **El Bitxo,** Verdaguer i Callis 9 (☎ **93-268-17-08**), serves outrageously imaginative dishes such as foie gras pâté with fig jam and goat's cheese with olive marmalade! It has a pretty good wine and *cava* selection too.

Finish off with a pudding course cour-tesy of Jordi Butrón at **Espai Sucre,** Calle Princesa 53 (☎ **93-268-16-30;** p. 133). Tales of his earthy Lapsang souchong tea ice cream go before him, and for many years his was the only pudding restau-rant in the world. Butrón can no longer claim that title, but this is still the ulti-mate end to a 21st-century tapas crawl.

selection of tasty sandwiches. There's also a wide choice of beers and wines, and the iced melon-flavored tea is a refreshing summer alternative. If you're lucky enough to get hold of a table, you'll find yourself lingering long after you planned to.

Plaça Vicenç Martorell 4. ⓒ **93-302-20-72.** www.barcelona-on-line.es/kasparo. Tapas 4.50€–10€. No credit cards. Daily 9am–midnight. Closed Dec 24–Jan 24. Metro: Plaça de Catalunya.

L'EIXAMPLE
Very Expensive

Beltxenea ★★ SPANISH   In a building originally designed in the late 19th century to house apartments, this restaurant celebrates fine Basque cuisine served in one of the most elegantly and comfortably furnished restaurants in the city. Schedule dinner for a special night—it's worth the money. The menu might include *merluza frito en ajo o con guarnición de almejas en caldo de pescado* (hake fried with garlic or garnished with clams and served with fish broth), *cordero asado* (roast lamb), *conejo a la plancha* (grilled rabbit), and *faisan* (pheasant). There's dining outside in the formal garden during the summer.

Majorca 275. ⓒ **93-215-30-24.** Reservations recommended. Main courses 22€–48€; tasting menu 80€. AE, DC, MC, V. Mon–Sat 1:30–3:30pm, 8:30–11:30pm. Closed Easter, 3 weeks in Aug, and Christmas week. Metro: Passeig de Gràcia or Diagonal.

Drolma ★★★ SPANISH   In business since 1999, this is one of Barcelona's best haute-cuisine restaurants. Fermin Puig is among Spain's most celebrated chefs, his culinary showcase found in the Hotel Majestic (p. 100). Only the freshest seasonal ingredients go into his luminous and carefully balanced dishes. Highlights are pheasant-stuffed cannelloni in a velvety foie gras sauce delicately sprinkled with the rare black truffle, *rodaballo* (wild turbot) served with fresh Catalan mushrooms, and *gambas* (prawns) with fresh asparagus tips in a virgin olive oil sauce. The *cordero* (lamb) is grilled with fresh herbs, and the bold yet delicate *chivo al horno* (baked goat) comes with potatoes and mushrooms.

Hotel Majestic, Passeig de Gràcia 70. ⓒ **93-496-77-10.** www.drolmarestaurant.cat/eng/index.htm. Reservations required. Main courses 38€–130€. AE, DC, MC, V. Mon–Sat 1–3:30pm, 8:30–11pm. Closed Aug. Metro: Passeig de Gràcia.

Jaume de Provença ★★★ FRENCH   This small, cozy restaurant is just a few steps from the Estació Central de Barcelona-Sants railway station, at the western end of L'Eixample. Named after its owner and chef, Jaume Bargués, it features modern interpretations of traditional Catalan and southern French cuisine. Dishes include gratin of clams with spinach, a salad of two different species of lobster, foie gras and truffles, and pigs' trotters with plums and truffles. Or order crabmeat lasagna, cod with saffron sauce, sole with mushrooms in port wine sauce, or an artistic dessert specialty of orange mousse.

Provença 88. ⓒ **93-430-00-29.** www.jaumeprovenza.com. Reservations recommended. Main courses 14€–38€; fixed-price menu 60€; tasting menu 80€. AE, DC, MC, V. Tues–Sat 1–3:45pm, 9–11:45pm; Sun 1–3:45pm. Closed Easter and Aug. Metro: Entença.

La Dama ★★★ SPANISH   One of the few restaurants in Barcelona that deserves, and gets, a Michelin star. In an elegant 1918 building designed by Manuel Sayrach, this stylish restaurant serves a clientele of local residents and civic dignitaries. Take the Art

L'Eixample Dining

Alkimia **14**	El Caballito Blanco **10**	L'Olivé **6**
Bar Turó **1**	Gaig **23**	Manairó **26**
Beltxenea **15**	Gorría **28**	Moo **13**
Can Ravell **21**	Gresca **9**	Neichel **1**
Casa Alfonso **24**	Hisop **18**	Quimet Quimet **20**
Casa Calvet **25**	Il Giardinetto **4**	Reno **3**
Casa Tejada **2**	Jaume de Provença **7**	Rosalert **16**
Cata 1.81 **19**	La Bella Napoli **20**	TapaÇ24 **22**
Cinc Sentits **8**	La Bodegueta **11**	Tapioles 53 **20**
Drolma **17**	La Dama **5**	Toc **27**
		Tragaluz **12**

Nouveau elevator up one flight to reach the dining room. Here chef Josep Bullich's specialties include salmon steak served with vinegar made from *cava* and onions, cream of potato soup flavored with caviar, a salad of *langostinos* (crayfish) with orange-flavored vinegar, an abundant platter of autumn mushrooms, and succulent preparations that include first-rate *cordero* (lamb), *ternera* (veal), and fresh *mariscos* (shellfish).

Diagonal 423. ✆ **93-202-06-86.** www.ladama-restaurant.com. Reservations required. Main courses 18€–40€; fixed-price menu 65€; tasting menus 75€ and 95€). AE, DC, MC, V. Daily 1:30–3:30pm, 8:30–11:30pm. Metro: Provença.

Expensive

Alkimia ★★ SPANISH Jordi Vilà's Alkimia is the type of restaurant that attracts other chefs to sample his singular style. He is a proponent of New Catalan cuisine, the culinary wave that started with Ferran Adrià (p. 300). For starters, try the deconstructed version of the traditional *pa amb tomàquet* (a slice of white bread rubbed with tomato pulp and olive oil), in which Vilà separates the juice from the tomato before adding the oil, crumbs of toasted bread, and a little pungent *lloganissa* salami. Many of his other dishes are also an offbeat take on traditional Catalan dishes: Tuna belly substitutes for Iberian ham in *faves a la catalana* (Catalan-style broad beans); truffle is added to a plate of cabbage, potato, and sausage; and fried eggs and Majorcan sausage are served with preserved quinces. There's an excellent wine cellar that includes many Spanish vintages.

Indústria 79. ✆ **93-207-61-15.** www.alkimia.cat. Reservations required. Main courses 15€–35€; tasting menus 45€ and 65€. DC, MC, V. Mon–Fri 1:30–4pm; Sat 8am–noon. Closed Easter and Aug 8–31. Metro: Sagrada Família.

Can Ravell ★ 🎁 SPANISH There's a good reason why Barcelona gourmets have tried—in vain—to keep this gem to themselves. Founded in 1929 by Ignasy Ravell and discreetly tucked away on the second floor of a deli, the restaurant is only accessible via a kitchen and spiral staircase. Chef Jesus Benavente, who's renowned for his divine creations, adjusts his menu according to season, so you never know quite what you're going to get until you arrive. A wonderful dish is *espalda de cerdo a horno con foie gras y guisantes* (braised pork shoulder with foie gras and young peas). The restaurant has a cellar of over 10,000 bottles, including *cavas* and champagnes.

Aragó 313. ✆ **93-457-51-14.** www.ravell.com. Reservations required. Main courses 25€–50€; tasting menu 45€. Tues–Wed 8:30am–9:30pm; Thurs–Fri 8:30am–10pm; Mon and Sat 9am–6pm. Metro: Gerona.

Casa Calvet ★★ MEDITERRANEAN Probably the most intimate Gaudían experience you can have in Barcelona is eating in this sumptuous dining room. The Casa Calvet was one of the architect's first commissions, built for textile magnate Pere Calvet. Now private apartments, the building is off-limits to the public, but a restaurant occupies Calvet's former ground-floor offices. Replete with velvet drapery, florid stained glass, attractive tiles, Gaudí-designed furniture, and other memorabilia, the only thing that jolts you back to the 21st century is the contemporary twist on Miguel Alija's excellent Catalan cuisine, such as giant prawns with rosemary-infused oil or duck liver with oranges. And although the setting ensures a fair share of tourists, Casa Calvet is also popular with locals.

Casp 48. ✆ **93-412-40-12.** www.casacalvet.es. Reservations recommended. Main courses 20€–40€; tasting menu 70€. AE, DC, MC, V. Mon–Sat 1–3:30pm and 8:30–11pm. Metro: Urquinaona.

Cata 1.81 ★★ 🛍 SPANISH   The dainty tapas-size dishes served here all look and taste innovative but many of the recipes are based on time-tested traditional stand-bys. These include *galtas de porc con nueces y higos* (pig's trotters with walnuts and fresh figs) with honey ice cream, and *calamar relleno de carne de cerdo picada en salsa almendrada de chocolate* (squid stuffed with minced pork and served with an almond-flavored chocolate sauce). Also popular are savory rice served with fresh asparagus and black truffles, and ravioli stuffed with codfish and minced smoked ham. There is a comprehensive and exemplary wine list.

Valencia 181. ☏ **93-323-68-18.** www.cata181.com. Reservations required. Tasting menu 35€ 9 dishes, 40€ 11 dishes; tapas 4€–9€. AE, DC, MC, V. Mon–Thurs 6pm–midnight; Fri–Sat 7pm–1am. Closed 3 weeks in Aug. Metro: Passeig de Gràcia or Hospital Clínic.

Cinc Sentits ★★ MEDITERRANEAN   This cutting-edge eatery aims to soothe the *cinc sentits* (five senses). Chef Jordi Artal offers a gourmet tasting menu of eight tapas-size dishes, which is diverse and delicious. Try a crème fraîche and caviar soup or a sliver of foie gras with violet-petal marmalade. Artal's cuisine is a combination of Catalan culinary know-how and new-world wit. An everyday white garlic soup is graced with pan-seared lobster, a monkfish sprinkled with bacon "dust," or a soft poached egg with tomato jam. My favorite dish was the smallest: A heavenly shot glass of *cava,* egg yolk, rock salt, and maple syrup. Cinc Sentits is an example of what fusion food can be like with a combination of the finest ingredients and intelligence.

Aribau 58. ☏ **93-323-94-90.** www.cincsentits.com. Reservations required. Main courses 14€–35€; tasting menu 50€ and 70€. AE, DC, MC, V. Mon 1:30–3:30pm; Tues–Sat 1:30–3:30pm and 8:30–11pm. Closed Easter and Aug 8–31. Metro: Passeig de Gràcia.

Gaig ★★★ SPANISH   One of the shining culinary showcases of Barcelona, Gaig was founded as an out-of-town *fonda* (small inn) in the late 19th century by the great-grandmother of present owner Carlos Gaig. Today it's a sleek deluxe downtown restaurant celebrated for the quality of its food. Eggs come from the chickens scratching on the patio, where customers dine al fresco in summer. Gaig's cuisine centers on traditional Catalan recipes transformed to suit light, modern palates. Among the stellar choices are *arroz del delta con pichón y zetas* (rice with partridge and mushrooms), and *els petits filet de vedella amb prunes i pinyons* (small veal filets with prunes and pine nuts). Desserts include *crema de Sant Joseph* (flan with wild strawberries on top), homemade chocolates, and a selection of tarts.

Aragó 214. ☏ **93-429-10-17.** www.restaurantgaig.com. Reservations recommended. Main courses 28€–50€; tasting menu 80€. AE, DC, MC, V. Mon–Sat 1:30–3:30pm and 9–11pm; Sun 9–11pm. Closed Easter and 3 weeks in Aug. Metro: Passeig de Gràcia.

Gorría ★ 🛍 SPANISH   This top Basque eating spot, within a stone's throw of La Sagrada Família, is run by Javier Gorría, who learned from his talented father master chef Fermin Gorría. Today it's Javier who pampers his clientele—many homesick expats from Navarra and the Basque country—with memories of home. No dish is finer than the herb-flavored baby lamb baked in a wood-fired oven. The classic Basque dish, hake, comes in a garlic-laced green herb sauce with fresh mussels and perfectly cooked asparagus on the side. Braised pork emerges from the wood-fired oven, and I could make a meal out of his *pochas* (white beans). Another favorite is a platter of artichokes stuffed with shrimp and wild mushrooms.

Diputació 421. © **93-245-11-64.** www.restaurantegorria.com. Reservations recommended. Main courses 18€–40€. AE, DC, MC, V. Mon–Sat 1–3:30pm and 9–11:30pm. Closed Aug. Metro: Monumental.

Gresca ★★ 🍴 SPANISH   Gifted Ferran Adrià disciple Rafael Peña runs this delightful little restaurant on the eastern edge of L'Eixample. A highly imaginative and inventive chef, Peña regularly entices elite noshers to road-test experimental dishes such as *higado de ternera con plátano y regaliz* (fresh calf's liver with plantains and lico-rice), *carpaccio de pulpo* (octopus carpaccio), and *butifarra negre con patatas fritas* (a very pungent black Catalan sausage served with fried potatoes—not for those on a diet!). Other pleasures include *anchoas en escabeche* (house-marinated fresh anchovies), *jamón Serrano con calamaritos fritos* (mountain ham served with fried baby squid), and *galtas de vacuno marinado en vino de Rioja* (tender beef cheeks braised in Rioja wine).

Provenza 230. © **93-451-61-93.** www.gresca.net. Reservations required. Main courses 16€–35€. MC, V. Mon–Fri 1:30–4pm, 8:30–11:30pm; Sat 8:30–11.30pm. Metro: Plaça de Catalunya or Hospital Clinic.

Hisop ★ SPANISH   In 2001, Guillem Pla and Oriol Ivem, two chefs formerly at prestigious Neichel (see below), launched this adventurous eating spot in the upper Diagonal where the emphasis of its new Catalan cuisine is on small understated dishes with a complexity of flavors. In a coolly minimalist setting of high wooden ceilings, red and black decor, and white walls lined with thin vases—each containing a single red rose—you can enjoy delicacies such as stone bass *suquet* with *trompet*, scallops with figs and Jabugo ham, and mouthwateringly rich desserts that include peach with ginger and fennel. There's an excellent wine list favoring top vintages from the Rioja and local Penedés vineyards.

Passatge Marimón 9. © **93-241-32-33.** www.hisop.com. Main courses 25€–32€. Tasting menu 55€. AE, DC, MC, V. Mon–Fri 1:30–4pm, 9pm–midnight; Sat 9pm–midnight. Closed Sundays and last 2 weeks in Aug. Metro: Hospital Clínic.

Moo ★★★ MEDITERRANEAN   The famed Roca brothers first launched their exquisite cuisine at **El Celler de Can Roca** (p. 283), a Michelin-starred eatery near Girona. Moo, their second restaurant, is located in Barcelona's applauded **Hotel Omm** (p. 100). All the dishes, from organic chicken with olives and mango to monkfish accompanied by wild mushrooms, are available in half-size portions, so you can create your own *menú de degustación*. Sample the set menu "Joan Roca"— five delightful dishes with wine recommended by Moo's talented sommelier Jordi Paronella. Start with a crescent of foie gras, followed by a lobster, rose, and licorice curry, and then a perfect filet of wild sea bass on a bed of snow peas and pine nuts. For dessert choose Bvlgari, a blend of Bergamot cream, lemon sorbet, and *pensam-iento* flowers, or chocolate cake, ginger, and 70% chocolate ice cream.

Rosselló 265. © **93-445-40-00.** www.hotelomm.es. Reservations recommended. Main courses 20€–35€; menu "Joan Roca" (with wine pairing) 95€; midday menu 55€. AE, DC, MC, V. Daily 1:30–4pm, 8:30–11pm. Closed Aug and Jan. 1. Metro: Diagonal.

Neichel ★★★ FRENCH   Alsatian-born owner Jean-Louis Neichel produces some of the most talked-about preparations of seafood, fowl, and desserts in Spain. Dinner could include a "mosaic" of foie gras with vegetables, strips of salmon marinated in sesame and served with vinaigrette sauce, or slices of raw and smoked salmon stuffed with caviar. The prize-winning terrine of sea crab floats on a bed of seafood sauce. Move onto *escalope* of turbot served with *coulis* of sea urchins, fricassee of Bresse chicken served with spiny lobsters, sea bass with a mousseline of truffles, or rack of lamb gratinéed in a herb-flavored pastry crust. The European cheeses and freshly made desserts are equally spectacular.

Beltrán i Rózpide 1-5. (Ⓒ **93-203-84-08.** www.neichel.es. Reservations required. Main courses 25€–40€; fixed-price lunch 48€; tasting menu 70€. AE, DC, MC, V. Tues–Sat 1:30–3:30pm, 8:30–11pm. Closed Aug. Metro: Palau Reial or María Cristina.

Reno ★ FRENCH   One of the finest and most enduring haute-cuisine restaurants in Barcelona, Reno sits behind sidewalk-to-ceiling windows hung with fine-mesh lace to shelter diners from prying eyes on the octagonal plaza outside. The impeccably mannered waiters are formal but not intimidating. Seasonal specialties can include partridge simmered in port sauce, a platter of assorted fish smoked on the premises, hake with anchovy sauce, or filet of sole stuffed with foie gras and truffles or grilled with anchovy sauce. An appetizing range of pastries is wheeled from table to table on a cart, or crèpes flambéed at your table.

Tuset 27. (Ⓒ **93-200-91-29.** Reservations recommended. Main courses 15€–35€; fixed-price lunch 38€; tasting menu 55€. AE, DC, MC, V. Mon–Sat 9–11:30pm; Mon–Fri 1–4pm. Closed Aug. Metro: Diagonal.

Moderate

Il Giardinetto ★ 🖻 ITALIAN   This eatery, a perennial favorite of the uptown arts crowd, won a major design award when it was opened in 1973, and the "fantasy forest" surroundings haven't dated one iota. It's split into two levels and dominated by columns decorated with leafy motifs. The walls are covered with foliage cutouts and the low ceilings sport swirls of pretty pale-green leaves. Indulge in one of the heady black or white seasonal truffle risottos or pastas, or a tuna *carpaccio*. The only letdown was dessert: The tiramisu was lacking in both coffee and amaretto flavors, but the sinful vanilla ice cream with bitter chocolate sauce made up for this lapse. There is a resident pianist in the evenings, and service is old-school without being stuffy.

La Granada del Penedès 22. (Ⓒ **93-218-75-36.** www.ilgiardinetto.es. Reservations recommended. Main courses 15€–30€; fixed-price lunch 21€. AE, DC, MC, V. Mon–Fri 1:30–4pm, 9pm–1:30am; Sat 9pm–1:30am. Closed Aug. Metro: Diagonal.

L'Olivé ★ SPANISH   Named after the owner, Josep Olivé, this restaurant is designed in modern Catalan style and the walls are adorned with reproductions of Miró, Dalí, and Picasso paintings. The overall feeling is one of elegance with a touch of intimacy; there are some discreet little corners in which to hide. You won't be disappointed by anything on the menu, especially *bacallà a la llauna* (baked salt cod) or *filet de vedella al vi negre al forn* (veal filets in a red-wine sauce). Monkfish flavored with roasted garlic is a palate pleaser, and you could finish with a *crema catalana* (creme caramel) or a delicious Catalan pastry.

Balmes 47. (Ⓒ **93-452-19-90.** www.rte-olive.com. Reservations recommended. Main courses 15€–28€; *menú completo* 45€. AE, DC, MC, V. Daily 1–4pm; Mon–Sat 8:30pm–midnight. Metro: Passeig de Gràcia.

Manairó ★★ SPANISH   Come for stylish but affordable haute cuisine at this highly inventive restaurant in the middle of L'Eixample and close to the bullring. Its creative takes on regional dishes are overseen by chef Jordi Herrera; his fabulous Catalan tasting menu features daring combinations such as local *botifarra* sausage with lobster and *empedrat de navajas con bacallá tibia* (razor shellfish with baked cod). The decor of the small but charming dining room is original and offbeat, including avant-garde cast-iron features, and the service couldn't be more friendly.

Diputació 424. ✆ **93-231-00-57.** www.manairo.com (in Catalan). Mon–Sat 1:30–3:30pm, 8:30–11pm. Main courses 22€; midday menu 35€; tasting menu 60€. Metro: Monumental.

Rosalert ★ SEAFOOD Situated at the corner of Carrer Napols close to La Sagrada Família, this restaurant has been the domain of Jordi Alert for more than 4 decades. He specializes in seafood, and his fish and crustaceans are simply grilled on a heated iron grill. This restaurant has Barcelona's most awesome fish tank, where you can choose tiny octopus, succulent mussels, fat shrimp, squid, fresh oysters, or langoustines. Begin with freshly made tapas, such as salt cod in vinaigrette or fava beans laced with garlic and virgin olive oil. Continue with the *parrillada* (assorted fish and shellfish from the grill). A delicious no-frills choice is *rodaballo a la plancha* (turbot cooked on the grill with potatoes and fresh mushrooms).

Diagonal 301. ✆ **93-207-19-48.** www.rosalert.com. Reservations recommended. Main courses 12€–25€; fixed-price lunch 22€; tasting menu 48€. AE, DC, MC, V. Tues–Sat noon–5pm, 8pm–2am; Sun noon–6pm. Closed Aug. Metro: Verdaguer or Sagrada Família.

Toc ★★ 📷 SPANISH This cool Eixample gourmet haven, run by genial maitre d' Sandra Baliarda and dynamic chef Santi Colominas, provides some of the most delicious traditional concoctions in Barcelona. Dishes range from mouth-watering entrees *esqueixada* (salad made from shreds of cod drenched in olive oil) and *escalivada* (a ratatouille-like blend of grilled peppers and eggplants/aubergine) to salmonetes con calçots i coliflor (red mullet with Catalan scallions and cauliflower) and *pechuga de pichón de sangre y pate trufado con queso* (white breast of pigeon with truffled pâté and cheese). For dessert try exquisite *pan y chocolate con aceite y sal* (bread and chocolate with olive oil and salt). There's a great wine selection, from vintage Riojas to lesser known Jumillas, supervised by top sommelier Ana López de Lamadrid.

Calle Girona 59. ✆ **93-488-11-48.** www.tocbcn.com. Main courses 28€–30€; tasting menu 50€. Mon–Fri 1–4pm, 8:30–11:30pm; Sat 8:30–11:30pm. Metro: Girona.

Tragaluz ★ MEDITERRANEAN This is the flagship restaurant of Barcelona's respected restaurateurs, Grupo Tragaluz. It offers three contemporary dining rooms on separate floors. Menus are derived from fresh seasonal ingredients, so, depending on the time of your visit, you could sample terrine of duck liver, Santurce-style hake (with garlic and herbs), filet of sole stuffed with red peppers, or beef tenderloin in a Rioja sauce. The vegetables are the freshest from the market that day. One of the tastiest desserts is a semi-soft slice of underbaked chocolate cake. Downstairs there is Tragarrapíd, a faster, more casual version of what's upstairs, and across the road is an enormously popular Japanese restaurant run by the same group.

Passatge de la Concepció 5. ✆ **93-487-06-21.** www.grupotragaluz.com. Reservations recommended. Main courses 18€–28€; fixed-price lunch 22€; tasting menu 55€. AE, DC, MC, V. Sun–Wed 1–4:30pm, 8:30pm–midnight; Thurs–Sat 1:30–4pm, 8:30pm–1am. Metro: Diagonal.

Inexpensive

El Caballito Blanco SEAFOOD This Barcelona standby is famous for seafood and popular with the locals. The "Little White Horse" is in the Passeig de Gràcia area and although the fluorescent-lit dining room does not offer much atmosphere, the food is good, varied, and relatively inexpensive (unless you order lobster!).

FAMILY-FRIENDLY restaurants

Granja Dulcinea This longtime favorite cafe and snack bar, at Petritxol 2 (✆ **93-302-68-24;** daily 9am–1pm, 5:30pm–midnight), makes a great refueling stop any time of day—guaranteed to satisfy all chocoholics. Lots of other sweet treats and drinks are on offer. (See also "Calling All Chocoholics!" earlier in this chapter.)

La Paradeta Fish and chips fun: Fish-loving kids get to choose what they want and see it being cooked. See p. 133.

Mesón David You don't have to worry about them making a noise here; the rest of the patrons and staff are just as ear-bursting. See p. 137.

Murivecchi Friendly, family-run Italian place with plenty of pasta dishes to suit the young ones. See p. 134.

Poble Espanyol A good introduction to Spanish food. All the restaurants in the "Spanish Village" serve comparable food at comparable prices—let the kids choose what to eat. See p. 188.

Dishes feature a huge selection of fish and shellfish, including *lubina santurce* (sea bass), *rape* (monkfish), *mejillones marinera* (mussels marinara), and *gambas ajillo* (shrimp with garlic). If you don't want fish, try the *chuletas de cordero a la plancha* (grilled lamb cutlets). Several different pâtés and salads are offered.

Mallorca 196. ✆ **93-453-96-16.** Main courses 10€–30€. AE, DC, MC, V. Tues–Sun 1–4pm; Tues–Sat 1–4pm, 8:45–11pm. Closed Aug. Metro: Hospital Clínic or Diagonal.

SNACKS, TAPAS & DRINKS

Bar Turó SPANISH Located in an affluent residential neighborhood close to the charming green oasis of Turó Park, north of the Old City, Bar Turó serves some of the best tapas in town. In summer you can sit outside or retreat to the narrow confines of the bar. Select from about 20 kinds of tapas, including *ensalada rusa* (Russian salad), *calamares romana* (rings of fried squid), and *jamón Serrano* (mountain ham).

Tenor Viñas 1. ✆ **93-200-69-53.** Tapas 3€–12€; main courses 8€–20€. MC, V. Mon–Sat 9am–midnight; Sun 9am–4pm. Closed weekends in Aug. Metro: Hospital Clínic.

Casa Alfonso SPANISH Spaniards love mountain ham, which comes from many different regions. The best of the best is *jamón Jabugo*, the only one sold at this traditional establishment. Entire hams hang from steel braces and they're taken down, carved, and trimmed into paper-thin slices in front of you. This particular form of cured ham, generically called *jamón Serrano*, comes from pigs fed on acorns in Huelva, in deepest Andalucia. Devotees of all things porcine will ascend to piggy-flavored heaven. The bar also offers salads and grilled meat dishes.

Roger de Llúria 6. ✆ **93-301-97-83.** Tapas 4.50€–14€; tasting menu 20€. AE, DC, MC, V. Mon–Tues 9am–midnight; Wed–Sat 9am–1am. Metro: Urquinaona.

Casa Tejada SPANISH Covered with rough stucco and decorated with hanging hams, Casa Tejada was established in 1964 and offers some of Barcelona's best tapas. Arranged behind a glass display case, they include marinated fresh tuna, German-style potato salad, ham salad, and five preparations of squid (including one that's stuffed). For variety, quantity, and quality, this place is hard to beat.

Tenor Viñas 3. ⓒ **93-200-73-41.** http://restcasatejada.restaurantesok.com. Tapas 3€-18€. MC, V. Mon-Thurs 9am-1am; Fri-Sun 9am-2am. Closed Aug 8-21. Metro: Hospital Clínic.

La Bodegueta SPANISH   Founded in 1940, this old wine tavern is one of the more authentic options on ritzy Rambla de Catalunya. It specializes in Catalan sausage (*botifarra*), salamis, and cheeses. Wash them all down with draft *vermut* or inexpensive Spanish wines from the barrel. It's loud, no-nonsense, and a favorite with students.

Rambla de Catalunya 100. ⓒ **93-215-48-94.** Tapas 2.50€-16€. No credit cards. Mon-Sat 8am-2am; Sun 6:30pm-1am. Closed Aug 8-22. Metro: Diagonal.

TapaÇ24 ★ SPANISH   Run by adventurous new-wave chef Carles Abellán, this is one of the city's newer and more interesting tapas bars. It seems outwardly traditional, but turns out fun and innovative dishes like "McFoie Burgers" and *tostadas con trufas* (truffle toast), alongside delicious homemade *croquetas de jamón* (ham croquettes), *albondigas* (meatballs), *callos* (tripe), and *rabo de buey* (oxtail) tidbits. It also serves great breakfasts.

Diputació 269. ⓒ **93-488-09-77.** www.carlesabellan.com/tapac24. Tapas 4€-14€. AE, DC, MC, V. Mon-Sat 8am-midnight. Metro: Passeig de Gràcia.

Sants, Paral.lel & Montjuïc
INEXPENSIVE
La Bella Napoli ITALIAN   This Poble Sec eatery underwent a paring-down facelift recently and now features stark brick walls, bare polished floorboards, and red-and-white gingham tablecloths. There's still plenty of original character in the food, which is authentic Italian from the lasagna to the tiramisu. Most people, however, come for the thin-crust pizzas, which are hauled out of a wood-fired oven, perfectly crisped and ready to go. Takeouts are available. Get here early, as it's amazingly popular.

Margarit 14. ⓒ **93-442-08-46.** www.bellanapoli.net. Reservations required. Main courses 14€-35€. AE, DC, MC, V. Daily 1:30-4pm, 8:30-midnight. Closed Aug and Christmas week. Metro: Paral.lel or Poble Sec.

La Bodegueta SPANISH   This popular bodega is typical of this working-class neighborhood. Even after its overhaul some years back, the period character remains, as does the original rose-petal-tiled floor. Owner Eva Amber is on hand to recommend her home cooking, which includes such favorites as lentils with chorizo and Catalan cannelloni. Meat *a al brasa* (grill-flamed) and *torrades* (toasted bread with charcuterie) are also on the agenda.

Blai 47. ⓒ **93-442-08-46.** www.labodeguetabcn.com. Tapas 3.50€-12€. MC, V. Mon-Fri noon-4pm, 7-10:30pm; Sat noon-4pm. Closed Aug. Metro: Poble Sec.

Quimet Quimet ★ SPANISH   This is a great tapas bar with the finest selection of cheeses in Barcelona. Built at the turn of the 20th century, the tavern in the Poble Sec sector is run by the fifth generation of Quimets, and their wine cellar is one of the best stocked of any tapas bar. If you're not watching the calories and cholesterol, try the prized four *quesos* (cheeses) on the same plate: *Nevat* (a tangy goat's cheese), *cabrales* (an intense Spanish blue cheese), *zamorano* (a hardy, nutty sheep's milk cheese), and *torta del Casar* (a soft, creamy farm cheese). Or chance the *tou dels tillers,* a cheese stuffed with trout roe and truffles. Other delights include *mejillones con confit de tomate y caviar* (mussels with tomato confit and caviar), *navajas* (razor clams), and even *esturión* (sturgeon).

Poeta Cabanyes 25. ✆ **93-442-31-42.** Tapas 3.50€–12€. MC, V. Mon–Fri noon–4pm, 7–10:30pm; Sat noon–4pm. Closed Aug. Metro: Paral.lel.

Tapioles 53 ★★★ 🔰MEDITERRANEAN   Australian chef Sarah Stothart's restaurant has only six tables, so eating here is like being in the stylish home of a friend who also happens to be a brilliant cook. Located in a former umbrella factory, the intimate and relaxed decor is by noted designer Ricardo Feriche. Chef Stothart's menus change nightly and, in my view, are the best dining deal in town. The dishes are created from fresh ingredients gathered every morning from the Santa Caterina market. Outstanding dishes include polenta with mozzarella, fresh tomatoes and basil, stuffed baby squid, and swordfish cooked in banana leaf with rice. All dishes for that day are explained to you at your table (there's no printed menu) and prepared in the open kitchen.

Carrer Tapioles 53. ✆ **93-329-22-38.** www.tapioles53.com. Reservations required. Fixed-price menu 26€–45€. MC, V. Tues–Sat 9pm–midnight. Metro: Poble Sec or Paral.lel.

BARRIO ALTO & GRÀCIA
Expensive

Botafumeiro ★★★ SEAFOOD   Although competition is strong, this classic *marisquería* consistently puts Barcelona's finest seafood on the table. Much of the allure comes from the solicitous attention of the white-jacketed staff. The restaurant is popular with international powerbrokers and also the King of Spain, and prides itself on its fresh- and saltwater fish, clams, mussels, lobster, crayfish, and scallops. There are also several varieties of crustaceans—such as *percebes* (goose barnacles)— that you may have never seen before. Stored live in holding tanks, most of the seafood is flown in daily from Galicia, homeland of owner Moncho Neira. With the 100 or so fish dishes, the menu lists only four or five meat dishes, including three kinds of steak. The wine list offers *cavas* from Catalonia and drinkable choices from Galicia, in particular the highly regarded Albariño white.

Gran de Gràcia 81. ✆ **93-218-42-30.** Reservations recommended for dining rooms. Main courses 25€–50€. AE, DC, MC, V. Daily 1pm–1am. Metro: Fontana.

Coure ★★ SPANISH   The specialty in this charming and elegant restaurant is chef/owner Albert Ventura's superb tasting menu. Be daring and try the *carpaccio de pies de cerdo,* a unique blend of pig's trotters with oysters, or the *tuna con sabor de lima y berengena ahumado* (fresh tuna flavored with lime and served with smoked eggplant/aubergine). For dessert, I recommend *helado de eucalipto* (eucalyptus ice cream).

Pasaje Marimón 20. ✆ **93-200-75-32.** Main courses 20€–35€; tasting menu 50€. V. Tues–Sat 1:30–3:30pm, 8:30–11:30pm. Closed Easter and Aug 3–10. Metro: Hospital Clínic.

El Mató de Pedralbes ★ SPANISH   *Mató* is Catalan for "cottage cheese"—in this case, prepared by nuns at the Monastery of Pedralbes (p. 193), just around the corner from this homely eating spot. Located in an old house in a relaxing residential corner of the city, it's high above the city's fumes and the hubbub of traffic, with a terrace offering fine views. It's the ideal spot for a relaxing traditional lunch. Sample Catalan dishes, from old standbys such as *truite de patata i cebra* (Spanish omelet with potatoes and onions) to more individual offerings *escudella barejada* (broth with chunks of veal) or *escargols a la llauna* (snails in oil, thyme, and garlic sauce).

Barrio Alto & Gràcia Dining

Botafumeiro **7**
Cantina Machito **9**
Coure **4**
El Mató de Pedralbes **1**
Flash-Flash Tortillería **5**
Folquer **10**
La Balsa **2**
Roig Robí **6**
Shojiro **8**
Via Veneto **3**

Bisbe Català 10. ℂ **93-204-79-62.** Main courses 15€–35€. AE, DC, MC, V. Mon–Sat 1–3:45pm, 8:30–11:45pm; Sun 1–3:45pm. Closed 15 days in Aug. Metro: Reina Elisenda.

Roig Robí ★ SEAFOOD   This restaurant—in Catalan, the name means "ruby red," the color of a perfectly aged Rioja—serves excellent food from an imaginative kitchen. Although I'm not as excited about it as I once was, it remains one of the city's most dependable choices. Order an aperitif at the L-shaped oak bar, and then head down a long corridor to a pair of flower-filled dining rooms. In warm weather, glass doors open onto a verdant walled courtyard. Seafood specialties include *bacalao a la "llauna"* (cod served with broccoli purée) and *rape y almejas con cebolla confitada* (monkfish with clams and onion confit). A mouthwatering dish is *tartare de lubina y langostinos con caviar de trucha* (sea bass and crayfish tartare with trout caviar).

Sèneca 20. ℂ **93-218-92-22.** www.roigrobi.com. Reservations required. Main courses 28€–50€; tasting menu 70€; fixed-price menu 50€. AE, DC, MC, V. Mon–Fri 1:30–4pm, 9–11:30pm; Sat 9–11:30pm. Closed Aug 8–21. Metro: Diagonal.

Shojiro ★ ASIAN   With Japanese restaurants now the norm in Barcelona, it was only a matter of time before Nippon cuisine was fused with Catalan. This quirky but brightly lit and functional-looking restaurant, led by Shojiro Ochi, a Japanese chef who arrived in Barcelona in 1979, does just that. Ochi presents his goodies in set-price four- and five-course menus. These delectable morsels include bonito (a type of tuna) preserved in a Catalan *escabeche*, tuna with a sherry reduction, or duck's breast with shiitake mushrooms. Desserts include more unconventional delights such as a foie bonbon.

Ros de Olano 11. ✆ **93-415-65-48.** Fixed-price lunch 18€; fixed-price dinner 50€. AE, DC, MC, V. Mon-Sat 1:30-3:30pm; Tues-Sat 9-11:30pm. Metro: Fontana or Joanic.

Moderate

Flash-Flash Tortillería 📷 FAST FOOD   Hamburgers, steaks, salads, and 70 types of tortillas are served up in a pop-art setting of funky black-and-white murals and white leather banquettes. Flash-Flash was opened in 1970 and the interior hasn't been altered since. The Twiggy-like model adorning the walls was the wife of Leopoldo Pomés, a well-known fashion photographer and part owner. Decor aside, the food is very good; the tortillas fly out fresh and fluffy and the bunless burgers are some of the best in town. It's a favorite with uptown business types, some of whom have been coming here since the place opened.

Granada de Penedès 25. ✆ **93-237-09-90.** Reservations recommended. Main courses 10€-28€. AE, DC, MC, V. Daily 1pm-1:30am. Metro: Diagonal. FGC: Gràcia.

Folquer 🍴 SPANISH   With its bright, sunny decor and animated local clientele, Folquer has an arty-bohemian feel. Rather secretively located at the southern end of Gràcia, it's a welcoming spot with inventive, tasty dishes using first-rate ingredients. There are two particularly good-value lunchtime menus. Regional dishes, meanwhile, dominate the a la carte list. Try the pungent *suquet de pop* (octopus stew).

Torrent de l'Olla 3. ✆ **93-217-43-95.** Main courses 16€-25€; set lunch 16€-28€; executive lunch 20€. AE, DC, MC, V. Mon-Fri 1-4pm, 9-11:30pm; Sat 9-11:30pm. Closed Sun and last 2 weeks of Aug. Metro: Diagonal or Verdaguer.

La Balsa SPANISH   Situated on the uppermost level of a circular tower, La Balsa offers a fine view over most of the surrounding cityscape. To reach it, climb to the rooftop, where you'll be greeted by owner and founder Mercedes López. Food emerges from a cramped but well-organized kitchen several floors below the dining room. The waiters are reputedly the most athletic in Barcelona, as they run up and down stairs carrying steaming platters. The restaurant serves simple but exquisite dishes such as a *judías verdes* (broad beans) with strips of salmon in lemon-flavored vinaigrette, *guiso de ternera* (stewed veal) with wild mushrooms, salad of warm lentils with anchovies, and pickled fresh salmon with chives. The restaurant is north of the city—you'll need a taxi—in Tibidabo. It's often booked out days in advance.

Infanta Isabel 4. ✆ **93-211-50-48.** www.labalsarestaurant.com. Reservations required. Main courses 12€-35€. AE, DC, MC, V. Mon-Sat 9-11:30pm; Tues-Sat 1:45-3:30pm. Aug buffet only, 9- 11:30pm. Closed Easter. Metro: Av. Tibidabo.

Via Veneto ★★★ SPANISH   Given its consistently well-prepared cuisine and overall class, this uptown restaurant mysteriously tends to fall under the radar. Not that this worries the management, who cater to regulars and visiting sports stars. The restaurant has a reputation for serving the finest *caza* (game) and fungi around, when in season. Look out for *rovellons* and *ceps,* both wild mushrooms from the Catalan forests, cooked to perfection in olive oil and rock salt. Other treats include *liebre* (hare) stuffed with foie gras and served on baked apples, and *patito* (baby duck), slow roasted and deboned at your table. The wine list is daunting as the cellar boasts over 10,000 bottles, so ask the sommelier for advice. Finish off with cheese or dessert such as chocolate mousse spiced with mixed peppers and cinnamon ice cream.

Ganduxer 10. © **93-200-72-44.** www.viavenetorestaurant.com. Reservations required. Main courses 20€–55€; tasting menu 90€. AE, DC, MC, V. Mon–Sat 8:30–11:30pm; Mon–Fri 1:15–4pm. Closed Aug 1-20. FGC: La Bonanova.

Inexpensive

Cantina Machito MEXICAN   This is considered to be the best Mexican restaurant in Barcelona. It's hard to get a table, especially when the cinema crowd from next door rolls in, but it's worth the wait. What they serve is far from the rudimentary Tex-Mex fare. The tacos and tortillas and a tangy guacamole are all present and correct, and so is a chicken *mole* (that's a hot sauce) and *sopa malpeña,* a warming soup of chickpeas, tomato, and chicken, plus an unusual lime and tequila mousse for dessert. The margaritas are renowned, as are their parties on Mexican national days and fiestas.

Torrijos 47. © **93-217-34-14.** Reservations recommended. Main courses 8€–15€; tasting menu 26€. MC, V. Daily 1–4:30pm, 7pm–12:30am. Metro: Fontana or Joanic.

BARCELONETA & VILA OLÍMPICA

Expensive

Anfiteatro ★ 📷 MEDITERRANEAN   In spite of the fashionable pedigree, it's amazing how this restaurant manages to elude so many—perhaps because it's tucked away on an underground level of a boulevard in the Olympic Village. Designed by the studio of Oriol Bohigas, the architects responsible for the Olympic Village itself, it features rationalist lines that are softened by an abundance of mosaics, and a central pond surrounded by tables. Within this setting of urban romanticism you can enjoy wild sea bass with grapes and a port sauce or cuttlefish and crab ravioli. If there is room for dessert, go for the mascarpone and vanilla ice cream with mango purée.

Parc del Port Olímpic, Av. Litoral 36 (opposite Calle Rosa Sensat). © **65-969-53-45.** www.anfiteatro-restaurante.com. Reservations recommended on weekends. Main courses 16€–38€; fixed-price lunch menu 30€; tasting menus 45€ and 60€. AE, MC, V. Tues–Sat 1:30–3:30pm, 8:30–11:15pm; Sun 1:30-3:30pm (also 8:30–11:15pm in summer). Closed Easter. Metro: Port Olímpic.

Can Costa ★ SEAFOOD   Established in the late 1930s, Can Costa is one of the oldest seafood restaurants in this seafaring city. It has two busy dining rooms, a practiced staff, and an outdoor terrace—although a warehouse blocks the view of the harbor. Fresh seafood prepared according to traditional recipes rules the menu, which includes the best *chipirones* (baby squid) in town, sautéed in a flash. A long-standing specialty is *fideuà de peix,* a relative of the classic Valencian shellfish paella, with noodles instead of rice. The yummy desserts are made fresh daily.

Passeig de Joan de Borbó 70. © **93-221-59-03.** www.cancosta.com. Reservations recommended. Main courses 16€–45€. MC, V. Daily 12:30–4pm; Thurs–Tues 8–11:30pm. Metro: Barceloneta.

EATING alfresco

Finding a terrace to sit out on in Barcelona is easier said than done. There are sidewalk cafes where you can drink your cappuccino to the roar of passing traffic, and tourist-filled plazas lined with restaurants serving microwaved paellas. But a tucked-away garden, a tranquil terrace, or a hideaway by the sea—that's another matter altogether.

The **Café de L'Acadèmia,** Calle Lledó 1 (© **93-319-82-53;** p. 125), is located on the one of the prettiest squares in Barcelona, Plaça Sant Just. It was on this square that the Romans executed the first Christians. Ghosts of the past aside, today it is one of the most peaceful and unspoiled plazas in the Old City. In the Born, the **Tèxtil Café,** Calle Mont-cada 12 (© **93-268-25-98;** p. 75), is an oasis of calm enclosed within the courtyard of an 18th-century palace. Providing you're not in a hurry (service is laid-back), it's an idyllic place in the inner city to fuel up on tea, coffee, or wholesome lunches in the shade of white parasols or the warmth of out-door gas fires in winter.

Barcelona's seafront has restaurant terraces aplenty, but for something a little more clandestine, continue along to the Parc del Port Olímpic, which straddles two busy highways. Here, sunk from view and traffic noise, is the gorgeous **Anfiteatro,** Avinguda Litoral 36 (© **65-969-53-45;** www.anfiteatro-restaurante.com; p. 151)—a smart restaurant serving creative Mediterranean dishes with a spacious terrace that wraps around an ornamental pool.

Another way to escape the crowds is to get up onto the rooftops at **La Miranda del Museu,** Museu d'Història de Catalunya, Plaça Pau Vila 3 (© **93-225-50-07**), which has fabulous views over the yachts in Port Vell. Frustratingly, the terrace is for drinks only, so go in time for an aperitif before lunch or linger over coffee afterward.

Heading further out and halfway up the hill to Montjuïc, **La Font del Gat,** Passeig Santa Madrona 28 (© **93-289-04-04**), is a secret garden and lunch spot chiseled out of the mountainside. The further out of town you go, the prettier the surroundings, and if it's real tranquillity and exclusivity you're seeking, the restaurants in the suburbs shine. In Horta, **Can Travi Nou,** Jorge Manrique, Parc de la Vall d'Hebron (© **93-428-04-34;** www.gruptravi.com), is a converted 14th-century farmhouse with sprawling grounds, two or three ample terraces, and gardens for strolling. It's great for long Sunday lunches or evenings under the stars, and serves pricey roast meats, fish dishes, and paella.

If you're looking to treat yourself, head for the **Restaurant L'Orangerie,** Gran Hotel La Florida, Carretera de Vallvidrera al Tibidabo 83–93 (© **93-259-30-00;** www.hotellaflorida.com). This fabulous spot is situated on the highest peak of the Collserola, with views over Barcelona, and its scented gardens and terraces make it one of the most spectacular dining destinations in the city.

Can Solé ★ SPANISH   Located in Barceloneta's harbor area, Can Solé still honors the traditions of this former fishing village. Many of the seafood joints here are too touristy for our tastes, but this is authentic and delivers good value. The decor is rustic and a bit raffish, with wine barrels, lots of noise, and excellent food. Begin with the sweet tiny clams or the cod cakes. *Langostinos* (king prawns) are an exquisite if expensive favorite, and everything is aromatically perfumed with fresh

Barceloneta Dining

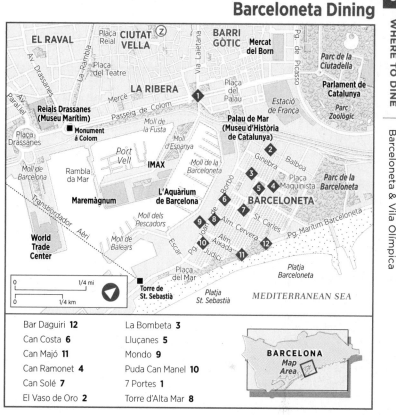

Bar Daguiri **12**	La Bombeta **3**
Can Costa **6**	Lluçanes **5**
Can Majó **11**	Mondo **9**
Can Ramonet **4**	Puda Can Manel **10**
Can Solé **7**	7 Portes **1**
El Vaso de Oro **2**	Torre d'Alta Mar **8**

BARCELONA
Map
Area

garlic. Try one of the seafood dishes such as *bacalao Serrallo* (cod with *romesco* sauce and gratinéed potatoes). Desserts are so good they're worth saving room for, especially the orange pudding or the praline ice cream.

Carrer Sant Carles 4. ✆ **93-221-50-12.** www.restaurantcansole.com. Reservations required. Main courses 12€–60€. AE, DC, MC, V. Tues–Sun 1:30–4pm; Tues–Sat 8:30–11pm. Closed 2 weeks in Aug. Metro: Barceloneta.

Els Pescadors ★★ SEAFOOD   This is acknowledged to be one of the best fish restaurants in Barcelona. The fact that it's located slightly out of the main drag, in the working-class beachside suburb of Poble Nou, should not stop you making the trip. The restaurant is divided into two *ambientes:* One is old-school—with marble tabletops and wooden beams—while the other is modern Mediterranean. But no one comes to gawk at the surroundings. The sole objective is to enjoy the freshest seafood in Barcelona, cooked in classical ways with surprising touches. Local *gambas* (prawns) are served with steaming garbanzos (chickpeas), or a baked *(al horno)* fish, such as *lubina* (sea bass) or *dorada* (bream)—whatever has been trawled that day.

Plaça Prim 1. ✆ **93-225-20-18.** www.elspescadors.com. Reservations recommended on weekends. Main courses 15€–50€. AE, DC, MC, V. Daily 1–3:45pm, 8–11:30pm. Closed Easter. Metro: Poble Nou.

Vila Olímpica Dining

Agua **2**
Anfiteatro **6**
Arola **3**
Bestial **1**
CDLC
 (Carpe Diem) **5**
Els Pescadors **7**
Talaia Mar **4**

Mondo ★ SEAFOOD   Yet another Catalan fishie haven, Mondo stands beside the sea at Port Olímpic, enjoying fabulous harbor and sea views from its terrace area. On summer nights this is one of the most evocative places to dine in the city. Top chef Ever Cubilla creates exquisite seafood dishes including fresh *percebes* (goose barnacles) and *veieras* (scallops) transported from Galicia's northwest Atlantic coast. Local Mediterranean specialties *espardenyas* (sea cucumbers in garlic and olive oil) and *gambas* (prawns) from Palamós also delight. His main-dish highlights include *paella marinera* and *lubina con ostras y lima kafir* (sea bass with oysters and lime dressing). Add to these mouthwatering *postres* such as tiramisu and *milhojas* (millefeuille pastry) created by desserts whiz David Martinez, and a list of over 100 quality wines, and you're set for an unforgettable meal under the stars. At night there's live music and dancing.

Imax Building, Moll d'Espanya, Maremagnum. ℂ **93-222-39-11.** www.mondobcn.com. Reservations required. Main courses 24€–38€. MC, V. Wed–Sun 1–4pm, 8–11pm. Metro: Drassanes.

7 Portes ★ 📷 SPANISH   Festive and elegant, 7 Portes has been around since 1836, making it one of the oldest and most prestigious restaurants in Barcelona. While these days it's more touristy than aristocratic, there is still enough authentic charm left in the decor (and patrons) to make it worth the visit. The white-aproned staff serve regional dishes, including fresh herring with onions and potatoes, daily paellas (with shellfish or rabbit), and a wide array of fresh fish, expertly fileted at the table. Order succulent oysters or an herb-laden stew of black beans with pork or white beans with sausage, which come in enormous portions. The restaurant's name means "Seven Doors," and it does indeed have seven doors, underneath charming porticoes typical of this portside pocket of Barcelona.

Passeig Isabel II 14. ✆ **93-319-30-33.** www.7portes.com. Reservations required. Main courses 18€–40€; group menus available. AE, DC, MC, V. Daily 1pm–1am. Metro: Barceloneta.

Torre d'Alta Mar MEDITERRANEAN   Alta Mar is sort of a mile-high gastro club. Its setting is the 75-m (250-feet)-high Torre de Sant Sebastián, one of the three towers that serves the port-crossing, tourist-carrying cable car (p. 189). Don't worry about rubbing shoulders with backpackers when you enter this exclusive eatery; patrons are whisked up in a private high-tech glass elevator to be greeted by a simply breathtaking 360-degree view of the city and sea. Once your jaw stops dropping and you are settled in the plush decor, dine in style from a predominantly fish menu that includes such inventions as a *merluza* (hake), porcini, and artichoke stir-fry, stewed *rape* (monkfish) in *romesco* sauce, or *rodaballo* (turbot) with pumpkin ravioli.

Passeig Don Joan Borbó Comte 88. ✆ **93-221-00-07.** www.torredealtamar.com. Reservations recommended. Main courses 22€–40€; lunch menu 70€; dinner menu 90€. Tues–Sat 1–4pm, 9–11:30pm; Sun–Mon 7:30–11:30pm. Metro: Barceloneta.

Moderate

Agua ★ MEDITERRANEAN   It bustles, it's hip, and it serves well-prepared fish and shellfish in a hyper-modern setting overlooking the Vila Olímpica beach. A terrace beckons, but if a chilly wind is blowing, retreat into the big-windowed blue-and-yellow dining room and order heaped portions of meats and fish to be grilled over an open fire. Favorite choices include *pollo* (chicken), *pez espada* (swordfish), *gambas* (prawns), and an especially succulent version of *calamares rellenos* (stuffed squid). They are served with as little culinary fanfare and as few sauces as possible, allowing the freshness and flavor of the ingredients to shine through. Risottos, some studded with fresh *almejas* (clams) and herbs, are usually winners, with vegetarian versions. The only problem here is popularity; make sure you book on the weekends.

Passeig Marítim de la Barceloneta 30. ✆ **93-225-12-72.** www.aguadeltragaluz.com. Reservations recommended. Main courses 12€–25€. AE, DC, MC, V. Daily 1–3:45pm (Sat–Sun until 4:30pm), 8–11:30pm (Fri–Sat until 12:30am). Metro: Ciutadella–Vila Olímpica.

Arola ★ SPANISH   Blessed with two Michelin stars, Catalan chef Sergi Arola is a rising star of Spain's culinary world. The setting for his first restaurant in Barcelona (the other, Sergi Arola Gastro, is in Madrid) is the luxury Hotel Arts (p. 115) in the Olympic Village. Amid a pop-art interior of purple and lime green, Arola starts off with hot or cold *picas* (nibbles) that range from artichoke hearts with garlic and parsley to *tacos de lubina* (chunks of sea bass) or *patatas bravas* arranged on the plate to look like tiny breasts. Main courses include Mediterranean standards imbued with Arola magic: *Mejillones* (mussels) with citrus juice and saffron, Gorgonzola cheese croquettes, grilled *gambas* (prawns) with potato cream, and *lubina* (sea bass) with an emulsion of watercress. The dessert of goat's cheese, macadamia nuts, tomato jelly, and quince cream will convince you of his talent.

Hotel Arts, Marina 19-21. © **93-483-80-90.** www.arola-arts.com. Reservations required. Main courses 10€-32€; tasting menu 50€. AE, DC, MC, V. Wed 1:30-3:30pm; Thurs-Fri 1:30-3:30pm, 8:30-11:30pm; Sat-Sun 2-4pm, 8:30-11pm. Month closed can vary each year, usually Jan. Metro: Ciutadella-Vila Olímpica.

Bestial ITALIAN A member of the famed Tragaluz group (p. 145), this modern Mediterranean eatery brings well-needed class to the gastronomically pedestrian Olympic Marina. The menu is an Italian-influenced alternative to the dozens of pedestrian paella restaurants in the vicinity. A typical tasty combination here is *caprese* salad of plump red tomato slices with *buffala* mozzarella, followed by seared tuna with black-olive risotto. The alfresco setting, with its spacious noise-absorbing wood decking and oversize umbrellas, is highly stylish, although the interior of the dining room has the disconcerting feel of a sci-fi bus station (a hangover, presumably, from its previous incarnation as Planet Hollywood).

Ramón Trias Fargas 30. © **93-224-04-07.** www.bestialdeltragaluz.com. Main courses 9€-24€; lunch menu 18€. AE, DC, MC, V. Mon-Fri 1-3:45pm, 8:30-11:30pm (Fri until 1am); Sat-Sun 1-4:30pm, 8pm-12:30am. Metro: Ciutadella-Vila Olímpica.

Can Majó ★★ SEAFOOD Set close to the harbor on the western edge of Barceloneta, this is one of the finest seafood restaurants in the city. In summer a terrace table here is much in demand. The interior decor, with its painting-lined walls, is in an inviting rustic-tavern style, and the staff is hospitable and friendly, although service is sometimes rushed. The restaurant is renowned for its *veieras* (scallops), *ostras* (oysters), and wide range of Mediterranean and Atlantic fish, all delivered fresh daily. Now into its fourth decade, Can Majó still serves as delicious a *bullabesa de mariscos* (shellfish bouillabaisse) as you'll find in the area. Also very good are the *calamares salteados* (sautéed squid) and *bacalao* (cod) served in a savory green sauce with baby clams in their shells.

Almirall Aixada 23. © **93-221-54-55.** www.canmajo.es. Reservations required. Main courses 14€-38€). AE, DC, MC, V. Tues-Sun 1-3:30pm; Tues-Sat 8-11:30pm. Metro: Barceloneta.

Can Ramonet ★ SEAFOOD This restaurant has been serving a large variety of fresh seafood in a Catalan-style villa near the seaport since 1763. The front room, with stand-up tables for seafood, tapas, beer, and regional wine, is often crowded. In the two dining rooms you can choose from a variety of marine dishes such as shrimp, hake, or monkfish. Other treats include pungent anchovies, grilled mushrooms, black rice, braised artichokes, tortilla with spinach and beans, and mussels "from the beach."

Carrer Maquinista 17. © **93-319-30-64.** www.elnouramonet.com. Reservations recommended. Main courses 12€-30€. DC, MC, V. Daily noon-midnight. Metro: Barceloneta. A new branch, El Nou Ramonet, with similar cuisine and service, has opened at nearby Calle Carbonell 5 (© **93-268-33-13**).

CDLC (Carpe Diem) MEDITERRANEAN Before its nightly transformation into a club for *gente guapa* (beautiful people), the beachside CDLC functions as a regular quality restaurant. The main attraction here is its sea-facing terrace rather than the food or impeccable service. Not that the cuisine, with its strong Thai and Japanese influence, is in any way unacceptable, but foodies may be suspicious when a plate of sushi can make it to your table in under 30 seconds. Perhaps better stick to the lunchtime menu, which includes reasonably priced salads, sandwiches, and burgers. The wine list includes some offerings priced to impress (you could, if money were no object, treat your date to a bottle of Cristal champagne or Saint Emilion Cheval Blanc), but a more affordable Spanish Albariño white or red Rioja usually suffices.

Passeig Marítim 32. ✆ **93-224-04-70.** www.cdlcbarcelona.com. Reservations required. Main courses 12€–30€; fixed-price lunch 20€. AE, DC, MC, V. Daily noon–1am (till 3am as a cocktail bar). Metro: Ciutadella–Vila Olímpica.

Lluçanes ★★ SEAFOOD   An alluring spot on the increasingly chic Barceloneta seafood gourmet scene, Lluçanes enjoys an enviable first-floor location inside Barceloneta market, with access to the freshest and most varied seafood in the city. There's also *paisano* (country-style) bread baked on the spot. The open-plan kitchen lets you see exactly what's going on. Talented chef Angel Pascual won the restaurant a Michelin star in 2008 for inventive dishes such as *suquet* shellfish stew; this classic Catalan dish is second to none. Some of his more adventurous offerings, including *salmonetes escabechados con vinagre de manzana frutas setas del tiempo y cebolla dulce* (soused red mullet with apple vinegar, fruit, fresh mushrooms and sweet onions!), are a whole new culinary experience. Savor this exhilarating food in a futuristic dining room of metallic gray-white. The service is a blend of efficient and informal.

Place de la Font, Mercat de la Barceloneta. ✆ **93-224-25-25.** www.restaurantllucanes.com. Main courses 32€–56€; minimalist menu 102€; tasting menu 73€; fixed-price menu 35€. AE, MC, V. Daily 1:30–3:30pm, 8:30–10:30pm. Metro: Barceloneta.

Puda Can Manel ★ SPANISH   One of the more annoying aspects of walking down Barceloneta's main boulevard is waiters trying to coax you into their overpriced outdoor restaurants. None of this goes on at Puda Can Manel as it's both a genuine local and a considerable cut above others along this touristy stretch. On Sunday afternoons you'll see people waiting patiently for a table while neighboring restaurants remain empty. They are lining up for succulent, tasty paellas and *fideuàs* (like paellas but with noodles instead of rice), rich *arroz negre* (rice cooked in squid ink), and *calamares* fried to perfection, all at excellent prices considering the standard.

Passeig Don Joan Borbó Comte 60. ✆ **93-221-50-13.** Reservations recommended. Main courses 10€–25€. AE, DC, MC, V. Tues–Sun 1–4pm, 7–11pm. Metro: Barceloneta.

Talaia Mar ★★ MEDITERRANEAN   This is the finest and most innovative restaurant at Port Olímpic, thanks to the sterling efforts of chef Javier Planes. His highly savory dishes are elegantly inventive, and his set *festival gastronómico* menu can include tuna tartare with guacamole and salmon eggs, or brochettes of lobster. Fresh fish arrives from the market daily and two of his top seafood specialties are *merluza al vapor* (steamed hake) in a balsamic reduction and *lubina a la plancha con gambas* (grilled sea bass with shrimp) flavored with asparagus juice. The increasingly rare black truffle also appears in some of his smooth and velvety risottos, and the roasted rack of lamb is excellent.

Marina 16. ✆ **93-221-90-90.** Reservations required. Main courses 19€–28€; weekday lunch menu 26€; tasting menu 55€. AE, DC, MC, V. Tues–Sun 1–4pm, 8pm–midnight. Metro: Ciutadella–Vila Olímpica.

SNACKS, TAPAS & DRINKS

Bar Daguiri CAFE   This bar-cafe with a bohemian vibe is right on the beach, an enviable location for many a restaurateur. It serves up light meals such as salads, dips, and sandwiches, plus coffee and drinks, to a reggae beat. The service can be irritatingly inept, but it's all part of the laid-back beach culture in this neck of the woods. A plus is the free Internet access—bring in your laptop and they will wire you up, and there is free live gig (mainly jazz and Latin music) on Thursday evenings. The large selection of daily foreign newspapers is also a welcome touch.

Grau i Torras 59. ℂ **93-221-51-09.** Snacks 8€–15€. MC, V. Daily 10am–midnight. Metro: Barceloneta.

El Vaso de Oro ★ SPANISH   This is a very good Barceloneta tapas bar that makes its own beer. Inside, the place is dauntingly narrow, making it a challenge not to elbow your neighbor as you raise your glass. Most people consider this part of the fun, though, as they tuck into a juicy *solomillo* (sirloin steak) served with *pimientos del padrón* (miniature green peppers), light *croquetas de jamón* (ham croquettes), or a shellfish and seafood salad. If you are on a budget, watch what you eat, as the portions here are small, and the bill adds up unexpectedly.

Balboa 7. ℂ **93-319-90-98.** Tapas 4.50€–16€. MC, V. Daily 9am–midnight. Closed 1st week in Sept. Metro: Barceloneta.

La Bombeta ★ SPANISH   A real slice of local life and one of the best tapas bars in the city, Bombeta is the modern version of a taverna. Its house specialty is *bombas,* deep-fried balls of fluffy mashed potato served with a spicy *brava* sauce. Other tapas include succulent mussels, either steamed or with a marinara sauce; giant grilled prawns; plates of paper-thin Serrano ham; and small chunks of deep-fried calamari called *rabas.* When washed down with a jug of their excellent sangria, this is a highly satisfying meal in itself.

Maquinista 3. ℂ **93-319-94-45.** Tapas 4.50€–14€. MC, V. Thurs–Tues 10am–midnight. Metro: Barceloneta.

OUT OF TOWN

Very Expensive

Can Fabes ★★★ MEDITERRANEAN   Located in a 300-year-old building in the provincial village of Sant Celoni, 52km (32 miles) north of Barcelona, this gourmet citadel is one of the greatest restaurants of Spain. Its dedicated owner, Santi Santamaría, who founded the restaurant in the 1980s, is regarded as one of the

---

📷 A Wine Taster's Haven

There are few better ways of enjoying a hedonistic afternoon of food and wine than on the street terrace of **La Vinya del Senyor,** Plaça Santa María 5 (ℂ **93-310-33-79**), where the view is dominated by the glorious Gothic facade of Santa María del Mar. The outstanding wine list includes Priorats, Riojas, and more than a dozen vintages of the legendary Vega Sicilia. In all, there are more than 300 wines and selected *cavas,* sherries, and *moscatells,* and the list is constantly rotated so you can always expect some new surprise on the *carte.* If you don't want a bottle, you'll find some two dozen wines offered by the glass, including a sublime 1994 Jané Ventura Cabernet Sauvignon. To go with your wine, tantalizing tapas are served. Tapas cost from 5€ to 10€ and credit cards are accepted. Opening hours are Tuesday through Saturday from noon to 1:30am and Sunday from noon to midnight. Metro: Jaume I or Barceloneta.

Barcelona's Vegetarian Scene

Being a "veggie" no longer means being an outsider in the Catalan capital.

You don't have to confine yourself to 100% veggie establishments to get the goods, either, as many standard Catalan eating spots offer a large choice of noncarnivorous *platos*.

Apart from the ubiquitous tortilla (made with eggs, Spanish-style, and not from cornmeal, Mexican-style), look for dishes like *escalivada* (grilled red and green pepper salad), *berengenas al horno* (eggplant/aubergine baked in the oven), *calabaza guisada* (stewed pumpkin), *setas al jerez* (mushrooms cooked in sherry), and *pisto* (Spain's answer to ratatouille—avoid the Manchego version, though, as this has ham in it). *Jamón Serrano* is not regarded as "real" meat in Spain and can appear in all sorts of dishes such as *caldo* (broth), so check with the waiter before you order.

Arabic, Indian, and Italian restaurants also serve vegetarian fare, with an inventive range of couscous, rice, and pasta-based dishes. If fish is an acceptable option, there are, of course, plenty of seafood restaurants to choose from, although these tend to be expensive.

country's key chefs, earning the place a Michelin three-star rating, the highest accolade of all, and rare in Spain. Each dish is inspired and carefully vetted. Two examples are hot-and-cold mackerel with cream of caviar and tender pigeon with duck tartare. Another heavenly concoction is spicy foie gras with Sauternes and a purée of sweet red and green peppers. Two different preparations of crayfish, each one a delight, come raw or cooked. Roast pigeon is prepared in ways that vary according to the "mood of the chef." For dessert, there's nothing finer than their "Festival of Chocolate."

Sant Joan 6 (Sant Celoni). ✆ **93-867-28-51.** www.canfabes.com. Reservations required. Main courses 30€–60€; tasting menu 140€; full menu 160€–270€. AE, DC, MC, V. Tues–Sun 1:30–3:15pm; Tues–Sat 8:30–10:30pm. Closed Jan 3–Feb 3. Take any RENFE train from the Passeig de Gràcia station, heading for France, disembarking at Sant Celoni.

Expensive

Sant Pau ★★★ SPANISH   If Picasso (who enjoyed his seafood) were around today, I bet he'd arrive at the doorstep of Carme Ruscalleda, Spain's leading female chef, who owns this fashionable eating spot in the charming Maresme resort of Sant Pol de Mar, a 45-minute drive north of Barcelona. Even some of the top chefs of France are crossing the Spanish border to sample her cuisine. Michelin grants her two stars, but I feel that she richly deserves three. Her virtuoso technique brings finesse to food and even a touch of fantasy to some of her dishes. I marvel at her ability to take the freshest of produce and add just the right spice or seasoning to maximize its flavor. Try her *raya sin cartilagos* (boneless skate) with courgettes and smoked red peppers and you'll see what all the fuss is about.

Carrer Nou 10 (Sant Pol de Mar). ✆ **93-760-06-62.** www.ruscalleda.com. Reservations required. Main courses 35€–85€. AE, DC, MC, V. Tues–Sun 1:30–3:30pm; Tues–Sat 9–11pm. Closed first 3 weeks in May and first 3 weeks in Nov. From Girona, take N-I about 55km (34 miles) south.

WHAT TO SEE & DO

For many visitors, Barcelona's most fascinating sights are in the Ciutat Vella (Old City). In the heart of the Ciutat Vella is the monument-filled Barri Gòtic, which effortlessly whisks us back across the centuries. Above this medieval world, in a sweeping arc that stretches up to the encompassing hills, is L'Eixample (Catalan for "extension"), which grew when the city was forced to expand beyond its confining city walls. It is, in contrast with the ultra-narrow lanes of the Ciutat Vella, a wide-open area of fine avenues and extraordinary 19th-century *moderniste* edifices.

But there's more to the city than an endless proliferation of buildings old and new. A welcome number of green belts soften the cityscape from Montjuïc and Tibidabo's high parklands to intimate hideaways like Ciutadella near the waterfront, which is in turn now a revitalized area of walkways, marinas, beaches, and top seafood eating spots. If sports are what you're after (p. 197), golf, horse riding, tennis, and swimming are within easy reach.

Given the complexity of Barcelona, getting around is surprisingly easy. An efficient system of subway and suburban trains and surface trams and buses will take you from one end of the city to the other for less than the price of a coffee, and bikes are increasingly used as a free means of transport (p. 11 of chapter 2, "Barcelona In Depth").

CIUTAT VELLA (OLD CITY)

The Ciutat Vella (Old City) is where the top attractions are, and if you are short of precious time, this is where you should spend most of it. The Gothic cathedral, the Roman foundations, and the earthy Raval and funky Ribera districts are all located within this large chunk of the city's landscape, which, due to its one-way and pedestrianized streets, is best visited on foot. It seems daunting at first, but striking landmarks such as the cathedral, the MACBA (Museum of Contemporary Art), and the Plaça del Rei will help you navigate around the maze. To make it easier, I have divided the attractions up into three sub-areas: The Barri Gòtic (east of La Rambla), El Raval (west of La Rambla), and La Ribera (west of Vía Laietana). For more information on these districts, see chapter 4.

Barri Gòtic ★★★

The old original Gothic quarter is Barcelona's greatest urban attraction. Most of it has survived intact from the Middle Ages. Spend at least 2 or 3 hours exploring its narrow streets and squares, which continue to form a vibrant, lively neighborhood. A nighttime stroll, when lanes and squares are atmospherically lit, takes on added drama. The buildings are austere and sober for the most part, the cathedral being the crowning achievement. Roman ruins and the vestiges of 3rd-century walls add further interest. This area is intricately detailed and filled with many attractions that are easy to miss. Follow Walking Tour 1 in chapter 8, "Strolling Around Barcelona," on p. 199, for a detailed rundown.

Catedral de Barcelona ★★★ Barcelona's cathedral is a celebrated example of Catalan Gothic architecture. Its spires can be seen from almost anywhere in the Barri Gòtic, and the large square upon which it resides, the Plaça de la Seu, is one of the neighborhood's main thoroughfares. The elevated site has always been Barcelona's center of worship: Before the present cathedral there was a Roman temple and later a mosque. Construction of the cathedral began at the end of the 13th century, under the reign of Jaume II. On the exterior of its southern transept, on the Plaça de Sant Lu, there is a portal commemorating the beginning of the work. The bishops of the time ordered a wide, single nave; 28 side chapels; and an apse with an ambulatory behind a high altar. Work was finally completed in the mid-15th century (although the west facade dates from the 19th century). The nave, cleaned and illuminated, has some splendid Gothic details.

With its large bell towers, blending of medieval and Renaissance styles, high altar, side chapels, handsomely sculptured choir, and Gothic arches, this ranks as one of the most impressive cathedrals in Spain. The most interesting chapel is the Cappella de Sant Benet, behind the altar, with its magnificent 15th-century interpretation of the crucifixion by Bernat Martorell. It is the cloister, however, that enthralls most visitors. Consisting of vaulted galleries enhanced by forged iron grilles, it is filled with orange, medlar, and palm trees; features a mossy central pond and fountain; and is (inexplicably) home to a gaggle of white geese. Underneath the well-worn slabs of its stone floor, key members of the Barri Gòtic's ancient guilds are buried. The historian Cirici called this "the loveliest oasis in Barcelona." On its northern side, the cathedral's chapter house houses the museum, where the highlight is the 15th-century *La Pietat* of Bartolomé Bermejo. Another pocket of the cathedral that is worth seeking out is the alabaster sarcophagus of Santa Eulàlia, the co-patroness of the city. The martyr, allegedly the virgin daughter of a well-to-do Barcelona family, was burned at the stake by the Roman governor for refusing to renounce her Christian beliefs. Take an elevator to the roof, where you get a wonderful view of Gothic Barcelona, but only Monday through Saturday. At noon on Sunday, you can see the *sardana*, a Catalonian folk dance, performed in front of the cathedral.

Plaça de la Seu s/n. ✆ **93-315-15-54.** www.catedralbcn.org. Free admission to cathedral; museum 1€. Elevator to roof 10:30am–1:30pm and 5–6pm; 2€. Global ticket for 1–4:30pm guided visit to museum, choir, rooftop terraces, and towers 5€. Cathedral daily 9am–1pm and 5–7pm; cloister museum daily 10am–1pm and 4–6:30pm. Metro: Jaume I or Liceu.

Barcelona Attractions

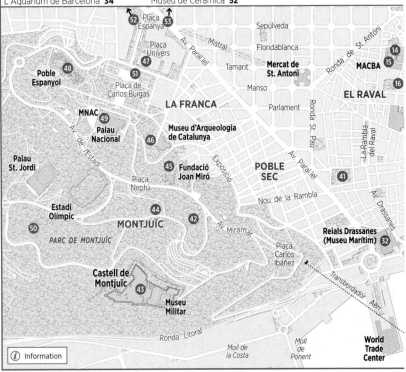

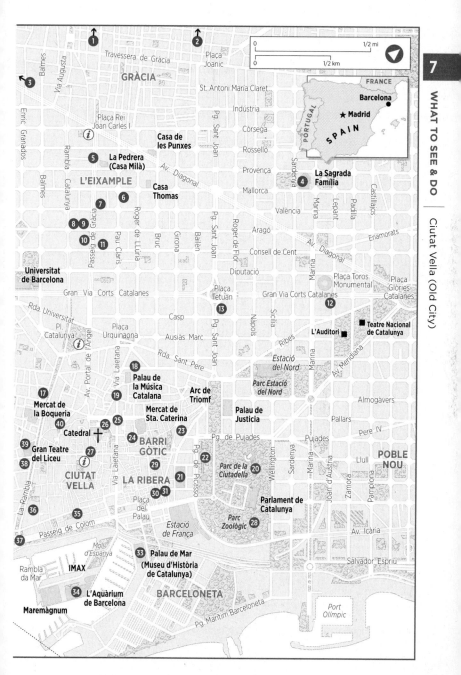

GRÀCIA

Travessera de Gràcia

Plaça Joanic

St. Antoni María Claret

Indústria

Còrsega

Rosselló

Provença

Mallorca

València

Aragó

Consell de Cent

Diputació

Gran Via Corts Catalanes

Casp

Ausiàs Marc

Plaça Tetuan

Balmes

Via Augusta

Enric Granados

Rambla Catalunya

Balmes

Plaça Rei Joan Carles I

Casa de les Punxes

La Pedrera (Casa Milà)

L'EIXAMPLE

Casa Thomas

Av. Diagonal

Passeig de Gràcia

Roger de Llúria

Pau Claris

Bruc

Girona

Bailèn

Pg. Sant Joan

Roger de Flor

Universitat de Barcelona

Pg. Sant Joan

Sardenya

La Sagrada Família

Marina

Lepant

Padilla

Castillejos

Av. Diagonal

Enamorats

Rda. Universitat

Pl. Catalunya

Plaça Urquinaona

Rda. Sant Pere

Av. Portal de l'Àngel

Via Laietana

Palau de la Música Catalana

Arc de Triomf

Mercat de la Boqueria

Catedral

Gran Teatre del Liceu

CIUTAT VELLA

Mercat de Sta. Caterina

BARRI GÒTIC

LA RIBERA

Plaça del Palau

Estació de França

La Rambla

Passeig de Colom

Moll d'Espanya

IMAX

Rambla da Mar

L'Aquàrium de Barcelona

Maremàgnum

Palau de Mar (Museu d'Història de Catalunya)

BARCELONETA

Pg. Marítim Barceloneta

Sicília

Nàpols

Ribes

Estació del Nord

Parc Estació del Nord

Palau de Justicia

Pg. de Pujades

Pg. de Picasso

Parc de la Ciutadella

Parlament de Catalunya

Parc Zoològic

Marina

Av. Meridiana

Plaça Toros Monumental

Gran Via Corts Catalanes

L'Auditori

Teatre Nacional de Catalunya

Almogàvers

Pallars

Pujades

Wellington

Sardenya

Marina

Joan d'Àustria

Zamora

Pamplona

Plaça Glòries Catalanes

Pere IV

Llull

POBLE NOU

Av. Icària

Salvador Espriu

Port Olímpic

0 ——————————— 1/2 mi

0 ——————————— 1/2 km

FRANCE

PORTUGAL

SPAIN

Barcelona

★ Madrid

Conjunt Monumental de la Plaça del Rei (Museu d'Història de la Ciutat & Palau Reial Major) ★★★ These two museums are viewed as a double act, and both reside in Plaça del Rei, which is nestled beneath a remaining section of the old city walls. Visitors enter through the Casa Clariana Padellàs, a Gothic mansion that was originally located on the nearby Carrer Mercaders and was moved here when the construction of the Vía Laietana ripped through the Barri Gòtic in the early 1930s. The ground floor is dedicated to temporary exhibitions on Iberian and Mediterranean culture, with a permanent virtual-reality display on the history of the city. The highlight, however, lies underground, underneath the Plaça del Rei itself. Excavation work carried out for the relocation of the Casa Clariana Padellàs unearthed a large section of Barcino, the old Roman city. Workers found a forum, streets, squares, family homes, shops, and even laundries and huge vats used for wine production. A clever network of walkways has been built over the relics, allowing you to fully appreciate the ebb and flow of daily life in old Barcino. Be on the lookout for a handful of beautiful mosaics, still *in situ*, from ancient Roman family homes.

The visit continues above ground in the medieval Royal Palace. The complex dates back to the 10th century, when it was the palace of the counts of Barcelona, then later became the residence of the kings of Aragón. The top step of its sweeping entrance is supposedly where King Ferdinand and Queen Isabella received Columbus after he returned from the New World in 1493. Immediately inside, the palace's chapel, the Capella de Santa Agüeda, is used for temporary exhibitions. Adjacent to the chapel is the Saló del Tinell, a massive, high-ceilinged Gothic banqueting hall and a key work of the period, featuring the largest stone arches to be found in Europe. Another palace highlight is the Mirador del Rei Martí (King Martin's Watchtower). Constructed in 1555, it is a later addition to the palace but in many ways one of its most interesting. King Martin was the last of the line of the city's count-kings, and this five-story tower was built to keep an eye on foreign invasions and peasant uprisings that often took place in the square below.

Plaça del Rei s/n. ✆ **93-315-11-11.** www.museuhistoria.bcn.cat. Admission 6€, free for children 16 and under. June–Sept Tues–Sat 10am–8pm; Oct–May Tues–Sat 10am–2pm and 4–8pm; year-round Sun 10am–3pm. Metro: Liceu or Jaume I.

La Mercè The church of La Mercè is dear to the heart of the people of Barcelona. Our Lady of Mercy (La Mercè) is the city's co-patron saint (the other is Santa Eulàlia; see below); she earned the privilege after supposedly diverting a plague of locusts in 1637. Thus, the city's main fiesta (Sept 24) is named in her honor, and

---

💬 **How the Egg Dances**

During the feast of Corpus Christi in June, a uniquely Catalan tradition can be seen in the cathedral's cloister. *L'ou com balla* (the egg that dances) consists of an empty eggshell placed on top of the fountain's spurts of water and left to "dance." Its origins go back to 1637, although its significance is disputed. Some say that the egg simply represents spring and the beginning of a new life cycle, others that its form represents the Eucharist.

BARCELONA'S patron saint: SANTA EULÀLIA

Barcelona's revered patron saint, Santa Eulàlia, was 13 years old when she died a virgin, having enraged the ruling Roman authorities by throwing sand at the altar of the Temple of Augustus after being ordered to honor it by ruthless local ruler Dacian. At the time the Roman Emperor Diocletian was persecuting Christians, so Eulàlia's act was insanely provocative. Dacian accused her parents, rich Sarrià merchants, of building up a fortune through the "sorcery" of their religion, so this was his chance to take revenge on their daughter. Her parents tried to protect Eulàlia from Dacian's wrath by retreating to their country home, but she bravely ran away to confront him in Barcelona, berating him in public for his cruelty to Christians. Her horrifically sadistic punishments included whippings; burnings with hot oil, lead, and braziers; burial in quicklime; and tearing of her flesh by hooks. After all these ordeals, which failed to shake her faith, she was paraded around the city three times on a cart. She died on the cross at Plaça San Pedro, where a monument records her martyrdom; her remains are buried in the crypt of the cathedral.

many Barcelona-born females are called Mercè (among males there is an abundance of Jordis—or George—Catalonia's patron saint).

The 18th-century church itself is the only one in the city with a baroque facade. Perched on top is a statue of the lady herself, a key feature of the city's skyline. The edifice resides on an elegant square with a central fountain of Neptune.

Plaça de la Mercè 1. ⓒ **93-315-27-56.** Free admission. Daily 10am–1pm and 6–8pm. Metro: Drassanes.

Mirador de Colón   This monument to Christopher Columbus was erected at Barcelona harbor on the occasion of the Universal Exhibition of 1888. It consists of three parts, the first being a circular structure raised by four stairways (6m/20 feet wide) and eight iron heraldic lions. On the plinth are eight bronze bas-reliefs depicting Columbus's principal feats. The originals were destroyed; these are copies. The second part is the base of the column, consisting of an eight-sided polygon, four sides of which act as buttresses; each side contains sculptures. The third part is the 50-m (164-feet)-high column, which is Corinthian in style. The capital boasts representations of Europe, Asia, Africa, and America—all linked together. Finally, over a princely crown and a hemisphere recalling the newly discovered part of the globe, is a 7.5-m (25-feet)-high bronze statue of Columbus—pointing supposedly to the New World, but in reality toward the Balearic Islands—by Rafael Ataché. Inside the iron column, a tiny elevator ascends to the *mirador*. From here, a panoramic view of Barcelona and its harbor unfolds.

Portal de la Pau s/n. ⓒ **93-302-52-24.** Admission 2.75€, 1.75€ children 4–12, free for children 3 and under. June–Sept 9am–8:30pm; Oct–May 10am–6:30pm. Metro: Drassanes.

Museu de Cera ☺   Madame Tussauds it may not be, but Barcelona's Wax Museum still has plenty of appeal. Located in a 19th-century building that used to be a bank, the winding staircase and frescoes are a fitting setting for the array of Catalan and Spanish historical and cultural personages plus Dracula, Frankenstein, and the usual suspects. Next door, the museum's cafe, El Bosc de les Fades, is fitted out "fairy-forest" style with magic mirrors, bubbling brooks, and secret doors, further adding to the fantastical experience.

Passatge de la Banca 7. ℂ **93-317-26-49.** www.museocerabcn.com. Admission 15€; 9€ children 5-11, students, and seniors. Oct-June Mon-Fri 10am-1:30pm and 4-7:30pm, Sat-Sun and holidays 11am-2pm and 4:30-8:30pm; July-Sept daily 10am-10pm. Metro: Drassanes.

Museu Frederic Marès ★★ One of the biggest repositories of medieval sculpture in the region is found in this interesting museum, situated behind the cathedral. Marès (1893–1991) was a sculptor and obsessive collector; the fruit of this passion is housed in an ancient palace with beautiful interior courtyards, chiseled stone, and soaring ceilings. He amassed a mind-boggling collection of religious sculpture and imagery. Downstairs, the pieces date from the 3rd and 4th centuries, then travel through to the fixating polychromatic crucifixes and statues of the Virgin Mary from the Romanesque and Gothic periods. Upstairs, the collection continues into the baroque and Renaissance before becoming the Museu Sentimental, a collection of everyday items and paraphernalia that illustrates life in Barcelona during the past 2 centuries. The "Entertainment Room" features toys and automatons, and the "Women's Quarter" has Victorian fans, combs, and other objects deemed for "feminine use only." Outside, the **Café d'Estiu** in the courtyard is an agreeable place to rest before moving on.

The Museum is closed for renovation work until the middle of 2011.

Plaça de Sant Iú 5-6. ℂ **93-310-58-00.** www.museumares.bcn.es. Admission 3€, free for children 15 and under. Tues-Sat 10am-7pm; Sun 10am-3pm. Free Wed 3-7pm. Metro: Jaume I.

Plaça Sant Jaume ★ The Plaça Sant Jaume is the political nerve center of Barcelona. Separated by a wide expanse of polished flagstones, the Casa de la Ciutat, home to the *ajuntament* (town hall), faces the Palau de la Generalitat, seat of Catalonia's autonomous government. The square itself frequently acts as a stage for protest gatherings, rowdy celebrations (such as when a local team wins a sporting event), and local traditions like the spectacular celebratory *castellers* (human towers) between mid-August and the end of October.

The buildings themselves are only infrequently open to the public, but if they are open when you are there, they are well worth visiting, especially the **Palau de la Generalitat** ★★. Although the governing body of Catalonia has its origins in 1283 under the reign of Pere II, it wasn't until the 15th century that it was given a permanent home. The nucleus spreads out from the **Pati de Tarongers (Courtyard of Orange Trees),** an elegant interior patio with pink Renaissance columns topped with gargoyles of historical Catalan folkloric figures.

Another highlight is the **Capella de Sant Jordi (Chapel of St. George),** which is resplendent with furnishings and objects depicting the legend of Catalonia's patron saint, whose image is a recurring theme throughout the Generalitat. The walls of the Gilded Hall are covered with 17th-century Flemish tapestries.

Across the square is the late-14th-century **Casa de la Ciutat** ★, corridor of power of the *ajuntament*. Behind its neoclassical facade is a prime example of Gothic civil architecture in the Catalan Mediterranean style. The building has a splendid courtyard and staircase. Its major architectural highlights are the 15th-century Salón de Ciento (Room of the 100 Jurors), with gigantic arches supporting a beamed ceiling, and the black-marble Salón de las Crónicas (Room of the Chronicles). The murals here were painted in 1928 by Josep María Sert, the Catalan artist who went on to decorate the Rockefeller Center in New York.

Capella de Sant Jordi: Plaça de Sant Jaume s/n. *℡* **93-402-46-17.** Free admission. 2nd and last Sun of each month, Apr 25, and Sept 24 10:30am–1:30pm. Casa de la Ciutat: Plaça de Sant Jaume s/n. *℡* **93-402-70-00.** Free admission. Sun 11am–3:30pm. Metro: Jaume I or Liceu.

Santa María del Pi   This church takes its name from the huge pine tree outside its main entrance. The church, built over a period of nearly 200 years between the early 14th and late 16th centuries, resides on one of the most charming squares (of the same name) in the Barri Gòtic. There is always something happening on this square, which merges into two other tiny plazas, whether it is an art market (Sun), a local cheese and artisan fair run by food hawkers (Thurs to Sat), street musicians strutting their stuff, or people milling around the plentiful outdoor cafes.

The church itself is a typical, if not the most complete, example of Catalan Gothic. Its wide, single nave spans nearly two-thirds of the building's length, lending

EL CALL: THE jewish QUARTER

Before the "Catholic Kings" Ferdinand and Isabella systematically set about persecuting Jewish communities in Iberia in the late 15th century, Barcelona's Jews had lived for centuries alongside Christians and enjoyed special status under the city's autonomous rule. Barcelona's Sephardic Jews flourished in the Middle Ages, reaching a population of four million people in the 13th century, 15% of the total population of the city. They were respected for their financial expertise, understanding of the law, and learned figures, including poet Ben Ruben Izahac and astronomer Abraham Xija. The community resided in the city neighborhood El Call (pronounced "kye"), reputedly from the Hebrew word *kahal*, which means "community" or "congregation." The area was bordered by old walls to the west and east, and its entrance was through the Plaça Sant Jaume. Today this tiny, ancient neighborhood is marked by atmospheric, narrow streets lined with 14th- to 16th-century buildings, some with vestiges of their former residents. The largest and most complete is the main synagogue in Calle Marlet, no. 5.

Consisting of two cellar-like rooms below street level, the space was virtually unknown, serving as a warehouse until 1995 when the building with its four floors added on top was put up for sale. It was acquired by the Asociación Call de Barcelona (see below), which embarked on a meticulous renovation.

On the same street, in the direction of the Arc de Sant Ramón, is a wall plaque dating from 1314 bearing the inscription (in Hebrew) "Holy Foundation of Rabbi Samuel Hassardi, whose life is never ending." The remains of the female Jewish public baths can be seen nearby in the basement of the pleasant Cafe Caleum at the intersection of the streets Banys Nous (which means "New Baths") and Palla. The men's baths are hidden in the rear of the furniture shop S'Olivier (Banys Nous 10); ask permission from the owner to take a peek.

Old Synagogue and Asociación Call de Barcelona: Marlet 5 (*℡* **93-317-07-90;** www.calldebarcelona.org). Free admission. Opening hours are Tuesday through Sunday 11am to 2:30pm and 4 to 7:30pm. Metro: Jaume I or Liceu.

the church its squat appearance. Above the main entrance is a gigantic rose window. Inside it's just as austere, although worth inspecting for the ingenious stone arch that has supported the structure's width for centuries.

Plaça del Pi 7. ✆ **93-318-47-43.** Free admission. Daily 9am–1pm and 4–9pm. Metro: Liceu.

La Ribera

Smaller than the Barri Gòtic, the La Ribera district boasts two major attractions: The Museu Picasso and the soaring Gothic church of Santa María del Mar. Additional smaller treasures abound in its atmospheric streets in the form of cafes, artisan workshops, and intimate boutiques. It's a wonderful place to stroll, window-shop, and grab a bite in its many outdoor cafes, and compact enough to cover in an afternoon. At night the bars and *coctelerías* open their doors and crowds roll in.

Mercat del Born   At the end of the Passeig del Born, the pretty promenade at the heart of the neighborhood, is the Mercat del Born, the city's steel-and-glass ode to the industrial age. Inspired by Les Halles in Paris, it acted as the city's wholesale market until 1973, and its closing marked the beginning of the neighborhood's decline before its current renaissance. Having lain abandoned for over 3 decades, a decision was taken in 2003 to turn the edifice into a library and cultural center. When the renovation work started, the remains of entire streets and homes from Phillipe V's demolition orders (see Parc de la Ciutadella, below) were discovered underneath. It's still in the process of being renovated at the time of writing (Sept 2010).

Carrer Comerç s/n. Interior closed to public.

Museu Barbier-Mueller d'Art Precolombí ★   Inaugurated in 1997, this museum is a smaller cousin to the museum of the same name in Geneva, which has one of the most important collections of pre-Columbian art in the world. In the restored Palacio Nadal, built during the Gothic period, the collection contains almost 6,000 pieces of tribal and ancient art. Josef Mueller (1887–1977) had acquired the first pieces by 1908; on his death his son-in-law Jean-Paul Barbier took over the running of both museums. The pre-Columbian cultures represented created religious, funerary, and ornamental objects of great stylistic variety by relatively simple means. Stone sculptures and ceramic objects are especially outstanding. For example, the Olmecs, who settled on the Gulf of Mexico at the beginning of the first millennium B.C, executed notable monumental sculptures in stone and magnificent figures in jade. Many exhibits focus on the Mayan culture, the most homogenous and widespread of its time; by 1000 B.C. their artisans had mastered painting, ceramics, and sculpture. Don't miss the work by the pottery makers of the Lower Amazon, particularly those from the island of Marajó, and the millennium-old gold adornments from northern Peru.

Carrer de Montcada 12-14. ✆ **93-310-45-16.** www.barbier-mueller.ch. Admission 3.50€, 1.70€ students, free for children 16 and under. Tues–Sat 10am–6pm; Sun 10am–3pm. Free 1st Sun of month. Metro: Jaume I.

Museu de Ciències Naturals de la Ciutadella (Geologia & Zoologia) These two museums, which can be viewed with the same ticket, reside inside the elegant Parc de la Ciutadella (see below). The most crowd-pleasing is the **Museu de Zoologia ★**, which is housed in a whimsical building designed by the *moderniste* architect Lluís Domènech i Montaner. It was created (but not finished in time) as a cafe for the 1887–88 World's Fair, which was largely centered around the park. Known at the time as the **Castell de Tres Dragons (Castle of the Three Dragons),** it is a daring example of medieval-inspired *modernisme,* with fortress-like towers featuring ceramic heraldry, *mudéjar* (mock-Arabic style) windows, and walls of exposed brick. The interior, although extremely altered, contains exhibits displayed in Victorian-style wooden and glass cabinets. Specimens include Goliath frogs, giant crabs, and a section on Catalan flora. Located in a colonnaded neoclassical structure, the setting for the **Museu Geològic** (Geological Museum) is slightly less inspiring. It was, however, the first building in the city to be constructed specifically for a museum, and it still holds the largest geology collection in the whole country. The left wing displays various granites, quartzes, and naturally radioactive rocks. The more interesting right wing is the area of fossils, with some nostalgic Jules Verne–type illustrations made in the 1950s, which depict prehistoric life.

Parc de la Ciutadella, Passeig Picasso 1. ℂ **93-319-68-95** (Museu de Geologia), ℂ **93-319-69-12** (Museu de la Zoologia). Admission (for both) 3.50€, children 16 and under free. Tues-Sat 10am-7pm; Sun 10am-3pm. Metro: Barceloneta or Arc de Triomf.

Museu de la Xocolata ★ ☺ Opened in 2000 in a former convent, this museum is an initiative from the city's chocolate and pastry makers. More like a giant, hands-on textbook, the exhibition takes you through the discovery of the cocoa bean by New World explorers, its commercialization, and chocolate as an art form. Every Easter, the museum is the venue for the annual *mona* competition. *Monas,* a Catalan invention, are elaborate chocolate sculptures, often of famous buildings, people, or cartoon characters. Chocolate makers display them in their windows during Easter Week and try to outdo each other with sheer creativity and inventiveness. Once your appetite has been whetted, you can enjoy a cup of hot chocolate or pick up some bonbons at the museum's cafe.

Antic Convent de Sant Augustí, Comerç 36. ℂ **93-268-78-78.** www.pastisseria.com. Admission 4.30€, seniors and students 15% discount, children 7 and under free. Mon-Sat 10am-7pm; Sun 10am-3pm. Metro: Jaume I or Arc de Triomf.

Museu Picasso ★★★ Five medieval mansions in a row contain a massive collection of the work of Pablo Picasso (1881–1973). The bulk of the art was donated by Jaume Sabartés y Gual, the Barcelona-born poet who was a lifelong friend of the artist. Although born in Málaga, Picasso moved to the Catalan capital in 1895 after his father was awarded a teaching job at the city's Fine Arts Academy in La Llotja. The family settled in the Calle Merce, and when Picasso was a bit older, he moved to the Nou de Les Ramblas in the Barrio Chino. Although he left Spain for good at the outbreak of the Civil War—and refused to return while Franco was in power— he was particularly fond of Barcelona, where he spent his formative years painting its seedier side and hanging around with the city's bohos. As a sign of his love for the city, and adding to Sabartés's enormous bequest, Picasso donated some 2,500 of his paintings, engravings, and drawings to the museum in 1970. All of these were executed in Picasso's youth (some were done when he was only aged nine), and the collection is particularly strong on his early Blue and Rose periods, painted before he left Barcelona for France. Many works show the artist's debt to van Gogh, El Greco, and Rembrandt.

The highlight of the collection is undoubtedly *Las Meninas,* a series of 59 inter-pretations of Velázquez's masterpiece of the same name. Another key work is *The Harlequin,* a painting clearly influenced by the time the artist spent with the Ballet Russes in Paris. It was his first bequest to Barcelona. Key works aside, many visitors are transfixed by his notebooks containing dozens of sketches of Barcelona street scenes and characters, proof of his extraordinary and often overlooked drawing tal-ents. Because the works are arranged in rough chronological order, you can get a wonderful sense of Picasso's development and watch as he discovered a trend or had a new idea, mastered it, grew bored with it, and then was off to something new. You'll learn that Picasso was a master portraitist and did many traditional representational works before his flights of fancy took off. The exhibits in the final section ("The Last Years") were donated by his widow Jacqueline and include ceramic and little-known collage work.

Montcada 15–23. ✆ **93-319-63-10.** www.museupicasso.bcn.es. Admission museum and temporary exhi-bition combined 9€, 6€ students and 25 and under, free for children 16 and under. Temporary exhibition 5.80€, 2.90€ students and those 25 and under. Tues–Sat 10am–8pm; Sun 10am–3pm. Metro: Jaume I, Liceu, or Arc de Triomf.

Museu Tèxtil i d'Indumentària   Located in the stunning Palau dels Marquesos de Lió, a Gothic mansion adjacent to the Museu Barbier-Mueller (see above), the city's textile museum is a slightly slapdash but overall interesting permanent display of fabric and lace-making techniques and costumes. The first floor covers periods from Gothic through to Regency, the latter consisting of crinoline skirts with bone-crushing bodices plus a wonderful selection of fans and opera glasses. Upstairs you find the 20th-century exhibits, which include ensembles from the Basque-born designer Cristóbel Balenciaga, Paco Rabanne, and Barcelona's own Pedro Rodríguez. Temporary exhibitions have ranged from Catalan jewelry to the outfits of Australian *enfant terrible* performer Leigh Bowery. The Tèxtil Café (p. 75) is in the courtyard and there is an above-average gift shop.

Montcada 12–14. ✆ **93-319-76-03.** Admission 5€, 3€ students and over 65s, free for children 16 and under. Tues–Sat 10am–6pm; Sun 10am–3pm. Metro: Jaume I.

Palau de la Música Catalana ★★★   Not strictly within the borders of La Ribera but north of the Calle Princesa in the La Pere district, the Palau de la Música is, for many, the most outstanding contribution of the *moderniste* movement. Declared a UNESCO World Heritage site in 1997, it was designed by Lluis Domènech i Montaner, a contemporary of Gaudí's also responsible for the magnifi-cent Hospital Sant Pau (p. 177).

In 1891 it was decided that the Orfeó Català (Catalan Choral Society) needed a permanent home. The Orfeó was a key player in *La Renaixença,* a heady political and cultural climate of renewed Catalan nationalism and artistic endeavor (with the two closely intertwined). The Orfeó, which still regularly performs at the Palau, had been touring Catalan rural areas, performing *catalanismo*-charged folk songs to much acclaim. The general opinion was that they deserved their own "Palace of Music." Domènech i Montaner obliged.

A riot of symbolism, the Palau de la Música Catalana, constructed between 1905 and 1908, is a feast for the senses. The facade features a rippling sculpture representing popular Catalan song and is crowned by an allegorical mosaic of the

Orfeó underneath, which displays busts of composers such as Bach, Beethoven, and the period's most popular composer, Wagner. The foyer, or vestibule, is linked to the street by an arcade and features dazzling columns of mosaic. It is the first-floor auditorium, however, where the excesses of *modernisme* run wild. Using the finest craftsmen of the day, Domènech i Montaner ordered almost every surface to be embellished with the most extraordinary detail. The ceiling features a stained-glass inverted dome with the auditorium's main light source, surrounded by 40 female heads, representing a choir. On the stage's rear wall are the *Muses del Palau*, a series of dainty, instrument-bearing maidens in terracotta and *trencadis* (broken mosaic collage). The *pièce de résistance* is the masterpiece proscenium that frames the stages. Executed by Pau Gargallo, on the left it features the Orfeó's director Josep Clavé bursting forth from the "Flowers of May," a tree representing a popular Catalan folk song. On the opposite side Beethoven peeks through a stampede of Wagner's Valkyries.

In 2003 local architect Oscar Tusquets completed his sensitive extension of El Palau, providing extra rehearsal space, a library, and another underground auditorium. It is worth checking their program when in town; concerts range from international orchestras and soloists to jazz and sometimes world music. Tickets for local acts are often very reasonably priced. If not, there are daily tours of the building (see below). Advance purchase for these is recommended.

Carrer de Sant Francesc de Paula 2. ☏ **93-295-72-00** for information; ☏ 902-442-882 to buy tickets. www.palaumusica.org. Tour 9€, 7.50€ students. Tickets can be bought up to 1 week in advance from the gift shop adjacent to the building. Guided tours daily, every half-hour 10am–3:30pm. Metro: Urquinaona.

Parc de la Ciutadella ★★ Barcelona's most formal park is also the one most steeped in history. The area was formerly a detested citadel (p. 16), built by Philip V after he won the War of the Spanish Succession (Barcelona was on the losing side). He ordered that the "traitorous" residential suburb be leveled. Between 1715 and 1718, over 60 streets and residences were torn down to make way for the structure, without any compensation to the owners (although many were relocated to the purpose-built neighborhood of Barceloneta). It never really functioned as a citadel, but was used as a political prison during subsequent uprisings and occupations. Once the decision to pull down the old city walls was made in 1858, the government decided that the citadel should go too (p. 16). Work on the park began in 1872, and in 1887 and 1888 the World's Fair was held on its grounds, with the nearby Arc de Triomf acting as the event's grandiose main entrance.

Today lakes, gardens, and promenades fill most of the park, which also holds a **Zoo** (see below). Gaudí contributed to the monumental Italianate fountain in the park when he was a student; the lampposts are also his. Other highlights include the Hivernacle, an elegant, English-style hothouse with an adjacent cafe, and the unusual Umbracle, a greenhouse that contains no glass but whose facades are of bare brick with wooden louvers. It's home to palm trees and tropical plants. Both these structures are on the Passeig de Picasso flank of the park. On the opposite side bordering Calle Wellington is the old arsenal, which now accommodates the parliament of Catalonia.

Entrances on the Passeig de Picasso and Passeig Pujades. Free admission. Daily sunrise–sunset. Metro: Arc de Triomf.

Parc Zoològic ★ ☺   A large chunk of the Parc de la Ciutadella is taken up with the city's well-matured zoo, whose age is softened by its attractive garden setting. Many of the enclosures are barless and the animals are kept in place via a moat. This seems humane until you realize how little running space the animals have on their "islands." Although it has its share of lions, hippos, bears, and primates, the greatest fun here for kids of all ages is provided by the dolphin show, in which these aquatically acrobatic mammals are put through their paces by enthusiastic trainers.

Parc de la Ciutadella. ⓒ **93-225-67-80.** www.zoobarcelona.com. Admission 16€, 9.50€ students, and 8.50€ seniors 65 and over and children 3-12. Open daily, summer 10am-7pm; off-season 10am-6pm; winter (Oct 26-Mar 15) 10am-5pm. Metro: Ciutadella or Arc de Triomf.

El Raval

El Raval is a neighborhood of contrasts. Here, imaginative new buildings and urban projects are continuously being created in the streets of the city's largest inner-city neighborhood. Historically working-class, the district is clearly being gentrified in many areas, while other neglected corners retain a markedly downtrodden air. For many, El Raval symbolizes progressive 21st-century Barcelona with a new multicultural blend of Catalan, Arabic, Middle Eastern, and South American cultures evident at every turn.

Centre de Cultura Contemporània de Barcelona (CCCB) ★   Adjacent to the MACBA (p. 173), the CCCB is a temporary exhibition space located in what was a 19th-century poorhouse. The building has been ingeniously adapted to its current function. The extension, built by prize-winning architects Helio Piñón and Albert Viaplana, is an impressive structure with sheer glass exterior walls supporting a large mirror that reflects the surrounding rooftops. You enter via a pretty courtyard, and there is an exterior garden that has an outside cafeteria.

Exhibitions here tend to focus on writers and the world of literature, or cultural and political movements such as Parisian surrealism. The setting is inundated in mid-June when **Sónar,** the annual dance music festival, stages its daytime events here, and other minifestivals such as alternative film and the plastic arts (p. 20) are also part of its vibrant calendar.

Montalegre 5. ⓒ **93-306-41-00.** www.cccb.org. Admission: 1 exhibition 4.50€, 3.50€ seniors and students; 2 exhibitions 6.50€, 4.50€ seniors and students; free for children 16 and under. Tues and Thurs-Fri 11am-2pm and 4-8pm; Wed (reduced rate 3.40€) and Sat 11am-8pm; Sun and holidays 11am-7pm. Metro: Plaça de Catalunya or Universitat.

Foment de les Arts i del Disseny (FAD)   FAD is the 100-year-old promotional board driving the city's active design culture, in charge of dishing out design and architecture awards and grants and promoting its artists to Spain and the rest of the world. Its headquarters, easily identifiable by the huge steel letters spelling its name outside the main entrance, are in a converted Gothic convent opposite the MACBA, and continuous exhibitions are held in the exposed brick nave. These range from the winners of their various competitions to more didactic shows—such as pirating in the design world—to everyday, utilitarian objects from around the world. Fun stuff includes the Tallers Oberts (open workshops), where artisans of the Raval show their work to the public, and *mercadillos,* where young designers sell their wares at cut prices.

Plaça dels Angels 5-6. ⓒ **93-443-75-20.** www.fadweb.org. Free admission. Mon-Sat 11am-8pm. Metro: Plaça de Catalunya or Universitat.

Gran Teatre del Liceu ★★   Barcelona's opera house, El Liceu, opened to great fanfare in 1847 and again in 2000, when a new and improved version was finished after a devastating fire had destroyed the original 6 years before. During its first life, El Liceu had been a symbol of the city's bourgeoisie, often provoking the wrath of the proletariat. (A telling note is that in 1893, an anarchist threw two bombs from a first-floor balcony into the audience, killing 22 people.) It was the principal venue for the Wagnerian craze that swept the city in the late 19th century. During its second life El Liceu consolidated its reputation as one of the finest opera houses in the world. The original design—based on La Scala in Milan—had a seating capacity of almost 4,000. The 1994 fire (started by sparks from the blowtorch of a stage worker) destroyed everything but the facade and members' room. The subsequent renovation saw the demolition of neighboring buildings for new rehearsal space and workrooms (much to the horror of neighborhood action groups, provoking a further backlash), and the auditorium returned to its former gilt, red velvet, and marble glory. Tickets to the concerts, at least the evening performances, are quite expensive, but, as with the Palau de la Música, tours of the edifice are available.

La Rambla 51-59. ✆ **93-485-99-00.** www.liceubarcelona.com. Guided tours depend on season; information available at the Espai Liceu, the theater's bookshop and cafe in the foyer. Prices vary from 20€–120€; expect to pay 40€–60€ for a good seat. Mon-Fri 8:30am-11:30pm; box office Mon-Fri 2-8pm, Sat-Sun 1 hr. before start of performance. Metro: Liceu.

Museu d'Art Contemporani de Barcelona (MACBA) ★★   A soaring white edifice in the once-shabby but rebounding Raval district, the Museum of Contemporary Art is to Barcelona what the Pompidou Center is to Paris. Designed by the American architect Richard Meier in 1995, the building is a work of art in itself, manipulating sunlight to offer brilliant, natural interior lighting. The permanent collection, which is expanding all the time, exhibits the work of modern international luminaries such as Broodthaers, Klee, Basquiat, and many others. Most of the museum, however, has been allotted to Catalan artistic movements, like the **Grup de Treball,** who were a bunch of reactionaries producing conceptual art criticizing Franco's dictatorship via enormous documents promoting independence for Catalonia. On a social level, photographs by Oriol Maspons and Leonardo Pómes illustrate Barcelona street life and the bohemians of the Gauche Divine (Divine Left) in the 1970s. **Dau al Set,** a surrealist movement led by the brilliant "visual poet" Joan Brossa, meanwhile, provokes thought and reflection through the juxtaposition of everyday items. Catalonia's most famous contemporary artists, Tàpies and Barceló, are both represented. Temporary exhibitions highlight international artists or a monographic show on a particular city or political movement. The museum has a library, a bookshop, and a cafeteria. Outside, the enormous square has become a meeting place for locals and international skateboarders who make use of the MACBA's sleek ramp, presumably with the management's blessing.

Plaça dels Angels 1. ✆ **93-412-08-10.** www.macba.cat. Museum and temporary exhibitions 8.50€, 6€ students, free for children 13 and under. Temporary exhibitions 6€, 4.50€ students. Wed 3€ for all. Mon and Wed-Fri 11am-7:30pm; Sat 10am-8pm; Sun 10am-3pm. Metro: Plaça de Catalunya or Universitat.

Palau de la Virreina   Built in the 1770s, this building was the former home of Manuel d'Amat, a wealthy viceroy who made his fortune in the Americas. Set back from the street, this grand structure is marked by typically Spanish top-heaviness. Inside there is a patio featuring columns, and a staircase to the right leads to the interior, most of which is not open to the public, as it is home to the city's cultural-events committee. On the left, a large space hosts a changing calendar of exhibitions, predominantly on aspects of Barcelona. One of the best, held in September, is the Fotomercè, amateur photographs of the previous year's Mercè festival. An excellent gift shop and cultural information point are on the ground floor.

Les Ramblas 99. ✆ **93-316-10-00.** www.bcn.cat/virreinacentredelaimatge. Admission 4€, seniors and students 2€, children 16 and under free. Tues–Sat 11am–8:30pm; Sun 11am–3pm. Metro: Plaça de Catalunya or Liceu.

Palau Güell ★★ This mansion is an important early work by Antoni Gaudí. Built between 1885 and 1889, it was the first major commission the architect received from Eusebi Güell i Bacigalupi (p. 192), the wealthy industrialist who went on to become Gaudí's lifelong friend and patron (p. 182).

A plot was chosen just off La Rambla in the lower Raval district, for its close proximity to Güell's father's residence, and Gaudí was given carte blanche. Although much of the marble for the house was supplied from Güell's own quarry, it is said that his accountants criticized the architect on more than one occasion for his free spending. Señor Güell himself, however, as much a lover of the arts as Gaudí, wished to impress his family and Barcelona's high society with an extravagant show-piece. He got his wish. Sometimes heavy-handed in detail, the work's genius lies in its layout and inspired interconnected spaces.

The facade of the building is Venetian in style and marked by two huge arched entrances protected by intricate forged iron gates and a shield of Catalonia, lending it a fortress-like appearance. The interior of the Palau Güell can only be viewed by guided tour. First you'll see the basement stables, which feature the nature-obsessed architect's signature columns with mushroom capitals; then you ascend again to view the interconnected floors. The first, the anteroom, is in fact four salons. Most of the surfaces are dark, lending the rooms a dour air, with Moorish-style detailing predominant throughout. Illumination comes in the form of an ingenious system that filters natural light via a constellation of perforated stars inlaid in a parabolic dome above the central hall. Also outstanding is the screened, street-facing gallery that sweeps the entire length of the facade, letting light into all salons except the "ladies room," where female visitors did their touch-ups before being received by Señor Güell. The ceilings of the first floor, in oak and bulletwood, are beautifully decorated with foliage, starting off as buds in the first room and in full bloom by the fourth. The dining room and the private apartments contain some original furniture, a sumptuous marble staircase, and a magnificent fireplace designed by architect Camil Oliveras, a regular collaborator with Gaudí. But visitors are usually most impressed by the roof, with its army of centurion-like, *trencadís* (mosaic)-covered chimneys. These chimneys, along with the rest of the building, were given an overhaul in the mid-1990s, and their tilework was restored; see if you can spot the one bearing a fragment of the Olympic mascot Cobi, the cartoon dog.

The palace is **closed** throughout 2010 while restoration work is completed. It is scheduled to reopen to the public in April 2011, when new entry prices and a visiting timetable will be announced.

Nou de la Rambla 3–5. ✆ **93-317-39-74.** www.palauguell.cat. Metro: Drassanes.

Sant Pau del Camp ★★ Architecture from the Romanesque period is rich in rural Catalonia and rare in the inner city. The name of this church ("Saint Paul of the Countryside") stems from the fact that it was once surrounded by green fields outside the city walls. It's the oldest church in Barcelona. Given its grand old age, Sant Pau is remarkably intact. Remains of the original 9th-century structure can be seen on the capitals and bases of the portal. The church was rebuilt in the 11th and 12th centuries and is shaped in the form of a Greek cross, with three apses. The western exterior door features a Latin inscription referring to Christ, Saint Peter, and Saint Paul. In the 14th-century chapter house is the tomb of Guífre Borrell, count of Barcelona in the early 10th century. The small cloister, however, is the highlight, with its Moorish arches and central fountain.

Sant Pau 99. ℭ **93-441-00-01.** Admission to cloister 3€. Mon–Fri 12 noon–2pm and 5–8pm. Metro: Paral.lel.

L'EIXAMPLE

Barcelona's "new town," its extension beyond the old city walls, actually contains a glorious grid of 18th- and 19th-century buildings, including the most vibrant examples of the *moderniste* movement. It is roughly divided into two areas: Dreta (right-hand), which is the southeast part of L'Eixample, and Esquerra (left-hand), meaning the northeastern side. The dividing line between the two is the Passeig de Gràcia. The famous **Quadrat d'Or (Golden Triangle),** an area bordered by the streets Bruc, Aribau, Aragó, and the Diagonal, has been named the world's greatest living museum of turn-of-the-20th-century architecture. Most of the key buildings are within these hundred-odd city blocks, including Gaudí's **La Pedrera** and the ultimate *moderniste* calling card, the **Manzana de la Discordia** (for both, see below). Many of these still serve their original use: Luxury apartments for the city's 19th-century nouveau riche. Others are office buildings and shops (the Passeig de Gràcia, the neighborhood's main boulevard, is the city's foremost shopping precinct). In case you were wondering, the marine-colored, hexagonal tiles on the footpaths are reproductions of ones used by Gaudí for La Pedrera and the Casa Batlló.

L'Eixample Dreta

La Pedrera (Casa Milà) ★★★ Commonly known as La Pedrera (The Quarry), the real name for this spectacular work of Antoni Gaudí's is the Casa Milà. The nickname stems from its stony, fortress-like appearance, much ridiculed at the time but today standing as the superlative example of *moderniste* architecture. The entire building was restored in 1996, the Espai Gaudí—a study area with maps and drawings of the building—was installed in the attic, and one of the apartments was refurbished to how it would have looked at the time of its early-20th-century residents.

The building was commissioned by Pere Milà i Camps, a rich developer who married an even richer widow. He wanted the most extravagant showpiece on the fashionable Passeig de Gràcia, so Gaudí, having just completed the Casa Batlló (see below), was the obvious choice.

La Pedrera occupies a corner block, and its sinuous, rippling facade is in sharp contrast to its neoclassical neighbors. In fact, it is unlike any piece of architecture anywhere in the world. La Pedrera seems to have been molded rather than built. Its massive, wavelike curtain walls are of Montjuïc limestone and the balconies' iron balustrades look like masses of seaweed. Inside, as outside, there is not one straight wall or right angle in the edifice, further adding to La Pedrera's cavelike appearance. (In a well-known anecdote, after French president Georges Clemenceau visited the building, he reported that in Barcelona they make caves for dragons.) The apartments (many still private homes) are centered on two courtyards whose walls are decorated with subtle, jewel-like murals. The high point of the visit (literally!) is the spectacular rooftop. It features clusters of centurion-like chimney stacks, artfully restored and residing on an undulating surface, mirroring the arches of the attic below, with outstanding views of the neighborhood, the Sagrada Família, and the port. In the summer months, jazz and flamenco concerts are held in this amazing setting. The entire first floor has been handed over as an exhibition space (past shows have included artists of the caliber of Dalí and Chillida). Admission is included in the La Pedrera entry.

Provença 261-265 (on corner of Passeig de Gràcia). ✆ **93-484-59-80** or 93-484-59-00. www. caixacatalunya.cat/obrasocial. Admission 10€, 5€ students, free for children 12 and under. Daily 10am–7:30pm; English tours Mon–Fri 6pm. Metro: Diagonal.

La Sagrada Família ★★★ 📷 Gaudí's incomplete masterpiece is one of the city's more idiosyncratic creations—if you have time to see only one Catalan landmark, you should make it this one. Begun in 1882 and incomplete at the architect's death in 1926, this incredible temple—the Church of the Holy Family—is a bizarre wonder. The languid, amorphous structure embodies the essence of Gaudí's style, often described as Art Nouveau run wild.

The Sagrada Família became Gaudí's all-encompassing obsession in the last years of his life. The commission came from the Josephines, a right-wing, highly pious faction of the Catholic Church. They were of the opinion that the decadent city needed an expiatory (atonement) temple where its inhabitants could go and do penance for their sins. Gaudí, whose view of Barcelona's supposed decadence largely coincided with that of the Josephines, was given a free hand; money was no object, nor was there a deadline to finish it. As Gaudí is known to have said, "My client [God] is in no hurry."

Dripping in symbolism, the Sagrada Família was conceived to be a "catechism in stone." The basic design followed that of a Gothic church, with transepts, aisles, and a central nave. Apart from the riot of stone carvings, it owes its grandeur to the elongated towers: Four above each of the three facades (representing the Apostles) at 100m (330 feet) high, with four more (the Evangelists) shooting up from the central section at a lofty 170m (560 feet). The words SANCTUS, SANCTUS, SANCTUS, HOSANNA IN EXCELSIUS (Holy, Holy, Holy, Glory to God in the Highest) are written on these, further embellished with colorful geometric tilework. The last tower, being built over the apse, will be higher still and dedicated to the Virgin Mary; it may be complete by 2014.

It is the two completed facades that are the biggest crowd pleasers. The oldest, and the only one to be completed while the architect was alive, is the **Nativity facade** on the Carrer Marina. So abundant in detail, upon first glance it seems like a wall of molten wax. As the name suggests, the work represents the birth of Jesus; its entire expanse is crammed with figurines of the Holy Family, flute-bearing angels, and an abundance of flora and fauna. Nature and its forms were Gaudí's passion; he spent hours studying its forms in the countryside of his native Reus, south of Barcelona, and much of his work is inspired by nature, so he added birds, mushrooms, and even a tortoise to the religious imagery on the facade. The central piece is the "Tree of Life," a Cyprus tree scattered with nesting white doves.

On the opposite side of the cathedral, the **Passion facade** is a harsh counterpart to the fluidity of the Nativity facade. It is the work of Josep M. Subirachs, a well-known Catalan sculptor whose highly stylized, elongated figures are of Christ's passion and death, from Last Supper to the crucifixion. The work, started in 1952, has been highly criticized. In the book *Barcelona,* art critic Robert Hughes called it "the most blatant mass of half-digested *moderniste* clichés to be plunked on a notable building within living memory." Despite his voice of dissent, work goes on.

In 1936 anarchists attacked the church (as they did many in the city), destroying the plans and models Gaudí had left behind. The present architects are working from photographs of these plans, aided by modern technology. The central nave is starting to take shape and the Glory facade is progressing well. It is estimated that the whole building will be completed by 2026 (the centenary of Gaudí's death), funded entirely by visitors and private donations. Another step in this direction will be the completion of the roof, hopefully due by early 2011 (at the time of writing).

Admission includes a 12-minute video on Gaudí's religious and secular works and entrance to the museum, where fascinating reconstructions of Gaudí's original models are on show.

Mallorca 401. ✆ **93-207-30-31.** www.sagradafamilia.org. Admission 12€, groups of 20 or more 10€ per person, guide/audio guide 4€, elevator to the top (about 60m/197 feet) 3€. Nov–Mar daily 9am–6pm; Apr–Sept daily 9am–8pm. Metro: Verdaguer or Sagrada Família.

L'Hospital de la Santa Creu i Sant Pau ★★★ The elegant pedestrianized boulevard of Avenida Gaudí stretches northward from the Sagrada Família, and at

🄾 GAUDÍ's resting PLACE

Before you leave the Sagrada Família, pay a visit to the crypt, Gaudí's resting place since his death in 1926. The architect spent the last days of his life on site, living a hermitlike existence in a workroom and dedicating all of his time to the project. Funds had dried up, and the *modernisme* movement had fallen out of fashion. In general, the Sagrada Família was starting to be viewed as a monumental white elephant.

In contrast to the rest of the Sagrada Família, the crypt is built in neo-Gothic style. The first part of the building to be completed, it is the work of Francesc de Villar, the architect who was originally commissioned for the project until Gaudí took over. Villar was a religious architect who studied at Madrid's prestigious Academia de San Fernando and whose important works included restoring the Barri Gòtic church of Santa María del Pi (p. 167) and building the apse in the mountaintop Monastery of Montserrat (p. 258). He quit the Sagrada Família project for unknown reasons and died in 1901. During 1936's "Tragic Week," when anarchists went on an anti-clerical rampage in the city, the crypt was ransacked. Ironically, the only artifact left intact was Gaudí's tomb.

La Manzana de la Discordia ★★★

The superlative showcase of the *moderniste* architecture is the **Manzana de la Discordia (Illa de la Discordia)**. The "Block of Discord," which is on the Passeig de Gràcia between Consell de Cent and Aragó, consists of three works by the three master architects of the movement: Josep Puig i Cadalfalch, Lluis Domènech i Montaner, and Antoni Gaudí. Although they are all quite different in style, they offer a coherent insight into the stylistic language of the period. The Casa Amatller houses the Centre del Modernismo, an information point on the *modernistes* and the movement.

the opposite end sits another key work of the *moderniste* movement, almost equal in vitality to Gaudí's. The Hospital Sant Pau (as it's more commonly known) is a remarkable work by the architect Domènech i Montaner. He is the second most important *moderniste* architect after Gaudí, and his magnificent Palau de la Música Catalana (p. 240) is one of the movement's most emblematic pieces.

The Hospital Sant Pau was commissioned by Pau Gil i Serra, a rich Catalan banker who wished to create a hospital based on the "garden city" model. While patients languished in turn-of-the-20th-century prisonlike edifices, Gil i Serra had the then-revolutionary idea of making their surroundings as agreeable as possible. He conceived a series of colored pavilions, each (like a hospital ward) serving a specific purpose, scattered among parkland. He only achieved half his vision. Although the first stone was laid in 1902, by 1911 funds ran out and only eight of the 48 projected pavilions were completed. Domènech himself died in 1930. After work subsequently carried out by his son, and economic intervention from another city medical institution, the Hospital Sant Pau was opened.

It's an inspiring place to visit (guided tours only; see below). The interiors of the pavilions are off-limits, but their gorgeous Byzantine- and Moorish-inspired facades and decoration, from gargoyles and angels to fauna and blossoming flora, greet you at every turn. The largest, the **Administrative Pavilion,** is also part of the tour. Its facade glows with mosaic murals telling the history of hospital care, and inside the building there are beautiful columns with floral capitals and a luxurious, dusty pink tiled ceiling.

Sant Antoni María Claret 167–171. ℂ **93-488-20-78.** www.santpau.es. Admission 5€, 3€ students, children 15 and under free. Guided tours daily in English 10:15am and 12:15pm. Metro: Hospital San Pau.

L'Eixample Esquerra

Casa Amatller ★★ Constructed in a cubic design with a Dutch gable, this building was created by Puig i Cadafalch in 1900 and was the first building on the Manzana de la Discordia. It stands in sharp contrast to its neighbor, the Gaudí-designed Casa Batlló (see below). The architecture of the Casa Amatller, imposed on an older structure, is a vision of ceramic, wrought iron, and sculptures. The structure combines grace notes of Flemish Gothic—especially on the finish of the facade—with elements of Catalan architecture. The gable outside is in the Flemish style. Look out for the sculptures of animals blowing glass and taking photos, both hobbies of the architect. They were executed by Eusebi Arnau, an artist much in demand by the *modernistes*. Check out the building's Centre de Modernisme (see below) for information on the whole *moderniste* scene.

Passeig de Gràcia 41. *𝄞* **93-487-72-17.** www.amatller.com. Admission 5€. Ground floor open to public Mon–Sat 10am–7pm; guided tours Mon–Fri noon. Metro: Passeig de Gràcia.

Casa Batlló ★★★   Next door to the Casa Amatller, Casa Batlló was designed by Gaudí in 1905 and is hands-down the superior of the three works in the *manzana*. Using sensuous curves in iron and stone and glittering, luminous *trencadís* (collage of broken tiles and ceramic) on the facade, the Casa Batlló is widely thought to represent the legend of Saint George (the patron saint of Catalonia) and his dragon. The balconies are protected by imposing skull-like formations and supported by vertebrae-like columns representing the dragon's victims, while the spectacular roof is the dragon's humped and glossy scaled back. Saint George can be seen in the turret, his lance crowned by a cross. Although the admission price may seem steep compared to many other Gaudí attractions, the interior of the building is just as extravagantly spectacular as the exterior, with sinuous staircases, flowing wood paneling, and a stained-glass gallery supported by yet more bone-like columns. Custom-made Gaudí-designed furniture is scattered throughout. Gaudí was strongly influenced by medieval French architect Viollet-le-Duc, who tried to design chairs and benches to fit the human anatomy (an early form of ergonomics?). His own furnishings were mainly constructed from wood or iron, with leather or velvet touches. The benches and upright chairs you see in Casa Batlló are functional, however, compared to his flamboyant chaise-longues and dressing tables in Palau Güell (which should be open to the public by 2011).

Passeig de Gràcia 43. *𝄞* **93-488-06-66.** www.casabatllo.cat. Admission 17.80€, 14€ and students, free for children of 7 and under. Mon–Sun 9am–8pm. Metro: Passeig de Gràcia.

Casa Lleó Morera ★★   The last building of the trio, on the corner of Carrer del Consell de Cent, is the Casa Lleó Morera. This florid work, completed by Domènech

THE *MODERNISTE* walk

As most of Barcelona's *moderniste* legacy is in the Eixample neighborhood, it makes sense to see it on foot. The **Centre del Modernisme** at the Casa Amatller, Passeig de Gràcia 41 (*𝄞* **93-488-01-39;** Mon–Sat 10am–7pm, Sun 10am–2pm; Metro: Gràcia), is a one-stop information point on the movement. They have devised the "modernism route," a tour of the city's 100 most emblematic Art Nouveau buildings. You can either pick up a free map or buy a well-produced, explanatory book (14€), which includes a book of coupons offering discounts of between 15% and 50% on attractions that charge

admission, such as Gaudí's Casa Batlló and La Pedrera.

If you wish to explore *modernisme* beyond the boundaries of Barcelona, the center supplies information on towns such as Reus (Gaudí's birthplace) and Terrassa, which has an important collection of *moderniste* industrial buildings. Tours are also offered. (See our recommended Walking Tour 4 in chapter 8, "Strolling Around Barcelona," p. 212.)

The Centre del Modernisme also has branches at the Hospital Sant Pau and the Finca Güell in Pedralbes.

7

WHAT TO SEE & DO

L'Eixample

i Montaner in 1906, is perhaps the least challenging of the three, as it represents a more international style of Art Nouveau. One of its quirkier features is the tiered wedding-cake-type turret and abundance of ornamentation: Comb the facade for a light bulb and telephone (both inventions of the period) and a lion and mulberry bush (after the owner's name: In Catalan, lion is *lleó,* and mulberry is *morera*). Tragically, the ground floor has been mutilated by its tenant, who stripped the lower facade of its detail and installed plate glass. The shop's interior, which fared no better, is the only part of the building open to the public.

Passeig de Gràcia 35. www.gaudiallgaudi.com/EA101.htm. Metro: Passeig de Gràcia.

Fundació Antoni Tàpies ★   This is the third most popular Barcelona museum, after the Miró and Picasso, to be devoted to the work of a single, prolific artist. In 1984 the Catalan artist Antoni Tàpies set up a foundation bearing his name, and the city of Barcelona donated an ideal site: The old Montaner i Simon publishing house. One of the city's landmark buildings, the brick-and-iron structure was built between 1881 and 1884 by that important exponent of Catalan *moderniste* architecture, Lluis Domènech i Montaner, also perpetrator of the Casa Lleó Morera around the corner (see above). The core of the museum is a collection of works by Tàpies (mostly contributed by the artist) covering stages of his career as it evolved into abstract expressionism. Here, you can see the entire spectrum of media in which he worked: painting, assemblage, sculpture, drawing, and ceramics. The largest of the works is on top of the building: A controversial gigantic sculpture, *Cloud and Chair,* made from 2,700m (8,900 feet) of metal wiring and tubing. The lower floor is used for temporary exhibitions, nearly always on contemporary art and photography, and the upper floor has a library with an extremely impressive section on Oriental art, one of the artist's inspirations.

Aragó 255. ℂ **93-487-03-15.** www.fundaciotapies.org. Admission 5€, 2.50€ students, free for children 16 and under. Tues–Sun 10am–8pm. Metro: Passeig de Gràcia.

Fundación Francisco Godia ★ 📷   In 2008, the museum moved to its new location in the heart of L'Eixample. This intriguing museum showcases the famous art collection of Francisco Godia Sales, the Catalan art lover and entrepreneur. It's one of the greatest displays in the country. Godia (1921–90) combined a desire for art with a head for business and a passion for motor racing. When he wasn't driving fast ("the most wonderful thing in the world"), he was amassing his collection. In gathering these treasures he showed exquisite taste and great sensitivity.

He collected a splendid array of medieval sculptures and ceramics but showed a keener instinct for purchasing great paintings. Godia acquired works by some of the most important Spanish and Catalan artists of the 20th century, including Julio González, María Blanchard, Joan Ponç, Antoni Tàpies, and Manolo Hugué, the latter a great friend of Picasso. From its earliest stages, Godia realized the artistic importance of Catalan *modernisme* and collected works by sculptors like Josep Llimona and celebrated *moderniste* painters Santiago Rusiñol and Ramón Casas. Godia also dipped deeper into the past, acquiring works of two of the most important artists of the 17th century, Jacob van Ruysdael and Luca Giordano, among others.

Diputació 250. ℂ **93-272-31-80.** www.fundacionfgodia.org. Admission 5€, 2.50€ students and seniors, free for children 5 and under. Wed–Mon 10am–8pm. Metro: Passeig de Gràcia.

Museu Egipci de Barcelona Spain's only museum dedicated to Egyptology contains more than 250 pieces from the personal collection of founder Jordi Clos (owner of the Hotel Claris). On display are sarcophagi, jewelry, hieroglyphics, sculptures, and artwork. Exhibits focus on ancient Egyptians' everyday life, including education, social customs, religion, and food. The museum has its own lab for restorations. A library with more than 3,000 works is open to the public.

Valencia 284. ℂ **93-488-01-88.** www.museuegipci.com. Admission 11€, 8€ students, children 5 and under free. Mon–Sat 10am–8pm; Sun 10am–2pm. Guided tours Sat. Metro: Passeig de Gràcia.

GRÀCIA

Located above the Diagonal and L'Eixample Esquerra, Gràcia is a large neighborhood, full of character and once a separate town from Barcelona. Although notable attractions here are not abundant, Gràcia is well worth visiting for a taste of authentic *barri* life. Shopping and cafe society are particularly good around the Calle Verdi and Plaça del Sol, and nocturnal activity here is lively, particularly in the summer at the famous **Fiesta Major de Gràcia.** Gràcia boasts a unique mixture of proud locals who have lived here all their lives and young, progressive urbanites. This melting pot is reflected in its street life.

Casa Vicens ★★ Although this early work of Gaudí's can only be viewed from the outside, the exuberance of its facade and form makes the trip well worth it. The architect accepted the commission for a summer residence from the tile manufacturer Manuel Vicens i Montaner in 1883, making the Casa Vicens one of the first examples of Art Nouveau not only in Barcelona but in the whole of Europe.

Since the house was designed to be an exponent of Señor Vicens's business, the entire facade is covered with florid, vividly colored tiles. At the time, Gaudí was deeply influenced by North African and Middle Eastern architecture, and this can be seen in the building's form. Its overall opulence and exoticism, with minarets and corbels, is reminiscent of the Indian Raj style. Inside, Ottoman, Koranic, and Andalucian influences can also be seen in eccentric touches such as the Turkish-style smoking room. The residence, on a narrow Gràcian street, is owned by descendants of Vicens and still a private home (although they seem to have no objections to camera-flashing tourists). The interior, however, has been well photographed and is always featured in books on the architect.

Carrer de les Carolines 18–24. No entry. www.gaudiallgaudi.com/EA004.htm. Metro: Fontana.

Parc Güell ★★★ After the abundant religious symbolism of the Sagrada Família and the heavy-handedness of the Palau Güell, Gaudí's whimsical Parc Güell often seems like light relief and is for many his best-loved and most accessible work. Although it's now officially a public park, in 1900 the Parc Güell began as a real estate venture for a friend, the well-known Catalan industrialist Count Eusebi Güell (see box below), who planned to make this a model garden-city community of 60 dwellings with its own market and church. It was never completed, and the city took over the property in 1926.

Spread over several acres of woodland high above central Barcelona, with wonderful views at every turn, the Parc Güell is one of the most unusual manmade landscapes on the planet. It is abundant with the architect's unique vision and expertise at finding creative solutions posed by the demands of the project.

Arriving at the main entrance in the Carrer d'Olot, you are greeted by two ginger-bread-style gatehouses. At the time they were built, Gaudí was working on some set designs for the opera *Hansel and Gretel* at the Liceu Opera House, so it is presumed that the inspiration for these whimsical structures came from that. Both shimmer with broken mosaic collage and are topped with chimneys in the shape of wild and toxic mushrooms. Much has been made of the Parc Güell's symbolism, and it has even been suggested that these toadstool chimneys reflect Gaudí's penchant for hallucinogenic substances. The fact is that mushroom gathering is a national pastime, and the work, as in most of Gaudí's cache, reflects a deep-rooted nationalism and respect for nature and Catalonia's history.

The main steps to the **Sala Hipóstila (marketplace)** feature a spectacular tiled lizard, the park's centerpiece. The covered would-be market supports a large platform with 86 Doric columns connected by shallow vaults. This pagan-looking space is thought to be inspired by Barcelona's Roman foundations (p. 21). The roof is embellished with four sun-shaped disks representing the seasons. In the elevated square above the marketplace, a sinuous bench, said to be the longest in the world, snakes its way around the perimeter. The decoration on this elaborate piece was carried out by architect and craftsman Josep Marià Jujol between 1911 and 1913. The story goes that the workers on the park were ordered to bring Jujol all the shards of broken crockery and glass they could lay their hands on, which accounts for the work's extraordinary mixture of colors and textures. Palm trees and vistas of the skyline add to the moment.

Three kilometers (2 miles) of rustic-inspired paths and porticoes using stone and earth quarried on site weave through the rest of the park, which is filled with Mediterranean vegetation. In typical Gaudí style, sculptures and figurines pop up in the most surprising places. Worth hunting out is the **Closed Chapel** at the highest point, a six-lobed structure crowned by a cross that may have taken inspiration from the ancient stone watchtowers common in the Balearic Islands.

Gaudí's Patron

Eusebi Güell i Bacigalupi, the man who launched Gaudí's career and became a lifelong friend, was a product of Barcelona's new, wealthy elite. He studied art, poetry, and theology in Paris and London and, upon returning to Barcelona, put his business sense into practice in the shipping, banking, railroad, and textile sectors—all the industries that drove Catalonia's industrial revolution in the late 1800s.

Enormously well respected, Güell was high-minded and took civic duty extremely seriously. He felt bound to improve the lives of his city's inhabitants (of all classes) through art and better working conditions. It seems Güell's first meeting with Gaudí was in the carpentry workshop Gaudí had designed as a showcase for a Barcelona glove shop, and shortly afterward Güell saw the work displayed at the 1878 International Exhibition in Paris. The fruit of the relationship materialized in such marvels as the Parc Güell, the Palau Güell, and the church for the ambitious Colònia Güell in outer Barcelona. Just before his death in 1918, Güell was made a count by King Alfonso XIII.

Only two houses were ever built in the colony, neither of them by Gaudí. One was designed by architect Ramón Berenguer and became Gaudí's residence in the latter part of his life. It is now the **Casa Museu Gaudí,** Carrer del Carmel 28 (© **93-219-38-11**), and contains furniture designed by the architect, drawings, and other personal effects, arranged as they were when the reclusive architect lived there.

Carrer d'Olot, Carretera del Carmel. © **93-413-24-00**. www.gaudiallgaudi.com/AA010.htm. Admission to park free. Open daily Nov–Feb 10am–6pm; Mar and Oct 10am–7pm; Apr and Sept 10am–8pm; May–Aug 10am–9pm. Admission to Casa Museu 4.50€, concessions 3€. Open Oct–Mar 10am–5:45pm; Apr–Sept 10am–7:45pm. Metro: Lesseps (then a 15-min walk). Bus: 24 or 25.

MONTJUÏC

For many visitors, and certainly those who arrive by sea, the mountain of Montjuïc is their first glimpse of Barcelona. Jutting out over the port on one side and facing the monumental Plaça Espanya on the other, Montjuïc is strategically placed as a pleasure ground, and a fortunate lack of a constant water source has deterred residential development. Instead it became the focal point of two of the city's key international events: The World's Fair of 1929, of which many structures still remain, and the 1992 Olympic Games.

The largest "green zone" in the city, Montjuïc's forests and parks have always been popular with joggers, cyclists, and strollers. In recent years the city council embarked on a project to spruce these up, install walkways and connecting escalators, and reclaim some forgotten gems in the process. One of these is the **Font del Gat,** Passeig Santa Madrona 28 (© **93-289-04-04**), a once-fashionable cafe built by *moderniste* architect Josep Puig i Cadafalch, which now acts as a Montjuïc information point and restaurant. Top-flight hillside museums such as the Fundacío Miró and the Museu Nacional d'Art de Catalunya (MNAC) are further good reasons to leave the bustle of the city behind and take the rewarding climb up here.

CaixaForum ★★ This is one of the city's more exciting contemporary art spaces, in terms of both its setting and what's inside. Opened in 2002 in the Casaramona, an old *moderniste* textile factory designed by Puig i Cadalfach that was used as police barracks in the 1930s, the vibrant edifice features a red-brick facade and singular turret, to which the Japanese architect Arata Isozaki added a daring walkway, courtyard, and entrance. Inside, after passing the huge abstract mural by Sol Lewitt, the elevator whisks you up to three exhibition spaces connected by exterior halls. These change constantly, meaning that three very diverse shows can be viewed at the same time. Traditional past exhibitions have ranged from Rodin's sculptures to Turner's Venice.

A leading exhibition on until spring 2011 covers a 25-year retrospective of work by Mallorcan expressionist artist Miquel Barceló, who died in 2009. He produced a variety of ceramics, sculptures, oil paintings, watercolors, and sketches based on his worldwide travel experiences. Cuban artist Jorge Pardo created the baroque setting for minimalist pieces from the CaixaForum's permanent collection. The foundation puts on a lively calendar of events and performances, the latter focusing on world music and modern dance. There is an excellent bookshop in the foyer, open daily from 10am to 8:30pm (10pm on Sat). Isozaki is also responsible for the Palau Sant Jordi, a major music and meeting venue further up the hill of Montjuïc. Built for the 1992 Olympics, it's a sprawling, metal-domed structure that hosts sporting events from basketball to tennis (including the 2009 Davis Cup) as well as big-scale pop concerts by the likes of Bruce Springsteen and Madonna.

Av. Marquès de Comillas 6-8. ⓒ **93-476-86-00.** www.obrasocial.lacaixa.es. Free admission. Tues–Sun 10am–8pm. Metro: Espanya. FGC: Espanya.

Fundació Joan Miró ★★★   Born in Mallorca in 1893, Joan Miró was one of Spain's greatest artists and, along with Tàpies (p. 180), the undisputed master of contemporary Catalan art. His work is known for its whimsical abstract forms, brilliant colors, and surrealism. Some 10,000 works, including paintings, graphics, and sculptures, are collected here. Constructed in the early 1970s, the building was designed by Catalan architect Josep Lluis Sert, a close friend of Miró's, who also designed the artist's workroom in Mallorca. Set in the parkland of Montjuïc, the museum consists of a series of white, rationalist-style galleries with terracotta floors. *Claraboias* (skylights) ensure that the space is bathed in natural light. Its hilltop setting affords some wonderful views of Barcelona, especially from the rooftop terrace that also serves as a sculpture garden.

The collection, donated by the artist himself, is so huge that only a portion of it can be shown at any one time. There is a gallery for temporary exhibitions, usually focusing on an aspect of Miró's work or a contemporary artist or movement. Concerts are held in the gardens in the summer months.

The first gallery holds two of the collection's treasures: The magnificent 1979 **Foundation Tapestry,** which Miró executed especially for the space, and the extraordinary **Mercury Fountain,** a work by his friend, the American sculptor Alexander Calder. In contrast to Miró's painting, which was nearly always carried out in a primary-color palette, there is a huge collection of drawings from his days as a student. Even as a young man, you can see his deep sense of national identity and Catalanism, which led to his extreme revulsion at the Civil War. The key work representing this sentiment is the powerful *Man and Woman in Front of a Pile of Excrement* (1935) in the Pilar Juncosa Gallery (Pilar was his wife), one of the "Wild Paintings." Much of Miró's work, however, is dreamlike and uplifting, with the sun, moon, and other celestial bodies represented again and again. Note the poetic *The Gold of the Azure* (1967) in the same gallery, a transfixing blue cloud on a golden background with dots and strokes for the planets and stars.

Even if you are already familiar with Miró's work, the excellent commentary provided via the audio guide (available at the ticket office) will supply you with special insight into this fascinating artist.

Parc de Montjuïc s/n. ⓒ **93-443-94-70.** www.fundaciomiro-bcn.org. Admission all exhibitions 8.50€, 6€ students, free for children 14 and under; temporary exhibitions 4€ adults, 3€ students. July–Sept Tues–Wed and Fri–Sat 10am–8pm; Oct–June Tues–Wed and Fri–Sat 10am–7pm; year-round Thurs 10am–9:30pm and Sun 10am–2:30pm. Bus: 50 or 55 at Plaça Espanya or 55. Funicular de Montjuïc.

Jardí Botànic ★   Just behind the Castell de Montjuïc, the city's Botanical Garden opened in 1999 and has steadily gathered international praise for its cutting-edge landscaping and concept. The foliage focuses on species of plants, flowers, and trees that flourish in a Mediterranean climate (all are clearly labeled in Latin, Catalan, Spanish, and English), and come from such far-flung destinations as Australia and California. The park is divided into sections representing each of these regions. The sci-fi telecommunications aerial you see a short distance away was designed by the Valencia-born architect Santiago Calatrava for the Olympic Games. This ingenious structure has a base decorated with broken tiles (a homage to Gaudí, one of the architect's main influences), and its position, leaning at the same angle as the hill's inclination, means that it also acts as a sundial.

Doctor Font i Quer s/n, Parque de Montjuïc. ✆ **93-426-49-35.** www.jardibotanic.bcn.cat. Admission 4€, 2€ students 25 and under, children 15 and under free. Open Nov–Jan 10am–5pm daily; Feb–Mar and Oct 10am–6pm daily; Apr–May and Sept 10am–7pm daily; June–Aug 10am–8pm daily. Transbordador Aeri (cable car; p. 189) from Barceloneta to Montjuïc, then an uphill walk. Bus: PM (Parc Montjuïc) departs from Plaça Espanya 8am–9:20pm Sat–Sun and public holidays. Metro: Paral.lel, then funicular (tram) 9am–8pm (until 10pm July–Sept).

Museu d'Arqueologia de Catalunya ★

The Archaeological Museum occupies the former Palace of Graphic Arts, which was built for the 1929 World's Fair. It has been attractively restored, with some rooms retaining their Art Deco flavor. The artifacts, which are arranged chronologically, reflect the long history of this Mediterranean port city and surrounding province, beginning with prehistoric Iberian artifacts. The collection includes articles from the Greek, Roman, and Carthaginian periods. Some of the more interesting relics were excavated in the ancient Greco-Roman city of Empúries (p. 294) in northern Catalonia. The Greeks in particular developed a strategic trading post here with other Mediterranean peoples, and the vessels, urns, and other everyday implements they left behind make fascinating viewing.

Undoubtedly the high point of this collection is the Roman artifacts. The Romans, using Empúries as their entry point, began their conquest of Iberia in 218 B.C., and the glassware, lamps, grooming aids, and utensils here are truly outstanding. The mosaics, many of them amazingly intact, have been laid into the floor, and visitors are invited to walk over them.

Passeig de Santa Madrona 39–41, Parc de Montjuïc. ✆ **93-424-65-77.** www.mac.cat. Admission 4€, 2.50€ students, free for children 16 and under. Tues–Sat 9:30am–7pm; Sun 10am–2:30pm. Metro: Espanya.

Museu Militar de Montjuïc ★

Although the collection at the city's museum is interesting enough, most people head up here for the views. Perched on the seafacing side of Montjuïc, this fortress (Castell de Montjuïc) dates back to 1640 and was rebuilt and extended during the mid-1800s. Its gloomy cells served as a military prison during the Civil War, earning it an indifferent, if not hostile, reputation among the people of Barcelona. While there have been noises from the local government about changing the focus of the museum to a more peaceful and reflective tone, it remains pretty much the same as when it was opened, shortly after the army moved out in 1960.

The collection itself contains the usual assortment of paintings marking military events and dozens of rooms of armor, uniforms, weapons, and the instruments of war. One of the more entertaining exhibits (Room 8) contains thousands of miniature figures forming a Spanish army division, which first went on show during the 1929 World's Fair.

The terraces and highest points of the star-shaped fortress-castle, and the walkways that surround it, offer some breathtaking views of the Barcelona skyline and the Mediterranean. If you don't mind an uphill stroll, the most spectacular way to get here is via the port-crossing cable car (see below). On the walk from the drop-off point, you will pass the famous statue of *La Sardana* by Josep Cañas, featuring the traditional Catalan dance that makes its appearance on so many postcards of Barcelona. Otherwise, grab the funicular from Paral.lel Metro station, which drops you off pretty much at the door.

Parc de Montjuïc s/n. ℂ **93-329-86-13.** Admission museum and castle 3€, castle and grounds 1.50€, free for children 7 and under. Nov–mid-Mar Tues–Sun 9:30am–5:30pm; mid-Mar–Oct Tues–Sun 9:30am–8pm. Transbordador Aeri (cable car; p. 189) from Barceloneta to Montjuïc, then uphill walk. Bus: PM (Parc Montjuïc); departs from Plaça Espanya Sat–Sun and public holidays 8am–9:20pm. Metro: Paral.lel, then funicular (tram) to top 9am–8pm (July–Sept until 10pm).

Museu Nacional d'Art de Catalunya (MNAC) ★★★ This museum is the major depository of Catalan art. Although its mammoth collection also covers the Gothic period and the 19th and 20th centuries, the MNAC is perhaps the most important center for Romanesque art in the world. The majority of the sculptures, icons, and frescoes were taken from dilapidated churches in the Pyrénées, restored, and mounted as they would have originally appeared in expertly reproduced domes and apses. Larger works are shown with a photograph of the church and a map pointing out its location, drawing you further into this fascinating and largely under-exposed 11th- to 13th-century movement. Simplistic yet mesmerizing, Romanesque art is marked by elongated forms, vivid colors, and expressiveness. Most outstanding is the **Apse of Santa María de Taüll** in Ambit V (Gallery V), with a serene, doe-eyed Christ surrounded by the apostles. Lapis lazuli was used to create the intense blue in the piece. Also look out for a series of ceiling paintings from an Aragónese chapter house in Ambit XI, echoing Tudor miniature painting. The entire collection is in chronological order, giving the viewer a tour of Romanesque art from its beginnings to the more advanced late Romanesque and early Gothic eras.

Sensory overload notwithstanding, the next section deals with the Gothic period, made up of pieces from the 13th to 15th centuries. All styles that were adopted in Catalonia are represented: Italianate Gothic, Flemish Gothic, and a more linear, local Gothic style. Look out for *retablos* by Jaume Huguet (Ambit XIII). The primary artist in the Catalan school, Huguet mixed Flemish and Italian influences with local Romanesque conventions. The Gothic collection also holds some Barcelonese Gothic Quarter artifacts such as giant signs made for an illiterate population that hung outside workshops (shoes, scissors, and such) and other decorative pieces. Among the Spanish, Italian, and Flemish Renaissance and baroque art is the Francesc Cambó Bequest, donated by the Catalan businessman, which contains glorious 14th- to 19th-century paintings including works by Cranach, Rubens, El Greco, and Goya.

Thanks to the MNAC's most recent acquisitions—19th- and 20th-century decorative art and painting, most stemming from the city's all-important *moderniste* movement—the collection now spans a millennium. While *moderniste* architecture in the city is abundant, the interiors of most buildings have been stripped bare of their mirrors, chandeliers, sculptures, and furnishings. Many of these were designed by the architects themselves. Until mid-2004 they were on display at the Museu d'Art Modern in the Parc de la Ciutadella. At the MNAC, they have a stunning new home.

Highlights of this collection, which spans the neoclassical, Art Nouveau (or *moderniste*), and subsequent *nou-centista* (or *fin-de-siècle*) movements, are numerous. Highlights include marquetry pieces by master *moderniste* carpenter Gaspar Homar and the Rodin-influenced sculptor Josep Clara. The superb private oratory by Joan Busquets will leave you breathless at the Art Nouveau movement's excesses and craftsmanship. There are also many pieces taken from the interiors of homes of the Manzana de la Discordia (p. 178).

A whole floor of MNAC is devoted to the Carmen Thyssen-Bornemisza Collection, previously kept in the Pedralbes Monastery (p. 193). This comprises more than 350 works of art from the Gothic period (13th–15th centuries) to rococo (16th–18th centuries), and includes key Italian paintings such as Fra Angelica's serene medieval *Madonna* and baroque landscape artist Giovanni Romanelli's *Return from the Flight into Egypt*.

Palau Nacional, Parc de Montjuïc. ☎ **93-622-03-60.** www.mnac.cat. Admission for combined permanent and temporary exhibits 8.50€ (valid for 2 days), 6€ students and youths 7-21, free for children 7 and under. Tues–Sat 10am-7pm; Sun 10am-2:30pm. Metro: Espanya.

Museu Olímpic i de l'Esport   One of the few museums in Europe devoted entirely to sports, the Museu Olímpic opened in 2007 opposite the Olympic Stadium. In addition to displaying the photos, costumes, and memorabilia contained in the former Galería Olímpica celebrating the 1992 games, the museum has added ceremonial costumes and personal memorabilia, such as soccer player Ronaldinho's boots. There are conference facilities, an auditorium, video recordings of athletic events, and archives. Most fun is pitting your skills against the top athletes in the hands-on interactive displays.

Av. Estadi. ☎ **93-292-53-79.** www.museuolimpicbcn.cat. Admission 4.50€, 2.50€ students, children 14 and under and seniors 65 and over free. Apr-Sept Tues–Sat 10am-8pm, Sun 10am-2:30pm; Oct-Mar Tues–Sat 10am-6pm, Sun 10am-2:30pm. Metro: Espanya, then 15-min walk, or take bus nos. 50, 55, or 61 from Plaça Espanya.

Pavelló Mies van der Rohe ★★   Directly across the road from the CaixaForum, this serene building stands in welcome contrast to the *moderniste* style of the Casaramona, constructed between 1909 and 1914, and the faux traditionalism of the

---

A Bicycle Built for Two

One of the star pieces of the MNAC's *moderniste* collection is a self-portrait of Ramón Casas and fellow Barcelona painter Pere Romeu riding a tandem. They both achieved fame in the early 1920s *moderniste* era. This iconic work was originally executed for **Els Quatre Gats** (p. 127), the tavern that served as a fraternity house for *moderniste* movers and shakers, bohemians, intellectuals, and poets. A young Picasso designed the menu (and held his first-ever exhibition there), and various other works donated to the owners still adorn the walls, although now most, such as Casas's pedaling portrait, are reproductions. The colorful Casas, who spent years in the artistic circles of Paris's Montmartre, was a perpetrator of the city's new-found modernity as well as a seminal artist. He specialized in portraits, caricatures, and political subjects such as street protests; his interpretations of *fin-de-siècle* Barcelona provide valuable insight into this heady time. Romeu was an extrovert and lively *animateur* at cabarets but a lesser artist, although his themes were similar.

Poble Espanyol (see below). Designed by German architect Mies van der Rohe, it was originally built as the German Pavilion for the 1929 World's Fair and was the last of the architect's works before he emigrated to the United States. It is a key work of both his and the International Style movement for which he and Frank Lloyd Wright, among others, became famous. The simple, horizontal structure contains his trademarks: Precision, fluidity of space, and abundance of "pure" materials, in this case different kinds of marble and glass. The structure is built around a shallow pool featuring a statue by Georg Kolbe, the German sculptor known for his female nudes. Inside is the original **Barcelona Chair** designed by van der Rohe and seen in reproduction throughout the city in reception areas. Although the pavilion now stands on its original location, this wasn't always the case. After the World's Fair, it was banished to an outer suburb, only to be rescued and reconstructed in 1985 thanks to an initiative by a group of the city's prominent architects.

Av. Marquès de Comillas s/n. ✆ **93-423-40-16.** www.miesbcn.com. Admission 3.50€, free for children 18 and under. Daily 10am–8pm. Metro: Espanya. FGC: Espanya.

Poble Espanyol ★★ ☺ This re-created Spanish village, built for the 1929 World's Fair, provokes mixed feelings: Purists see it as the height of kitsch, while others delight in its open spaces and Disneyland feel. But the question remains: Where else would you find over 100 styles of Spanish vernacular architecture crammed into one very pleasant spot? From the Levante to Galicia, from Castilian high Gothic to the humble whitewashed dwellings of the south and to colorful Basque homes, it's all here. At the entrance stands a facsimile of the gateway to the grand walled city of Avila. This leads you to the center of the village, with an outdoor cafe; there are other venues throughout the village, including the excellent flamenco taverna **Tablao de Carmen** (p. 241), and a couple of other trendy nightspots. The big names of July's El Grec festival (p. 236) also play here, in the main plaza just inside the gates. As was originally intended, numerous shops sell provincial crafts and souvenirs, and in some you'll see artists at work, printing fabric, making pottery, and blowing glass. If you are lucky, your visit may coincide

🄾 THE MAGIC fountain

Without a doubt, the most popular attraction for young and old alike in the Montjuïc area is the **Font Màgica (Magic Fountain).** During the day, the grandiose fountain at the base of the staircase to the MNAC seems like any other, but at night it takes on a different personality. At regular intervals, the fountain puts on a spectacular show. Music, from pop ballads to classics, belts out from loudspeakers, and different colored lights are beamed from inside the fountain itself. The fountains of water, controlled by computer, "dance" to the mixture of light and sound. Supposedly the only one of its kind in the world, the fountain was designed by the visionary engineer Carles Buïgas for the 1929 World's Fair, predating similar Vegas-type attractions by decades. It's free and never fails to enthrall. Grab a seat at one of the nearby outdoor cafes and enjoy. It's at Plaça Carles Buïgas 1 (Metro: Espanya). The sound and light shows run from May to early October, Thursday through Sunday at 9:30, 10, 10:30, 11, and 11:30pm. The rest of the year, they are held on Friday and Saturday at 7, 7:30, 8, and 8:30pm.

Swinging over the Port

Unless you suffer from vertigo, the most spectacular way to reach the Castell and other attractions at Montjuïc is via the cable car that crosses the port. **The Transbordador Aeri** starts at Torre de Sant Sebastiá at the end of the Passeig de Joan de Borbó in Barceloneta (bus: 17, 64, or 39), stops at the World Trade Center on the way, and finishes at the peak of Montjuïc. The cable car runs every 15 minutes daily—from 10am to 8pm June 19 to September 14, 10am to 6pm October 20 to February 28, and 10:45am to 7pm the rest of the year.

Cost is 9€ one-way, 12.50€ round-trip. Call ✆ **93-430-47-16** or 93-441-50-71 for more information.

If you're afraid of heights, take the **Telefèric de Montjuïc** (✆ **93-441-48-20;** www.tmb.net/en_US/turistes/busturistic/teleferic.jsp), a funicular-style, land-based service that climbs the hillside from Paral.lel Metro station in Poble Sec, and makes a final stop immediately below the castle at the top of Montjuïc. It costs 6.30€, 4.80€ children 4 to 12 one-way, and 9€ adults, 6.50€ children 4 to 12 round-trip.

with a wedding at the Sant Miquel monastery, one of the most popular places in the city to get married. In 2001, the Poble Espanyol opened the **Fundació Fran Daural** (✆ **93-423-41-72;** www.fundaciofrandaurel.com; open daily 10am–7pm), a collection of contemporary Catalan art with works by Dalí, Picasso, Barceló, and Tàpies. Many families delight in the faux-Spanish atmosphere, but the more discriminating find it a bit of a tourist trap.

Av. Marquès de Comillas s/n, Parc de Montjuïc. ✆ **93-508-63-00.** www.poble-espanyol.com. Admission 8.90€, 5.60€ children 4–12, free for children 4 and under; 20€ family ticket; 2€ guided tours. Mon 9am–8pm; Tues–Thurs 9am–2am; Fri-Sat 9am–5am; Sun 9am–11pm. Metro: Espanya, then 10-min. walk uphill, or take bus no. 13 or 50 from Plaça Espanya.

THE HARBORFRONT

For a city that for centuries "lived with its back to the sea," Barcelona now sports a spectacular harborfront, the busiest leisure port in the Mediterranean, and kilometers of urban beaches. The relocation of the commercial port and coastal main road, and the demolition of industrial buildings and eyesores that blocked the view of the sea, were pushed ahead for the 1992 Olympic Games. Without a doubt, the reclaiming of the city's coast has been the most life-enhancing change Barcelona has seen in the last century. Starting at the Columbus Monument (p. 165), follow the coastal stretch via boardwalks and esplanades to the Olympic Village and beyond. Along the way you will pass the modern marina, the Port Vell, and the old fisherman's district of La Barceloneta, and end at Frank Gehry's famous fish sculpture at the Olympic Port.

L'Aquàrium de Barcelona ★★   One of the most impressive testimonials to sea life anywhere opened in 1996 in Barcelona's Port Vell, a 10-minute walk from the bottom of La Rambla. One of the largest aquariums in Europe, it contains 21 glass tanks positioned along either side of a wide curving corridor. Each tank depicts a different marine habitat, containing multicolored fish and corals, seagoing worms, and sharks. The highlight is a huge "oceanarium" representative of the Mediterranean as a self-sustaining ecosystem. View it from the inside of a glass tunnel running along its entire length, with fish, eels, and sharks swimming all around you. Kids can let off some steam in the **Explora** section, a collection of touchy-feely educational exhibits on Catalonia's Costa Brava and Ebro Delta.

Moll d'Espanya-Port Vell. ℭ **93-221-74-74.** www.aquariumbcn.com. Admission 17.50€, 13€ seniors 60 and over, 14.50€ children 4–12, free for children 3 and under. July–Aug daily 9:30am–11pm; Sept–June Mon–Fri 9:30am–9pm, Sat–Sun 9:30am–9:30pm. Metro: Drassanes or Barceloneta.

Museu d'Història de Catalunya ★   The Catalan History Museum is located in the Palau del Mar, a huge warehouse dating from the late 19th century. Many similar buildings stood alongside it before this side of the port was redeveloped for the 1992 Olympic Games, creating the marina and recreational area that surrounds it.

The museum, divided into eight sections, provides a stroll through Catalan history. It's a sometimes exhausting, highly didactic tour of the region. **Roots, Birth of a Nation,** and **Our Sea** look at Catalonia's ancient ancestors, the flourishing Romanesque period, and the Catalan-Aragónese sea trade. **On the Periphery of an Empire, Bases of the Revolution,** and **Steam and Nation** study Catalonia's decline under Hapsburg rule and the subsequent economic and cultural recovery in the industrial age. Finally, **The Electric Years** (which is one of the more entertaining parts of the exhibit) and **Defeat and Recovery** deal with the 20th century, the Civil War, Catalonia during Franco's dictatorship, and the first democratic elections after his death.

It's a lot to cover and the museum uses a mixture of multimedia, re-creations, models, and other interactive devices as their media, most of the time with effective results. As the accompanying explanations are in Catalan, you are provided with a translation (in book form) at the entrance.

The temporary exhibitions on the ground floor are less ponderous and have included some excellent shows on Mediterranean cultures and on the relationship between the famed poet Federico García Lorca and Salvador Dalí. Exhibitions in 2010 covered a variety of subjects from paintings by disabled artists to an appraisal of traditional Catalan songs and a display of early-20th-century photos of the then distinctly untouristy Costa Brava.

After all this you need a break. The museum's **cafe** offers great food and an excellent view of the port; also on the port side are a handful of outdoor seafood restaurants. **Puda Can Manel** (see chapter 6, "Where to Dine," p. 120) is one of the most reliable and popular spots.

Plaça de la Pau Vila 3. ℭ **93-225-47-00.** www.mhcat.net. Admission 4€, 3€ children 7–18, students, and seniors 65 and over. Free 1st Sun of month. Tues–Sat 10am–7pm (until 8pm Wed); Sun 10am–2:30pm. Metro: Barceloneta.

Museu Marítim ★★★ ☺   In the former Royal Shipyards (Drassanes Reials), the city's Maritime Museum is the finest of its kind in Spain. The seafaring cities of Venice, Genoa, and Valencia all had impressive arsenals, but only vestiges remain. In contrast, Barcelona's shipyards with their majestic arches, columns, and gigantic vaults are a preciously intact example of medieval civic architecture. This complex, which sat right on the water's edge before the coastline receded, was used to dry-dock, construct, and repair ships for the Catalan-Aragónese rulers. During the 18th century, the yards went into decline, mainly due to the dissolution of naval construction. Right up until the Civil War, it served as an army barracks until it opened as a museum in the 1970s.

The collection titled **The Great Adventure of the Sea** is homage to Catalonia's maritime history. The most outstanding exhibit occupies an entire bay. It is a reconstruction of La Galería Real of Don Juan of Austria, a lavish royal galley. In 1971, following extensive documentation, this model was built in celebration of the vessel's most glorious achievement 400 years earlier. The ship headed an alliance of Spanish, Venetian, Maltese, and Vatican vessels in a bloody battle against a Turkish squadron. The "Holy League" won, effectively ending Ottoman rule in the Mediterranean. On board the ship, there is an excellent film re-creating the battle, and you can view the galley's elaborate hull, hold, and deck, complete with 59 oars.

Other exhibits chart traditional fishing techniques and sailing as sport through neat little caravels and draggers, snipes, and sloops. The art of wooden shipbuilding, the charting of the oceans, and the launch into the steam age are also covered. Particularly fine is the collection of late-19th-century mastheads, navigational instruments, and models of the Compañía Trasmediterránea's fleet (this local company still operates the Barcelona–Balearic Islands route). The collection also boasts a small model of *Ictíneo,* one of the world's first submarines, designed by the Catalan visionary Narcís Monturiol; it made its first underwater trip in 1859.

Av. de les Drassanes s/n. ✆ **93-342-99-20.** www.museumaritimbarcelona.com. Admission 6.50€, 5.20€ youths 11–25 and seniors 65 and over, 3.25€ children 6–10. Daily 10am–8pm. Metro: Drassanes.

BARCELONA OUTSKIRTS

Barcelona's outer suburbs are largely residential. Once they were country areas, annexed over the years by the city's continuing sprawl. Thus there are a handful of notable buildings that once stood in a village or country estate. The *barri* of Sarrià, easily reached by the FGC station of the same name, has retained a particularly authentic, villagey feel. Located at the foot of Tibidabo, it's a pleasant place to wander around and take in some clean air.

Colònia Güell ★★ For many, Gaudí's most prolific work lies not within Barcelona, but outside. He designed the church for the Colònia Güell, an ambitious plan of Eusebi Güell's that lies 20 minutes by train inland from the city. Güell was a progressive man and wished to set up a colony for the workers of his textile mill, which was being transferred here from central Barcelona. The colony would contain a hospital, library, residences, theater, and church. Only the crypt was completed before Güell's death.

The haunting grotto-like structure stands on an elevated part of the *colònia* surrounded by a pine forest. Its cavernous dimensions and stone-forest interior are the result of an ingenious method that the architect also employed in the planning stages of the Sagrada Família and La Pedrera. He devised the models for his work using lengths of string attached to weights, with the weights taking the tension, photographed the pieces, and then inverted the photos. What was concave became convex, as in an arch. Thus he was able to measure the angles, build the scaffolding and envisage the forms, and predate three-dimensional computer drawing by a hundred years. The work at Colònia Güell is Gaudí's most organic: Walls bend and curve at impossible angles, and windows open out like beetles' wings.

It's worth taking a walk around the rest of the colony. The red-brick *moderniste* buildings were designed by architects Francesc Berenguer and Joan Rubió Bellver. Most of these are now private residences, but many of the factories and warehouses have been abandoned, which gives the place a ghost-town-like ambience.

Claudi Güell s/n, Santa Coloma de Cervelló. ✆ **93-630-58-07.** www.gaudiallgaudi.com/EA007.htm. Admission Colònia Güell and crypt 10€, 7€ seniors. Guided tour of crypt 5[eu], non-guided visit to crypt 4€, free for children 10 and under. Mon–Sat 10am–2pm and 3–7pm; Sun 10am–3pm (Mass at 11am and 1pm). FGC: Colònia Güell, lines S33, S34, S8, or S7 (all leave from Plaça Espanya).

CosmoCaixa (Museu de la Ciència) ★★★ ☺ This spectacular science museum is an enlarged, much-improved version of the 1980 original. Funded by a major bank (La Caixa), the Museu de la Ciència closed in 1998 and embarked on a 6-year overhaul. The result is the best, most high-tech, and certainly most hands-on science museum in Europe.

Like the original, El Museu de la Ciència occupies a *moderniste* building (originally a poorhouse) at the foot of Tibidabo, but with a daring underground extension and renovation of the original edifice, effectively quadrupling its exhibition space to 3,700 sq m (39,800 sq feet).

As well as the additional new bio-research center, the permanent collection has been completely overhauled and, through an imaginative combination of original material and multimedia, takes the novice on a comprehensive tour of scientific principles. The collection is divided into four categories: **Inert Materials** (*Materia inerte*) deals with the big-bang theory up to the first signs of life, **Living Materials** (*Materia viva*) focuses on the birth of mankind, **Intelligent Materials** (*Materia inteligente*) looks at the development of human intelligence, and **Civilized Materials** (*Materia civilizada*) explores history and science from pioneers to the computer age.

The biggest crowd pleaser is **The Flooded Forest** (*El Bosque Inundado*), a living, breathing Amazonian rainforest *inside* the museum, with over 100 species of animal and plant life. Kids come into close contact with fauna in the *Toca Toca* section, which has rats, frogs, spiders, and other natives from diverse ecosystems, some of which can be touched. There is a 3D planetarium and the extraordinary **Geological Wall** (*El Muro Geológico*) that explains, through an interactive route, the history of the world from a geological perspective. All in all, the new Science Museum is a highly entertaining window on the world of science.

Teodor Roviralta 47. ✆ **93-212-60-50.** www.obrasocial.lacaixa.es. Admission 3€, 2€ students and seniors 65 and over, free for children 2 and under; planetarium 2€; Toca Toca (children come into contact with animals) 2€. Tues–Sun 10am–8pm. FGC: Avinguda Tibidabo (then 10-min. walk). Bus: 17, 22, 58, or 73.

Finca Güell ★ The Finca Güell, the country estate of Eusebi Güell (p. 182), features three works by Gaudí, the industrialist's favorite architect. Still on a private estate, they can only be viewed from the street, but that doesn't detract from the impact they have upon the viewer. Eusebi Güell asked Gaudí to create an entrance gate, a gatehouse, and stables. The gate is one of the most stunning pieces of wrought-iron work in the world. Locally known as the Drac de Pedralbes (the Dragon of Pedralbes), a huge reptile appears to jump out, tongue extended and ready to attack. The dwellings are no less powerful. Like **Casa Vicens** (p. 181), they were designed early in Gaudí's career when he was influenced by Islamic architecture, and feature turrets and white walls contrasted with brightly colored tiles. The pavilion on the right houses a library and Gaudían research center.

Gaudí took inspiration for the *finca* from the Greek myth of Hesperides. The ominous dragon is a metaphor for the beast that Hercules battled, and although they are a tad run-down, the gardens behind the gate used to be lush and full of citrus trees—the legendary gardens of Hesperides themselves.

Av. Pedralbes 7. Metro: Palau Reial.

Monestir de Pedralbes ★★   The oldest building in Pedralbes (the city's wealthiest residential area) is a monastery founded in 1326 by Elisenda de Montcada, Jaume II's queen. It housed the nuns of the Order of Saint Clare (who now live in a small building adjacent), and after the king's death Queen Elisenda took up residence in the convent. She is buried in the Gothic church next door (where the nuns sing their vespers) in a beautiful tomb surrounded by angels.

Beyond the threshold is a serene cloister with a central fountain, well, herb gardens, and other greenery. There are nearly two dozen elegant arches on each side of the cloister, rising three stories high. Immediately to your right is a small chapel containing the chief treasure of the monastery, the intact Capellà de Sant Miquel. Inside, it is decorated with murals by Ferrer Bassa, a major artist of Catalonia in the 1300s, depicting the Passion of Christ.

The original nuns' residence houses an exhibition re-creating the monastic life of the 14th century: What they ate, how they dressed, the hours of prayer, and their general comings and goings. Some of the day chambers contain original artifacts of the *monestir*, although the most evocative rooms are the kitchen and refectory and the communal dining room where the Mother Superior broke her vow of silence with mealtime Bible readings from the wooden pulpit.

Baixada del Monestir 9. ℂ **93-203-92-82.** www.museuhistoria.bcn.es. Admission 5€, 3.50€ students and seniors, free for children 12 and under. Tues–Sun 10am–2pm. Free 1st Sun of month. FGC: Reina Elisenda. Bus: 75.

Museu de les Arts Decoratives/Museu de Ceràmica ★   The city's museums of decorative arts and ceramics occupy the Palau de Pedralbes and can be seen together. The palace is set in an elegant garden once belonging to the Finca Güell (see above), the country estate of Gaudí's patron and friend Eusebi Güell.

The neoclassical residence was taken over by King Alfonso XIII in 1920, who handed it over to the local government 10 years later. It was then turned into an exhibition space for the decorative arts. During the dictatorship, General Franco made this his Barcelona home, before the building finally regained its status as a museum in 1960.

Inside, the lavish halls with their gilt, marble, and frescoes make a picturesque backdrop for both collections. By far the superior is the Ceramic Museum, where collections are arranged regionally and span from the 11th century to the present. Particularly striking are the *mudéjar* and metallic inlay work from the south and the baroque and Renaissance pieces from Castile. One extraordinary exhibit from Catalonia is an enormous plaque from the 18th century depicting a chocolate feast in the countryside.

Compared to the collection of decorative arts at the MNAC (p. 186), the small exhibition here is a slight letdown. The name is somewhat deceiving, as the focus is

MES QUE UN *club* (MORE THAN A CLUB)!

After the Museu Picasso, the most visited museum in the city is the **Museu FC Barcelona** (www.fcbarcelona.cat), the museum of the city's revered football (soccer) team, Barça. It's inside their home ground, Camp Nou, the largest stadium in Europe, with a capacity of 120,000 and built in 1997. Despite its size, tickets to matches are as scarce as hens' teeth. Most of the seats are taken by *socis* (members) of the richest soccer club in the world. As their slogan goes, Barça is *mes que un club* ("More than a club"). Membership is handed down through the generations and is a mark of *Catalanismo* (Catalan identity). During the Franco dictatorship, the war was played out on the soccer field, with Madrid's team seen as representative of the hated central government. Madrid is still Barça's arch-enemy (old grudges die hard in soccer) and when the two meet at Camp Nou, the whole city stops.

Along with the museum, you can choose to see the (empty) stadium, the chapel where players say a prayer before a big match, the club and pressrooms, and the tunnel leading onto the field. The collection consists of photos, trophies, documents, kit, and other paraphernalia telling the emotive history of the club from its beginnings in 1899 to the present. It makes for some light relief from other heady cultural offerings.

Planned work by Sir Norman Foster is on hold at the time of writing (Sept 2010) for financial reasons, although it's hoped his radical plans for giving the stadium a facelift will get the go-ahead by 2012.

Camp Nou stadium, access door nos. 7 and 9. Arístides Maillol s/n (✆ **93-496-36-00;** www.fcbarcelona.cat). Admission museum and stadium: 18€, 13€ children 14 and under. Tickets for matches 19€–88€. April 14 to October 12 Monday to Saturday 10am to 8pm, Sunday 10am to 2:30pm; rest of year Monday to Saturday 10am to 6:30pm, Sunday 10am to 2:30pm. Metro: Collblanc.

really on design. That said, Catalonia's design heritage is an important one, and there are many pieces here from the city's design boom of the 1980s and early 1990s, featuring top names such as Javier Mariscal and Oscar Tusquets. In the future, this collection may form part of the projected Design Museum, but there are no firm plans at the time of writing.

Av. Diagonal 686. ✆ **93-280-16-21.** www.museuceramica.bcn.cat. www.museuartsdecoratives.bcn.es. Admission (for both) 5€, 3€ students, free for children 16 and under. Tues–Sat 10am–6pm; Sun 10am–3pm. Free 1st Sun of month. Metro: Palau Reial.

Parc d'Atraccions Tibidabo ★★ ☺   The mountain of Tibidabo has been a popular retreat for Barcelonese since 1868 when a road was built connecting it to the city. You arrive there on the creaky old funicular—or, less dramatically, by bus—to find an amusement park combining tradition with modernity. In summer, the place takes on a carnival-like atmosphere, and most of the credit for this can go to a wealthy pill manufacturer by the name of Dr. Andreu, who believed (quite sensibly) that fresh mountain air was good for your health. He created the Sociedad Anónima de Tibidabo, which promoted the slopes as a public garden and was instrumental in installing both the Tramvía Blau (Blue Tram) and the funicular up to Tibidabo (p. 48).

Some of the attractions in the park date from Andreu's time. **L'Avio,** for example, is a replica of the first plane that served the Barcelona–Madrid route. In the Tibidabo version, you are treated to a whisk over the summit in a toy-like craft suspended from a central axis. Another dated attraction designed to scare you out of your wits is **Aeromàgic,** an exhilarating cable-car ride covering the whole park, with amazing views of the city and the coastline below. On a more relaxed level, you can also visit a charming museum of period automatons.

SMALL IS GOOD: OTHER BARCELONA
museums

There are dozens of small private museums in Barcelona, some the fruit of a collector's obsessive passion, others that display an ancient guild's craft. Many are free; others charge a minimal entrance fee or ask for a donation. The charming **Museu de Calçat,** Plaça Sant Felip Neri 5 (✆ **93-301-45-33;** 2.50€; Tues–Sun 11am–2pm; Metro: Liceu), is housed in the ancient headquarters of the city's shoemaker guild. The collection ranges from Roman sandals to the boots of famous Catalan cellist Pablo Casals. The **Museu de Carrosses Fúnebres (Museum of Funeral Carriages),** Sancho d'Avila 2 (✆ **93-484-17-00;** free admission; Mon–Fri 10am–1pm and 4–6pm, Sat–Sun 10am–1pm; Metro: Marina), has an unusual location: The basement of the city's morgue.

Although bullfighting is not popular in Catalonia and will be banned in 2012 (p. 59), La Monumental, Barcelona's bullring, is an exotic structure that houses the **Museu Tauri,** Gran Vía 749 (✆ **93-245-58-03;** 5€ adults, 4€ children; Apr–Sept Tues–Sat 10:30am–2pm and 4–7pm, Sun 10am–1pm; Metro: Monumental), a small museum of memorabilia, costumes, and other bull-ish items. The most sacred of cultures around the world are explored in the **Museu Etnològic,** Passeig de Santa Madrona s/n (✆ **93-424-64-02;** www.museuetnologic.bcn.es; 3€, free for children 16 and under and seniors 65 and over; Tues–Sun 10am–2pm; Metro: Espanya). In a similar vein, ethnographic pieces collected by Capuchin nuns in the Amazon region can be viewed in their convent at the **Museu Etnogràfic Andino-Amazónic,** Cardenal Vives i Tutó 2-16 (✆ **93-204-34-58;** www.museuetnologic.bcn.es; by appointment only; Metro: María Cristina). In 1982 the prominent Barcelonese doctor Melcior Colet donated his home, a *moderniste* dwelling designed by Puig i Cadafalch, and his amassed sporting memorabilia to the city. The result, the **Museu de L'Esport Dr. Melcior Colet,** Buenos Aires 56–58 (✆ **93-419-22-32.** Free admission. Mon–Fri 10am–2pm and 4–8pm; bus: 7, 15, 33, 34, or 59), is a collection of artifacts relating to Catalan sporting achievements.

In an outer Barcelona park, an extraordinary collection of period carriages, adornments, and uniforms worn by coachmen is found at the **Museu de Carruatges,** Plaça Josep Pallach 8 (✆ **93-427-58-13;** Mon–Fri 10am–1pm; Metro: Mundet). One of the prettiest of all the city's private museums is at the rear of a perfume shop. The **Museu del Perfum,** Passeig de Gràcia 39 (✆ **93-216-01-21;** www.museudelperfum.com; 5€, 3€ students and seniors; Mon–Fri 10:30am–1pm and 5–8pm, Sat 11am–1:30pm; Metro: Passeig de Gràcia), holds over 5,000 examples of perfume bottles, vials, and paraphernalia from Egyptian times to the present day. Watch out for the Dalí-designed Le Roi de Soleil.

The church next door to the amusement park is **Temple de Sagrat Cor,** an ugly and highly kitsch building dating from 1902, meant to provide Barcelona with its own Sacré Coeur. Its distinctive mountaintop silhouette can be seen from all over the city.

Plaça Tibidabo 3. ✆ **93-211-79-42.** www.tibidabo.es. 25.20€ for unlimited rides, 11€ students, 9€ seniors 60 and over, 9€ children 1.2m (4 feet) tall and under, free for children 3 and under. Summer daily noon–10pm; off-season Sat–Sun noon–7pm. Bus: 58 to Avinguda Tibidabo Metro, then take the Tramvía Blau, which drops you at the funicular. Round-trip 4.10€.

PARKS & GARDENS

Contrary to first impressions, Barcelona is not solely a city of concrete squares and stone streets. In a fine Mediterranean climate, life takes place outside in parks and gardens, some designed by the city's top architects for the Olympic renewal frenzy. The most popular are the leafy and formal **Parc de la Ciutadella** (p. 171), Gaudí's visionary **Parc Güell** (p. 181), and the mountain of **Montjuïc** (p. 183). But there are plenty more parks, gardens, and leafy hideaways for a bit of solitude or one-on-one with nature. Most parks open 9am to sunset.

Not strictly a park but a large open square, one of the city's most famous "hard plazas," the **Parc de Joan Miró,** Aragó 1 (Metro: Espanya), occupies an entire L'Eixample block that was once the city's slaughterhouse. Its main features are an esplanade and pond from which a towering sculpture by Miró, *Woman and Bird,* rises. Palm, pine, and eucalyptus trees, as well as playgrounds and pergolas, complete the picture. Nearby, the enormous **Parc de l'Espanya Industrial**, next to the Sants train station (near the Plaça dels Països Catalans entrance to the Metro station), is a surrealist landscape of amphitheater-type seating, watchtowers, and postmodern sculpture juxtaposed with greener parkland at the rear. On the opposite side of L'Eixample, the **Parc de L' Estació del Nord,** Nápoles 70 (Metro: Arc de Triomf or Marina), is a whimsical piece of landscape gardening featuring sculptures and land art by U.S. artist Beverly Pepper.

Another daring urban space is the **Parc de la Crueta del Coll** near the Parc Güell, Castellterçol 24 (Metro: Penitents). Located in a former quarry, this urban playground features a manmade pool and an enormous oxidized metal sculpture, the *Elogia del Agua* by Basque sculptor Eduardo Chillida. Looking somewhat like a huge claw, it is theatrically suspended from a cliff face. Further north is **Collserola** (p. 81), a natural parkland of nearly 1,800 hectares (4,400 acres). Urbanites come up here in droves on the weekend to cycle, stroll, or have a picnic. Get here on the FGC from Plaça de Catalunya to either Baixador de Vallvidrera (which has an information office about the park) or Les Planes.

For those who like their parks more traditional, the romantic **Parc del Laberint,** Passeig de Castanyers s/n (Metro: Mundet), in the outer suburb of Horta, is the oldest and most established in the city. As the name suggests, there is a central maze of cyprus trees, and the rest of the site is laid out over terraces with Italianate-style statues and balustrades.

One of the new parks to appear in 2009 was the **Parc Central de Poble Nou,** Avinguda Diagonal 130 (bus: 7, 40, 42, and 71), designed by the controversial French architect Jean Nouvel. The park is designed in a spartan futuristic style that's more a modern-art creation—with its cratered moonscape and sporadic plants, all enclosed by flowered covered walls—than a place to relax and enjoy a picnic. Created by Enric Miralles (who designed the notorious Scottish Parliament in the 1990s), the **Parc de la Diagonal Mar,** Llull 362 (Metro: Selva de Mar), is another green zone developed around the same time. It also lies close to Poble Nou and has a small lake bordered by a blend of futuristic-looking metallic tubes and flowery areas.

OUTDOOR & SPORTING PURSUITS

Golf

One of the city's best courses, **Club de Golf Vallromanes,** Afueras s/n, Vallromanes (✆ **93-572-90-64;** www.clubdegolfvallromanes.com), is 20 minutes north of the city center by car. Non-members who reserve tee times in advance are welcome to play. The green fee is 100€ on weekdays, 180€ on weekends. The club is open Wednesday through Monday from 9am to 9pm. Established in 1972, it is the site of the Spanish Open Golf Tournament.

   Reial Club de Golf El Prat, El Prat de Llobregat (✆ **93-379-02-78**), is a prestigious club that allows non-members to play under two conditions: They must have a handicap issued by the governing golf body in their home country, and they must prove membership of a golf club at home. The club has two 18-hole, par-72 courses. Greens fees are 125€ Monday through Friday. Weekends are for members only. From Barcelona, follow Avinguda Once de Septiembre past the airport to Barrio de San Cosme. From there follow the signs along Carrer Prat to the golf course.

Horseback Riding

Set high above the city on the mountain of Montjuïc, this is a perfect setting for a riding school. The **Escola Municipal d'Hípica La Foixarda,** Avinguda Muntayans 1 (✆ **93-426-10-66;** Metro: Espanya), has classes for all ages and skills, from 18€ per hour.

Surfing & Windsurfing

When the wind blows, Barcelona's beaches offer good conditions for wind- and kite-surfing and regular surfing, and the latter is really taking off. **Wind 220°,** on the corner of Passeig Marítim and Pontevedra (✆ **93-221-47-02;** www.box220.com; Metro: Barceloneta), right on the beach at Barceloneta, has all the equipment you need for rent, plus storage facilities, a cafe, information, and courses for all standards.

Swallow Boats

Las Golondrinas (**Swallow Boats;** ✆ **93-442-31-06;** www.lasgolondrinas.com) are pretty little double-deckers that take you on a leisurely cruise of the city's port, or port and northern coast combined. Boats depart from the port side of the Plaça Portal de la Pau, directly in front of the Columbus column. The port-only tour leaves every hour (weekends only) between 11:45am and 6pm, and the port and coast excursion daily at 11am and 12:20, 1:15, and 3:30pm. Prices for adults are 6.50€ for

Happy, Happy, Joy, Joy!

Happy Parc (www.happyparc.com) is the perfect solution for kids who need to let off steam. It's a huge, covered, labyrinth-type set-up full of bouncy, touchy, feely, jumpy, rubbery contraptions for little darlings to romp around on. Monitors are on hand and there is a special enclosed area for tiny tots.

There are two in Barcelona: One at Comtes de Bell-lloc 74–78 (② 93-490-08-35; Metro: Sants) and the other at Pau Claris 97 (② 93-317-86-60; Metro: Urquinaona). Both are open Monday to Friday 5 to 9pm and weekends 11am to 9pm. Cost is 4.50€ per hour for children, free for adults.

port-only and 13.50€ for port and coast as far as the Forum; children 4 to 14 pay 2.60€ and 5€ for these respective tours.

Swimming

Swim at **Piscina Bernardo Picornell,** Avinguda de Estadí 30–40, Montjuïc (② 93-423-40-41), where Olympic events took place in 1992. Adjacent to the Olympic Stadium, it incorporates two of the best swimming pools in Spain (one indoor, one outdoor). Custom-built for the Olympics, they're open to the public Monday through Friday from 7am to midnight, Saturday from 7am to 9pm, and Sunday from 7am to 4pm. Entrance costs 8€ for adults and 4€ for children and allows full use throughout the day plus the gymnasium, sauna, and whirlpools. Bus no. 61 makes frequent runs from Plaça Espanya.

Tennis

The **Centre Municipal de Tennis,** Passeig Vall d'Hebron 178 (② 93-427-65-00; Metro: Montbau), has been the training ground for some of the country's top players. It has 17 clay and 7 grass courts set over beautiful grounds, but you need to supply your own racket and balls. Court hire is 10€ an hour for clay courts and 14€ an hour for grass courts.

STROLLING AROUND BARCELONA

Spain's second-largest city is also its most cosmopolitan and avant-garde, a rich repository of landmark buildings and world-class cultural centers that range from its famed *moderniste* Sagrada Família and great medieval Gothic cathedral to the MNAC's Romanesque treasures and Picasso Museum's cubist masterpieces.

Cutting through the heart of its emblematic Old Quarter is the tree-lined promenade of La Rambla, a former riverbed that today is a vibrant, colorful thoroughfare perennially packed with visitors of all nations. Three of our walking tours take you on strolls through the medieval labyrinths on either side of this emblematic *paseo*. The fourth leads you out into the spacious Eixample to explore its long, wide boulevards and surreal 19th-century edifices

WALKING TOUR 1: BARRI GÒTIC (THE GOTHIC QUARTER)

START:	**Plaça Nova (Metro: Jaume I).**
FINISH:	**Same point at Plaça Nova, or Vía Laietana opposite Port Vell (Metro: Barceloneta).**
TIME:	**2 to 3 hours.**
BEST TIMES:	**Any sunny day or early evening.**

This walk will take you through the core of medieval Barcelona, down narrow lanes, across tiny plazas, and past some of the city's oldest and most imposing palaces and religious centers.

Walking Tour 1: Barri Gòtic (The Gothic Quarter)

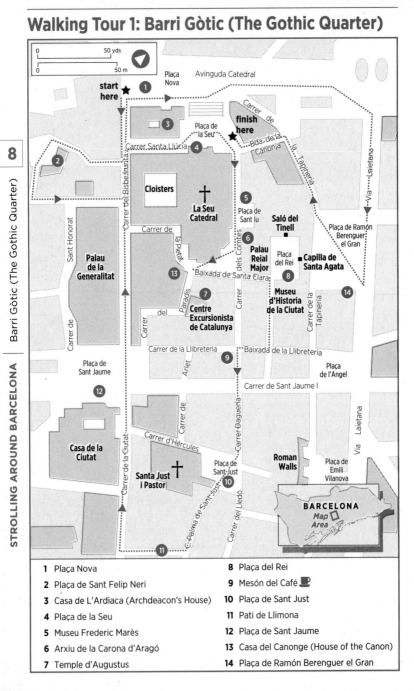

1 Plaça Nova

2 Plaça de Sant Felip Neri

3 Casa de L'Ardiaca (Archdeacon's House)

4 Plaça de la Seu

5 Museu Frederic Marès

6 Arxiu de la Carona d'Aragó

7 Temple d'Augustus

8 Plaça del Rei

9 Mesón del Café

10 Plaça de Sant Just

11 Pati de Llimona

12 Plaça de Sant Jaume

13 Casa del Canonge (House of the Canon)

14 Plaça de Ramón Berenguer el Gran

1 Plaça Nova

Set within the shadow of the cathedral, this is the largest open-air space in the Gothic Quarter. Behind you, the facade of the **Collegi de Architects,** the city's architecture school, features a frieze designed (but not executed by) Picasso. From Plaça Nova, climb the incline of the narrow asphalt-covered street (Carrer del Bisbe).

At the approach of the first street on the right, the Carrer de Montjuïc del Bisbe de Santa Llúcia, turn right and follow this winding street to the:

2 Plaça de Sant Felip Neri

This small square is often cited as the most charming in the Barri Gòtic. Although none of the buildings are in fact Gothic (and some were moved from other parts of the city in the 18th and 19th centuries), the central fountain, majestic trees, and overall tranquillity more than qualify it for the status of "urban oasis." The holes you see in the stonework of the lower facade of the 17th-century church (which unfortunately lost many of its baroque features in the late 18th century) were caused by a bomb dropped by Fascist troops that killed 20 children from the adjoining school in 1937. On the opposite side, the oldest building is Renaissance in style and serves as the headquarters of the shoemakers' guild, with the Museu de Calçat (Shoe Museum, p. 195) inside.

Walk back to the Carrer del Bisbe. Backtrack left, then take the immediate right, Carrer de Santa Llúcia. This will lead you to:

3 Casa de L'Ardiaca (Archdeacon's House)

Constructed in the 15th century as a residence for Archdeacon Despla, the Gothic building has sculptural reliefs with Renaissance and early-20th-century motifs. In its cloister-like courtyard are a fountain and a palm tree. Notice the mail slot, designed by the *moderniste* architect Domènech i Montaner, where five swallows and a turtle carved into stone await the arrival of important messages. This beautiful setting now holds the city's archives and is not open to the public, but you are free to inspect the courtyard and exterior.

As you exit the Archdeacon's House, continue in the same direction several steps until you reach the:

4 Plaça de la Seu

This square is in front of the main entrance to the **Catedral de Barcelona** (p. 161). If you are here in the first couple of weeks of December, your visit will coincide with the lively Fira de Santa Lucía, an outdoor market selling Christmas trees, decorations, and figurines such as the "pooping Catalan," the *caganer* (p. 37).

After touring the cathedral (about 40 minutes), exit and turn right onto Carrer dels Comtes, admiring the gargoyles on the exterior walls along the way. After about 100 paces on the left, you'll approach the:

5 Museu Frederic Marès ★★

This wonderful museum (p. 166) holds an extraordinary collection of Romanesque and Gothic religious artifacts. Even if you don't go in, the courtyard of the 13th-century former bishop's palace is well worth a peek. The outdoor Café d'Estiu is a relaxing spot to take a coffee break. The museum is closed until mid-2011.

Exit and continue your promenade in the same direction. You'll pass the portal on the cathedral's right side, where the heads of two rather abstract angels flank the throne of a seated female saint. A few paces farther, on the left, notice the stone facade of the:

6 Arxiu de la Carona d'Aragó

The Arxiu is the former archives center of the crown of Aragón and Catalunya. Once known as the **Palau del Lloctinent (Deputy's Palace),** this Gothic building was the work of Antonio Carbonell. It is not open to the public, but you can get a glimpse of its patios and upper arcades, admiring the century-old grapevines.

As you exit from the courtyard, you'll find yourself back on Carrer dels Comtes. Take the street in front of you, the Carrer de la Pietat, which follows the rear facade of the cathedral, and then the first street on your left, the Carrer del Paradis. At no. 10 is one of the Barri Gòtic's best-kept secrets, the:

7 Temple d'Augustus

Inside the courtyard of this medieval building, four majestic Corinthian columns are all that remain of Roman Barcelona's main temple. Most historians believe that it was dedicated to Emperor Caesar Augustus, hence its name. What is certain is that, on the highest point of the city, known as Mons Taber, it was the prominent feature of the Roman Forum. Admission is free. From June to September, the temple is open Tuesday to Saturday from 10am to 8pm, and Sunday 10am to 2pm; the rest of the year, it's open Tuesday to Saturday from 10am to 2pm and 4pm to 8pm, and Sunday 10am to 2pm.

Retrace your steps along the Carrer de la Pietat to the Palau del Lloctinent. Continue in the same direction on the same street and it will bring you to the most famous squares of the Gothic Quarter:

8 Plaça del Rei

The Great Royal Palace, an enlarged building of what was originally the residence of the counts of Barcelona, dominates this square. Here you can visit both the **Palau Reial** and the **Museu d'Història de la Ciutat** (p. 164). On the right side of the square stands the **Palatine Chapel of Santa Agata,** a 14th-century Gothic temple that is part of the Palau Reial. Preserved in this chapel is the altarpiece of the Lord High Constable, a 15th-century work by Jaume Huguet.

9 Mesón del Café 🍵

Llibrería 16 (📞 93-315-07-54), founded in 1909, specializes in coffee and cappuccino. It is one of the oldest coffeehouses in the neighborhood, sometimes crowding 50 people into its tiny precincts. Regulars perch on stools at the bar and order breakfast. Coffee costs 1.20€, and a cappuccino goes for 2.10€. The cafe is open Monday to Saturday from 7am to 9:30pm.

Exit the Plaça del Rei on its southern side. Turn left into the steep Baixada de Llibretería. At no. 7 you will see the beautiful candle shop, the Cereria Subira, the oldest
continuous retail establishment in Barcelona. A few paces on, turn left and cross over
the busy Carrer Ferran. Continue along the Carrer de la Dagueria. This will lead you to:

10 Plaça de Sant Just

The square is dominated by the entrance to the **Església dels Sants Just i
Pastor.** Above the entrance portal, an enthroned virgin is flanked by a pair of
protective angels. The Latin inscription hails her as VIRGO NIGRA ET PULCHRA,
NOSTRA PATRONA PIA (Black and Beautiful Virgin, Our Holy Patroness). This
church dates from the 14th century, although work continued into the 16th.
Some authorities claim that it is an earlier, 4th-century manifestation of the
present structure, the oldest in Barcelona. You'll find that its doors are usually
closed except during Sunday Mass.

Opposite the church, at Plaça de Sant Just 4, is the 18th-century **Palau
Moxó,** (✆ **93-315-22-38;** www.palaumoxo.com) an aristocratic town house
covered with faded but still elegant frescoes of angels cavorting among gar-
lands. At its base is a public well, the oldest water source in the city.

Continue walking in the same direction down the Carrer de la Dagueria, which
changes its name to the Carrer de Lledó. If you like, take a detour to the street
parallel on your left, the Carrer del Sots-Tinent Navarro; here you will see the
remains of the old Roman city walls. If not, take the second street on your right,
the Carrer Cometa (so named for a sighting of a comet here in 1834). Turn right
again onto the Carrer del Regomir. At no. 3 is the:

11 Pati de Llimona

This lively community center, named after its interior patio and lemon tree,
has a beautiful 15th-century gallery, and vestiges of the old Roman sewer
system, displayed underneath glass in the floor. Check out www.bcn.cat/
centrecivicpatillimona to see which exhibitions are on in the center; they are
normally by local artists and photographers. Next door, the tiny 16th-century
open **Chapel of Saint Christopher** is protected from the street by an iron
gate. Admission is free; go in and explore.

Continue walking up the Carrer Regomir (which changes its name to the Carrer de la
Ciutat) until you reach the:

12 Plaça de Sant Jaume

In many ways, this plaza is the political heart of Catalan culture. Across this
square, constructed at what was once a major junction for two Roman streets,
politicians and bureaucrats rush around intent on Catalonian government
affairs. On Sunday evenings you can witness the *sardana,* the national dance of
Catalonia. There are plenty of bars and restaurants on the side streets leading
from this square.

Standing in the square, with your back to the street just left (Carrer de la
Ciutat), you'll see, immediately on your right, the Doric portico of the **Palau
de la Generalitat,** the parliament of Catalonia. Construction of this exquisite
work, with its large courtyard and open-air stairway, along with twin-arched

galleries in the Catalonian Gothic style, began in the era of Jaume I. A special feature of the building is the Chapel of St. George, constructed in Flamboyant Gothic style between 1432 and 1435 and enlarged in 1620 with the addition of vaulting and a cupola with hanging capitals. The back of the building encloses a courtyard, begun in 1532, full of orange trees. In the Gilded Hall, the Proclamation of the Republic was signed. Across the square are the Ionic columns of the **Casa de la Ciutat/Ayuntamiento,** the town hall of Barcelona. Both these buildings are only periodically open to the public (p. 166).

With your back to the Casa de la Ciutat, cross the square to the right and turn left once again into the Carrer del Bisbe. On your immediate right is the:

13 Casa del Canonge (House of the Canon)

This series of buildings, once a group of canons' houses, dates from the 14th century and was restored in 1925; escutcheons from the 15th and 16th centuries remain. Notice the heraldic symbols of medieval Barcelona on the building's stone plaques—twin towers supported by winged goats with lion's feet. On the same facade, you'll see the depiction of twin angels. The building is used today as the town residence of the President of the Generalitat.

Connecting it to the Palau de la Generalitat across the road is a charming bridge carved into lacy patterns of stonework, also dating from the 1920s.

Continue walking along Carrer del Bisbe until you reach your starting place, the Plaça Nova. If you wish to continue your walk, cross the square to the right to the busy Vía Laietana. Here you will see:

14 Plaça de Ramón Berenguer el Gran

This equestrian statue is dedicated to a local hero, the Count of Barcelona (1082–1131), who won battles against the Moors and expanded his kingdom to include Tarragona. It is ringed by a semicircular park, which has a backdrop of ancient walls from a Roman fort and, nearby, a Gothic tower. Keep walking down the Vía Laietana toward the port and you will see more Roman walls; they were constructed between A.D. 270 and 310. They followed a rectangular course and were built so that their fortified sections faced the sea. By the 11th and 12th centuries, Barcelona had long outgrown its confines. Jaume I ordered the opening of the Roman walls, and the burgeoning growth that ensued virtually destroyed them, except for the foundations you see today.

The nearest Metro stop is at Jaume I or Barceloneta.

WALKING TOUR 2: **LA RIBERA (EL BORN & SANT PERE)**

START:	**Plaça de l'Angel (Metro: Jaume I).**
FINISH:	**Arc de Triomf at northern end of Parc de la Ciutadella (Metro: Arc de Triomf).**
TIME:	**2 to 3 hours.**
BEST TIMES:	**Any sunny day or early evening.**

This tour continues your exploration of the Old Quarter, concentrating on the eastern corner, formerly an area of tradesmen and artisans but today filled with top museums and trendy cafes.

Begin at the:

1 Plaça de l'Angel

Known in medieval times as the Plaça del Blat ("Square of Wheat"), since all grain sales were made here, this small, atmospheric square stands at the busy junction of Jaume I and Laietana on the eastern edge of the Barri Gòtic.

From the Plaça de l'Angel take Carrer Boria right; then turn left into Carrer Mercaders and immediately right again to Plaça Santa Caterina and the:

2 Mercat de Santa Caterina

This is the oldest working market in the area. It occupies the original site where the medieval convent of Santa Caterina once stood, and provides the usual rich cornucopia of Mediterranean produce. In 2005, after a protracted period of renovation, the market was reopened with a stunning new *moderniste* design (by the late Enric Miralles), whose colorful waved roof owes more than a little to Gaudí. It's open every day except Sunday.

From the south-facing side of the market take Carrer Sant Jacint, turn right into Carrer Corders, and then south into the Placeta d'en Marcus.

3 Capella d'en Marcus

Well worth a peek is this diminutive 12th-century chapel nestling in the tiny Placeta d'en Marcus, near the junction of calles Montcada and Carders (the latter means "Woolcomber's Street"). Originally conceived by one Bernat Marcus as a sanctuary for luckless travelers who reached the city after the gates had been closed, the chapel may have been headquarters of the country's very first postal service.

Continue south across Carrer Princesa to reach:

4 Carrer Montcada

Named after a powerful merchant, Guillem de Montcada, who in 1153 built a long-since-disappeared palace here, this charming medieval street would be interesting enough to stroll along even if it didn't contain three of the city's most interesting museums (to which, alas, you won't be able to do justice if you're to finish this walk the same day). The elegant buildings lining the street are reminders of the time it was a wealthy trading center; vast fortunes were made here by adroit and ambitious merchants.

5 Museu Picasso ★★★

Located in no fewer than five former palaces in Carrer Montcada, the Picasso (p. 169) is generally rated the most popular museum in town. In essence it covers the artist as a young man, and even the older works on display were created when the Malagueño was a mere 20-something. Exhibits range from notes and rough

Walking Tour 2: La Ribera (El Born & Sant Pere)

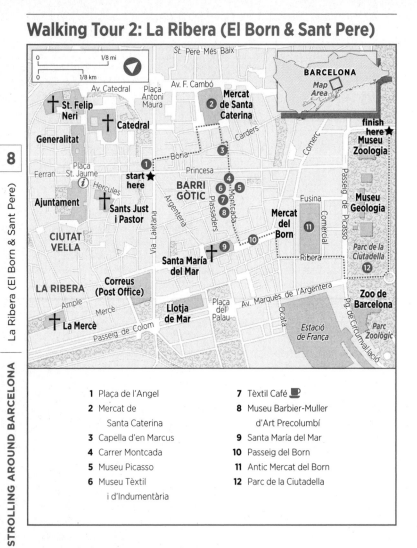

1 Plaça de l'Angel
2 Mercat de Santa Caterina
3 Capella d'en Marcus
4 Carrer Montcada
5 Museu Picasso
6 Museu Tèxtil i d'Indumentària
7 Tèxtil Café
8 Museu Barbier-Muller d'Art Precolumbí
9 Santa María del Mar
10 Passeig del Born
11 Antic Mercat del Born
12 Parc de la Ciutadella

sketches to lithographs, ceramics, and oil canvases. Highlights are *Las Meninas* (his take on Velázquez's painting of the same name) and *The Harlequin;* although time will be short, keep an eye open for *La Ciencia y la Caridad* (Science and Charity), a masterpiece created while Picasso was at school.

On the same street is:

6 Museu Tèxtil i d'Indumentària

Over 1,000 years of fashion fill the salons of this extraordinary museum (p. 170), which spreads throughout a fine period house, the Palau dels Marquesos de Llió, and features the original medieval ceilings. The oldest exhibits date from early Egypt, but it's the flamboyant baroque, Regency, and 20th-century styles that really catch the eye.

7 Tèxtil Café ☕

Carrer Montcada (☎ 93-268-25-98) is a convenient spot for a break between museums. This chic little cafe is tucked away in a secluded, cobbled courtyard on the grounds of the Museu Tèxtil itself. Ideal for relaxing over a *café llet (café con leche)* and Danish pastry.

On the same street is the:

8 Museu Barbier-Mueller d'Art Precolombí

Atmospherically housed in the 15th-century Palau Nadal, close to the above two museums, this branch of the great Geneva museum offers one of the best displays of pre-Columbian art and has been drawing in the crowds ever since it opened in 1997. Among its highlights is a dazzling selection of gold, jewelry, and masks (p. 168).

Continue down Carrer Montcada to the Passeig del Born. Turn right onto Carrer de Santa María.

9 Santa María del Mar

Built in the 14th century during a period of just over 50 years (quick for the time), this grandiose, high-vaulted basilica, honoring the patron saint of sailors, used to stand on the city's shore when the sea reached further inland. As the welfare of sailors mainly depended on the clemency and protection of "Our Lady of the Sea," in those days large numbers of penniless people helped without pay on its construction. Bronze figures of two porters on the door commemorate this, and the west portal is flanked by statues of Peter and Paul.

Today it's one of Barcelona's most imposing Gothic structures, noted for its soaring columns and uncluttered aura of space. Look out for the superb stained-glass windows, particularly the 15th-century rose-shaped one above the main entrance. A belated 1997 addition to this is, in contrast, jarringly unimpressive. You'll want to return for an evening concert—particularly a performance of Handel. In such a timeless setting it's an unforgettable experience.

Go back again to the:

10 Passeig del Born

This short wide *paseo,* or avenue, was once a center for tournaments and jousting events. (The name "Born" in Catalan means, among other things, the point of a jousting lance.) In medieval times, when Catalonia was a major naval power, the *paseo's* fame was such that the saying *Roda el món i torna al Born* ("Go around the world and return to the Born") became widespread. It was the spiritual heart of the city from the 13th century right up to the 18th century, when La Rambla took over the number-one spot. Today the Born's revelry assumes a more modern nocturnal form, centered mainly around the countless bars and cafes filling the bustling side streets.

At the end of the avenue is the:

11 Antic Mercat del Born

This massive building, with its wrought-iron roof, was formerly one of the city's biggest wholesale markets. Closed since the 1970s, during renovations a number of excavations were discovered, which can be viewed through glass flooring. It is scheduled to reopen as a museum and cultural center, but as yet there is no firm date for reopening; 2012 looks like the earliest.

Cross the Passeig de Picasso just past the eastern end of the market and you enter the:

12 Parc de la Ciutadella ★★

Built on the site of a much-hated 18th-century Bourbon citadel, which was destroyed in 1878 (p. 16), this 30-hectare (75-acre) oasis of relaxing greenery came about in the late 1890s after serving as the site for the Universal Exhibition. Its many highlights include statues, fountains (one designed by a young Gaudí), a boating lake, a waterfall (La Cascada) with a giant hairy mammoth sculpture, the Domènech i Muntaner–designed Castell dels Tres Dragons (Castle of Three Dragons), which houses the zoological museum, two arboretums, and a small botanical garden. There's also a science museum and—last, but not least—the Catalan parliament, which is located in the former citadel's arsenal and can be visited by appointment (p. 171). Stroll to the northern end of the park to view the *moderniste*-cum-neo-*mudéjar*–style Arc de Triomf, which served as the entrance to the Universal Exhibition.

There are Metro stops at Arc de Triomf and Jaume I.

WALKING TOUR 3: **EL RAVAL**

START:	**Monumento de Colom (Metro: Drassanes).**
FINISH:	**Universitat (Metro: Universitat).**
TIME:	**2 to 3 hours.**
BEST TIMES:	**Any sunny day or early evening.**

This tour takes you through El Raval, a once run-down and deprived corner of Old Barcelona that has reinvented itself as an earthy cosmopolitan quarter with international eating spots and cutting-edge cultural centers.

Walk north up the main La Rambla *paseo* and then turn left onto the Carrer Nou de la Rambla. Almost immediately on your left is:

1 Palau Güell

Gaudí's first architectural creation (p. 174)—in reality an extension of his parents' old house, which has since been turned into a hotel—was this citadel-like *moderniste* building located just a stone's throw from La Rambla. Partial renovation work has been completed, but the whole place won't be totally finished until 2012. In the meantime you can enjoy free entrance to the ground floor and admire its Venetian facade, entrance archways, and rooftop array of bizarre chimneys from the street.

Continue along Carrer Nou de la Rambla. When you reach the wide, busy Avinguda del Paral.lel, turn right onto Carrer de l'Abat Safont and then right again onto Carrer de Sant Pau. On your immediate right is:

Walking Tour 3: El Raval

1 Palau Güell
2 Església de Sant Pau del Camp
3 Rambla de Raval
4 Antic Hospital de Santa Cruz
5 Carrer d'en Robador
6 Gran Teatre del Liceu
7 Mercat de la Boqueria
8 La Boqueria ☕

9 Palau de la Virreina
10 MACBA (Museu d'Art
    Contemporani de Barcelona)
11 FAD (Foment de les
    Arts i del Disseny)
12 CCCB (Centre de Cultura
    Contemporània
    de Barcelona)

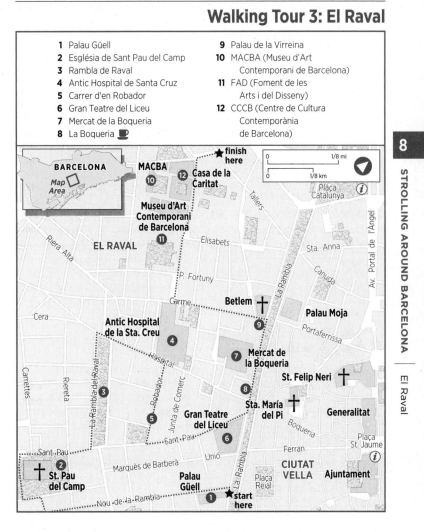

2 Església de Sant Pau del Camp

This rare urban example of Romanesque architecture (officially declared a national monument) is in fact Barcelona's grandaddy of all churches (p. 175), filled with fascinating small sculptures and grotesque figures. When it was originally built by monks in the 9th century, the surrounding area consisted of fields and woodlands (hence its name, "Saint Paul of the Countryside"). Today's rather squat building is a delightfully intact blend of 11th- to 14th-century styles, including some Visigothic decor, and highlighted by a beautiful, tiny cloister with Moorish archways and a stone fountain.

209

Continue along Carrer de Sant Pau to the:

3 Rambla de Raval

This is one of the city's newest *paseos,* created in 2000 when a large quadrangle of congested alleyways and insalubrious tenements was removed as part of a commendable and necessary "Raval open to the heavens" plan. Today it's a sunny, pedestrianized area where children play and locals can relax in the shade of the palm trees. Surrounded by a new blend of nifty hotels and eating spots—including various ethnic cafes and restaurants owned by immigrants—it exudes an international atmosphere, although some of the earlier grittiness remains. Similar changes are continuing to take place as the area becomes increasingly gentrified and cosmopolitan. Look for the huge black *Gat* (cat) statue at the southern end of the Rambla.

At the northern end of the Rambla de Raval, turn right into Carrer de l'Hospital.
Ahead on your left is the:

4 Antic Hospital de Santa Cruz

The name is misleading, as the famed former hospital—one of Spain's biggest in the Middle Ages—ceased to cater to the bodily sick and needy over 80 years ago, when one of its last patients was the dying Gaudí. Today, instead, it provides sustenance for the mind. Its blend of Gothic, baroque, and neoclassical styles is spread throughout several buildings, which were converted in 2001 into a variety of cultural institutions including the main Catalan National Library and the Massana Art School (© **93-485-99-13**).

On the right of the Antic Hospital is the:

5 Carrer d'en Robador

This narrow, winding, and sunless street in the heart of the old *Barrio Chino* (or Barri Xino, as it's known today) was once the notorious focus not of robbers (*robadors),* but of posturing prostitutes of all shapes and sizes who filled every doorway and lined every corner. Today it's more low-key, a mildly risqué corner of unadorned medieval Barcelona; just take sensible precautions when walking here at night.

At the end of Carrer d'en Robador, turn right onto Sant Pau and continue to the end, where you meet La Rambla and the:

6 Gran Teatre del Liceu

Tragically destroyed over a decade ago by fire, this magnificent, traditional opera house (p. 240) overlooking La Rambla has risen phoenix-like from the ashes and today once more hosts some of the best classical performances in the world. Its new facade belies the opulent interior of rich, dark colors and intricate carvings where a 19th-century setting has been revived alongside various modern accoutrements.

Carry on left up La Rambla to:

7 Mercat de la Boqueria ★★★

In a class all its own, this ever-colorful, ever-dynamic food market is among the biggest and best in Europe. Under its high, wrought-iron ceilings (p. 226), countless stalls sell a kaleidoscopic mix of Atlantic and Mediterranean seafood,

Castilian meat, Valencian fruit, and local vegetables. The picture-postcard stalls at the front tend to be more expensive, so take an admiring look and then head farther back for the better-value stuff.

8 La Boqueria 🍽

Inside the market you'll also find several good-value bars and cafes where locals come for early breakfasts or a snifter, or where chefs from top restaurants pause for a *cafe solo* between their purchases. These outwardly unassuming bars serve some of the best coffee and tapas in the city. Look out in particular for Pinotxo and El Quim.

Almost adjoining the Boqueria is the:

9 Palau de la Virreina

Built in 1770, this classical baroque palace (p. 173) is named after the widow of a wealthy former viceroy of Peru. Today it's a cultural-events center, mainly private but with occasional public exhibitions dedicated to Barcelona history and traditions. The downstairs photographic displays are usually worth a look. You can also buy souvenirs here, and consult the information desk for up-to-date cultural events.

Turn left away from La Rambla along Carrer Carmé and take the fourth left onto Carrer del Angel, to arrive at the Plaça dels Angels, where you'll see a trio of avant-garde arts centers. Straight in front of you across the square is the:

10 MACBA (Museu d'Art Contemporani de Barcelona)

Opened in 1995 with a rather tentative display, this American-designed, glass-walled contemporary art museum (p. 173)—with its bright white walls, intricately planned ramps, and triple atrium—illuminates its now adventurous collection of modern-art masterpieces with natural light. Alongside international favorites such as Klee, there's a strong presence of Catalan artists, reflecting various reactionary movements in both painting and photography. Displays are constantly changing and temporary exhibitions feature new creative works.

To your left is the:

11 FAD (Foment de les Arts i del Disseny)

Located in the old Convent dels Angels (p. 172), opposite the MACBA, this essentially administrative body, which promotes talented artists and awards grants to promising newcomers, organizes many exhibitions of its own. Workshops and art markets also give burgeoning artists a chance to sell their own offerings.

Behind the MACBA, reached by Carrer Montealegre, is the:

12 CCCB (Centre de Cultura Contemporània de Barcelona)

Built on the site of a spacious former *casa de caritat* (almshouse), this is Spain's biggest cultural center (p. 172). Its design—by Viaplana and Piñon, who also created the Maremagnum commercial center by the port—is mainly a modern conglomeration of steel and glass, although the patio and facade of the former building remain. It offers an eclectic blend of movie and video shows, art exhibitions, conferences and courses, music and dance performances, and even organized walks around offbeat areas of the city. There's also a well-stocked bookstore and a bar/restaurant.

Turn right onto Carrer Valldoncella and then left along Carrer dels Tallers past Plaça de Castella for Plaça de la Universitat and the Metro stop.

WALKING TOUR 4: *MODERNISTE* ROUTE (L'EIXAMPLE)

START:	**Plaça Urquinaona (Metro: Urquinaona).**
FINISH:	**Plaça de Catalunya (Metro: Plaça de Catalunya).**
TIME:	**2 to 3 hours.**
BEST TIMES:	**Any sunny day or early evening, although some shops close in the afternoon.**

This stroll explores the wide-laned, 19th-century-inspired Eixample (or "extension") of the city, where fine *moderniste* buildings stand alongside some of the city's most elegant shops and cafes.

Start at Plaça Urquinaona and head down to Carrer Sant Francesc de Paula to the:

1 Palau de la Música Catalana ★★★

This haven for Barcelona music lovers, designed by Domènech i Muntaner and tucked away just above La Ribera, is well worth a slight detour before you begin your meander up into L'Eixample. Ornately extravagant, its highlights include busts of Palestrina, Bach, and Beethoven; multicolored mosaics and columns; and a large allegorical frieze of the Orfeó Català (Catalan Choral Society) by Lluis Bru. The thing to do, of course, is to come back one evening to enjoy a concert in the magnificent interior (p. 170).

Return to Urquinaona and walk right along Carrer Ausiàs March to no. 31, where you'll find:

2 Farmacia Nordbeck

Built in 1905, this is one of the best examples of pharmacies built in a complete *moderniste* style, with stained-glass windows and dark mellow wood. Throughout L'Eixample you'll notice similarly exotic chemists—such as the Argelaguet in Carrer Roger de Llúria—emphasizing this balm-like link between curing the body and satisfying the soul.

And three buildings down the street (on the same side), you'll see:

3 Cases Tomàs Roger

This duo of houses at nos. 37 and 39, designed by Enric Sagnier at the end of the 19th century, is noted for its fine archways and well-restored *sgraffito* on the facades.

Return to Plaça Urquinaona and head north up Carrer Roger de Llúria. At no. 85 you'll find:

Walking Tour 4: *Moderniste* Route (L'Eixample)

1 Palau de la Música Catalana
2 Farmacia Nordbeck
3 Cases Tomàs Roger
4 Queviures Murrià
5 Café Baume
6 BD Barcelona Design
7 Casa de les Punxes
   (Casa Terrades)
8 Casa Comalat
9 Palau de Baró de Cuadras
10 La Pedrera (Casa Milà)
11 Manzana de la Discordia

4 Queviures Murrià

Run by the same family for more than 150 years, this marvelous grocery store is also an impressive work of art. The array of goodies inside is complemented by a lavish exterior by the *moderniste* painter Ramón Casas.

5 Café Baume 🍵

(Roger de Llúria 124. ✆ 93-459-05-66), is a traditional cafe where you can put your feet up on one of the old-fashioned, well-worn leather chairs and enjoy a morning coffee or tea during the exhausting business of checking out the area's artistic attractions. On Sundays it's particularly popular with locals, who come to relax and browse the latest scandals and spats with Madrid in *La Vanguardia*.

Continue up Roger de Llúria to Carrer de Mallorca. Turn right and proceed to no. 291 to find:

6 BD Barcelona Design

One of the classiest interior-design shops you'll find anywhere, this stylish building—known as Casa Tomas—was designed by several key *moderniste* architects, including the great Domènech i Muntaner. Browse through the (expensive) selection of chic reproductions and furnishings based on work by the likes of Dalí and Gaudí.

Continue farther up Roger de Llúria and then turn right onto the wide Avinguda Diagonal. On the opposite (north) side of the road at nos. 416 to 420 is the:

7 Casa de les Punxes (Casa Terrades)

Known locally as the "House of Spikes" because of its sharply pointed turrets, this neo-Gothic, castle-like eccentricity built by Puig i Cadafalch in 1905 has four towers and a trio of separate entrances (one for each of the family's daughters). Its ceramic panels have patriotic motifs. Controversial in the past (a then-prominent politician, Alejandro Lerroux, called it "a crime against the nation"), it's regarded today as one of *modernisme*'s great landmark facades.

Farther along the Avinguda Diagonal at no. 442 is:

8 Casa Comalat

Designed by the Gaudí-influenced architect Salvador Valeri i Popurull, this unusual house has two different facades, formal at the front, more playful at the back. The former has a dozen curvy stone balconies with wrought-iron railings; the latter, which opens onto Carrer Corséga, features polychrome ceramic work and wooden galleries. It's not open to the public but well worth a look from the outside.

Now walk left along the avenue to:

9 Palau de Baró de Cuadras

Built in 1904 to a design by the ubiquitous Puig i Cadafalch, this mansion features a unique double facade that combines Plateresque and Gothic styles on the Diagonal-facing side; the more staid rear facade reflects the fact that the building was essentially a mere block of apartments overlooking Carrer Rosselló. Inside, the decor is predominantly Arabic, with a wealth of mosaics, *sgraffito,* and polychrome woodwork. It houses the **Casa Asia** exhibition (*C* **93-368-08-36;** www.casaasia.es), which aims to foster cultural and economic relations between Asia and Europe.

Continue to Passeig de Gràcia and turn left to reach:

10 La Pedrera (Casa Milà) ★★★

Created between 1905 and 1910, this building is, after La Sagrada Família, Gaudí's most extraordinary work (p. 176). **Casa Milà**—the building's original name—may baldly be a block of apartments, but it's like none other on earth. The highly sculpted, undulating limestone facade earned the place its nickname, **La Pedrera** (stone quarry), while its stunning wrought-iron balconies, parabolic arches, and gnarled, fairy-tale chimneys evoke a fantasy. The rooftop is spellbinding, even more so than the views it affords, and concerts are held here on summer weekends.

The fourth floor comprises an entire *moderniste* apartment, the Pis de Pedrera—*pis* means "apartment" in Catalan—where rooms are laden with wondrous knick-knacks and antiques. In the attic you can see the **Espai Gaudí** (Gaudí Space), which comprehensively summarizes Gaudí's style of working.

Continue a few blocks left down Passeig de Gràcia to:

11 Manzana de la Discordia ★★★

This small zone of L'Eixample is the highlight of any *moderniste* enthusiast's visit (p. 178). Here you have, almost on top of each other, works by not just one great architect but three. (*Manzana,* incidentally, means both "plot of land" and "apple" in Spanish, so its double meaning hints at the Greek myth in which Paris has to choose which beauty wins the coveted Apple of Discord.)

If there is a single victor here it's generally acknowledged to be Gaudí's exotically curvaceous **Casa Batlló** (no. 43). Permanently illuminated at night, it's known affectionately by Catalans as the "Casa dels Ossos" (House of Bones)—and sometimes alternatively the "Casa del Drach" (House of the Dragon)—and it features an irregular blend of mauve, green, and blue fragmented tiles topped by a bizarre azure chimney-filled roof, which is also open to the public (p. 179).

Next comes Puig i Cadalfach's cubical-style **Casa Amatller** (no. 41), with its gleaming ceramic facade, Flemish Gothic pediments, and small, bizarre Eusebio Arnau–sculpted statues of precociously talented animals (one of them blowing glass). Finally, there is Domènech i Muntaner's **Casa Lleó Morera** (no. 35), whose dominant turret resembles a melting, pale-blue wedding cake atop a sea of esoteric ornamentation that includes models of a lion (*lleo*) and mulberry bush (*morera*).

From here it's a 5-minute stroll right down the Passeig de Gràcia to Plaça de Catalunya and the Metro stop.

8

STROLLING AROUND BARCELONA | Moderniste Route (L'Eixample)

SHOPPING

The shopping scene in Barcelona—long a trader's haven thanks to its richly varied shipping imports, wealth of local products, and innate commercial savvy—is wide enough to satisfy the most demanding consumer.

The city has an impressive ability to move with the times, and Barcelona today offers a fascinating blend of centuries-old shops and dynamic *última moda* stores run by fashionistas who have a tendency to look outward for trend inspiration, rather than toward the rest of Spain. Keen shoppers have at their disposal a time-straddling gamut of traditional *colmados* (small grocery shops), family-run *tiendas*, polished specialty stores, colorful covered markets replete with Mediterranean fare, pristine modern malls, designer showcases, and top-name boutiques. Some of the leading global fashion names (Zara, Mango, and Camper, to name a few) are in fact Spanish, and stock a large range of their offerings at competitive prices.

With the pound and dollar currently weaker against the euro than in previous years, and Spanish sales tax (IVA) at 18% on most goods (food is 8%), shopping in Barcelona isn't quite the bargain it once was. There's certainly a superabundance of goodies to tempt you, though, as long as you don't get too carried away.

THE SHOPPING SCENE

L'Eixample's elegant Passeig de Gràcia contains some of the most expensive retail space in Spain. Here the big guns of fashion have set up shop in gorgeous 19th- and 20th-century buildings: Chanel, Max Mara, and Loewe jostle for your attention alongside Benetton, Zara, Mango, Custo Barcelona, and Diesel. All along the avenue there are dozens of outdoor cafes for resting up, enjoying a tapas or two, and examining your booty. The Rambla de Catalunya, which runs parallel to the Passeig de Gràcia, has lesser-known—but equally glitzy—establishments with more of a focus on housewares, books, and beauty.

Don't bypass the cross-streets that run between the two, as they are also scattered with some of the city's top shopping, particularly Valencia, Provença, and Consell de Cent; the latter is renowned for its expensive antiques shops and art galleries. The top end of the Passeig de Gràcia intersects El Diagonal, one of the city's main arteries. Here you will find housewares giant Habitat, the megamall L'Illa, and various other boutiques in between, such as homegrown fashion gurus Adolfo Dominguez, Josep Font, and Antonio Miró. The Metro only services this part of town sparsely and the shops are spread out, but don't worry: The *tombus* is a comfortable minibus that does the "shopping line" along the Diagonal; hop on at any regular bus stop.

The older, more traditional shops and one-of-a-kind retailers are mostly to be found in the Ciutat Vella (El Raval, El Born, and the Barri Gòtic). Here in the Old City, you will also find intimate boutiques and galleries. One promising new hub is around the MACBA (p. 173), the city's museum of contemporary art in El Raval. Smaller galleries come and go here, and there are fashion and design shops springing up all the time. Two of the most enticing are Gimenez y Zuazo and Como Agua de Mayo. In the direction of the port, shops on the streets running off La Rambla (particularly Carme and Hospital) reflect the melting-pot nature of the neighborhood: Wine shops sit side by side with halal butchers and traditional Catalan bakers; others seem to have survived for centuries selling scissors. This is where you see the dusty old emporiums of yesteryear, ones that have, sadly, largely disappeared from cities like London and New York.

Even though the Barri Gòtic is home to many traditional stores, there's no shortage of trendy spots at the top end of the area. Here, throngs hit the Portal d'Angel and Portaferrisa on Friday evenings and Saturdays, seeking out new arrivals in fashion from the top high-street names such as H&M, Levi's, Benetton, and other global fashion labels. With the major department store El Corte Inglés in the immediate vicinity, these two streets (which cross each other) make up another of the city's convenient and central shopping hubs.

Opening Hours

Catalonia has resisted the lure of Sunday trading, mainly at the insistence of the trade unions. Apart from Barcelona's coin and stamp markets, which open on Sundays, most stores shut on Sundays and many also close on Saturday afternoon. The good news is that most shops in the center stay open through the lunch hour and generally don't close until 9pm, even on Saturdays, with department stores extending this to 10pm. As a general rule of thumb, smaller shops are open Monday through Saturday 9:30 or 10am to 1:30 or 2pm, and then open again in the afternoon from 4:30 or 5pm to 8:30pm. You will always find exceptions to this, especially as the tourist trade fans out over the city. You may come across some that, frustratingly, take Monday morning off, or decide to take a long siesta, but even that adds to the unique experience of Barcelona being a modern city that has retained its retro feel.

Credit cards are accepted nearly everywhere, even for small purchases. You must show a form of photo ID (passport or photo driver's license) when making a purchase with your credit card. Don't be offended when the assistant asks for ID; it is an effective guard against fraudulent credit card use.

Sales tax is called IVA. In July 2010 it rose to 8% for food items and 18% for most other goods. Cash register receipts will show this as a separate charge. If you see a "Tax-Free Shopping" sticker displayed in a shop you can request a tax-free receipt on purchases of over 90.16€. Get this stamped at any airport Customs (in Barcelona-Prats it's in Terminal 2A) when you depart Spain and you can claim a cash refund from the banks in the airport. Refunds can be made to your credit card or by check. For more information see www.globalrefund.com.

Sales (*rebajas* or *rebaixes*) start in early July and early January. Discounts at the sales are extraordinary, often starting at 50%. On the whole, shopping in Barcelona is a genteel affair; small business and trading has historically been a major backbone of its economy, and many establishments here still feel like a piece of living history, in terms of both service and presentation.

What to Buy

Stylish clothing, shoes, and leatherwear are the items to go for in Barcelona. Leather shoes, belts, jackets, and coats are particularly good buys; whether you want a high-end store such as Loewe or succumb to the leather hawkers on La Rambla, the quality and value of leather goods is superb. Barcelona is renowned for its expertise in design and has a vibrant design culture supported by the local government. Decorative objects and housewares here are original and well made and can be found in the shops around the MACBA and the Museu Picasso. Artisan pieces, such as ceramic tiles and gifts and earthenware bowls and plates, are cheap and plentiful. Cookware, crockery, wine glasses, and utensils in general are a great buy; a poke around a humble hardware store can unearth some great finds, too.

What follows is a limited selection from the hundreds of shops in Barcelona.

SHOPPING A TO Z
Antiques

Serious collectors should check out the maze of streets around the Calle Palla near the Plaça de Pi in the Barri Gòtic; while there are few bargains to be had you will find everything from bric-a-brac to old posters and lace. Consell de Cent in L'Eixample houses a range of shops selling fine antiques and antiquities. Every Thursday, many of these traders set up stalls outside the cathedral, transferring to Port Vell (the port end of La Rambla) at the weekend.

Angel Batlle ★★ 📖 This shop has an unbeatable collection of old posters from travel to advertising and music to sport, as well as postcards, engravings, maps, prayer cards—really, anything that's printed. They make wonderful souvenirs; take home a 1950s' sherry poster or a Picasso or Miró print. Palla 23. ✆ **93-301-58-84.** Metro: Liceu.

Artur Ramón Art ★★ One of the finest antiques and art dealers in Barcelona, found in a three-level emporium. Set on a narrow, flagstone-covered street near Plaça del Pi (the center of the antiques district), it stands opposite the tiny Placeta al Carrer de la Palla. The store, which has been operated by four generations of the Ramón family (all called Artur), also has branches nearby and is known for its 18th- and 19th-century decorative arts, 20th-century paintings and sculpture, rare ceramics, porcelain, and glassware. Prices are high, as you'd expect, but it's high quality and lasting value. Palla 25. ✆ **93-302-59-70.** www.arturamon.com. Metro: Liceu.

Bulevard dels Antiquaris This 70-unit indoor market just off one of Barcelona's most aristocratic avenues has a huge collection of art, antiques, bric-a-brac, and junk assembled in a series of stands and small shops. It's great for browsing, although the erratic opening hours may drive you mad. Passeig de Gràcia 55. ✆ **93-215-44-19.** www.bulevarddelsantiquaris.com. Metro: Passeig de Gràcia.

L'Arca de l'Avia ★★ 📷 This gorgeous shop sells lace and linen bedspreads and curtains, petticoats and handkerchiefs, and other assorted textiles from the 18th to early 20th centuries. Some of the sequined numbers worn by Kate Winslet in the film *Titanic* were snapped up from their collection of period clothing. Prices aren't cheap, but the quality is unsurpassed. Banys Nous 20. ✆ **93-302-15-98.** www.larcadelavia.com. Metro: Liceu.

Urbana 🏛 Urbana sells an array of architectural remnants (often from torn-down mansions), antique furniture, and reproductions of brass hardware. There are antique and reproduction marble mantelpieces, wrought-iron gates, and garden seats, even carved wooden fireplaces with the *modernisme* look. It's an impressive, albeit costly, array of merchandise. Còrsega 258. ☎ **93-218-70-36.** Metro: Hospital Sant Pau. There's another branch at Seneca 13. ☎ **93-237-36-44.** Metro: Diagonal.

Books

Altaïr This is an excellent travel bookstore with helpful staff, and the wide selection of books—mainly in Spanish but with some in English—covers nature, anthropology, history, and global travel. There's a good choice of material on Barcelona, of course, as well as kids' books, comics, CDs, and DVDs. Gran Vía de les Corts Catalanes 616. ☎ **93-342-71-71.** www.altair.es. Metro: Universitat.

BCN Books The main content of this English-language bookshop is language-learning material, including basic grammar and phrasebooks plus a wide range of dictionaries. There's also a good selection of travel books, contemporary fiction, and classic novels. Roger de Llúria 118. ☎ **93-457-76-92.** www.bcnbooks.com. Metro: Girona. Other branches at Riera d'Horta 32. ☎ **93-476-33-43.** Metro: La Pau; and Amigó 81. ☎ **93-200-79-53.** Metro: Llucmajor.

Buffet y Ambigú 🏛 In among the deli stalls at the back of the Boqueria market is a unique book outlet. The stall sells cookbooks catering to all tastes, from the best tapas recipes to manuals for chefs and special editions such as El Bulli's encyclopedia showcasing Catalan super-chef Ferran Adrià's (p. 300) cooking techniques. Many of the books are in English. Mercat de la Boqueria, Parada 435. ☎ **93-243-01-78.** Metro: Liceu.

Casa del Libro 🖋 This huge book barn covers all genres, from novels to self-help, travel to technical. There are sections with foreign-language books, including English, and cover prices here are what you would pay back home. Passeig de Gràcia 62. ☎ **93-272-34-80.** www.casadellibro.com. Metro: Passeig de Gràcia.

Cooperativa d'Arquitectes Jordi Capell For books on Barcelona's architects and interior designers, head to the basement of the city's architecture school. This bookstore has a huge range of technical books for architects as well as monographs and photographic books of the work of leading architects, from Gaudí to Gehry. Plaça Nova 5. ☎ **90-299-89-93.** www.eupalinos.com. Metro: Liceu.

FNAC 🖋 The Plaça de Catalunya branch of this music-and-entertainment megastore has a solid section of English-language books. Most of the novels are bestsellers, and current travel guides to Barcelona and the rest of Spain are available. If you are here to learn Spanish, there is a dictionary and language textbook section. El Triangle, Plaça de Catalunya 4. ☎ **93-301-99-02.** www.fnac.es. Metro: Plaça de Catalunya.

Hibernian Books This friendly second-hand English-language bookstore, a mainstay of the Gràcia literary scene, is a favorite with residents and visitors alike. The books cover topics ranging from health to hobbies; exchanges and generous discounts are available. The shop also gives you the lowdown on Anglo-Irish social and cultural goings-on in Barcelona. A kids' corner and tea and coffee service add to the atmosphere, and there are armchairs in which to sit and browse before you buy. Carrer de Montseny. ☎ **93-217-46-96.** www.hibernian-books.com. Metro: Fontana.

Laie ★★ A good selection of English-language books, including contemporary literature, travel maps, and guides. The bookstore has an upstairs cafe with international newspapers, and a terrace. It serves breakfast, lunch (at the salad bar), and dinner. The cafe is open Monday through Saturday from 9am to 1am. The shop schedules cultural events, including art exhibits and literary presentations. Pau Claris 85. ℭ **93-318-17-39.** www.laie.es. Metro: Plaça de Catalunya or Urquinaona.

Chocolates & Cakes

Cacao Sampaka ★★   If there were such a thing as *haut chocolat,* this establishment would be its Christian Dior. Using the finest cacao available, a mind-boggling selection of confectionery is categorized into exotic collections. The sleek packaging turns the chocolates into true objects of desire, and there is a bar-cafe where you can enjoy a cup of creamy hot chocolate, pastries, and high-cholesterol sandwiches, at prices not dissimilar to more pedestrian places. Consell de Cent 292. ℭ **93-272-08-33.** www.cacaosampaka.com. Metro: Passeig de Gràcia.

Escribà ★ 👜   You may have already seen the glittering facade of this beautiful Art Nouveau shop on postcards. But far from a curious relic, it sells the products of one of the city's finest chocolate and cake makers. Pop in for a coffee and croissant (outside tables in the summer) or pick up a box of bonbons or a bottle of dessert wine to take home. At Easter, the windows display *monas,* elaborate chocolate sculptures decorated with jewels and feathers. La Rambla 83. ℭ **93-301-60-27.** www.escriba.es. Metro: Liceu. Other branches at Gran Vía 546. ℭ **93-454-75-35.** Metro: Universitat; and Ronda Litoral 42. ℭ **93-221-07-29. Bus: 36.**

Granja Dulcinea ★   Here at Barcelona's number-one chocolate mecca you can buy *melindros* (sugar-topped soft biscuits) and drink hot chocolate that's as richly viscous as a melted bar of the real stuff. The place is both a genial cafe (p. 128) and a traditional shop selling a scrumptious variety of chocs as well as pastries such as the sinfully high-caloried *ensaimada* from Mallorca. Carrer de Petritxol 2. ℭ **93-302-68-24.** Metro: Liceu.

Xocoa ★   In the same street as Granja Dulcinea, brothers Marc and Miguel Escurell have modernized their century-old family business by employing top graphic artists to design their packaging and diversifying with chocolate candles, incense, and even a CD for chocolate lovers. Try the house specialty, the *Ventall,* a scrumptious cake of almond pastry and chocolate truffle. Petritxol 11. ℭ **93-301-11-97.** www.xocoa-bcn.com. Metro: Liceu. Other branches at Roger de Llúria. ℭ **93-487-24-99;** and Casp 33. ℭ **93-304-03-00.** Metro: Girona for both.

Department Stores

El Corte Inglés   The main Barcelona branch of Spain's largest department store chain sells a wide variety of merchandise, ranging from traditional handicrafts to high-fashion items, and from Spanish CDs to food. The store has a restaurant and cafe and offers consumer-related services, such as a travel agency. You can also get your purchases mailed straight home. Not only that, but you can have shoes re-heeled, get hair and beauty treatments, or relax in the rooftop cafe. The basement supermarket (Plaça de Catalunya branch only) is the best place to pick up wines and other foodstuffs to take home. Open Monday through Saturday from 10am to 10pm. Plaça de Catalunya 14. ℭ **93-306-38-00.** www.elcorteingles.es. Other branches at Av. Diagonal 617–619. ℭ **93-366-71-00.** Metro: María Cristina; and Av. Diagonal 471. ℭ **93-493-48-00.** Metro: Hospital Clínic.

Designer Homewares

BD Barcelona Design ★★★ Started by a group of prominent Catalan architects, this gorgeous gallery-shop, housed in a sumptuous *moderniste* edifice, offers the best contemporary pieces alongside reproductions of work by the likes of Gaudí, Dalí, and Mackintosh. Artwork by Oscar Tusquets, one of the shop's founders and a leading Catalan designer, is also a good investment. Goodies range from furniture, fittings, and rugs to easily packed items such as kitchenware and decorative objects. Sleek and serious, BD is Barcelona's bastion of design culture. Casa Tomás, Mallorca 291. *93-458-69-09.* www.bdbarcelona.com. Metro: Passeig de Gràcia.

Gotham Although the fad for retro design pieces is well and truly established in Spain, this shop was a pioneer. You'll find furniture from the 1950s and 1960s, as well as ceramics, crockery, vases, lights, and other items hailing from the same epoch. Prices aren't cheap, but most of the stock has been restored or is in faultless condition. Cervantes 7. *93-412-46-47.* www.gotham-bcn.com. Metro: Jaume I.

Ici et Là ★ Craftsmanship and quirky design characterize the pieces on display in this charming showroom located right next to the Palau de la Música (p. 240). Most pieces are limited editions by local artists, but they also receive regular shipments of Nepalese chairs, African baskets, and Indian textiles. Glass features strongly, from candleholders to delicately embossed wine glasses. Nearly everything in this shop could be described as "conversation pieces." It's only open from Tuesday to Thursday. Pasaje Sert 5. *93-268-78-43.* www.icietla.com. Metro: Urquinaona.

Vinçon ★★ Fernando Amat's Vinçon is the best design emporium in the city, with 10,000 products—everything from household items to the best in Spanish contemporary furnishings. Its mission is to purvey good design, period. Housed in the former home of artist Ramón Casas—a contemporary of Picasso's during his Barcelona stint—the showroom is filled with the best Spain has. The creative window displays alone are worth the trek. Expect *anything.* Passeig de Gràcia 96. *93-215-60-50.* www.vincon.com. Metro: Diagonal.

Vitra ★★ The famed Swiss contemporary design company has a formidable two-story showcase in Barcelona, featuring unique pieces by Charles and Ray Eames, Phillipe Starck, Alväro Siza, and Frank Gehry. The prices are restrictive and most of them won't fit into hand luggage, but it's okay to dream, isn't it? Plaça Comercial 5. *93-268-72-19.* www.vitra.com. Metro: Jaume I or Arc de Triomf.

Fabrics, Textiles & Trimmings

Antiga Pasamaneria J. Soler If fringes, ribbons, braids, tassels, and cords are what you're after, look no further. This place has been selling them since 1898 and has a wall-to-wall display of everything from dainty French grosgrain ribbons to thick tapestry braids and borders. Plaça del Pi 2. *93-318-64-93.* Metro: Liceu.

Coses de Casa ★ Appealing fabrics and weavings are displayed in this 19th-century store. Many of the textiles are hand-woven in Mallorca, their boldly geometric patterns inspired by Arab motifs of centuries ago. The fabric, for the most part, is 50% cotton, 50% linen; much of it would make excellent upholstery material. Cushions, spreads, and throws can be made to order. Plaça Sant Josep Oriol 5. *93-302-73-28.* www.cosesdecasa.com. Metro: Jaume I or Liceu.

Gastón y Daniela ★★   This 100-year-old company originally hails from Bilbao, although these days its name is synonymous with fine fabrics for upholstery and drapery all over Spain. Every one of their damasks, polished cottons, brocades, and tapestries is lush, suited to a time when children's fingerprints and cat hair were not an issue. It's great for browsing, even if it's just for a new cushion cover. Pau Claris 171. ℭ **93-215-32-17.** www.gastonydaniela.com. Metro: Diagonal.

Fashion

Adolfo Domínguez ★   This is one of many outlets across Spain and Europe, and displays the fashion that has earned the store the appellation of the "Spanish Armani." There's one big difference: Domínguez's clothes for women and men, unlike Armani's, are designed for those with hips and limited budgets. And they cover all ages at their stores, including the youth market. As one fashion critic said of their offerings: "They are austere but not strict, forgivingly cut in urbane earth tones." Passeig de Gràcia 32. ℭ **93-487-41-70.** www.adolfodominguez.com. Metro: Passeig de Gràcia. Several other branches throughout the city.

Antonio Miró ★   This shop is devoted exclusively to Miró's fashionable men's and women's clothing designs. Since winning the Balenciaga designer's award in 1987 he has notched up several notable commissions, including creating the official wardrobe for the city's Olympics 5 years later. He was also awarded top prize for his 2001 collection at the Cibeles showrooms in Madrid. Consell de Cent 349. ℭ **93-487-06-70.** www.antoniomiro.es. Metro: Passeig de Gràcia.

Comité 🛍   This store is typical of the inventive fashion shops that have sprouted in the streets around the MACBA. Inside is a charmingly naive decor of pastel colors and white curtains, and much of the clothing is made of recycled items: An embroidered sheet or tablecloth is transformed into a wrap skirt or dress, or a striped men's shirt is reworked into a blouse. Notariat 8. ℭ **93-317-68-83.** www.comitebarcelona.com. Metro: Plaça de Catalunya or Liceu.

Como Agua en Mayo ★   A delightful Ciutat Vella boutique selling chic clothes and accessories, with Josep Font and other well-known labels among them. The shop's name translates as "Like Rain in May," summing up the refreshing feel of its wide range of brightly colored gear. The shop is located in trendy El Born near the iconic Santa María del Mar church and lots of stylish bars and shops. Carrer Argenteria 43. ℭ **93-310-64-41.** Metro: Jaume I.

Custo-Barcelona ★   First it was Hollywood, with the likes of Julia Roberts and Drew Barrymore seen sporting Custo T-shirts. Now they have taken over the world, with stores from Chicago to Perugia to Shanghai. As the name suggests, these tops and shirts, skirts, and trousers in mad mixes of fabrics and emblazoned with 1960s' retro motifs are a homegrown product and have become a symbol of "Cool Barcelona." Plaça de les Olles 7. ℭ **93-268-78-93.** www.custo-barcelona.com. Metro Jaume I or Liceu. Another branch at Calle Ferran 36. ℭ **93-342-66-98.** Metro: Jaume I or Barceloneta.

Du Pareil au Même   One for families traveling with trendy nippers, this switched-on member of the popular French chain provides very stylish gear for young 'uns from tiny tots to slim pre-pubescents. Perky, attractive clothing at (by today's standards) affordable prices. It's located in a lively street in the upper Eixample. Rambla de Catalunya 95. ℭ **93-487-14-49.** www.dpam.com. Metro: Diagonal.

El Mercadillo   This is Barcelona's temple to alternative culture, with dozens of stalls selling urban and club wear, leather and suede jackets, records, and second-hand clothes. The kids love it, but you may have a hard time of it if you have a post-teenage body size. Portaferrisa 17. ✆ **93-301-89-13.** Metro: Liceu.

Giménez & Zuazo ★   Quirky, colorful, and very Barcelonese, designer duo Giménez & Zuazo's creations are characterized by daring prints and unusual fabrics. Their skirts may have a female silhouette splashed across the front, or a shirt collar bordered in contrasting cross-stitch. Their BoBa T-shirts, with hand-painted imagery, are a cult item. Elisabets 20. ✆ **93-412-33-81.** www.boba.es. Metro: Plaça de Catalunya or Liceu. Another branch at Rec 42. ✆ **93-310-67-43.** Metro: Jaume I or Barceloneta.

Jean-Pierre Bua ★★   Another pioneer, this boutique was the first to import big-name Parisian fashion labels to Barcelona. There is a large stock of Gaultier (the French *enfant terrible* and Bua are friends), Comme des Garçons, and Spain's most international designer, Sybilla; Brussels is represented by Dries van Noten. Despite the price tags, the staff is laid-back and no one minds if you spend time simply looking. Diagonal 469. ✆ **93-439-71-00.** www.jeanpierrebua.com. Metro: Hospital Clínic.

Josep Font ★★   With a masterful eye for fabrics and attention to detail that recalls vintage St. Laurent, Catalan designer Josep Font is in a class of his own. His sumptuous shop retains many original Art Nouveau features, customized with his inherent quirkiness. Bold yet feminine, with a slight nod to trends, his designs are timeless. Provença 304. ✆ **93-487-21-10.** www.josepfont.com. Metro: Passeig de Gràcia.

La Boutique del Hotel   In the lobby of Hotel Axel (p. 106), the Boutique stocks the best and brightest names in menswear: John Richmond, Helmut Lang, and Rykiel Homme, to name just a few. In a city that is somewhat lacking in cutting-edge menswear stores, this one is frequented by homo-, hetero-, and metrosexuals alike. Aribau 33. ✆ **93-323-93-98.** www.axelhotels.com. Metro: Passeig de Gràcia.

La Commercial ★   This French-owned boutique stocks beautifully detailed and highly feminine clothing for day and evening by the likes of Cacharel, Paul & Joe, Comme des Garçons, and Spain's own Jocomomola. There is also a selection of artisan Parisian perfumes and accessories by the bijoux jewelry brand Scooter. A menswear outlet is located across the street. Calle Rec 52. ✆ **93-268-33-67.** www.lacomercial.info. Metro: Jaume I or Barceloneta.

Loft Avignon   Relocated to the wide-avenued Eixample from its original cozy Ciutat Vella address in 2009, this emporium is one of Barcelona's key fashion meccas. The clothes for men and women feature Vivienne Westwood, Gaultier, and Dirk Bikkembergs. Be warned, however: Staff are masters of subtle manipulation, and you may find yourself handing over your credit card for a jumpsuit you didn't mean to purchase. Muntaner 99. ✆ **93-453-15-46.** www.loftavignon.com. Metro: Diagonal.

Mango ✦   Apart from Zara (see below), Spain's other main fashion export is Mango, which in some countries goes by the name MNG. Young, trendy, and midpriced is the deal here, and although the range isn't as extensive as their main competitors (nor do they do men's or children's wear), it's a sad day in Retail Land when you won't find something to pop on for that special evening out. If your visit coincides with the winter season, their suede and leather coats and jackets are definitely worth considering. Portal de l'Angel 7. ✆ **93-317-69-85.** www.mango.es. Metro: Plaça de Catalunya. Other branches all over Barcelona.

On Land 🗡 Although On Land is surrounded by hyper-trendy boutiques, the men's and women's clothing here is highly wearable; it's cross-generational without forfeiting a cutting edge. Their own label produces some well-cut trousers and jackets, and when complemented by one of Monte Ibáñez's hand-painted T-shirts, you have a distinctive outfit. Prices are good and sizes (mercifully) generous. Princesa 25. ℰ **93-310-02-11.** www.on-land.com. Metro: Jaume I. Another branch at Calle Valencia, L'Eixample. ℰ **93-215-56-25**. Metro: Passeig de Gràcia.

Suite 🎁 It's worth taking a trip up to Gràcia to check out this contemporary boutique owned by fashion luminary Marta R. Gustems. The shop features stylish clothes and shoes by new Spanish designers such as Espera Drap as well as a range of sketches, watercolors, and other works of art by the owner herself. You'll find one of the city's best original-language cinemas (The Verdi, p. 240) in the same street, incidentally. Carrer Verdi 3–5, Gràcia. ℰ **93-213-19-93.** www.martargustems.com. Metro: Fontana.

Tèxtil i d'Indumentària Operated as a showcase for Catalonian design and ingenuity by Barcelona's Museu Tèxtil i d'Indumentària (p. 170), this shop proudly displays and sells clothing and accessories for men, women, and children, all of which are designed or at least manufactured within the region. Inventories include shoes, men's and women's sportswear and formalwear, jewelry, teddy bears, suitcases and handbags, umbrellas,

THE zaravolución

Many visitors to Spain are familiar with the **Zara** clothing label. Now with over 1,000 (2,500, counting the Zara offshoot brands) outlets in 70 countries, including megastores in the fashion capitals of Milan, Paris, London, and New York, Zara is hard to ignore. But not everybody is aware that Zara is Spanish-owned.

Zara was started back in the early 1970s by an industrious young Galician called Amancio Ortega; he's now the richest man in Spain. He spotted a need for stylish housecoats for the women in his rural village, and out of that an empire grew. Today, Zara is one of the few fashion empires in the world that vertically controls the entire process, from textile manufacture to design to retail. Using a global network of buyers and trend-spotters, they interpret hot-off-the-catwalk pieces for men, women, and children at astoundingly affordable prices. They appeal to the full cross-generational demographic gamut, from urban tribes to executives.

Zara's calendar doesn't just consist of four seasons; clothing is produced and distributed all year round from their behemoth headquarters in Ortega's native Galicia. New, never-to-be-repeated styles arrive every day, meaning converts return again and again.

A revolution needs a charismatic leader and Ortega is no exception. Until he took the company public in 2001, the press possessed only one photo of a man estimated to be worth €7.5 billion. He imposes a strict "no-press" policy on his staff and never gives interviews or accepts any of the dozens of accolades awarded to him in person. What he has done is, in less than a generation, democratized fashion and made it possible to dress like a film star for a song. *¡Viva la revolución!*

Located at Pelayo 58 (ℰ **93-301-09-78;** www.zara.com; Metro: Plaça de Catalunya), Passeig de Gràcia 16 (ℰ **93-318-76-75;** Metro: Passeig de Gràcia), and all over the city.

and towels, each created by up-and-coming Catalans. Two of the most famous designers include menswear specialist Antonio Miró (see above) and women's clothing designer Lydia Delgado. Montcada 12. ✆ **93-256-23-00.** www.museutextil.bcn.cat. Metro: Jaume I.

Fine Food & Wine

Caelum 🏛 Everything in this shop has been produced in monasteries and nunneries throughout Spain: Preserved fruit, marzipan and liquors, and quality cakes and cookies, some with cheeky names. (The delicious holy honey cake is one of the more innocently named products.) The ornate packaging makes them great gifts, and there is a cafe downstairs where you can sample before you buy. Palla 8. ✆ **93-302-69-93.** Metro: Liceu.

Casa Gispert If you have trouble finding this shop behind Santa María del Mar church, simply follow your nose. Coffee and nuts are roasted daily (go for the almonds straight from the oven) and are sold alongside dried and candied fruit of all descriptions: Turkish figs, apricots, currants, and raisins, and French *marron glacé*. Sometimes the lines spill out onto the street, such is the quality of everything this ancient shop sells. Sombrerers 23. ✆ **93-319-75-35.** www.casagispert.com. Metro: Jaume I.

La Botifarreria de Santa María ★ If you haven't already noticed that when faced with a rib-eye filet and a *botifarra* (sausage), Catalans will opt for the latter, then you should visit the shop opposite the Gothic Santa María del Mar church. As well as making their own *botifarras* (reputed to be the finest in the land) on the premises, they sell the richest *jamón Jabugo* (acorn-fed ham), rare cheeses, sweet *fuet* (a thin salami) from central Catalonia, and other meaty delicacies. They will vacuum-pack your edibles for traveling (check if you can bring it back to your home country), or you can take some of their produce to the nearby Parc de la Ciutadella for a picnic. Santa María 4. ✆ **93-319-91-23.** www.labotifarreria.com. Metro: Jaume I or Barceloneta.

Lavinia ★★ A sort of wine megastore, Lavinia makes selection easy as all their products are displayed according to country of origin, from Germany to Uruguay, Australia to California. As expected, the Spanish section is the biggest, bulging with Riojas, Priorats, *cavas*, Albariños, and sherries. There is a pack-and-send service, which is handy, as most bottles come cheaper by the dozen (check your country's laws about what/how much you can send back). Diagonal 605. ✆ **93-363-44-45.** www.lavinia.es. Metro: María Cristina.

Origens 99.9% ★ Purveyors of fine, exclusively Catalan foodstuffs (0.1% being the margin of error, presumably), this shop sells olive oils from Lleida, *mató* (a fresh, ricotta-like cheese) from the mountains, and wines from the Penedès and Priorat regions. There is a cafe next door where you can try before you buy. This is a good place to pick up presents for foodies back home. (Check regulations on what you can legally bring back to your country!) There's also an adjoining restaurant. Muntaner 409. ✆ **93-201-45-79.** www.origen99.com. Metro: Jaume I or Barceloneta. There are several branches throughout Barcelona.

Vila Viniteca ★★ This awesome wine shop in the heart of the El Born neighborhood supplies most of the restaurants around it. The selection here can be frightening for the non-vinicultured among us, but those in the know rave about it. There are 4,500 different wines, sherries, *cavas*, liquors, and spirits from all over Spain, many of which are exclusive to the shop. Check out the bargain basket at the counter, where the last in the crates are sold for a song. Agullers 7–9. ✆ **90-232-77-77** or 93-310-19-56. www.vilaviniteca.es. Metro: Jaume I or Barceloneta.

LA BOQUERIA: ONE OF THE WORLD'S
finest food MARKETS

The **Boqueria market,** La Rambla 91–101 (📞 **93-318-20-17;** www.boqueria.info; Mon–Sat 8am–8pm; Metro: Liceu), is the largest market in Europe (and probably the greatest in the world) and a must-see in the Catalan capital. It's located right in the middle of the famous boulevard La Rambla. While many markets have little to offer a visitor in terms of practical shopping, the Boqueria displays great produce, boasts some of the best bars and cafes in the city, and offers a chance to rub shoulders with the movers and shakers who have put the city at the forefront of world gastronomy.

It owes its central location to an historical twist of fate. In the mid-1800s, the demolition of the city's medieval walls began. *Pageses* (Catalan peasants) had been touting their bounty on the spot of the present market (originally one of the city's gates) and around the

perimeter of the neighboring Convent de Sant Josep for centuries, and the authorities saw no reason to move them when the work began. When the convent burned to the ground in 1835, the market expanded, and 30 years later, the engineer Miquel de Bergue finished his plans for a grandiose, wrought-iron market of five wings supported by metal columns, a project that wasn't finished until 1914. The official name of the market is Mercat de Sant Josep (a reference to the Capuchin nuns' old dwelling), although the term *boqueria* (meaning abattoir or butcher shop in Catalan) has stuck since the 13th century, when the site was a slaughterhouse.

The Boqueria's 330 stalls are a living testament to the fertility of the peninsula (Spain produces the widest variety of farm produce in all Europe) and its surrounding seas. What lies inside is a

Galleries

Despite producing some of the world's great artists, small galleries have a notoriously hard time surviving in Barcelona. This could be due to the fickleness of the scene. At the moment, gallery hubs include the streets around the Museu Picasso, the MACBA, and Calle Petritxol in the Barri Gòtic.

Art Picasso Here you can get good lithographic reproductions of works by Picasso, Miró, and Dalí, as well as T-shirts and tiles emblazoned with the masters' designs. Tapinería 10. 📞 **93-310-49-57.** Metro: Jaume I.

Galeria Toni Tàpies The son of Catalonia's most famous living painter, Antoni Tàpies (p. 180), runs this elegant gallery in the heart of L'Eixample. It's featured an eclectic blend of international work by such contemporary artists as Sol de Witt and João Onofre since its opening in 1994, and offers innovative exhibitions whose contributors change from season to season. Consell de Cent 282. 📞 **93-487-64-02.** www.tonitapies.com. Metro: Passeig de Gràcia.

Iguapop 🎁 The Iguapop company is one of the leading promoters of contemporary music in Barcelona. Hardly surprising, then, that the emphasis is firmly on youth culture in their first gallery. Graffiti, video art, magazine design, and contemporary photography by young people from both Spain and abroad is exhibited in their gastronomic cornucopia that changes its palette from season to season. Early fall sees the hues of burnt yellow, orange, and brown in the cluster of stalls selling the dozens of varieties of *bolets,* wild mushrooms from the hills and forests of Catalonia. In spring, the candy colors of fresh strawberries and plump peaches, and in early summer the greens of a dozen different lettuces, from curly bunches of escarole to pert little heads of endives and *cogollos* (lettuce hearts), make an appearance.

The fish and seafood section takes prime place in a central roundabout known as the *Isla del Pescado* (Island of Fish), a pretty marble and shiny steel affair dating from the Boqueria's overhaul back in 2001, which brought more natural light to the market and provided more space for customers. The variety of produce is awesome—from giant carcasses

of tuna that send Japanese tourists into a camera-flashing frenzy to the ugly but tasty scorpionfish, prawns the size of bananas, live crayfish, octopi, bug-eyed grouper, and countless other species. Other stalls range from game and delicatessens to bewildering businesses specializing in one product, be it lettuce, potatoes, or smoked salmon.

If you are up early, visit the Boqueria in the early morning as it is being hurled into life. Cartloads of produce are dragged to the stalls to be arranged into patterns and combinations that border on food art. Have breakfast at **Pinotxo** (© **93-317-17-31**) on the right of the main entrance. Here you will rub shoulders with the city's innovative chefs before they embark on their daily sourcing spree. If shopping yourself, avoid the stalls at the front unless you want to pay "tourist" prices.

airy, white space near the Parc Ciutadella. An adjoining shop sells cult streetwear and accessories. Comerç 15.© **93-310-07-35.** www.iguapop.net. Metro: Jaume I.

Sala Parés ★★   Established in 1840, this is a Barcelona institution. The Maragall family promotes the work of Spanish and Catalan painters and sculptors, many of whom have gone on to acclaim. Paintings are displayed in a two-story amphitheater, with high-tech steel balconies supported by a quartet of steel columns evocative of Gaudí. Exhibitions of the most avant-garde art in Barcelona change about every 3 weeks. Petritxol 5.© **93-318-70-20.** www.salapares.com. Metro: Plaça de Catalunya.

Hats

Sombrería Obach 👔   This reassuringly old-fashioned hat shop in El Call (the old Jewish quarter; p. 167) stocks the largest color range of *barrets* (berets) on earth, as well as Panamas, Kangol flat caps, straw sun hats, and a host of other headgear for men and women. Check out the classic Mexican sombrero: Wide-brimmed, black, and very stylish. Carrer del Call 2.© **93-318-40-94.** Metro: Jaume I or Liceu.

Herbs & Health Foods

Comme-Bio   Comme-Bio is one-stop shopping for organic fruit and vegetables, health foods, tofu and other meat substitutes, and natural cosmetics. Don't get a shock at the prices; demand here for whole foods is just starting to take off, so expect to pay more than in the U.K. or the States. Next to the supermarket is a juice bar and restaurant open for lunch and dinner, although the food is a bit pedestrian. Vía Laietana 28. ☎ **93-319-89-68.** Metro: Jaume I.

Manantial de Salud This herbalist delight is one of eight enticing branches around the city. Dried medicinal herbs, aromatic pills and potions, and its own range of natural beauty products are all displayed in pretty, pale-green glass cabinets or large ceramic urns. Locals pop in for a natural cure to their ailments. The staff are extremely knowledgeable and used to dealing with foreigners, although you could look up a few key words in your dictionary beforehand. Xucla 23. ☎ **93-301-14-44.** www.manantialdesalud.com. Metro: Liceu.

Jewelry

Forvm Ferlandina ★★ Contemporary jewelry and accessories from over 50 designers are on display in tiny cubist cases that give this tiny shop, just opposite the MACBA (p. 173), the feel of a contemporary gallery. Silversmithing, enamel work, beading, and glassware are featured among many other creations. Particularly lovely are the felt flower-bouquet brooches, rings, and hair ornaments produced in the workroom. Ferlandina 31. ☎ **93-441-80-18.** Metro: Liceu or Plaça de Catalunya.

Platamundi ✦ The string of Platamundi stores offers highly affordable, high-quality pieces in silver, both imported and by local designers such as Ricardo Domingo, head of the jewelry wing of FAD, the city's design council (p. 172). Check out the pieces combining silver with enamel work in Mediterranean colors. Hospital 37. ☎ **93-317-13-89.** Metro: Liceu. There are several branches throughout the city.

Tous Depending on your point of view, the jewelry made by this Catalan family is either must-have or too twee to contemplate. Tous's leitmotif is the teddy bear, and the little fellow features on everything from earrings to keyrings to belts and bracelets. They are adored by the city's VIP set, and their popularity has grown to such an extent that you now see pirated versions. Everything in Tous is produced to a very high standard in precious metals and semiprecious stones. Passeig de Gràcia 75. ☎ **93-488-15-58.** www.tous.es. Metro: Passeig de Gràcia.

Leather

Acosta ★ Started in the 1950s, this chain selling stylish Spanish leather belts and bags now has 37 shops all over Spain and one each in Lisbon and Brussels. It's still a family-run affair, which is perhaps why everything sold has the air of being lovingly and meticulously produced. Prices are excellent, given the overall quality. Diagonal 602. ☎ **93-414-32-78.** Bus: 5, 7, 15, 33, or 34.

Loewe ★★★ Barcelona's biggest branch of this prestigious Spanish leather-goods chain is in one of the best-known *moderniste* buildings in the city. Everything is top-notch, from the elegant showroom to the expensive merchandise to the helpful salespeople. The company exports its goods to branches throughout Asia, Europe, and North America. With creative director Stuart Vevers now at the helm, their clothing line continues the good work started by their previous top man, designer Jose Enrique Ona Selfa. Passeig de Gràcia 35. ☎ **93-216-04-00.** www.loewe.com. Metro: Passeig de Gràcia.

Lupo ★★ The current name in deluxe leather goods. Trading from a minimalist silver-and-white shop in L'Eixample, Lupo's bags and belts stretch the limits of the craft by molding and folding leather into incredible shapes and using new dyeing techniques to create vivid colors. The world is taking notice, and the company is now exporting to the States, the rest of Europe, and Japan. Majorca 257, Bajos. ✆ **93-487-80-50.** www.lupo.es. Metro: Passeig de Gràcia.

Linen & Towels

El Indio 🎁 Established in 1870 and easily recognizable by the florid facade and arched windows, this emporium sells all sorts of textiles from sheets to tea towels to tablecloths. The service and wood-lined surroundings are charmingly old-school and the range mind-boggling, from cheap polyester sheets to the finest linen napkins. If they don't have it, it probably doesn't exist. Carme 24. ✆ **93-317-54-42.** Metro: Liceu.

Ràfols ★ Beautiful, made-to-order, and hand-embroidered bed linens, towels, tablecloths, and other items for your trousseau. The nimble-fingered staff will whip up any design you like, and the pure cottons and linens used are heavenly. Bori i Fontestà 4. ✆ **93-200-93-52.** Metro: Diagonal.

Lingerie

Le Boudoir 🎁 This may look like an upmarket sex shop, but in reality the scarlet-red walls house a gorgeous collection of silk and lace lingerie and racy bedroom accessories, from furry handcuffs to music CDs designed to "get you in the mood" and other objects for intimate moments. In summer, they bring in an exclusive range of swimwear. Naughty, but very, very nice. Canuda 21. ✆ **93-302-52-81.** www.leboudoir.net. Metro: Plaça de Catalunya.

Women'sSecret 🔥 This chain of lingerie, underwear, and sleepwear stores will make you want one in your hometown. The prints are hip and colorful, the designs funky, and the prices highly palatable. Even their basics range from pure cotton bras and nighties to striped PJs, matching slippers and toiletry bags; this is concept retailing at its cleverest. Portaferrisa 7-9. ✆ **93-318-92-42.** www.womensecret.com. There are several branches throughout Barcelona.

Maps

Llibreria Quera 🎁 This establishment was started in 1916 by the legendary adventurer Josep Quera, who pretty much covered every square inch of Catalonia and Andorra in his lifetime. Whether you are going hiking in the Pyrénées, motoring along the coast, or rock climbing in the interior, you can plan your trip here with their selection of specialized books and maps. Petritxol 2. ✆ **93-318-07-43.** www.llibreriaquera.com. Metro: Liceu.

Music

Casa Beethoven 🎁 Established in 1920, this store carries the most complete collection of sheet music in town. The collection focuses on the works of Spanish and Catalan composers. Music lovers often make rare discoveries. La Rambla 97. ✆ **93-301-48-26.** www.casabeethoven.com. Metro: Liceu.

Discos Castelló With six shops around Barcelona, Castelló pretty much has the CD market sewn up. Half of them are located in the Calle Tallers, a street of door-to-door music and vinyl shops. Opened in 1934, their flagship store at no. 7 is mainly pop rock. Next door, "Overstocks" has more of the same plus sections on jazz,

TO MARKET, TO market . . .

There are lots of outdoor markets held in the streets of Barcelona. Practice your bartering skills before heading for **El Encants flea market,** held every Monday, Wednesday, Friday, and Saturday in Plaça de les Glòries Catalanes (Metro: Glòries). Go anytime during the day to survey the selection of new and used clothing, period furniture, and out-and-out junk (although the traders will try to convince you otherwise). **Coins** and **postage stamps** are traded and sold in Plaça Reial on Sunday from 10am to 8pm. It's off the southern flank of La Rambla (Metro: Drassanes). A **book** (mainly Spanish-language) **and coin market** is held at the Ronda Sant Antoni every Sunday from 10am to 2pm (Metro: Universitat), with a brisk trade in pirated software and DVDs around the periphery. Fine-quality **antiquarian** items can be found at the **Mercat Gòtic** every Thursday 9am to 8pm, on the Plaça Nova outside the city's

main cathedral (Metro: Liceu), but don't expect any bargains. More like a large **flea market** is the **Encants del Gòtic,** Plaça George Orwell, Saturday 11am to 4pm (Metro: Drassanes). The wide promenade of the Rambla del Raval (Metro: San Antoni) is taken over by hippie-type traders all day every Saturday, hawking **handmade clothing, jewelry,** and boho crafts. Nearby, the **vintage and retro clothing traders** of the Riera Baixa (Metro: San Antoni) hawk their goods on the street (some real bargains are to be found here). Over 50 painters set up shop every weekend in the pretty Plaça del Pi (Metro: Liceu) in a **Mostra d'Art** that is of a surprisingly high standard. If food is your thing, over a dozen purveyors of artisan cheese, honey, cookies, olives, chocolate, and other **Catalan delicacies** can be found in the Plaça del Pi, on the first and third weekend of every month from 10am to 10pm.

world, Spanish, and country music. Classical music is sold at no. 3. Calle Tallers. ℭ **93-318-20-41.** www.castellodiscos.com. Metro: Plaça de Catalunya.

FNAC 🖉 If you don't want anything too out of the mainstream, the best place to pick up music is the FNAC megastore (p. 219). The second floor has CDs of all kinds—rock, pop, jazz, classical, and a selection of not-quite-current releases of current artists at rock-bottom prices. You can ask to listen before buying, which is handy for making purchases of Spanish music and flamenco. It's open Monday through Saturday 10am to 10pm. Plaça de Catalunya 4. ℭ **93-344-18-00.** www.fnac.es. Metro: Plaça de Catalunya.

Outlets & Seconds

Contribución y Moda 👔 This large split-level store sells men's and women's designer clothing from last season and beyond. It's the sort of place where you could pick up a pair of Vivienne Westwood trousers on the cheap. That said, you will normally find at least one item to your taste and budget (especially at the beginning of the season), although the different size ranges can make you want to scream. Riera de Sant Miquel 30. ℭ **93-218-71-40.** Metro: Diagonal.

La Roca Village Only true bargain hunters will make the trip to this outer Barcelona "outlet village." But if you do, the savings are legendary; you'll be rewarded with up to 60% off over 50 brands, including high-fashion labels such as Roberto Verino, Versace, and Carolina Herrera, shoes from Camper, luxury leather goods from Loewe and

Mandarina Duck, and sportswear from Billabong and Timberland. The setting is reasonably pleasant, with a playground for kids and cafes. Open daily from 11am to 9pm. Santa Agnés de Malanyanes, La Roca del Vallès. ✆ **93-842-39-00**. www.larocavillage.com. By car: Take the AP-7 to Exit 12, head to Cardedeu, and then to the Centre Comercial. By train: Take the train from Sants Station to Granollers Center (trains leave every half-hour; trip time: 35 min.); from the station, a bus leaves for La Roca Village every hour at 23 min. past; a taxi will cost you 15€. By bus: Sagalés (✆ **93-870-78-60**) runs buses directly to La Roca village from the Fabra i Puig bus terminal (Passeig Fabra i Puig, next to the Metro entrance); buses (5.50€ round-trip) leave Mon–Fri at 9am, noon, and 4 and 8pm (trip time: 50 min).

MNG Outlet 🗡 MNG is Mango (p. 223), one of the biggest chains in Spain for young fashion. Their outlet store has items with *taras* (faults—of varying dimensions) and last season's stock at the silliest of prices. It's not unusual to pick up a pair of jeans here for 14€ or a T-shirt for as low as 8€. There is also a good selection of shoes and bags at rock-bottom prices. It gets frustratingly busy on Saturday. A few other outlet stores are located in the immediate vicinity. Girona 37. ✆ **93 412 29 35.** www. mango.com. Metro: Tetuan or Urquinaona.

112 🗡 People with a foot fetish will love this Barrio Alto shop selling last year's shoes, boots, and bags at 50% off. Marc Jacobs, Givenchy, Emma Hope, Emilio Pucci, Robert Clergerie, and Rossi are just some of the names. Laforja 105. ✆ **93-414-55-13.** FGC: Gràcia.

Perfume & Cosmetics

La Galería de Santa María Novella 🎁 This is the Barcelona outlet of the famed Officina Profumo–Farmaceutica di Santa María Novella in Florence, the oldest and most luxurious apothecary in the world. The perfumes and colognes are unadulterated scents of flowers, spices, and fruits; the soaps handmade; and the packaging seemingly unchanged since the 18th century. Prices are high. Espasería 4-8. ✆ **93-268-02-37.** www.lagaleriadesantamarianovella.com. Metro: Jaume I or Barceloneta.

Regia ★ This high-end perfume and cosmetics shop has a secret: Wander through the racks stacked with Dior and Chanel and you reach a small door that leads to a unique museum (free admission). There are over 5,000 examples of perfume bottles and flasks from Grecian times to the present day. The star of the collection is the dramatic Le Roy Soleil by Salvador Dalí. Passeig de Gràcia 39. ✆ **93-216-01-21.** www.regia.es. Metro: Passeig de Gràcia.

Sephora Cosmetics addicts may be forgiven for thinking they have died and gone to heaven when they enter this beauty megastore. All the desired brands are here: Clarins, Dior, Arden, Chanel, and so on—plus hard-to-finds such as Urban Decay and Phytomer. The house brand's range of makeup is a great buy. El Triangle, Pelai 13-17. ✆ **93-306-39-00.** www.sephora.es. Metro: Plaça de Catalunya.

Porcelain

Kastoria This large store near the cathedral is an authorized Lladró dealer and stocks a big selection of the famous porcelain. It also carries many kinds of leather goods, including purses, suitcases, coats, and jackets. Av. Catedral 6-8. ✆ **93-319-55-90.** Metro: Plaça de Catalunya.

Pottery

Artesania i Coses If you are in the vicinity of the Museu Picasso, pop into this jumble sale of a shop selling pottery and porcelain from every region of Spain. Most of the pieces are heavy and thick-sided, and you can pick up a coffee mug for a couple of euros. Placeta de Montcada 2. ✆ **93-319-54-13.** Metro: Jaume I.

Baraka   Baraka's owner regularly raids the *souks* of Morocco and brings back the booty to this small shop in trendy El Born. There is a lovely range of brightly colored and patterned pottery and ceramics, plus traditional *dhurries* (woven rugs), *bubucha* slippers, earthenware *tagines,* lamps, and other North African paraphernalia. Canvis Vells 2. ✆ **93-268-42-20.** www.barakaweb.com. Metro: Jaume I.

Itaca 🎁   Here you'll find a wide array of handmade pottery from Catalonia and other parts of Spain, plus Portugal, Mexico, and Morocco. The merchandise has been selected for its basic purity, integrity, and simplicity. There is a wide range of Gaudí-esque objects, inspired by trademark *trencadis* (broken-tile) work. Ferran 26. ✆ **93-301-30-44.** www.itacas.com. Metro: Liceu.

Scarves, Shawls & Accessories

Alonso   If you fancy a classy silk or mohair scarf, this is the place to come. Fashionable Catalan ladies have been frequenting Alonso's for over a century for the scarves, ultrasoft lace gloves, and delicately ornate fans. A true original in dedicating itself to Hispanic traditions, the store also sells *mantillas* (Spanish shawls) and castanets. The shop nestles behind a suitably impressive *moderniste* facade in the heart of the Barri Gòtic. Santander 27. ✆ **93-317-60-85.** www.tiendacenter.com. Metro: Liceu.

Mina Madhu ★★   Formerly known as Rafa Teja Atelier but unchanged in its essential character, this friendly shop next to Santa María del Mar church has a sublime collection of wool, cotton, and silk scarves and shawls from India, Asia, and Spain, all neatly hung on wooden rails or folded into glorious, multicolored stacks. They produce a limited range of clothing, showcasing evening coats in Chinese brocades or sarong-style skirts in Indonesian batiks. Santa María 18. ✆ **93-310-27-85.** Metro: Jaume I or Barceloneta.

Shoes

Camper ★★   Made on the island of Mallorca, Camper shoes have conquered the world. Their distinctive molded shapes in unusual colors are seen treading the streets of New York and Sydney, but Barcelona has the biggest range at the best prices. The shop interiors, often kitted out by quirky Catalan designer Martí Guixe, reflect the brand's wholesome yet hip culture. Valencia 249. ✆ **93-215-63-90.** www.camper. es. Metro: Passeig de Gràcia. There are several branches throughout Barcelona.

Casas ★★   If you are serious about footwear, this is the only name you need to know. With three shops in central Barcelona, Casas is a one-stop shoe store for the most prominent Spanish brands (Camper, Vialis, Dorotea) and coveted imports from Clergerie, Rodolfo Zengarini, and Mare, plus sports and walking shoes. La Rambla 125 (✆ **93-302-45-98**); Portaferrisa 25 (✆ **93-302-11-32**); Portal de l'Angel 40 (✆ **93-302-11-12**). Metro: Plaça de Catalunya or Liceu.

Czar   For sports shoes and sneakers, look no further than Czar. They have everything from Converse, Le Coq Sportif, and Adidas classics to more bizarre creations by Diesel, W&LT, Asics, and other cult labels. Passeig del Born 20. ✆ **93-310-72-22.** Metro: Jaume I or Barceloneta.

La Manual Alpargatera 🎁   The good people at this Ciutat Vella shop have been making espadrilles here for nearly a century. As well as the classic slip-on variety, you

The streets around the Barri Gòtic are packed with traditional establishments specializing in everything from dried cod to dancing shoes, some of them remnants from the days when trading was Barcelona's lifeblood. If you see a shop window that entices, don't be shy; most shopkeepers welcome curious tourists, and a brief exchange with them may be one of those fleeting traveler's experiences you cherish long after it's over.

Dating from 1761, **Cereria Subira,** Baixada de Llibretería 7 (℘ **93-315-26-06**), has the distinction of being the oldest continuous shop in Barcelona. It specializes in candles, from long and elegant white ones used at Mass to more fanciful creations. Magicians and illusionists love the **Rey de la Magia,** Princesa 11 (℘ **93-319-39-20;** www.elreydelamagia.com), a joke and magic shop dating from 1881. Behind the ornate Art Nouveau facade of **Alonso,** Santa Ana 27 (℘ **93-317-60-85;** www.tradecenter.com), lie dozens of gloves, from dainty calfskin to more rugged driving gloves, plus pretty fans and lace *mantillas* (Spanish shawls).

More traditional Spanish garb is to be found at **Flora Albaicín,** Vallirana 71–73 (℘ **93-418-23-09;** www.flora-albaicin.com), which specializes in flamenco dancing shoes and spotty, swirly skirts and dresses. The **Herboristeria del Rei,** del Vidre 1 (℘ **93-318-05-12**), is another shop steeped in history; it has been supplying herbs, natural remedies, cosmetics, and teas since 1823. **Casa Colomina,** Cucurulla 2 (℘ **93-317-46-81**), makes its own *turrones,* slabs of nougat and marzipan that are a traditional Christmas treat. Nimble fingers will love the **L'Antiga Casa Sala,** Call 8 (℘ **93-318-45-87;** www.antigacasasala.com), which has an enormous range of beads and trinkets begging to be turned into an original accessory. In the old Born food hub, **Angel Jobal,** Princesa 38 (℘ **93-319-78-02**), is the city's most famed spice merchant, selling everything from Spanish saffron to Indian pepper and oregano from Chile. **Ganiveteria Roca,** Plaça del Pi 3 (℘ **93-302-12-41;** www.ganiveteriaroca.com), has a range of knives, blades, scissors, and all sorts of special-task cutting instruments. **Xancó Camiseria,** La Rambla 78–80 (℘ **93-318-09-89**), is one of the few period shops remaining on La Rambla; they have been making classic men's shirts in cottons, wools, and linens since 1820. And finally, you never know when you may need a chicken feather: the **Casa Morelli,** Banys Nous 13 (℘ **93-302-52-94**), has sacks of them, for stuffing pillows or decorating a party outfit.

will find the Catalan *espadenya,* which has ribbon ankle-ties, wedge-heeled versions in fashion colors, toasty lamb's wool slippers, and other "natural" footwear. Clients have included Michael Douglas and the Pope. Avinyó 7. ℘ **93-301-01-72.** www.lamanual.net. Metro: Jaume I or Liceu.

Lottusse These Mallorcan cobblers are revered for their extraordinary quality. The brogues, loafers, T-bars, and other classic styles for men and women actually look and feel handmade. They won't make you stand out in a crowd, but are liable to last you a lifetime. Lottusse also sells bags, wallets, and belts. Rambla de Catalunya 103. ℘ **93-215-89-11.** www.lottusse.com. Metro: Passeig de Gràcia.

Muxart ★★ Hermenegildo Muxart knows how to make heels that appeal, offering sexy, cutting-edge shoes and handbags from his Eixample shop. A pair of black stilettos may feature a red bead on the toe or metallic silver and electric-blue leather plaited together with straw to form an intricate tapestry. While this may sound a bit faddy, Muxart knows when to draw in the reins, making a pair of his shoes an investment buy rather than an expensive whim. Rosselló 230. ℂ **93-488-10-64.** www.muxart.net. Metro: Diagonal. Another branch at Rambla de Catalunya 47. ℂ **93-467-74-23**. Metro: Passeig de Gràcia.

Shopping Centers & Malls

Shopping malls are a contentious topic in Catalonia. Many small traders feel they are squeezing them out of the market. The local government has reacted by limiting their construction, especially in central Barcelona. But there are still enough in existence to appease any mall fan.

Centre Comercial Glòries Built in 1995, part of a huge project to rejuvenate a downtrodden part of town, this three-story emporium has more than 230 shops, a few posh and others far from it. Most people head here for the Carrefour department store, the cheaper cousin of El Corte Inglés that sells electrical and home goods. Although there's a typical shopping-mall anonymity to this place, it's great for kids, with lots of open spaces and bouncy things to jump on. Open Monday to Saturday from 10am to 10pm. Av. Diagonal 208. ℂ **93-486-04-04.** www.lesglories.com. Metro: Glòries.

Diagonal Mar This is one of the city's largest malls, part of an urban project that has breathed residential and commercial life into the city's still developing northern coastline. Reflecting the surrounding property prices, shops are mid- to high-end. All the fashion staples are here, plus a branch of the music and entertainment megastore FNAC, and a movie theater. Open Monday to Saturday from 10am to 10pm. Av. Diagonal 3. ℂ **93-567-76-30** or **90-253-03-00**. www.diagonalmar.com. Metro: Maresme/Forum, Selva de Mar, or Besós-Mar.

L'illa Diagonal Located in an expensive part of town, shopping here is mainly high-end. This two-story mall has stores mainly devoted to fashion products: Lacoste, Diesel, Custo Barcelona, Miss Sixty, as well as a scattering of home, gift, and toy boutiques. The first level has a huge supermarket and food hall selling everything from handmade chocolates to dried cod. Open Monday through Saturday 10am to 9:30pm. Av. Diagonal 557. ℂ **93-444-00-00.** www.lilla.com. Metro: María Cristina.

Pedralbes Centre This two-story arcade focuses mainly on fashion. Check out the street and club wear from E4G and ZasTwo, froufrou party frocks by Puente Aereo, and the brightly colored quirky clothes of Agata Ruiz de la Prada. Other highlights include a Lavinia wine store and a branch of El Corte Inglés. Diagonal 609–615. ℂ **93-410-68-21.** www.pedralbescentre.com. Metro: María Cristina.

Sporting Goods

Decathlon 🔔 If you plan to take some physical activity in Barcelona beyond a stroll down La Rambla, Decathlon is the only name you need to know. Every single sport is covered in this French-owned megastore, from soccer and tennis to *jai-alai* (Basque handball) and ping-pong. There is swimwear, clothing for jogging, aerobics, cycling hats (and bicycles), ski gear, hiking boots, and wetsuits. Their prices are pretty much unbeatable, especially on their own-brand items. Canuda 20. ℂ **93-342-61-61.** www.decathlon.es. Metro: Plaça de Catalunya or L'illa. Another location at Diagonal 557. ℂ **93-444-01-65.** Metro: María Cristina.

BARCELONA AFTER DARK

B arcelona is a great night-time city, and the array of after-dark diversions is staggering. There is something to interest almost everyone and to fit most wallets. Fashionable **bars** and **clubs** operate in every major district of the city, and when one closes down, another opens within weeks.

Locals sometimes opt for an evening in the *tascas* **(taverns),** or perhaps settle in for a bottle of wine at a cafe, an easy and inexpensive way to spend an evening people-watching. The legal age for drinking is 18, but is rarely enforced with much vigor.

A haze of cigarette smoke has always been an inevitable part of the Barcelona night scene despite bars being required to have a nonsmoking area since legislation was passed in 2006. However, new restrictions will transform the scene in January 2011 when a law is scheduled to be passed banning smoking in all public areas. It'll doubtless outrage a majority of the population but the times they are a-changing, even for diehard Spanish puffers.

If the weather is good (which is most of the time) the city's outdoor squares are at least half-filled with as many tables and chairs as can reasonably fit.

Alfresco drinking has become so popular that complaining neighbors have forced the local government to restrict hours in some areas—around midnight, it's commonplace to be asked to finish your drinks or to go inside. Particularly good places to sit and see the world go by are **Plaça del Sol** in Gràcia and **Passeig del Born, Plaça del Pi,** and **Plaça Reial** in the Ciutat Vella. These squares are also popular drinking haunts for groups of teenagers, but their tipple tends to be more of the supermarket-bought variety. The old Spanish tradition of the *botellón*, whereby groups of young people sit around on the ground swilling beer or wine, is treated as a nuisance by the local government and noise-sensitive neighbors. Despite cracking down on the practice, it persists, especially in the summer.

People-watching of a more flesh-exposed nature can be done down at the beach in the summer. Between May and October, a line of *chiringuitos* (beach bars) opens for nighttime frivolity in the sands along Barcelona's urban beaches, from Barceloneta to Poble Nou. Each one has its own flavor—some play chill-out music; others have live DJs or bands. Owners, names, and styles change from year to year, but generally they open at lunchtime (or late breakfast) and stay open until 2 or 3am.

Also down near the sands, there are plenty of bars and restaurants around the Olympic marina and port. This, as well as Maremagnum, the entertainment and leisure complex, and the port end of La Rambla cater more for tourists by offering punters international beers, lagers, and cocktails rather than Spanish brands.

Other areas filled with bars include the **Carrer Avinyó** in the Barri Gòtic, the **Rambla del Raval** in El Raval, and the streets of **El Born** in La Ribera—just walk around and see where the noise is coming from. There are plenty of local secrets to uncover if you follow the crowd for a while.

Joining In Barcelona Nightlife

Nightlife begins for many Barcelonese with a *paseo* (promenade) from about 8 to 9pm. Then things quiet down a bit until a second surge of energy brings out the post-dinner crowds from 11pm to midnight. Serious drinking in the city's pubs and bars usually begins by midnight. For the most fashionable places, Barcelonese will delay their entrances until at least 1am—meeting friends for the first drink of the evening after midnight certainly takes some getting used to. If you want to go on to a club, be prepared to delay things even longer—most clubs don't open until around 2am, and they will be mostly empty for the first half-hour or so until the bars close at 3am. Many clubs stay open as late as 6am. Most of them will have free entrance or discount flyers available in bars or given out on the streets, saving you between 5€ and 12€, which is the normal club entrance price. This will largely depend on the night, the DJ, and what the doorman thinks you look like. The price of a mixed drink (such as a *cuba libre*, rum and coke) hovers between 6€ and 14€. This may seem pricey, but drinks in Barcelona come *strong*. If you are charged an admission fee, ask if it's *amb consumició* (drink included). If so, take your ticket to the bar to get the first drink free.

Barcelona is a fast-moving city and the clubbing scene is notoriously fickle. New venues come up and others disappear. Although I've recommended places that have been around for a while, don't be too surprised if names and styles have changed when you roll up.

Barcelona & Music

Most famous international names, from the Rolling Stones to Mika and Jamie Cullum, include Barcelona in their tours. The biggest concerts take place at the **Palau Sant Jordi** (p. 166) on Montjuïc, a flexible and cavernous space that's also used to host the city's basketball games. In a city where the cult of the DJ reigns, Barcelona is short of small and midsize live-music venues (although some clubs do both, with a concert taking place before the club kids roll in).

One of the best places to see people playing instruments (as opposed to spinning records) is the street. In the summer you'll see plenty of free entertainment—everything from opera to Romanian gypsy music—by walking around the Barri Gòtic. Festivals such as **El Grec** (July–Aug) and **La Mercè** (late Sept) are when the biggest musical offering tends to take place.

To find out what's going on in the city, the best source of local information is a little magazine called ***Guía del Ocio,*** which previews "La Semana de Barcelona"

KEEP IT down

Although Spain is one of the last countries on earth you'd think of as being intolerant of noise, mumblings are growing over the decibels surging from the pleasure spots of city centers where many people still live. Placards and banners pleading for more consideration hang across the narrow lanes and squares of Barcelona's Ciutat Vella, with disconcerting signs like *Estem farts* (which means "we're fed up" in Catalan). One result has been a tentative crackdown on culprits making the loudest sounds, from top disco La Terrrazza in the Poble Espanyol to the veteran Bar Pastis in Poble Sec. La Terrrazza was closed for just over a year, so the gesture has been made and steps apparently taken to diffuse the din in both these establishments, as well as in other spots where similar problematic situations have arisen. Whether or not the noise has abated sufficiently for locals to get a decent night's sleep in those offending areas is, however, debatable.

(This Week in Barcelona). It's in Spanish, but most of its listings will be comprehensible. Every news kiosk along La Rambla carries it. If you have Internet access, *Le Cool* magazine (www.lecool.com) carries an English summary of some of the more alternative options each week.

If you've been scared off by press reports about La Rambla between the Plaça de Catalunya and the Columbus Monument, the area's been cleaned up in the past decade. Still, you will feel safer along the Rambla de Catalunya, north of the Plaça de Catalunya in L'Eixample. This street and its offshoots are lively at night, with many cafes and bars.

The main area where things feel a little uneasy is in El Raval, or the Barrio Chino—that is, the lower half of the right-hand side of La Rambla as you walk toward the port. But despite (or because of?) this, a lot of the new trendy bars are appearing there (such as Bar Pastis; p. 249). There are some great bars and venues down there, but do use caution, especially when withdrawing money from a cash machine (although more and more of these are locked at night anyway).

THE PERFORMING ARTS

Culture is deeply ingrained in the Catalan soul, and the performing arts are strong. Long a city of the arts, Barcelona experienced a cultural decline during the Franco years, but now it is filled once again with the best opera, symphonic, and choral music. At the venues listed here, unless otherwise specified, ticket prices depend on the event. Tickets can be bought at the venues, but it's often more convenient and easier to use one of the special ticket services or buy online. The bank Caixa Catalunya sells *entradas* for many events, and it also has the wondrous **Servi-Caixa**—an automated machine that dispenses theater and cinema tickets—in many of its branches. **Tel-entrada** (② **90-233-22-11**) lets you buy over the phone with your credit card.

Cabaret, Jazz & Blues

Espai Barroc ★★★   One of Barcelona's most culture-conscious (and slightly pretentious) nightspots occupies some of the showplace rooms of the Palau Dalmases, a stately Gothic mansion in La Ribera. In a room lined with grand *objets d'arts,* flowers, and large platters of fruit, you can listen to recorded arias and sip glasses of beer or wine. The most appealing night is Thursday—beginning at 11pm, 10 singers perform a roster of arias from assorted operas, one of which is invariably *Carmen.* Almost everyone around the bar apparently has at least heard of the world's greatest operas, and some can even discuss them more or less brilliantly. Montcada 20. ℂ **93-310-15-17.** Metro: Jaume I.

Harlem Jazz Club ★★   On a quiet street in the Ciutat Vella, this is one of Barcelona's oldest and finest jazz clubs. It's also one of the smallest, with just a handful of tables that get cleared away when the set ends so that people can dance. No matter how many times you've heard "Black Orpheus" or "The Girl from Ipanema," they always sound new here. Music is viewed with a certain reverence; no one talks when the performers are on. Live jazz, blues, tango, Brazilian funk, Romanian gypsy music, African rhythms—the sounds are always fresh. Most gigs start around 10pm, slightly later on the weekends. Comtessa de Sobradiel 8. ℂ **93-310-07-55.** www.harlemjazzclub.es. Free admission Mon–Thurs, 8€ Fri–Sat. 1-drink minimum. 2 sessions starting 10:30pm and midnight. Closed first 2 weeks in Aug. Metro: Jaume I.

Jamboree ★★   This has long been one of the city's premier locations for good blues and jazz, although it doesn't feature jazz every night. Sometimes a world-class performer will appear here, but most likely it'll be a younger group. The crowd knows its stuff and demands only the best talent. On my last visit, I was entertained by an evening of Chicago blues, but you might also find a Latin dance band performing. As it gets late, the music changes and the place opens up as a nightclub for a young crowd, with hip-hop featuring downstairs and a more world-music vibe upstairs. Most shows begin at about 11pm and end at 5am. Plaça Reial 17. ℂ **93-319-17-89.** www.masimas.com/jamboree. Admission (includes 1 drink) 8€–10€; shows 9€–12€. Metro: Liceu.

Luz de Gas ★★   This theater is renowned for Latino jazz. The place itself is a turn-of-the-20th-century delight, with colored glass lamps, red drapery, and other details, but it's also a world-class live-music venue. It was once a theater, and its original seating has been turned into different areas, each with its own bar. The lower two levels open onto the dance floor and stage. If you'd like to talk, head for the top tier, which has a glass enclosure. Call to see what the lineup is on any given night: Jazz, pop, soul, rhythm and blues, salsa, bolero, whatever. Be warned that the management can be somewhat snooty, so go with attitude. Muntaner 246. ℂ **93-209-77-11.** www.luzdegas.com. Cover (includes 1 drink) usually 20€–25€. Bus: 6, 27, 32, or 34. Metro: Diagonal.

Marulla Café   An offshoot of the popular Madrid club, this bouncy venue plays highly danceable DJ pop stuff from the likes of Mika and Shakira. Live-music night is Saturday, when the place gets even more packed than usual and Spanish groups like The Presidentes and Julio Marks belt out their versions of pop, soul, and funk. You'll find it nestling in one of the Barri Gòtic's narrowest and liveliest streets. Escudellers 49. ℂ **93-318-76-90.** www.marulacafe.com. Cover (includes 1 drink) 10€. Metro: Liceu.

23 Robador ★   This seedily raucous and atmospheric Raval rendezvous features an eclectic and varied selection of live musical soirées on Wednesdays (jazz sessions) and

Sundays (traditional Andalucian flamenco). At other times there's loud disco music played by whoever the DJ of the evening deems suitable. Graffiti-style murals give it a certain semi-underground urban cred, as does the fact that it has neither a direct phone nor a website. Just turn up and enjoy it. Robador 23. No credit cards. Metro: Liceu.

Cinema

In Barcelona there's a good choice of cinemas showing original-language (*versió original*) movies—mostly in English—with Spanish subtitles. Some offer Monday and Wednesday discounts. Weekends are popular (and crowded), with most movie houses also featuring late-night shows that start at 1am. Check the *Guía del Ocio, Metropolitan-Barcelona,* and local papers such as *El País* and *La Vanguardia* for information on showings, times, and screenings of special programmes.

Boliche   Standard four-screen movie house that shows mainstream films in their original version. One of the more recent venues to make the move from dubbing its celluloid epics in Castilian or Catalan, it's located in the upper part of L'Eixample, below Gràcia. Av. Diagonal 508. ☎ **93-218-17-88.** www.ecartelera.com/cines. Tickets Mon–Tues, Thurs 6.80€, Wed 5.50€, Fri–Sat 7€. Metro: Diagonal.

Casablanca-Kaplan   This modern multiplex shows a variety of up-to-date mainstream and art releases. Some find its minimalist-style seats distractingly hard, especially if the film you're watching doesn't keep you hooked. Passeig de Gràcia 115, L'Eixample. ☎ **93-218-43-45.** www.ecartelera.com/cines. Tickets 7.40€. 4 showings a day. Metro: Diagonal.

Cinemes Méliès   Two screens here provide a blend of art-house and standard commercial releases. Anything from classics to contemporary work is shown, sometimes with special seasons focusing on particular directors or stars. The program is constantly changing, so it's well worth keeping an eye on this place if you're in town for a while. Villaroel 10, L'Eixample. ☎ **93-451-00-51.** www.cinesmelies.net. Tickets Mon 4€, Tues–Sun 6€. 8 programs a week. No credit cards. Metro: Urgell.

Filmoteca de la Generalitat de Catalunya (Cine Aquitania)   Funded by the Catalan government, this *cineaste's* haven shows classics and lesser-known esoteric works. It offers special seasons devoted to famous and not-so-famous directors, and you can buy bargain block-purchasing booklets of 20 or more tickets, which bring the already low entry price down even further. Occasional children's shows are another attraction. A bargain. Av. Sarrià 33. ☎ **93-410-75-90.** www.filmotecadelageneralitat decatalunyacineaquita.es.visualnet.com. Tickets 3.50€. Metro: Hospital Clínic.

Icária Yelmo Cineplex   Located in a large mall down in the Port Olímpic area, this large, 15-screen multiplex features popular mainstream releases as well as the occasional offbeat European movie. Seats are numbered at the weekend when crowds flock in, so it's a safer bet to book your seat on their website. Salvador Espriu 61, Vila Olímpica. ☎ **93-221-75-85.** www.yelmocineplex.es. Tickets Mon 5€, Tues–Sun 7.50€. Late shows Fri and Sat. Metro: Ciutadella–Vila Olímpica.

Renoir Floridablanca   One of the city's most centrally located cinemas, the Renoir Floridablanca features conventional—but totally up-to-date—releases on a quartet of small screens. Usually there's a choice of eight different films on any given day. Its sister movie house, the Renoir Les Corts, offers a similar program. Floridablanca: Floridablanca 135. ☎ **93-228-93-93.** Metro: Sant Antoni. Les Corts: Eugenie d'Ors 12.

Metro: Les Corts. For both: www.cinesrenoir.com. Tickets Tues–Sun 7.50€, Mon 5€. Late shows Fri–Sat.

Verdi Cozily situated in the heart of Gràcia, this five-screen movie house—the very first in town to feature original-version movies—is a recognized institution in Barcelona. Films shown tend to be more adventurous and radical than the norm, and its popularity is demonstrated by long lines at weekends. Get there early, then, or book in advance. Its four-screen annex, Verdi Park, is close by. Verdi 32 and Verdi Park, Torrijos 49, Gràcia. **93-238-79-90.** www.cines-verdi.com/Barcelona. Tickets 7.50€. Late shows Fri–Sat. Metro: Fontana.

Classical Music

Gran Teatre del Liceu ★★★ This monument to Belle Epoque extravagance is one of the grandest opera houses in the world. It was designed by the Catalan architect Josep Oriol Mestes. In 1994, a disastrous fire gutted the opera house, but it was quickly rebuilt, and today it stands as a beloved citadel of the Catalan classical-music scene. The 2,300-seat theater boasts re-created ornate classical carvings, along with additional modern touches including international subtitles on the chair backs. Other amenities include a quiet cafe and an extensive shop in the basement, open during the day. Each show offers a couple of performances where tickets are half-price (or close to it). It's very easy to find, halfway down La Rambla; guided tours of the edifice (lasting about an hour) are also available daily 10am to 6pm. Rambla dels Caputxins 51–59. **93-485-99-13.** www.liceubarcelona.com. Metro: Liceu.

La Casa dels Músics Pianist Luis de Arquer has established a small chamber company in his 19th-century Gràcia home. It's called "the smallest opera house in the world," and that's probably right since the performers are almost sitting on your lap as they do small-scale productions of *opera buffa* and *bel canto*. Shows usually begin at 9pm, but call to confirm. For the true music lover, this could be your most charming evening in Barcelona. Encarnació 25. **93-284-99-20** (call 5–9pm only). www.lacasadelsmusics.com. Tickets 30€. Metro: Fontana.

L'Auditori ★★ This is the newest of the city's classical-music bastions, designed as a permanent home for the Orfeó Català choral society and the OBC (Barcelona's symphony orchestra), although top-flight international names perform here as well. The building was designed by award-winning Spanish architect Rafael Moneo, and its state-of-the-art acoustics are among the best in town. Lepant 150. **93-247-93-00.** www.auditori.org. Metro: Glòries.

Palau de la Música Catalana ★★★ In a city chock-full of architectural highlights, this one stands out. In 1908 Catalan architect Lluís Domènech i Montaner designed this structure as a home for the choral society Orfeó Català, using stained glass, ceramics, statuary, and ornate lamps, among other elements. It stands today as the lushest example of *modernisme*. Concerts (mainly classical but also jazz, folk, and other genres) and leading recitals take place here, as do daily guided tours of the buildings. But they say you only really appreciate it when enjoying a concert. An extension called Petit Palau includes a luxury restaurant. Open daily from 10am to 3:30pm; box office open Monday through Saturday from 10am to 9pm. Sant Pere Mès Alt s/n. **93-295-72-00,** bookings **902-442-882.** www.palaumusica.org. Metro: Urquinaona.

Flamenco

Though flamenco isn't the rage here that it is in Seville and Madrid, it has its devotees. It's not a Catalan tradition, but Barcelona has an active Andalucian population and dancers with as much verve and color as you'd find farther south.

El Tablao de Carmen ★★★   This club presents a highly rated flamenco cabaret in the re-created imitation "typical Spanish artisan village" of Poble Espanyol on the side of the Montjuïc hill. Go early to explore the village, or even have dinner there as the sun sets. This place has long been a tourist favorite. The club is open Tuesday through Sunday from 8pm to past midnight—around 1am on weeknights, often until 2 or 3am on weekends, depending on business. The first show is always at 9:30pm; the second at 11:30pm on Tuesday, Wednesday, Thursday, and Sunday, or midnight on Friday and Saturday. Reservations are recommended. Av. Marquès de Comillas, Poble Espanyol de Montjuïc. ✆ **93-325-68-95.** www.tablaodecarmen.com. Dinner and show 75€–90€; drink and show 40€. Metro: Espanya.

Los Tarantos ★★   Established in 1963, this first-floor club is the oldest flamenco club in Barcelona, with a rigid allegiance to the tenets of Andalucian flamenco. Its roster of artists changes regularly. Performers often come from Seville or Córdoba, stamping out their well-rehearsed passions in ways that make the audience appreciate the arcane nuances of Spain's most intensely controlled dance idiom; other nights it could be a lesser-known local artist or a percussion show. No food is served. The place resembles a cabaret theater, where up to 120 people at a time can drink, talk quietly, and savor the nuances of a dance that combines elements from medieval Christian and Muslim traditions. Shows are sporadic, so check before you roll up. Plaça Reial 17. ✆ **93-319-17-89.** www.masimas.com/tarantos. Cover (includes 1 drink) around 25€. Metro: Liceu.

Tablao Flamenco Cordobés ★   At the southern end of La Rambla, close to the harborfront, you'll hear the strum of the guitar, the sound of rhythmic clapping, and the haunting sound of flamenco, a tradition here since 1968. Head upstairs to an Andalucian-style room where performances take place with the traditional *cuadro flamenco*—singers, dancers, and guitarist. Cordobés is said to be the city's best flamenco showcase. Three shows are offered nightly with dinner, at 7, 8:30, and 10pm. Reservations required. La Rambla 35. ✆ **93-317-57-11.** www.tablaocordobes.com. Dinner and show 50€–60€; 1 drink and show 30€–35€. Metro: Liceu or Drassanes.

Tiritïtran   A flamenco restaurant run by genuine *gitanos,* the background music, the pictures on the wall, and the menu all sing of the same passionate musical tradition. In the basement they have a small stage and music, and late on weekends, groups of Andalucians often come by to strum a guitar and drink some hard liquor. The atmosphere is friendly, and although you won't see many beautifully dressed dancers or roses between the teeth, they know their flamenco as well as anyone. Buenos Aires 28. ✆ **93-363-05-91.** Admission 8€. Metro: Hospital Clínic.

Theater

The majority of theater in Barcelona is presented in Catalan by Spanish production companies. Avant-garde theater and comedy is particularly strong; La Fura dels Baus is an internationally renowned troupe, El Comedients and La Cubana draw on local folklore and popular culture to make us laugh, and El Tricicle is a well-loved trio of comedians whose medium is mime. The Catalan director Calixto Bieito is one of the world's leading directors, renowned for his contemporary and often violent versions of Shakespeare's work.

Institut del Teatre ★★★   This grand new theatrical complex is where the city's theater and dance schools are located. There are three auditoriums of varying capacities, and performances range from student showcases to cutting-edge international companies or 24-hour circus "marathons." Plaça Margarida Xirgú s/n. ✆ **93-227-39-00.** www.institutdelteatre.org. Metro: Espanya.

L'Antic Teatre 🎒   This is an on-trend small theater near the Palau de la Música Catalana (see above), which hosts touring companies as well as locals. You never know what to expect, so it's worth reading through the schedules on the door, if you can understand them—one night it's Belgian mime, the next South American circus skills, the next a Jamaican documentary. Tickets are always excellent value, whatever you end up seeing. Verdaguer I Callís 12. ✆ **93-315-23-54.** www.lanticteatre.com. Metro: Urquinaona.

Mercat de Les Flors ★★   Housed in a building constructed for the 1929 World's Fair at Montjuïc, this is the other major Catalan theater. Peter Brook first used it as a theater for a 1983 presentation of *Carmen*. The theater focuses on innovators in drama, dance, and music, as well as European modern-dance companies. It also often features avant-garde art festivals. The 999-seat house has a restaurant overlooking the city rooftops. Lleida 59. ✆ **93-426-18-75.** www.mercatflors.org. Metro: Espanya or Poble Sec.

Teatre Lliure   The theater has two stages, one large and one small, on which plays by the likes of Tennessee Williams and Samuel Beckett are performed. Run by the

---

📷 I Could Have Danced All Weekend

Although the city caters to music lovers of most tastes, the really big thing in Barcelona is electronic dance music. DJs are the new rock heroes, and the Woodstock of this generation is called **Sónar** (www.sonar.es). The festival began in 1996 in a small, outside venue, as a way of showcasing some of the more unusual experimental music coming out of Europe. Now it takes over a significant part of the city for a long weekend in mid-June, drawing people from far and wide. It's now really two festivals, held in two separate locations. During the day, it's held at a number of stages around the MACBA and CCCB in El Raval. At night, it moves to a huge congress and trade-fair hall outside the center, with a special bus shuttling punters between the two areas. Tickets are sold separately for the day and night gigs, although you can buy a pass to the whole thing. Recent Sónar night-time headliners have included Dizzee Rascal and the Chemical Brothers, but the daytime music is much more open and eclectic, often accompanied by strange visuals. Of course, this being Barcelona, there's also a string of unofficial festivals running at the same time, all of which are much cheaper (or sometimes free); find out about them from posters and fliers in bars. This, claim the purists, is where you find the true experimental music, Sónar having sold out to the big sponsors years ago. The best thing is probably to enjoy both—but if you want to go to the official Sónar festival, buy your tickets (and book your room) well beforehand.

young and energetic director Alex Rigola, it's one of the most popular venues in the theater-oriented Poble Sec area, and also features regular dance performances. Plaça Margarita Xirgú 1. ℂ **93-289-27-70.** www.teatrelliure.com. Metro: Poble Sec.

Teatre Nacional de Catalunya   Josep María Flotats heads this major company in a modern, mock-Roman building inaugurated in 1997 and a little out of the center near L'Auditori (see above). The actor/director trained in the tradition of theater repertory, working in Paris at Théâtre de la Villa and the Comédie Française. His company presents both classic and contemporary plays, in two venues: The *Sala Gran* (Large Salon) and *Sala Petita* (Small Salon). Plaça de les Arts 1. ℂ **93-306-57-00.** www.tnc.cat. Metro: Glòries.

Teatre Victòria   Situated in the once gritty (and now only slightly more trendy) Poble Sec district, this lively, large-capacity theater was remodeled in 1992 on the site of the original 19th-century theater. It specializes now in hosting big-scale productions, usually musical spectaculars or comedies. Paral.lel 65. ℂ **93-329-91-89.** www. teatrevictoria.com. Metro: Paral.lel.

BEST BARS & PUBS

- **Best Champagne Bar:** Sparkling wine in Spain is called *cava,* and often there is very little difference between the local version and what you get north of the border in France. **El Xampanyet,** Montcada 22 (ℂ **93-319-70-73**), a tiny, ceramic-lined *cava* bar opposite the Picasso Museum, has been serving up its house variety for eons and is one of the more atmospheric places to down a bottle or two. See p. 255.

- **Best Bar View:** The trek up to the peak of Tibidabo is worth it for **Mirablau,** Plaça Doctor Andreu s/n (ℂ **93-418-58-79**), a chic bar that provides an unparalleled panoramic view of the city from its floor-to-ceiling glass windows. See p. 254.

- **Best Bar for Pre-Dinner Drinks:** Strategically located just off the top end of La Rambla, **Boadas,** Tallers 1 (ℂ **93-318-95-92**), is another historic watering hole, this time with its roots in Havana. Predictably, *mojitos* and daiquiris are a specialty, and it's relaxed enough that you can wander in casually dressed. See p. 244.

- **Best Tapas Bar:** For a great all-round choice of tasty morsels from Catalonia the **Taller de Tapas** ("Tapas Workshop") at L'Argenteria 51 (ℂ **93-268-85-59;** www.tallerdetapas.com) is hard to beat. Local juicy prawns, marinated anchovies, and *esqueixat* (shredded salt cod in olive oil) head the list of goodies. It's my favorite of the five bars in this Barcelona chain. See p. 135.

BARS, CAFES, PUBS & CLUBS
Ciutat Vella
BARS, CAFES & PUBS

Almirall ★   Quiet and dimly lit, this bar might help you imagine what a late-19th-century Barcelona bohemian artists' hangout might have looked like. A huge Art Nouveau mirror behind the bar completes the picture. The crowd is still bohemian

In Barcelona, it's not unusual for places to have several personalities. During the day, that peaceful cafe is the perfect place to sit and read a book or enjoy a fresh croissant. Then, as night falls, the staff changes, the music is turned up, and suddenly you might look up from your book and find yourself in a cool bar surrounded by a loud group of trendy young things. If you wait longer, you might find yourself moved from your table as the furniture is stored away so that the DJ can turn the music up loud and people can dance.

and it's a good place to pop in for a pre-club drink. Joaquín Costa 33, El Raval. ✆ **93-318-99-17.** Metro: Sant Antoni or Universitat.

Barcelona Rouge 🏨 Hidden in the gritty but increasingly inventive Poble Sec, this tiny, scarlet-red bar serves unique cocktails (including some with absinthe) and has an overstuffed collection of furniture to cozy up in, making the overall look one of a turn-of-the-20th-century bordello. There are sporadic performances (of the legal nature) of anything from Argentine tango to acrobats. The music is more of the old-school variety, and regulars tend to shimmy up and ask you to dance. Poeta Cabanyes 21. ✆ **93-442-49-85.** Free admission. Metro: Poble Sec.

The Black Horse This is where many of the neighborhood expats hang out. It has a traditional old pub feel and offers classic British beers on draft. It also shows all the major soccer games and even has a bilingual pub quiz on Sundays. A good place to hear what the situation in the city is from those who've been living here for years. Allada Vermell 16, La Ribera. ✆ **93-268-33-38.** www.pubblackhorse.com. Metro: Jaume I.

Borneo The name is a pun on the area it's in, known as El Born, but the only concession to the historical theme is a slide show straight from the pages of *National Geographic*. Otherwise what you have is a spacious, relaxed bar with an upstairs area for those who want to escape for a while. Rec 49. ✆ **93-268-23-89.** www.barborneo.com. Metro: Jaume I.

Café Bar Padam One of the new breed of chic bars in a down-at-heel part of town, the clientele and decor here are modern and hip. The only color in the black-and-white rooms comes from fresh flowers and modern paintings. French music is featured as well as art expositions. Rauric 9, El Raval. ✆ **93-302-50-62.** Metro: Liceu.

Café Zurich 🍴 At the top of La Rambla overlooking Plaça de Catalunya, this is a traditional meeting point in Barcelona, and it's also great for the passing parade around Catalonia's most fabled boulevard. If the weather is fair, opt for an outdoor table, enjoying a cold beer and the gaiety, which often includes live music. Launched in the early 1920s, the cafe was moved out as they built the Triangle shopping center, and then swiftly moved back in the late 1990s after a renovation. Despite the high prices, grumpy waiters, and rudimentary tapas, it's been going strong ever since. Location says it all. Plaça de Catalunya 1. ✆ **93-317-91-53.** Metro: Catalunya.

Cocktail Bar Boadas ★ This intimate, conservative bar is usually filled with regulars. Established in 1933, it is the city's oldest cocktail bar. It's located at the top end of La Rambla, and many visitors stop in for a pre-dinner drink and snack before wandering to one of the area's many restaurants. It stocks a wide array of Caribbean rums, Russian vodkas, and English gins, and the skilled bartenders know how to mix them all. You won't regret trying a daiquiri. Tallers 1, El Raval. ℰ **93-318-95-92.** Metro: Catalunya.

El Born Facing a rustic-looking square, this former fish store has been cleverly converted. There are a few tables near the front, but our preferred spot is the inner room decorated with rattan furniture and modern paintings. The music might be anything from Louis Armstrong to classic rock 'n' roll. The upstairs buffet serves dinner; although the room is somewhat cramped, you'll find a simple collection of tasty fish, meat, and vegetable dishes, all carefully laid out. Passeig del Born 26, La Ribera. ℰ **93-319-53-33.** Metro: Jaume I.

El Bosc de les Fades 👔 This is the most bizarre bar/cafe in Barcelona, evoking a fairy-tale forest, or at the least trying to. It's brought to you by the same people who created the Museu de Cera (Wax Museum; p. 165), which is next door. Expect "unreal trees" and the whispering sound of waterfalls, plus a "gnome" or two—and a magic mirror that merits 30 seconds' closer inspection. At night the place attracts essentially a young crowd that enjoys the faux woodland dell, the loud background music, and the drinks. Pasaje de la Banca 7, Barri Gòtic. ℰ **93-317-26-49.** www.museocerabcn. com. Metro: Drassanes.

El Café Que Pone Muebles Navarro 👔 This strange little bar has genial aspirations to trendiness. Its name, which means "The Bar Where They Put Navarro Furniture," stems from the days when it was an old furniture storeroom, and it does feel a little like you're sitting in an old-fashioned Ikea as you sip your *fino seco* or gin and tonic. Good music, though. Riera Alta 4–6, El Raval. ℰ **60-718-80-96.** Metro: San Antoni.

Fonfone This is a great example of a bar that fits as many in as it can when the music gets them dancing. The colorful, lighting-based decor is particularly original, and the dance music is always of high quality for those that like modern, accessible electronica. This isn't a place to stand and talk, but rather a good place to fill in those awkward hours when you're ready to go out but it's still too early to hit the clubs. The location is perfect for finding your way anywhere in the Ciutat Vella later on. Escudellers 24, Barri Gòtic. ℰ **93-317-14-24.** Metro: Drassanes.

Ginger ★★ This is a stylish, split-level cocktail, wine, and tapas bar on a pretty Barri Gòtic square. The well-mixed cocktails (including a rarity—a traditional Pimms) make it worth hunting out, as do the tasty snacks, which include imaginative morsels such as sausages flamed-cooked in *orujo* and grilled foie. It's the sort of place you pop in for 1 hour and stay for 3. Palma de Sant Just 1. ℰ **93-310-53-09.** www. ginger.cat. Metro: Jaume I.

Guru White walls, tables, and pillars bedeck this luminous Raval after-dark rendezvous, beloved by the chic and would-be chic alike. Its rather stark futuristic look is softened by a few indoor palms. Not as slinky as it thinks it is but the eclectic sounds from salsa to funk are great. Nou de la Rambla 22. ℰ **93-318-08-40.** www.guru-bcn. com. Free admission. Metro: Liceu.

Hivernacle 👔 This is an airy bar/cafe luring a young, hip crowd to a setting of towering palms in a 19th-century greenhouse. The location is just inside the gates of the Ciutadella Park, but it stays open after the park is closed (the entrance is down one side, on Passeig Picasso). A fashionable crowd likes to come here to "graze" upon the tapas. A restaurant adjoins and there is live music during the summer months. Passeig Picasso s/n, La Ribera. ✆ **93-295-40-17.** Metro: Arc de Triomf.

La Concha 👬 There aren't many bars that have a Moroccan gay-kitsch feeling, but this place does, and it's great fun to hang out while staring at the walls filled with color-treated photos of Spain's starlet from the 1960s, Sara Montiel. One part of the bar becomes a tiny dance floor at weekends. This bar is a Barrio Chino institution and it's still a bit hairy, but perfect to experience an authentic slice of bohemia. Guàrdia 14, El Raval. ✆ **93-302-41-18.** Metro: Drassanes.

La Fianna 👬 With its Moroccan feel, this is a perfect spot to lie back and relax if it's raining or when you don't want a night that's too wild. It houses a restaurant at the back and some normal tables and barstools, but the best thing is to come early and secure one of the cushion-filled platforms—the coziest place to curl up with a few drinks and a friend or three. They also do big American-style Sunday brunches. Banys Vells 15, La Ribera. ✆ **93-315-18-10.** www.lafianna.com. Metro: Jaume I.

La Ovella Negra 🍺 An Old City classic, "The Black Sheep" is like a hidden beer hall. The crowd is young—it's a student favorite—and the drinks are great value. Noisy, friendly, with a beer-stained pool table and a remarkable cave-like setting, this is a fun place for young people to order jugs of cheap sangria and meet some people. There will almost certainly be a line at the table soccer game. Sitges 5, El Raval. ✆ **93-317-10-87.** www.ovellanegra.com. Metro: Plaça de Catalunya.

L'Ascensor ★ "The Elevator" has an entrance just like you'd think—you pass through (rather than go up or down in) an old European sliding-door-style elevator to get into this very local bar so well known for its *mojitos* (Cuban rum cocktails) that it has a line of mint-and-sugared glasses waiting to be filled on order. Bellafila 3, Barri Gòtic. ✆ **93-318-53-47.** Metro: Jaume I.

Margarita Blue ★ They may try to cram in a few too many tables in the Mexican restaurant part, but if you can find a corner to stand in, then the bar is well worth visiting. The music's good, the crowd is lively, and the cocktails are great, especially the eponymous Blue Margarita. For over-30s. Josep Anselm Clavé 6, Barri Gòtic. ✆ **93-412-54-89.** www.margaritablue.com. Metro: Drassanes. They also have a sister club called Rita Blue, Plaça Sant Agustí 3, Barri Gòtic, ✆ **93-342-40-86.** Metro: Liceu.

Molly's Fair City The hangout of expats, plus visiting Brits and Irishmen, this beer hall is incredibly popular. The sound of English voices is heard throughout the pub, growing louder as the evening wears on—and that can get very late. Expect blaring music, loud voices, and beer flowing like a river. Plus, if there's a major soccer game, a lot of friendly shouting. Ferran 7, Barri Gòtic. ✆ **93-342-40-26.** Metro: Liceu.

Nao Colón ★ Located opposite the Estación de Francia at the southern end of El Born, the Nao Colón is a chic designer restaurant for the first half of the week. Then from Thursdays to Sundays it gestates into a club playing funk, soul, and house. If you dine there on a Thursday, they also provide live jazz from 10pm with the meal. Marquès de l'Argentera 19, La Ribera. ✆ **93-268-76-33.** Daily during the day as restaurant, Thurs–Sat as nightclub 12:30–3am. Metro: Barceloneta.

Pitin Bar Easy to spot thanks to the lit-up stars over the door, this is a great place to sit with friends. The bar downstairs may not look anything special, and the patio,

DANCING WITH THE green fairy

If you're feeling adventurous, go to **Bar Marsella**, Sant Pau 65 (✆ **93-442-72-63**; nightly 6pm–2:30am or so; Metro: Liceu) for its specialty: Absinthe (absenta). Picasso and Dalí may have been regulars here and it looks like they haven't dusted the bottles since. The bar's said to be Barcelona's oldest and has been around since 1820, serving the homemade drink that's made the place famous. Absinthe is an impossibly strong, aniseed-tasting concoction (the bane of Vincent van Gogh, among others) made, in part, with the herb wormwood. Some countries ban it for its alleged hallucinogenic qualities, which led to it being called "the green fairy."

Here they serve it the traditional way: With a fork, a small bottle of water, and a sugar cube. Place the sugar on the fork prongs, and balance it over the rim of your glass. Then slowly drip a little of the water (not too much!) over the sugar so that it slowly dissolves into the drink. Wait for it to sink in, and then keep adding drips of water so that the sugar has nearly all dripped into your glass. Then mix the last of the sugar into your glass with the fork, and drink. One glass won't do you much harm, but you can see those around the bar who've had at least a few by their glassy expressions and loose jaws.

though nice, is fairly standard, but if you brave the small spiral staircase, upstairs is a cozy, beamed Old-City room with some funky decorations. It's a great place to sit and talk while watching people through the windows—but tall people may have trouble with the low roof! Passeig del Born 34, La Ribera. ✆ **93-319-50-87.** Metro: Jaume I.

Travel Bar The place for the solo backpacker to start. The main aim of this friendly English-speaking place is to help introduce the city to those who are passing through. Nothing particularly Spanish about the atmosphere—it's simply an easygoing, unpretentious, and convenient bar where you can get a sandwich or a beer, find out what you need to know, or hook up with others for a night of exploring. If you need some guidance on where to go, the bar also runs its own nightly bar crawls around local haunts. Boqueria 27, Barri Gòtic. ✆ **93-342-52-52.** www.travelbar.com. Metro: Liceu.

CLUBS

Apolo ★★ This is a multifaceted venue located in a turn-of-the-20th-century ballroom—Tuesdays it's an alternative cinema, Thursdays it's a funk club, sometimes they have rock concerts, Sundays they have a hugely popular gay night, and on Fridays and Saturdays it's a dance club called Nitsa. Check out listings to find out what's going on when you're in town. Nou de la Rambla 113, Poble Sec. ✆ **93-441-40-01.** www.sala-apolo.com. Metro: Paral.lel.

Aurora ★ Located in the heart of Raval, a stone's throw from the barrio's polyglot early-hours food spots, this intimate, dimly lit spot has a tiny dance floor where you can get up close and personal, plus a welcoming staff and good cocktails. The music ranges from laid-back reggae to lively house sounds. Aurora 7. ✆ **680-518-250.** Metro: Liceu.

Café Royale ★★ Right next to Plaça Reial, this trendy bar is a place for beautiful people—grungy students may have problems getting past the bouncer. But if you can, it's worth it for the subtle gold lighting, the in-house DJs, and the comfortable seating all around the small dance floor. A classic central location for local trendies and models. Nou de Zurbano 3, Barri Gòtic. ✆ **93-412-14-33.** Metro: Liceu.

Club 13 ★★   This club is a favorite of the trendy set. The meeting point for those who like to see and be seen in the heart of Plaça Reial, it gets few tourists, so the majority of those striking a pose are local. Don't be fooled by how small it looks upstairs—all the real action, and the very loud music, happens in the basement where two rooms—one small, one large—house the dancing masses and the cool cats until late. The music is usually electronic dance. Plaça Reial 13, Barri Gòtic. ✆ **93-317-23-52.** Metro: Liceu or Drassanes.

Diobar   One of seaside Barceloneta's favorite clubs and located in the basement of a lively Greek restaurant. No bouzoukis, retsina, or plate-throwing here though. Just a chummy, packed-to-the-gills nightspot that features an enthusiastically eclectic range of Latin and soul sounds from Thursdays to Saturdays, plus funk when the DJ's mood is right (which is most of the time). Carrer Marquès de l'Argentera 27. ✆ **93-319-56-19.** Metro: Barceloneta.

Dot   Anyone who's both a hard-core dance-music fan and a *Star Trek* geek will love this small bar/club. The music is loud and rhythmical, but by far the best thing about the place is the transporter-style doorway between the bar and dance floor. Beam me up. Nou de Sant Francesc 7, Barri Gòtic. ✆ **93-302-70-26.** Metro: Drassanes.

La Luz de Luna ★   For lovers of music a little more Latin, La Luz de Luna ("The Light of the Moon") is a friendly place that specializes in salsa. Don't worry about making a fool of yourself on the dance floor if you don't know the moves—but if you do, you'll find no end of partners who also really know where to put their feet and at what point to twirl you around. Comerç 21, La Ribera. ✆ **93-310-75-42.** Admission after 2am 6€. Metro: Jaume I.

Magic   Make devil horns with your hands and rock your sweaty mullet at this hard-rock/metal club. It's all harmless fun, though, and tourists are more than

---

Old-Time Dancing

Plenty of nightclubs claim to be "classics," but none can beat **La Paloma, Tigre 27** (✆ **93-301-68-97** and 93-317-79-14; admission 10€; Metro: Universitat)—more than 105 years young and still going strong. The name means "The Pigeon" and it opened as a ballroom in 1903, with its famous murals and chandelier added in 1919. It's a part of Barcelona's history—Pablo Picasso met one of his long-term girlfriends here, and Dalí used to sit in a box by the long balcony and sketch the people who came in. During Franco's draconian regime,

someone called "El Moral" was employed to make sure that couples didn't get too close to each other. But there's none of that now. During the early evening, the venue opens as a ballroom for lovers of foxtrot, tango, and bolero, accompanied by a live orchestra. But, late at night from Thursday to Sunday, the place undergoes a transformation and becomes a hip and happening nightclub from 2:30 to 5am. From its incredible decor to the mime artists that stand outside trying to keep punters quiet, this place is an original.

Do you long to check out the seedy part of Barcelona that writer Jean Genet (p. 77) brought so vividly to life in his books? Much of it is gone forever, but *la Vida* nostalgically lives on in pockets like the **Bar Pastis,** Carrer Santa Mónica 4 (℗ **93-318-79-80;** www.barpastis.com; Mon–Fri noon–2:30am, weekends 7pm–3am; 7€; Metro: Drassanes). Valencianos Carme Pericás and Quime Ballester opened this tiny bar just off the southern end of La Rambla in 1947, making it a shrine to Edith Piaf, and her songs still play on an old phonograph behind the bar. The decor consists mostly of paintings by Ballester, who had a dark, rather morbid vision of the world. The house

special, naturally, is the French aniseed-flavored drink pastis (to be drunk straight or with a mixer), and you can order four kinds of pastis in this dimly lit "corner of Montmartre."

Outside the window, check out the view—often a parade of transvestite hookers. The bar crowd can include anyone, especially ageing bohemians. The bar features live music of the French, tango, and folk variety, squeezed into one corner.

A while ago, some people rallied to shut down Pastis due to its noisiness, but the management toned down the din, objections dwindled, and the bar lived to fight on. Today, more low-key or not, its popularity continues unabated.

10

welcome, as long as they can mosh with the best of them. Passeig Picasso 40, La Ribera. ℗ **93-310-72-67.** www.magic-club.net. Metro: Barceloneta.

Moog ★ This is where lovers of techno music and hard pumping beats gather to crash heads. The music is heavy but the people are friendly. Upstairs is a much smaller space where, strangely, 1980s' disco (including a wide selection of Abba) is played and the flamboyant DJ himself is part of the experience. Arc del Teatre 3, El Raval. ℗ **93-301-72-82.** www.masimas.com/moog. Admission 10€. Metro: Drassanes.

New York Talk about late, late nightlife in Barcelona. The gang of 20-something patrons who like this club don't show up until 3am. It's a former strip joint, and the red lights and black walls still evoke its heyday when the women bared all. Recorded music—mainly hip-hop and soul/funk—is heard in the background. Carrer Escudellers 5, Barri Gòtic. ℗ **93-318-87-30.** Admission 6€, after 2am (includes 1 drink) 10€. Metro: Drassanes.

BEACH CLUBS, PORT CLUBS & BEACH BARS

Baja Beach Club If you want to dance to classic disco tracks, there's no place quite like Baja. It can feel a bit like a meat market and it's as far from the sophisticated trendy club or upmarket cocktail bar as you can possibly go, but if you don't mind topless waiters and bikini-clad waitresses, and want a night dancing to cheesy songs you can sing along to from the 1980s and 1990s, then this is probably the place to head. You won't find many other places where the entrance is a giant beach ball and the DJ is standing in a speedboat on the dance floor! It's located right on the beach and does reasonably priced food during the day. Passeig Maritim 34. ℗ **93-225-91-00.** www.bajabeach.es. Metro: Ciutadella–Vila Olímpica.

Carpe Diem Lounge Club ★★   People on a budget should avoid the dress-code-conscious CDLC. Prices are high and so is the snob factor at this achingly cool bar on the edge of the beach. The VIP section is a favorite of famous soccer players, but if you want to join them on the comfortable-looking white chill-out beds, you'll have to buy a 150€ bottle of champagne. It has a large outside terrace for passersby to gawk at the beautiful people. The trendy night is Sunday, when chill-out music plays around 11pm for those cool enough to not have to wake up first thing on Monday. Paseo Marítimo 32.℃ **93-224-04-70.** www.cdlcbarcelona.com. Metro: Ciutadella–Vila Olímpica.

Club Catwalk   This huge disco has two dance areas. Upstairs in the Sky Room they're usually belting out hip-hop or R'n'B, while downstairs in the livelier Main Room you're more likely to be deafened by an ear-splitting selection of electronic sounds played by resident DJs. Its hip young crowd likes to dress up, so best to come suitably attired. Carrer Ramón Trias Vargas s/n. ℃ **93-221-61-61.** www.clubcatwalk.net. Metro: Ciutadella–Vila Olímpica.

The Fastnet Bar ★★   Out of the dozens of Irish pubs and bars in the city, this is the only one that seems to have realized that it is situated in Mediterranean climes and not wet and windy Dublin. Located on a boulevard overlooking the marina, the bar has an ample terrace, which fills up on days when soccer or rugby games are being shown on the large-screen TV that faces the street. The rest of the time it is frequented by Anglo-Saxon yachties, who pop in for a Guinness and bacon-and-egg breakfast. Passeig Joan de Borbó 22.℃ **93-295-30-05.** Daily midday–2am. Metro: Barceloneta.

Le Kasbah ★   Situated next to the Olympic port in the old Palau del Mar building now occupied by the Museu de Catalunya (p. 185), this cool little bar/dance floor plays projections on the wall, has cushions on the benches, and offers good dance music both inside and outside on the terrace. Great place to head to on a hot evening. Plaça Pau Vila 1.℃ **93-238-07-22.** Metro: Barceloneta.

Sala Monasterio ★   Not particularly monastic but chock-full of atmosphere, this ever-popular subterranean hideaway reverberates to a knock-out sound system covering a wide range of live and recorded music. Each night offers something different, from Monday's *catautores* (singer–song writers) and Wednesday's exotic Brazilian themes to Saturday night's all-out, mind-blowing electronic rhythms, and Sunday's cool jazz sessions. Passeig Isabel II 4.℃ **61-628-71-97.** www.salamonasterio.com. Metro: Barceloneta.

Shôko ★   This Asian restaurant-cum-club has an annoying faux-spiritual decor that doesn't sit well with its high drink prices and fashionable clientele, many of whom spill over from the neighboring über-trendy nightspot CDLC. That said, it's a nice place to boogie with the bright young things, and the VIP lounge is open to anyone willing to splash out on champagne. Passeig Marítim 36.℃ **93-225-92-00.** www.shoko.biz. Metro: Ciutadella–Vila Olímpica.

L'Eixample

BARS, CAFES & PUBS

The bars and clubs of L'Eixample tend to attract a slightly more mixed age group than those of the Old City, and more of a classic nature. They are also more spread out, so you may find yourself hopping in and out of cabs if you plan to barhop.

Antilla BCN Latin Club ★★★   Catering to Barcelona's sizeable Latin American and Caribbean community, this is the city's biggest salsa club. Some of the biggest

THE village PEOPLE

During the day it's dedicated to small artisan shops, market stalls, and street theater (see "Montjuïc" in chapter 7, "What to See & Do"), but at night **Poble Espanyol,** Avinguda Marquès de Comillas s/n (✆ **93-508-63-00;** www.poble-espanyol.com; Metro: Espanya), turns into a party town. Built as a "typical" Spanish village for the Universal Exhibition in 1929, it may look old, but the whole place—right down to the huge fortified towers that dominate the entrance—is fake. At night, it makes the perfect location to party, as no one actually lives inside and the gates are strictly guarded. You have a couple of options. One is to buy a 3€ ticket and enter the village to pass the night in three or four small bars which offer drinks, Spanish pop music, and outside tables to watch the partygoers pass by. The other, more expensive option is to pay for a ticket (20€–24€) *outside* to one of the clubs that lie *inside* the walls (entrance to the village is included in your ticket price). The main, and by far the best, venue is **La Terrrazza** (www.laterrrazza.com), rated by many as the liveliest summertime nightspot in Barcelona. It's an outdoor-only club that's open from May to October—again, trendy dance music and a great place to dance the night away until the sun comes up (but not so much when it's raining). If you stay the distance (until 6am on a weekend), look for fliers, and sometimes even buses, to take you to "after parties," situated a little out of town and open until noon.

names in salsa, merengue, mambo, rumba, and all their derivatives have passed through, and when there's not live music, the recorded variety is just as stomping. If you are unsure of how to shake your booty, the club runs a dance school on Monday and Wednesday to Friday between 9 and 11:30pm (cost 80€–125€ per week), and on Tuesday classes are free when you've paid your entrance fee. Open late at weekends. Aragó 141. ✆ **93-451-45-64** or **93-451-21-51.** www.antillasalsa.com. Admission (includes 1 drink) 10€. Metro: Urgell.

City Hall ★ This dark, busy club has a small, cool VIP room upstairs and a reasonably sized dance floor downstairs. The music is usually the standard electronic dance-music fare, but there's also a small, urban chill-out garden with a bar outside at the back. If you get one of the comfortable seats out there, it can be difficult to get up. The other big advantage of this place is that it's situated very close to Plaça de Catalunya—convenient for taxis and many hotels. Discount fliers can be found in many bars. Rambla de Catalunya 2-4. ✆ **93-317-21-77** or **93-238-07-22.** www.grupo-ottozutz.com. Admission (includes 1 drink) 10€. Metro: Plaça de Catalunya.

Costa Breve ★ Sitting uptown, this is a decent disco playing a mixture of Spanish and European commercial music, with the odd surprise thrown in such as a stripper or live gig. Hugely popular with office workers in the area, and young *picos* (yuppies), the vibe is different from the Old City clubs but its tourist-free clientele makes a nice change. Thursday nights are popular with university students, so be warned. Aribau 230. ✆ **93-414-71-95.** www.grupocostabreve.com. Admission 10€. Metro: Diagonal. FGC: Gràcia.

Nick Havanna ★★   Started in 1987, this was one of the first of the city's "designer bars"—that is, postmodern drinking palaces that spent more on decor than practicalities (such as plumbing). It's still very stylish, although in a more retro sort of way, with projections, a dome over the dance floor, uncomfortable metal seating, and some of the most highly designed toilets in the city. Rosselló 208. ℂ **93-215-65-91.** www.nickhavanna.com. Metro: Diagonal.

Toscano Antico ★   A noisy Italian cocktail bar that's a million miles away from the slickness you might expect. They serve all the cocktails in the same style of glass, the music is loud, and the decor rough. But the drinks are excellent and they offer free Italian food on the bar before 10:30pm. The place is all staffed and owned by Italians (the name means "Old Tuscany") and is so Italian that it even has its own ice cream shop a few blocks down, which stays open until 1am on summer weekends; ask at the bar for the *cremería*. Aribau 167. ℂ **93-532-15-89.** Metro: Diagonal.

Gràcia

Alhough the area is filled with small squares and hidden corners, the center of the Gràcia world is Plaça del Sol. In the summer, it's the best place to head to meet young Catalans and to watch people on their way to party. Just as many take their own cans of beer as buy from the bars around the square—the atmosphere is noisy and fun and drives the neighbors mad.

Alfa   A great club if you like indie and rock music. The walls are filled with framed covers of classic albums from bands like U2 and the Smiths, which gives you a good idea of the music. It's as local as you can get (its location in a quiet, shop-filled street means there aren't many passing tourists) and the enormous candles dripping wax onto the bar just add to the atmosphere. It's not a big place, nor a particularly clean one, but it does what it does just fine. Gran de Gràcia 36. ℂ **93-415-18-24.** Metro: Fontana.

Café del Sol   The center of the young Catalan scene, this bar is filled with bohemians, pro-independence Catalan youth, and people who just go to enjoy the tapas and the view over the plaza and its people from the outside tables. An eclectic blend of nightly sounds carries on well into the early hours, with resident DJs at weekends. Wintertime visitors can also enjoy piano evenings on Sundays. Plaça del Sol 16. ℂ **93-415-56-63.** www.cafedelsol.org. Metro: Fontana.

Heliogabal ★★   A cherished member of the Gràcia's cultural and arts scene, this classy, low-key venue is a world away from the raucous, in-your-face urban ambience of central discos and nightspots. Here you have jazz groups, solo singer-songwriters, indie movies, and even poetry-reading evenings. There's a dense, ever-changing program of events so check the website for the latest news. Ramón y Cajal 80, Gràcia. No phone. www.heliogabal.com. Admission up to 10€. Metro: Joanic.

KGB   If the dance music is getting you down, KGB is the place where independent pop acts (metal, reggae, hip-hop) come to find people of their own kind—and to play at them, very loudly. Usually pop rock on Thursdays and a variety of gigs at weekends. Alegre de Dalt 55. ℂ **93-210-59-06.** www.salakgb.net. Admission 12€. Metro: Joanic.

Barrio Alto

Barrio Alto is sometimes seen as a world of its own. Here is where all the rich families live, in houses no less (something unheard of down in the city), and many of

After a long night out, the one thing you need is food—and the greasier the better. If you're out of the center, you might come across a traveling *churros* stand, selling fresh potato chips, long strips of greasy fried donut dough, and sometimes cups of hot chocolate to dip them into. Some tapas bars are open late or very early, such as **El Reloj** (Vía Laietana 47). If it's any early morning but Sunday, the markets usually have bars open too—the local favorite is **Bar Pinotxo** ((℡ **93-317-17-31**) in the Boqueria Market on La Rambla. Also open very early is the real local secret: The croissant factory hidden on the small Carrer Lancaster on the Raval side of La Rambla near the corner of Nou de la Rambla. It opens at about 5am and, for 2.80€, you can buy a box of greasy, chocolate cream-filled doughy croissants that you'll be hard-pressed to finish.

them never leave their enclave. The same applies to going out—rich kids aplenty, alongside some normal types—flood the area. The main bars and clubs are concentrated around a street called Marie Cubí, around 10 minutes' walk from the nearest metro stops of María Cristina and Les Corts or FGC suburban line stations such as Gràcia. They're all very quiet during the week, though.

CLUBS & BARS

Bikini ★★★   A classic of the Barcelona nightlife scene, this venue opened first as an outdoor bar and minigolf course in the 1950s, then reopened in the mid-1990s. It is now a venue for live music and for lively dancing. One room is Latin rhythms, another disco/punk/rock/whatever's going, plus a chill-out cocktail bar tucked away as well. It's also one of the better places to hear live music; when the gig's over, the walls roll back and disco rules. Deu i Mata 105. ℡ **93-322-08-00.** www.bikinibcn.com. Admission (includes 1 drink) 15€. Metro: Les Corts.

Elephant   Located high above the city in the stylish suburb of Pedralbes, the bizarrely named Elephant is located in a trendily converted old house with a thronged dance floor and outdoor terrace. The mood is as elegantly downbeat as its well-heeled customers, and the music, even when it's house sounds, is relaxingly subdued. Here's a nightspot where you can kick back and have a conversation without wincing at the din. Thank the neighbors for that: They signed the petition that keeps noise to a bearable level. Passeig dels Tillers 1, Pedralbes. ℡ **93-334-02-58.** www.elephant.bcn.com. Metro: Palau Reial.

Gimlet ★★★   In this stylish uptown cocktail bar, the lights are low, the music is jazz, and the measures are generous. Sit at the tables or head for the bar at the back and chat with the bartenders as they shake and mix the drinks, pour them into retro glasses, and place them on cute little coasters. There's nothing they can't whip up, and everything they do, they do with admirable style. Santaló 46. ℡ **93-201-53-06.** There's another branch in La Ribera: Rec 24. ℡ **93-310-10-27.** www.gimletbcn.com. Metro: Arc de Triomf (or Jaume 1 for La Ribera branch).

Otto Zutz ★★★   If you're anyone who's anyone in Barcelona, you'll have one of Otto Zutz's gold VIP cards, which allows you access to the bar and small dance area on the top floor, where you can watch all the trendy wannabes down below strutting their stuff and, if the whim takes you, go down and invite one of them up to join you on the balcony. For mere mortals and those from out of town, the dance floor is a good size and the small stage often features club dancers who pose and pout almost as much as those upstairs. There's no shortage of discount cards in bars all over town, but its location means that it can be hard to get home afterward if you're staying in the Ciutat Vella. Lincoln 15. ✆ **93-238-07-22.** www.ottozutz.es. Admission 15€. FGC: Gràcia.

Up and Down ★ The chic atmosphere here attracts elite Barcelonans of all ages. The more mature patrons, specifically the black-tie, post-theater crowd, head upstairs, leaving the downstairs section to loud music and flaming youth. Up and Down is the most cosmopolitan disco in Barcelona, with impeccable service, sassy waiters, and a welcoming atmosphere. Technically, this is a private club—you can be turned away at the door. Numància 179. ✆ **93-205-51-94.** Admission (includes 1 drink) 12€–18€. Metro: María Cristina.

Outer Barcelona
CLUBS & BARS
Mirablau It's all about the location at Mirablau. Although there are worse disco/bars in the city, there are certainly better ones too. But you don't go for the music, the bar prices, or the crowd—you go for the view, as Mirablau is situated right next to the funicular near the top of Tibidabo hill and has a huge window overlooking the twinkling lights of the entire city, from the hill to the sea. It's open during the day for coffee, but the view at night is something else entirely. If it's pretty enough to help tune out the music, all the better. Plaça Doctor Andreu 2. ✆ **93-418-58-79.** www.mirablaubcn.com. Admission 7€. FGC: Tibidabo, then Tramvía Blau.

Razzmatazz ★ Five clubs in one (Razz, Loft, Pop Bar, Rex Room, and Lolita), each with its own style of music. The venue is an enormous multilevel warehouse, and it's not unusual to have a big-name DJ playing the main stage while upstairs, oblivious, a group of goths and rock chicks mosh themselves into a frenzy. If you can't find music you like here, you probably don't like music very much. The crowd can be dominated by students, but it depends very much on the night. One ticket gets you entry to all the venues, so intrepid dancers can spend the night trying them all. Almogàvers 122/Pamplona 88. ✆ **93-320-82-00.** www.salarazzmatazz.com. Mon–Sun (concerts) 9:30pm; Fri–Sat (club) 1–5am. Admission (except for special concerts) 12€–15€. Metro: Bogatell.

CHAMPAGNE BARS

The Catalans call their own version of sparkling wine *cava* and it comes from the nearby Penedès region (p. 276). In Catalan, champagne bars are called *xampanyerias*. With more than 50 Catalan companies producing *cava,* and each bottling up to a dozen grades of wine, the best way to learn about Catalan "champagne" is to sample the products at a *xampanyeria.*

Champagne bars usually open at 7pm and stay open until midnight or later. They serve a small range of tapas, from caviar to smoked fish to frozen chocolate truffles. The traditional local time to go is on a Sunday afternoon, when entire families will have a pre-lunch sip. Most establishments sell only a limited array of house *cavas* by the glass, and more esoteric varieties by the bottle. You'll be offered a choice of *brut* (slightly sweeter), *brut nature,* or *rosat* (rosé, or pink champagne).

Can Paixano 🍾 If you want to sample the cheapest *cava* in town alongside a bewildering selection of sandwiches, this is the best place to go. It's a rowdy *cava* bar where a *copa* is about 1.50€ and the most expensive Can Paixano bottle is a little over 7€. There are no seats, though. If you go at lunchtime, you'll be able to find some space to enjoy your drink—but if you go at night, expect the place to be crammed full. It's a good way to get tipsy early, but don't say I didn't warn you about the evenings—anytime after 7pm the bar will start to get very, very full. It's compulsory to order two mini-sandwiches with the first bottle you buy. Reina Cristina 7. ⓒ **93-310-08-39.** www.canpaixano.com. Closed Feb 14–21, Aug 17–Sept 7. Metro: Barceloneta.

El Xampanyet ★★★ This little champagne bar, my favorite in Barcelona, has been operated by the same family since the 1930s. When the Museu Picasso opened nearby, its popularity was assured. On this ancient street, the tavern is adorned with colored tiles, antique curios, marble tables, and barrels. With your sparkling wine, you can order fresh anchovies in vinegar, impressively fat green olives, or other tapas. If you don't want the *cava*, you can order fresh cider at the old-fashioned zinc bar. Montcada 22. ⓒ **93-319-70-03.** Closed Aug. Metro: Jaume I.

Xampanyeria Casablanca Someone had to fashion a champagne bar after the Bogart–Bergman film, and this is it. There's decor based on the evergreen 1940s' hit and the joint serves four kinds of house *cava* by the glass, plus a good selection of tapas, especially pâtés. Bonavista 6. ⓒ **93-237-63-99.** 8am–3am. Metro: Diagonal.

Xampú Xampany At the corner of the Plaça de Tetuan, this *xampanyeria* offers a variety of hors d'oeuvres in addition to wine. Abstract paintings, touches of high tech, and bouquets of flowers break up the pastel color scheme, and it opens early and closes late. Gran Vía de les Corts Catalanes 702. ⓒ **93-265-04-83.** Metro: Girona or Tetuan.

GAY & LESBIAN BARS

The city has a vibrant, active gay nightlife, with bars and clubs to suit all tastes. The best thing to do is to walk around the area known locally as "Gayxample"—a part of the left side of L'Eixample, more or less between Carrer Sepulveda and Carrer Aragón, and Carrer Casanova and Plaça Urquinaona. By no means is every bar there a gay bar, but many are—and all of the trendy-looking ones almost certainly will be. Most bars welcome people of any persuasion—but hetero couples should be prepared to be discreet.

Aire Lesbians aren't so well served by the city, but this is the classic club of note for everyone, from fashionable young things to older women. It's a large venue with a big dance floor, a pool table, and a buzzing bar. Gay boyfriends are also welcome. Valencia 236. ⓒ **93-454-63-94.** www.arenadisco.com. Admission (includes 1 drink) 6€. Metro: Passeig de Gràcia.

Café Dietrich ★ As if you didn't already know by its namesake, this cafe stages the best drag strip shows in town, a combination of local and foreign divas "falling in love again" like the great Marlene herself. It remains Barcelona's most popular gay haunt. The scantily clad bartenders are hot, and the overly posh decor lives up to its reputation as a "divinely glam musical bar/disco." Many of the drag queens like to fraternize with the handsomest of the patrons, to whom they offer deep kisses on the mouth. So be warned. Consell de Cent 255. ⓒ **93-451-77-07.** Metro: Universitat.

D-Boy ★   This leading gay dance club has been going strong since 1999. It's still the flashiest dive on the see-and-be-seen circuit, and a good place to wear your see-through clothing, especially under those pink lasers. There are two rooms devoted to different types of music, the first with house music and DJs and the other with more commercial and "soapy" themes. The waiters are probably the most sensual, handsome, and muscular in town. Look your most gorgeous if you want to get past the notoriously selective doorman. Ronda de Sant Pere 19-21. © **93-318-06-86.** Metro: Urquinaona.

Medusa   This minimalist-decorated bar draws a trendy young crowd, mainly of cute boys. "The cuter you are, the better your chances of getting in if we get crowded as the night wears on," I was assured by one of the staff members. A super-trendy place, Medusa draws the fashionistas and its DJs are among the best in town. The place gets very cruisy after 1am. Casanova 75. © **93-454-53-63.** Metro: Urgell.

Metro   Still one of the most popular gay discos in Barcelona, Metro attracts a diverse crowd—from young fashion victims to more rough-and-ready macho types. One dance floor plays contemporary house and dance music, and the other traditional Spanish music mixed with Spanish pop. This is a good opportunity to watch men of all ages dance the *sevillanas* together with a surprising degree of grace. The gay press in Barcelona accurately dubs the backroom here as a "notorious, lascivious labyrinth of lust." One interesting feature appears in the bathrooms, where videos have been installed in quite unexpected places. Sepulveda 185. © **93-323-52-27.** Admission 10€. Metro: Universitat.

New Acid Oxide   If you've done all the hot spots and find you're still on your lonesome, head for this very companionable after-hours haven. Its notorious "dark room" is the darkest in town. Joaquín Costa 61. © **93-268-10-19.** Admission (includes 1 drink) 10€. Metro: Universitat.

New Chaps   Gay Barcelonese refer to this saloon-style watering hole as Catalonia's premier leather-and-denim bar, mainly patronized by "mature" clients (30- to 50-somethings) . In fact, the dress code usually is leather of a different stripe: More boots and jeans than leather and chains. Behind a pair of swinging doors evocative of the old American West, New Chaps contains two different bar areas. Some of Barcelona's horniest guys flock to the downstairs darkroom in the wee hours. Diagonal 365. © **93-215-53-65.** www.newchaps.com. Metro: Diagonal.

New Kiut   This intimate, discreetly lit all-ages favorite has video screens showing blends of beach house and standard pop. Considerately, for a nightspot, it had smoking and non-smoking areas even before the ban came in January 2011. Thursday is "straight nite," when heteros mingle with the lesbian regulars. Consell de Cent 280. © **687-394-627** (mobile). Admission free for women, 10€ for men. Metro: Passeig de Gràcia.

Punto BCN   Barcelona's largest gay bar attracts a mixed crowd of young "hotties" and foreigners. Always crowded, it's a good base to start your evening. There is a very popular happy hour on Wednesday from 6 to 9pm. Free passes to other bars are available from the bar. Muntaner 63-65. © **93-453-61-23.** www.arenadisco.com. Metro: Universitat.

SIDE TRIPS IN CATALONIA

About six million people live in Catalonia, and twice that many visit every year, flocking to the beaches along the Catalan *costas* (coasts), the area of Spain that practically invented package tourism. Though some areas—such as Lloret de Mar—have become overdeveloped, there are many unspoiled little seaside spots to be found.

Three of the most attractive resorts are on the **Costa Brava (Rugged Coast)**, 100km (60 miles) north of Barcelona: The southerly town of **Tossa de Mar,** with its walled Ciutat Vella; the idyllic coastal village of **Calella de Palafrugell;** and the northerly whitewashed fishing village of **Cadaqués,** up near the French border.

Inland from the latter lies **Figueres,** low-key capital of Girona province's northerly Alt Empordà region, birthplace of the father of surrealism, Salvador Dalí, and home to his eccentric museum, which enthralls everyone from art lovers to the downright curious. The capital of the whole province, including the lower Baix Empordà region, is **Girona,** an ancient town steeped in history, with a magnificent Old Quarter and cathedral.

South of Barcelona, along the **Costa Daurada (Golden Coast),** the beaches are wide and sandy. **Sitges,** a fine resort town that has a huge gay following, and **Tarragona,** the UNESCO-classified capital of the region, are the two destinations to visit here, the latter for its concentration of Roman vestiges and architecture.

Away from the coast, amid attractive wooded hills and fertile valleys at the meeting point of Tarragona and Lleida provinces, is a fine trio of small Cistercian monasteries—**Poblet, Santes Creus,** and **Vallbona de les Monges**—all dating from the 12th century.

These are eclipsed, however, by the greatest monastery of them all: **Montserrat,** a hugely popular day excursion to the northwest of Barcelona. The serrated outline made by the sierra's steep cliffs led the Catalonians to call it *montserrat* (saw-toothed mountain). Today this Benedictine sanctuary remains the religious center of Catalonia, and thousands of pilgrims annually visit the monastery complex to see its Black Virgin.

Due northeast of Barcelona, the atmospheric Romanesque towns of **Vich, Ripoll,** and **Camprodón**—each one more charmingly compact as you approach the Pyrénées—are well worth an off-the-beaten-track tour.

MONTSERRAT ★★

56km (35 miles) NW of Barcelona, 592km (368 miles) E of Madrid

The monastery at **Montserrat,** which sits atop a 1,200-m (3,900-feet)-high mountain, 11km (7 miles) long and 5.5km (3½ miles) wide, is one of the most important pilgrimage spots in Spain. It ranks alongside Zaragoza and Santiago de Compostela in Galicia, at the end of the pilgrimage route of St. James. Thousands travel here every year to see and touch the medieval statue of La Moreneta (The Black Virgin), the most important religious icon in Catalonia. Many newly married couples flock here for her blessing.

Avoid visiting on Sunday, especially if the weather is good, as thousands of locals pour in. At all times, remember to take along warm sweaters or jackets, since it can get cold in the evening.

Essentials

GETTING THERE   The best and most exciting way to go is via the Catalan **railway.** Ferrocarrils de la Generalitat de Catalunya (⟨© 93-205-15-15; www.fgc. es) to Montserrat-Aeri leaves every hour from Plaça Espanya in Barcelona. The train connects with a high-tech funicular (Aeri de Montserrat), which leaves every 15 minutes.

Although the train, with its funicular tie-in, has taken over as the preferred and cheapest means of transport, a long-distance **bus** service is also provided by Autocares Julià in Barcelona (⟨© 93-490-40-00 or 90-240-00-80; www.autocaresjulia. es). A daily service from Barcelona is available, with departures near the Estació de Sants on the Plaça de Països Catalans. Buses leave at 9:15am, returning at 5pm, and at 6pm in July and August; the round-trip ticket costs 10€ on weekdays and 12€ on weekends.

To **drive** to Montserrat, exit via the Avinguda Diagonal, then take the A-2 (exit Martorell). The signposts and exit to Montserrat will be on your right. From the main road, it's 15km (9⅓ miles) up to the monastery through eerie rock formations and dramatic scenery.

VISITOR INFORMATION   The **tourist office** is at the Plaça de la Creu (⟨© 93-877-77-77; www.manresaturisme.cat/montserrat-cataluna.phb), open daily from 8:50am to 7:30pm. This office can provide maps with walks around the mountain.

Exploring Montserrat

Among the monastery's noted attractions is the 50-member **Escolanía ★★**, one of the oldest and most renowned boys' choirs in Europe, dating from the 13th century. At 1pm daily (noon on Sun) you can hear them singing "Salve Regina" and the "Virolai" (hymn of Montserrat) in the basilica. The basilica is open Monday to Friday from 7:30am to 7:30pm, and Saturday and Sunday from 7:30pm to 8:30pm. Admission is

Catalonia

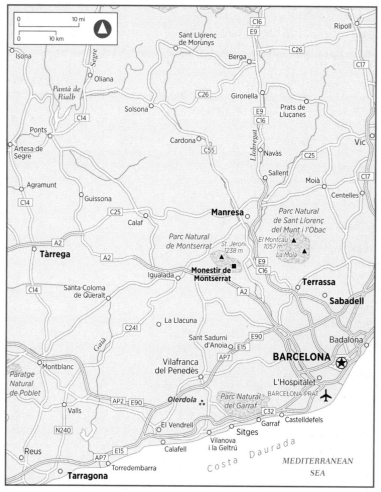

free. To view the Black Virgin, a statue from the 12th or 13th century, enter the church through a side door to the right. She was found in one of the mountain caves in the 12th century (p. 260) and is said to have been carved by St. Luke himself.

At the Plaça de Santa María you can also visit the **Museu de Montserrat** (✆ **93-877-77-77;** www.abadiamontserrat.net), known for its collection of ecclesiastical paintings, including works by Caravaggio and El Greco. Modern Spanish and Catalan artists are also represented (see Picasso's early *El Viejo Pescador,* 1895). Works by Dalí and French Impressionists Monet, Sisley, and Degas are shown. The collection of ancient artifacts is quite interesting; look for the crocodile mummy, which is at least 2,000 years old. The museum is open Monday through Friday from 10am to 6pm, and Saturday and Sunday from 9:30am to 6:30pm, charging 5€ for adults and 3.50€ for children and students.

The 9-minute **funicular ride** (Aeri de Montserrat; ✆ **93-237-71-56;** www. aeridemontserrat.com) to the 1,236-m (4,055-feet)-high peak, Sant Joan, makes for a panoramic trip. The funicular operates about every 20 minutes daily from 9:25am to 1:45pm and 2:20 to 6:45pm March through October, and 10:10am to 1:45pm and 2:20 to 5:45pm (or 6:45pm on public holidays) November through February. The cost is 8.20€ round-trip, 5.15€ one-way. From the top on a clear day you'll see most of Catalonia and the Pyrénées plus—if you're very lucky—the islands of Majorca and Ibiza.

Make an excursion to **Santa Cova (Holy Grotto),** the alleged site of the discovery of the Black Virgin. The grotto dates from the 17th century and was built in the shape of a cross. Go halfway by funicular and complete the trip on foot. The grotto is open year-round, daily from 10am to 1pm and 2 to 5:45pm. The funicular operates every 20 minutes daily from 11am to 6pm at a round-trip cost of 2.90€ adults, 1.60€ children. For more information, visit www.cremallerademontserrat.com.

Where to Stay & Dine

Few people spend the night here, but most visitors want at least one meal. There is only one restaurant on Montserrat (see below). Maybe bring a picnic lunch from Barcelona instead?

MODERATE

Abat Cisneros   This modern hotel on the main square of Montserrat offers few pretensions and a history of family management from 1958. The small rooms are simple and clean, each with a comfortable bed, and en-suite bathrooms. Rudimentary regional dishes are served in the in-house restaurant. The hotel's name is derived from a title given to the head of any Benedictine monastery during the Middle Ages.

Plaça de Montserrat s/n, 08199 Montserrat. ✆ **93-877-77-01.** Fax 93-877-77-24. www.interhotel.com/ spain/es/hoteles/1829.html. 82 units. 60€–115€ double. Rates include breakfast. Main courses in restaurant 12€–18€. AE, DC, MC, V. Parking 10€. Bus: Autocares Julià from Plaça Espanya in Barcelona. Train: Montserrat line from Estació de Sants and then Ferrocarril. **Amenities:** Restaurant; bar; lounge. *In room:* TV, Wi-Fi (free).

TARRAGONA ★★

97km (60 miles) S of Barcelona, 554km (344 miles) E of Madrid

The ancient Roman port city of **Tarragona,** on a rocky bluff above the Mediterranean, is one of the grandest but most unfairly neglected sightseeing centers in Spain. Honoring its abundance of Roman and medieval remains, UNESCO

ROUTE OF THE CISTERCIAN monasteries

Near the medieval town of **Montblanc,** 113km (70 miles) west of Barcelona in the heart of Tarragona province, is a little-known trio of small but exquisite monasteries, all founded in the 12th century by Benedictine monks from Cite-aux, or Cistercium, in Burgundy, France, with the purpose of returning to a simple lifestyle of austerity and unworldliness detached from material concerns.

The oldest and largest of them, **Santa María de Poblet** (Oficina Comarcal de Turisme, Monasterio de Poblet. (C) **97-787-00-89;** www.poblet.cat; Mon–Fri 10am–12:30pm and 3–6pm, closes at 5:30pm in winter; 6€, 3.50€ seniors, students, and children 18 and under), nestles on the wooded slopes of the Prades Mountains. Its name derives from the Latin *populetum,* meaning "white poplar". Founded in 1151, and continuously expanded and reconstructed over the centuries, its styles range from Romanesque (13th-century St. Catherine's chapel) to Gothic (15th-century St. George's chapel) and baroque. In its great, high-vaulted chapter house the kings of Catalonia and Aragón are laid to rest in (restored) tombs. The present active community of monks originates from 1945 when the Poblet Brotherhood was created.

The nearby, smaller **Monestir de Santes Creuses** ((C) **97-763-83-29;** Mar 16–Sept 15 10am–1:30pm and 3–7pm, Sept 16–Jan 15 10am–1:30pm and 3–5:30pm, Jan 16–March 15 10am–1:30pm and 3–6pm; 4€) is set in a secluded, wooded valley beside the River Gaia. Founded 7 years after Poblet, it also underwent transitional work as recently

as the 18th century. Its highlights are the ancient Trinitat chapel and 14th-century Gothic cloister with a striking Romanesque octagonal pavilion.

The convent of **Santa María de Vallbona de les Monges** ((C) **97-333-02-66;** www.vallbona.com; Tues–Sat 10am–1:30pm and 4:30–6:45pm, Sun and holidays noon–1:30pm and 4:30–6:45pm, closed Mon; 3€) lies just inside neighboring Lleida province in a fertile valley noted for its excellent olive oil. Founded by the Cistercians' female branch in the 12th century, it originally housed daughters of noble families from the House of Aragón. Today it still has a resident community of some 30 nuns as well as an active cultural and spiritual center. Romanesque styles predominate, especially in the north transcept doors, the south and east wings of the superb cloister, and the 14th-century bell tower.

These three monasteries can all be visited with a combined 9€ ticket, which you can purchase at Santa María de Poblet monastery.

Montblanc itself is atmospheric enough to warrant an overnight stay. It was once the center of a thriving Jewish community, as the scenic Carrer Jeues (Street of Jews) testifies. Two-thirds of the surrounding 13th-century walls are still intact and the Palau Reial (Royal Palace) is a standout. Book a room at the two-star **Fonda Cal Blasi,** which is located in a converted 19th-century house in the town center at Carrer Alenyá 11 ((C) **97-786-13-36;** www.fondacalblasi.com); a double goes for 90€ to 125€.

A romanesque ROUTE TO THE PYRÉNÉES

Barcelona's Museu Nacional d'Art de Catalunya (MNAC; p. 186) houses one of the finest Romanesque collections in Europe, with many of its sculptures and icons transferred from churches or monasteries high in the Pyrénées. Yet those mountains and their foot-hills still contain a countless host of Romanesque treasures, and a most enjoyable way of seeing some of them in their natural setting is to explore a trio of towns lying northeast of Barcelona. You can do this reason-ably effectively by public transporta-tion, although this is one occasion where renting a car would help you to do the area full justice.

VIC   The first stop is **Vic,** a fascinat-ing town that's surprisingly little known to outside visitors. Its arcaded **Plaça Mayor,** whose fine *moderniste* building, **Casa Comella,** features a four-seasons *sgraffito* by Gaità Buigas, designer of Barcelona's Columbus Monument, is the setting for an impressive Saturday mar-ket. The neoclassical **Catedral de Sant Pere,** founded in the 9th century and "renovated" from 1781 onward, boasts a magnificent, seven-story Lombar-dian bell tower, and together with the **Museu Episcopal** contains fine exam-ples of Romanesque works. Stay at

the central, three-star **Hotel J. Balmes Vic,** Francesc Pla el Vigatá 6 (© **93-889-12-72;** www.hoteljbalmes.com; double 90€–105€), or out of town at the deluxe, four-star **Parador de Tur-ismo de Vic,** Carretera de Roda de Ter 14 (© **93-812-23-23;** www.paradores. es; double 160€–190€). The top local choice for a meal is the traditional **Car-dona 7,** Cardona 7 (© **93-883-28-45;** www.restaurantesvic.com/restaurant/cardona-7). The local *salchichones* (sausages) are legendary here.

Vic is about 65km (40 miles) from Barcelona on the C-17 Puigcerda road. You can travel there by bus with Empresa Sagalés (© **93-231-27-56;** www.sagales.com) from Barcelona's Fabra i Puig bus station (Avinguda Meridiana 392. Metro: Fabra i Puig), by a RENFE train from Sants main railway station (www.renfe.es), or by car. For more information on Vic, contact the **Oficina de Turismo de Vic,** Carrer Ciutat 4 (© **93-886-20-91;** www. victurisme.cat).

RIPOLL   Continue on to **Ripoll,** a small town with narrow, medieval streets, virtually in the foothills of the Pyrénées. Few towns of its size—even in Catalonia—can boast such a wealth of history. Dominating everything is the

included Tarragona's entire "archeological ensemble" on its prestigious World Heritage list in 2000.

The Romans captured Tarragona *(Tarraco)* in 218 B.C., and during their rule the city sheltered one million people behind 64-km (40-mile)-long city walls. One of the four capitals of Catalonia when it was an ancient principality, and once the home of Julius Caesar, Tarragona today consists of an Old Quarter filled with interesting buildings, particularly the houses with connecting balconies. The upper walled town is mainly medieval; the town below is newer.

In the new town, explore the **Rambla Nova,** the city's main artery and a fashion-able, wide boulevard. Running parallel to the Rambla Nova to the east is the **Rambla** astounding Benedictine monastery of **Santa María de Ripoll** (www.romanico catalan.com/Ripolles/Ripoll/ripoll.htm), founded in the 9th century by the formidable Wilfred the Hairy (p. 13), whose remains are entombed here. Like Vic cathedral, it has a seven-story bell tower, but this and its evocative cloisters and Lombardian apses are eclipsed by the incomparable exterior and interior Romanesque carvings and sculptures, the finest outside those on display in the MNAC. The nearby monastery of **Sant Joan de les Abadesses** (www.monestirs. cat/monst/ripoll/crp14abad.htm), with its splendid Gothic bridge, was also founded by Wilfred the Hairy and is well worth the 10-km (6¼-mile) detour. Stay at the **Pensió Trobada,** Passeig Honorat Vilamanya 4 ((℮ **97-270-23-53;** http:// pension-la-trobada-en--girona.buscalis. com/f/ripoll/72404.html**;** double 70€– 75€). Eat out at the traditional **Hostal del Ripollès,** Plaça Nova 11 ((℮ **97-270-02-15;** www.hostaldelripolles.com).

Ripoll is 104km (65 miles) from Barcelona on the C-17 Puigcerda road. You can travel there by TEISA bus from the corner of Carrer Pau Claris and Carrer Consell de Cent in Barcelona ((℮ **97-220-48-68;** www.teisa-bus.com), by train from Sants or Plaça de Catalunya

station (www.renfe.es), or by car. Journey time is approximately 2 hours. For more information on Ripoll, contact the **Oficina de Turisme de Ripoll,** Plaça Abat Oliva 1 ((℮ **97-270-23-51;** www. ripoll.cat).

CAMPRODÓN High up in the heart of the Pyrénées is the charming township of **Camprodon,** birthplace of Catalan composer Isaac Albeñiz, whose Alpine-style birthplace you can view from outside (but can't visit). Its **Sant Pere** church, built in the shape of a Latin cross, is the sole remaining part of the original 9th-century Cistercian monastery. The most remarkable structure intact today is the 14th-century Romanesque **Pont Nou,** which straddles the fast-flowing river Ter as it cascades down from the surrounding mountains. Stay at the **Hotel Güell,** Plaça Espanya 8 ((℮ **97-274-00-11;** double 75€). Dine out at the **Nuria Restaurant,** Plaça Espanya 11 ((℮ **97-274-00-24).**

To visit Camprodón, follow the route to Ripoll (see above) and then take the C-26 via Sant Joan de les Abadesses. Journey time is approximately 2½ hours. For more information, contact the **Oficina de Turisme de Camprodón,** Plaça Espanya 1 ((℮ **97-274-00-10;** www.valldecamprodon.org).

Vella, which marks the beginning of the Old Town. The city has a bullring, good hotels, and some beaches, particularly the Platjes del Miracle and del Cossis.

After seeing the attractions listed below, cap off your day with a stroll along the **Balcó del Mediterráni (Balcony of the Mediterranean),** where the vistas are especially beautiful at sunset.

Essentials

GETTING THERE There are daily basic commuter **trains** every 15 to 45 minutes making the 1-hour trip to and from Barcelona-Sants station; the fare is 6.40€ one-way. Slightly faster and far more comfortable long-distance Euromed, Talgo, and

Tarragona

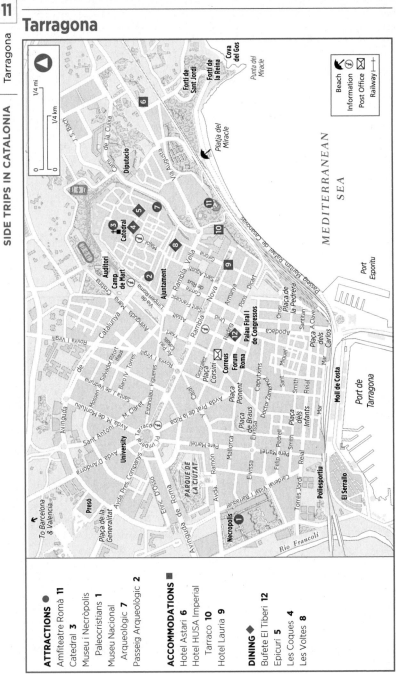

ATTRACTIONS ●
Amfiteatre Romà **11**
Catedral **3**
Museu i Necròpolis
 Paleocristians **1**
Museu Nacional
 Arqueològic **7**
Passeig Arqueològic **2**

ACCOMMODATIONS ■
Hotel Astari **6**
Hotel HUSA Imperial
 Tarraco **10**
Hotel Lauria **9**

DINING ◆
Bufete El Tiberi **12**
Epicuri **5**
Les Coques **4**
Les Voltes **8**

Alaris trains stopping here charge between 17.80€ and 19.80€ one-way. In Tarragona, the RENFE office is in the train station at Plaça Pedrera s/n (© **90-224-02-02;** www.renfe.com).

From Barcelona to Tarragona (1½ hours), there are eight **buses** per day from Monday to Saturday and two on Sunday and bank holidays, run by Plana (© **97-721-44-75;** www.itenewebs.com/autocaresplana). Another company, Hispania (© **97-775-41-47**) also operates a service that continues to Reus. All buses leave from the María Cristina Metro station and cost 8.95€ one-way.

To **drive,** take the A-2 southwest from Barcelona to the A-7, via Vilafranca. The route to Tarragona is well marked.

VISITOR INFORMATION The **tourist office** is at Carrer Major 39 (© **97-725-07-95;** www.tarragonaturisme.cat). It's open July to September Monday to Friday from 9am to 9pm, Saturday 9am to 2pm and 4 to 9pm, and Sunday 10am to 2pm; the rest of the year, it's open Monday to Saturday 10am to 2pm and 4 to 7pm, and Sunday 10am to 2pm.

Exploring the Town

Amfiteatre Romà ★   At the foot of Miracle Park and dramatically carved from a cliff that rises from the beach, this Roman amphitheater recalls the days in the 2nd century when thousands gathered here to be entertained by games and gladiator fights.

Parc del Milagro s/n. © **97-724-25-79.** Admission 2.45€, 1.25€ students and seniors. Mar–Sept Tues–Sat 9am–9pm, Sun 9am–3pm; Oct–Feb Tues–Sat 9am–5pm, Sun 10am–3pm. Closed Dec 25, Jan 1, and Jan 6. Bus: 2.

Catedral ★★   At the highest point of Tarragona is the 12th-century cathedral, whose architecture represents the transition from Romanesque to Gothic. It has an enormous vaulted entrance, fine stained-glass windows, Romanesque cloisters, and an open choir. In the main apse, observe the altarpiece of Santa Tecla, the patron saint of Tarragona, carved by Pere Joan in 1430. Two flamboyant doors open into the chevet. The east gallery contains the **Museu Diocesà** (www.museu.diocesa. arquebisbattarragona.cat), with a collection of Catalan art.

Plaça de la Seu s/n. © **97-723-72-69.** Admission to cathedral and museum 3.50€, 2.50€ students and seniors, free for children 16 and under. Mar–May daily 10am–1pm and 4–7pm; June–Sept daily 10am–7pm; Oct–Feb daily 10am–2pm. Bus: 1.

Museu i Necròpolis Paleocristians ★   This is one of the most important burial grounds in Spain, used by Christians from the 3rd to the 5th century. It stands outside town next to a tobacco factory whose construction led to its discovery in 1923. While on the grounds, visit the **Museu Paleocristià,** which contains a number of sarcophagi and other objects discovered during the excavations.

Av. de Ramón y Cajal 80. © **97-723-62-09.** Admission to museum, necropolis, and Museu Nacional Arqueològic 2.50€, 1.25€ students, free for seniors and children 18 and under. June–Sept Tues–Sat 10am–1:30pm and 4–7pm, Sun and holidays 10am–2pm; Oct–May Tues–Sat 10am–1:30pm and 3–5:30pm, Sun and holidays 10am–2pm. Bus: 4.

Museu Nacional Arqueològic ★   Overlooking the sea, the Archaeology Museum houses a collection of Roman relics—mosaics, ceramics, coins, silver, sculpture, and more. The outstanding attraction here is the mosaic *Head of Medusa* ★★, with its penetrating stare.

CATALONIA remembers PABLO CASALS

Fleeing from Franco and the fascist regime, the world's greatest cellist, Pablo Casals, left his homeland in 1939. Today his body has been returned to El Vendrell, 72km (45 miles) south of Barcelona, where he is remembered with a museum in his honor. The museum is installed in the renovated house where he lived until he went into self-imposed exile.

Seventeen rooms are filled with Casals' memorabilia, including his first cello, photographs and films of his performances, the Peace Medal awarded by the United Nations in 1971, and photographs of the artist with famous people including John F. Kennedy, who awarded him the Medal of Freedom.

Casals died in Puerto Rico in 1973 at the age of 96, and he was finally returned to his beloved Catalonia in 1979, where he is buried at the El Vendrell graveyard.

The **Museu Pau Casals** lies at Avinguda Palfuriana 59–61, in Sant Salvador–El Vendrell (© **97-768-42-76;** www.paucasals.org). From September 16 to June 14 it is open Tuesday through Friday from 10am to 2pm and 4 to 6pm, Saturday from 10am to 2pm and 4 to 7pm, and Sunday from 10am to 2pm. From June 15 to September 15 it's open Tuesday through Saturday from 10am to 2pm and 5 to 9pm, and Sunday from 10am to 2pm. Admission is 8€ for adults; 4€ for children, students, and seniors; and free for children 8 and under. Allow 1 hour.

To reach El Vendrell from Barcelona, head south along the C-32 until you come to the El Vendrell exit just past Calafell.

Plaça del Rei 5. © **97-723-62-09.** www.mnat.es. Admission for museum and Museu i Necròpolis Paleocristians 2.50€, 1.25€ students, free for seniors and children 18 and under. June–Sept Tues–Sat 10am–8pm, Sun 10am–2pm; Oct–May Tues–Sat 10am–1:30pm and 4–7pm, Sun 10am–2pm. Bus: 8.

Passeig Arqueològic ★★ At the far end of the Plaça del Pallol, an archway leads to this .8km (½-mile) walkway along the ancient ramparts, built by the Romans on top of gigantic boulders. The ramparts have been much altered over the years, especially in medieval times and in the 1600s. There are scenic views from many points along the way.

El Portal del Roser s/n. © **97-724-57-96.** Admission 2.50€, 1.25€ students and seniors, free for children 16 and under. Oct–Mar Tues–Sat 9am–7pm, Sun and holidays 10am–3pm; Apr–Sept Tues–Sat 9am–9pm, Sun and holidays 9am–3pm. Bus: 2.

Theme Park Thrills

A 10-minute ride from the heart of Barcelona, the **PortAventura Park,** Port Aventura (© **97-777-90-90;** www.portaventura.es), is Spain's biggest theme park. Universal Studios has acquired a prime stake in it and has plans to make it even larger; it looks like some progress may be made on this in 2011. On a vast 809 hectares (1,999 acres), it will be expanded to become Europe's largest entertainment center. Since its inauguration in 1995, it has already become one of the Mediterranean's favorite family destinations.

The park is a microcosm of five distinct worlds, with full-scale re-creations of classic villages ranging from Polynesia to Mexico, from China to the old American West. It also offers a thrilling variety of roller-coaster and white-water rides, all centered on a lake you can travel to via the deck of a Chinese junk.

The park is open daily March 18 to June 19 from 10am to 8pm, June 20 to September 13 from 10am to midnight, September 14 to January 8 from 10am to 8pm. It's closed January 9 to March 17. A 1-day pass costs 44€ adults, 35€ children, 22€ visitors with disabilities; a 2-day pass costs 66€ adults, 52.50€ children, 33€ visitors with disabilities. Nighttime admission, available only in summer months, is 28€ adults, 23€ children, 16€ visitors with disabilities. The fee includes all shows and rides.

Where to Stay
MODERATE
Hotel HUSA Imperial Tarraco ★★ Just south of the cathedral, atop an oceanfront cliff, which has panoramas including sweeping views of the sea and the Roman ruins, this hotel is the finest in town. It was designed in the form of a crescent and has guest rooms that may angle out to sea and almost always include small balconies. The rooms, all with en-suite bathrooms, are comfortably furnished and decorated with dark-wood headboards, patterned bedspreads, and a warm autumnal russet-and-ocher decor. The public rooms display lots of polished white marble, Oriental carpets, and leather furniture. The staff cheerfully handle the demands of both business travelers and art lovers on sightseeing excursions.

Passeig Palmeras s/n, 43003 Tarragona. *②* **97-723-30-40.** Fax 97-721-65-66. www.hotelhusaimperial tarraco.com. 170 units. 100€–150€ double; 175€–220€ suite. AE, DC, MC, V. Free parking on street; Mon–Fri parking lot 15€ per day. Bus: 1. **Amenities:** Snack bar; babysitting; outdoor pool; room service; tennis court; Wi-Fi. *In room:* A/C, TV, hair dryer, minibar.

INEXPENSIVE
Hotel Astari 🏄 Travelers in search of peace and quiet on the Mediterranean come to the Astari, which opened in 1959. This resort hotel on the Barcelona road offers fresh and airy accommodations in compact, neatly furnished rooms, each with cream walls, wooden bedsteads, dark-blue bedcovers, and drapes. The Astari has long balconies and terraces, one favorite spot being the outer flagstone terrace with its umbrella-shaded tables set among willows, orange trees, and geranium bushes. This is the only hotel in Tarragona with garage space for each guest's car.

Vía Augusta 95-97, 43003 Tarragona. *②* **97-723-69-00.** Fax 97-723-69-11. www.hotelastari.com. 81 units. 80€ double; 105€ business suite. AE, DC, MC, V. Parking 8€. Bus: 9. **Amenities:** Restaurant; bar; pool; room service. *In room:* A/C, TV, hair dryer, minibar, Wi-Fi (free).

Hotel Lauria ★ Less than half a block north of the town's popular seaside promenade (Passeig de les Palmeres), beside the tree-lined Rambla, this government-rated three-star hotel offers unpretentious rooms, each of which has been recently modernized. They all feature comfortable beds, gaily patterned bedspreads and colorful bedsteads, dressing tables, and warmly carpeted floors. The rooms at the back open onto a view of the sea.

Rambla Nova 20, 43004 Tarragona. © **97-723-67-12.** Fax 97-723-67-00. www.hotel-lauria.com. 72 units. 85€ double. AE, DC, MC, V. Parking 10€. Bus: 1. **Amenities:** Bar; outdoor pool; room service; Wi-Fi (free). *In room:* A/C, TV, hair dryer.

Where to Dine
EXPENSIVE

Les Coques ★ 🍴 MEDITERRANEAN   A real discovery in the historic core of the Old Town, this sophisticated eating spot specializes in quality fare from both land and sea. They prepare the best grilled octopus (the miniature variety) in town. I tasted virgin olive oil and garlic, but the chef prefers to keep his other flavors "secret." They also offer marvelously tender and succulent lamb chops flavored with rich burgundy sauce. The specialties depend on whatever is good in any season. Their selection of wild mushrooms *(seta)* can be prepared in almost any style without losing their marvelously woodsy taste.

Carrer Nou Patriarca 2 bis. © **97-722-83-00.** Reservations required. Main courses 18€–28€. AE, DC, MC, V. Mon–Sat 1–3:45pm and 9–10:45pm. Closed 1 week in Feb and July 24–Aug 14.

MODERATE

Bufete El Tiberi ★ SPANISH   It may be named after Rome's legendary river but the grub in this superior self-service establishment is definitely produced in dear old Catalonia. Local delights such as *exqueixada* (shredded salt cod salad) and *galtas de porc* (pig's cheek) temptingly bedeck the elegant central table, around which diners gyrate before making their choice. Desserts include delicious marinated fruits, and there's a good selection of wines to accompany your dishes. Although it's near the heart of town, the restaurant looks like it's part of an old country house, enticingly rural with its alcoves and ceramic-covered walls. The fixed menu is particularly good value as there's no limit on the amount you eat!

Carrer Marti d'Ardenya 5, Tarragona. © **97-723-54-03.** www.eltiberi.com. AE, DC, MC, V. Menu 14€. Sun–Mon 1:30–4pm, Tues–Sat 1:30–4pm and 8–11:30pm.

Epicurí ★★ 🍷 SPANISH   In 2002 this long-established restaurant was bought by chef Javier Andrieu. Within a cozy dining room, where the decor falls midway between the organic *modernisme* of Gaudí and the Art Nouveau opulence of turn-of-the-20th-century Paris, you'll be presented with a choice of two set menus, the more lavish version featuring an aperitif plus six courses. Cuisine is based on securing the best market-fresh ingredients in town. The most intriguing dishes include half-cooked foie gras served with grapes, a succulent entrecôte of veal with artichokes, steamed veal cutlets with lemon sauce, maigret of duckling with tiny Catalan mushrooms known as *moixernons,* and a heaven-sent filet of turbot with an almond-flavored saffron sauce.

Mare de Deú de la Mercè s/n. © **97-724-44-04.** Reservations required. Main courses 10€–20€, set dinner menu 25€–38€. AE, DC, MC, V. Mon–Sat 8pm–12:30am. Closed Dec 25–Jan 2.

Les Voltes ★ 🍴 MEDITERRANEAN   This excellent restaurant lies within the vaults of the Roman Circus Maximus. Chiseled stone from 2,300 years ago abides harmoniously with thick plate glass and polished steel surfaces. A large 250-seat restaurant, Les Voltes offers a kitchen of skilled chefs turning out a flavorful and

THE beaches OF THE COSTA DAURADA

Running along the entire coastline of the province of Tarragona for 211km (131 miles), from Cunit as far as Les Cases d'Alcanar, is a series of excellent beaches and impressive cliffs, along with beautiful pine-covered headlands. In the city of Tarragona itself is **El Milagre** beach, and a little farther north are the beaches of **L'Arrabassade, Savinosa, dels Capellans,** and the **Llarga.** At the end of the latter stands **La Punta de la Mora** with its 16th-century watchtower. The small towns of **Altafulla** and **Torredembarra,** both complete with castles, stand next to these beaches and are the location of many hotels and urban developments.

Farther north again are the two magnificent beaches of **Comarruga** and **Sant Salvador.** The first is particularly cosmopolitan; the second is more secluded. Last come the beaches of **Calafell, Segur,** and **Cunit,** all with modern tourist complexes. You'll also find the small towns of **Creixell, Sant Vicenç de Calders,** and **Clarà,** which have wooded hills as a backdrop.

South of Tarragona, the coastline forms a wide arc that stretches for miles and includes **La Piñeda** beach. **El Recó** beach fronts the Cape of Salou where, in among its coves, hills, and hidden-away corners, many hotels and residential centers are located. The natural port of **Salou** is nowadays a center for international, family-oriented package tourism but is pleasant enough if you don't mind the crowds and noisy night scene.

Continuing south toward Valencia, you next come to **Cambrils,** a maritime town with an excellent beach and an important fishing port. In the background stand the impressive Colldejou and Llaberia mountains. Farther south are the beaches of **Montroig** and **L'Hospitalet,** as well as the small town of **L'Ametlla de Mar** with its small fishing port.

After passing the Balaguer massif, you eventually reach the delta of the River Ebro, a wide lowland area covering more than 480km (300 miles), opening like a fan into the sea. This is an area of rice fields crisscrossed by branches of the Ebro and by an enormous number of irrigation channels. There are also some lagoons that, because of their immense size, are ideal as hunting and fishing grounds. Moreover, there are some beaches several miles in length and others in small hidden estuaries. Two important towns in the region are **Amposta,** on the Ebro itself, and **Sant Carles de la Ràpita,** an 18th-century port town favored by King Carlos III.

The Costa Daurada extends to its most southwesterly point at the plain of **Alcanar,** a large area given over to the cultivation of oranges and other similar crops. Its beaches, along with the small hamlet of **Les Cases d'Alcanar,** mark the end of the Tarragona section of the Costa Daurada.

well-seasoned Mediterranean cuisine. The menu features time-tested favorites such as a succulent baked lamb from the neighboring hills. *Rape* (monkfish) deserves special billing, served with roasted garlic in a cockle and mussel sauce.

Carrer Trinquet Vell 12. © **97-723-06-51.** Reservations recommended. Main courses 9€–25€. DC, MC, V. Tues–Sun 1–4pm, Tues–Sat 8:30–11:30pm. Closed Dec 25–Jan 2.

Sitges

| Beach |
| Campground |
| Information |
| Parking |
| Post Office |
| Railway |

To Vilafranca del Penedès **1**

To Barcelona & Tarragona

Avinguda de Ronda

Carrer Campmanar

Carrer

Pilar Franquet

POBLE SEC

0   1/10 mi
0   100 m

SINIA MORERA

C. Josep Vidal

Avinguda de les Flors

Carrer

Sant

Ignasi

Carrer Àngel Guimerà

Carrer Josep Miró

SANT CRISPI

Carrer Sn. a Morera

Vilanova

Av. Artur Carbonell

Plaça de E. Maristany

Train Station

C. Hospital

Carretera de les Costes

PARC FACUNDO BACARI MASSÓ

Passeig de Vilanova

2

P

C. Esparter

3

C. Sant

C. St. Gaudenci

C. Illa

St. Isidre

Jesus

C. Emili Pico

Carrer Sant Honoral

Carrer M. Casanovas

Carrer Tarragona

Plaça d'Espanya **P**

Carrer

C. ST.

Carrer St.

C. de Cuba

Carrer

Rafael

C. Marqués de Montroig

de Maig

C. Sant Josep

Parellades

C. Angel

Vidal

Carrer

Carrer St.

Sebastia

Carrer

Joan

Maragall

Carrer Sant Antoni

Carrer Espanya

Carrer Bonaire

C. St. Pau

6

Carrer

Major

Port Alegre

Platja del St. Sebastià

Avinguda de Sofia

Carrer Sant Mus

Passeig Maritim

12

11

Passeig de la Ribera

10

7

9 8

Platja del Ribera

Platja del Fragata

Plaça del Baluard

Platja del Bassa Rodona

13

14

MEDITERRANEAN SEA

ATTRACTIONS ●
Museu Cau Ferrat **8**
Museu Maricel **9**
Museu Romàntic ("Can Llopis") **4**

ACCOMMODATIONS ■
Hotel El Cid **2**
Hotel Noucentista **1**
Hotel Romàntic de Sitges **5**
Meliá Gran Sitges **14**
Terramar **13**

DINING/CLUBS ◆
Al Fresco **6**
El Tambucho **7**
El Velero **11**
Fragata **10**
Mare Nostrum **12**
Mediterráneo **3**

SPAIN   Sitges

PORTUGAL   ★ **Madrid**

SITGES ★★

40km (25 miles) S of Barcelona, 596km (370 miles) E of Madrid

Sitges is one of the most popular resorts in southern Europe and the brightest spot on the Costa Daurada. It's especially crowded in summer, mostly with affluent young northern Europeans, many of them gay. Throughout the 19th century, the resort largely drew prosperous middle-class industrialists and traders (known as *indios* since they made their fortunes in the Americas), and many of their stately homes still stand along the sea-facing promenade, the Passeig Marítim. Today, Sitges easily accommodates a mixed crowd of affluent residents, vacationing families and couples, and swarms of day-trippers from Barcelona.

Sitges has long been known as a city of culture, thanks in part to resident artist, playwright, and bohemian dandy Santiago Rusiñol. The 19th-century *modernisme* movement was nurtured in Sitges, and the town remained the scene of artistic encounters and demonstrations long after the movement waned. Sitges continued as a resort of artists, attracting such giants as Salvador Dalí and poet Federico García Lorca. The Spanish Civil War (1936–39) erased what has come to be called the "golden age" of Sitges. Although other artists and writers arrived in the decades to follow, none had the impact of those who had gone before.

Essentials

GETTING THERE RENFE runs trains from Barcelona-Sants and Passeig de Gràcia stations to Sitges, a 30- to 40-minute trip. Call *©* **90-224-02-02** or visit www.renfe.com for information about schedules. If you plan to stay late, check what time the last train leaves once in Sitges, as they vary.

Sitges is a 45-minute **drive** from Barcelona along the C-246, a coastal road. There is also an express highway, the A-7, which passes through the Garraf Tunnels. The coastal road is more scenic, but it can be extremely slow on weekends because of the heavy traffic, as all of Barcelona seemingly heads for the beaches.

VISITOR INFORMATION The **tourist office** is at Carrer Sínea Morera 1 (*©* **93-894-42-51**; www.sitges.org). From June to September 15, it's open daily from 9am to 9pm; from September 16 to May, hours are Monday through Friday from 9am to 2pm and 4 to 6:30pm, and Saturday from 10am to 1pm.

SPECIAL EVENTS The **Carnaval** at Sitges is one of the outstanding events on the Catalan calendar and frankly makes all other Carnaval celebrations in the region look lame. For more than a century, the town has celebrated the days before the

---

HERE COME THE boys

Along with Ibiza and Mikonos, Sitges has established itself firmly on the "A" list of gay resorts. It's a perfect destination for those who want a ready-made combination of beach and bars, all within a few minutes' walk of each other. It works well as a temporary, calmer alternative to Barcelona, which is about 30 minutes away by train, and so is great for a day trip or a few days out of the city. In the off-season, it's pretty quiet on the gay front apart from the Carnaval in February, when hordes of gays and lesbians descend from Barcelona and the party really begins.

Summer, however, is pure hedonistic playtime, and the town draws males in from all over Europe. Sitges is never going to tax the intellect, but it might well exhaust the body. There's a gay beach crammed with the usual overload of muscles and summer accessories in the middle of the town, in front of the Passeig Marítim. The other beach is nudist and farther out of town, between Sitges and Vilanova. The best directions are to go as far as the L'Atlántida disco and then follow the train track to the farther of the two beaches. The woods next to it are, unsurprisingly, packed with playful wildlife sporting short hair and deep tans.

beginning of Lent. Fancy dress, floats, feathered outfits, and sequins all make this an exciting event. The party begins on the Thursday before Lent with the arrival of the king of the Carnestoltes and ends with the burial of a sardine on Ash Wednesday. Activities reach their flamboyant best on Sant Bonaventura, where gays hold their own celebrations. During the week of Corpus Christi in June, blankets of flowers are laid in the streets of the Old Town, and on the night of June 23, the feast of Sant Joan, the beach lights up with fireworks and bonfires.

Fun on & off the Beach

The old part of Sitges used to be a fortified medieval enclosure. The castle is now the seat of the town government. The local parish church, called **La Punta (The Point)** and built next to the sea on top of a promontory, presides over an extensive maritime esplanade, where people parade in the early evening. Beside the church are the Museu Cau Ferrat and the Museu Maricel (see "Museums," below).

Most people are here to hit the beach. The beaches have showers, bathing cabins, and stalls; kiosks rent motorboats, watersports equipment, beach umbrellas, and sunbeds. Beaches on the eastern end and those in the town center are the most peaceful—for example, **Aiguadolç** and **Els Balomins. Playa San Sebastián, Fragata Beach,** and the **"Beach of the Boats"** (below the church and next to the yacht club) are the area's family beaches. A young, happening crowd heads for the **Playa de la Ribera** to the west.

All along the coast, women can and certainly do go topless. Farther west are the most solitary beaches, where the scene grows racier, especially along the **Playas del Muerto,** where two tiny nude beaches lie between Sitges and Vilanova i la Geltrú. A shuttle bus runs between the church and the Hotel Terramar. From here, go along the road to the club L'Atlántida, then walk along the railway. The first beach draws nudists of every sexual persuasion, and the second is almost solely gay. Be advised that lots of action takes place in the woods at the back of these beaches.

Museums

Beaches aside, Sitges has some choice museums, which shouldn't be missed. Visit all three on a combined 6.40€ ticket obtainable at Museu Cau Ferrat.

Museu Cau Ferrat ★★ 📷   The Catalan artist Santiago Rusiñol combined two charming 16th-century cottages to make this house, where he lived and worked; upon his death in 1931 he willed it to Sitges along with his art collection. More than anyone else, Rusiñol made Sitges a popular resort. The museum's immense and cluttered collection boasts two paintings by El Greco and several small Picassos, including *La Corrida (The Bullfight)*. A number of Rusiñol's works are on display, along with his prolific collection of wrought-iron artifacts and a dazzling display of Mediterranean tilework. The edifice, with its dramatic sea views from tiny windows, is worth the visit alone. At the time of writing (2010) the museum is closed for restoration work.

Carrer Fonollar s/n. ℭ **93-894-03-64.** www.mnac.es/museus/mus_ferrat.jsp?lan=003. Admission 3.50€, 1.75€ students, free for children 12 and under. June 15-Sept Tues-Sun 10am-2pm and 5-9pm; Oct-June 14 Tues-Fri 10am-1:30pm and 3-6:30pm, Sat 10am-7pm, Sun 10am-3pm.

Museu Maricel ★   Opened by the king and queen of Spain, the Museu Maricel contains art donated by Dr. Jesús Pérez Rosales. The palace, built by American Charles

Deering right after World War I, is made up of two parts connected by a small bridge. The museum has a good collection of Gothic and Romantic paintings and sculptures, as well as many fine Catalan ceramics. There are three noteworthy works by Santiago Rebull and an allegorical painting of World War I by José María Sert.

Carrer del Fonollar s/n. ⓒ **93-894-03-64.** www.sitges.cat. Admission 3.50€, 1.75€ students, free for children 12 and under. June 15–Sept Tues–Sun 10am–2pm and 5–9pm; Oct–June 14 Tues–Fri 10am–1:30pm and 3–6:30pm, Sat 10am–7pm, Sun 10am–3pm.

Museu Romàntic ("Can Llopis") This museum re-creates the daily life of a Sitges' land-owning family, the Llopis, in the 18th and 19th centuries. The family rooms, furniture, and household objects are interesting. Upstairs, you'll find wine cellars and an important collection of antique dolls.

Sant Gaudenci 1. ⓒ **93-894-29-69.** Admission (including guided tour) 3.50€, 1.75€ students, free for children 12 and under. June 15–Sept Tues–Sun 10am–2pm and 5–9pm; Oct–June 14 Tues–Fri 10am–1:30pm and 3–6:30pm, Sat 10am–7pm, Sun 10am–3pm.

Where to Stay

Sitges is packed to the gills in July and August, and you'll be hard-pressed to find accommodations here if you're planning to stay a few days, but by mid-October everything—including hotels, restaurants, and bars—quietens down considerably and life assumes a more leisurely pace. In many ways winter is an ideal time to visit the town.

EXPENSIVE

Meliá Gran Sitges ★ Designed with steeply sloping sides reminiscent of a pair of interconnected Aztec pyramids, this hotel was originally built to house spectators and participants for the 1992 Barcelona Olympics. Its marble lobby boasts what feels like the largest window in Spain, with a view of the mountains. Each of the midsize rooms comes with a large furnished veranda for sunbathing. Many guests are here to participate in the conferences and conventions held frequently in the battery of high-tech convention facilities. It's about a 15-minute walk east of the center of Sitges, near the access roads leading to Barcelona.

Joan Salvat Papasseit 38, Puerto de Aiguadolç, 08870 Sitges. ⓒ **93-811-08-11** (hotel) or 90-214-44-44 (reservations). Fax 93-894-90-34. www.solmelia.com. 307 units. 105€–250€ double; 290€ suite. Some rates include breakfast. AE, DC, MC, V. Parking 10€. **Amenities:** Restaurant; bar; babysitting; health club; 2 pools; room service; sauna. *In room:* A/C, TV, hair dryer, minibar, Internet access.

MODERATE

Hotel Noucentista ★ ⬧ This is a winning choice. The name means "1900," the year of the building's original construction. The interior is quite stunning, a statement of *modernisme* with much use of antiques. The small to midsize bedrooms are stylishly and comfortably furnished with ample closet space and bathrooms, each with a shower. Some of the accommodations open onto small private balconies. The inn is a 10-minute walk from the beach. The hotel is also graced with a small courtyard garden, and guests have access to the swimming pool and restaurant of the Hotel El Xalet across the road.

Illa de Cuba 21, 08870 Sitges. ⓒ **93-811-00-70.** Fax 93-894-55-79. www.elxalet.com. 12 units. 65€–120€ double; 90€–150€ suite. AE, DC, MC, V. **Amenities:** Restaurant; pool. *In room:* A/C, TV, hair dryer, minibar.

Hotel Romàntic de Sitges ★ 👬 Made up of three beautifully restored 19th-century villas, this hotel is only a short walk from the beach and the train station. The romantic bar is an international rendezvous, and the public rooms are filled with artworks. You can have breakfast in the dining room or in a garden filled with mulberry trees. The rooms, reached by stairs, range from small to medium and are well maintained, with good beds, and most have bathrooms with shower stalls. Overflow guests are housed in a nearby annex, the Hotel de la Renaixença.

Sant Isidre 33, 08870 Sitges. ✆ **93-894-83-75.** Fax 93-894-81-67. www.hotelromantic.com. 60 units. 80€–120€ double without bathroom; 90€–125€ double w/shower/bathroom. Rates include breakfast. AE, MC, V. Closed Nov–Mar 15. **Amenities:** Restaurant; cocktail bar; buffet breakfast; babysitting. *In room:* A/C, TV, hair dryer, Wi-Fi (free).

Terramar ★★ 👬 Facing the beach in a residential area of Sitges, a short walk from the center, this resort hotel, one of the first "grand hotels" along the coast, is a Sitges landmark. Its balconied facade evokes a multi-decked yacht and the interior, renovated in the 1970s, is a near-perfect example of retro design. The foyer has a quirky marine theme, the floors and wall panels are lined with marble, and the ladies' restroom is hot pink. The spacious and comfortable guest rooms contain the same sort of eccentric detailing.

Passeig Marítim 80, 08870 Sitges. ✆ **93-894-00-50.** Fax 93-894-56-04. www.hotelterramar.com. 209 units. 120€–175€ double; 160€–180€ suite. Rates include breakfast buffet. AE, DC, MC, V. Closed Nov–Mar. **Amenities:** 2 restaurants; 2 bars; babysitting; bike rental; outdoor pool; 2 tennis courts; room service. *In room:* A/C, TV, hair dryer, minibar.

INEXPENSIVE

Hotel El Cid ★ El Cid's very name evokes Castile, although the white-walled facade, with its bright-orange sun canopies, suggests yet another stylish summery Sitges hideaway. Inside, however, you'll find beamed ceilings, natural stone walls, heavy wrought-iron chandeliers, and leather chairs. The same theme is carried out in the rear dining room and in the pleasantly furnished rooms, which, although small, are quite comfortable, with fine beds and bathrooms containing shower stalls. Breakfast is the only meal served. El Cid is off the Passeig de Vilanova in the center of town.

Sant Josep 39B, 08870 Sitges. ✆ **93-894-18-42.** Fax 93-894-63-35. www.hotelsitges.com. 77 units. 55€–90€ double. Rates include continental breakfast. MC, V. Closed Oct–Apr. **Amenities:** Bar; babysitting; outdoor pool.

Where to Dine
EXPENSIVE

El Velero ★ SEAFOOD This is one of Sitges's leading restaurants, positioned along the beachside promenade. The most desirable tables are found on the glass greenhouse terrace, opening onto the esplanade, though there's a more glamorous restaurant inside. Try the soup, such as clam and truffle or whitefish, followed by a main dish of paella marinara (with seafood) or suprême of salmon in pine-nut sauce.

Passeig de la Ribera 38. ✆ **93-894-20-51.** www.restaurantevelero.com. Reservations required. Main courses 18€–38€; tasting menu 40€; gastronomic menu 55€. AE, DC, MC, V. Tues–Sun 1:30–4pm and 8:30–11:30pm. Closed Dec 22–Jan 6.

MODERATE

Al Fresco ★★ 🍴 ASIAN   Many people, especially the gay community, reckon this is the best bet in Sitges; perhaps because it is more like an eatery you would encounter in Sydney. Owned by an Australian couple, the eclectic menu draws heavily on Asian influences. Upstairs there is a cheaper cafe, an enormously popular breakfast spot; here, you can feed your hangover on such un-Spanish fare as blueberry pancakes, fresh muesli, and muffins, or choose from a selection of salads such as Thai beef or Caesar for lunch.

Pau Barrabeig 4. ⓒ **93-894-06-00.** www.alfrescorestaurante.es. Reservations recommended. Main courses 12€–30€. MC, V. May-Sept Tues-Sun 8:30am-midnight; Oct-Apr Wed-Sun 8:30am-midnight. Closed Dec 20-Jan 20.

El Tambucho SEAFOOD   This little family-run eating spot nestles in one of Sitges's quieter corners on Sant Sebastian beach, directly overlooking the Mediterranean and close to the church and Museu Maricel. A seafood lovers' dream, it specializes in the sort of dishes you'd expect to find in such a nautical setting, from local *paellas* like *arroz negre* (made with black rice), fresh shellfish like *navajas* (razor clams) and *mejillones* (mussels), local *sopa de pescado* (seafood broth), and Basque-style *merluza* (hake). The atmosphere's relaxing and the staff friendly and obliging. It gets really noisy and crowded on fiesta days.

Carrer Port Alegre 49, 08870 Sitges. ⓒ **93-894-79-12.** Main courses 15€–25€; menus 18€–20€. DC, MC, V. Tues-Sun 1:30-4pm, 8:30-11:30pm. Closed Nov.

Fragata ★ SEAFOOD   Though its simple interior offers little more than well-scrubbed floors, tables with crisp linens, and air-conditioning, some of the most delectable seafood specialties in town are served here, and hundreds of loyal customers come to enjoy the authentic cuisine. Specialties include seafood soup, a mixed grill of fresh fish, cod salad, mussels marinara, several preparations of squid and octopus, plus some flavorful meat dishes such as grilled lamb cutlets.

Passeig de la Ribera 1. ⓒ **93-894-10-86.** www.restaurantefragata.com. Reservations recommended. Main dishes 12€–28€. AE, DC, MC, V. Daily 1-4:30pm and 8:30-11:30pm.

Mare Nostrum ★★ SEAFOOD   This landmark dates from 1950, when it opened in what had been a private home dating from the 1890s. The dining room has a waterfront view, and in warm weather tables are placed outside. The menu includes a full range of seafood dishes, among them grilled fish specialties and steamed hake with champagne. The fish soup is particularly delectable. Next door, the restaurant's cafe serves ice cream, milk shakes, sandwiches, tapas, and three varieties of sangria, including one with champagne and fruit.

Passeig de la Ribera 60. ⓒ **93-894-33-93.** www.restaurantmarenostrum.com. Reservations required. Main courses 12€–28€. AE, DC, MC, V. Thurs-Tues 1-4pm and 8-11pm. Closed Dec 15-Feb 1.

Sitges After Dark

One of the best ways to pass an evening in Sitges is to walk the waterfront esplanade, have a leisurely dinner, then retire at about 11pm to one of the dozens of open-air cafes for a nightcap and some serious people-watching.

cava COUNTRY

The Penedès region is Catalonia's wine country, the place where the crisp whites, hearty reds, and sparkling *cava* that you've tried in Barcelona's restaurants are produced. After years of being thought of solely as an agrarian region, wine tourism is starting to take off in the villages and rolling vineyards of this delightful destination.

The capital is Vilafranca del Penedès, a bustling provincial town that has a fine outdoor market on Saturday mornings and is famous for its local *castellers* (human towers) team. The **Vinseum,** Plaça Jaume I 5 (☏ **93-890-05-82;** www.vinseum.cat), has a collection of viniculture equipment and memorabilia considered to be the best of its kind in Europe. If you are curious to know more, the Museu de Vilafranca, located next door, has a collection of works by artists on wine-related themes and a gorgeous collection of Spanish and Catalan ceramic work from the 15th century onward. If you have time, the Basílica de Santa María, in Plaça Sant Jaume, is a Gothic church dating from the 15th century. Ascend the 52-m (171-feet)-high bell tower for a panoramic view of the town and surrounding area.

Nothing, however, beats the hands-on experience of seeing the process of winemaking from start to finish. A handful of bodegas (wineries) are open to the public, the best being the estate of **Codorníu** (☏ **93-818-32-32;** www. codorniu.es), the top *cava* maker in Catalonia. Their magnificent winery is located 10km (6¼ miles) from Vilafranca in the village of Sant Sadorni d'Anoia. Designed at the end of the 19th century by Josep María Puig i Cadafalch (a master architect of the

modernisme movement), his beautiful project reflects the luxurious product made within; the complex is replete with Art Nouveau touches and details and 15km (9⅓ miles) of sinuous underground tunnels where the product is aged. Another highlight is a museum containing gorgeous past advertising posters of the product, many by renowned artists of the period. Codorníu is open to the public Monday through Friday 9am to 5pm and Saturday 9am to 1pm. A minitrain whisks you around the estate, including the vineyards, and a *cava* tasting nicely rounds up your visit.

Another sumptuous *moderniste* wine palace is that of **Freixenet,** Avinguda Casetas Mir s/n (☏ **93-891-70-25;** www.freixenet.es), Codorníu's main competition. Freixenet's landmark bodega, located right beside the train station of Sant Sadorni d'Anoia, also gives tours of its headquarters (by appointment) on Saturday from 10am to 1pm. Its colorful, florid facade is one of the area's landmarks.

The **tourist office** in Vilafranca del Penedès is located at Carrer de la Cort 14 (☏ **93-892-03-58;** www.turisme vilafranca.com). It's open Tuesday to Friday from 9am to 1pm and 4:30 to 7pm, and Saturday 10am to 1pm. **RENFE** (☏ **90-224-02-02;** www.renfe. es) runs dozens of trains a day (trip time: 55 minutes) from Barcelona to Vilafranca del Penedès and Sant Sadorni d'Anoia, leaving from Plaça de Catalunya station. If you're driving, head west out of the city via the A-7. Follow the signs to Sant Sadorni d'Anoia and then stay on the same highway to Vilafranca.

If you're straight, you may have to hunt to find a late-night bar in the center of town that isn't predominantly gay. For the locations of Sitges's gay bars, look for a pocket-size map that's distributed in most of the gay bars—you can pick it up in the Parrot's Pub (in the Plaça de la Industria) or it can be downloaded on **www.gaymap.info.** Nine of these bars are concentrated on **Carrer Sant Bonaventura,** a 5-minute walk from the beach (near the Museu Romàntic). If you grow bored with the action in one place, you just have to walk down the street to find another. Drink prices run about the same in all the clubs.

Mediterráneo   The largest gay disco/bar in Sitges, Mediterráneo sports a formal Iberian garden and sleek modern styling. And upstairs in this restored 1690s' house just east of the Plaça Espanya are pool tables and a covered terrace. On summer nights, the place is filled to overflowing. Sant Bonaventura 6. ☏ **93-894-12-90**.

Pacha Sitges   This chain of nightclubs was founded way back in the swinging 1960s, and is the grandaddy of many Spanish discos; it's a must for any clubber worth his salt. It's not stuck in the past, though, and like its namesakes elsewhere offers the latest in electronic sounds and lighting effects, plus a spectrum of music raging from funk to soul played by top international DJs. Carrer Didac s/n. ☏ **93-894-22-98**. www.pachasitges.com.

GIRONA ★★

97km (60 miles) NE of Barcelona, 90km (56 miles) S of the French city of Perpignan

Girona, one of the top 10 important historical sites in Spain, was founded by the Romans. Later, it became a Moorish stronghold and, later still, it reputedly withstood three invasions by Napoleon's troops in the early 1800s. For that and other past aggressions, Girona is often called the "City of a Thousand Sieges." These days, residents go about their daily business happy in the knowledge that their city is constantly rated among the top three in the country in terms of quality of life. Its prime contenders are Vitoria and Oviedo, located in the Basque Country and Asturias, respectively.

Split by the Onyar River, this bustling, provincial city often only gets a nod from the crowds of tourists who use its airport as a springboard for the resorts and beaches of the Costa Brava. When you arrive, make your way to the narrow lanes and hidden staircases of the Old Town and El Call, the remains of the sizeable Jewish community, via the ancient stone footbridge across the Onyar. From here, you'll have the finest view of ocher-colored town houses on each side. Bring walking shoes, as you will want to circumnavigate the old town walls to take in the splendid stone edifices and lush countryside of its surrounds. Much of Girona can be appreciated from the outside, but there are some important attractions you'll want to see on the inside.

Essentials

GETTING THERE   More than 26 **trains** per day run between Girona and Barcelona-Sants or Passeig de Gràcia station. Trip time is 1 to 1½ hours, and one-way

The Costa Brava

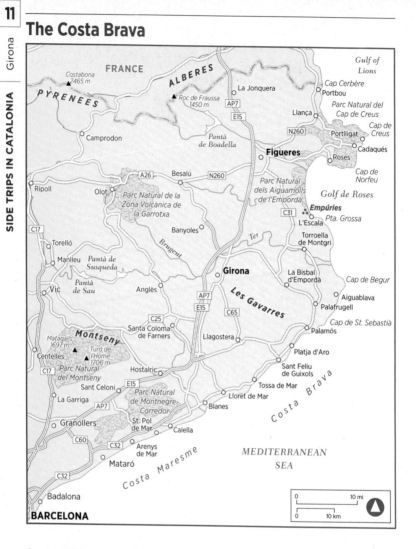

fare is 6.50€ to 8.80€ depending on the train. Trains arrive in Girona at the Plaça Espanya (ⓒ **97-220-70-93;** www.renfe.com).

By **car** from Barcelona, take the A-7 at Ronda Litoral and head north via the A-7.

VISITOR INFORMATION The **tourist office** at Rambla de la Libertat 1 (ⓒ **97-222-65-75;** www.ajuntament.gi) is open Monday through Friday from 8am to 8pm, Saturday from 8am to 2pm and 4 to 8pm, and Sunday from 9am to 2pm.

Girona

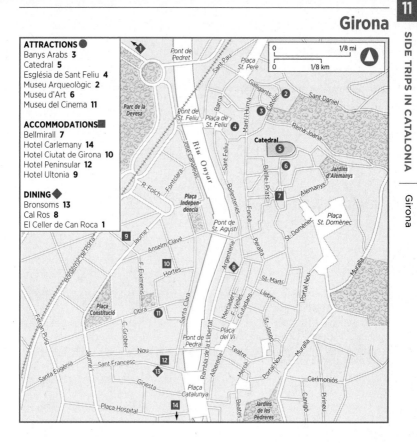

ATTRACTIONS ●
Banys Arabs **3**
Catedral **5**
Església de Sant Feliu **4**
Museu Arqueològic **2**
Museu d'Art **6**
Museu del Cinema **11**

ACCOMMODATIONS ■
Bellmirall **7**
Hotel Carlemany **14**
Hotel Ciutat de Girona **10**
Hotel Peninsular **12**
Hotel Ultonia **9**

DINING ◆
Bronsoms **13**
Cal Ros **8**
El Celler de Can Roca **1**

Exploring the Medieval City

Banys Arabs ★   These 12th-century Arab baths, an example of Romanesque civic architecture, are in the Old Quarter of the city. Visit the **caldarium (hot bath),** with its paved floor, and the **frigidarium (cold bath),** with its central octagonal pool surrounded by pillars that support a prism-like structure in the overhead window. Although the Moorish baths were heavily restored in 1929, they'll give you an idea of what the ancient ones were like.

Carrer Ferran el Catòlic s/n. ✆ **97-221-32-62.** www.banysarabs.org. Admission 2€, 1€ students, free for seniors and children 16 and under. Apr–Sept Mon–Sat 10am–7pm, Sun 10am–2pm; Oct–Mar Tues–Sun 10am–2pm. Closed Jan 1, Jan 6, Easter, and Dec 25–26.

Catedral ★★★   Girona's major attraction is its magnificent cathedral, reached by climbing a 17th-century baroque staircase of 90 steep steps. The 14th-century cathedral represents many architectural styles, including Gothic and Romanesque, but it's most notably Catalan baroque. The facade you see as you climb those long stairs dates from the 17th and 18th centuries; from a cornice on top rises a bell tower crowned by a dome with a bronze angel weathervane. Enter the main door of the cathedral and go into the Gothic nave, which, at 23m (75 feet), is the broadest example of its type in the world.

The cathedral contains many works of art, displayed for the most part in its museum. Its prize exhibit is a **tapestry of the Creation,** a unique piece of 11th- or 12th-century Romanesque embroidery depicting humans and animals in the Garden of Eden. The other major work displayed is one of the world's rarest manuscripts—the 10th-century *Códex del Beatus,* which contains an illustrated commentary on the Revelation. From the cathedral's **Chapel of Hope,** a door leads to a **Romanesque cloister** from the 12th and 13th centuries, with an unusual trapezoidal layout. The cloister gallery, with a double colonnade, has a series of biblical scenes that are the prize jewel of Catalan Romanesque art. From the cloister you can view the 12th-century **Torre de Carlemany (Charlemagne's Tower).**

Plaça de la Catedral s/n. (*) **97-221-44-26.** www.catedraldegirona.org. Free admission to cathedral; nave, cloister, and museum 4€, 3€ students and seniors; all free on Sun. Cathedral daily 9am–1pm and during cloister and museum visiting hours. Cloister and museum July–Sept Tues–Sat 10am–8pm, Sun 10am–2pm; Oct–Feb Tues–Sat 10am–2pm and 4–6pm, Sun 10am–2pm; Mar–June Tues–Sat 10am–2pm and 4–7pm, Sun 10am–2pm.

Església de Sant Feliu ★ This 14th- to 17th-century church was built over what may have been the tomb of Feliu of Africa, martyred during Diocletian's persecution at the beginning of the 4th century. Important in the architectural history of Catalonia, the church has pillars and arches in the Romanesque style and a Gothic central nave. The **bell tower**—one of the Girona skyline's most characteristic features—has eight pinnacles and one central tower, each supported on a solid octagonal base. The main facade of the church is baroque. The interior contains some exceptional works, including a 16th-century **altarpiece** and a 14th-century alabaster *Christo Recostado (Reclining Christo).* Notice the eight pagan and Christian **sarcophagi** set in the

EL call

The Jewish diaspora made an indelible mark on the city of Girona. A sizeable chunk of the Old Town is taken up with the remains of **El Call,** once Spain's biggest Jewish quarter. From 20-odd families who arrived at the end of the 9th century, the community grew to nearly 2,000, with three synagogues, butchers, bakers, and other mercantile activity taking place in the neighborhood's cobbled streets. In 1492, along with other Jewish communities on the Peninsula (including Barcelona and Majorca), they were blamed for the spread of the plague and unceremoniously ousted by Catholic powers. The **Centre Bonastruc Ca Portal,** Calle La Force 8 ((*) **97-221-67-61**), in the heart of El Call, contains exhibitions on medieval Jewish life and customs, with an emphasis on the cohabitation of Jews and Christians, as well as exhibitions by contemporary Jewish artists. It also conducts special-interest tours of the area and courses on Jewish culture and history. It's open Monday to Saturday 10am to 8pm, Sunday 10am to 3pm. Admission is 2€.

walls of the presbytery, the two oldest of which are from the 2nd century A.D. One shows Pluto carrying Persephone off to the depths of the earth.

Pujada de Sant Feliu s/n. ✆ **97-220-14-07.** Free admission. Daily 8am-7:45pm.

Museu Arqueològic ★   Housed in a Romanesque church and cloister from the 11th and 12th centuries, this museum illustrates the history of the region from the Paleolithic to the Visigothic periods, using artifacts discovered in nearby excavations. The monastery itself ranks as one of the best examples of Catalan Romanesque architecture. In the cloister, note some Hebrew inscriptions from gravestones of the old Jewish cemetery.

Sant Pere de Galligants, Santa Llúcia 1. ✆ **97-220-26-32.** www.mac.cat. Admission 2€, 1.50€ students, free for seniors and children 16 and under. Oct-May Tues-Sat 10am-2pm and 4-6pm, Sun 10am-2pm; June-Sept Tues-Sat 10am-1:30pm and 4-7pm, Sun 10am-2pm.

Museu d'Art ★   In the Romanesque and Gothic former episcopal palace (Palau Episcopal) next to the cathedral, this museum displays artworks (once housed in the old diocesan and provincial museums) spanning 10 centuries. Stop in the throne room to view the **altarpiece of Sant Pere of Púbol** by Bernat Martorell and the **altarpiece of Sant Miguel de Crüilles** by Luis Borrassa. Both of these works, from the 15th century, are exemplary pieces of Catalan Gothic painting. The museum is also proud of its **altar stone** of Sant Pere de Roda, from the 10th and 11th centuries; this work in wood and stone, depicting figures and legends, was once covered in embossed silver. The 12th-century *Crüilles Timber* is a unique piece of Romanesque polychrome wood. *Nuestra Señora de Besalù (Our Lady of Besalù),* from the 15th century, is one of the most accomplished depictions of the Virgin carved in alabaster.

Pujada de la Catedral 12. ✆ **97-220-38-34.** www.museuart.com. Admission 2€, 1.50€ students, free for seniors and children. Mar-Sept Tues-Sat 10am-7pm, Sun 10am-2pm; Oct-Feb Tues-Sat 10am-6pm, Sun 10am-2pm. Closed Jan 1, Jan 6, Easter, and Dec 25-26.

Museu del Cinema ★★   Film buffs flock to this museum, the only one of its kind in Spain. It houses the Tomàs Mallol collection of some 25,000 cinema artifacts, going all the way up to films shot as late as 1970. Many objects are from the "pre-cinema" era, plus other exhibits from the early days of film. The museum even owns the original camera of the pioneering Lumière brothers. Fixed images such as photographs, posters, engravings, drawings, and paintings are exhibited along with some 800 films of various styles and periods. There's even a library with film-related publications.

Sèquia 1. ✆ **97-241-27-77.** www.museudelcinema.org. Admission 5€, 2.50€ students and seniors, free for children 16 and under. May-Sept Tues-Sun 10am-8pm; Oct-Apr Tues-Fri 10am-6pm, Sat 10am-8pm, Sun 11am-3pm. Closed Jan 1, Jan 6, and Dec 25-26.

Where to Stay
MODERATE
Hotel Carlemany ★   In a commercial area only 10 minutes from the historic core, this 1995 hotel is often cited as the best in town. A favorite of business travelers, the facilities are top-class. Its soundproofed rooms are comfortably spacious and the cool, sober gray-black decor is lightened by pinewood bedsteads and working areas with desks. All have adjoining tiled bathrooms.

Plaça Miquel Santaló s/n, 17002 Girona. ✆ **97-221-12-12.** Fax 97-221-49-94. www.carlemany.es. 90 units. 125€ double; 190€ suite. AE, DC, MC, V. Parking 12€. **Amenities:** Restaurant; 2 bars; room service. *In room:* A/C, TV, hair dryer, minibar, Wi-Fi (free).

Hotel Ciutat de Girona ★   This hip and high-tech four-star hotel is located right in the town center and is a good choice for people who prefer mod cons to rustic charm. Opened in 2003, all the rooms are decked out in *diseño catalán* style in tones of taupe and cream with dramatic swaths of red, and all have Internet connections (you can even get your own PC upon request). The classy cocktail bar in the foyer clinches the stylish deal.

Nord 2, 17001 Girona. ✆**97-248-30-38.** Fax 97-248-30-26. www.hotel-ciutatdegirona.com. 44 units. 125€–210€ double; 155€–240€ triple. AE, DC, MC, V. Parking 14€. **Amenities:** Restaurant; bar; room service. *In room:* A/C, TV, hair dryer, free minibar, Wi-Fi (free).

Hotel Ultonia   This small hotel lies a short walk from the Plaça de la Independencia. Since the late 1950s it has been a favorite with business travelers, but today it attracts a wider range of visitors, as it's close to the historical district. The cosy, subtly lit rooms have brightly patterned walls and bedspreads and polished parquet floors with en-suite bathrooms. Double-glazed windows help ensure that your stay's a peaceful one. Some of the rooms opening onto the avenue have tiny balconies. You can cross the Onyar into the medieval quarter in just a few minutes. Guests can enjoy a breakfast buffet (not included in the rates quoted below), but no other meals are served.

Av. Jaume I 22, 17001 Girona. ✆ **97-220-38-50.** Fax 97-220-33-34. www.hotelhusaultonia.com. 45 units. 80€–140€ double. AE, DC, MC, V. Parking 10€. **Amenities:** Breakfast bar. *In room:* A/C, TV, minibar, Wi-Fi (free).

INEXPENSIVE

Bellmirall ★★ 📷   Across the Onyar, this little discovery lies in the heart of the old Jewish quarter. It's one of the best values in the Old Town. The building itself, much restored and altered over the years, dates originally from the 14th century. Bedrooms are small to midsize and are decorated in part with antiques set against brick walls. Some of these walls are adorned with paintings; others come with carefully selected ceramics. Each room comes with a small bathroom with shower. In summer, it's possible to order breakfast outside in the courtyard.

Carrer Bellmirall 3, 17004 Girona. ✆ **97-220-40-09.** 7 units. 65€–80€ double; 90€–100€ triple. Rates include breakfast. No credit cards. Free parking (hotel provides permit). Closed Jan–Feb.

Hotel Peninsular ★   Devoid of any significant architectural character, this modest hotel provides clean but unremarkable accommodations near the cathedral and the river. The small rooms are scattered over five floors. All units contain neatly kept bathrooms with showers. The hotel is better for short-term stopovers than for prolonged stays. Breakfast is the only meal served (and is not included in the rates quoted below).

Av. Sant Francesc 6, 17001 Girona. ✆ **90-273-45-41.** Fax 97-221-04-92. www.novarahotels.com. 47 units. 80€) double. AE, DC, MC, V. Parking nearby 10€. **Amenities:** Breakfast bar. *In room:* TV, hair dryer.

Where to Dine

EXPENSIVE

El Celler de Can Roca ★★★ SPANISH   A little way out of the center of Girona, El Cellar de Can Roca is the best of the new spate of Catalonian restaurants and represents the success of the campaign to transform Girona into one of the most fashionable cities in Spain. Run by three young brothers (one of whom now heads the fashionable Moo Restaurant in Barcelona; p. 143), the restaurant is intimate, with only 12 tables. The cuisine is an interesting combination of traditional Catalan dishes creatively transformed into contemporary Mediterranean fare. Start with an avocado purée, and for dessert you can't pass up the mandarin sorbet with pumpkin compote.

Can Sunyer 48. ℂ **97-222-21-57.** www.cellercanroca.com. Reservations recommended. Main courses 16€–40€; fixed-price menu 70€. AE, DC, MC, V. Tues–Sat 1–4pm and 9–11pm. Closed Dec 22–Jan 6 and June 23–July 14. Bus: 5.

MODERATE

Bronsoms ★ SPANISH   In the heart of the Old Town, in an 1890s' building that was once a private home, this restaurant is one of the most consistently reliable in Girona. Praised by newspapers as far away as Madrid, it has been under its present management since 1982. It's perfected the art of serving a Catalan-based *cocina del mercado*—that is, cooking with whatever market-fresh ingredients are available. House specialties include fish paella, *arroz negro* (black rice, tinted with squid ink and studded with shellfish), white beans, and several preparations of Iberian ham.

Av. Sant Francesc 7. ℂ **97-221-24-93.** Reservations recommended. Main courses 8€–24€; fixed-price menu 12€. AE, MC, V. Mon–Sun 1–4pm; Mon–Sat 8–11:30pm.

Cal Ros SPANISH   In the oldest part of Girona, near the Plaça de Catalunya, this restaurant thrives as a culinary staple and has done so since the 1920s. It was named after a long-ago blond-haired owner, although exactly who that was, no one today seems to remember. You'll be seated in one of four rustic dining rooms, each with heavy ceiling beams, exposed stone and plaster, and a sense of old Catalonia. Menu items include savory *escudilla*, made with veal, pork, local herbs, and vegetables; at least four kinds of local fish, usually braised with potatoes and tomatoes; tender fried filets of veal with mushrooms; and flaky homemade pastries, some of them flavored with anise-flavored cream. Kosher and halal dishes are also prepared.

Cort Reial 9. ℂ **97-221-91-76.** www.calros-restaurant.com. Reservations recommended. Main courses 8€–28€. AE, DC, MC, V. Tues–Sun 1–4pm; Tues–Sat 8–11pm. Closed Sun evening and Mon.

Shopping

There are some interesting shops to be found around El Call and the Old Town. Look out for little specialty shops selling local wares such as beige- and yellow-colored ceramic cookware, and more upmarket designer joints. The famous Barcelonese design and furniture emporium BD has a branch here at Plaça dels Països Catalans 1 (ℂ **97-22-43-39;** www.bdgirona.com), one of a handful of design stores on the same medieval street. There are also a couple of open-air artisan

GARDEN OF SEA &myrtle

The **Jardí Botànic Marimurtra,** with its meandering paths and white clifftop pergolas, towers beside the fishing town of Blanes at the southern extremity of the Costa Brava. You'd be hard-pressed to find a more lovely evocation of nature in the whole Mediterranean than this 16-hectare (40-acre) Garden of Eden, with its 200,000 species of plants and shrubs from the five continents. Long declared an Area of National Cultural Interest, it was founded by biologist Karl Faust at the beginning of the 20th century as a research center for universal flora. Allow an hour for a full stroll, longer if you feel like soaking up the atmosphere and meditating in some quiet corner like the tiny Plaça de Goethe. Jardí Botànic Marimurtra is at Passeig de Carles Faust 9, Blanes (✆ 97-233-08-26; www.marimurtra. cat). Admission is 6€ (groups 5€) and it's open April to October daily 9am to 6pm (until 8pm in midsummer), November to March 10am to 5pm, year-round weekends and holidays 10am to 2pm.

markets on Saturday, at the Pont de Pedra (stone bridge) and in the Plaça Miquel Santaló and Plaça de les Castanyes.

Girona After Dark

Central Girona has a good number of tapas bars and cafes. Many of them are scattered along **Les Ramblas,** around the edges of the keynote **Plaça de Independencia,** and within the antique boundaries of the **Plaça Ferran el Católic.** Moving at a leisurely pace from one to another is considered something of an art form. Some animated tapas bars in the city center are **Bar de Tapes,** Carrer Barcelona 13 (✆ 97-222-87-81), near the rail station, and **Tapa't,** Plaça de l'Oli s/n (no phone), which is noteworthy for its old-fashioned charm. Also appealing for its crowded conviviality and its impressive roster of shellfish and seafood tapas is **Bar Boira,** Plaça de Independencia 17 (✆ 97-220-30-96). In a street that is the hub of Girona's bar culture, **Zanpanzar,** Cort Real 10–12 (✆ 97-221-28-43), pulls in the crowds for its mouthwatering Basque-style *pintxos.* **La Sala del Cel,** Pedret 118 (✆ 97-221-46-64), Girona's "palace of techno," is located in an old convent with outdoor gardens. The DJs, both local and international, are top-class. Be prepared for long waits and a *very* late night out. Slightly more subdued is the **Sala de Ball,** Paseo de la Deversa 21 (✆ 97-220-14-39), an elegant, old-style dance hall that aims to please most tastes, from hip-hop to house and salsa, depending on the night.

LLORET DE MAR

100km (62 miles) S of the French border, 68km (42 miles) N of Barcelona

Although it has a superb half-moon-shaped sandy beach, **Lloret de Mar** is neither chic nor sophisticated, and most people who come here are Europeans on inexpensive package tours. The competition for cheap rooms is fierce.

Lloret de Mar has grown at a phenomenal rate from a small fishing village with just a few hotels to a bustling resort with more hotels than anyone can count. And more keep opening, although there never seem to be enough in July and August. The accommodations are typical of those in other Costa Brava towns, running the gamut from impersonal, modern, box-type structures to vintage flowerpot-adorned, white-washed buildings on the narrow streets of the Old Town. There are even a few pockets of posh. The area has rich vegetation, attractive scenery, and a mild climate.

Essentials

GETTING THERE From Barcelona, take a **train** to Blanes station (4.65€ one-way); from there take the quarter-hourly **bus** 8km/5 miles (2€) to Lloret. If you **drive,** head north from Barcelona along the A-19.

VISITOR INFORMATION The **tourist office** at Plaça de la Vila 1 (*C* **97-236-47-35;** www.lloret.org) is open Monday to Friday 9am to 1pm and 4 to 7pm, Saturday 10am to 1pm.

Where to Stay

Many of the hotels—particularly the government-rated three-star places—are booked solid by tour groups. Here are some possibilities if you reserve in advance.

EXPENSIVE

Guitart Gran Hotel Monterrey ★★ Ranked just beneath the Roger de Flor Palace (see below), this five-star hotel is similar to a deluxe country club in a large park. It's a short walk from the casino, town center, and beaches. The hotel opened in the 1940s and has been partly renovated almost every year since. It's well known as a retreat for those who want to recharge their batteries. The interior areas have big windows with expansive views. The spacious and luxurious guest rooms have mellow, cream-and-brown decor and polished parquet flooring; most have lounge areas or balconies with sea or garden views.

Carretera de Tossa, 17310 Lloret de Mar. *C* **97-236-40-50.** Fax 97-236-35-12. www.ghmonterrey.com. 225 units. 120€–195€ double; 140€–205€ suite. AE, DC, MC, V. Free parking. Closed Oct–Mar. **Amenities:** Restaurant; 3 bars; babysitting; casino; 3 tennis courts; health club; 2 pools (1 indoor); spa; room service. *In room:* A/C, TV, DVD player, hair dryer, minibar, Wi-Fi (free).

Hotel Santa Marta ★★ 📖 This tranquil hotel, a short walk above a crescent-shaped bay favored by swimmers, is nestled in a sun-flooded grove of pines. Both public rooms are attractively paneled and traditionally furnished The spacious and comfortable bedrooms have leather bedside chairs and tiled floors, as well as private balconies overlooking the Mediterranean or the hotel's charming gardens. The neighborhood is quietly relaxing, and located about 2km (1¼ miles) west of the commercial center of town.

Playa de Santa Cristina, 17310 Lloret de Mar. *C* **97-236-49-04.** Fax 97-236-92-80. www.hstamarta.com. 78 units. 150€–275€ double; 250€–390€ suite. AE, DC, MC, V. Free parking. Closed Dec 23–Jan 31. **Amenities:** 2 restaurants; 2 bars; babysitting; outdoor pool; spa; room service. *In room:* A/C, TV, hair dryer, minibar, Wi-Fi (free).

MODERATE

Hotel Vila del Mar This century-old hotel is located close to Lloret's main bus station and the town center, only a few minutes' walk away from the resort's superb beach. Over the years it has been regularly refurbished and today's soundproofed guest rooms are well equipped and pleasantly decorated with comfortable beds, gleaming white walls, and traditional tiled floors. Many of them have first-rate sea views, and all feature adjoining en-suite bathrooms with hydromassage baths. Service is friendly and efficient.

Calle de La Vila 55, 17310 Lloret de Mar. ℰ**97-234-92-92.** Fax 97-237-11-68. 36 units. 80€–160€ double. AE, DC, MC, V. Parking 12€. **Amenities:** Restaurant; bar; babysitting; health club; sauna; outdoor pool. *In room:* A/C, TV, hair dryer, minibar, high-speed Internet access.

Roger de Flor Palace ★★ This much-enlarged old hotel, some of which is reminiscent of a private villa, is a pleasant diversion from the aging slabs of concrete filling other sections of the resort. Set at the eastern edge of town, it offers the most pleasant and panoramic views of any hotel. Potted geraniums, climbing bougainvillea, and evenly spaced rows of palms add elegance to the combination of new and old architecture. The bright, comfortable rooms are high-ceilinged and exquisitely furnished in traditional style. They all have views of either the sea or the mountains.

Turó de l'Estelat s/n, 17310 Lloret de Mar. ℰ**97-236-48-00.** Fax 97-237-16-37. www.hotelrogerdeflor. com. 93 units. 80€–150€ double; 155€–200€ suite. Rates include breakfast. AE, DC, MC, V. Free parking. **Amenities:** Restaurant; 2 bars; babysitting; fitness center; saltwater pool; 2 tennis courts; limited room service. *In room:* A/C, TV, hair dryer, minibar.

INEXPENSIVE

Hotel Best Western Excelsior This hotel attracts a beach-oriented clientele from Spain and northern Europe. It sits almost directly on the beach, rising six floors above the esplanade. Rooms are bright and neatly furnished with good-sized beds and all enjoy full or side views of the Mediterranean. During midsummer, half-board is obligatory. Even though the hotel is modest, one of the Costa Brava's greatest restaurants, Les Petxines, is located here (see below).

Passeig Mossèn Jacinto Verdaguer 16, 17310 Lloret de Mar. ℰ**97-236-41-37.** Fax 97-237-16-54. www. bestwesternhotelexcelsior.com. 45 units. July–Sept 90€ per person double; Oct–June (including breakfast) 60€ per person double. AE, DC, V. Parking 10€. Closed Nov 1–Mar 21. **Amenities:** 2 restaurants; bar; babysitting; spa. *In room:* A/C, TV, Wi-Fi (free).

Where to Dine
EXPENSIVE

El Trull SEAFOOD   Food lovers from all over come to this prestigious eating spot to enjoy both the food and the spectacular views. Set 3km (2 miles) north of the center in the modern suburb of Urbanización Playa Canyelles, El Trull positions its tables within view of a well-kept garden and a (sometimes crowded) pool. The food is some of the best in the neighborhood. Menu items focus on seafood and include fish soup; fish stew heavily laced with lobster; many variations of hake, monkfish, and clams; and an omelet "surprise." (The waiter will tell you the ingredients if you ask.)

Cala Canyelles s/n. ℰ**97-236-49-28.** www.eltrull.com. Main courses 25€–50€; fixed-price menu 16€, 40€, and 70€. AE, DC, MC, V. Daily 1–4pm and 8–11pm.

Les Petxines ★★★ MEDITERRANEAN   The resort's most carefully orchestrated food is served within the Franco-era (ca. 1954) dining room of the Hotel Best Western Excelsior (see above). The dining room is intimate, seating 30 at a time, with lots of big windows. The cuisine varies with the season, the inspiration of the chef, and the availability of ingredients in local markets, but you can always expect superlatively fresh fish and shellfish (*petxines* in Catalan). The best examples include several versions of fish soup, some of them with a confit of lemons and shrimp-stuffed ravioli; and an extremely succulent ragout of fish and shellfish. Meat eaters appreciate seasonal, flavorful versions of pigeon, one stuffed with foie gras.

In the Hotel Excelsior, Passeig Mossèn J. Verdaguer 16. $\mathcal{C}$ **97-236-41-37.** Reservations required. Main courses 20€–40€; fixed-price menu 34€); six-course "surprise menu" 80€. AE, DC, MC, V. Tues–Sun 1:15–3:35pm, Tues–Sat 8:30–11pm; July–Aug Sun nights.

Restaurante Santa Marta ★ SPANISH   Set in the hotel of the same name about 2km (1¼ miles) west of the commercial center of town (p. 285), this pleasantly sunny enclave offers well-prepared food and a sweeping view of the beaches and the sea. Menu specialties vary with the seasons but might include pâté of wild mushrooms, smoked salmon with hollandaise on toast, medallions of monkfish with a mousseline of garlic, ragout of shrimp with broad beans, filet of beef Stroganoff, or a regionally inspired cassoulet of chicken prepared with cloves.

In the Hotel Santa Marta, Playa de Santa Cristina. $\mathcal{C}$ **97-236-49-04.** Reservations recommended. Main courses 20€–40€; fixed-price menu 45€. AE, DC, MC, V. Daily 1:30–3:30pm and 8:30–10:30pm. Closed Dec 15–Jan 31.

Lloret de Mar After Dark

At the **Casino Lloret de Mar,** Carrer Esports 1 ($\mathcal{C}$ **97-236-61-16**), games of chance include French and American roulette, blackjack, and chemin de fer. There's a restaurant, buffet dining room, bar-boîte, and dance club, along with a pool. The casino is southwest of Lloret de Mar, beside the coastal road leading to Blanes and Barcelona. Drive or take a taxi at night and bring your passport for entry. Hours are Sunday through Thursday from 5pm to 3am, Friday and Saturday from 5pm to 4am (30 min. later in summer). Admission is 6€.

The dance club **Hollywood,** Carretera de Tossa ($\mathcal{C}$ **97-236-74-63;** www.disco hollywood.es), at the edge of town, is the place to see and be seen. Look for it on the corner of Carrer Girona. It's open nightly 10pm to 5am.

TOSSA DE MAR ★★

90km (56 miles) N of Barcelona, 12km (7½ miles) NE of Lloret de Mar

The gleaming white town of **Tossa de Mar,** with its 12th-century walls, labyrinthine Vila Vella, fishing boats, and fairly good sand beaches, is perhaps the most attractive base for a Costa Brava vacation. Its character and *joie de vivre* come midway between the devil-may-care excesses of Lloret and laid-back aplomb of Sant Feliu de Guíxols just up the coast (p. 291). The battlements and towers of Tossa were featured in the 1951 Ava Gardner and James Mason movie *Pandora and the Flying Dutchman*. A life-size bronze statue of the screen goddess herself in evening dress, erected in 1998 and facing a stone inscription of an Omar Khayyam quote from the movie, overlooks the bay from a high vantage point in the Vila Vella.

In the 18th and 19th centuries, Tossa survived as a port center, growing rich on the cork industry. But that declined in the 20th century, and many of its citizens emigrated to America. In the 1950s, thanks in part to the Ava Gardner movie, tourists began to discover the charms of Tossa, and a new industry was born.

To experience these charms, walk through the 12th-century walled town, known as **Vila Vella,** built on the site of a Roman villa from the 1st century A.D. Enter through the Torre de les Hores.

Tossa was once a secret haunt for artists and writers—Marc Chagall called it a "blue paradise." It has two main beaches, **Mar Gran** and **La Bauma.** The coast near Tossa, north and south, offers even more possibilities.

As one of the few resorts that have withstood exploitation and retain most of their allure, Tossa enjoys a broad base of international visitors—so many, in fact, that it can no longer shelter them all. In spring and fall, finding a room may be a snap, but in summer it's next to impossible unless reservations are made far in advance.

Essentials

GETTING THERE   Direct **bus** service is offered from Blanes and Lloret. Tossa de Mar is also on the main Barcelona–Palafrugell route. Service with Sarfa (✆ **90-230-20-25;** www.sarfa.com) from Barcelona is daily from 8:15am to 8:15pm, taking 1½ hours; the one-way fare is 10.60€. For information call ✆ **90-226-06-06** or 93-265-65-08. **Drive** north from Barcelona on the A-19.

VISITOR INFORMATION   The **tourist office** is at Avinguda El Pelegrí 25 (✆ **97-234-01-08;** www.infotossa.com). In April, May, and October, it's open Monday to Saturday 10am to 2pm and 4 to 8pm, Sunday 10:30am to 1:30pm; November to March it's open Monday to Saturday 10am to 1pm and 4 to 7pm; June to September it's open Monday to Saturday 9am to 9pm, Sunday 10am to 2pm and 5 to 8pm.

Where to Stay
VERY EXPENSIVE
Grand Hotel Reymar ★   A triumph of engineering—the hotel occupies a position on a jagged rock above the sea edge—this graceful building, a 10-minute walk southeast of the historic walls, was constructed in the 1960s. The Reymar has several levels of expansive terraces, ideal for sunbathing away from the crowds below. The bedrooms are bright and spacious, with cream walls, white drapes, and a mix of modern wood-grained and painted furniture. All have balconies and splendid Mediterranean views.

Platja de Mar Menuda, 17320 Tossa de Mar. ✆ **97-234-03-12.** Fax 97-234-15-04. www.bestwestern ghreymar.com. 148 units. 130€–275€ double; 330€–395€ suite. Rates include breakfast. AE, DC, MC, V. Parking 10€. Closed Nov–Apr 17. **Amenities:** 4 restaurants; 3 bars; babysitting; health club; outdoor pool; room service; spa. *In room:* A/C, TV, hair dryer, minibar, Internet access.

MODERATE
Best Western Hotel Mar Menuda ★★ 🛍   This hotel is a gem, a real Costa Brava hideaway surviving amid tawdry tourist traps and fast-food joints. Its terrace is the area's most panoramic, overlooking the sea and the architectural highlights of the town. The guest rooms range from midsize to spacious, each tastefully furnished, and most have views across the beach to the sea and scattered rocky inlets. The staff are helpful in arranging many watersports, such as scuba diving, windsurfing, and sailing. The cuisine served here is first-class.

Platja de Mar Menuda, 17320 Tossa de Mar. ✆ **97-234-10-04.** Fax 97-234-00-87. www.hotelmar menuda.com. 50 units. 160€–200€ double w/breakfast; 220€ suite. AE, DC, MC, V. Free parking. Closed Nov–Dec. **Amenities:** Restaurant; bar; babysitting; tennis courts; children's playground; limited room service; spa. *In room:* A/C, TV, hair dryer, minibar, Wi-Fi (free).

INEXPENSIVE

Canaima ☺ Lacking the charm of Hotel Diana (see below), this little inn is the resort's bargain. It lies in a tranquil zone in a residential area just a few steps from the beach. The palm trees in this sector of Tossa evoke a real Mediterranean setting. Most of the midsize guest rooms, each very plainly furnished, have a balcony opening onto a view. Since some of the accommodations have three beds, the Canaima is also a family favorite. In lieu of its lack of amenities, it has a public phone, a bar with a TV, and a hotel safe.

Av. La Palma 24, 17320 Tossa de Mar. ℂ/fax **97-234-09-95.** www.hotelcanaima.com. 17 units. 60€–90€ double. Rates include continental breakfast. AE, MC, V. Parking 8€. **Amenities:** Restaurant; bar.

Hotel Cap d'Or ★ 🛍 Perched on the waterfront on a quiet edge of town, this 1790s' building nestles against the stone walls and towers of the village castle. Built of rugged stone itself, the Cap d'Or is a combination of old country inn and seaside hotel. The guest rooms come in different shapes and sizes but are decently maintained, each with a good bed and a small bathroom with a shower stall. Although the hotel is a bed-and-breakfast, it does have a terrace on the promenade offering a quick meal.

Passeig de Vila Vella 1, 17320 Tossa de Mar. ℂ/fax **97-234-00-81.** www.hotelcapdor.com. 11 units. 70€–100€ double. Rates include breakfast. MC, V. Closed Nov–Mar. **Amenities:** Restaurant; bar. *In room:* A/C, TV, hair dryer.

Hotel Diana ★ Set back from the esplanade, this two-star hotel is a former villa designed in part by students of Gaudí. It boasts the most elegant fireplace on the Costa Brava. An inner patio—with towering palms, vines, flowers, and fountains—is almost as popular with guests as the sandy front-yard beach. The spacious rooms contain fine traditional furnishings and bathrooms with shower stalls; many open onto private balconies.

Plaça Espanya 6, 17320 Tossa de Mar. ℂ **97-234-18-86.** Fax 97-234-18-86. www.diana-hotel.com. 21 units. 70€–140€ double; 120€–180€ suite. Rates include breakfast. AE, DC, MC, V. Closed Nov–Apr. **Amenities:** Restaurant; bar; room service (breakfast). *In room:* A/C, TV, hair dryer, minibar.

Hotel Neptuno The popular Neptuno sits on a quiet residential hillside northwest of Vila Vella, somewhat removed from the seaside promenade and the bustle of Tossa de Mar's inner core. Built in the 1960s, the hotel was renovated and enlarged in the late 1980s. Inside, antiques are mixed with modern furniture. The beamed-ceiling dining room is charming. The guest rooms are tastefully lighthearted and modern, each with a good bed and a small bathroom with shower. This place is a longtime favorite with northern Europeans, who book it solid in July and August.

La Guardia 52, 17320 Tossa de Mar. ℂ **97-234-01-43.** Fax 97-234-19-33. www.ghthotels.com. 124 units. June–Sept 70€–130€ per person double; off-season 50€–60€ per person double. Rates include breakfast. AE, DC, MC, V. Free parking. Closed Nov–Mar. **Amenities:** Restaurant; bar; outdoor pool. *In room:* A/C, TV, hair dryer.

Hotel Tonet Opened in the early 1960s, in the earliest days of the region's tourist boom, this simple, family-run pension is one of the resort's oldest. Renovated since then, it's on a central plaza surrounded by narrow streets and maintains the ambience of a country inn, with upper-floor terraces where you can relax amid potted vines and other plants. The small guest rooms are rustic, with wooden headboards, simple furniture, and bathrooms equipped with shower stalls. The Tonet maintains its own brand of Iberian charm.

Plaça de l'Església 1, 17320 Tossa de Mar. © **97-234-02-37.** Fax 97-234-30-96. www.hoteltonet.com. 36 units. 75€ double; 100€ triple. Rates include breakfast. AE, DC, MC, V. Parking nearby 10€. **Amenities:** Bar; Internet access; solarium. *In room:* A/C, TV.

Where to Dine
EXPENSIVE

Bahía ★SPANISH   Adjacent to the sea, Bahía is well known for a much-awarded chef and a history of feeding hungry vacationers since 1953. Menu favorites are for the most part based on time-honored Catalan traditions and include *simitomba* (a grilled platter of fish), *brandade* of cod, baked monkfish, and an array of grilled fish—including *salmonete* (red mullet), *dorada* (gilthead sea bream), and *calamares* (squid)—depending on what's available.

Passeig del Mar 29. © **97-234-03-22.** Reservations recommended. Main courses 14€–38€; *menú del día* 16€–35€. AE, DC, MC, V. Daily 1–4:30pm and 7:30–11:30pm.

La Cuina de Can Simon ★★★SPANISH   Some of the most sought-after dining tables in Tossa de Mar are found within this charming, cozy, and intimate establishment containing only 18 seats. The antique, elegantly rustic stone-sided dining room was originally built in 1741. During the colder months, a fire might be burning in the stately fireplace. Most diners select the *menú gastronómico*, consisting of six small courses, which might include oven-roasted duckling with a sweet-and-sour sauce, crayfish-stuffed ravioli with Beluga caviar and truffle oil, or a monkfish supreme with scalloped potatoes and golden-fried sweet onions. One of the desserts we particularly fancied was an artfully arranged platter of ice cream, pastries, sauces, and tarts, each of which factored seasonal red fruits (strawberries, whortleberries, and currants) into its composition.

Portal 24. © **97-234-12-69.** www.lacuinadecansimon.es. Reservations required. Main courses 18€–55€; price-fixed menus 50€–80€. AE, DC, MC, V. Wed–Mon 1–4pm and 8–11pm.

Sa Muralla ★★SEAFOOD   Beautifully located in the heart of Tossa's tiny Ciutat Vella (Old City), this atmospheric gem dates back to the time of Tossa's earliest international tourists, when it served as a fishermen's tavern. Today its intimate roof-beamed interior shelters one of the town's prime seafood spots, where specialties like *suquet La Muralla* (a saffron-flavored stew containing sea bream, prawns, and other local fish) and *rodaballo a la plancha* (grilled turbot) draw in the eager crowds. Its prized dish, *cim i tomba* (highly seasoned grouper served on thinly sliced potatoes), is made from an old fishermen's recipe and unique to Tossa. In fine weather, eat outside and sun yourself as you watch the world go by.

Carrer Portal 16, 17320 Tossa de Mar. © **97-234-11-28.** www.samuralla.com. Main courses 15€–30€; menu 18€. AE, DC, MC, V. Daily 12:30–4:30pm and 7–11pm. Closed Dec 9–Jan 19.

Tossa de Mar After Dark

Tossa de Mar is pretty low-key at night. People come to relax rather than party and those who do get the urge, once the sun's gone down, to gyrate to hot music beneath the flashing lights tend to head for nearby Lloret (p. 284), where they're spoiled for choice. One solid favorite in Tossa, though, is the **Ely Club,** Carrer Bernat 2 (© **97-234-00-09**). Fans from all over the Costa Brava actually come *here* to dance to its latest sounds. Daily hours are from 10pm to 5am between April 1 and October 15 only. In July and August, there's a one-drink minimum policy. The Ely Club is in the center of town between the two local cinemas.

SANT FELIU DE GUÍXOLS

110km (68 miles) N of Barcelona, 35km (22 miles) SE of Girona

Sant Feliu de Guíxols has a quiet dignity that befits its role as the official capital of the Costa Brava. Trade with Italy in past centuries may have given it what the late Catalan scribe Josep Pla described as an Italianite look, though—as he pointed out—it lacks the brighter colors of its Ligurian coastal counterparts. The once lucrative local activities of sardine fishing and cork production (with the natural product taken straight from the cork trees of the inland Gavarres forests) have waned, but it still gives the rare impression of a town that has a life of its own outside tourism. High-rise buildings have been kept to a commendable minimum and the elegant, wide Passeig Marítim, facing its enclosed sandy bay, is lined with a blend of stylish cafes and impressive *moderniste* buildings. For lovers of culture and architecture, the town's historic highlight is the 10th-century **Monasterio Benedictino (Benedictine Monastery)** (reconstructed in 1723) at the southern end of the town, whose **Porta Ferrada** has three archways. The **Centre Cultural (Cultural Center)** and **Museu de la Historia de la Ciutat (History Museum)** exhibits recall Sant Feliu's prosperous 19th-century cork-and-sardine days. Outside town, just off the Tossa road to the south, the charming 19th-century **Capellà de Sant Elm (Chapel of Sant Elm)** offers splendid panoramic coastal views.

Meanwhile, 3km (2 miles) to the north, the crescent-shaped sandy area of Sant Pol adjoins the exclusive hotel resort area of S'Agaró and the marvelous Cami de Ronda coastal path, which leads past Sa Conca (another gem of a beach) to over-developed Platja d'Aro and then on as far as the sprawling port-resort of Palamós.

Essentials

GETTING THERE The **bus** company Sarfa (© **90-230-20-25;** www.sarfa.com) runs services from Plaça Urquinaona and the Estación Nort in Barcelona starting at 8:15am and operating a service of eight buses a day until 8:30pm. Traveling time is 1 hour 35 minutes and the one-way fare is 13.50€. From June to September coastal *cruceros* **(pleasure cruisers)** take the scenic sea route here from Blanes, Lloret, and Tossa. If you're renting a **car** and fancy an adrenaline-charging drive, try the clifftop coastal route from Tossa; it's 20km (12 miles) of twists and turns through pine-wooded headlands, past dozens of tiny hidden coves. Movie buffs should check out *Pandora and the Flying Dutchman* (p. 25) and a lesser-known black-and-white 1950s' thriller, *Chase a Crooked Shadow,* starring Anne Baxter and Richard Todd, for an idea of the thrills and spills involved.

VISITOR INFORMATION The **tourist office** is at Plaça del Mercat 28 (© **97-282-00-51;** www.infotossa.com). It's open Monday through Saturday 10am to 1pm and 4 to 7pm, Sunday 10am to 2pm.

Where to Stay

VERY EXPENSIVE

Hostal de la Gavina ★★★ This very chic Costa Brava hostelry is the grandest address in the northeast corridor of Spain. Since it opened in the early 1980s, the Hostal de la Gavina has attracted the rich and glamorous, including King Juan Carlos, Elizabeth Taylor, and a host of celebrities from northern Europe. It's on a peninsula jutting seaward from the center of S'Agaró, within a thick-walled Iberian villa built as the home of the Ansesa family (the hotel's owners) in 1932. Most of the accommodations are in the resort's main building, which has been enlarged and modified. The spacious guest rooms are the most sumptuous in the area, with elegant appointments and deluxe fabrics.

Plaça de la Rosaleda, 17248 S'Agaró (Girona). ℂ**97-232-11-00.** Fax 97-232-15-73. www.lagavina.com. 74 units. 250€–395€ double w/balcony; 300€–950€ suite. AE, DC, MC, V. Free parking outside, garage 20€. Closed Nov–Apr. **Amenities:** 4 restaurants; 2 bars; babysitting; health club; outdoor pool; tennis courts; room service; sauna; stores. *In room:* A/C, TV, hair dryer, minibar, Wi-Fi (free).

EXPENSIVE

Curhotel Hipócrates ★ Located halfway between Sant Feliu and S'Agaró and enjoying easy access to coastal walks, this large hotel prides itself on superb facilities, which range from steam baths to a well-equipped "aquagym." With over 2 decades of experience in the field of health treatments and therapies, it's an ideal place to relax and get in shape. Service is friendly and attentive and the comfortable rooms, each with en-suite bathroom with tub and shower, all have sea or mountain views.

Carretera Sant Pol 229, Sant Feliu de Guíxols (Girona). ℂ**97-232-06-62.** www.hipocratescurhotel. com. 92 units (88 doubles plus 4 suites). 150€–250€ double; 230€–420€ suite. AE, DC, MC, V. Free parking. **Amenities:** Restaurant; health-food bar; gym; health center; outdoor pool; room service; spa. *In room:* A/C, TV, hair dryer, minibar, Wi-Fi (free).

A ROOM WITH A view

Radiating out around the hilltop town of **Begur,** just 6km (3¾ miles) to the north of Palafrugell, is a series of idyllic sandy coves that epitomize the very best the "Rugged Coast" has to offer: Pines, rocks, secluded inlets with hidden caves that can, even now, only be reached by boat, and tiny resorts with evocative names like **Sa Tuna, Aigua Xelida,** and **Aigua Blava** that vie with the Palafrugell resorts for the title of most beautiful spot on the coast. Access is difficult unless you have a car, with only occasional buses running from Bagur. Should you decide to stay overnight, don't miss the chance to stay at one of the most dramatically located hotels in Spain: The clifftop **Parador Hotel de Aiguablava** (ℂ **97-262-21-62;** www.parapromotions-spain.com/parador/spain/aiguablava. html), where a double will cost from 175€ to 270€ and the Mediterranean vistas through the surrounding pines are out of this world. Book well ahead. Mod cons include, of course, the now indispensable free Wi-Fi connection.

Nature on the Costa Brava

The **Illes Medes,** located a mile offshore from the small fishing port–turned–pop resort of **Estartit,** are a miniature archipelago of seven limestone islets and one lighthouse whose surrounding waters are a protected ecosystem. Here, divers can search for coral and rich aquatic life that includes lobsters and octopus. In summer you can take trips by glass-bottom boat from Estartit. For more information, contact the **Estartit–Medes Islands Water Sports Station** (*℡* 97-275-06-99; www.enestartit.com).

Further north on the Costa Brava, above the ancient Roman town of Empúries, is another wildlife sanctuary: The 4,800-hectare (11,900-acre) **Aiguamolls de l'Empordà** natural park (*℡* 97-245-42-22; www.parcsde catalunya.net), located near the town of **Sant Pere Pescador.** Amateur ornithologists should note that it's the best area in Catalonia for bird-watching. The watery areas also shelter turtles and otters.

Where to Dine
EXPENSIVE
Casa Buxó 🍴 CATALAN   Open to a grateful public since 1931, this welcoming, family-run establishment in the center of Sant Feliu is now under its third generation of ownership. The kitchen is famed for its traditional Catalan starters such as *torrada amb escalivada i anxovies* (anchovy and pepper salad on toast) and first-rate main-course paella and *bacallà* (cod) dishes, all best accompanied by the house white Penedès wine.

Carrer Mayor 18, Sant Feliu de Guíxols (Girona).*℡* **97-232-01-87.** Main courses 15€–30€. AE, DC, MC, V. Daily 1–4pm and 8–11pm.

PALAFRUGELL & BEACHES
124km (77 miles) N of Barcelona, 36km (22 miles) E of Girona

The prosperous but laid-back junction town of **Palafrugell** is noted for three things. First, it's the birthplace of Catalonia's most famous 20th-century regional chronicler, Josep Pla (to check out the rather esoteric literary route named after him, visit the **Fundació Josep Pla,** Carrer Nou 49–51; *℡* **97-230-55-77;** www.fundaciojosep pla.cat). Second, the town's Sunday open **market** is one of the best on the coast.

Third, and of more interest to hedonistically minded visitors, it's close to three of the coast's most exquisite beach resorts, where the clear waters are a paradise for snorklers. **Calella de Palafrugell** is a whitewashed former fishing town with many attractive summer villas, located just north of the charming **Cap Roig** gardens. From beneath the 19th-century archways of its diminutive Ses Voltes *paseo,* you look out past a series of sandy inlets and jutting rocks to the tiny offshore **Illes Formigues.** A

GREEKS & ROMANS IN empúries

Close to the fishing port of **L'Escala,** a 20-minute stroll along the shore of the wide Bay of Rosas, is **Empúries,** evocative site of the best Greco-Roman remains in Spain. It dates back to 600 B.C., when it was founded by Phoenicians, shortly to be followed by the Greeks, who built a town they called Neapolis (replacing their initial settlement of Paleopolis, which is now covered by the sea). The township flourished until the Romans arrived in A.D. 2, but as Barcino (Barcelona) and Tarraco (Tarragona) assumed more importance, its decline began. Today you can clearly see traces of the shoreside Greek agora harbor and fish-salting area, and the impressive Roman walls, amphitheater, forum, and Paleochristian basilica. You may even feel nostalgic for a past you never knew as you wander among its crumbling pillars, fading mosaics, and paved walkways, enjoying the timeless environment of land, sea, and sky. Modern amenities include a museum and small cafe, plus an information booth beside the parking lot where you can get an audio guide to the site. For more information, visit www.cbrava.com/empuries/empuries.uk.htm.

15-minute coastal walk north around the headland brings you to the sister resort of **Llafranch** with its single beach and yachting marina nestled below the clifftop lighthouse of San Sebastian. A couple of kilometers further north, isolated from these twin resorts, is one of Pla's favorite spots, **Tamariu,** a small sandy cove backed by delectable seafood restaurants.

Essentials

GETTING THERE   The **bus** company Sarfa (✆ **90-230-20-25;** www.sarfa.com) runs services from Plaça Urquinaona and Estación Nort in Barcelona starting at 8:15am and offering a service of eight buses a day until 8:30pm. Travel time is 2 hours 15 minutes and the one-way fare is 16.15€. From Palafrugell bus station, there are half a dozen daily buses that run to Calella and Llafranch. A separate service runs three times a day to Tamariu. Each costs 1.25€ one-way and takes 10 to 15 minutes.

VISITOR INFORMATION   The **tourist office** is at Carrilet 2 (✆ **97-230-02-28;** www.turismepalafrugell.org). It's open daily from 10am to 1pm and 4 to 7pm.

Where to Stay

VERY EXPENSIVE

Mas de Torrent ★★★   Just a few minutes' drive inland from **Palafrugell,** this hotel, elegantly created from a 1751 farmstead (*masía*) in the hamlet of Torrent, is one of the best hotels in Spain. Try for one of the 10 rooms in the original farmhouse, with their massive beams and spacious bathrooms with deep tubs and power showers. The rooms in the more modern, bungalow-style annex are just as comfortable but lack the mellow old atmosphere. From the rooms' stone balconies, you can enjoy vistas of the countryside, with Catalonian vineyards in the distance. In the restaurant, the chef focuses mainly on classic local dishes, including monkfish in saffron or fine noodles simmered in fish consommé and served with fresh shellfish.

Afueras de Torrent, Torrent 17123 (Girona). © **90-255-03-21.** www.mastorrent.com. 39 units. 295€–405€ double; 475€–650€ suite. Rates include breakfast. AE, DC, MC, V. Free parking. **Amenities:** 2 restaurants; 2 bars; babysitting; tennis court; pool; room service. *In room:* A/C, TV, hair dryer, minibar, Wi-Fi (free).

EXPENSIVE

El Far de Sant Sebastià ★   This highly individual little hotel stands next to a restored medieval watchtower and an 18th-century hermitage on a promontory overlooking both Calella de Palafrugell and Llafranc. Named after the lighthouse that towers amid the wooded hills on the cliff edge above, the hotel is an ideal spot for relaxing and enjoying the best of Costa Brava coastal scenery. It's open year-round and has a fine restaurant where you can sample typical Empordà cuisine, ranging from fresh seafood to hearty stews.

Platja de Llafranc s/n, Llafranc (Girona). © **97-230-16-39.** www.elfar.net. 10 units (9 doubles and 1 suite). 160€–225€ double; 275€ suite. AE, DC, MC, V. **Amenities:** Restaurant; babysitting; spa. *In room:* A/C, TV, hair dryer, minibar, Wi-Fi (free).

Where to Dine

EXPENSIVE

La Casona   This well-regarded restaurant is situated in the heart of the town and is a favorite with visitors and locals alike thanks to its homely, down-to-earth setting and highly attentive and friendly service. Here you can enjoy genuine gourmet Catalan specialties at reasonable rates. Look out in particular for the delicious *suquet de peix* (a seafood stew with rich ingredients, including monkfish, sea bass and mussels) and *pollastre pagès amb sepia i escarlamans* (a country-style chicken dish that also has salty marine additions such as squid and langoustines). End your meal with a scrumptious homemade fig flan served with an aromatic almond sauce. If you're thinking of dining here at the weekend or during fiestas, be sure to book ahead.

Paratge de la Sauleda 4, Palafrugell (Girona). © **97-230-36-61.** Main courses 22€–35€. Lunch only on Sun. Closed Mon.

FIGUERES

36km (24 miles) N of Girona, 136km (85 miles) N of Barcelona

The sleepy, laid-back capital of the northerly Alt Empordà sub-region of Girona province, **Figueres** once played a role in Spanish history. Philip V wed María Luisa of Savoy here in 1701 in the church of San Pedro, thereby paving the way for the War of the Spanish Succession. But that historical fact is nearly forgotten today: The town is better known as the birthplace of surrealist artist Salvador Dalí in 1904. In view of the lack of other worthy sights in the town, most people stay only a day in Figueres, using Girona, Cadaqués, or any of the other towns along the Costa Brava as a base.

Essentials

GETTING THERE   RENFE has an hourly **train** service between Barcelona and Figueres, stopping off at Girona along the way. Traveling times range from 2 hours to 2 hours 30 minutes and one-way fares from 9.40€ to 12.80€. All trains between Barcelona and France stop here as well, including the faster and more comfortable Talgo, which charges 20€ one-way.

THE MAD, MAD world OF SALVADOR DALÍ

Salvador Dalí (1904–89) was a leading exponent of surrealism, depicting the irrational imagery of dreams and delirium in a unique, meticulously detailed style. Famous for his eccentricity, he was called "outrageous, talented, relentlessly self-promoting, and unfailingly quotable." At his death at age 84, he was the last survivor of the three famous *enfants terribles* of Spain (the poet Federico García Lorca and the filmmaker Luis Buñuel were the other two).

For all his international renown, Dalí was born in Figueres and died in Figueres. Most of his works are in the eponymous theater-museum there, built by the artist himself around the former theater where his first exhibition was held. Dalí is also buried in the theater-museum, next door to the church that witnessed both his christening and his funeral—the first and last acts of a perfectly planned scenario.

Salvador Felipe Jacinto Dalí i Domènech, the son of a highly respected notary, was born on May 11, 1904, in a house on Carrer Monturiol in Figueres. In 1922 he registered at the School of Fine Arts in Madrid and went to live at the prestigious Residencia de Estudiantes. There, his friendship with García Lorca and Buñuel had a more enduring effect on his artistic future than his studies at the school. As a result of his undisciplined behavior and the attitude of his father, who clashed with the Primo de Rivera dictatorship over local elections, the young Dalí spent a month in prison.

In the summer of 1929, artist René Magritte and poet Paul Eluard and his wife, Gala, came to stay at Cadaqués; their visit caused sweeping changes in Dalí's life. The young painter became enamored of Eluard's wife, leaving his family and fleeing with Gala to Paris, where he became an enthusiastic member of the surrealist movement. Some of his most famous paintings—*The Great Masturbator, Lugubrious Game,* and *Portrait of Paul Eluard*—date from his life at

Figueres is about a 2-hour **drive** from Barcelona. Take the excellent north–south A-7 and exit at the major turnoff to Figueres.

VISITOR INFORMATION   The **tourist office** is at Plaça del Sol s/n (© 97-250-31-55; www.figueresciutat.com). On weekdays it's open year-round from 8:30am to 3pm, and in summer also from 4:30pm till 8:30 pm (until 9pm in July and Aug). Saturday opening times vary from 9:30am to 1:30 and 3:30pm to 6:30pm (winter) to 9am to 9pm (summer). On Sunday it's open from 9am to 3pm in midsummer only.

Visiting Dalí

Casa-Museu Castell Gala Dalí ★★ 🎁   For additional insights into the often bizarre aesthetic sensibilities of Spain's most famous surrealist, consider a 40-km (25-mile) trek from Figueres eastward along highway C-252, following the signs to Parlava. In the village of **Púbol,** where the permanent population almost never exceeds 200, you'll find the Castell de Púbol. Dating from A.D. 1000, the rustic stone castle was partially in ruins when bought by Dalí as a residence for his estranged wife, Gala, in 1970, on the condition that he'd come visit when she invited him. (She almost never did.) After her death in 1982, Dalí moved in for 2 years, moving

Port Lligat, the small Costa Brava town where he lived and worked off and on during the 1930s.

Following Dalí's break with the tenets of the surrealist movement, his work underwent a radical change, with a return to classicism and what he called his mystical and nuclear phase. He became one of the most fashionable painters in the United States and seemed so intent on self-promotion that the surrealist poet André Breton baptized him with the anagram "Avida Dollars." Dalí wrote a partly fictitious autobiography titled *The Secret Life of Salvador Dalí*, and *Hidden Faces*, a novel containing autobiographical elements. These two short literary digressions earned him still greater prestige and wealth, as did his collaborations in the world of cinema (such as the dream set for Alfred Hitchcock's *Spellbound*, 1945) and in those of theater, opera, and ballet.

On August 8, 1958, Dalí and Gala were married according to the rites of the Catholic Church, in a ceremony performed in the strictest secrecy at the shrine of Els Angels, just a few miles from Girona.

During the 1960s, Dalí painted some very large works, such as *The Battle of Tetuán*. Another important work of this period is *Railway Station at Perpignan*, a painting that relates this center of Dalí's mythological universe to his obsession with painter Jean-François Millet's *The Angelus*.

In 1979 Dalí's health began to decline, and he retired to Port Lligat in a state of depression. When Gala died, he moved to Púbol, where, obsessed by the theory of catastrophes, he painted his last works, until he suffered severe burns in a fire that nearly cost him his life. Upon recovery, he moved to the Torre Galatea, a building he had bought as an extension to the museum in Figueres. Here he lived for 5 more years, hardly ever leaving his room, until his death in 1989.

on to other residences in 1984 after his bedroom mysteriously caught fire one night; he was seriously hurt and never recovered his health. Quieter, more serious, and much less surrealistically flamboyant than the other Dalí buildings in Port Lligat and Figueres, the castle is noteworthy for its severe Gothic and Romanesque dignity and for furniture and decor that follow the tastes of the surrealist master. Don't expect a lot of paintings—that's the specialty of the museum at Figueres—but do expect a fascinating insight into one of the most famous muses of the 20th century.

Plaza Gala Dalí s/n, 17120 Púbol-La Pera.© **97-248-86-55.** www.salvador-dali.org/museus. Admission 7€, 5€ students, free for children 9 and under. June 15-Sept 15 Tues-Sun 10:30am-8pm; Mar 13-June 14 and Sept 16-Nov 1 Tues-Sun 10:30am-6pm; Nov 2-Dec 31 Tues-Sun 10am-5pm. Closed Jan 1-Mar 12.

Teatre-Museu Dalí ★★★   Dalí was as famous for his surrealist and often erotic imagery as he was for his flamboyance and exhibitionism. At the Figueres museum, in the center of town beside the Rambla, you'll find paintings, watercolors, gouaches, charcoals, and pastels, along with graphics and sculptures, many rendered with seductive and meticulously detailed imagery. His wide-ranging subject matter encompassed such repulsive issues as putrefaction and castration. You'll see, for instance, **The Happy Horse,** a grotesque and lurid purple beast the artist painted during one of his long exiles at Port Lligat. A tour of the museum is an experience.

When a catalog was prepared, Dalí said, with a perfectly straight face, "It is necessary that all of the people who come out of the museum have false information."

Plaça Gala-Salvador Dalí 5, 17600 Figueres. ✆ **97-267-75-00.** www.salvador-dali.org. Admission 11€ adults, 7€ groups, free for children 9 and under. Daily 10:30am–6pm, later in summer. Oct–May closed Mon.

Where to Stay & Dine

MODERATE

Duran ★★   Most stopover visitors to Figueres tend to be business-oriented, and hotels cater for them accordingly. Duran is a magnificent exception: A bargain hotel of character, dating from 1855, whose illustrious guests have included Salvador Dalí (he used to meet regularly with fellow bohemians in the hotel's highly regarded restaurant). While retaining its original interior furnishings and ambience, the hotel has deftly incorporated the latest 21st-century features from satellite TV to Wi-Fi. The guest rooms are compact and well furnished with pristine polished parquet floorboards. All have delicately pale-pink tiled en-suite bathrooms. The restaurant is one of the best in town, offering a fine range of traditional specialties.

Carrer Lausaca 5, 17600 Figueres. ✆97-250-12-50. www.hotelduran.com. 65 units. Doubles 80€–110€. Main courses in restaurant 12€–20€. AE, DC, MC, V. Parking free. **Amenities:** Restaurant; bar. *In room:* A/C, TV, hair dryer, Wi-Fi (free).

CADAQUÉS ★★

196km (122 miles) N of Barcelona, 31km (19 miles) E of Figueres

Cadaqués is still relatively unspoiled and remote, despite the publicity it received when Salvador Dalí lived in the next-door village of Port Lligat in a split-level house surmounted by a giant egg. The last resort on the Costa Brava before the French border, Cadaqués is reached by a small, winding road, twisting over the mountains from Rosas, the nearest major center. The town winds around half a dozen small coves, with a narrow street running along the water's edge.

Scenically, Cadaqués is a knockout: Crystal-blue water, fishing boats on the sandy beaches, old whitewashed houses, narrow twisting streets, and a 16th-century parish up on a hill. (Like most Catalan seaside towns it's tourist-packed in July and Aug, however, and that tortuous road can get choked with traffic. Avoid it if you can.)

Essentials

GETTING THERE   There are three **buses** per day from Figueres to Cadaqués (11am, 1pm, and 7:15pm). Trip time is 1¼ hours and the fare is 4.80€ one-way. The service is operated by Sarfa (✆ **97-225-87-13;** www.sarfa.com), which also runs a twice-daily service directly from Barcelona; journey time is a smooth 2¼ hours along the inland highway and the one-way fare is 21.35€.

VISITOR INFORMATION   The **tourist office,** Cotxe 2A (✆ **97-225-83-15;** www.visitcadaques.org), is open Monday through Saturday from 10:30am to 1pm and 4:30 to 7:30pm.

What to See

Casa-Museu Salvador Dalí Portlligat ★★ 📷   This fascinating private-home-turned-museum completes (along with the Teatre-Museu Dalí and the

Casa-Museu Castell Gala Dalí) the touted "Dalían Triangle" of northern Catalonia. The structure, home to the Dalís for over 40 years, lies in the tiny fishing port of Port Lligat and is surrounded by the eerie rock and coastal formations that feature heavily in his work. Walking from the town center, 15 minutes away, your first glimpse of the museum will be of the oversize white eggs that adorn the roof. Inside, the house has been pretty much left as it was when it was inhabited, with the expected eclectic collections of Dalían objects, art, and icons thrown together in surrealist fashion. The swimming pool and terrace, where Dalí threw many of his legendary parties in the 1970s, is the highlight. The museum doesn't have a proper address, but you can't miss it.

Port Lligat.© **97-225-10-15.** www.salvador-dali.org/museus. Admission 10€, 8€ students and seniors, free for children 9 and under. Mid-Mar–mid-June and mid-Sept–Jan 6 Tues–Sun 10:30am–6pm; mid-June–mid-Sept daily 9:30am–9pm. Closed Jan 7–mid-Mar.

Where to Stay
EXPENSIVE

Rocamar ★★   On the beach, this three-star hotel is one of the better choices in town, attracting a fun-loving crowd of young northern Europeans in the summer. All the accommodations are well furnished, with rustic yet comfortable pieces, along with small and neatly kept bathrooms. The rooms at the front have balconies opening onto the sea; those at the back have balconies with views of the mountains and beyond. The hotel is known for its good food served at affordable prices.

Dr. Bartomeus s/n, 17488 Cadaqués.© **97-225-81-50.** Fax 97-225-86-50. www.rocamar.com. 71 units. 100€–195€ double; 200€–295€ suite. Rates include breakfast. DC, MC, V. Free parking. **Amenities:** Restaurant; bar; babysitting; bike rental; golf; indoor and outdoor pools; room service; spa; tennis court. *In room:* A/C, TV.

MODERATE

Hotel Playa Sol ★   In a relatively quiet section of the port along the bay, this 1950s' hotel offers a great view of the stone church that has become the town's symbol; it's located at the distant edge of the harbor and overlooks the bay of Cadaqués. Many of the rooms have balconies looking right onto the bay (specify when booking) and the smallish rooms are comfortably furnished. The hotel doesn't have an official restaurant, but it does offer lunch from June 15 to September 15 and breakfast all year round. The swimming pool is a definite plus.

Platja Planch 3, 17488 Cadaqués.© **97-225-81-00.** Fax 97-225-80-54. www.playasol.com. 50 units. 110€–200€ double. AE, DC, MC, V. Parking 10€. Closed Jan–Feb. **Amenities:** Restaurant (summer only); bar; bike rental; breakfast room; outdoor pool; tennis court; limited room service. *In room:* A/C, TV, hair dryer, Wi-Fi (free).

Llane Petit ★★ 🦪   This is a little inn of considerable charm lying below the better-known Rocamar (see above), and opening right onto the beach. A hospitable place, it offers decent-sized and well-maintained bathrooms with both tubs and showers. All accommodations open onto a little terrace. The owners keep the hotel under constant renovation during the slow months so it's always fresh again when the summer hordes descend. Try to patronize the hotel's little dinner-only restaurant, as the cuisine is well prepared and most affordable.

FAREWELL TO FERRAN—THE "MOSTfamous chef IN THE WORLD"

Ferran Adrià was hailed not just as the most exciting chef in Spain, but also in the entire world. The press dubbed him the "Salvador Dalí of the kitchen" because of his creative, wholly high-tech approach to cookery that challenged the concept of food as we know it, seizing the world's attention with his initial, mold-breaking "foam" and "air" dishes.

All the more reason now for lamenting the impending 2011 closure of his famed de luxe restaurant El Bulli, a culinary mecca which was originally converted from an old farmhouse in Montjoi cove near Roses. In its heyday, Michelin granted it three stars, an accolade most often reserved for the top restaurants of Paris, and its *menú de degustación* was a major highlight for visiting gourmets.

He's not completely saying goodbye to the culinary world, though. Adrià's plan now is to take a 2-year tour of Asian countries, after which—replete with new ideas—he'll reopen El Bulli as a private training school for restaurateurs. Though the public will, alas, no longer be able to dine at this temple of good taste, they can sample the fare served in eating spots run by his many disciples, such as Ramón Freixa and Sergi Arola, both of whom have top Michelin-rated restaurants in Spain's two main cities. His name and influence live on—and not only in revered establishments providing exclusive 150€ tasting menus, but also in more modest places such as the ubiquitous bright minimalist-style "Fast Good," eating spots which serve quality "fast food" versions of Adrià-influenced dishes at around a tenth of El Bulli prices. (There's a branch at Calle Balmes 127 in Barcelona ✆ 93-452-2374. See www.fast-good.com.) The legacy he's left caters for all pockets.

Platja Llane Petit s/n, 17488 Cadaqués. ✆**97-225-10-20.** Fax 97-225-87-78. www.llanepetit.com. 37 units. 80€–160€. AE, DC, MC, V. Rates include breakfast in off-season. Free parking. Closed Jan 9–Feb 21. **Amenities:** Restaurant; bar; outdoor pool; limited room service. *In room:* A/C, TV, Wi-Fi (free).

INEXPENSIVE

Misty As peaceful a retreat as you'll find in this relaxing corner of the coast, the German-run Misty is a hacienda-style hotel located on the outskirts of Cadaqués beside a winding road that leads to Dalí's home hamlet of Port Lligat. It stands in verdant gardens beside a tree-shaded swimming pool with a BBQ area, backed by a landscape of olive-tree-dotted hills. The centrally heated accommodations range from atmospheric rooms with slate walls and floors, wooden roof beams, and modest but charming rustic-style furnishing to newer, sunny, whitewashed rooms opening onto the garden. Communal areas include a cozy lounge with a piano and pool table.

Carretera Port Lligat. ✆**97-225-89-62.** www.hotel-misty.com. 60€–100€ double. AE, DC, MC, V. Parking. **Amenities:** Bar; cafe; outdoor pool; tennis court. *In room:* A/C, TV.

Where to Dine
EXPENSIVE

Es Trull 🍴 SEAFOOD   On the harborside street in the center of town, this cedar-shingled cafeteria is named after the ancient olive press dominating the interior. A filling fixed-price meal is served. According to the chef, if it comes from the sea and can be eaten, he'll prepare it with that special Catalan flair. You might try mussels in marinara sauce, grilled hake, or natural baby clams. Rice dishes are a specialty—not only paella but also black rice colored with squid ink and rice with calamari and shrimp.

Port Ditxòs s/n.✆ **97-225-81-96.** Reservations recommended in high season. Main courses 10€–35€. AE, DC, MC, V. Daily 12:30–4pm and 7–11pm. Closed Nov–Easter.

La Galiota ★★ SPANISH   Dozens of surrealist paintings, including some by Dalí, adorn the walls of this award-winning restaurant, the finest in town. On a sloping street below the cathedral, the place has a downstairs sitting room and a dining room converted from what was a private house. Dalí himself was a patron (his favorite meal was cheese soufflé and chicken roasted with apples), and the chef's secret is in selecting only the freshest of ingredients and preparing them in a way that enhances their natural flavors. Roast leg of lamb flavored with garlic is a specialty. The marinated salmon is also excellent, as are the sea bass and the sole with orange sauce.

Carrer Narcis Monturiol 9.✆ **97-225-81-87.** Reservations required. Main courses 18€–34€. AE, DC, MC, V. Daily 1:30–3:30pm and 8:30–10:30pm. Closed Oct–mid-June.

A SIDE TRIP TO MALLORCA

12

Mallorca is the most popular of Spain's beautiful quartet of Balearic Islands, which also includes Minorca, Ibiza, and Formentera. One of the Mediterranean's great tourist success stories, this island of just 800,000 inhabitants currently (2010) attracts around 10 million visitors annually, who come to enjoy its fine climate and multitude of holiday attractions. But visitors also come to savor its unexpectedly unspoiled and peaceful areas. The mountainous northwest is covered with untouched olive groves, and the fertile central flatlands, which are dotted with windmills, boast millions of almond trees that burst into a sea of white blossoms in early spring.

About 209km (130 miles) from Barcelona and 145km (90 miles) from Valencia, Mallorca has a coastline 500km (310 miles) long. Palma is the charming, monument-filled capital, flanked by the Bay of Palma. The golden sands of Mallorca are famous, with highly overbuilt pleasure beaches such as El Arenal and Magaluf spreading out in separate bays on either side of Palma. These tend to be chock-full of sun worshippers on package tours, while more isolated inlets, such as Cala de San Vicente, a pine-shrouded cove overlooked by high precipices 6.5km (4 miles) from Port of Pollença, offers relaxation and semi-seclusion.

> ### Not an Island for All Seasons
>
> **July and August are high season for Mallorca; don't even think of coming then without a reservation. It's possible to swim comfortably from June to October; but after that, it's prohibitively cold.**

Island Essentials

GETTING THERE   Make the trip to Mallorca by boat or plane, but if you are thinking of traveling to Palma in July and August, book your ferry or air tickets way ahead of time. You won't be able to get there without advance reservations.

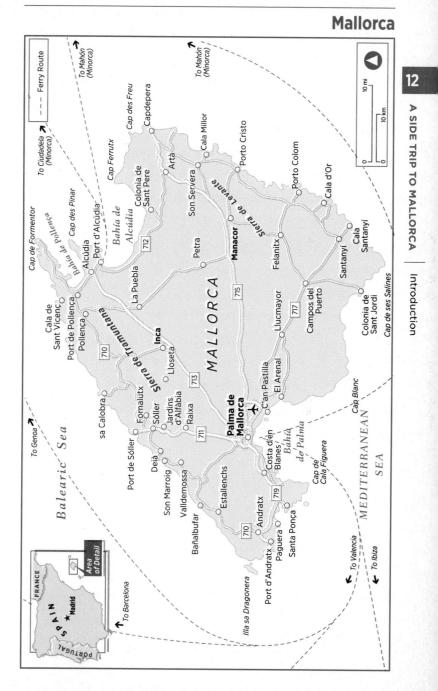

Iberia (© **90-240-05-00;** www.iberia.com) flies to Palma's Aeroport Son Sant Joan (© **97-178-90-00**) from Barcelona, Valencia, and Madrid. There are daily planes from Madrid and Barcelona year-round, with increased numbers in summer. **Spanair** (© **90-213-14-15;** www.spanair.com) flies into Palma from Barcelona and from Madrid, Bilbao, Minorca, Santiago de Compostela, Málaga, and Tenerife. **Air Europa** (© **90-240-15-01;** www.aireuropa.com) also flies to Palma from Barcelona up to twice a day during peak season. There are flights to the island from Madrid, Minorca, Ibiza, and Seville, plus countless charter flights.

From Palma de Mallorca–Son San Joan airport, bus no. 1 takes you to Plaça Espanya in the center of Palma every 15 minutes from 5:30am to 2:15pm daily; the trip takes about 30 minutes and costs 3€. A metered cab charges from 28€ for the 25-minute drive into the city.

Trasmediterránea, Estació Marítim, Palma (© **90-245-46-45;** www. trasmediterranea.es), operates a daily **ferry** from Barcelona, taking 8 hours and costing from 80€ one-way. Tickets can be booked at the Trasmediterránea office at Estació Marítim in Barcelona (© **90-245-46-45**). Any travel agent in Spain can book you a seat. Schedules and departure times (subject to change) should always be checked and double-checked.

GETTING AROUND At the tourist office in Palma, pick up a **bus** schedule that explains island routes. Or contact **Empresa Municipal de Transports** (© **97-175-22-45** or 90-250-78-50; www.emtpalma.es), the company that runs city buses from its main terminal, Estació Central d'Autobus, Plaça Espanya. The standard one-way fare is 1.25€ within Palma; at the station you can buy a booklet good for 10 rides, costing 8€. For buses covering the whole island, contact **TIB** (Transport de les Illes Balears; © **97-117-77-77;** tib.caib.es). Buses leave the d'Eusebi Estada station in Calle d'Eusebi Estada, which adjoins the Plaza España for towns all over the island, including Manacor and Porto Cristo (for the Caves of Drach) in the east, to Deya (45 min), Valldemossa (30 min), Sóller, and Pollença (1 hr. each) in the north and northwest. Fares range from 3€ to 8€ one-way, depending on the distance.

Ferrocarril de Sóller, Carrer Eusebio Estada 1 (© **97-175-20-51;** www. trendesoller.com), off Plaça Espanya, is a **train** service operating between Palma and Sóller that makes for an unforgettable journey, passing through majestic mountain scenery. Trains run from 8am to 7pm, and a ticket costs 10€ one-way or 17€ round-trip.

Another train runs to Inca; it's often called the "Leather Express" because most passengers are onboard to buy inexpensive leather goods in the Inca shops. **Servicios Ferroviarios de Mallorca** leaves from Plaça Espanya (© **97-175-22-45;** www.sfm.cat for more information and schedules). The train ride is only 40 minutes, with 40 departures per day Monday through Saturday and 32 per day on Sunday. A one-way fare costs 3.50€. For a **taxi,** call © **97-175-54-40,** flag one down in the street, or look for a rank. To book online, go to www.palmataxi.com for taxis from the airport or www.mallorcataxi.com for anywhere else.

If you plan to stay in Palma, you don't need a car. The city is extremely traffic-clogged, and parking is scarce. However, if you do choose to **drive,** you can rent cars at such companies as **Europcar,** at the airport terminal (© **95-615-01-38;** www. europcar.com), where rentals range from 60€ to 120€ per day, though lower rates can usually be arranged off-season. Both **Atesa** (www.atesa.es) and **Avis** (www.avis.es) maintain offices at the airport. Reservations should always be made in advance.

PALMA DE MALLORCA ★★

Palma, on the southern tip of the island, is the seat of the autonomous government of the Balearic Islands, as well as the center for most of Mallorca's hotels, restaurants, and nightclubs. Founded by the Romans in 123 B.C., it was later rebuilt by the Moors in the style of a Kasbah, or walled city. Its foundations are still visible, although obscured by the high-rise hotels that line the Paseo Maritimo.

Old Palma is characterized by the area immediately surrounding the cathedral. Mazes of narrow alleys and cobblestone streets recall the era when Palma was one of the chief ports in the Mediterranean.

Today the Mallorcan capital is a bustling city whose massive tourist industry has more than made up for its decline as a major seaport. It's estimated that 500,000 people live in Palma, which is nearly half of Mallorca's population. Somehow the city has miraculously managed to retain much of its original charm and character. The islanders call Palma simply *Ciutat* (City), and as the largest of the Balearic ports, its bay is often clogged with yachts. Arrival by sea is impressive, with the skyline dominated by the turrets of Bellver Castle (p. 308) and the cathedral's Gothic bulk (p. 308).

Essentials

VISITOR INFORMATION The **tourist office** in Palma is at Plaça Reyna 2 (© **97-171-22-16;** www.palmademallorca.es). It's open Monday to Friday 9am to 8pm, and Saturday 9am to 2pm. The website for information on Mallorca is www.mallorcaonline.com.

GETTING AROUND In Palma, you can get around the Old Town and the Paseo Maritimo on foot. Otherwise, you can make limited use of taxis, or take one of the buses that cut across the city. Out across the island, you'll have to depend mainly on buses or rented cars.

FAST FACTS The **U.S. Consulate,** Edificio Reina Constanza, Porto Pi, 8, 9D (© **97-140-37-07;** www.embusa.es), is open Monday to Friday from 10:30am to 1:30pm. The **British Consulate,** Plaça Mayor 3D (© **97-171-24-45;** www.ukinspain.fco.gov.uk), is open Monday to Friday from 9am to 2pm.

In an **emergency,** dial © **112.** If you fall ill, head to **Clínica Rotger,** Calle Santiago Rusiñol 9 (© **97-171-66-00**), or **Clínica Juaneda,** Calle Son Espanyolet 55 (© **97-173-16-47**). Both clinics are open 24 hours.

For **Internet access,** go to Babaloo, Calle Verja 2 (© **97-195-77-25;** www.babalointernet.com), just off Calle Sant Magi. It charges 2.50€ per hour and is open Monday to Saturday 10am to 10pm and Sunday 3 to 10pm.

Mallorca observes the same **holidays** as Barcelona (p. 34) but also celebrates June 29, the Feast of Saint Peter, the patron saint of all fishers.

The central **post office** is at Constitución 6 (© **97-172-70-54** or 90-219-71-97; www.correos.es). Hours are Monday to Friday 8:30am to 8:30pm, and Saturday 9:30am to 2pm.

Palma de Mallorca

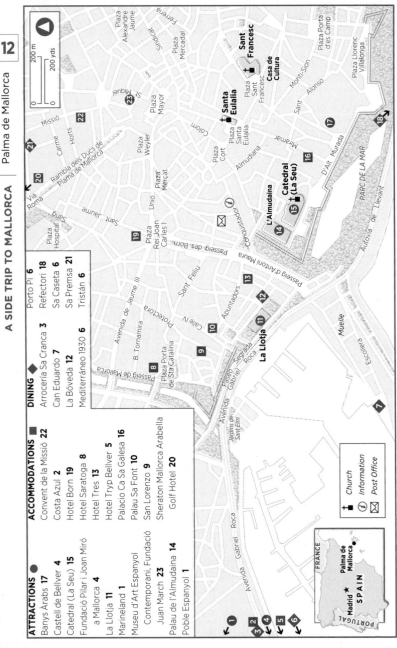

ATTRACTIONS ●
Banys Àrabs **17**
Castell de Bellver **4**
Catedral (La Seu) **15**
Fundació Pilar i Joan Miró
a Mallorca **4**
La Llotja **11**
Marineland **1**
Museu d'Art Espanyol
Contemporani, Fundació
Juan March **23**
Palau de l'Almudaina **14**
Poble Espanyol **1**

ACCOMMODATIONS ■
Convent de la Missió **22**
Costa Azul **2**
Hotel Born **19**
Hotel Saratoga **8**
Hotel Tres **13**
Hotel Tryp Bellver **5**
Palacio Ca Sa Galesa **16**
Palau Sa Font **10**
San Lorenzo **9**
Sheraton Mallorca Arabella
Golf Hotel **20**

DINING ◆
Arrocería Sa Cranca **3**
Can Eduardo **7**
La Bóveda **12**
Mediterráneo 1930 **6**

Porto Pi **6**
Refectori **18**
Sa Caseta **6**
Sa Premsa **21**
Tristán **6**

Church
Information
Post Office

Fun on & off the Beach

There is a beach fairly close to the cathedral in Palma, but some people have been discouraged from swimming here because of fears over the cleanliness of the water. The wide sweep of Palma Bay boasts better beaches. Take the 30-minute bus journey east to the excellent long, sandy stretch of **Playa de Palma,** which links **C'an Pastilla** with **El Arenal;** it's very well equipped with tourist facilities. To the west you'll find the good, but smaller and often crowded, coves of **Cala Mayor**, **Sant Agustí,** and **Illetas.**

You can swim from late June to October; don't believe the promoters who try to sell on the promise of mild Mallorcan winters in January and February—it can get downright cold. Only spartan Scandinavians might be seen taking a dip then. Spring and fall can be heaven-sent, sun- and temperature-wise, and in summer the coastal areas are pleasantly cooled by sea breezes.

GOLF   Mallorca is a golfer's dream. The best course is Son Vida Club de Golf, Urbanización Son Vida, about 13km (8 miles) east of Palma along the Andraitx Highway. This 18-hole course is shared by the guests of the island's two best hotels, Arabella Golf Hotel and Son Vida, and is also open to any players who call for reservations (© **97-179-12-10;** www.sonvidagolf.com). Greens fees for 18 holes range from 65€ to 100€ for hotel guests and 120€ for nonguests. Golf-cart rentals are also available for 50€.

There are many more golf courses on the island. For information about them, contact **Federación Balear de Golf,** Avinguda Jaime III 17, Palma (© **97-172-27-53;** www.fbgolf.com).

HIKING   The mountains of northwest Mallorca, the Serra de Tramuntana, are the best for hiking. The tourist office (see above) can provide a free booklet called *20 Hiking Excursions on the Island of Mallorca.* For hiking information, contact **Grup Excursionista de Mallorca,** the Mallorcan hiking association, at Carrer dels Horts 1 baixos, Palma (© **97-171-88-23;** www.gemweb.org).

TENNIS   If your hotel doesn't have a court, head for the **Club de Tenis,** Carrer Sil s/n, Santa Ponsa (© **97-169-22-61**), half an hour's drive or bus trip west of Palma.

WATERSPORTS   You can hire surfboards, water skis, canoes, and dinghies on most beaches. Try **Escola d'Esports Nàutics,** Paseo Playa d'en Repic, Port de Sóller (© **97-163-30-18;** www.nauticsoller.com).

Shopping

Stores in Palma offer handicrafts, elegant leather goods, Mallorcan pearls, and fine needlework. The best shopping is on the following streets: San Miguel, Carrer

Sindicato, Jaume II, Jaume III, Carrer Platería, Vía Roman, and Passeig des Borne, plus the streets radiating from the Borne all the way to Plaça Cort, where the city hall stands. Most shops close on Saturday afternoon and Sunday.

The famous **Casa Bonet ★★★**, Plaça Federico Chopin 2 (© **97-172-21-17**), founded in 1860, sells finely textured needlework. The sheets, tablecloths, napkins, and pillowcases are made in Mallorca from fine linen or cotton. Many are hand-embroidered using traditional designs and motifs popularized by this store.

Loewe, Avinguda Jaume III 1 (© **97-171-52-75**), offers fine leather, elegant accessories for men and women, luggage, and chic apparel for women.

Perlas Majorica, Avinguda Jaume III 11 (© **97-171-21-59**), is the authorized agency for authentic Mallorcan pearls. The pearl producers offer a decade-long guarantee for their products. Pearls come in varied sizes and settings.

Palma's leading department store, **El Corte Inglés,** Avinguda Jaume III 15 (© **97-177-01-77;** www.elcorteingles.es), stocks an exceptional collection of delicate Mallorcan needlework and hand-embroidered napkins and tablecloths.

Seeing the Sights

Most visitors don't spend much time exploring the historic sights in Palma, but it is a fascinating, historic city, well worth making the effort to explore. Here are some suggestions for sightseeing in Palma:

Banys Àrabs   These authentic Moorish baths date from the 10th century. They are the only complete remaining Moorish-constructed buildings in Palma. One room contains a dome supported by 12 columns.

Carrer Serra 7. ©**97-172-15-49.** Admission 2€. Apr–Sept daily 9am–7pm; Oct–Mar daily 9am–6pm. Bus: 15.

Castell de Bellver ★   Erected in 1309, this round hilltop castle was once the summer palace of the kings of Mallorca—during the short period between 1231 and 1344 when there were kings of Mallorca! The castle, which was a fortress with a double moat, is well preserved and now houses the Museu Municipal, devoted to archeological objects and old coins. It's really the view from here, however, that is the chief attraction. In fact, the name, Bellver, means "beautiful view."

Btw. Palma and Son Armadams. ©**97-173-06-57.** Admission 2.50€; 1€ children 14–18, students, and seniors; free for children 14 and under. Apr–Sept Mon–Sat 8am–8:30pm, Sun 10am–5pm; Oct–Mar Mon–Sat 8am–7:15pm, Sun 10am–5pm. Museum closed Sun. Bus: 3 or 15.

Catedral (La Seu) ★★   This Catalonian Gothic cathedral, known as La Seu, stands in the Old Town overlooking the seaside. It was begun during the reign of Jaume II (1276–1311) and completed in 1601. Its central vault is 43m (141 feet) high, and its columns rise 20m (66 feet). There is a wrought-iron *baldachin* (canopy) by Gaudí over the main altar. The treasury contains supposed pieces of the True Cross and relics of San Sebastián, patron saint of Palma. Museum and cathedral hours often change; call ahead to make sure they're accepting visitors before you go.

Carrer Palau Reial. © **97-172-31-30.** www.catedraldemallorca.info. Free admission to cathedral; museum, and treasury 4€. Apr–May and Oct Mon–Fri 10am–5:15pm; Nov–Mar Mon–Fri 10am–3:15pm; June–Sept Mon–Fri 10am–6:15pm; year-round Sat 10am–2:15pm. Bus: 15.

Fundació Pilar i Joan Miró a Mallorca ★   The great artist Joan Miró and his wife, Pilar Juncosa, donated four workshops to the city of Palma; he worked on the island from 1956 until his death in 1983. They are at Miró's former estate; rotating exhibitions devoted to his life and work are presented along with a permanent collection of his art and sculptures. You can also see his studio as it was at the time of his death.

Carrer Joan de Saridakis 29.℡ **97-170-14-20.** http://miro.palmademallorca.es. Admission 6€, 3€ children and seniors. Mid-May to mid-Sept Tues–Sat 10am–7pm; off-season Tues–Sat 10am–6pm; year-round Sun 10am–3pm. Bus: 3 or 6.

La Llotja ★   This 15th-century Gothic structure is a leftover from the wealthy mercantile days of Mallorca. La Lonja (its Spanish name) was, roughly, an exchange or guild. Exhibitions here are announced in local newspapers.

Plaça de la Llotja.℡ **97-171-17-05.** Free admission. Tues–Sun 11am–2pm; Tues–Sat 5–9pm. Bus: 15.

Marineland ☺   Some 18km (11 miles) west of Palma, just off the coast road en route to Palma Nova, Marineland offers dolphin, sea lion, and parrot shows. The daily dolphin shows are at 11:45am and 3:15pm; the parrot shows at 10:30am, 12:30pm, and 4:30pm. There's also a Polynesian pearl-diving demonstration and a small zoo. There's a cafeteria, picnic area, and children's playground, plus beach facilities.

Costa d'en Blanes.℡ **97-167-51-25.** www.marineland.es. Admission 22.50€, 16.50€ children 3–12, free for children 2 and under. Mar 17–Nov 30 daily 9:30am–6pm. Direct bus, marked MARINELAND, from Palma rail station.

Museu d'Art Espanyol Contemporani, Fundació Juan March ★   The Juan March Foundation's Museum of Spanish Contemporary Art houses a collection representing one of the most fertile periods of 20th-century art, with canvases by Picasso, Miró, Dalí, and Juan Gris, as well as Antoni Tàpies, Carlos Saura, Miquel Barceló, Lluis Gordillo, Susana Solano, and Jordi Teixidor. There is a room devoted to temporary exhibits; one series featured 100 Picasso engravings from the 1930s. The oldest and best-known work in the museum is Picasso's *Head of a Woman,* from his cycle of paintings known as *Les Demoiselles d'Avignon.* These works form part of the collection that the Juan March Foundation began to amass in 1973.

Carrer Sant Miquel 11. ℡ **97-171-35-15.** www.march.es. Free admission. Mon–Fri 10am–6:30pm; Sat 10:30am–2pm. Bus: 2.

Palau de l'Almudaina   Long ago, Muslim rulers erected this splendid fortress surrounded by Moorish-style gardens and fountains opposite the cathedral. During the short-lived reign of the kings of Mallorca, it was converted into a royal residence that evokes the Alcázar at Málaga, with its Arabic-style archways, turrets, and fortified walls. Now it houses a museum displaying antiques, artwork, suits of armor, and Gobelin tapestries. You'll get panoramic views of Palma's harbor from here.

Carrer Palau Reial.℡ **97-121-41-34.** Admission 4€ adults, 2.70€ children; free Wed. Mon–Fri 10am–2pm and 4–6:30pm; Sat 10am–1:15pm. Closed holidays. Bus: 15.

Poble Espanyol ★   This is a touristy collection of buildings evoking Spain in miniature and is similar to the Poble Espanyol in Barcelona (p. 188). Bullfights are held in its *corrida* on summer Sundays. There are mock representations of such famous structures as the Alhambra in Granada, the Torre de Oro in Seville, and El Greco's House in Toledo.

Carrer Pueblo Español s/n. ℂ **97-173-70-75.** Admission 9€, 5.50€ students, 6€ children 7-12. Mon 9am-8pm; Tues-Thurs 9am-2pm; Fri 9am-4pm; Sun 9am-midnight. Bus: 5.

There are plenty of options for exploring the rest of Mallorca too. **Viajes Sidetours,** Passeig Marítim 19 (ℂ **97-128-39-00;** www.sidetours.com), offers numerous full- and half-day excursions in Palma and throughout the surrounding countryside. The full-day excursion to Valldemossa and Sóller takes visitors through the **Cartoixa Reial** monastery, where former island residents Frédéric Chopin and his lover, George Sand, spent their scandalous winter in 1838–39. After leaving the monas- tery, the tour explores the peaks of the Sierra Mallorquina, and then makes its way to the seaside town of Sóller. Call ahead for ticket prices.

Another full-day tour of the mountainous western side of the island is conducted by train and boat, including a ride on one of Europe's oldest railways to the town of Sóller and the Monasterio de Lluch, as well as a boat ride between the ports of Sóller and La Calobra. The eastern coast of Mallorca is explored in the Caves of Drach and Hams tour. A concert on the world's largest underground lake (Lake Martel), tours through the caves, a stop at an olive-wood works, and a visit to the Majorica Pearl Factory are all covered. Times of departure may vary.

Balearic Discovery, Calle Jaime Solivellas 11, Selva (ℂ **97-187-53-95;** www. balearicdiscovery.com), offers tailor-made tours around Mallorca. The company can arrange everything from art tours to windsurfing excursions.

Where to Stay in Palma

If you go in high season, reserve well in advance—Mallorca's staggering number of hotels is still not enough to hold the August crowds. Some of our hotel recommenda- tions in Palma are in El Terreno, the heart of the local nightlife; don't book these hotels unless you like plenty of action, continuing until late at night.

Palma's suburbs, notably Cala Mayor, about 4km (2½ miles) from the center, and San Agustín, about 5km (3 miles) from town, continue to sprawl. In El Arenal, there is a huge concentration of hotels but the long, white sandy beach that curves round the bay from here to C'an Pastilla, backed by gardens and a maritime promenade, is one of the cleanest and best on the island.

VERY EXPENSIVE

Hotel Tryp Bellver ★ Set on Palma's superb Passeig Marítim right below the emblematic Bellver Castle (p. 308), this prominent member of the distinguished Tryp chain enjoys some of the best yachting-harbor views of any Palma hotel. The spacious rooms are light, sunny, and furnished in a comfortable modern style with whitewashed walls and mellow wooden headboards and dressing tables. Some are equipped for disabled guests, and all have balconies ensuring you get the very best out of the privileged location. Come off-season to take advantage of some bargain rates (roughly half what you'd pay in summer).

Av. Gabriel Roca (Passeig Marítim) 11, 07014 Palma de Mallorca. ℂ**97-122-22-40.** www.solmelia.com. 384 units. 175€–200€ double. AE, DC, MC, V. **Amenities:** Restaurant; bar; lounge; gym; outdoor pool; room service. In room: A/C, TV, minibar, Wi-Fi (free).

Palacio Ca Sa Galesa ★★ 🎁 This place is a delight and far more personal than the bigger chain hotels. For generations the 15th-century town house languished as a decaying apartment building facing the side of the cathedral. In 1993 an entrepreneurial couple from Cardiff, Wales, began restoring the place, salvaging the original marble floors and stained-glass windows, sheathing the walls of the public areas with silk, and adding modern amenities. Today, the hotel is the most alluring in Palma, loaded with English and Spanish antiques and paintings. Most rooms overlook an enclosed courtyard draped with pot plants and climbing vines. The guest rooms are quite opulent, with antiques and Persian rugs. There's no restaurant, but a hearty buffet is served each morning (for an extra charge).

Carrer de Miramar 8, 07001 Palma de Mallorca. ©**97-171-54-00.** Fax 97-172-15-79. www.palaciocasa galesa.com. 12 units. 340€ double; 375€–500€ suite. AE, MC, V. Parking 15€. **Amenities:** 2 lounges; babysitting; sauna; spa; room service. In room: A/C, TV, hair dryer, minibar, Wi-Fi.

Sheraton Mallorca Arabella Golf Hotel ★★★ ☺ The natural environment surrounding this hotel has been fiercely protected. Don't come here expecting raucous good times on the beach; the resort is elegant and rather staid. There's no health club and no shuttle to the beach; many visitors drive to the several nearby beaches, but it does boast one of the only hotel bullrings in Spain. The low-rise complex is intensely landscaped and offers views over the lush green grounds (not of the sea) from many of its good-size rooms. Accommodations have white walls, dark-stained furnishings, carpeting, en-suite bathrooms, and, in the more expensive rooms, balconies or verandas.

Carrer de la Vinagrella, 07013 Palma de Mallorca. ©**800/325-3535** in the U.S. or 97-178-71-00. Fax 97-178-72-00. www.starwoodhotels.com. 93 units. 350€–500€) double; 1,200€–1,600€ suite. Rates include breakfast. AE, DC, MC, V. Free parking. Bus: 7. **Amenities:** 2 restaurants; bar; babysitting; children's programs; fitness center; golf course; 3 tennis courts; 2 pools (1 indoor); sauna; room service. In room: A/C, TV, hair dryer, minibar, high-speed Internet access.

EXPENSIVE

Convent de la Missió ★★ 🎁 This magnificent 17th-century convent is hidden away in the Ciutat Vella (Old City) amid narrow streets and plant-filled patios, and adjoins a church of the same name. Missionaries are no longer taught here, for the building has been massively restored and turned into a hotel with many amenities, including a solarium and whirlpool. The guest rooms, which range from small to spacious, are comfortably furnished and smartly minimalist in style, with white and sand the predominant colors. Suites are equipped with Jacuzzis, while some standard doubles have only a shower.

Carrer de la Missió, 07003 Palma de Mallorca. ©**97-122-73-47.** Fax 97-122-73-48. www.conventde lamissio.com. 4 units. 250€ double; 300€ junior suite; 375€ suite. Rates include buffet breakfast. AE, DC, MC, V. Parking 12€. **Amenities:** Restaurant; bar; babysitting; sauna; solarium; room service. In room: A/C, TV, hair dryer, minibar.

Hotel Tres ★★ 🎁 Located right in the heart of Ciutat Vella, this one-of-a-kind character hotel is a tasteful blend of two well-preserved old palaces. Guests enjoy an infinity splash pool, as well as sweeping vistas of Palma and its port, and walk across a linking bridge from one roof terrace to another. The midsize bedrooms are minimalist in decor but comfortably and attractively furnished, with wood floors, lots of glass and white surfaces, fresh cotton sheets, plush sofas in flamboyant colors, and superb bathrooms. A suite boasts its own private terrace and Jacuzzi. A romantic stone courtyard, with a towering palm tree, is an idyllic place for breakfast or for a glass of wine before dinner.

Calle Apuntadores 3, 07012 Palma de Mallorca.© **97-171-73-33.** Fax 97-171-73-72. www.hoteltres. com. 41 units. 220€–300€ double; 340€ junior suite; 575€ suite. Rates include breakfast. AE, DC, MC, V. No parking. **Amenities:** Restaurant; bar; outdoor pool; room service. *In room:* A/C, TV, hair dryer, minibar, Wi-Fi.

Palau Sa Font ★ ▮▮   This 16th-century palace has been successfully converted into one of Mallorca's most charming boutique hotels. It's located a 3-minute walk from the harbor and 15 minutes from the cathedral. The atmosphere is a bit funky unless you like jelly-bean colors. Distressed iron and island stone add more traditional notes. Especially popular with English visitors, this has been called the hippest and most atmospheric place to stay in the Old Town. Designers transformed the guest rooms into a blend of modern and traditional, each with a sleek bathroom. Plump comforters, linen curtains, rustic iron furnishings, and plain walls lend style and grace. The breakfast is one of the reasons to stay here, featuring such delights as smoked salmon, Serrano ham, tortillas, and fresh fruit.

Carrer Apuntadores 38, Barrio Antiguo, 07017 Palma de Mallorca.© **97-171-22-77.** Fax 97-171-26-18. www.palausafont.com. 19 units. 160€–225€ double; 250€ junior suite. Rates include buffet breakfast. AE, DC, MC, V. No parking. Closed Jan. **Amenities:** Breakfast lounge; bar; babysitting; outdoor pool. *In room:* A/C, TV, hair dryer, minibar, Wi-Fi (free).

MODERATE

Hotel Saratoga ★   The entrance to the hotel is under an arcade beside the Old Town's medieval moat. The hotel features bright, well-furnished guest rooms, many with balconies or terraces with views of the bay and city of Palma. Decor varies from room to room but most have cream-colored walls, comfortable furnishings, and either warmly carpeted or polished wooden floors. One of the hotel's most attractive features is a cafe-bar on the seventh floor, enjoying Mediterranean vistas.

Passeig Mallorca 6, 07012 Palma de Mallorca.© **97-172-72-40.** Fax 97-172-73-12. www.hotelsaratoga. es. 187 units. 150€–175€ double; 200€–250€ suite. Rates include breakfast. AE, DC, MC, V. Parking 10€. Bus: 3, 7, or 15. **Amenities:** Restaurant; cafe/bar; gym; 2 outdoor pools; fitness center; room service; sauna. *In room:* A/C, TV, Wi-Fi, hair dryer, minibar, Wi-Fi (free).

San Lorenzo ★★   This historic hotel and romantic oasis occupies the center of the maze of winding streets that form Palma's Old Town. The building is 18th-century, and the decor is a pleasant mix of modern and traditional Mallorcan styles. The fixtures in its Art Deco bar once decorated a saloon in Paris. All guest rooms are comfortable, airy, and gleaming white, with beamed ceilings. While some have balconies, the more luxurious rooms offer fireplaces and private terraces. This hotel is perfect for relaxing after a day of sightseeing or shopping; it's peaceful and atmospheric, conjuring up a bygone age.

San Lorenzo 14, 07012 Palma de Mallorca.© **97-172-82-00.** Fax 97-171-19-01. www.hotelsanlorenzo. com. 6 units. 135€–210€ double; 250€ suite. AE, DC, MC, V. No parking. **Amenities:** Bar; babysitting; outdoor pool; room service. *In room:* A/C, TV, hair dryer, minibar, Wi-Fi (free).

INEXPENSIVE

Costa Azul ⚓ This established waterfront hotel, located right beside Palma Bay, offers reasonable rates and superb views of the yachts in the harbor. In short, if location is your top priority, it's a bargain. The bright, sunny rooms are neatly if modestly furnished and spotlessly clean, with white walls, mellow wooden floorboards, and large windows that flood the room with light. It's a short stroll into town along the *paseo* or up the hill behind the hotel to the bars and clubs of Plaça Gomila in El Terreno.

Av. Gabriel Roca (Passeig Marítim) 7, 07014 Palma de Mallorca. © **97-173-19-40.** Fax 97-173-19-71. www.esperanzahoteles.com. 126 units. 95€–135€ double. MC, V. Parking 12€. **Amenities:** Restaurant; bar; outdoor pool; room service; sauna. *In room:* A/C, TV, Internet access (Wi-Fi in some rooms).

Hotel Born ★ ⚓ If you'd like to stay within Palma itself, there is no better bargain than this two-star hotel in the city's center. A 16th-century palace, it once belonged to the Mallorcan aristocrat, Marqués de Ferrandell. It was vastly altered and extended in the 18th century with the addition of a Mallorcan courtyard shaded by a giant palm tree. Today it's a small, cozy inn with all the modern amenities, and it retains many of its original architectural features, such as Romanesque arches. Guest rooms are mostly spacious and well equipped, with neatly tiled bathrooms with shower. Off Plaça Rei Juan Carlos, the hotel opens onto a tranquil side street.

Carrer Sant Jaume 3, 07012 Palma de Mallorca. © **97-171-29-42.** Fax 97-171-86-18. www.hotelborn. com. 30 units. 80€–120€ double; 135€ suite. Rates include breakfast. AE, DC, MC, V. No parking. **Amenities:** Bar; bike rentals. *In room:* A/C, TV.

Where to Stay in Illetas

This built-up resort-suburb of Palma lies 8km (5 miles) west of the center, beside a series of intimate coves.

EXPENSIVE

Meliá de Mar ★★ Built in 1964, Meliá de Mar is one of the most comfortable (albeit expensive) hotels in Palma. This seven-story hotel is close to the beach and sports a large garden. The marble-floored lobby and light, summery furniture offer a cool refuge from the sun. Guest rooms, mainly midsize, have many fine features, including original art, terracotta-tiled balconies, marble or wrought-iron furnishings, and excellent beds. Marble-clad bathrooms come with deluxe toiletries and dual basins.

Paseo de los Illetas 7, 07015 Calvia. © **97-140-25-11.** Fax 97-140-58-52. www.solmelia.com. 144 units. 190€–350€ double; from 375€ suite. AE, DC, MC, V. Free parking. **Amenities:** 3 restaurants; bar; babysitting; 2 pools (1 indoor); room service; spa; tennis court. *In room:* A/C, TV, hair dryer, minibar, Wi-Fi (free).

INEXPENSIVE

Hotel Bonsol ★ ☺ Set across from the beach, this four-star hotel was built in 1953 and has been renovated frequently since then. It charges less than hotels with similar amenities, and the on-site swimming facilities make it quite popular with vacationing families, who dine in the airy, somewhat spartan dining room. The core is a four-story, white-sided masonry tower; some of the suites are clustered into simple, outlying villas. The hotel overlooks a garden, adjacent to the sea. The midsize rooms are larger than you might expect, efficient but comfortable and well suited to beachfront vacations.

Paseo de Illetas 30, 07181 Illetas. ℂ **97-140-21-11.** Fax 97-140-21-11. www.hotelbonsol.es. 147 units. 100€–160€ double. Rates include breakfast. MC, V. Free parking. Closed Nov 20–Dec 20. **Amenities:** 2 restaurants; lounge; babysitting; fitness center; Jacuzzi; sauna; room service; outdoor pool; 2 tennis courts. *In room:* A/C, TV, hair dryer, minibar.

Where to Stay in Costa d'en Blanes

Located at the western end of Palma Bay, 9km (5⅔ miles) from the capital, this hotel enjoys a privileged position in the sheltered resort of Costa d'en Blanes, a 10-minute drive from the center of Palma.

INEXPENSIVE

H10 Punta Negra Resort ★★   In an exclusive enclave, this two-story hotel is surrounded by two Mediterranean beaches and an array of golf courses. Elegant and posh, it's constructed in classic Mallorcan style with white walls, antique furnishings, tiled floors, and panoramic views of either the sea or pine forests. The hotel is only 1.5km (1 mile) from the yachting port of Puerto Portals. Spacious and beautifully furnished rooms have creamy walls, pristine white bedspreads, and traditional tiled floors. Some rooms have terraces.

Carretera Andaitz Km 12, Costa d'en Blanes, 07181 Mallorca.ℂ **97-168-07-62.** Fax 97-168-39-19. www. h10.es. 137 units. 120€–240€ double; 175€–275€ suite. Rates include continental breakfast. AE, DC, MC, V. Free parking. **Amenities:** 2 restaurants; bar; babysitting; 3 pools (1 indoor); room service; spa; tennis courts. *In room:* A/C, TV, hair dryer, minibar, Wi-Fi (free).

Where to Dine in Palma

Mallorca's most typical main dish is *lomo,* or pork loin, the specialty in any restaurant offering local cuisine. *Lomo con col* is prepared with the loin wrapped in cabbage leaves and served with a sauce of tomatoes, grapes, pine nuts, and bay leaf.

A local sausage, *sobrasada,* is made with pure pork and red peppers. Paprika gives it its characteristic bright red color. *Sopa mallorquina* can mean almost anything, but basically it is mixed greens in a soup flavored with olive oil and thickened with bread. When garbanzos (chickpeas) and meat are added, it becomes a meal in itself.

The best-known vegetable dish is *el tumbet,* a kind of cake with a layer of potato and another of lightly sautéed eggplant (aubergine). Everything is covered with a tomato sauce and peppers, then boiled. Eggplant, often served stuffed with meat or

---

A Special Treat

Dating from 1700, **Can Joan de S'aigo,** Carrer Can Sanç 10 (ℂ **97-171-07-59;** www.canjoandesaigo.webs-sites.com), is the oldest ice-cream parlor on the island. Correspondingly elegant and Old World, it serves its homemade ice creams (try the almond), pastries, cakes, *ensaimadas* (light-textured and airy specialty cakes of Palma), fine coffee, and several kinds of hot chocolate in a setting of marble-top tables, beautiful tiled floors, and an indoor garden with a fountain. It's open Monday to Saturday.

fish, is one of the island's vegetable mainstays. *Frito mallorquín* is basically a traditional country dish of fried onions and potatoes, mixed with red peppers, diced lamb liver, "lights" (lungs), and fennel. It's hearty, unsophisticated, and filling.

In the Balearic Islands, only Mallorca produces wine in any quantity, although Ibiza and Formentera have their own tiny output. It is exported in small quantities to major Spanish cities like Barcelona and Madrid. The red wines from Felanitx and Binissalem tend to be the best, and you could add Franja Roja and Viña Paumina to your list. Most of the wine, however, comes from mainland Spanish areas such as Rioja and Penedès. *Café carajillo*—coffee with cognac—is a Spanish specialty particularly enjoyed by Mallorcans.

EXPENSIVE

Mediterráneo 1930 ★ MEDITERRANEAN   Named after the Art Deco, 1930s-era styling that fills its interior, this is a well-managed, artfully hip restaurant. One of Palma's top eating spots, with a sense of chic defined by its cosmopolitan owners Juan and Mary Martí, it has a beige-and-white decor accented by verdant plants and Art Deco sculptures. The menu relies heavily on seafood, with special emphasis on fish slowly baked in a salt crust, a process that adds a light-textured flakiness to even the most aromatic fish. Another specialty is beef steak cooked on a hot stone, carried directly to your table, and served with béarnaise, pepper, or port sauces.

Av. Gabriel Roca (Passeig Marítim) 33. ℰ **97-173-03-77.** www.mediterraneo1930.com. Reservations recommended. Main courses 18€–38€; fixed-price lunch 30€; fixed-price dinner 40€. AE, DC, MC, V. Daily 1–4pm and 8–11:30pm. Bus: 1.

Porto Pi ★ MEDITERRANEAN   This restaurant, a favorite of King Juan Carlos, occupies an elegant 19th-century mansion above the yacht harbor at the western end of Palma. Contemporary paintings complement the decor, and there is an outdoor terrace. The food has a creative Mediterranean influence. Specialties change with the season but might be house-style fish *en papillote,* angelfish with shellfish sauce, or quail stuffed with foie gras cooked in a wine sauce. Game is a specialty in winter.

Joan Miró 174. ℰ **97-140-00-87.** Reservations required. Main courses 20€–35€. AE, DC, MC, V. Mon–Fri 1–3:30pm; daily 7:30–11:30pm. Bus: Palma–Illetas or 3.

Refectori ★★★ MEDITERRANEAN   Jaime Oliver—no relation to *The Naked Chef*—is one of the island's most celebrated chefs, and his superb kitchen on the ground floor of the Convent de la Missió (see "Where to Stay in Palma," above) offers the island's most creative cuisine. Book well ahead to enjoy it, especially if you're aiming for an open-air terrace table. First-rate seasonal produce and a wide-ranging wine list await diners, who can also sit in the main room decorated with black-and-white photographs of Mallorcan salt mounds. Oliver's delectable dishes range from the deceptively simple poached eggs and mushrooms with crème and soy emulsion to the exquisite lamb in a crust of basil and goat's cheese. For something more challenging try the candied-style squid, stuffed with shrimp and pine-nut praline. The menu changes frequently and the desserts are the most sumptuous on the island.

Carrer de la Misión de San Diego 7. ℰ **97-122-73-47.** www.conventdelamissio.com. Reservations required way in advance. Main courses 25€–32€. AE, DC, MC, V. Mon–Fri 1–3:30pm; Mon–Sat 8–11pm. Bus: 20.

Tristán ★★★ MEDITERRANEAN   Southwest of Palma, Tristán overlooks the marina of Port Portals. This is the finest restaurant in the Balearics, winning a coveted two stars from Michelin, a designation previously unheard of in the archipelago. The sophisticated menu varies, depending on what's best in the market each day. Selections may be pigeon in rice paper, a medley of Mediterranean vegetables, or the catch of the day, usually prepared Mallorcan style. But this recitation doesn't prepare you for the exceptional bursts of flavor you'll sample in chef Gerhard Schwaiger's creations.

Port Portals 1, Portals Nous. © **97-167-55-47.** www.grupotristan.com. Reservations required. Main courses 35€–60€; special menus 120€–150€; gourmet tapas menu 155€. AE, DC, MC, V. Daily 1–3:30pm and 8:30–11:30pm. Closed Jan 7–Feb 28. Bus: 22.

MODERATE

Arrocería Sa Cranca SEAFOOD   This sophisticated restaurant, which specializes in seafood dishes (in many cases, mixed with rice), has an ideal setting overlooking the port. The best way to appreciate its offbeat charm is to begin your meal with grilled baby sardines or a well-seasoned version of *buñuelos de bacalau* (minced and herb-laden cod patties). Either of these might be followed by a *parrillada*—an array of grilled fish and shellfish—or a rice casserole. Two of the best are black rice with squid and squid ink, and a particularly succulent one with spider crabs, clams, and mussels. Other variations include vegetables, roasted goat, or hake with tomatoes and garlic.

Passeig Marítim 13. © **97-173-74-47.** www.sacranca.com. Reservations recommended. Main courses 16€–38€. AE, DC, MC, V. Tues–Sun 1–4pm; Tues–Sat 8pm–midnight. Bus: 1.

Can Eduardo ★★ SEAFOOD   Thriving since the 1930s, this no-frills restaurant serves the catch of the day, taken directly from boat to kitchen. Specialties include seafood paella and *zarzuela* (fish stew). It's also possible to get fresh lobster. The rest of the menu consists of various fish, most prepared in the Mallorcan style. Situated at the very heart of the harbor alongside the fishing boats that bring in their daily catch, this is the most atmospheric restaurant in town to sample seafood.

3º Travesía Contrameulle Industria Pesquera 4, Es Mollet. © **97-172-11-82.** www.caneduardo.com. Reservations required. Main courses 15€–35€. AE, MC, V. Tues–Sat 1–3:30pm and 8–11pm; Sun 1–3pm. Bus: 1 or 4.

Sa Premsa ★ SPANISH   A genuine culinary institution, this huge, vault-like eating spot is lined with wine barrels, fading pictures of the island, and hanging garlic, and serves up traditional specialties like *sopa mallorquín* (deceptively simple but delicious local soup made from bread and vegetables) and *tumbet* (a sort of Balearic ratatouille). The Basque style *bacalao* (cod) and Galician *pulpo* (octopus) are delicious. Top fare among its meaty delights is *lechona* (suckling pig), which is melt-in-your-mouth tasty. Although the restaurant is usually packed, the hard-working waiters are genially efficient. The lunchtime (weekday) menu is really good value at 14€.

Plaça Bisbe Berenguer de Palau 8. © **97-172-35-99.** www.cellersapremsa.com. Main courses 9€–16€. AE, DC, MC, V. Mon–Sat noon–4pm and 4:30–11:30pm. Bus: 3.

INEXPENSIVE

La Bóveda SPANISH   Set in the oldest part of Palma, a few steps from the cathedral, this rustic-looking restaurant maintains a busy tapas bar near the entrance, and no more than 14 tables set near the bar or in the basement. The menu lists predictable Spanish staples, each well prepared, including roasted or fried veal, pork, chicken, and fish, served with fresh greens, potatoes, or rice. Any of the roster of tapas from the bar (fava beans with ham, spinach tortillas, grilled or deep-fried calamari, and shrimp with garlic sauce) can be served while you're at your table, along with bottles of full-bodied red or more delicate white wines. A worthy and particularly refreshing dessert consists of freshly made sorbet, sometimes garnished with a shot of vodka or bourbon, depending on the flavor of the sorbet.

Calle Botería 3. ✆ **97-171-48-63.** www.restaurantelaboveda.com. Reservations recommended for a table in the restaurant, not necessary for the tapas bar. Main courses 12€–30€. AE, MC, V. Mon–Sat 1:30–4pm and 8:30pm–midnight. Bus: 7 or 13.

Sa Caseta ★★ 🍴SPANISH   For some of the best-tasting regional cuisine, head west of the city to the village of Gènova. Here, in the attractive dining rooms of a hacienda, enjoy typical local cuisine served by a helpful staff. *Sopa mallorquina* (the island's famed vegetable soup) begins many a meal here. The chef loves *bacalao* (cod), and cooks it superbly in at least 10 different preparations. If you're dining with friends, order some of the best suckling pig or roast baby lamb in Mallorca. On hotter days, you may prefer one of the local fish dishes, including (our favorite) *rape* (monkfish) in a shellfish sauce. Paella is served with dried salt cod and vegetables, an unusual variation on this classic dish. A series of homemade desserts, including ice cream, is a special feature. Most dishes are priced at the lower end of the scale.

Carrer Alférez Martínez Vaquer 1, Gènova. ✆**97-140-26-40.** www.sacaseta.com. Reservations recommended. Main courses 12€–34€; tasting menu 45€. AE, DC, MC, V. Daily 1pm–midnight. Bus: 46.

Palma After Dark

Palma is packed with bars and dance clubs. Sure, there are some fun hangouts along Mallorca's northern tier, but for a rocking, laser- and strobe-lit club, you'll have to boogie in Palma.

ABACO   This just might be the most opulently decorated nightclub in Spain—a cross between a harem and a czarist Russian church. The bar is decorated with a trove of European decorative arts. The place is always packed, with many customers congregating in a beautiful courtyard which contains exotic caged birds, fountains, more sculpture than the eye can absorb, extravagant bouquets, and hundreds of flickering candles. All this exoticism is enhanced by the lushly romantic music (Ravel's *Boléro*, at our last visit) piped in through the sound system. Whether you view this as a bar, a museum, or a sociological survey, be sure to go. The bar is open Sunday to Thursday 8pm to 1am, Friday and Saturday 8pm to 3am, from February to December only. Wandering around is free; however, the lethal cocktails are 16€. Carrer Sant Joan 1. ✆97-171-49-39. www.bar-abaco.com.

Atlántico   This large, dimly lit place in the heart of old Palma is filled with graffiti-covered walls and nostalgic 1960s' decor, and echoes to the sounds of the Stones and Jimi Hendrix. It's a must for diehard rock 'n' roll lovers. It used to be a dive called Texas Jack, much frequented by U.S. sailors when the fleet was in; something of that sleazy ambience still remains today, making it a blend of curiosities little seen today in Palma's other nightspots. Sample a caipirinha cocktail as you listen to the music. Drinks 5€ to 7€. Carrer Sant Feliu 12. ✆**97-172-28-82.** www.atlanticocafe.com.

B.C.M. Planet Dance   The busiest and most cosmopolitan disco in Mallorca. Boasting high-tech strobe lights and lasers, this sprawling, three-story venue offers a different sound system on each floor, giving you a wide variety of musical styles. If you're young, eager to mingle, and like to dance, this place is for you. The cover charge of 14€ includes your first drink and entitles you to party until 7am. Av. Olivera s/n, Magaluf.© **97-113-26-09.** www.bcm-planetdance.com.

Bodeguita del Medio   In this genial bar you can enjoy a Caribbean cocktail with one of Palma's more charismatic bar owners, Pasqual, who just might invite you to dance a bit of salsa. The music is Latin-inspired and the crowd is a mix of locals and visitors from almost everywhere. Try their delicious *mojito* cocktail, more potent than it tastes, costing 6€. Inside is rustic in tone; outside is more intimate and romantic, with Chinese lanterns illuminating a garden that overlooks the sea. The bar is open from Sunday to Thursday 8pm to 1am, Friday and Saturday 8pm to 3am. Carrer Vallseca 18.© **97-171-78-32.** www.labodegadelmedio.es.

Gran Casino Mallorca   The island's gambling mecca is enviably located right on the harborfront promenade beside the twinkling lights of Palma Bay. You'll need a passport—plus a shirt and tie for the gents—to enter, and must pay a 6€ admission charge. Inside, play American or French roulette, blackjack, dice, or the slot machines. The casino is open daily 5pm to 5am. Av. Gabriel Roca 4.© **97-113-00-00.** www.casinodemallorca.com.

Jazz Voyeur Club   Formerly Bar Barcelona, this popular jazz club evokes its namesake city with its spiral staircase and atmospheric, subdued lighting. Despite its location in the heart of Palma's busiest nightlife area, it attracts a predominantly local crowd that comes to enjoy live jazz every night from 11pm to 3am. There is no admission, and drinks are reasonably priced, making this one of Palma's best values for a night out. Opening hours are Sunday to Thursday 8:30pm to 1am; on Friday and Saturday, it's 8:30pm to 3am. Carrer Apuntadores 5.© **97-171-35-57.** www.jazzvoyeur.com.

Tito's ★   Set directly on the beach, close to a dense concentration of hotels, this iconic nightspot charges a cover of 15€ to 20€ including the first drink. A truly international crowd mingles on a terrace overlooking the Mediterranean. This club is the most popular, panoramic, and appealing disco on Mallorca. If you visit only one nightclub during your time on the island, this should be it. Opening hours are June and September, nightly 11pm to (at least) 6am; and October to May, Thursday to Sunday 11pm to 6am. Passeig Marítim.© **97-173-00-17.** www.titosmallorca.com.

Footnote: Although Mallorca is generally a permissive place, it doesn't have a gay scene to match that of Barcelona.

VALLDEMOSSA & DEIÀ

Valldemossa is the site of the **Cartoixa Reial ★**, Plaça de las Cartujas s/n (© **97-161-21-06**), where George Sand and the tubercular Frédéric Chopin wintered in 1838 and 1839. The monastery was founded in the 14th century, but the present buildings are from the 17th and 18th centuries. After monks abandoned the dwelling, the cells were rented to guests, which led to the appearance of Sand and Chopin, who managed to shock the conservative locals by their unconventional behavior. They occupied cell nos. 2 and 4. The only belongings left are a small painting and a French piano. The peasants, fearing they'd catch Chopin's tuberculosis, burned most of the rest after the couple returned to the mainland. The cells may be visited November to February, Monday to Saturday 9:30am to 4:30pm, Sunday 10am to 1:30pm; and March to October, Monday to Saturday 9:30am to 6pm. Admission is 10€, free for children 10 and under.

From Valldemossa continue through the mountains, following the signposts for 11km (6¾ miles) to Deià. Before the village, consider a stopover at **Son Marroig** (© **97-163-91-58;** www.sonmarroig.com), at Km 26 on the highway. Now a museum, this was once the estate of Archduke Luis Salvador. Born in 1847, he tired of court life in his early 20s and found refuge here with his young bride in 1870. A tower on the estate is from the 1500s. Many of the archduke's personal furnishings and mementos, such as photographs and his ceramic collection, are still here. The estate is surrounded by lovely gardens leading to the cliff edge, and the property has many panoramic views, including one of the striking, rocky Na Foradada headland with its keyhole gap in the middle. It is open Monday to Saturday 9:30am to 6:30pm (to 5:30pm in winter). Admission is 4€.

There are more tributes to the Austrian archduke at **Costa Nord,** Avinguda Palma 6 (© **97-161-24-25**), a cultural center opened by actor Michael Douglas, who has a home in the area. A life-size reproduction of the archduke's yacht is on exhibit and a 15-minute film, narrated by Douglas, covers the history and geography of this corner of the island. Classical music and flamenco shows are performed in the auditorium during summer on Friday and Saturday nights. Admission is 8€, 6.50€ for seniors and students, 5€ for ages 7 to 12, and free for ages 6 and under. Summer hours are daily 10am to 6pm; off-season visits are possible daily 9am to 5pm.

Set against the backdrop of olive-green mountains, **Deià (Deyá)** is a peaceful and serene village, with its stone houses and creeping bougainvillea. In its beautiful setting, with steep olive-tree-covered slopes plunging down to a small, rocky, clear-watered cove, the village has long had a special meaning for artists. Robert Graves, the English poet and novelist (*I, Claudius* and *Claudius the God*), lived in Deià, and died here in 1985. He is buried in the local cemetery. His house, **Ca N'Alluny ★,** Carretera de Sóller Km 1 (© **97-163-61-85;** www.lacasaderobertgraves.com), a 5-minute stroll from the village center, has been restored to how it was when Graves returned to the island in 1946, with the original furnishings and even the electrical fittings. Visitors can explore the studies of Robert Graves and his wife, Laura, an American poet, and visit the kitchen and dining room.

Essentials

VISITOR INFORMATION The **Tourist Information Office** is in Avinguda Palma 7 (© **97-161-20-19;** turismevalldemossa@yahoo.es). This office also provides information about Deià.

GETTING AROUND The L210 **bus** service operates 11 times a day to Valldemossa and 7 times a day to Deià from Palma (see www.caib.es for timetable). One-way fares are 3.75€ (Valldemossa) and 4.25€ (Deià).

Where to Stay

Deià offers some of the most tranquil and stunning retreats on Mallorca and a number of inexpensive little boarding houses as well.

VERY EXPENSIVE

La Residencia ★★★ Launched by Virgin Airlines owner Richard Branson, this stylish and expensive hilltop property is something of an elitist celebrity haven. Guests have included everyone from Queen Sofía of Jordan to the emperor of Japan and America's rock 'n' roll elite. Surrounded by 12 hectares (30 acres) of rocky Mediterranean gardens, the hotel's two sprawling 16th- and 17th-century stone mansions offer guests every conceivable luxury. Spacious rooms are outfitted with rustic antiques, terracotta floors, romantic four-poster beds, and, in some cases, beamed ceilings, all with luxurious appointments. Open hearths, deep leather sofas, wrought-iron candelabras, and a supremely accommodating staff make this hotel internationally famous. Although it's technically defined as a four-star resort, only the lack of certain luxuries prevents it from reaching five-star status.

Camino Son Canals s/n, 07179 Deià. © **97-163-90-11.** Fax 97-163-93-70. www.hotel-laresidencia.com. 59 units. 355€–505€ double; 525€–775€ junior suite; 625€–1,095€ suite; 1,200€–2,750€ suite w/private pool. Rates include breakfast. AE, DC, MC, V. Free parking. **Amenities:** 2 restaurants; 2 bars; babysitting; fitness center; 3 pools (1 indoor); room service; spa; 2 tennis courts. *In room:* A/C, TV, DVD player, hair dryer, minibar, Wi-Fi (free).

EXPENSIVE

Hotel Es Molí ★★ One of the mostly highly recommended and spectacular hotels on Mallorca originated in the 1880s as a dignified manor house in the rocky highlands above Deià, home of the landowners who controlled access to the town's freshwater springs. In 1966, two annexes were added to the manor house and it was transformed into a luxurious four-star hotel. Guest rooms are beautifully furnished and impeccably maintained, with pinewood bedsteads and dressing tables and elegant chintzy chairs; some have access to a private veranda overlooking the gardens or the faraway village. Hardy souls make it a point to hike for 30 minutes to the public beach at Deià Bay; others wait for the shuttle bus to take them to the hotel's private beach, 6km (3¾ miles) away.

Carretera Valldemossa s/n, 07179 Deià. © **97-163-90-00.** Fax 97-163-93-33. www.esmoli.com. 87 units. 150€–190€ double; 160€–250€ junior suite; 190€–220€ suite. Rates include breakfast; half-board 21€ extra per person per day. AE, DC, MC, V. Free parking. Closed early Nov to late Apr. **Amenities:** Restaurant; bar; babysitting; lounge; outdoor pool; room service; tennis court. *In room:* A/C, TV, hair dryer, minibar, Wi-Fi (free).

Where to Dine

EXPENSIVE

Ca'n Quet ★ MEDITERRANEAN This restaurant, belonging to the Hotel Es Molí (see above), is one of the most sought-after dining spots on the island. Set on a series of terraces above a winding road leading out of town, the building is modern and stylish, with an undeniably romantic air. Cascades of pink geraniums adorn its terraces, and if you wander along the sloping pathways you'll find groves of orange and lemon trees, roses, and a swimming pool ringed with neoclassical balustrades. There's a spacious and sunny bar, an elegant indoor dining room with a blazing fire in winter, and alfresco dining on the upper terrace under an arbor. The food is well prepared and the portions generous. Meals might include a salad of marinated fish, terrine of fresh vegetables, fish crepes, shellfish stew, duck with sherry sauce, or an ever-changing selection of fresh fish.

Carretera Valldemossa–Sóller. ✆**97-163-91-96.** www.esmoli.com. Reservations required. Main courses 20€–45€; tasting menus 60€–75€. AE, MC, V. Tues–Sun 1–4pm and 8–11pm. Closed Nov–Mar. Bus: L210.

El Olivo ★★MEDITERRANEAN   A 30- to 40-minute drive north of Palma, this is one of the island's most elegant and upscale restaurants, visited by pop stars and royalty from Sting and Bruce Springsteen to the king and queen of Spain. It's set inside a thick-walled, centuries-old olive press in the gardens of La Residencia (see above). Much of the illumination comes from theatrical-looking candelabras placed on every table, from which flickering light throws shadows against thick ceiling beams, antique accessories, and very formal table settings. The cuisine is modern and subtly flavored. The chefs know how to take classic dishes and add inventive tastebud-stimulating touches. Menu items include a salad of red mullet with julienne of vegetables and vinaigrette, roasted rack of lamb with tomato and herb sauce, baked hake with a seafood risotto, and a dessert specialty of almond soufflé.

In La Residencia Hotel, Camino Son Canals. ✆**97-163-93-92.** www.hotel-laresidencia.com. Reservations recommended. Main courses 35€–85€; fixed-price menu 90€; tasting menu 100€–120€. AE, DC, MC, V. Summer daily 1–3pm and 8–11pm; winter Wed–Sun 1–3pm and 7:30–9:30pm. Bus: L210.

PORT DE POLLENÇA/ FORMENTOR

Beside a sheltered bay and between Cape Formentor to the north and Cape del Pinar to the south is Port de Pollença, 65km (40 miles) north of Palma. The inland market town of Pollença is located 4km (2½ miles) inland from the port and overlooked by two hills: **Calvary** to the west and **Puig** to the east. A cypress-lined stone stairway leads to the chapel that tops the former, while the longer pathway to the latter winds through pine woods to reach a monastery, the Santuari del Puig de María (Carrer Puig de María s/n, Pollença; ✆ **97-118-41-32**), which provides ultra-cheap dormitory accommodations. Both hills enjoy splendid views of the northern coastline and surrounding countryside.

The port's low-rise hotels, private homes, restaurants, and snack bars line the very attractive beach, which is somewhat narrow at its northwestern end but has some of the island's finest, whitest sand and warmest, clearest water; the area also has excellent water-skiing and sailing facilities. For several miles along the bay there is a pleasant pedestrian promenade. There is only one luxury hotel in the area, however: The Barceló Formentor (see below) is out on the peninsula of the same name.

Tons of fine white sand were imported to the beach at the southeastern end of Pollença Bay to create a broad ribbon of sunbathing space that stretches for several miles along the bay. Windsurfing, water-skiing, and scuba-diving are among the watersports offered in the area.

Cabo de Formentor ★, "the devil's tail," can be reached from Port de Pollença via a spectacular road, twisting along to the lighthouse at the cape's end. Formentor is Mallorca's fjord country—a dramatic landscape of mountains, pine trees, rocks, and sea, plus some of the best beaches on the island. In Cape Formentor you'll see *miradores*, lookout terraces providing panoramic views.

Essentials

GETTING THERE Five **buses** a day leave Plaça Espanya in Palma, pass through Inca, and continue on to Port de Pollença; a one-way fare is 6€. You can continue on from Deià (see above) along the C-710, or from Inca on the C-713, all the way to Pollença.

VISITOR INFORMATION The **tourist information office,** on Carrer Monges, Port de Pollença (*©* **97-186-54-67**), is open Monday to Saturday 8am to 3pm and 5 to 7pm.

Where to Stay

VERY EXPENSIVE

Barceló Formentor ★★★   Built in 1929 by an Argentinian entrepreneur, Alan Diehl, and owned today by the prestigious Barceló chain, this famous secluded, cliffside hotel on the island's northernmost peninsula is a gleaming white rectangular gash amid the greenery of the surrounding pines, nestling above one of the island's most idyllic beaches. In the 1940s it hosted many famous guests, from Sir Winston Churchill to Charlie Chaplin, but today focuses its attention more on business conferences. Unlike many hotels this side of the island, the Formentor is a year-round destination and, after periodic innovative refurbishments, its once rather somber rooms have a perennially warm aura, thanks to their glowing ocher decor, light summery furnishings, and traditional tiled floors. Its chefs also deserve high praise for their combination of international and Mediterranean cuisine.

Playa Formentor, 07470 Port de Pollença.*©* **97-189-91-01.** Fax 97-186-51-55. www.barceloformentor. com. 131 units. 210€–520€ double; 550€–775€ junior suite. Rates include breakfast. AE, DC, MC, V. Free parking. **Amenities:** 3 restaurants; 3 bars; babysitting; boating; horseback riding; gym; 2 outdoor pools; room service; 5 tennis courts; windsurfing. *In room:* A/C, TV, hair dryer, minibar, Wi-Fi (free).

EXPENSIVE

Hotel Illa d'Or ★   Built in the same year as the Formentor, and enlarged and improved several times since then, this four-story hotel sits on the seashore at the northwestern edge of Port de Pollença, enjoying fabulous views across the bay to Alcudia. Decorated in a mixture of colonial Spanish and English reproductions, it offers a seafront terrace with a view of the mountains, and airy, simply furnished spaces. Guest rooms are midsize to spacious, each with comfortable furnishings, including good beds. The beach is just a few steps away.

Passeig Colón 265, 07470 Port de Pollença.*©* **97-186-51-00.** Fax 97-186-42-13. www.hotelillador.com. 120 units. 125€–245€ double; 280€–550€ suites. Rates include breakfast. DC, V. Free parking. Closed Dec–Jan 9. **Amenities:** Restaurant; 2 bars; bikes; fitness center; 2 pools (1 indoor); room service; sauna; spa; tennis court. *In room:* A/C, TV, hair dryer, minibar, Wi-Fi (free).

MODERATE

Hotel Juma ★   A genuinely family-run hotel built in 1907 and set in the middle of Port Pollença town, this is a tiny, enchanting alternative to the usual beachside choices. It's squeaky-clean, relaxing (apart from fiesta nights when you can get noise from the adjoining main square), and very friendly. Rooms are immaculate and quietly atmospheric, furnished in a modestly traditional style with high wooden bedsteads and old-style wardrobes. Its cafe has, over the years, hosted informal *tertulias* (conversation evenings) and get-togethers of local singers and artists such as María del Mar Bonet and Jordi Savall, little known outside Spain but cultural icons in their homeland.

Plaça Major 1. ✆ **97-153-50-02.** www.hoteljuma.com. 6 units. 90€–130€ double including breakfast. DC, MC, V. Closed Nov 15–Dec 15. **Amenities:** Cafe-lounge where breakfast is served. *In room*: A/C, TV, hair dryer, Wi-Fi (free).

Where to Dine
EXPENSIVE
Restaurant Clivia ★ SPANISH The best and most appealing restaurant in Pollença, the Clivia is always busy. The restaurant, in a century-old house in the heart of town, is composed of two dining rooms scattered with antique furniture, and an outdoor patio. Its discreet, well-organized staff produces a limited list of meats (veal, chicken, pork, and beef) and a more appealing roster of seafood prepared with skill and finesse. Specialties depend on the availability of fish, such as cod, monkfish, dorado, eel, squid, and whitefish, either baked in a salt crust or prepared as part of a succulent *parrillada* (platter) of shellfish that's among the freshest anywhere. Begin with a spicy fish soup and accompany it with fresh vegetables, such as asparagus or spinach. The restaurant's name derives from the variety of bright red flowers (*las clivias*) planted profusely beside the patio, that bloom throughout the summer.

Av. Pollentia 7, 07460 Pollença. ✆ **97-153-36-35.** Reservations recommended. Main courses 15€–28€. AE, DC, MC, V. Year-round daily 1–3pm and 7–11pm (May–Oct closed Mon and Wed afternoons). Closed Nov 15–Dec 15. Bus: 340, 341, and 342.

FAST FACTS

BARCELONA

American Express   There are two American Express offices in Barcelona: One at Passeig de Gràcia 101 (☏ **93-415-23-71**) and the other at La Rambla 74 (☏ **93-301-11-66**).

Area Codes   The area code for Barcelona is **93.**

ATM Networks   Maestro, Cirrus, and Visa cards are readily accepted at all ATMs. See also "Money & Costs" in chapter 3, "Planning Your Trip To Barcelona," p. 49.

Babysitters   Most major hotels can arrange for babysitters, called *canguros* (literally, kangaroos) or *niñeras*. Rates vary considerably but are usually reasonable.

Business Hours   Banks are open Monday through Friday from 8:30am to 2pm. Most offices are open Monday through Friday from 9am to 6 or 7pm. In July this changes from 8am to 3pm for many businesses, especially those in the public sector. In August, businesses are on skeleton staff if they are not closed altogether. In restaurants, lunch is usually from 2 to 4pm and dinner from 9 to 11:30pm or midnight. There are no set rules for the opening of bars and tavernas. Many open at 8am, others at noon, and most stay open until midnight or later. Major stores are open Monday through Saturday from 9:30 or 10am to 8pm; smaller establishments, however, often take a siesta, doing business from 9:30am to 2pm and 4:30 to 8 or 8:30pm. Hours can vary from store to store. Opening hours of bars and establishments selling liquors vary widely. They can open as early as 6am and close as late as 2am. Nightclubs, late-night bars, and after-hours establishments fill the remaining hours up to and after dawn.

Car Rentals   See "Websites," p. 329.

Drinking Laws   The legal age for drinking is 18. Alcoholic drinks are available in practically every bar, hotel, and restaurant in the city, and by law cannot be served to minors under 18. Generally, you can purchase alcoholic beverages in almost any market; supermarkets sell alcoholic drinks from 9 or 10am until closing time around 9 or 10pm.

   Breathalyzers are now used more frequently than in the past and drivers may be subject to spot-checks, whether or not they've just had an accident or broken the law. The official permitted limit for drinking is the equivalent of one glass of wine, two *cañas* (small glasses) of beer, or one glass of spirits.

Driving Rules   See "Getting There & Getting Around," in chapter 3, "Planning Your Trip To Barcelona."

Electricity   Hotels have 220 volts AC (50 cycles). Carry a two-pin adapter with you, and always check at your hotel desk before plugging in any electrical appliance. Most hotels have hair dryers, so no need to pack yours.

Embassies & Consulates If you lose your passport, fall seriously ill, get into legal trouble, or have some other serious problem, your embassy or consulate can help. These are the Barcelona addresses and hours:

The **United States Consulate,** Passeig de Reina Elisenda 23 (© **93-280-22-27;** www. barcelona.usconsulategov; FGC: Reina Elisenda), is open Monday through Friday from 9am to 1pm.

The **Canadian Consulate,** Carrer de Elisenda Pinós 10 (© **93-204-27-00.** www.canada international.gc.ca; FGC: Reina Elisenda), is open Monday through Friday from 10am to 1pm.

The **United Kingdom Consulate-General,** Diagonal 477 (© **93-366-62-00;** www. ukinspain.fco.gov.uk/en/about-us/; Metro: Hospital Clínic), is open Monday through Friday from 9:30am to 3pm.

The **Republic of Ireland** has a small consulate at Gran Vía Carles III 94 (© **93-491-50-21;** Metro: María Cristina), open Monday through Friday from 10am to 1pm.

In the adjacent building is the **Australian Consulate,** Gran Vía Carles III 98 (© **93-490-90-13;** www.dfat.gov.au/missions/countries/esba.html; Metro: María Cristina), open Monday through Friday from 10am to noon.

Citizens of **New Zealand** have a consulate at Travesera de Gràcia 64 (© **93-209-03-99;** no website: check with Australian Consul; FGC: Gràcia), open Monday through Friday from 9am to 4:30pm and 4 to 7pm.

Emergencies For an ambulance dial © **061;** for fire dial © **080.**

Gasoline/Petrol The price of unleaded petrol (used in practically all vehicles now), ranges from 1.15€ to 1.27€ per liter at the time of writing (Nov 2010). These prices cover, respectively, the "Normal 95" and Super 98" versions. In petrol stations look for "sin plomo" (unleaded) signs.

Holidays See "Barcelona Calendar of Events" in chapter 3, "Planning Your Trip To Barcelona."

Hospitals/Clinics In Barcelona, the **Centre d'Urgències Perecamps,** located near La Rambla at Avinguda de las Drassanes 13–15 (© **93-441-06-00**), is a good bet. *Farmacias* (pharmacies) are everywhere, and they usually have highly trained staff and can often replace a trip to the doctor (most drugs are available over the counter). Pharmacies work on a shift basis; when one is closed they display a list of nearby 24-hour or extended-hour pharmacies on their front doors.

Hotlines Call the tourist information service at © **010** for opening and closing times of attractions, special events, and other hard-to-find info.

Insurance Since Spain for most of us is far from home, and a number of things could go wrong—lost luggage, trip cancellation, a medical emergency—consider the following types of insurance.

For travel overseas, most **U.S.** health plans (including Medicare and Medicaid) do not provide coverage, and the ones that do often require you to pay for services upfront and reimburse you only after you return home. As a safety net, you may want to buy travel medical insurance. If you require additional medical insurance, try **MEDEX Assistance** (© **410/453-6300;** www.medexassist.com) or **Travel Assistance International** (© **800/821-2828;** www.travelassistance.com; for general information on services, call the company's **Worldwide Assistance Services, Inc,** at © **800/777-8710**).

Canadians should check with their provincial health plan office or call **Health Canada** (© **866/225-0709;** www.hc-sc.gc.ca) to find out the extent of their coverage and what documentation and receipts they must take home if they are treated in Spain.

Travelers from the **U.K.** should carry their European Health Insurance Card (EHIC) as proof of entitlement to free/reduced-cost medical treatment abroad (© **0845/606-2030;**

www.ehic.org.uk). Note, however, that the EHIC only covers "necessary medical treatment," and for repatriation costs, lost money, baggage, or cancellation, travel insurance from a reputable company should always be sought (www.travelinsuranceweb.com).

Travel Insurance   The cost of travel insurance varies widely, depending on the destination, the cost and length of your trip, and your age and health. You can get estimates from various providers through **InsureMyTrip.com**. Enter your trip cost and dates, your age, and other information for prices from more than a dozen companies.

Families who make more than one trip abroad per year may find an annual travel insurance policy works out cheaper. Check **www.moneysupermarket.com**, which compares prices across a wide range of providers for single-trip and multitrip policies.

Most big travel agents offer their own insurance and will try to sell you their package when you book a holiday. Think before you sign. Britain's **Consumers' Association** recommends that you insist on seeing the policy and reading the fine print before buying travel insurance. The **Association of British Insurers** (✆ 020/7600-3333; www.abi.org.uk) gives advice by phone and publishes *Holiday Insurance*, a free guide to policy provisions and prices. You might also shop around for better deals: Try **Columbus Direct** (✆ 0870/033-9988;** www.columbusdirect.net).

Trip-Cancellation Insurance   Trip-cancellation insurance will help you retrieve your money if you have to back out of a trip or come home early, or if your travel supplier goes bankrupt. You won't get back 100% of your prepaid trip cost, but you'll be refunded a substantial portion.

Internet Access

Internet access is plentiful, both in cybercafes and in hotels. The **Bornet Internet Café** (Barra del Ferro 3, Born; ✆ **93-268-15-07;** www.bornet-bcn.com) has 16 terminals and charges 2.80€ per hour. For music while you catch up on your e-mail, try **Alsur Café,** Carders 17 (✆ **93-182-54-07;** www.alsurcafe.com), with two branches, one in the Sant Pere district, the other next to the Palau de la Música.

Language

There are two official languages in Catalonia: Castilian Spanish *(Castellano)* and Catalan. After years of being outlawed during the Franco dictatorship, Catalan has returned to Barcelona and Catalonia, with the language and its derivatives spoken throughout the *Països Catalans* (Catalan Countries), namely Catalonia, Valencia, the Balearic Islands (including Mallorca, even though natives there will tell you they speak *Mallorquín*), and pockets of Southern France and Aragón. Although street signs and most media is in Catalan, no tourist is expected to speak it, although you will be met with delight if you can at least master a few phrases. Descriptions in museums are in both Catalan and Spanish, with some also in English. Most restaurants have an English menu.

Laundromats

There are a few self-service and serviced laundromats in the Ciutat Vella, including **Tigre,** Carrer de Rauric 20, and **Lavamax,** Junta de Comerç 14. Some dry cleaners *(tintorerías)* also do laundry.

Legal Aid

Should you happen to break the law and be arrested, you will be assigned an *abogado de oficio* or duty solicitor free of charge at the police station. You'll also be allowed to phone your consulate, who can put you in touch with an English-speaking lawyer.

Lost & Found

Tell all of your credit card companies the minute you discover your wallet has been lost or stolen and file a report at the nearest police station. Your credit card company or insurer will require a police report number or record of the loss. Most credit card companies have an emergency toll-free number to call if your card is lost or stolen; they may be able to wire you a cash advance immediately or deliver an emergency credit card in a day or two.

Visa's emergency number in Spain is ✆ **90-099-11-24** (www.visaeurope.es). **American Express** cardholders and traveler's check holders call ✆ **90-237-56-37** (www.americanexpress.com) in Spain. **MasterCard** holders call ✆ **90-097-12-31** (www.mastercard.com) in Spain.

Mail   The local postage system is both reliable and efficient, though services such as FedEx are available if you prefer to use them. To send an airmail letter or postcard to the United States costs .78€ for up to 20 grams. Airmail letters to Britain or other E.U. countries cost .62€ for up to 20 grams; letters within Spain cost .39€.

Post your letters in the post office itself or in yellow mailboxes called *buzones.* Buy stamps in an *oficina de correos* (post office) or in an *estanco* (a government-licensed tobacconist, easily recognized by its brown and yellow logo).

Postcards have the same rates as letters. Allow about 8 days for airmail delivery to North America, generally less to the U.K.; in some cases, letters take 2 weeks to reach North America. As for surface mail to North America, forget it. Chances are you'll be home long before your letter arrives.

For further information, check the Spanish post office website, www.correos.es.

Barcelona's central post office is in Plaza San Antonio López, past the southern end of El Born (✆ **93-486-80-50**); the nearest Metro station is Barceloneta.

Maps   See chapter 3, "Planning Your Trip To Barcelona," for information on where to get maps of the Metro. Maps are available of the combined metro and FGC suburban railway line systems.

Measurements   See the chart on the inside front cover of this book for details on converting metric measurements to nonmetric equivalents.

Newspapers & Magazines   Foreign newspapers and magazines are available on the newsstands along La Rambla. The Paris-based *International Herald Tribune,* which sometimes includes an English-language version of *El País* (see below), is sold at most newsstands in the tourist districts, as are *USA Today,* the *Wall Street Journal,* and European editions of *Time* and *Newsweek,* for U.S. travelers; and *The Guardian, The Times,* the *Financial Times,* and the *Telegraph,* for U.K. visitors. Top Catalan newspapers are *La Vanguardia* and *Avui* (the latter is in Catalan), while major national Spanish newspapers are *El País, El Mundo, ABC,* and *La Razón.*

Catalonia Today is a free newsletter in English published by the Catalan newspaper *El Punt. Barcelona Metropolitan* is a monthly magazine in English with loads of information on events as well as features on Barcelona living. You can pick it up in bars and pubs or read it online at www.barcelona-metropolitan.com. The *Guía del Ocio* is the most comprehensive "What's On." There is a small section at the back in English. **Free** Spanish newspapers giving you a brief rundown on what's going on both in the city and around the world are handed out at the entrances to Metro stations. These publications include *Metro, Qué,* and *20 Minutos.*

Passports   The websites listed provide downloadable passport applications and fees for processing applications.

For Residents of Australia   Call the Australian Passport Information Service (APIS) at ✆ **131-232**, or download at www.passports.gov.au.

For Residents of Canada   Call the **Passport Office,** Department of Foreign Affairs and International Trade, Ottawa, K1A 0G3 at ✆ **800/567-6868**, or download at www.ppt.gc.ca.

For Residents of Ireland   Call the **Passport Office,** Setanta Centre, Molesworth Street, Dublin 2 on ✆ **01/671-1633**, or download from www.irlgov.ie/iveagh.

For Residents of New Zealand Call the **Passports Office, Level 3, Boulcott House, Wellington 6011** at ✆ **0800/225-050** or 04/474-8100, or download from www.passports.govt.nz.

For Residents of the United Kingdom Call the **United Kingdom Passport Service (UKPS)** at ✆ **0870/521-0410** or search its website at www.ips.gov.uk., which gives 22 passport office addresses to contact throughout the USA.

Police In an emergency, dial ✆ **112.**

Smoking At the time of writing, smoking restrictions currently apply to all working and most public places, though most bars and cafes still allow smoking except in certain categorized "non smoking zones."

However, things look set for a really radical change. The first stage of a new bill to ban smoking in *all* public places (especially restaurants and hotels) was approved by a vast majority in Madrid's Congreso de Diputados (Parliament) on June 23, 2010. The aim is for the final law to be passed by January 1, 2011, following the other European examples of Italy, Ireland, and even Turkey, formerly one of the world's most avid smoking countries. (If Turkey can do it, surely so can Spain!)

Restaurants are concerned that this new bill may become law and they're afraid of losing customers, and **hoteliers** are even more worried. From having a few rooms set aside for nonsmokers—as is the case in some of the better hotels at present—**all** will be for **nonsmokers.** Open-air terrace smoking in both will still be allowed.

Taxes Sales tax is called IVA. In July 2010 it rose to 8% for food items and 18% for most other goods. Cash-register receipts will show this as a separate charge. If you see a "Tax-Free Shopping" sticker displayed in a shop you can request a tax-free receipt on purchases of over 90.16€. Get this stamped at airport Customs (Terminal 2A) when you depart Spain and you can claim a cash refund from one of the banks in the airport. Refunds can be made to your credit card or by check. For more information see www.globalrefund.com.

Telephones See "Staying Connected" in chapter 3, "Planning Your Trip To Barcelona."

Time Spain is 6 hours ahead of Eastern Standard Time in the United States, 1 hour ahead of Greenwich Mean Time in the U.K., 6 hours behind Perth and 9 hours behind Sydney (both in Australia). **Daylight saving time** is in effect from the last Sunday in March to the last Sunday in October.

Tipping More expensive restaurants add a 10% tax to the bill and cheaper ones incorporate it into their prices. This is *not* a service charge, and a tip of 5% is acceptable in these establishments if the full service charge is not included (see below). For coffees and snacks most people just leave a few coins or round up to the nearest euro.

Don't over-tip. The government requires restaurants and hotels to include their service charges—usually around 15% of the bill. However, that doesn't mean you should skip out of a place without dispensing an extra euro or two. For cab drivers, add about 10% to the fare shown on the meter.

In both restaurants and nightclubs, a service charge is added to the bill. To that, add another 3% to 5% tip, depending on the quality of the service. Waiters in deluxe restaurants and nightclubs are accustomed to the extra 5%, which means you'll end up tipping around 20%.

Toilets There aren't many public toilets in Barcelona. The best places to find them are bus and train stations (where their conditions vary greatly) or more pleasantly in public parks like La Ciutadella and big stores like El Corte Inglés (p. 220). Ask in bars and cafes before using their facilities, or at least buy a coffee.

Visas These are not required for Australian, American, British, Canadian, or New Zealand visitors. (See "Entry Requirements" in chapter 3, "Planning Your Trip To Barcelona.")

Water Although the water in Barcelona is safe to drink, most people find the taste unpleasantly chlorinated and instead buy bottled water.

WEBSITES

CAR RENTAL AGENCIES

Advantage
www.advantage.com

Auto Europe
www.autoeurope.com

Avis
www.avis.com

Budget
www.budget.com

Enterprise
www.enterprise.com

Europcar
www.europcar.com

Hertz
www.hertz.com

National
www.nationalcar.com

Thrifty
www.thrifty.com

MAJOR INTERNATIONAL HOTEL & MOTEL CHAINS

Best Western International
www.bestwestern.com

Four Seasons
www.fourseasons.com

Hilton Hotels
www.hilton.com

Holiday Inn
www.holidayinn.com

Hyatt
www.hyatt.com

InterContinental Hotels & Resorts
www.ichotelsgroup.com

Marriott
www.marriott.com

Radisson Hotels & Resorts
www.radisson.com

Ramada Worldwide
www.ramada.com

Renaissance
www.marriott.com

Sheraton Hotels & Resorts
www.starwoodhotels.com/sheraton

Westin Hotels & Resorts
www.starwoodhotels.com/westin

USEFUL TERMS & PHRASES

I n Barcelona and Catalunya province both Castilian Spanish and the local Catalan language are spoken and understood. The latter has become increasingly important for Catalunya since the death of Franco, symbolizing the region's drive for independence—even possibly separation—from the rest of Spain.

The Catalan lingo sounds blunter and harsher than the flowery, often hyperbolic national tongue. Like the Catalans themselves it cuts out waffle and gets to the point. Don't believe Castilian purists from Burgos, Valladolid, and—especially—arch-rival Madrid when they tell you it's just a dialect. Catalan is a long-established language in its own right, with a rich literature that goes back to pre-medieval times. Its roots are French, Provençal, Latin, and modern Italian, as you may intimate from words like *formatge* (cheese) and *gelat* (ice cream). (The respective Castilian equivalents are *queso* and *helado*, by the way.) However there are some strange examples of Catalan spelling. A prime example of the weirdness of Catalan spelling is the area of "Paral.lel" in Barcelona. Other Catalan words such as *parcel.la* (plot of land) and *capil.lar* (capillary) have the same spelling format, so this is not unique. In Catalan words containing double "l"s, the "l"s are separated by a dot when a slight pause is necessary between them. However, in a word like *capellà* (chapel), no such pause is needed so no central separating dot is required.

Most Catalans are both pleased and patient with foreigners who try to speak their language. For English speakers, the pronunciation is a lot easier than Castilian Spanish, so give it a go. (And if it doesn't come off, most good restaurants and hotels have staff on hand who can give you a helping hand in English.)

USEFUL WORDS & PHRASES

English	Spanish/Catalan	Pronunciation
Good day/Good morning	**Buenos días/Bon dia**	*bweh*-nohs *dee*-ahs/bohn *dee*-ah
How are you?	**¿Cómo está?/Com està?**	*koh*-moh es-*tah*/com ehs-*tah*

English	Spanish/Catalan	Pronunciation
Very well	**Muy bien/Molt bé**	mwee byehn/mohl beh
Thank you	**Gracias/Gràcies**	*grah*-syahs/*grah*-syahs
You're welcome	**De nada/De res**	deh *nah*-dah/duh ress
Goodbye	**Adiós/Adéu**	ah-*dyos*/ah-*deh*-yoo
Please	**Por favor/Si us plau**	por fah-*vohr*/see yoos plow
Yes	**Sí/Sí**	see
No	**No/No**	noh
Excuse me	**Perdóneme/Perdoni'm**	pehr-*doh*-neh-meh/per-*don*-eem
Where is . . . ?	**¿Dónde está . . . ?/On és . . . ?**	*dohn*-deh es-*tah*/ohn ehs
the station	**la estación/la estació**	lah es-tah-*syohn*/la es-tah-*cyo*
a hotel	**un hotel/l'hotel**	oon oh-*tehl*/ehl ho-*tehl*
the market	**el mercado/el mercat**	ehl mehr-*kah*-doh/ehl mehr-*kah*
a restaurant	**un restaurante/un restaurant**	oon rehs-tow-*rahn*-the/oon rehs-tow-*rahn*
the toilet	**el baño/el lavabo**	ehl *bah*-nyoh/ehl lah-*vah*-boh
a doctor	**un médico/un metge**	oon *meh*-dee-koh/oon meht-*jah*
the road to . . .	**el camino a/al cami per**	ehl kah-*mee*-noh ah/ahl kah-*mee* pehr
To the right	**A la derecha/A la dreta**	ah lah deh-*reh*-chah/ah lah *dreh*-tah
To the left	**A la izquierda/A l'esquerra**	ah lah ees-*kyehr*-dah/ahl ehs-kee-*ra*
I would like . . .	**Quisiera/Voldría**	kee-*syeh*-rah/vohl-*dree*-ah
I want . . .	**Quiero/Vull**	*kyeh*-roh/*boo*-wee
to eat	**comer/menjar**	ko-*mehr*/mehn-*jahr*
a room	**una habitación/un habitación**	*oo*-nah ah-bee-tah-*syohn*/oon ah-bee-tah-*syohn*
Do you have . . . ?	**¿Tiene usted?/Té?**	*tyeh*-neh oo-*sted*/the
a book	**un libro/un llibre**	oon *lee*-broh/oon *yee*-breh
a dictionary	**un diccionario/un diccionari**	oon deek-syoh-*nah*-ryoh/oon deek-syoh-*nah*-ree
How do you say it in Catalan?	**Como se dice eso en Catalan?/Com se diu aixóen Català?**	*coh*-mo say *dith*-ay *es*-so en Cah-tah-*lan*?/comm say *dee*-oh esh-*aw* en Cah-tah-*là*?
How much is it?	**¿Cuánto cuesta?/Quant es?**	*kwahn*-toh *kwehs*-tah/kwahnt ehs?
When?	**¿Cuándo?/Quan?**	*kwahn*-doh/kwahn
What?	**¿Qué?/Com?**	keh/cohm
There is (Is there . . . ?)	**(¿)Hay (. . . ?)/Hi ha? *or* Hi han?**	aye/ee ah/ee ahn
What is there?	**¿Qué hay?/Que hi ha?**	keh aye/keh ee ah
Yesterday	**Ayer/Ahir**	ah-*yehr*/ah-*yeer*
Today	**Hoy/Avui**	oy/ah-*wee*
Tomorrow	**Mañana/Demá**	mah-*nyah*-nah/deh-*mah*
Good	**Bueno/Bon**	*bweh*-noh/bohn

14

USEFUL TERMS & PHRASES | Useful Words & Phrases

English	Spanish/Catalan	Pronunciation
Bad	**Malo/Mal**	*mah*-loh/mahl
Better (Best)	**(Lo) Mejor/Millor**	(loh) meh-*hohr*/mee-*yohr*
More	**Más/Mes**	mahs/mehss
Less	**Menos/Menys**	*meh*-nohs/*meh*-nyus
Hot	**Caliente/Calent**	cah-lee-*yen*-tay/cah-*lent*
Cold	**Frío/Fred**	*free*-yoh/fred
To rent	**Alquilar/Lloguer**	*all*-kee-lar/lyogg-*air*
Do you speak English?	**¿Habla inglés?/Parla anglès?**	ah-blah een-*glehs*/ pahr-lah ahn-*glehs*
I speak a little Spanish/ Catalan	**Hablo un poco de español/ Parlo una mica de Català**	ah-*bloh* oon *poh*-koh deh es-pah-*nyol*/*pahr*-loh oo-nah *mee*-kah *deh* kah-tah-*lahn*
I don't understand	**No entiendo/No comprenc**	noh ehn-*tyehn*-doh/ noh cohm-*prehnk*
What time is it?	**¿Qué hora es?/ Quina hora és?**	keh *oh*-rah ehss/ *kee*-nah *oh*-rah ehss
The check, please	**La cuenta, por favor/ El compte, si us plau**	lah *kwehn*-tah pohr fah-*vohr*/ ehl *cohmp*-tah see yoos plow

NUMBERS

Number	Spanish	Catalan
1	**uno** (*oo*-noh)	**un** (oon)
2	**dos** (dohs)	**dos** (dohs)
3	**tres** (trehs)	**tres** (trehs)
4	**cuatro**(*kwah*-troh)	**quatre** (*kwah*-trah)
5	**cinco** (*seen*-koh)	**cinc** (sink)
6	**seis** (says)	**sis** (sees)
7	**siete** (*syeh*-the)	**set** (seht)
8	**ocho** (*oh*-choh)	**vuit** (vweet)
9	**nueve** (*nweh*-beh)	**nou** (noo)
10	**diez** (dyehs)	**deu** (*deh*-yoo)
11	**once** (*ohn*-seh)	**onze** (*ohn*-zah)
12	**doce** (*doh*-seh)	**dotze** (*doh*-tzah)
13	**trece** (*treh*-seh)	**tretze** (*treh*-tzah)
14	**catorce** (kah-*tohr*-seh)	**catorza** (kah-*tohr*-zah)
15	**quince** (*keen*-seh)	**quinza** (*keen*-zah)
16	**dieciséis** (dyeh-see-*says*)	**setze** (*seh*-tzah)
17	**diecisiete** (dyeh-see-*syeh*-the)	**disset** (dee-*seht*)
18	**dieciocho** (dyeh-*syoh*-choh)	**divuit** (dee-*vweet*)

Number	Spanish	Catalan
19	**diecinueve** (dyeh-see-*nweh*-beh)	**dinou** (dee-*noo*)
20	**veinte** (*bayn*-the)	**vint** (vehnt)
30	**treinta** (*trayn*-tah)	**trenta** (*trehn*-tah)
40	**cuarenta** (kwah-*rehn*-tah)	**quaranta** (kwah-*rahn*-tah)
50	**cincuenta** (seen-*kwehn*-tah)	**cinquanta** (theen-*kwahn*-tah)
60	**sesenta** (seh-*sehn*-tah)	**seixanta** (see-*shahn*-tah)
70	**setenta** (seh-*tehn*-tah)	**setanta** (seh-*tahn*-tah)
80	**ochenta** (oh-*chehn*-tah)	**vuitanta** (vwee-*tahn*-tah)
90	**noventa** (noh-*behn*-tah)	**noranta** (noh-*rahn*-tah)
100	**cien** (*syehn*)	**cent** (sent)

Index

Accommodations

Restaurants